PENGUIN  CLASSICS

THE ESSAYS: A SELECTION

'Dr Screech's principal achievement has been to render Montaigne into contemporary English without quaintness, but also without sacrifice of that flavour of the sixteenth century which is implicit in Montaigne's thinking . . . We want the essence of the man in a form accessible to modern readers, and that is what the translator has so gracefully given us' – Robertson Davies

'[Screech] is the master of Montaigne' – Roy Porter on *Kaleidoscope*, BBC Radio Four

'Of [the translation's] limpidity and charm there can be no question' – Simon Raven in the *Guardian*

'[The commentary] constitutes a fascinating sixteenth-century *honnête homme*'s library. For this reason the French reader will turn to the translation of M. A. Screech, who takes his place among those who, crossing cultural boundaries, enable each country to rediscover its writers in a new light' – Jean-Robert Armogathe in *Bibliothèque d'Humanisme et Renaissance*

'This thinking tome, edited by a fine scholar, is utterly readable as fine scholars should be' – Anthony Blond in the *Evening Standard*

'Anglophones of the next century will be deeply in [Dr Screech's] debt' – Gore Vidal in *The Times Literary Supplement*

MICHEL EYQUEM, Seigneur de Montaigne, was born in 1533, the son and heir of Pierre, Seigneur de Montaigne (two previous children dying soon after birth). He was brought up to speak Latin as his mother tongue and always retained a Latin turn of mind; though he knew Greek, he preferred to use translations. After studying law he eventually became counsellor to the *Parlement* of Bordeaux. He married in 1565. In 1569 he published his French version of the *Natural Theology* of Raymond Sebond; his *Apology* is only partly a defence of Sebond and sets sceptical limits to human reasoning about God, man and nature. He retired in 1571 to his lands at Montaigne, devoting himself to reading and reflection and to composing his *Essays* (first version, 1580). He loathed the fanaticism and cruelties of the religious wars of the period, but sided with Catholic orthodoxy and legitimate monarchy. He was twice elected Mayor of Bordeaux (1581 and 1583), a post he held for four years. He died at Montaigne in 1592 while preparing the final, and richest, edition of his *Essays*.

M. A. SCREECH is an Honorary Fellow of Wolfson College and an Emeritus Fellow of All Souls College, Oxford (Fellow and Chaplain, 2001–3), a Fellow of the British Academy and of the Royal Society of Literature, a Fellow of University College London and a Corresponding member of the Institut de France. He long served on the committee of the Warburg Institute as the Fielden Professor of French Language and Literature in University College London, until his election to All Souls in 1984. He is a Renaissance scholar of international renown. He has edited and translated the complete *Essays* for Penguin Classics and, in a separate volume, Montaigne's *Apology for Raymond Sebond*. His other books include *Erasmus: Ecstacy and the Praise of Folly* (Penguin, 1988), *Rabelais* (Duckworth, 1979), and *Montaigne and Melancholy* (Penguin, 1991), and, most recently, *Laughter at the Foot of the Cross* (Allen Lane, 1998); all are acknowledged to be classic studies in their fields. He worked with Anne Screech on *Erasmus' Annotations on the New Testament*. Michael Screech was promoted Chevalier dans l'Ordre du Mérite in 1982 and Chevalier dans la Légion d'Honneur in 1992. He was ordained, in Oxford, deacon in 1993 and priest in 1994.

MICHEL DE MONTAIGNE

The Essays

A Selection

Translated and Edited with an Introduction and Notes by
M. A. SCREECH

PENGUIN BOOKS

PENGUIN BOOKS

Published by the Penguin Group

Penguin Books Ltd, 80 Strand, London WC2R 0RL, England

Penguin Group (USA) Inc., 375 Hudson Street, New York, New York 10014, USA

Penguin Group (Canada), 90 Eglinton Avenue East, Suite 700, Toronto, Ontario, Canada M4P 2Y3
(a division of Pearson Penguin Canada Inc.)

Penguin Ireland, 25 St Stephen's Green, Dublin 2, Ireland (a division of Penguin Books Ltd)

Penguin Group (Australia), 707 Collins Street, Melbourne, Victoria 3008, Australia
(a division of Pearson Australia Group Pty Ltd)

Penguin Books India Pvt Ltd, 11 Community Centre, Panchsheel Park, New Delhi – 110 017, India

Penguin Group (NZ), 67 Apollo Drive, Rosedale, Auckland 0632, New Zealand
(a division of Pearson New Zealand Ltd)

Penguin Books (South Africa) (Pty) Ltd, Block D, Rosebank Office Park,
181 Jan Smuts Avenue, Parktown North, Gauteng 2193, South Africa

Penguin Books Ltd, Registered Offices: 80 Strand, London WC2R 0RL, England

www.penguin.com

The Complete Essays published by Allen Lane The Penguin Press 1991
This selection published in Penguin Books 1993
Reprinted in Penguin Classics with a new Chronology 2004

036

Filmset in Bembo Monophoto
Typeset by Datix International Limited, Bungay, Suffolk
Printed in England by Clays Ltd, St Ives plc

ISBN: 978-0-140-44602-9

www.greenpenguin.co.uk

In Memory of

PHILIP EVELEIGH

*Wit, poet, scholar
killed during the Allied
landings in Italy*

Table of Contents

===

THE ESSAYS: A SELECTION

BOOK I

BOOK II

BOOK III

Introduction

===

Many who write or talk about themselves are bores: Montaigne is not. He remains utterly readable. His book certainly affords delight and many men and women who experience that delight feel wiser for having done so.

'I myself am the subject of my book.' Despite the wide variety of topics treated in these *Essays*, Montaigne is quietly stating a fact.

He is one of a select band of authors: he leads us to feel that we know him – not partially, as an author, but fully, as an individual person. Only a residual respect for convention stopped him from portraying himself in his native simplicity, 'whole, and wholly naked'. Thank goodness he did not worry over-much about taboos of language or of topic; as a result we know the form of his mind better than that of anybody who wrote before him.

Montaigne himself judged that he and his book were 'of one substance' with each other. Within his covers we find not merely a wise book but a wise man. That once neat and clever little French nobleman who had grown wise and rancid with age came from a not very ancient family; his forebears were at home among wholesale traders and professional men. Montaigne was no don *manqué*, yet he changed the way we think about ourselves and about mankind. He achieved that revolution not by hectoring or by preaching, not by political manœuvring or by academic brilliance, but by writing about subjects which interested him, so letting us see the slant of his mind.

Much of what he published has profound implications for what we should trust in and how we should live, yet he avoids technicalities. He made excellent use of the rhetorical techniques favoured in his day in order to set forth his ideas clearly, persuasively and often humorously. He wrote with a simple directness which won him readers far beyond the formally educated few: he was read and admired by statesmen such as Henry of Navarre (the future *Henri Quatre* for whom Paris was well worth a Mass). One of his valets realized the cash value of his writings and stole the only copy of one of his chapters (it has never resurfaced). He was much admired by noblewomen too. His longest chapter, *An apology for Raymond Sebond* (II, 12) was probably undertaken for Margaret of France, the future wife of Henry of Navarre, and certainly for some great lady; his very personal chapter *On educating children* (I, 26) is dedicated to Diane de Foix, the countess of Gurson; towards the end of the Second Book, when writing *On the resemblance of children to their fathers* (II, 37), he broke off at one point in order to address directly Madame de Duras, who had just called on him at Montaigne. It was his widow and his *fille d'alliance*, Marie de Gournay, who contributed to the editing of the posthumous printed text of 1595, taking into account the hundreds of additions and changes which he had made in the wide margins of the copy of the 1588 edition now in Bordeaux.

Montaigne did not have a firm plan when he set about writing his *Essays*. His book and his aims changed and grew as he changed and grew in wisdom. That he was original and challenging is not, in retrospect, all that surprising. As a boy and man he had never been just another provincial gentleman. His father, possibly under the influence of the ideas of the Humanist theologian Erasmus of Rotterdam, arranged for Latin to be his native tongue. A special tutor was brought from Germany; his parents and the servants learned sufficient Latin to speak to him in nothing but that language. He lost his fluency in speaking Latin when his father, getting cold feet, sent him to board at the Collège de Guyenne in Bordeaux, but he never ceased to read it with ease and delight. Even his Greek philosophers he read (as Renaissance scholars often did) in Latin translation. Latin was the language of educated men, still the dominant language of school, university and learning generally. In addition to Latin, Montaigne also had to learn French: in his region the language was Gascon.

Montaigne's judgement is so balanced and wise that it may come as a surprise that the whole undertaking of writing the *Essays* arose out of a crisis of melancholy. When his father died in June 1568 Montaigne, as his son and heir, resigned his legal office in the *Parlement* of Bordeaux and withdrew to his estates. His closest of friends, Etienne de la Boëtie, had died unexpectedly some four years earlier (August 1563), leaving a yearning gap in Montaigne's life which nothing was ever completely to fill. They had spent very little time actually together, but they felt great joy in each other's company and in their conversation; Montaigne was convinced that their friendship was of the rarest kind which occurs but once in a few centuries. He was devastated by his friend's death. Devastated too by the death of the man whom he acknowledged to be the best of fathers.

In between those two grievous bereavements Montaigne had married Françoise de Chassaigne. His withdrawal to his estates was not, therefore, a hermit's withdrawal into literal solitude; it was, however, a conscious rejection of *negotium* in favour of *otium*, of, that is, a busy preoccupation with affairs in favour of learned leisure. In this Montaigne was following the practice and counsel of many a sage in Classical and Christian antiquity. Both Seneca and Augustine of Hippo would have appreciated his aim. He covered his library with quotations from Greek and Latin texts (including some Biblical ones) to mark this withdrawal and to declare his philosophy to himself and to his visitors.

Such learned leisure was a great ideal, but, for Montaigne, it did not turn out well in practice. Instead of finding peace and mental repose he fell into *chagrin* (a melancholic depression). He experienced the kind of anguish which Milton describes in *Il Penseroso* and in his *Ode to Melancholy*. Where he had hoped that his mind would be content with a private, bookish idleness he found that it 'bolted off like a runaway horse', giving birth to 'chimeras and fantastic monstrosities'. It was in order to contemplate at his ease 'their oddness and their strangeness' that he began to write them down (I, 8).

That helps to explain the nature of the chapters which he wrote first – which are not always the chapters which we now read first. (Montaigne decided the order of his chapters on aesthetic and philosophical grounds.) Before that access of melancholy he had apparently intended to write short discourses on matters of war and high policy – matters which directly concerned him as a gentleman who fought in the civil wars. He stood both for the Old Religion and, where the French monarchy was concerned, for the legitimate succession to the throne (which, for him, was independent of the religion of the heir). The military discourses which Montaigne wrote in those early days are strongly marked by *pro et contra* arguments. Montaigne delights in showing how easy it is to be wise after the event. Afterwards, convincing arguments can be marshalled to justify any outcome: but in real life, where decisions have to be actually taken, strong cases can be made to justify opposing courses of action. The wise commander needs judgement – and luck – if he can choose aright between equally persuasive arguments.

Under the influence of his bout of melancholy he began to deal also with such matters as death, sadness, idleness and those 'ecstatic' emotions which melancholics were held to be particularly prone to when they were 'beside themselves'. Such considerations did not take him right away from war to battle, since there is such a thing as 'mad' bravery on the field or 'mad' anger in political debate. The causes of such actions and emotions were classified under the general heading of melancholy.

In fact all the chapters of the first two Books are marked to some extent by that access of melancholy or by the remembrance of it. That is to be expected. Montaigne's native complexion was a balanced mixture of humours, of the melancholy and the sanguine (II, 17). It was a good one to have: ever since the *Problems* of Aristotle (or Pseudo-Aristotle), that or a similar complexion was seen as the basis of all genius. But it was also a worrying one to have: the same *Problems* (30–1) also declared it to be potentially the sole basis of many distressing kinds of madness. An increase in melancholy humour risked making Montaigne 'unbalanced', as the equilibrium of the melancholy and the sanguine in his complexion was broken and toppled suddenly towards the melancholy.

One of the marked features of Montaigne's writings as a younger man is a preoccupation with death – not with being dead but with the act of dying. By the time he had reached his full maturity his mind was centred not on dying but on living. His book shows us why. And it shows us how he dissipated his melancholy humours.

The title *Essays* is one of striking modesty. It is nearer to 'assay' than to 'essay' as used today. The term was used of schoolboys' 'attempts' or 'exercises'; it was used when apprentices tried out their skills, well before producing their masterpiece; it was used when gold or silver was 'assayed' to find out its worth. What Montaigne was 'assaying' was both his 'self' and his opinions. He realized virtually from the outset that, since he was not a past master in any of the arts or sciences, he was not stating conclusions but exploring opinions – his opinions. Since he was writing philosophy, he could normally leave revelation aside and concentrate on whatever fell within the fields of human intellect and emotion. That distinction was well understood and had been so for centuries. Montaigne held more than most that theology was best when reigning apart in glory: lesser subjects such as philosophy were subordinate to it, but did not have to have it forever in sight. Philosophy could treat of natural religion, and even trespass into the territory of theology, provided always that it was exploring problems, not resolving them to the detriment of revelation. Reason might go her way and revelation hers, provided that, in the end, reason gave way to properly established revelation as authorized by the Church.

His apparent subjects did not really matter to him: he could write, he said, about a fly! Whatever the subject of a chapter, Montaigne was really 'assaying' himself. He was breaking one of Europe's greatest taboos by writing thus about himself. (Nobody had ever done so before – not even Saint Augustine, whose *Confessions* are more a work of theology than of moral philosophy.) Montaigne was not at first fully conscious that he was doing so, but he was quickly aware of the strangeness of his enterprise:

... unless I am saved by oddness and novelty ... I shall never extricate myself from this daft undertaking ...

It was a melancholy humour (and therefore a humour most inimical to my natural complexion) brought on by the chagrin caused by the solitary retreat I plunged myself into a few years ago which first put into my mind this raving concern with writing.

(II, 8)

An account of his opinions – a book telling others not what he knew from authority but what he opined as an individual inexpert man – was in fact a self-portrait. So it is as a self-portrait that he offers his book first to his relations and then to a wider public. Had he been a great clerk or statesman or general, he might have written memoirs; but he was not.

Finding myself quite empty, with nothing to write about, I offered my self to myself as theme and subject matter.

(II, 8)

He found his enterprise to be 'wild and monstrous' or, on second thoughts, 'wild and fantastically eccentric'. But he soon concluded that he was producing a self-portrait, analogous to the self-portraits which artists were increasingly painting in their studios. The portrait was, at first, mainly that of his *forma mentis*, the slant of his mind. (A sustained concern with his body came much later.) It portrays for us the way he thought and felt and, therefore, acted. There was at the outset little or no claim to reach unshakeable conclusions. But unlike the artist in his studio who catches in pencil or paint a fixed likeness of himself and of his character, Montaigne discovered that he could never pin down a stable 'I' which he could study: his 'I' as the writer was ever-changing; his 'I' as the subject was ever-changing too. And French, unlike Latin, promised no stability either.

Others form Man; I give an account of Man and sketch a picture of a particular one of them who is very badly formed ... I am unable to stabilize my subject: it staggers confusedly along with a natural drunkenness. I grasp it as it is now, at this moment when I am lingering over it. I am not portraying being but becoming.

(III, 2)

Montaigne's method of avoiding the perils of pure introspection was to turn his gaze outward on to events, people or books and then to bring the subjects back to himself to find what his opinions about them really were. He did this with increasing confidence once he found that men may differ in degree but not in kind.

> You can attach the whole of moral philosophy to a commonplace private life
> just as well as to one of richer stuff. Every man bears the whole Form of the
> human condition.
>
> (III, 2)

Aristotle had convinced untold generations of thinkers that all human
beings had identical versions of the same 'form': the form (soul and mind)
of Man. Philosophers had striven to find what that form of Man was like
and then to apply their knowledge to individuals – to identical examples of
that form, every one of which was profoundly modified by its attachment
to matter (to its individual body). Montaigne, quite revolutionarily, started
from the other end: he studied his own mind, his own form, and, since he,
like anyone else, bore the whole form of the human condition, he applied
his knowledge of himself to anyone he met in life, by report or in books.
Recent changes in the way Aristotle was interpreted greatly helped him in
his enterprise. Traditionally, strict Aristotelians allowed there to be nothing
but absolute identity between all human forms. Individual differences arose
not in the form but in the complex linking of soul (form) with its body
(matter). Renaissance theologians (and many moral philosophers) insisted,
on the contrary, that just as there are many shades of white which still
nevertheless remain white, so there are many grades of human soul which
still remain human souls. Some are greater or higher than others: some are
baser and lower. All remain human. Montaigne accepts that view. So even
a mediocre human soul and a splendid one remain, as it were, in touch
with each other. Each can understand the other. Even a base soul can, in
some circumstances, attain momentarily to the calm virtue which Socrates
could sustain throughout his adult life.

Many also held that a man could see his soul rise to a higher rank –
to that of a hero or an angel. Montaigne came to believe that no man
ever ceased to be Man – not even Socrates, not even Homer. Similarly,
men were never so wicked or evil that other men ceased to have
cousinage with them. He also came to be convinced that, since Man is
body and soul, to portray only the soul is signally inadequate: human
beings are 'wondrously corporeal' (III, 8). The soul can influence the
body, but the body can also influence the soul! That is how it should
be: the body has its rights, its joys, its pabulum and its duties; they may
be less valid and less enduring than those of the soul but they have their
place within the wise and moral life of Man. Only saints, under grace,
may rightly neglect the body as their enraptured souls enjoy an ecstatic
foretaste of future joy. The rest of us must keep our feet on the ground,

teaching the body and soul to live wedded together in mutual harmony, until death them do part.

And if that was not revolutionary enough, Montaigne discovered that men have more in common with women than was usually thought. The greatest women, indeed, surpassed their own menfolk in stoic virtue (*On three good wives*, II, 35). And in matters sexual and social women were unfairly judged by men – who make all the rules: Montaigne enjoys what seem today to be bar-room tales but which were *exempla* forming part of established moral 'facts' about women. He draws a startling conclusion from a consideration of his own and women's sexuality:

> I say that male and female are cast in the same mould: save for education and custom the difference between them is not great. It is far more easy to charge one sex than to discharge the other.

That is the conclusion which he reached in 1588 at the end of a long chapter devoted to sex and poetry and which has its fair share of misogynistic *exempla* and stories. In the final version it is even more striking, since judgements are interpolated from two of the philosophers whom Montaigne most admired:

> In *The Republic* Plato summons both men and women indifferently to a community of all studies, offices and vocations both in peace and war; and Antisthenes the philosopher removed any distinction between their virtue and our own.
>
> (III, 5)

Reading Montaigne is like following a delightful course in moral philosophy. Delightful, since Montaigne held that philosophy should be delightful. He saw no need for it to be severe and forbidding. He was deeply influenced by the Ancient Stoics. His own sceptical turn of mind was reinforced by his discovery of authentic Ancient scepticism in the works of Pyrrho. His taste for life was partly guided by the Epicureans. It is sometimes suggested that he was first a Stoic, then a Sceptic, then an Epicurean. In fact he held those and other philosophies in easy harmony. Ancient philosophers easily swayed him, but one did not replace another completely. Increasingly he came to appreciate, however, the humanity of Socrates, the calm judgement of Plutarch and, despite his verbosity and vanity, the wisdom of Cicero, who attached a real and solid importance to the body within our common humanity.

Plutarch enjoyed a place apart because of Bishop Amyot's excellent translation of his works into French. (English readers can enjoy a second-hand taste of Amyot, since North's *Plutarch* was translated from Amyot's version, not from the original Greek.) The wider background to much of Montaigne's moral thought is provided by Aristotle's *Nicomachaean Ethics*. For Montaigne – an outstanding pupil of the School of Athens – Aristotle and the Peripatetics were the Ancients who were most concerned with civility. Plato, though admired, sought to rise too high and was anyway outstripped by his master, Socrates, who was content to 're-form' his soul and to remain a man. Yet no man, no author, not even the greatest, ever provides the last word on anything. Men are 'vain authorities who can resolve nothing' (II, 13).

Montaigne's natural and acquired scepticism were both greatly increased by the vast new horizons of the Renaissance, which had opened up the riches of Ancient thought and more modern science, at the same time as the discovery of more and more new peoples and new lands put established 'certainties' to the test. Montaigne came to understand the 'barbarity' of the Incas: he found it preferable to the cruelty and compromises of the Europe of his own times.

All about him the old order was being challenged and fought over. The year that Montaigne began to write, 1572, is that of the Massacre of Saint Bartholomew's Day and of the beginning of the Fourth Civil War in France. 1580, the year of the original edition of the *Essays*, is the year of the Seventh Civil War, in southern France. 1588, the year of what seemed at first to be the definitive edition of the *Essays*, saw the Guises entering Paris; King Henry III fleeing; the invincible Armada blown to perdition by what Protestant Europe saw as the breath of God; and the murder of Henri de Guise and of his brother the Cardinal at the instigation of their King. When Montaigne died in 1592 civil war was still raging, with peasants having recently revolted in Brittany while the English supported *Henri Quatre* in Normandy. Those events eroded not only political and ecclesiastical systems; they eroded the very basis of law and morality. But 'suffering is good for poets', and momentous events form a rich backcloth for a man like Montaigne, who can be seen not merely talking as a philosopher but acting as one. He is sometimes presented as a bookworm: in fact he was anything but that. He tells us that he rarely spent more than an hour at a time with a book; but there are many hours in a lifetime and many an hour for reflections upon one hour's reading.

His sheet anchor remained his Church. He was a firm Roman Catholic. It was his faith in his Church which enabled him to enjoy his universal doubt and to remain himself.

This very awareness of my mutability has had the secondary effect of engendering a certain constancy in my opinions. I have hardly changed any of my first and natural ones, since whatever likelihood novelty may appear to have, I do not change easily, for fear of losing in the exchange. As I do not have the capacity for making a choice myself, I accept Another's choice and remain where God put me. Otherwise I would not know how to save myself from endlessly rolling.

(II, 12)

He could ask deep questions, and revel in his doubt. Where he was wrong the Church could correct him if she would. He accepted her right to censure and to censor (I, 56). But that right was not unlimited; nor was it granted to just any clergyman. When he was in Rome a friendly and powerful cleric, the Maestro di Palazzo of the Vatican, read the *Essays* and suggested changes, leaving Montaigne to do what he thought right. Some changes Montaigne made; in other cases he strengthened his argument, or made his position clearer. But when 'the magistrate' overstepped the mark, rebuking him for having judged that Beza (the successor to Calvin) was an excellent Latin poet, Montaigne stood his ground. He opposed the New Religion, just as he opposed innovation within the State, but he did so without hatred and anger:

I absolutely condemn such defective arguments as, 'He belongs to the League, because he admires the grace of Monsieur de Guise'; 'He is a Huguenot: the activity of the King of Navarre sends him into ecstasies'; 'He finds such-and-such lacking in the manner of the King: at heart he is a traitor.' I did not concede to the magistrate himself that he was right to condemn a book for having named a heretic among the best poets of the age.

(III, 10)

It was this gentleness and reasonableness which won Montaigne deep respect wherever French was read, not least in Anglican England. But he won even greater respect for the guidance which he gave to men and women in search of a sound, wise and moral way to live. As Marc Fumaroli of the Collège de France has so cogently argued, there was a widespread desire in Roman Catholic circles in France – and, one could add, in Anglican circles in England – for a liberal spirituality, free from the constraints of the traditional clerical models and adapted to the circumstances of the independent lives of the laity. Montaigne began with his own self during a period of personal strain and peril: he ended up confidently seeking how men should (by the canons of natural reason and natural wisdom) live well and die well. His *Essays* show us not only what he thought but how he reached his poise and contentment, despite the plague, despite the suicidal pains of the stone, despite the collapse of the State and despite the din of conflicting opinions and the marauding bands around him.

Montaigne's book is not a series of essays but a series of chapters. He first wrote two Books divided into fifty-seven and thirty-seven chapters. The longer chapters contain several 'essays' of his thoughts and opinions. In 1588 he republished his first two Books, making numerous modifications, and added a third one. But he was never satisfied: his *Essays* are not a static work but a process. No sooner had he published those three Books than he set about changing a little and adding much. Death overtook him before he could send his final text to the printer, but it was virtually ready for publication.

In this edition we have a selection of his chapters chosen to give a taste of his thought, style, wit and wisdom. The text follows the practice of French editions and shows how his work progressed; the signs [A] and '80; [A1] and '82; [B] and '88; [C]; and finally ['95] indicate the different layers of his writing, as listed in the *Explanation of the Symbols* at the end of this Introduction. The selection also aims to give some idea of the structure of the *Essays* as a whole. For example, the first and last chapters are given in the case of both Book One and Book Two; all four contribute to the flavour and to the structure of the *Essays* as Montaigne first conceived them. Long before he came to write Book Three Montaigne had abandoned the very short chapter: he found that he could make more satisfactory 'assays' of himself in longer chapters which gave him more scope and allowed for greater depth. The last pages of the last chapter, *On Experience*, represent the sum of his wisdom and the end of his long quest. Those last pages were intended to be read last: they correct, resume, modify or emphasize such glimpses of wisdom as Montaigne had discovered. They tell us how he – and we – can enjoy living richly as human beings into a serene and grateful old age.

Before reaching that great final chapter we are treated to Montaigne's distinguishing between true repentance and mere regret; to insights into his three chief social delights (decent friends, women and books); to his outspoken and at times humorous reflections on sexuality in the surprisingly named chapter *On some lines of Virgil* (III, 5); and to reflections on greed, cruelty and European barbarity when considering the Indies of the Conquistadores in the chapter *On coaches* (III, 6).

On the lame (III, 11) takes us into the ways in which men and women can deceive themselves, using their reason to find 'causes' for phenomena which simply do not exist:

[B] I was recently letting my mind range wildly (as I often do) over our human reason and what a rambling and roving instrument it is. I realize that if you ask people to account for 'facts' they usually spend more time finding reasons for them than finding out whether they are true. They ignore the *whats* and expatiate on the *whys*.   [C]   Wiseacres!

(III, 11)

That is not only an amiable folly: it leads to wretched old women convincing their judges – and themselves – that they are maleficent witches. Opinion, after all, is not certainty; surmises are hazardous and subjective.

[B] There is nothing over which men usually strain harder than when giving free run to their opinions: should the regular means be lacking, we support them with commands, force, fire and sword ... There is a kind of ignorance, strong and magnanimous, which in humour and courage is in no wise inferior to knowledge ... After all, it is to put a very high value on your surmises to roast a man alive for them.

(IV, 11)

But if reason is fallible so too is experience. This very fallibility leads anyone who would be wise to cultivate judgement and to be tentative, circumspect and moderate.

On experience gives us the fruit of Montaigne's judgement on the place of our humanity in the life of every one of us. Montaigne firmly anchors his last chapter in an Aristotelian context. The first sentence of that final chapter echoes the first sentence of one of the most famous of all books. (That sentence was known by heart by schoolboys, let alone by dons and dominies; it comes from Aristotle's *Metaphysics*.)

[B] No desire is more natural than the desire for knowledge.

For Aristotle that truth pointed the way to the mastering of all those arts which are based not on high reason but on lowly experience. Experience (which included experimentation) underlies medicine and common law, which are the 'arts' *par excellence*. Montaigne however is not convinced that experience, without sound judgement, is any better than wayward reason:

[B] Reason has so many forms that we do not know which to resort to: experience has no fewer.

The opening sentence of Aristotle's *Metaphysics* had long been used to prove the existence of an afterlife. Mankind has been given by Nature a desire to know. In this life that desire is never satisfied. Since Nature does

nothing without a cause, there must be a life after this one in which that
desire can indeed be satisfied. By implication Montaigne accepts that
argument: he soon reaches the conclusion that 'there is no end to our
inquiries: our end is in the next world'. Yet, despite his owing much to
Aristotle, Montaigne does not believe that the experience which lies behind
the *Metaphysics* or the *Physics* is in any way a substitute for his own:

> Whatever we may in fact get from experience, such benefit as we derive
> from others' examples will hardly provide us with an elementary education if
> we make so poor a use of such experience as we have presumably enjoyed
> ourselves: that is more familiar to us and certainly enough to instruct us in
> what we need.
>   I study myself more than any other subject. That is my metaphysics; that is
> my physics.
>
> (III, 13)

Montaigne had a very large library, not least for a minor country
nobleman. He delighted in possessing books; he liked being able to turn to
them whenever the spirit moved him. But he had no desire to be learned
for its own sake. His reading, like his reflections upon his experience, had
utilitarian aims: first and always, to afford him pleasure; secondly, and
when possible, to instruct him in ethics:

> From books all I seek is to give myself pleasure from an honourable pastime:
> or if I do study, I seek only that branch of learning which deals with
> knowing myself and which teaches me how to live and die well.
>
> (II, 10)

What a very small number of his books taught him – and what his
experience of himself and of others confirmed – is that our bodies play a
large part in that marriage of body and soul which constitutes the 'being'
of each one of us. But just as in a good marriage each partner must love the
other and tend to the other's necessities, so, too, bodies and souls should
share each other's pains and joys, allowing each to see that its necessities are
duly catered for. A few souls, privileged by grace to have a rapturous
foretaste of God's presence, can virtually ignore their bodies; no one else
should; no one else, with impunity, can. Not even Plato. Not even
Socrates.

Our 'being' consists of body plus soul. Each part has its own dignity. For
the vast majority of mankind wisdom does not consist in trying to send the
soul sallying forth from its body in rapture: it consists in binding the two

together. To act otherwise is to court madness. Anyway, our gross humanity will accompany us everywhere in this life:

Upon the highest throne in the world, we are seated, still, upon our arses.

Within that general rule Montaigne found that each person was wise to live, as far as proper and as far as possible, *secundum se* (in accordance with his own inborn characteristics). He might, if he follows Socrates, strive to re-form his soul: what he will not do is to strive, unaided, to live like an angel. If he does, he will sink to the level of the beast.

Life gives us much to live for; such good things include the Muses. Readers of Montaigne cannot for long ignore his passionate love of poetry. On virtually every page he surprises us with entertaining and apt quotations from poets great and minor. Yet he never crushes us with learning: for erudition you must 'go where such fish are to be caught'.

Montaigne set out to discover himself. He did more than that: he discovered what makes the human race fully human.

ALL SOULS COLLEGE
OXFORD

WHIT SUNDAY 1992

POSTSCRIPT

Since my ordination by the Bishop of Oxford in 1993 I am often asked if I find Montaigne's arguments for his Church still convincing. Clearly not: I was not ordained in his Church; but I do think that Montaigne can still succeed in getting many to take Christianity – and religion in general – seriously.

ALL SOULS COLLEGE
OXFORD

JUNE 2003

Note on the Text

There is no such thing as a definitive edition of the *Essays of Michel de Montaigne*. One has to choose. The *Essays* are a prime example of the expanding book.

The text translated here is an eclectic one, deriving mainly from the corpus of editions clustering round the impressive *Edition municipale* of Bordeaux (1906–20) edited by a team led by Fortunat Strowski. This was further edited and adapted by Pierre Villey (1924); V.-L. Saulnier of the Sorbonne again revised, re-edited and adapted the work for the Presses Universitaires de France (1965). Useful editions were also published by J. Plattard (Société 'Les Belles Lettres', 1947) as well as by A. Thibaudet and M. Rat for the Pléiade (1962). These editions largely supersede all previous ones and have collectively absorbed their scholarship.

I have also used the posthumous editions of 1595, 1598 and 1602 and, since it is good and readily available at All Souls, the *Edition nouvelle* procured in 1617 by Mademoiselle Marie de Gournay, the young admirer and bluestocking to whom Montaigne gave a quasi-legal status as a virtually adopted daughter, a *fille d'alliance*.

The numbering of the essays selected here remains the same as in *The Complete Essays*, since the selection aims to give some idea of the structure of the *Essays* as a whole.

The Annotations

Marie de Gournay first contributed to the annotation of Montaigne by tracing the sources of his verse and other quotations, providing translations of them, and getting a friend to supply headings in the margins.

From that day to this, scholars have added to them. The major source has long been the fourth volume of the Strowski edition, the work of Pierre Villey. It is a masterpiece of patient scholarship and makes recourse to earlier editions largely unnecessary. Most notes of most subsequent editions derive from it rather than from even the fuller nineteenth-century editions subsumed into it. This translation is no exception, though I have made quite a few changes and added my own. Montaigne knew some of his authors very well indeed, but many of his *exempla* and philosophical sayings were widely known from compendia such as Erasmus' *Adages* and *Apophthegmata*. His judgements on women and marriage are sometimes paralleled in a widely read legal work on the subject, the *De legibus connubialibus* of Rabelais' friend Andreas Tiraquellus. Similarly some of his classical and scriptural quotations and philosophical arguments in religious contexts are to be found in such treatises as the *De Anima* of Melanchthon or in the theological books of clergymen of his own Church writing in his own day. I have taken care to point out some of these possible sources, since Montaigne's ideas are better understood when placed in such contexts.

References to Plato, Aristotle, Cicero and Seneca are given more fully than usual. Although Montaigne read Plato in Latin, references are given to the Greek text since most readers will not have access to Ficino's Latin translation. References to Aristotle too are always given to the Greek: that will enable them to be more easily traced in such bilingual editions as the Loeb Classics. For Plutarch's *Moralia* detailed references are given to the first edition of Amyot's translation (*Les Oeuvres morales et meslées*, Paris, 1572); for Plutarch's *Lives* however only general references are given under their English titles (many may like to read them in North's *Plutarch*).

For historical writers of Montaigne's own time only brief references are given. All of them derive from Pierre Villey's studies in which the reader will find much relevant detail: *Les Livres d'histoire modernes utilisés par*

Montaigne, Paris, 1908, and *Les sources et l'évolution des Essais de Montaigne*, Paris, 1908 (second edition 1933). Those books are monuments of scholarship and have not been superseded.

The classical quotations (which from the outset vary slightly from edition to edition of the *Essays*) are normally given as they appear in the Villey/Saulnier edition: most readers discover that the quickest way to find a passage in another edition or translation is to hunt quickly through the chapter looking for the nearest quotation. Once found in the Villey/Saulnier edition a passage can be followed up in the Leake *Concordance* and traced to other standard editions.

My studies of Montaigne have been greatly helped by the kindness of the Librarian of University College London, the Reverend Frederick Friend, who has authorized several volumes to be made available to me on a very long loan. I am most grateful to him and to University College London.

Note on the Translation

═══

I have tried to convey Montaigne's sense and something of his style, without archaisms but without forcing him into an unsuitable, demotic English. I have not found that his meaning is more loyally conveyed by clinging in English to the grammar and constructions of his French: French and English achieve their literary effect by different means. On the other hand I have tried to translate his puns: they clearly mattered to him, and it was fun doing so. Montaigne's sentences are often very long; where the sense does not suffer I have left many of them as they are. It helps to retain something of his savour.

It is seldom possible to translate one word in one language by one only in another. I have striven to do so in two cases vital for the understanding of Montaigne. The first is *essai*, *essayer* and the like: I have rendered these by *essay* or *assay* or the equivalent verbs even if that meant straining English a little. The second is *opinion*. In Montaigne's French, as often in English, *opinion* does not imply that the idea is true: rather the contrary, as in Plato.

Montaigne's numerous quotations are seldom integrated grammatically into his sentences. However long they may be we are meant to read them as asides – mentally holding our breath. I have respected that. To do otherwise would be to rewrite him.

When in doubt, I have given priority to what I take to be the meaning, though never, I hope, losing sight of readability.

Of versions of the Classics Jowett remarked that, 'the slight personification arising out of Greek genders is the greatest difficulty in translation.' In Montaigne's French this difficulty is even greater since his sense of gender enables him to flit in and out of various degrees of personification in ways not open to writers of English. Where the personification is certain or a vital though implied element of the meaning I have sometimes used a capital letter and personal pronouns, etc., to produce a similar effect.

Explanation of the Symbols

===

[A] or '80: all that follows is (ignoring minor variations) what Montaigne published in 1580 (the first edition).

[A1]: all that follows was added subsequently, mainly in 1582 and in any case before [B].

[B] or '88: all that follows shows matter added or altered in 1588, the first major, indeed massive, revision of the *Essays*, which now includes a completely new Third Book.

[C]: all that follows represents an edited version of Montaigne's final edition being prepared for the press when he died. The new material derives mainly from Montaigne's own copy, smothered with additions and changes in his own hand and now in the Bibliothèque Municipale of Bordeaux.

'95: the first posthumous edition prepared for the press by Montaigne's widow and by Marie de Gournay. It gives substantially the text of [C] but with important variants. (The editions of 1598 and 1617 have also been consulted, especially the latter, which contains most useful marginal notes as well as French translations, also by Marie de Gournay, of most of Montaigne's quotations in Classical or foreign languages.)

Summary of the Symbols

[A] and '80: the text of 1580

[A1]: the text of 1582 (plus)

[B] and '88: the text of 1588

[C]: the text of the edition being prepared by Montaigne when he died, 1592

'95: text of the 1595 posthumous printed edition

In the notes there is given a selection of variant readings, including most abandoned in 1588 and many from the printed posthumous edition of 1595.

By far the most scholarly account of the text is that given in R. A. Sayce, *The Essays of Montaigne: A Critical Exploration*, 1972, Chapter 2, 'The Text of the *Essays*'.

Chronology

1477 Raymond Eyquem, a rich merchant in Bordeaux trading in wines and salt fish, purchases the estates of Montaigne.

1497 Birth of Pierre Eyquem (Montaigne's father) at the family estates.

1519 Pierre Eyquem, as a result of deaths in the family, inherits the estates at Montaigne and leaves to fight in Italy, entailing an absence of several years.

1528 Pierre Eyquem marries Antoinette de Louppes, of a rich and politically influential family. The Louppes, a pious Christian family, were descended from Iberian Jews.

1530 Pierre Eyquem is *premier jurat* (first magistrate) and Provost of Bordeaux. Birth of Etienne de la Boëtie.

1533 *28 February*: birth of Michel Eyquem de Montaigne at the family estates.

1534 A brother, Thomas, is born.

1535 Montaigne's German tutor's aim is to make Latin his first language. This continues his father's scheme from the outset.
Another brother, Pierre, is born.

1536 A sister, Jeanne, is born.

1539/40 Montaigne enters the Collège de Guyenne at Bordeaux, where the tutors include Mathurin Cordier, Buchanan (the humanist playwright and future Scottish Reformer) and Elie Vinet. He stays there for six years. His understanding tutors encouraged his delight in Latin poetry. He acquired some Greek, but Latin was his literary language.

1546 Montaigne probably studies philosophy in the Faculty of Arts at Bordeaux.

1548 Civil disobedience and riots in Bordeaux, fiercely suppressed. Mayors now to be elected for periods of two years only. The Huguenots become established and numerous in the City and its environs.

1552 Birth of Montaigne's second sister, Lénor.

1554 Michel follows his father and becomes counsellor at the Cour des Aides at Périgueux. This Cour is suppressed three years later and the counsellors join the Parlement of Bordeaux. His father becomes Mayor of Bordeaux.
Birth of third sister, Marie.

1557/8 Montaigne meets Etienne de la Boëtie, also a member of the Parlement de Bordeaux; their deep and special friendship begins.

1559 Montaigne visits Paris, and follows King Francis II to Bar-le-Duc. Amyot's translation of Plutarch: it greatly influences Montaigne both in thought and style.

1560 Birth of Montaigne's brother Bertrand.

1561 Second visit to Paris and the Royal Court, partly in connection with the serious religious strife in Guyenne.

1562 Proclamation of the *Edict of the Seventeenth of January 1562* granting limited rights of assembly to members of the 'so-called Reformed Church'. In June, Etienne de la Boëtie writes a *mémoire* on that Edict. Montaigne, still in Paris, makes a public profession of Roman Catholicism before the First President of the Parlement de Paris. In October he follows the Royal Army when Rouen is retaken from the Huguenots; he meets there Indians from Brazil. Massacre of Huguenots at Wassy.

1563 *February*: Montaigne returns to Bordeaux.

18 August: death of La Boëtie at Germinant at the home of Montaigne's brother-in-law, Lestonnat. Montaigne writes of it to his father.

Assassination of François de Guise.

1564 *16 October*: Montaigne finishes reading the *De Rerum Natura* of Lucretius and notes at the end the date and 31 (his age). The flyleaves are all covered with dense Latin notes. Several topics in the *Essays* go back to that initial reading. On a subsequent reading Montaigne made many notes on the pages of the text in French. This edition of Lucretius by Lambinus had been published either late in 1563 or early in 1564.

1565 *January*: visit of Charles IX to Bordeaux.

Marriage of Montaigne to Françoise de la Chassaigne, the daughter of a colleague in the Parlement de Bordeaux.

1568 Death of Montaigne's father, Pierre. Montaigne becomes Seigneur de Montaigne and inherits the domain. (Difficulties with his mother over the inheritance.)

1569 Montaigne publishes his French translation of the *Theologia Naturalis* of Raymond Sebond (Raymundus de Sabunde), with the printer G. Chaudière of Paris.

1570 Montaigne sells his counsellorship of the Parlement de Bordeaux. Goes to Paris to publish works left by Etienne de la Boëtie (Latin, then French).

Birth of his first daughter, Toinette, who dies three months later.

1571 Montaigne returns to his estates, to consecrate his life to the Muses: to scholarship, philosophy and reflection. He receives the Ordre de Saint-Michel and is named Gentleman of the Chamber by Charles IX.

Birth of Léonor (the only one of his six daughters to live).

1572 *24 August*: massacre of Saint Bartholomew's Day. Uprisings at La Rochelle (a stronghold of the Reformed Church).

Publication of the French translation of the *Moral Works* of Plutarch by Bishop Amyot. It joins other authors studied by Montaigne in the tower of his château.

1572–4 During the civil wars Montaigne joins the royalist forces. Montaigne dispatched to Bordeaux to advise the Parlement to strengthen their defences.

1574 Anonymous publication (adapted to Reformed propaganda) of La Boëtie's short treatise *De la Servitude volontaire*.

1575 Reads Sextus Empiricus' *Hypotyposes*.

1576 Strikes a medal with the Greek motto *I abstain*. He is working on his *Apology of Raymond Sebond*.

1577 Henri de Navarre names Montaigne Gentleman of the Chamber.

About this time suffers his first attack of the stone.

1580–81 *1 March*: publication of the *Essays* (Simon Millanges, Bordeaux).

Montaigne leaves on his travels. At Paris he offers his book to Henri III, who is delighted with it. On his travels (partly to take the waters) Montaigne visits Plombières, Mülhauser, Basle, Baden, Augsburg, Munich, Innsbruck, the Tyrol, Padua, Venice, Ferrara and Rome (which was reached on 30 November). At Rome his books are impounded, but relations are good. The maestro di Palazzo offers suggestions for changes to be made by Montaigne in his *Essays*, without further interference. Montaigne has an audience of the Pope, Gregory XIII. On his way back he makes a pilgrimage to Loretto and has medals of the Virgin blessed for his wife and daughter as well as himself. Travels via Florence and Pisa and the baths at Lucca.

17 September: leaves on learning that royal approval requires him to become Mayor of Bordeaux.

30 September: arrives home.

1582 Second edition of the *Essays* published with the same publisher.

Gregory XIII reforms the calendar, a reform accepted in France, but not in England.

1583 Montaigne re-elected Mayor of Bordeaux for a further two years.

1582–5 During his Mayoralty Montaigne visits Paris and often stays on his estates. Henri de Navarre, now heir to the throne, visits Montaigne and stays in his château. Montaigne is concerned with high politics as well as local affairs. In 1585 the plague ravages Bordeaux. Montaigne, absent, does not return to the town: he and his family are forced to leave their home, Montaigne, and wander about in search of a safe lodging.

1587 *24 October*. The King of Navarre dines at Montaigne.

1588 *16 February*: Montaigne, en route for Paris, is attacked and robbed by soldiers of *La Ligue*. His goods and freedom are restored to him. His third edition of the *Essays* is published in Paris by L'Angelier.

Mlle de Gournay sends him greetings from her lodgings in Paris. Montaigne visits her. She becomes eventually his *fille d'alliance*, virtually an adopted daughter.

June: publication of the greatly expanded edition of the *Essays*, which now includes a new third book (Paris, L'Angelier).

10 July: Montaigne is arrested in Paris and sent to the Bastille apparently to serve as a hostage. He is restored to freedom the same day by order of Catherine de' Medici.

1589 *2 August*: death of Henri III.

Montaigne begins working on a further expanded edition of the *Essays*.

1590 *18 June*: marriage of Montaigne's daughter Léonor to François de La Tour. Though ill, Montaigne writes to Henri de Navarre (now Henri IV), who replies to him (20 July) and invites him to come as (probably) his adviser.

1591 Birth of Françoise de La Tour, Montaigne's grand-daughter.

1592 *13 September*. death of Montaigne during a Mass said in his bed-chamber.

1595 Montaigne's widow, Pierre de Brach and Marie de Gournay produce the first posthumous edition of the *Essays*, incorporating Montaigne's last additions and changes.

1601 Death of Montaigne's mother.

1613 John Florio's translation of the *Essays*.

The Essays: A Selection

=

To the Reader

═══

[A] You have here, Reader, a book whose faith can be trusted, a book which warns you from the start that I have set myself no other end but a private family one. I have not been concerned to serve you nor my reputation: my powers are inadequate for such a design. I have dedicated this book to the private benefit of my friends and kinsmen so that, having lost me (as they must do soon) they can find here again some traits of my character and of my humours. They will thus keep their knowledge of me more full, more alive. If my design had been to seek the favour of the world I would have decked myself out [C] better and presented myself in a studied gait.[1] [A] Here I want to be seen in my simple, natural, everyday fashion, without [C] striving[2] [A] or artifice: for it is my own self that I am painting. Here, drawn from life, you will read of my defects and my native form so far as respect for social convention allows: for had I found myself among those peoples who are said still to live under the sweet liberty of Nature's primal laws, I can assure you that I would most willingly have portrayed myself whole, and wholly naked.

And therefore, Reader, I myself am the subject of my book: it is not reasonable that you should employ your leisure on a topic so frivolous and so vain.

Therefore, Farewell:

From Montaigne;
this first of March, One thousand, five hundred and eighty.[3]

---

1. '80: myself out, *with borrowed beauties, or would have tensed and braced myself in my best posture.* Here I want . . .
2. '80: Without *study* or artifice . . .
3. Date as in [A] and [C]. In [B]: 12 June 1588.

1. We reach the same end by discrepant means

================

[This first chapter treats of war and history, subjects appropriate to a nobleman. Montaigne introduces the irrational (astonishment, ecstasy and the fury of battle) and shows how unpredictable are the reactions of even great, brave and virtuous men. The verb to assay is used three times; explanations of motives are mere conjecture – what 'could be said'; [A] cites the exemplum *of Conrad III from the foreword to Bodin's* Method towards an Easy Understanding of History, *which Montaigne was reading about 1578. In [B] he adds his own reactions.]*

[A] The most common way of softening the hearts of those we have offended once they have us at their mercy with vengeance at hand is to move them to commiseration and pity [C] by our submissiveness. [A] Yet flat contrary means, bravery and steadfastness,[1] have sometimes served to produce the same effect.

Edward, Prince of Wales[2] – the one who long governed our Guyenne and whose qualities and fortune showed many noteworthy characteristics of greatness – having been offended by the inhabitants of Limoges, took their town by force. The lamentations of the townsfolk, the women and the children left behind to be butchered crying for mercy and throwing themselves at his feet, did not stop him until eventually, passing ever deeper into the town, he noticed three French noblemen who, alone, with unbelievable bravery, were resisting the thrust of his victorious army. Deference and respect for such remarkable valour first blunted the edge of his anger; then starting with those three he showed mercy on all the other inhabitants of the town.

1. '80: means, bravery, steadfastness *and resolution*, have . . .
2. The Black Prince (Limoges, 1370). Sources include Froissart, Paolo Giovio, *Vita di Scanderbeg*; Jean Bodin, *Methodus* (Preface); Plutarch (tr. Amyot), *Comment on peut se louer soy mesme*; *Dicts notables des Roys . . .*; *Instruction pour ceux qui manient les affaires d'estat*; Diodorus Siculus (tr. Amyot), *Histoires*; and Quintus Curtius, *Life of Alexander the Great*.

Scanderbeg, Prince of Epirus, was pursuing one of his soldiers in order to kill him. The soldier, having assayed all kinds of submissiveness and supplications to try and appease him, as a last resort resolved to await him, sword in hand. Such resolution stopped his Master's fury short; having seen him take so honourable a decision he granted him his pardon. (This example will allow of a different interpretation only from those who have not read of the prodigious strength and courage of that Prince.)

The Emperor Conrad III had besieged Guelph, Duke of Bavaria; no matter how base and cowardly were the satisfactions offered him, the most generous condition he would vouchsafe was to allow the noblewomen who had been besieged with the Duke to come out honourably on foot, together with whatever they could carry on their persons. They, with greatness of heart, decided to carry out on their shoulders their husbands, their children and the Duke himself. The Emperor took such great pleasure at seeing the nobility of their minds that he wept for joy and quenched all the bitterness of that mortal deadly hatred he had harboured against the Duke; from then on he treated him and his family kindly.

[B] Both of these means would have swayed me easily, for I have a marvellous weakness towards mercy and clemency – so much so that I would be more naturally moved by compassion than by respect. Yet for the Stoics pity is a vicious emotion: they want us to succour the afflicted but not to give way and commiserate with them.

[A] Now these examples seem to me to be even more to the point in that souls which have been assaulted and assayed by both those methods can be seen to resist one without flinching only to bow to the other.

It could be said that for one's mind to yield to pity is an effect of affability, gentleness – and softness (that is why weaker natures such as those of women, children and the common-people are more subject to them) – whereas, disdaining [C] tears [A] and supplications[3] and then yielding only out of respect for the holy image of valour is the action of a strong, unbending soul, reserving its good-will and honour for stubborn, masculine vigour. Yet ecstatic admiration and amazement can produce a similar effect in the less magnanimous. Witness the citizens of Thebes: they had impeached their captains on capital charges for having extended their mandates beyond the period they had prescribed and preordained for them; they were scarcely able to pardon Pelopidas, who, bending beneath the weight of such accusations, used only petitions and supplications in his defence, whereas on the contrary when Epaminondas

3. '80: disdaining *prayers* and . . .

came and gloriously related the deeds he had done and reproached the people with them proudly [C] and arrogantly, [A] they had no heart for even taking the ballots into their hands: the meeting broke up, greatly praising the high-mindedness of that great figure.

[C] The elder Dionysius had captured, after long delays and extreme difficulties, the town of Rhegium together with its commander Phyton, an outstanding man who had stubbornly defended it. He resolved to make him into a terrible example of vengeance. Dionysius first told him how he had, the previous day, drowned his son and all his relations. Phyton merely replied that they were happier than he was, by one day. Next he had him stripped, seized by executioners and dragged through the town while he was flogged, cruelly and ignominiously, and plied with harsh and shameful insults. But Phyton's heart remained steadfast and he did not give way; on the contrary, with his face set firm he loudly recalled the honourable and glorious cause of his being condemned to death – his refusal to surrender his country into the hands of a tyrant – and he threatened Dionysius with swift punishment from the gods. Dionysius read in the eyes of the mass of his soldiers that, instead of being provoked by the taunts which this vanquished enemy made at the expense of their leader and of his triumph, they were thunder-struck by so rare a valour, beginning to soften, wondering whether to mutiny, and ready to snatch Phyton from the hands of his guards; so he brought Phyton's martyrdom to an end and secretly sent him to be drowned in the sea.

[A] Man is indeed an object miraculously vain, various and wavering. It is difficult to found a judgement on him which is steady and uniform. Here you have Pompey pardoning the entire city of the Mamertines, against whom he was deeply incensed, out of consideration for the valour and great-heartedness of Zeno,[4] a citizen who assumed full responsibility for the public wrong-doing and who begged no other favour than alone to bear the punishment for it. Yet that host of Sylla showed similar bravery in the city of Perugia and gained nothing thereby, neither for himself nor for the others.

[B] And, directly against my first examples, Alexander, the staunchest of men and the most generous towards the vanquished, stormed, after great hardship, the town of Gaza and came across Betis who commanded it; of his valour during the siege he had witnessed staggering proofs; now Betis was alone, deserted by his own men, his weapons shattered; all covered with blood and wounds, he was still fighting in the midst of several

4. Not Zeno, Stheno.

Macedonians who were slashing at him on every side. Alexander was irritated by so dearly won a victory (among other losses he had received two fresh wounds in his own body); he said to him: 'You shall not die as you want to, Betis! Take note that you will have to suffer every kind of torture which can be thought up against a prisoner!' To these menaces Betis (not only looking assured but contemptuous and proud) replied not a word. Then Alexander, seeing his haughty and stubborn silence, said: 'Has he bent his knee? Has he let a word of entreaty slip out? Truly I will overcome that refusal of yours to utter a sound: if I cannot wrench a word from you I will at least wrench a groan.' And as his anger turned to fury he ordered his heels to be pierced[5] and, dragging him alive behind a cart, had him lacerated and dismembered.

Was it because [C]   bravery was so usual for him[6] that   [B]   he was never struck with wonder by it and therefore respected it less?   [C]   Or was it because he thought bravery to be so properly his own that he could not bear to see it at such a height in anyone else without anger arising from an emotion of envy; or did the natural violence of his anger allow of no opposition? Truly if his anger could ever have suffered a bridle it is to be believed that it would have done so during the storming and sack of Thebes, at seeing so many valiant men put to the sword, men lost and with no further means of collective defence. For a good six thousand of them were killed, none of whom was seen to run away or to beg for mercy; on the contrary all were seeking, here and there about the streets, to confront the victorious enemy and to provoke them into giving them an honourable death. None was so overcome with wounds that he did not assay with his latest breath to wreak revenge and to find consolation for his own death in the death of an enemy. Yet their afflicted valour evoked no pity; a day was not long enough to slake the vengeance of Alexander: this carnage lasted until the very last drop of blood remained to be spilt; it spared only those who were disarmed – the old men, women and children – from whom were drawn thirty thousand slaves.

5. '80: pierced, *a rope threaded through them*, and, . . .
6. '80: because *strength of courage was so natural and usual to* him . . .

8. On idleness

===

[The Essays *were started to tame melancholic delusions induced by Montaigne's withdrawal to his estates, when his thoughts galloped away with him much as Milton later describes in* Il Penseroso *as being typical of the melancholic in his lonely tower.]*

[A]   Just as fallow lands, when rich and fertile, are seen to abound in hundreds and thousands of different kinds of useless weeds so that, if we would make them do their duty, we must subdue them and keep them busy with seeds specifically sown for our service; and just as women left alone may sometimes be seen to produce shapeless lumps of flesh but need to be kept busy by a semen other than her own in order to produce good natural offspring: so too with our minds.[1] If we do not keep them busy with some particular subject which can serve as a bridle to reign them in, they charge ungovernably about, ranging to and fro over the wastelands of our thoughts:

> [B]   *Sicut aquae tremulum labris ubi lumen ahenis*
> *Sole repercussum, aut radiantis imagine Lunae*
> *Omnia pervolitat late loca jamque sub auras*
> *Erigitur, summique ferit laquearia tecti.*

[As when ruffled water in a bronze pot reflects the light of the sun and the shining face of the moon, sending shimmers flying high into the air and striking against the panelled ceilings.][2]

[A]   Then, there is no madness, no raving lunacy, which such agitations do not bring forth:

> *velut ægri somnia, vanæ*
> *Finguntur species.*

[they fashion vain apparitions as in the dreams of sick men.][3]

---

1. The human egg not yet having been discovered, many believed with Galen that children were produced by an intermingling of a (weaker) female semen with the male's. By itself the female semen could at times produce *moles*, a misshapen lump. (Montaigne found the idea developed in Plutarch's *Matrimonial Precepts*, which La Boëtie translated, and which Montaigne published in 1571.)
2. Virgil, *Aeneid*, VIII, 22.
3. Horace, *Ars poetica*, 7.

When the soul is without a definite aim she gets lost; for, as they say, if you are everywhere you are nowhere.

[B]   *Quisquis ubique habitat, Maxime, nusquam habitat.*

[Whoever dwells everywhere, Maximus, dwells nowhere at all.][4]

Recently I retired to my estates, determined to devote myself as far as I could to spending what little life I have left quietly and privately; it seemed to me then that the greatest favour I could do for my mind was to leave it in total idleness, caring for itself, concerned only with itself, calmly thinking of itself. I hoped it could do that more easily from then on, since with the passage of time it had grown mature and put on weight.

But I find –

Variam semper dant otia mentis

[Idleness always produces fickle changes of mind][5]

– that on the contrary it bolted off like a runaway horse, taking far more trouble over itself than it ever did over anyone else; it gives birth to so many chimeras and fantastic monstrosities, one after another, without order or fitness, that, so as to contemplate at my ease their oddness and their strangeness, I began to keep a record of them, hoping in time to make my mind ashamed of itself.[6]

4. Martial, VII, lxxiii.
5. Lucan, *Pharsalia*, IV, 704.
6. Montaigne's terms are the technical ones of melancholy madness. Cf. for example Milton's *Ode to Melancholy*, where the English equivalents occur.

16. On punishing cowardice

[Renaissance Jurisconsults such as Tiraquellus were concerned to temper the severity of the Law by examining motives and human limitations. Montaigne does so here in a matter of great concern to gentlemen in time of war.]

[A] I once heard a prince, a very great general, maintain that a soldier should not be condemned to death for cowardice: he was at table, being told about the trial of the Seigneur de Vervins who was sentenced to death for surrendering Boulogne.

In truth it is reasonable that we should make a great difference between defects due to our weakness and those due to our wickedness. In the latter we deliberately brace ourselves against reason's rules, which are imprinted on us by Nature; in the former it seems we can call Nature herself as a defence-witness for having left us so weak and imperfect. That is why a great many[1] people believe that we can only be punished for deeds done against our conscience: on that rule is partly based the opinion of those who condemn the capital punishment of heretics and misbelievers as well as the opinion that a barrister or a judge cannot be arraigned if they fail in their duty merely from ignorance.

Where cowardice is concerned the usual way is, certainly, to punish it by disgrace and ignominy. It is said that this rule was first introduced by Charondas the lawgiver, and that before his time the laws of Greece condemned to death those who had fled from battle, whereas he ordered that they be made merely to sit for three days in the market-place dressed as women:[2] he hoped he could still make use of them once he had restored their courage by this disgrace — [C] 'Suffundere malis hominis sanguinem quam effundere.' [Make the blood of a bad man blush not gush.][3]

[A] It seems too that in ancient times the laws of Rome condemned deserters to death: Ammianus Marcellinus tells how the Emperor Julian

---

1. Until [C] the misprint peu de gens (for prou de gens) made this read: few people (which inverts the sense).
2. Diodorus Siculus, Histoires (tr. Amyot), XII, ix.
3. Tertullian, cited by Justus Lipsius, Adversus dialogistam, III.

condemned ten of his soldiers to be stripped of their rank and then suffer death, 'following,' he said, 'our Ancient laws'. Elsewhere however Julian for a similar fault condemned others to remain among the prisoners under the ensign in charge of the baggage.[4] [C] Even the harsh sentences decreed against those who had fled at Cannae and those who in that same war had followed Gnaeus Fulvius in his defeat did not extend to death.

Yet it is to be feared that disgrace, by making men desperate, may make them not merely estranged but hostile.

[A] When our fathers were young the Seigneur de Franget, formerly a deputy-commander in the Company of My Lord Marshal de Châtillon, was sent by My Lord Marshal de Chabannes to replace the Seigneur Du Lude as Governor of Fuentarabia; he surrendered it to the Spaniards. He was sentenced to be stripped of his nobility, both he and his descendants being pronounced commoners, liable to taxation and unfit to bear arms. That severe sentence was executed at Lyons. Later all the noblemen who were at Guyse when the Count of Nassau entered it suffered a similar punishment; and subsequently others still.[5]

Anyway, wherever there is a case of ignorance so crass and of cowardice so flagrant as to surpass any norm, that should be an adequate reason for accepting them as proof of wickedness and malice, to be punished as such.

4. Ammianus Marcellinus, *Res gestae*, XXIV, iv, and XXV, i.
5. The Du Bellay *Mémoires*, II, 52; VII, 217.

18. On fear

===

[Montaigne discusses fear, partly in the light of his own experience in war, partly from exempla. He sees it as often leading to mad, ecstatic behaviour: it was indeed to be classed as a case of rapture or of madness, the frightened man being 'beside himself'.]

[A] *Obstupui, steteruntque comae, et vox faucibus haesit.*

[I stood dumb with fear; my hair stood on end and my voice stuck in my throat.][1]

I am not much of a 'natural philosopher' – that is the term they use; I have hardly any idea of the mechanisms by which fear operates in us; but it is a very odd emotion all the same; doctors say that there is no emotion which more readily ravishes our judgement from its proper seat. I myself have seen many men truly driven out of their minds by fear, and it is certain that, while the fit lasts, fear engenders even in the most staid of men a terrifying confusion.

I leave aside simple folk, for whom fear sometimes conjures up visions of their great-grandsires rising out of their graves still wrapped in their shrouds, or else of chimeras, werewolves or goblins; but even among [C] soldiers,[2] [A] where fear ought to be able to find very little room, how many times have I seen it change a flock of sheep into a squadron of knights in armour; reeds or bulrushes into men-at-arms and lancers; our friends, into enemies; a white cross into a red one.

When Monsieur de Bourbon captured Rome, a standard-bearer who was on guard at the Burgo San Pietro was [C] seized by [A] such terror[3] at the first alarm that he leapt through a gap in the ruins and rushed out of the town straight for the enemy still holding his banner; he thought he was running into the town, but at the very last minute he just managed to see the troops of Monsieur de Bourbon drawing up their ranks ready to

---

1. Virgil, *Aeneid*, II, 774.
2. '80: even among *warriors* where . . . (Many melancholics were prone to visions of chimeras and bugaboos).
3. '80: was *held* by such terror . . . (Du Bellay, *Mémoires*, III, 75.)

resist him (it was thought that the townsfolk were making a sortie); he realized what he was doing and headed back through the very same gap out of which he had just made a three-hundred-yards' dash into the battlefield.

But the standard-bearer of Captain Juille was not so lucky when Saint-Pol was taken from us by Count de Bures and the Seigneur de Reu; for fear had made him so distraught that he dashed out of the town, banner and all, through a gun-slit and was cut to pieces by the attacking soldiers. There was another memorable case during the same siege, when fear so strongly seized the heart of a certain nobleman, freezing it and strangling it, that he dropped down dead in the breach without even being wounded.[4]

[C] Such fear can sometimes take hold of a great crowd. [B] In one of the engagements between Germanicus and the Allemani two large troops of soldiers took fright and fled opposite ways, one fleeing to the place which the other had just fled from.[5]

[A] Sometimes fear as in the first two examples puts wings on our heels; at others it hobbles us and nails our feet to the ground, as happened to the Emperor Theophilus in the battle which he lost against the Agarenes; we read that he was so enraptured and so beside himself with fear, that he could not even make up his mind to run away: [B] *'adeo pavor etiam auxilia formidat'* [so much does fear dread even help].[6] [A] Eventually Manuel, one of the foremost commanders of his army, shook him and pulled him roughly about as though rousing him from a profound sleep, saying, 'If you will not follow me I will kill you; the loss of your life matters less than the loss of the Empire if you are taken prisoner.'

[C] Fear reveals her greatest power when she drives us to perform in her own service those very deeds of valour of which she robbed our duty and our honour. In the first pitched battle which the Romans lost to Hannibal during the consulship of Sempronius, an army of ten thousand foot-soldiers took fright, but seeing no other way to make their cowardly escape they fought their way through the thick of the enemy, driving right through them with incredible energy, slaughtering a large number of

4. Du Bellay, *Mémoires*, VIII, 255.
5. '88: Such *madness* can sometimes take hold of *entire armies*; – [B] (until [C]): Allemani, *fear being spread among their army*, two . . . (Tacitus, *Hist.*, I, lxiii.)
6. Quintus Curtius, III, ii. The general account is from Joannes Zonaras, *Historia*, III.

Carthaginians but paying the same price for a shameful flight as they should have done for a glorious victory.[7]

It is fear that I am most afraid of. In harshness it surpasses all other mischances.   ['95]   What emotion could ever be more powerful or more appropriate than that felt by the friends of Pompey who were aboard a ship with him and witnessed that horrible massacre of his forces? Yet even that emotion was stifled by their fear of the Egyptian sails as they began to draw nearer; it was noticed that his friends had no time for anything but urging the sailors to strive to save them by rowing harder; but after they touched land at Tyre their fear left them and they were free to turn their thoughts to the losses they had just suffered and to give rein to those tears and lamentations which that stronger emotion of fear had kept in abeyance.

Tum pavor sapientiam omnem mihi ex animo expectorat.

[Then fear banishes all wisdom from my heart.][8]

[C]   Men who have suffered a good mauling in a military engagement, all wounded and bloody as they are, can be brought back to the attack the following day; but men who have tasted real fear cannot be brought even to look at the enemy again. People with a pressing fear of losing their property or of being driven into exile or enslaved also lose all desire to eat, drink or sleep, whereas those who are actually impoverished, banished or enslaved often enjoy life as much as anyone else. And many people, unable to withstand the stabbing pains of fear, have hanged themselves, drowned themselves or jumped to their deaths, showing us that fear is even more importunate and unbearable than death.

The Greeks acknowledged another species of fear over and above that fear caused when our reason is distraught; it comes, they say, from some celestial impulsion, without any apparent cause.[9] Whole peoples have been seized by it as well as whole armies. Just such a fear brought wondrous desolation to Carthage: nothing was heard but shouts and terrified voices; people were seen dashing out of their houses as if the alarm had been sounded; they began attacking, wounding and killing each other, as though they took each other for enemies come to occupy their city. All was

7. Livy, *Annal.*, XXI, lvi.
8. Cicero: *Tusc. disput.*, III, xxvii, 66. (The event figures in Shakespeare's *Antony and Cleopatra*.) Then ibid., IV, viii, 19, citing Ennius.
9. Diodorus Siculus, XV, vii.

disorder and tumult until they had calmed the anger of their gods with prayer and sacrifice.

Such outbursts are called 'Panic terrors'.[10]

10. Cf. Erasmus, *Adages*, III, VIII, III, *Panicus casus*; also *Apophthegmata*, V; *Epaminondas*, I.

20. To philosophize is to learn how to die

[*Montaigne comes to terms with his melancholy, now somewhat played down. He remains preoccupied with that fear of death — fear that is of the often excruciating act of dying — which in older times seems to have been widespread and acute. His treatment is rhetorical but not impersonal. The [C] text may be influenced by the advice of the Vatican censor. The philosophical presuppositions of this chapter are largely overturned at the end of the Essays (in III, 13, 'On experience'). Montaigne is on the way to discovering admirable qualities in common men and women. His starting-point here is Socratic: philosophy (by detaching the soul from the body) is a 'practising of death'; [C] introduces an Epicurean concern with pleasure.*]

[A] Cicero says that philosophizing is nothing other than getting ready to die.[1] That is because study and contemplation draw our souls somewhat outside ourselves, keeping them occupied away from the body, a state which both resembles death and which forms a kind of apprenticeship for it; or perhaps it is because all the wisdom and argument in the world eventually come down to one conclusion; which is to teach us not to be afraid of dying.

In truth, either reason is joking or her target must be our happiness; all the labour of reason must be to make us live well, and at our ease, as Holy [C] Scripture [A] says.[2] All the opinions in the world reach the same point, [C] that pleasure is our target [A] even though they may get there by different means; otherwise we would throw them out

---

1. Cicero, *Tusc. disput.*, I, xxx, 74–xxxi, 75. In Plato (*Phaedo* 67D) for Socrates, whom Cicero is following, *to philosophize* is *to practise dying*. However, Cicero translates 'practice' not by *meditatio*, which means that, but by *commentatio*, which means a careful preparation. Montaigne is here echoing Cicero, not Socrates directly, and so lessens the element of ecstasy implied by Socrates.

2. '80: as the Holy *Word* says . . .

Montaigne is at best paraphrasing not citing Scripture: cf. Ecclesiastes 3:12; 5:17; 9:7; also Ecclesiasticus 14:14 (no New Testament text is relevant). Several inscriptions in Montaigne's library prove that he was citing either or both of Ecclesiastes and Ecclesiasticus from some untraced intermediary source.

immediately, for who would listen to anyone whose goal was to achieve for us   [C]   pain and suffering?[3]

In this case the disagreements between the schools of philosophy are a matter of words. 'Transcurramus solertissimas nugas.' [Let us skip quickly through those most frivolous trivialities.][4] More stubbornness and prickliness are there than is appropriate for so dedicated a vocation, but then, no matter what role a man may assume, he always plays his own part within it.

Even in virtue our ultimate aim — no matter what they say — is pleasure. I enjoy bashing people's ears with that word which runs so strongly counter to their minds. When pleasure is taken to mean the most profound delight and an exceeding happiness it is a better companion to virtue than anything else; and rightly so. Such pleasure is no less seriously pleasurable for being more lively, taut, robust and virile. We ought to have given virtue the more favourable, noble and natural name of pleasure not (as we have done) a name derived from vis (vigour).[5]

There is that lower voluptuous pleasure which can only be said to have a disputed claim to the name not a privileged right to it. I find it less pure of lets and hindrances than virtue. Apart from having a savour which is fleeting, fluid and perishable, it has its vigils, fasts and travails, its blood and its sweat; it also has its own peculiar sufferings, which are sharp in so many different ways and accompanied by a satiety of such weight that it amounts to repentance.[6]

Since we reckon that obstacles serve as a spur to that pleasure and as seasoning to its sweetness (on the grounds that in Nature contraries are enhanced by their contraries) we are quite wrong to say when we turn to virtue that identical obstacles and difficulties overwhelm her, making her austere and inaccessible, whereas (much more appropriately than for voluptuous pleasure) they ennoble, sharpen and enhance that holy, perfect pleasure which virtue procures for us. A man is quite unworthy of an acquaintance with virtue who weighs her fruit against the price she exacts; he knows neither her graces nor her ways. Those who proceed to teach us

3. '80: for us our torment. Now there are no means of reaching this point, of fashioning a solid contentment, unless it frees us from the fear of death.   [A]   That is why . . .
4. Seneca, Epist. moral., CXVII, 30.
5. On Cicero's authority (Tusc. disput., II, xviii, 43), virtus, the Latin word for virtue, was normally derived from vir (man) not from vis, (strength). True virtue, in this sense, was 'manliness'. (Same etymology: Essays, II, 7.)
6. Philosophical pleasure (quite ascetic in Epicurus) is contrasted here with sexual pleasure.

that the questing after virtue is rugged and wearisome whereas it is delightful to possess her can only mean that she always lacks delight.[7] (For what human means have ever brought anyone to the joy of possessing her?) Even the most perfect of men have been satisfied with aspiring to her – not possessing her but drawing near to her. The contention is wrong, seeing that in every pleasure known to Man the very pursuit of it is pleasurable: the undertaking savours of the quality of the object it has in view; it effectively constitutes a large proportion of it and is consubstantial with it. There is a happiness and blessedness radiating from virtue; they fill all that appertains to her and every approach to her, from the first way in to the very last barrier.

Now one of virtue's main gifts is a contempt for death, which is the means of furnishing our life with easy tranquillity, of giving us a pure and friendly taste for it; without it every other pleasure is snuffed out. [A]   That is why all rules meet and concur in this one clause.[8]   [C]   It is true that they all lead us by common accord to despise pain, poverty and the other misfortunes to which human lives are subject, but they do not do so with the same care. That is partly because such misfortunes are not inevitable. (Most of Mankind spend their lives without tasting poverty; some without even experiencing pain or sickness, like Xenophilus the musician, who lived in good health to a hundred and six.) It is also because, if the worse comes to worse, we can sheer off the bung of our misfortunes whenever we like: death can end them.[9] But, as for death itself, that is inevitable.

> [B]   *Omnes eodem cogimur, omnium*
> *Versatur urna, serius ocius*
> *Sors excitura et nos in æter-*
> *Num exitium impositura cymbæ.*

[All of our lots are shaken about in the Urn, destined sooner or later to be cast forth, placing us in Charon's skiff for everlasting exile.][10]

7. In the great myth of Hesiod, the father of Greek mythology (*Works and Days*, 289), the upward path to Virtue is steep and rugged: once attained, her dwelling-place is a delightful plateau. (Cf. Rabelais, *Quart Livre*, LVII, Joachim Du Bellay, *Regrets*, TLF, 3. 3.) Montaigne is rare in challenging the truth of the myth: most accepted it, often with a Christian sense.

8. '80: That is why all *Schools of Philosophy* meet and concur in this one clause, *teaching us to despise it* [i.e., death]. It is true . . .

9. The last resort of the Stoic: suicide. (Xenophilus' longevity was proverbial.)

10. Horace, *Odes*, II, iii, 25.

[A]   And so if death makes us afraid, that is a subject of continual torment which nothing can assuage.   [C]   There is no place where death cannot find us – even if we constantly twist our heads about in all directions as in a suspect land: *'Quae quasi saxum Tantalo semper impendet.'* [It is like the rock for ever hanging over the head of Tantalus.]¹¹   [A]   Our assizes often send prisoners to be executed at the scene of their crimes. On the way there, take them past fair mansions and ply them with good cheer as much as you like –

> [B]   . . . *non Siculæ dapes*
> *Dulcem elaborabunt saporem,*
> *Non avium cytharæque cantus*
> *Somnum reducent –*

[even Sicilian banquets produce no sweet savours; not even the music of birdsong nor of lyre can bring back sleep] –

[A]   do you think they can enjoy it or that having the final purpose of their journey ever before their eyes will not spoil their taste for such entertainment?

> [B]   *Audit iter, numeratque dies, spacioque viarum*
> *Metitur vitam, torquetur peste futura*

[He inquires about the way; he counts the days; the length of his life is the length of those roads. He is tortured by future anguish.]¹²

[A]   The end of our course is death.¹³ It is the objective necessarily within our sights. If death frightens us how can we go one step forward without anguish? For ordinary people the remedy is not to think about it; but what brutish insensitivity can produce so gross a blindness? They lead the donkey by the tail:

> *Qui capite ipse suo instituit vestigia retro.*

[They walk forward with their heads turned backwards.]¹⁴

---

11. Cicero, *De finibus*, I, xviii, 60; Erasmus, *Adages*, II, IX, VII, *Tantali lapis* (a boulder was ever about to fall on Tantalus' head but never did, keeping him in suspense for all eternity).
12. [A] until [C]: past *all* fair mansions of *France*, and ply them . . . (Horace, *Odes*, I, xviii; Claudian, *In Ruffinum*, II, 137.)
13. Contrast III, 12, in which Montaigne denies that death is the end to which our life aims (its *'but'*) but merely its ending (*'bout'*).
14. Lucretius, IV, 472.

No wonder that they often get caught in a trap. You can frighten such people simply by mentioning death (most of them cross themselves as when the Devil is named); and since it is mentioned in wills, never expect them to draw one up before the doctor has pronounced the death-sentence. And then, in the midst of pain and terror, God only knows what shape their good judgement kneads it into!

[B] (That syllable 'death' struck Roman ears too roughly; the very word was thought to bring ill-luck, so they learned to soften and dilute it with periphrases. Instead of saying *He is dead* they said *He has ceased to live* or *He has lived*. They [C] found consolation in [B] living, even in a past tense! Whence our 'late' (*feu*) So-and-So: 'he was' So-and-So.)[15]

[A] Perhaps it is a case of, 'Repayment delayed means money in hand', as they say; I was born between eleven and noon on the last day of February, one thousand five hundred and thirty-three (as we date things nowadays, beginning the year in January);[16] it is exactly a fortnight since I became thirty-nine: 'I ought to live at least as long again; meanwhile it would be mad to think of something so far off.' – Yes, but all leave life in the same circumstances, young and old alike. [C] Everybody goes out as though he had just come in. [A] Moreover, however decrepit a man may be, he thinks he still has another [C] twenty years [A] to go[17] in the body, so long as he has Methuselah ahead of him. Silly fool, you! Where your life is concerned, who has decided the term? You are relying on doctors' tales; look at facts and experience instead. As things usually go, you have been living for some time now by favour extraordinary. You have already exceeded the usual term of life; to prove it, just count how many more of your acquaintances have died younger than you are compared with those who have reached your age. Just make a list of people who have ennobled their lives by fame: I wager that we shall find more who died before thirty-five than after. It is full of reason and piety to take as our example the manhood of Jesus Christ: his life ended at thirty-

15. Montaigne believed that *feu* ('the late') derived from *fut* ('he was'). That is a false etymology. But the Romans could indeed say *vixit* ('he has lived') to mean, 'he is dead' or 'he has died'.

[B]: They *were happy with* living . . .

16. Traditionally the year began at Easter (or thereabouts). Dating the year from the first of January, a Roman practice, was decreed in France in 1565 and generally applied in 1567.

17. '80: another *year more* to go . . .

three.[18] The same term applies to Alexander, the greatest man who was simply man.

Death can surprise us in so many ways:

> *Quid quisque vitet, nunquam homini satis*
> *Cautum est in horas.*

[No man knows what dangers he should avoid from one hour to another.][19]

Leaving aside fevers and pleurisies, who would ever have thought that a Duke of Brittany was to be crushed to death in a crowd, as one was during the state entry into Lyons of Pope Clement, who came from my part of the world! Have you not seen one of our kings killed at sport? And was not one of his ancestors killed by a bump from a pig? Aeschylus was warned against a falling house; he was always on the alert, but in vain: he was killed by the shell of a tortoise which slipped from the talons of an eagle in flight. Another choked to death on a pip from a grape; an Emperor died from a scratch when combing his hair; Aemilius Lepidus, from knocking his foot on his own doorstep; Aufidius from bumping into a door of his Council chamber. Those who died between a woman's thighs include Cornelius Gallus, a praetor; Tigillinus, a captain of the Roman Guard; Ludovico, the son of Guy di Gonzaga, the Marquis of Mantua; and – providing even worse examples – Speucippus the Platonic philosopher, and one of our Popes.[20]

Then there was that wretched judge Bebius; he was just granting a week's extra time to a litigant when he died of a seizure: his own time had run out. Caius Julius, a doctor, was putting ointment on the eyes of a patient when death closed his.[21] And if I may include a personal example, Captain Saint-Martin, my brother, died at the age of twenty-three while playing tennis; he was felled by a blow from a tennis-ball just above the right ear. There was no sign of bruising or of a wound. He did not even sit

18. Christ incarnate was God and Man, immortal as touching his Godhead, mortal as touching his Manhood. (Thirty-three is a traditional age of Christ at the Crucifixion.)

19. Horace, *Odes*, II, xiii, 13–14.

20. Lists like these were common in Renaissance compilations and handbooks. Montaigne is partly following here Ravisius Textor's *Officina* ('Workshop'). The lecherous Pope was Clement V (early fourteenth century); the French king killed in a tournament (1559) was Henry II; his ancestor killed by a pig was Philip, the crowned son, who never reigned, of Louis the Fat.

21. Two *exempla* from Pliny, VII, liii.

down or take a rest; yet five or six hours later he was dead from an apoplexy caused by that blow.

When there pass before our eyes examples such as these, so frequent and so ordinary, how can we ever rid ourselves of thoughts of death or stop imagining that death has us by the scruff of the neck at every moment?

You might say: 'But what does it matter how you do it, so long as you avoid pain?' I agree with that. If there were any way at all of sheltering from Death's blows – even by crawling under the skin of a calf – I am not the man to recoil from it. It is enough for me to spend my time contentedly. I deal myself the best hand I can, and then accept it. It can be as inglorious or as unexemplary as you please:

> *prætulerim delirus inersque videri,*
> *Dum mea delectent mala me, vel denique fallant,*
> *Quam sapere et ringi.*

[I would rather be delirious or a dullard if my faults pleased me, or at least deceived me, rather than to be wise and snarling.][22]

But it is madness to think you can succeed that way. They come and they go and they trot and they dance: and never a word about death. All well and good. Yet when death does come – to them, their wives, their children, their friends – catching them unawares and unprepared, then what storms of passion overwhelm them, what cries, what fury, what despair! Have you ever seen anything brought so low, anything so changed, so confused?

We must start providing for it earlier. Even if such brutish indifference could find lodgings in the head of an intelligent man (which seems quite impossible to me) it sells its wares too dearly. If death were an enemy which could be avoided I would counsel borrowing the arms of cowardice. But it cannot be done. [B] Death can catch you just as easily as a coward on the run or as an honourable man:

> [A] *Nempe et fugacem persequitur virum,*
> *Nec parcit imbellis juventæ*
> *Poplitibus, timidoque tergo;*

[It hounds the man who runs away, and it does not spare the legs or fearful backs of unwarlike youth;]

22. Horace, *Epistles*, II, ii, 126–8.

[B]   no tempered steel can protect your shoulders;

> *Ille licet ferro cautus se condat ære,*
> *Mors tamen inclusum protrahet inde caput;*

[No use a man hiding prudently behind iron or brass:
Death will know how to make him stick out his cowering head;][23]

[A]   we must learn to stand firm and to fight it.

To begin depriving death of its greatest advantage over us, let us adopt a way clean contrary to that common one; let us deprive death of its strangeness; let us frequent it, let us get used to it; let us have nothing more often in mind than death. At every instant let us evoke it in our imagination under all its aspects. Whenever a horse stumbles, a tile falls or a pin pricks however slightly, let us at once chew over this thought: 'Supposing that was death itself?' With that, let us brace ourselves and make an effort. In the midst of joy and feasting let our refrain be one which recalls our human condition. Let us never be carried away by pleasure so strongly that we fail to recall occasionally how many are the ways in which that joy of ours is subject to death or how many are the fashions in which death threatens to snatch it away. That is what the Egyptians did: in the midst of all their banquets and good cheer they would bring in a mummified corpse to serve as a warning to the guests:[24]

> *Omnem crede diem tibi diluxisse supremum.*
> *Grata superveniet, quæ non sperabitur hora.*

[Believe that each day is the last to shine on you. If it comes, time not hoped for will be welcome indeed.][25]

We do not know where death awaits us: so let us wait for it everywhere. To practise death is to practise freedom. A man who has learned how to die has unlearned how to be a slave. Knowing how to die gives us freedom from subjection and constraint.   [C] Life has no evil for him who has thoroughly understood that loss of life is not an evil.   [A] Paulus Aemilius was sent a messenger by that wretched King of Macedonia who was his prisoner, begging not to be led in his triumphant procession. He replied: 'Let him beg that favour from himself.'

It is true that, in all things, if Nature does not lend a hand art and

---

23. Horace, *Epistles*, III, ii, 14–17; Propertius, IV, xviii, 25.
24. Plutarch (tr. Amyot), *Banquet des Sept Sages*, 1515A.
25. Horace, *Epistles*, I, iv, 13–14. Then echoes of Seneca's *Epist. moral.*, I, lxxxviii, 25, and of Plutarch's *Life of Paulus Aemilius.*

industry do not progress very far. I myself am not so much melancholic as an idle dreamer: from the outset there was no topic I ever concerned myself with more than with thoughts about death – even in the most licentious period of my life.

> [B] *Jucundum cum aetas florida ver ageret.*
>
> [When my blossoming youth rejoiced in spring.]²⁶

[A]   Among the games and the courting many thought I was standing apart chewing over some jealousy or the uncertainty of my aspirations: meanwhile I was reflecting on someone or other who, on leaving festivities just like these, had been surprised by a burning fever and   [C]   his end,   [A]   with his head²⁷ full of idleness, love and merriment – just like me; and the same could be dogging me now:

> [B] *Jam fuerit, nec post unquam revocare licebit.*
>
> [The present will soon be the past, never to be recalled.]²⁸

[A]   Thoughts such as these did not furrow my brow any more than others did. At first it does seem impossible not to feel the sting of such ideas, but if you keep handling them and running through them you eventually tame them. No doubt about that. Otherwise I would, for my part, be in continual terror and frenzy: for no man ever had less confidence than I did that he would go on living; and no man ever counted less on his life proving long. Up till now I have enjoyed robust good health almost uninterruptedly: yet that never extends my hopes for life any more than sickness shortens them. Every moment it seems to me that I am running away from myself.   [C]   And I ceaselessly chant the refrain, 'Anything you can do another day can be done now.'

[A]   In truth risks and dangers do little or nothing to bring us nearer to death. If we think of all the millions of threats which remain hanging over us, apart from the one which happens to appear most menacing just now, we shall realize that death is equally near when we are vigorous or feverish, at sea or at home, in battle or in repose.   [C]   '*Nemo altero fragilior est*:

---

26. Catullus, LXVIII, 26. On Montaigne's melancholic humour, which was modified by the sanguine, cf. II, 17. (His comportment corresponds to the symptoms associated with melancholy.)
27. '80: fever and *death*, with his head . . .
28. Lucretius, III, 195.

nemo in crastinam sui certior.' [No man is frailer than another: no man more
certain of the morrow.][29]

[A]   If I have only one hour's work to do before I die, I am never sure I
have time enough to finish it. The other day someone was going through
my notebooks and found a declaration about something I wanted done
after my death. I told him straight that, though I was hale and healthy and
but a league away from my house, I had hastened to jot it down because I
had not been absolutely certain of getting back home.   [C]   Being a man
who broods over his thoughts and stores them up inside him, I am always
just about as ready as I can be: when death does suddenly appear, it will
bear no new warning for me.   [A]   As far as we possibly can we must
always have our boots on, ready to go; above all we should take care to
have no outstanding business with anyone else.

> [B]   *Quid brevi fortes jaculamur ævo*
> *Multa?*

[Why, in so brief a span, do we find strength to make so many projects?][30]

[A]   We shall have enough to do then without adding to it.

One man complains less of death itself than of its cutting short the course
of a fine victory; another, that he has to depart before marrying off his
daughter or arranging the education of his children; one laments the
company of his wife; another, of his son; as though they were the principal
attributes of his being.

[C]   I am now ready to leave, thank God, whenever He pleases,
regretting nothing except life itself – if its loss should happen to weigh
heavy on me. I am untying all the knots. I have already half-said my adieus
to everyone but myself. No man has ever prepared to leave the world
more simply nor more fully than I have. No one has more completely let
go of everything than I try to do.

> [B]   *Miser o miser, aiunt, omnia ademit*
> *Una dies infesta mihi tot præmia vitæ.*

['I am wretched, so wretched,' they say: 'One dreadful day has stripped me of all
life's rewards.']

[A]   And the builder says:

29. Seneca, *Epist. moral.*, XCI, 16.
30. Horace, *Odes*, II, xvi, 17.

> *Manent opera interrupta, minaeque*
> *Murorum ingentes.*

[My work remains unfinished; huge walls may fall down.][31]

We ought not to plan anything on so large a scale – at least, not if we are to get all worked up if we cannot see it through to the end.

We are born for action:[32]

> *Cum moriar, medium solvare inter opus.*

[When I die, may I be in the midst of my work.]

I want us to be doing things,   [C]   prolonging life's duties as much as we can;   [A]   I want Death to find me planting my cabbages, neither worrying about it nor the unfinished gardening. I once saw a man die who, right to the last, kept lamenting that destiny had cut the thread of the history he was writing when he had only got up to our fifteenth or sixteenth king!

> [B]   *Illud in his rebus non addunt, nec tibi earum*
> *Jam desiderium rerum super insidet una!*

[They never add, that desire for such things does not linger on in your remains!][33]

[A]   We must throw off such humours; they are harmful and vulgar.

Our graveyards have been planted next to churches, says Lycurgus, so that women, children and lesser folk should grow accustomed to seeing a dead man without feeling terror, and so that this continual spectacle of bones, tombs and funerals should remind us of our human condition:[34]

> [B]   *Quin etiam exhilarare viris convivia cæde*
> *Mos olim, et miscere epulis spectacula dira*
> *Certantum ferro, sæpe et super ipsa cadentum*
> *Pocula respersis non parco sanguine mensis;*

[It was once the custom, moreover, to enliven feasts with human slaughter and to entertain guests with the cruel sight of gladiators fighting: they often fell among the goblets, flooding the tables with their blood;]

---

31. Lucretius, III, 898–9 (Lambin); Virgil, *Aeneid*, IV, 88.
32. [A] until [C]: for action: *and I am of the opinion that not only an Emperor, as Vespasian said, but any gallant man should die on his feet:* Cum moriar . . . Then Ovid, *Amores*, II, x, 36.
33. Lucretius, III, 900.
34. By 'churches' here Montaigne means pagan temples. Then, Silius Italicus, *The Punic War*, XI, li.

[C]   so too, after their festivities the Egyptians used to display before their guests a huge portrait of death, held up by a man crying, 'Drink and be merry: once dead you will look like this';[35]   [A]   similarly, I have adopted the practice of always having death not only in my mind but on my lips. There is nothing I inquire about more readily than how men have died: what did they say? How did they look? What expression did they have? There are no passages in the history books which I note more attentively.   [C]   That I have a particular liking for such matters is shown by the examples with which I stuff my book. If I were a scribbler I would produce a compendium with commentaries of the various ways men have died. (Anyone who taught men how to die would teach them how to live.) Dicearchus did write a book with some such title, but for another and less useful purpose.[36]

[A]   People will tell me that the reality of death so far exceeds the thought that when we actually get there all our fine fencing amounts to nothing. Let them say so: there is no doubt whatsoever that meditating on it beforehand confers great advantages. Anyway, is it nothing to get even that far without faltering or feverish agitation?

But there is more to it than that: Nature[37] herself lends us a hand and gives us courage. If our death is violent and short we have no time to feel afraid: if it be otherwise, I have noticed that as an illness gets more and more hold on me I naturally slip into a kind of contempt for life. I find that a determination to die is harder to digest when I am in good health than when I am feverish, especially since I no longer hold so firmly to the pleasures of life once I begin to lose the use and enjoyment of them, and can look on death with a far less terrified gaze. That leads me to hope that the further I get from good health and the nearer I approach to death the more easily I will come to terms with exchanging one for the other. Just as I have in several other matters assayed the truth of Caesar's assertion that things often look bigger from afar than close to,[38] I have also found that I was much more terrified of illness when I was well than when I felt ill. Being in a happy state, all pleasure and vigour, leads me to get the other state quite out of proportion, so that I mentally increase all its discomforts by half and imagine them heavier than they prove to be when I have to bear them.

35. Herodotus, II, lxxviii; Erasmus, *Apophthegmata*, VI; *varie mixta*, LXXXIV.
36. Cicero, *De officiis*, II, V, 16. Dicearchus' book was called *The Perishing of Human Life*. It has not survived.
37. '80: than that. *I realize from experience that* Nature . . .
38. Caesar, *Gallic Wars*, VII, lxxxiv.

I hope that the same will apply to me when I die. [B] It is normal to experience change and decay: let us note how Nature robs us of our sense of loss and decline. What does an old man still retain of his youthful vigour and of his own past life?

> *Heu senibus vitae portio quanta manet.*

[Alas, what little of life's portion remains with the aged.][39]

[C] When a soldier of Caesar's guard, broken and worn out, came up to him in the street and begged leave to kill himself, Caesar looked at his decrepit bearing and said with a smile: 'So you think you are still alive, then?'[40]

[B] If any of us were to be plunged into old age all of a sudden I do not think that the change would be bearable. But, almost imperceptibly, Nature leads us by the hand down a gentle slope; little by little, step by step, she engulfs us in that pitiful state and breaks us in, so that we feel no jolt when youth dies in us, although in essence and in truth that is a harsher death than the total extinction of a languishing life as old age dies. For it is not so grievous a leap from a wretched existence to non-existence as it is from a sweet existence in full bloom to one full of travail and pain.

[A] When our bodies are bent and stooping low they have less strength for supporting burdens. So too for our souls: we must therefore educate and train them for their encounter with that adversary, death; for the soul can find no rest while she remains afraid of him. But once she does find assurance she can boast that it is impossible for anxiety, anguish, fear or even the slightest dissatisfaction to dwell within her. And that almost surpasses our human condition.

> [B] *Non vultus instantis tyranni*
> *Mente quatit solida, neque Auster*
> *Dux inquieti turbidus Adriæ,*
> *Nec fulminantis magna Jovis manus.*

[Nothing can shake such firmness: neither the threatening face of a tyrant, nor the South Wind (that tempestuous Master of the Stormy Adriatic) nor even the mighty hand of thundering Jove.][41]

---

39. Pseudo-Gallus, *Elegies*, I, 16. (Like his contemporaries Montaigne attributed to Cornelius Gallus poems later attributed to Maximianus.)
40. Seneca, *Epist. moral.*, LXXVII, 19. The Emperor was Gaius Caesar (Caligula), not Julius Caesar.
41. Horace, *Odes*, III, iii, 3–6.

[A]   She has made herself Mistress of her passions and her lusts, Mistress of destitution, shame, poverty and of all other injuries of Fortune. Let any of us who can gain such a superiority do so: for here is that true and sovereign freedom which enables us to cock a snook at force and injustice and to laugh at manacles and prisons:

> in manicis, et
> Compedibus, sævo te sub custode tenebo.
> Ipse Deus simul atque volam, me solvet: opinor,
> Hoc sentit, moriar. Mors ultima linea rerum est.

['I will shackle your hands and feet and keep you under a cruel gaoler.' – 'God himself will set me free as soon as I ask him to.' (He means, I think, 'I will die': for death is the last line of all.)][42]

Our religion has never had a surer human foundation than contempt for life; rational argument (though not it alone) summons us to such contempt: for why should we fear to lose something which, once lost, cannot be regretted? And since we are threatened by so many kinds of death is it not worse to fear them all than to bear one?[43]   [C]   Death is inevitable: does it matter when it comes? When Socrates was told that the Thirty Tyrants had condemned him to death, he retorted, 'And nature, them!'[44]

How absurd to anguish over our passing into freedom from all anguish. Just as our birth was the birth of all things for us, so our death will be the death of them all. That is why it is equally mad to weep because we shall not be alive a hundred years from now and to weep because we were not alive a hundred years ago. Death is the origin of another life. We wept like this and it cost us just as dear when we entered into this life, similarly stripping off our former veil as we did so. Nothing can be grievous which occurs but once; is it reasonable to fear for so long a time something which lasts so short a time? Living a long life or a short life are made all one by death: *long* and *short* do not apply to that which is no more. Aristotle says that there are tiny creatures on the river Hypanis whose life lasts one single day: those which die at eight in the morning die in youth; those which die at five in the evening die of senility.[45] Which of us would not laugh if so momentary a span counted as happiness or unhappiness? Yet if we compare our own span against eternity or even against the span of mountains, rivers, stars, trees or, indeed, of some animals, then saying *shorter* or *longer* becomes equally ridiculous.

42. Horace, *Epistles*, I, xvi, 76–9.
43. St Augustine, *City of God*, I, xi.
44. Erasmus, *Apophthegmata*, III; *Socratica*, LII.
45. Cicero, *Tusc. disput.*, I, xxxix, 94.

[A]   Nature drives us that way, too:[46] 'Leave this world,' she says, 'just as you entered it. That same journey from death to life, which you once made without suffering or fear, make it again from life to death. Your death is a part of the order of the universe; it is a part of the life of the world:

> [B]   *inter se mortales mutua vivunt . . .*
> *Et quasi cursores vitaï lampada tradunt.*

[Mortal creatures live lives dependent on each other; like runners in a relay they pass on the torch of life.][47] –

[A]   Shall I change, just for you, this beautiful interwoven structure! Death is one of the attributes you were created with; death is a part of you; you are running away from yourself; this *being* which you enjoy is equally divided between death and life. From the day you were born your path leads to death as well as life:

> *Prima, quae vitam dedit, hora, carpsit.*

[Our first hour gave us life and began to devour it.]

> *Nascentes morimur, finisque ab origine pendet.*

[As we are born we die; the end of our life is attached to its beginning.][48]

[C]   All that you live, you have stolen from life; you live at her expense. Your life's continual task is to build your death. You are *in* death while you are *in* life: when you are no more *in* life you are after death. Or if you prefer it thus: after life you are dead, but during life you are dying: and death touches the dying more harshly than the dead, in more lively a fashion and more essentially.

[B]   'If you have profited from life, you have had your fill; go away satisfied:

> *Cur non ut plenus vitae conviva recedis?*

[Why not withdraw from life like a guest replete?]

But if you have never learned how to use life, if life is useless to you, what does it matter if you have lost it? What do you still want it for?

46. The main source of what follows is Nature's soliloquy in Lucretius, III.
47. Lucretius, II, 76 and 79; cf. Erasmus, *Adages*, I, II, XXXVIII, *Cursu lampada tradunt.*
48. Seneca (the dramatist), *Hercules furens*, III, 874; Manilius, *Astronomica*, IV, xvi.

> *Cur amplius addere quæris*
> *Rursum quod pereat male, et ingratum occidat omne?*

[Why seek to add more, just to lose it again, wretchedly, without joy?][49]

[C] Life itself is neither a good nor an evil: life is where good or evil find a place, depending on how you make it for them.[50]

[A] 'If you have lived one day, you have seen everything. One day equals all days. There is no other light, no other night. The Sun, Moon and Stars, disposed just as they are now, were enjoyed by your grandsires and will entertain your great-grandchildren:

> [C] *Non alium videre patres: aliumve nepotes*
>   *Aspicient.*

[Your fathers saw none other: none other shall your progeny discern.][51]

[A] And at the worst estimate the division and variety of all the acts of my play are complete in one year. If you have observed the vicissitude of my four seasons you know they embrace the childhood, youth, manhood and old age of the World. Its [C] play [A] is done.[52] It knows no other trick but to start all over again. Always it will be the same.

> [B] *Versamur ibidem, atque insumus usque;*

> [We turn in the same circle, for ever;]

> *Atque in se sua per vestigia volvitur annus.*

> [And the year rolls on again through its own traces.]

[A] I have not the slightest intention of creating new pastimes for you.

> *Nam tibi præterea quod machiner, inveniamque*
> *Quod placeat, nihil est, eadem sunt omnia semper*

[For there is nothing else I can make or discover to please you: all things are the same forever.][53]

Make way for others as others did for you. [C] The first part of equity is equality. Who can complain of being included when all are included?[54]

---

49. Lucretius, III, 938; 941–2.
50. Seneca, *Epist. moral.*, XCIX, 12.
51. Manilius cited by Vives (Commentary on St Augustine's *City of God*, XI, iv).
52. '80: Its *role* is done . . .
53. Lucretius, III, 1080; Virgil, *Georgics*, II, 402; Lucretius, III, 944–5.
54. Seneca, *Epist. moral.*, XXX, 11.

[A] 'It is no good going on living: it will in no wise shorten the time you will stay dead. It is all for nothing: you will be just as long in that state which you fear as though you had died at the breast;

> *licet, quod vis, vivendo vincere secla,*
> *Mors æterna tamen nihilominus illa manebit.*

[Triumph over time and live as long as you please: death eternal will still be waiting for you.]

[B] And yet I shall arrange that you have no unhappiness:

> *In vera nescis nullum fore morte alium te,*
> *Qui possit vivus tibi te lugere peremptum,*
> *Stansque jacentem.*

[Do you not know that in real death there will be no second You, living to lament your death and standing by your corpse.]

"You" will not desire the life which now you so much lament.

> *Nec sibi enim quisquam tum se vitamque requirit . . .*
> *Nec desiderium nostri nos afficit ullum.*

[Then no one worries about his life or his self; . . . we feel no yearning for our own being.]

Death is less to be feared than nothing – if there be anything less than nothing:

> *multo mortem minus ad nos esse putandum*
> *Si minus esse potest quam quod nihil esse videmus.*

[We should think death to be less – if anything is "less" than what we can see to be nothing at all.][55]

[C] 'Death does not concern you, dead or alive; alive, because you are: dead, because you are no more.

[A] 'No one dies before his time; the time you leave behind you is no more yours than the time which passed before you were born;[56] [B] and does not concern you either:

> *Respice enim quam nil ad nos ante acta vetustas*
> *Temporis æterni fuerit.*

55. Lucretius, III, 1090 (within a wider Lucretian context); III, 885 (adapted); III, 919; 922; 926.
56. Seneca, *Epist. moral.*, LXIX, 6; then Lucretius, III, 972–3.

[Look back and see that the aeons of eternity before we were born have been nothing to us.]

[A] 'Wherever your life ends, there all of it ends. [C] The usefulness of living lies not in duration but in what you make of it. Some have lived long and lived little. See to it while you are still here. Whether you have lived enough depends not on a count of years but on your will.

[A] 'Do you think you will never arrive whither you are ceaselessly heading? [C] Yet every road has its end. [A] And, if it is a relief to have company, is not the whole world proceeding at the same pace as you are?

[B]   *Omnia te vita perfuncta sequentur.*

[All things will follow you when their life is done.]⁵⁷

[A] Does not everything move with the same motion as you do? Is there anything which is not growing old with you? At this same [C] instant [A] that you die⁵⁸ hundreds of men, of beasts and of other creatures are dying too.

[B]   *Nam nox nulla diem, neque noctem aurora sequuta est,*
        Quæ non audierit mistos vagitibus ægris
        Ploratus, mortis comites et funeris atri.

[No night has ever followed day, no dawn has ever followed night, without hearing, interspersed among the wails of infants, the cries of pain attending death and sombre funerals.]⁵⁹

[C] 'Why do you pull back when retreat is impossible? You have seen cases enough where men were lucky to die, avoiding great misfortunes by doing so: but have you ever seen anyone for whom death turned out badly? And it is very simple-minded of you to condemn something which you have never experienced either yourself or through another. Why do you complain of me⁶⁰ or of Destiny? Do we do you wrong? Should you

---

57. Several echoes of Seneca: *Epist. moral.*, LXXVII, 20, 13 (etc.); XLIX; LXI, LXXVII. Then, Lucretius, III, 968.
58. '80: same *hour* that you die . . .
    Further borrowings, Seneca, *Epist. moral.*, LXXVII.
59. Lucretius, II, 578–80.
60. Nature is still speaking and the inspiration is still Senecan; cf. *Epist. moral.*, XCIII, 2 ff.

govern us or should we govern you? You may not have finished your stint but you have finished your life. A small man is no less whole than a tall one. Neither men nor their lives are measured by the yard. Chiron refused immortality when he was told of its characteristics by his father Saturn, the god of time and of duration.[61]

'Truly imagine how much less bearable for Man, and how much more painful, would be a life which lasted for ever rather than the life which I have given you. If you did not have death you would curse me, for ever, for depriving you of it.

'Seeing what advantages death holds I have deliberately mixed a little anguish into it to stop you from embracing it too avidly or too injudiciously. To lodge you in that moderation which I require of you, neither fleeing from life nor yet fleeing from death, I have tempered them both between the bitter and the sweet.

'I taught Thales, the foremost of your Sages, that living and dying are things indifferent. So, when asked "why he did not go and die then," he very wisely replied: "Because it *is* indifferent."[62]

'Water, Earth, Air and Fire and the other parts of this my edifice are no more instrumental to your life than to your death. Why are you afraid of your last day? It brings you no closer to your death than any other did. The last step does not make you tired: it shows that you are tired. All days lead to death: the last one gets there.'

[A] Those are the good counsels of Nature, our Mother.[63]

I have often wondered why the face of death, seen in ourselves or in other men, appears incomparably less terrifying to us in war than in our own homes – otherwise armies would consist of doctors and cry-babies – and why, since death is ever the same, there is always more steadfastness among village-folk and the lower orders than among all the rest. I truly believe that what frightens us more than death itself are those terrifying grimaces and preparations with which we surround it – a brand new way of life: mothers, wives and children weeping; visits from people stunned and beside themselves with grief; the presence of a crowd of servants, pale and tear-stained; a bedchamber without daylight; candles lighted; our bedside besieged by doctors and preachers; in short, all about us is horror and terror. We are under the ground, buried in our graves already!

61. Cf. Lucian, *Dialogues of the Dead*, XXVI; Ovid, *Metamorphoses*, II, 649 ff.
62. Diogenes Laertius, *Life of Thales*, XXX.
63. Seneca, *Epist. moral.*, CVII, and CXX. The entire speech of Nature, who adds her arguments to Reason's in support of 'our religion's contempt for life' is a patchwork of quotation, at first from Lucretius and subsequently from Seneca.

Children are frightened of their very friends when they see them masked.
So are we. We must rip the masks off things as well as off people. Once
we have done that we shall find underneath only that same death which a
valet and a chambermaid got through recently, without being afraid.[64]
Blessed [65] the death which leaves no time for preparing such gatherings of
mourners.

64. Seneca, *Epist. moral.*, XXIV, 14.
65. [A] until [C]: Blessed, *and thrice blessed*, the death ... (Doubtless an echo of
Aeneas' evocation in Virgil, *Aeneid*, I, 94.)

26. On educating children

[*The previous chapter,* On schoolmasters' learning, *was read in manuscript by visitors. Montaigne was encouraged to write at greater length on how to bring up boys. He had no son of his own but wrote partly for his friend and admirer Diane de Foix (who married in 1579 and was pregnant, hoping for a son and heir). Montaigne tells of his own upbringing by the best of fathers. Emphasizing the importance of things over words brings him to write of his own 'brain-child': the* Essays, *a matter of words. Thinking of his father's gentle methods based on exciting a child's love and enthusiasm for learning and good morals, he makes a diversion on kings and magistrates, who as 'fathers of the people', ought to use similar methods. The additions marked* [C] *show his new and growing respect for Plato (for whom books were indeed the preferred 'children' of superior minds). Montaigne launches a frontal attack (without naming him) on Hesiod, who made the path to virtue sweaty, painful and rough. For Montaigne, even children can find the paths to virtue lovely and delightful.*]

For Madame Diane de Foix, Countess of Gurson

[A]   I have never known a father fail to acknowledge his son as his own, no matter how   [C]   scurvy or crook-backed   [A]   he may be.[1] It is not that he fails to see his infirmities (unless he is quite besotted by his affection): but the thing is his, for all that! The same applies to me: I can see – better than anyone else – that these writings of mine are no more than the ravings of a man who has never done more than taste the outer crust of knowledge – even that was during his childhood – and who has retained only an ill-formed generic notion of it: a little about everything and nothing about anything, in the French style. For, in brief, I do know that there is such a thing as medicine and jurisprudence; that there are four parts to mathematics: and I know more or less what they cover.   [C]   (Perhaps I do also know how the sciences in general claim to serve us in our lives.)   [A]   But what I have definitely not done is to delve deeply into them, biting my nails over the study of Aristotle,[2]   [C]   that monarch of

1. '80: how *crooked-back or lame* he may be . . .
2. [A] until [C]: study of *Plato or* Aristotle . . . (A significant deletion).

the doctrine of the Modernists,[3]   [A]   or stubbornly persevering in any field[4] of learning.   [C]   I could not sketch even the mere outlines of any art whatsoever; there is no boy even in the junior forms who cannot say he is more learned than I am: I could not even test him on his first lesson, at least not in detail. When forced to do so, I am constrained to extract (rather ineptly) something concerning universals, against which I test his inborn judgement – a subject as unknown to the boys as theirs is to me.[5]

I have fashioned no sustained intercourse with any solid book except Plutarch and Seneca; like the Danaïdes I am constantly dipping into them and then pouring out: I spill some of it on to this paper but next to nothing on to me.[6]

[A]   My game-bag is made for history [C] rather, [A] or poetry, which I love, being particularly inclined towards it;[7] for (as Cleanthes said) just as the voice of the trumpet rings out clearer and stronger for being forced through a narrow tube so too a saying leaps forth much more vigorously when compressed into the rhythms of poetry, striking me then with a livelier shock. As for my own natural faculties which are being assayed here, I can feel them bending beneath their burden. My concepts and judgement can only fumble their way forward, swaying, stumbling, tripping over; even when I have advanced as far as I can, I never feel satisfied, for I have a troubled cloudy vision of lands beyond, which I cannot make out. I undertake to write without preconceptions on any subject which comes to mind, employing nothing but my own natural resources: then if (as happens often) I chance to come across in excellent authors the very same topics I have undertaken to treat (as I have just done recently in Plutarch about the power of the imagination) I acknowledge myself to be so weak, so paltry, so lumbering and so dull compared with such men, that I feel scorn and pity for myself. I do congratulate myself,

---

3. *Modernists* (often a pejorative term, as in Spiegel's *Lexicon Juris Civilis*) was applied to Nominalists – neo-Aristotelians who refused to seek philosophical truths in revelation, restricting revealed truth to Christian theology.

4. [A] until [C]: any *solid* field. . .

5. Celio Calcagnini stressed that the young can be knowledgeable about 'universals' but not about 'particulars', which depend on experience. Cf. also Aristotle, *Nicomachaean Ethics*, VI, 8, 5–8.

6. Those daughters of Danaus who killed their husbands and were condemned to fill a leaky jar with water in Hades.

7. [A] until [C]: made, *where books are concerned*, for history, or poetry . . .
   Then, Cleanthes in Seneca, *Epist. moral.*, CVIII, 10.

however, that my opinions frequently coincide with theirs [C] and on the fact that I do at least trail far behind them murmuring 'Hear, hear'. [A] And again, I do know (what many do not) the vast difference there is between them and me. What I myself have thought up and produced is poor feeble stuff, but I let it go on, without plastering over the cracks or stitching up the rents which have been revealed by such comparisons.[8] [C] You need a strong backbone if you undertake to march shoulder to shoulder with fellows like that.

[A] Those rash authors of our own century who scatter whole passages from ancient writers throughout their own worthless works, seeking to acquire credit [C] thereby,[9] [A] achieve the reverse; between them and the Ancients there is an infinite difference of lustre, which gives such a pale sallow ugly face to their own contributions that they lose far more than they gain.

– [C] There were two opposing concepts. Chrysippus the philosopher intermingled not merely passages from other authors into his writings but entire books: in one he cited the whole of the *Medea* of Euripides! Apollodorus said that if you cut out his borrowings his paper would remain blank. Epicurus on the other hand left three hundred tomes behind him: not one quotation from anyone else was planted in any of them.[10] –

[A] The other day I chanced upon such a borrowing. I had languished along behind some French words, words so bloodless, so fleshless and so empty of matter that indeed they were nothing but French and nothing but words. At the end of a long and boring road I came upon a paragraph which was high, rich, soaring to the clouds. If I had found a long gentle slope leading up to it, that would have been pardonable: what I came across was a cliff surging up so straight and so steep that I knew I was winging my way to another world after the first half-a-dozen words. That was how I realized what a slough I had been floundering through beforehand, so base and so deep that I did not have the heart to sink back into it.

If I [C] were to stuff one of my chapters with such rich spoils, that chapter [A] would reveal[11] all too clearly the silliness of the others.

---

8. '80: comparisons; *for otherwise I would have given birth to monstrosities, as do* those rash authors . . .
9. '80: credit *by their theft* achieve . . .
10. Diogenes Laertius, *Life of Chrysippus* and *Life of Epicurus*.
11. '80: If I *used such rich paintings as make-up for a chapter of mine that* would reveal . . .

[C] Reproaching other people for my own faults does not seem to me to be any more odd than reproaching myself for other people's (as I often do). We must condemn faults anywhere and everywhere, allowing them no sanctuary whatsoever. Yet I myself know how valiantly I strive to measure up to my stolen wares and to match myself to them equal to equal, not without some rash hope of throwing dust in the eyes of critics who would pick them out (though more thanks to the skill with which I apply them than to my skill in discovering them or to any strengths of my own). Moreover I do not take on those old champions all at once, wrestling with them body to body: it is a matter of slight, repeated, tiny encounters. I do not cling on: I merely try them out, going less far than I intended when haggling with myself over them. If I should prove merely up to sparring with them it would be a worthy match, for I only take them on when they are toughest.

But what about the things I have caught others doing? They bedeck themselves in other men's armour, with not even their fingertips showing. As it is easy for the learned to do on some commonplace subject, they carry through their projected work with bits of what was written in ancient times, patched together higgledy-piggledy. In the case of those who wish to hide their borrowings and pass them off as their own, their action is, first and foremost, unjust and mean: they have nothing worthwhile of their own to show off so they try to recommend themselves with someone else's goods; secondly it is stupid to be satisfied with winning, by cheating, the ignorant approbation of the crowd while losing all credit among men of understanding: their praise alone has any weight, but they look down their noses at our borrowed plasterwork. For my part there is nothing that I would want to do less: I only quote others the better to quote myself.

None of this applies to *centos* published as such; I have seen some very ingenious ones in my time, including one under the name of Capilupi, not to mention those of the ancients. Their authors show their wits in both this and other ways, as did Justus Lipsius in his *Politics*, with its industriously interwoven erudition.[12]

12. A *cento* was a literary poem, entirely, and often ingeniously, composed of lines from other authors and made to apply to a different subject. Lelio Capilupi's *cento* was a work on monks, entirely composed of lines of Virgil. Justus Lipsius, an author much admired by Montaigne, who knew his *Politics* well and borrowed much from it, did not write *centos* but did at times make his works into a patchwork of borrowings from ancient writers, especially the Stoics.

[A] Be that as it may; I mean that whatever these futilities of mine may be, I have no intention of hiding them, any more than I would a bald and grizzled portrait of myself just because the artist had painted not a perfect face but my own. Anyway these are *my* humours, *my* opinions: I give them as things which *I* believe, not as things to be believed. My aim is to reveal my own self, which may well be different tomorrow if I am initiated into some new business which changes me. I have not, nor do I desire, enough authority to be believed. I feel too badly taught to teach others.

Now in my home the other day somebody read the previous chapter and told me that I ought to spread myself a bit more on the subject of children's education. If, My Lady, I did have some competence in this matter I could not put it to better use than to make a present of it to that little man who is giving signs that he is soon to make a gallant sortie out of you. (You are too great-souled to begin other than with a boy.) Having played so large a part in arranging your marriage I have a rightful concern for the greatness and prosperity of all that springs from it, quite apart from that long enjoyment you have had of my service to you, by which I am indeed bound to desire honour, wealth and success to anything that touches on you. But in truth I know nothing about education except this: that the greatest and the most important difficulty known to human learning seems to lie in that area which treats how to bring up children and how to educate them.

[C] It is just as in farming: the ploughing which precedes the planting is easy and sure; so is the planting itself: but as soon as what is planted springs to life, the raising of it is marked by a great variety of methods and by difficulty. So too with human beings; it is not much trouble to plant them, but as soon as they are born we take on in order to form them and bring them up a diversity of cares, full of bustle and worry. [A] When they are young they give such slight and obscure signs of their inclinations, while their promises are so false and unreliable, that it is hard to base any solid judgement upon them. [B] Look at Cimon, Themistocles and hundreds of others; think how unlike themselves they used to be! Bear-cubs and puppies manifest their natural inclinations but humans immediately acquire habits, laws and opinions; they easily change or adopt disguises.[13]

[A] Yet it is so hard to force a child's natural bent. That explains why, having chosen the wrong route, we toil to no avail and often waste years training children for occupations in which they never achieve anything. All

13. Cimon and Mnesiphilus Themistocles were, as young men, 'debauched and dissolute', then they reformed: Plutarch (tr. Amyot), *Si l'homme sage doit entremettre et mesler des affaires publiques*, 186v°.

the same my opinion is that, faced by this difficulty, we should always guide them towards the best and most rewarding goals, and that we should attach little importance to those trivial prognostications and foretellings we base on their childish actions. [C] Even Plato seems to me to give too much weight to them in his *Republic*.

[A] Learning, My Lady, is a great ornament and a useful instrument of wondrous service, especially in those who are fortunate to live in so high an estate as yours. And in truth she does not find her true employment in hands base and vile. She is far more proud to deploy her resources for the conducting of a war, the commanding of a nation and the winning of the affection of a prince or of a foreign people than for drawing up dialectical arguments, pleading in a court of appeal or prescribing a mass of pills. And, therefore, My Lady, since I believe you will not overlook this aspect of the education of your children, you who have yourself tasted its sweetness and who belong to a family of authors – for we still possess the writings of those early de Foix, Counts from whom both the present Count, your husband, is descended and you yourself, while your uncle François, the Sieur de Candale, gives birth every day to new ones, which will spread an awareness of this family trait to many later centuries[14] – I want to tell you of one thought of mine which runs contrary to normal practice. That is all I am able to contribute to your service in this matter.

The responsibilities of the tutor you give your son (and the results of the education he provides depend on your choice of him) comprise many other elements which I do not touch upon since I have nothing worthwhile to contribute; as for the one subject on which I do undertake to give him my advice, he will only accept what I say insofar as it seems convincing to him. The son of the house is seeking book-learning[15] not to make money (for so abject an end is unworthy of the grace and favour of the Muses and anyway has other aims and depends on others) nor for external advantages, but rather for those which are truly his own, those which inwardly enrich and adorn him. Since I would prefer that he turned out to be an able man not an erudite one, I would wish you to be careful to select as guide for him a tutor with a well-formed rather than a well-filled brain. Let both be looked for, but place character and intelligence before knowledge; and let him carry out his responsibilities in a new way.

---

14. Gaston III, Count de Foix, had published (c.1510) a book on hunting, *Phébus*; François de Candale, Bishop of Aire, translated Hermes Trismegistus and Euclid in 1578–9.
15. [A] until [C]: book-learning *and instruction*, not . . .

Teachers are for ever bawling into our ears as though pouring knowledge down through a funnel: our task is merely to repeat what we have been told. I would want our tutor to put that right: as soon as the mind in his charge allows it, he should make it show its fettle by appreciating and selecting *things* – and by distinguishing between them; the tutor should sometimes prepare the way for the boy, sometimes let him do it all on his own. I do not want the tutor to be the only one to choose topics or to do all the talking: when the boy's turn comes let the tutor listen to his pupil talking. [C] Socrates and then Arcesilaus used to make their pupils speak first; they spoke afterwards. *'Obest plerumque iis qui discere volunt authoritas eorum qui docent.'* [For those who want to learn, the obstacle can often be the authority of those who teach.][16]

It is good to make him trot in front of his tutor in order to judge his paces and to judge how far down the tutor needs to go to adapt himself to his ability. If we get that proportion wrong we spoil everything; knowing how to find it and to remain well-balanced within it is one of the most arduous tasks there is. It is the action of a powerful elevated mind to know how to come down to the level of the child and to guide his footsteps. Personally I go uphill more firmly and surely than down.

Those who follow our French practice and undertake to act as schoolmaster for several minds diverse in kind and capacity, using the same teaching and the same degree of guidance for them all, not surprisingly can scarcely find in a whole tribe of children more than one or two who bear fruit from their education.

[A] Let the tutor not merely require a verbal account of what the boy has been taught but the meaning and the substance of it: let him judge how the child has profited from it not from the evidence of his memory but from that of his life. Let him take what the boy has just learned and make him show him dozens of different aspects of it and then apply it to just as many different subjects, in order to find out whether he has really grasped it and made it part of himself, [C] judging the boy's progress by what Plato taught about education. [A] Spewing up food exactly as you have swallowed it is evidence of a failure to digest and assimilate it; the stomach has not done its job if, during concoction, it fails to change the substance and the form of what it is given.[17]

16. For the importance of *things* not *words*, cf. Erasmus, *Apophthegmata*, III, *Socratica*, LXXXIII; then, Cicero, *De natura deorum*, I, v, 10.
17. '80: given. *They are only seeking a reputation for erudition. When they can say 'He's a learned man', they think they have said it all. Their souls* . . .

Our [B] souls are moved only at second-hand, being shackled and constrained to what is desired by someone else's ideas; they are captives, enslaved to the authority of what they have been taught. We have been so subjected to leading-reins that we take no free steps on our own. Our drive to be free has been quenched. [C] 'Nunquam tutelae suae fiunt.' [They are never free from tutelage.]¹⁸ [B] In Pisa I met, in private, a decent man who is such an Aristotelian that the most basic of his doctrines is that the touchstone and the measuring-scale of all sound ideas and of each and every truth lie in their conformity with the teachings of Aristotle, outside of which all is inane and chimerical: Aristotle has seen everything, done everything. When that proposition was taken too widely and unfairly interpreted, for a long time he had a great deal of trouble from the Roman Inquisition.¹⁹

[A] Let the tutor pass everything through a filter and never lodge anything in the boy's head simply by authority, at second-hand. Let the principles of Aristotle not be principles for him any more than those of the Stoics or Epicureans. Let this diversity of judgements be set before him; if he can, he will make a choice: if he cannot then he will remain in doubt. [C] Only fools have made up their minds and are certain:

[A1]   *Che non men che saper dubbiar m'aggrada.*

[For doubting pleases me as much as knowing.]²⁰

For if it is by his own reasoning that he adopts the opinions of Xenophon and Plato, they are no longer theirs: they are his. [C] To follow another is to follow nothing: '*Non sumus sub rege: sibi quisque se vindicet.*' [We are under no king: let each man act freely.]²¹ Let him at least know what he does know. [A] He should not be learning their precepts but drinking in their humours. If he wants to, let him not be afraid to forget where he got them from, but let him be sure that he knows how to appropriate them. Truth and reason are common to all: they no more belong to the man who first put them into words than to him who last did so. [C] It

18. Seneca, *Epist. moral.*, XXXIII, 10.
19. Known from Montaigne's *Journal de Voyage* to be Dr Girolamo Borro, released from the prisons of the Inquisition on Papal authority. He wrote important books on motion and on the tides.
20. Dante, *Inferno*, XI, 93.
21. Seneca, *Epist. moral.*, XXXIII, 4 (adapted). Romans hated kings: here Seneca virtually means, 'We are under no despot.'

is no more *secundum Platonem* than *secundum me*: Plato and I see and understand it the same way. [A] Bees ransack flowers here and flowers there: but then they make their own honey, which is entirely theirs and no longer thyme or marjoram. Similarly the boy will transform his borrowings; he will confound their forms so that the end-product is entirely his: namely, his judgement, the forming of which is the only aim of his toil, his study and his education.

[C] Let him hide the help he received and put only his achievements on display. Pillagers and borrowers make a parade of what they have bought and built not of what they have filched from others! You never see the 'presents' given to a Parliamentary lawyer: what you see are the honours which he obtains for his children, and the families they marry into. Nobody puts his income on show, only his possessions. The profit we possess after study is to have become better and wiser.

[A] As Epicharmus said, that which sees and hears is our understanding; it is our understanding which benefits all, which arranges everything, which acts, which is Master and which reigns.[22] We indeed make it into a slave and a coward by not leaving it free to do anything of itself. Which tutor ever asks his pupil what he thinks about [B] rhetoric or grammar or [A] this or that statement of Cicero? They build them into our memory, panelling and all, as though they were oracles, in which letters and syllables constitute the actual substance. [C] 'Knowing' something does not mean knowing it by heart; that simply means putting it in the larder of our memory. That which we rightly 'know' can be deployed without looking back at the model, without turning our eyes back towards the book. What a wretched ability it is which is purely and simply bookish! Book-learning should serve as an ornament not as a foundation – following the conclusion of Plato that true philosophy consists in resoluteness, faithfulness and purity, whereas the other sciences, which have other aims, are merely cosmetic.

[A] Take Palvel and Pompeo, those excellent dancing-masters when I was young: I would like to have seen them teaching us our steps just by watching them without budging from our seats, like those teachers who seek to give instruction to our understanding without making it dance – [C] or to have seen others teach us how to manage a horse, a pike or a lute, or to sing without practice, as these fellows do who want to teach us

22. Plutarch (tr. Amyot), *De la Fortune ou vertu d'Alexandre*, 313E (cf. *Quels animaux*, 508H).

to judge well and to speak well but who never give us exercises in judging or speaking. [A] Yet for such an apprenticeship everything we see can serve as an excellent book: some cheating by a page, some stupidity on the part of a lackey, something said at table, all supply new material.

For this purpose mixing with people is wonderfully appropriate. So are visits to foreign lands: but not the way the French nobles do it (merely bringing back knowledge of how many yards long the Pantheon is, or of the rich embroidery on Signora Livia's knickers); nor the way others do so (knowing how much longer and fatter Nero's face is on some old ruin over there compared with his face on some comparable medallion) but mainly learning of the humours of those peoples and of their manners, and knocking off our corners by rubbing our brains against other people's. I would like pupils to be taken abroad from their tenderest years, mainly (so as to kill two birds with one stone) to any neighbouring peoples whose languages, being least like our own, are ones which our tongue cannot get round unless you start bending it young. And, besides, it is a universally received opinion that it is not sensible to bring up a boy in the lap of his parents. Natural affection makes parents too soft, too indulgent – even the wisest of them. They are incapable of either punishing his faults or of bringing him up as roughly and as dangerously as he ought to be. They could not bear to see him riding back from his training all dirty and sweaty, [C] drinking this hot, drinking that cold, [A] nor to see him on a fractious horse, or up against a tough opponent foil in hand, nor with his first arquebus. But there is no other prescription: anyone who wants to be absolutely certain of making a real man of him must not spare his youth and must frequently flout the laws of medicine.

> [B] *vitamque sub dio et trepidis agat*
> *In rebus.*

[Let him camp in the open, amidst war's alarms.][23]

[C] Nor is it enough to toughen up his soul: you must also toughen up his muscles.[24] The Soul is too hard-pressed if she is not seconded. She has too much to do herself to think of taking on the duties of both. I know how my own soul groans in her fellowship with a body so soft and sensitive to pain and which relies too heavily on her; and I have noticed in my reading that in their writings my moral guides pass off as examples of greatness of soul or strength of mind things which really belong to a tough

23. Horace, *Odes*, III, ii, 5.
24. Cf. Erasmus, *Apophthegmata*, VII, *Plato*, XVII.

skin or to strong bones. I have known men, women and children who are so constituted that a good beating means less to them than a pinch does to me, and who stir neither tongue nor eyebrow under the blows. When athletes play the philosopher in endurance it is strength of muscle rather than strength of mind. Now learning to endure toil is learning to endure pain: *'labor callum obducit dolori'* [toil puts callouses on our minds, against pain].[25] Pain and discomfort in training are needed to break him in for the pain and discomfort of dislocated joints, of the stone and of cauterizings – and of dungeons and tortures as well, for, seeing the times we live in, those two may concern the good man as much as the bad. We are experiencing that now: whoever bears arms against Law threatens the best of men with the cat-o'-nine-tails and the rope.

[A] And then the authority of the tutor, which must be sovereign for the boy, is hampered and interrupted by the presence of his parents. Add to which the respect paid to the boy by his household and his awareness of the resources and dignity of his family are not in my opinion trivial disadvantages at that particular age.

Yet in the school of conversation among men I have often noticed a perversion: instead of learning about others we labour only to teach them about ourselves and are more concerned to sell our own wares than to purchase new ones. In our commerce with others, silence and modesty are most useful qualities. Train the lad to be sparing and reticent about his accomplishments (when he eventually has any) and he will not take umbrage when unlikely tales and daft things are related in his presence – for it is unmannerly and impolite to criticize everything which is not to our liking. [C] Let him be satisfied with correcting himself without being seen to reproach others for doing things he would not do himself and without flouting public morality: *'Licet sapere sine pompa, sine invidia.'* [One should be wise without ostentation or ill-will.][26] Let him shun any semblance of impolitely laying down the law, as well as that puerile ambition to wish to appear clever by being different or to earn a name for criticizing or flaunting novelties. It is only appropriate for great poets freely to break the rules of poetry: similarly it is intolerable for any but great and illustrious souls to give themselves unaccustomed prerogatives: – *'Si quid Socrates et Aristippus contra morem et consuetudinem fecerint, idem sibi ne arbitretur licere: magnis enim illi et divinis bonis hanc licentiam assequebantur.'* [Although Socrates and Aristippus sometimes

25. Cicero, *Tusc. disput.*, II, xv, 36.
26. Seneca, *Epist. moral.*, CIII, 5.

flouted normal rules and customs, one should not feel free to do the same: they obtained that privilege by qualities great and sublime.][27]

[A]   The boy will be taught not to get into a discussion or a quarrel except when he finds a sparring-partner worth wrestling with – and even then not to employ all the holds which might help him but merely those which help him most. Teach him a certain refinement in sorting out and selecting his arguments, with an affection for relevance and so for brevity.

Above all let him be taught to throw down his arms and surrender to truth as soon as he perceives it, whether that truth is born at his rival's doing or within himself from some change in his ideas. He will never be up in a pulpit reading out some prescribed text: he only has to defend a case when it has his approbation. He is not going to take up the kind of profession in which freedom to think again, or to admit mistakes, has been traded for ready cash.   [C]   *'Neque, ut omnia que præscripta et imperata sint defendat, necessitate ulla cogitur.'* [He is under no obligation to support all precepts and assertions.][28]

If the tutor's complexion is like mine he will so form the will of the boy that he will become a loyal subject of his monarch as well as a devoted and brave one, but he will throw cold water on any desire to be attached to him except through public service. Apart from several other disadvantages which cripple our freedom, when a man's judgement is pledged and purchased by private obligations, either it is partial and less free or else he can be taxed with unwisdom and ingratitude. A courtier can have neither the right to speak nor the desire to think other than favourably of a Master who from among so many thousands of his subjects has chosen to favour him with his own hand and to elevate him. Not unreasonably such favour and preferment will corrupt his freedom and dazzle him. That is why what that lot have to say on the topic is habitually at variance with all others in the State and little to be trusted.

[A]   As for our pupil's talk, let his virtue and his sense of right and wrong shine through it   [C]   and have no guide but reason.   [A]   Make him understand that confessing an error which he discovers in his own argument even when he alone has noticed it is an act of justice and integrity, which are the main qualities he pursues;   [C]   stubbornness and rancour are vulgar qualities, visible in common souls whereas to think again, to change one's mind and to give up a bad case in the heat of the argument are rare qualities showing strength and wisdom.

27. Cicero, *De officiis*, I, xli, 148.
28. Cicero, *Academica*, II (*Lucullus*), iii, 8 (adapted).

[A] When in society the boy will be told to keep his eyes open: I find that the front seats are normally taken as a right by the less able men and that great inherited wealth is hardly ever associated with ability; while at the top end of the table the talk was about the beauty of a tapestry or the bouquet of the malmsey, I have known many witty remarks at the other end pass unnoticed. He will sound out the capacity of each person: of a herdsman, a mason, a wayfarer: he must use what he can get, take what a man has to sell and see that nothing goes wasted: even other people's stupidity and weakness serve to instruct him. By noting each man's endowments and habits, there will be engendered in him a desire for the good ones and a contempt for the bad.

Put into his mind a decent, careful spirit of inquiry about everything: he will go and see anything nearby which is of singular quality: a building, a fountain, a man, the site of an old battle, a place which Caesar or Charlemagne passed through:

> [C]   *Quæ tellus sit lenta gelu, quæ putris ab æstu,*
> *Ventus in Italiam quis bene vela ferat.*

[what land is benumbed with the cold, which dusty with heat, which favourable winds blow sails towards Italian coasts.][29]

[A] He will inquire into the habits, means and alliances of various monarchs, things most pleasant to study and most useful to know. In his commerce with men I mean him to include – and that principally – those who live only in the memory of books. By means of history he will frequent those great souls of former years. If you want it to be so, history can be a waste of time: it can also be, if you want it to be so, a study bearing fruit beyond price –   [C]   the only study, Plato said, which the Spartans kept as their share.[30]   [A]   Under this heading what profit will he not get out of reading the *Lives* of our favourite Plutarch! But let our tutor remember the object of his trust, which is less to stamp   [C]   the date of the fall of Carthage on the boy as the behaviour of Hannibal and Scipio; less to stamp   [A]   the name of the place where Marcellus died as how his death there showed him unworthy of his task. Let him not so much learn what happened as judge what happened.   [C]   That, if you ask me, is the subject to which our wits are applied in the most diverse of manners. I have read hundreds of things in Livy which another has not found there. Plutarch found in him hundreds of things which I did not see

29. Propertius, IV, iii, 39–40.
30. Plato, *Greater Hippias* (beginning).

(and which perhaps the author never put there). For some Livy is purely a grammatical study; for others he is philosophy dissected, penetrating into the most abstruse parts of our nature. [A] There are in Plutarch developed treatises very worth knowing, for he is to my mind the master-craftsman at that job; but there are also hundreds of points which he simply touches on: he merely flicks his fingers towards the way we should go if we want to, or at times he contents himself with a quick shot at the liveliest part of the subject: those passages we must rip out and put out on display. [B] For example that one saying of his, 'that the inhabitants of Asia were slaves of one tyrant because they were incapable of pronouncing one syllable: NO,' may have furnished La Boëtie with the matter and moment of his book *De la Servitude volontaire*.[31] [A] Seeing Plutarch select a minor action in the life of a man, or an apparently unimportant saying, is worth a treatise in itself. It is a pity that intelligent men are so fond of brevity: by it their reputation is certainly worth all the more, but we are worth all the less. Plutarch would rather we vaunted his judgement than his knowledge, and he would rather leave us craving for more than bloated. He realized that you could say too much even on a good subject, and that Alexandridas rightly criticized the orator whose address to the ephors was good but too long, saying, 'Oh, Stranger, you say what you should, but not the way that you should!'[32] [C] People whose bodies are too thin pad them out: those whose matter is too slender pad it out too, with words.

[A] Frequent commerce with the world can be an astonishing source of light for a man's judgement. We are all cramped and confined inside ourselves: we can see no further than the end of our noses. When they asked Socrates where he came from he did not say 'From Athens', but 'From the world'.[33] He, whose thoughts were fuller and wider, embraced the universal world as his City, scattered his acquaintances, his fellowship and his affections throughout the whole human race, not as we do who only look at what lies right in front of us. When frost attacks the vines in my village my parish priest talks of God being angry against the human race: in his judgement the Cannibals are already dying of the croup! At the sight of our civil wars, who fails to exclaim that the world is turned upside

---

31. Plutarch (tr. Amyot), *De la mauvaise honte*, 79B. La Boëtie's book circulated under the title of *Contr'un* (*Against* [the rule of] One) after his death and was used as Protestant propaganda against the French King.

32. Plutarch (tr. Amyot), *Dicts notables des Lacedaemoniens*, 214F.

33. Plutarch (tr. Amyot), *Du bannissement, ou de l'exil*, 125D–E.

down and that the Day of Judgement has got us by the throat, forgetting that many worse events have been known in the past and that, in thousands of parts of the world, they are still having a fine old time!   [B]   Personally I am surprised that our wars turn out to be so mild and gentle, given their unpunished licentiousness.   [A]   When the hail beats down on your head the entire hemisphere seems stormy and tempestuous. Like that peasant of Savoy who said that if only that silly King of France had known how to use his luck properly he could have become the Duke's chief steward eventually! His mind could not conceive of any degree of grandeur above that of his Duke.   [C]   We are all caught in that same error without realizing it: a harmful error of great consequence.   [A]   Only a man who can picture in his mind the mighty idea of Mother Nature in her total majesty; who can read in her countenance a variety so general and so unchanging and then pick out therein not merely himself but an entire kingdom as a tiny, faint point: only he can reckon things at their real size. This great world of ours (which for some is only one species within a generic group) is the looking-glass in which we must gaze to come to know ourselves from the right slant. To sum up then, I want it to be the book which our pupil studies. Such a variety of humours, schools of thought, opinions, laws and customs teach us to judge sanely of our own and teach our judgement to acknowledge its shortcomings and natural weakness. And that is no light apprenticeship. So many revolutions, so many changes in the fortune of a state, teach us to realize that our own fortune is no great miracle. So many names, so many victories and conquests lying buried in oblivion, make it ridiculous to hope that we shall immortalize our names by rounding up ten armed brigands or by storming some hen-house or other known only by its capture. The proud arrogance of so many other nations' pomp and the high-flown majesty of the grandeur of so many courts strengthen our gaze to look firmly and assuredly, without blinking, at the brilliance of our own. So many millions upon millions of men dead and buried before us encourage us not to be afraid of going to join such a goodly company in the world to come.

And so on.

[C]   Our life, said Pythagoras,[34] is like the vast throng assembled for the Olympic Games: some use their bodies there to win fame from the contests; others come to trade, to make a profit; still others – and they are by no means the worst – seek no other gain than to be spectators, seeing

---

34. Erasmus, *Apophthegmata*, VII, *Pythagoras* VII (from Cicero, *Tusc. disput.*, V, iii, 9).

how everything is done and why; they watch how other men live so that they can judge and regulate their own lives. [A] All the most profitable treatises of philosophy (which ought to be the touchstone and measure of men's actions) can be properly reduced to examples. Teach the boy this:

> [B]   *quid fas optare, quid asper*
> *Utile nummus habet; patriæ charisque propinquis*
> *Quantum elargiri deceat: quem te Deus esse*
> *Jussit, et humana qua parte locatus es in re;*
> *Quid sumus, aut quidnam victuri gignimur;*

[what he may justly wish for; that money is hard to earn and should be used properly; the extent of our duty to our country and to our dear ones; what God orders you to be, and what place He has assigned to you in the scheme of things; what we are and what we shall win when we have overcome;][35]

teach him [A] what knowing and not knowing means (which ought to be the aim of study); what valour is, and justice and temperance; what difference there is between ordinate and inordinate aspirations; slavery and due subordination; licence and liberty; what are the signs of true and solid happiness; how far we should fear death, pain and shame:

> [B]   *Et quo quemque modo fugiatque feratque laborem;*

[How we can flee from hardships and how we can endure them;][36]

[A] what principles govern our emotions and the physiology of so many and diverse stirrings within us. For it seems to me that the first lessons with which we should irrigate his mind should be those which teach him to know himself, and to know how to die ... and to live. [C] Among the liberal arts, start with the art which produces liberal men. All of them are of some service in the regulation and practice of our lives, just as everything else is; but let us select the one which leads there directly and professes to do so.

If we knew how to restrict our life's appurtenances to their right and natural limits, we would discover that the greater part of the arts and sciences as now practised are of no practical use to us, and that, even in those which are useful, there are useless wastes and chasms which we would do better to leave where they are; following what Socrates taught, we should set limits to our study of subjects which lack utility.

35. Persius, *Satires*, III, 69–73.
36. Virgil, *Aeneid*, III, 459.

> [A]   *sapere aude,*
> *Incipe: vivendi qui recte prorogat horam,*
> *Rusticus expectat dum defluat amnis; at ille*
> *Labitur et labetur in omne volubilis ævum.*

[Dare to be wise. Start now. To put off the moment when you will start to live justly is to act like the bumpkin who would cross but who waits for the stream to dry up; time flows and will flow for ever, as an ever-rolling stream.][37]

There is great folly in teaching our children

> [B]   *quid moveant Pisces, animosaque signa Leonis,*
> *Lotus et Hesperia quid Capricornus aqua,*

[what influences stem from Pisces and the lively constellation of Leo or from Capricorn which plunges into the Hesperian Sea,][38]

about the heavenly bodies   [A]   and the motions of the Eighth Sphere before they know about their own properties.

> *Τί πλειάδεσσι χἀμοί;*
> *Τί δ' ἀστράσι βοώτεω!*

[What do the Pleides or the Herdsman matter to me!][39]

[C]   Writing to Anaximenes, Pythagoras asked: 'What mind am I supposed to bring to the secrets of the heavens, having death and slavery ever present before my eyes?' (At that time the kings of Persia were preparing for war against his country.)[40] We could all ask the same: 'Assaulted as I am by ambition, covetousness, rashness and superstition, and having such enemies to life as that within me, should I start wondering about the motions of the Universe?'

[A]   Only after showing the boy what will make him a wiser and a better man will you explain to him the elements of Logic, Physics, Geometry and Rhetoric. Since his judgement has already been formed he will soon get to the bottom of any science he chooses. His lessons will sometimes be discussion, sometimes reading from books; at times the tutor will provide him with extracts from authors suited to his purposes: at others the tutor will pick out the marrow and chew it over for him. If the

---

37. Horace, *Epistles*, I, ii, 40–3.
38. Propertius, IV, i, 85–6.
39. In Ptolomaic astronomy, the Eighth Sphere contained the fixed stars (Anacreon, *Odes*, XVII, x).
40. Diogenes Laertius, *Life of Anaximenes*.

tutor is not sufficiently familiar with those books to find the discourses in them which serve his purposes you could associate with him a scholar who could furnish him, as the need arises, with material for him to arrange and dispense to the growing boy.

Who can doubt that such lessons will be more natural and easy than those in Theodore Gaza,[41] whose precepts are prickly and nasty, and whose words are hollow and fleshless, with nothing to get hold of or to quicken the mind. Here then is nourishment for the soul to bite on. The fruit is incomparably more plentiful and will ripen sooner.

Oddly, things have now reached such a state that even among men of intelligence philosophy means something fantastical and vain, without value or usefulness, [C] both in opinion and practice. [A] The cause lies in chop-logic which has captured all the approaches. It is a great mistake to portray Philosophy with a haughty, frowning, terrifying face, or as inaccessible to the young. Whoever clapped that wan and frightening mask on her face! There is nothing more lovely, more happy and gay – I almost said more amorously playful. What she preaches is all feast and fun. A sad and gloomy mien shows you have mistaken her address.

Some philosophers were sitting together in the temple at Delphi one day. 'Either I am mistaken,' said Demetrius the grammarian, 'or your calm happy faces show that you are not having an important discussion.' One of them, Herakleon of Megara, retorted: 'Furrowed brows are for grammarians telling us whether *ballō* takes two *l*s in the future, researching into the derivation of the comparatives *keiron* and *beltion* and of the superlatives *keiriston* and *beltiston*: philosophical discussions habitually make men happy and joyful not frowning and sad.'[42]

> [B]   *Deprendas animi tormenta latentis in ægro*
> *Corpore, deprendas et gaudia: sumit utrumque*
> *Inde habitum facies.*

[You can detect in a sickly body the hidden torments of the mind; you can detect her joys as well: the face reflects them both.][43]

[A] The soul which houses philosophy must by her own sanity make for a sound body. Her tranquillity and ease must glow from her; she must fashion her outward bearing to her mould, arming it therefore with gracious pride, a spritely active demeanour and a happy welcoming

41. Author of a fifteenth-century Greek grammar.
42. Plutarch (tr. Amyot), *Des oracles qui ont cessé*, 338A.
43. Juvenal, *Satires*, IX, 1879.

face. [C] The most express sign of wisdom is unruffled joy: like all in the realms above the Moon, her state is ever serene. [A] *Baroco* and *Baralipton* have devotees reeking of filth and smoke.[44] She does not. They know her merely by hearsay. Why, her task is to make the tempests of the soul serene and to teach hunger and fever how to laugh – not by imaginary epicycles but by reasons, [C] natural and palpable.[45] Her aim is virtue, which is not (as they teach in schools) perched on the summit of a steep mountain, rough and inaccessible. Those who have drawn nigh her hold that on the contrary she dwells on a beautiful plateau, fertile and strewn with flowers; from there she clearly sees all things beneath her; but if you know the road you can happily make your way there by shaded grassy paths, flower-scented, smooth and gently rising, like tracks in the vaults of heaven.[46]

This highest virtue is fair, triumphant, loving, as delightful as she is courageous, a professed and implacable foe to bitterness, unhappiness, fear and constraint, having Nature for guide, Fortune and Pleasure for her companions: those who frequent her not have, after their own weakness, fashioned an absurd portrait of her, sad, shrill, sullen, threatening and glowering, perching her on a rocky peak, all on her own among the brambles – a spectre to terrify people.

This tutor of mine, who knows that his duty is to fill the will of his pupil with at least as much love as reverence for virtue, will know how to tell him that our poets are following commonplace humours: he will make him realize that the gods place sweat on the paths to the chambers of Venus rather than of Pallas.[47] And when he comes to know his own mind and is faced with a choice between Bradamante to court and enjoy or Angelica[48] – one with her natural beauty, active, noble, virile though not mannish, contrasting with the other's beauty, soft, dainty, delicate and all artifice; the one disguised as a youth with a shining helmet on her head, the other robed as a maiden with pearls in her headdress: then his very passion will be deemed manly if he chooses flat contrary to that effeminate Phrygian

44. Mnemonics representing by their vowels: i) the fourth mood of the Second figure of syllogisms; ii) the first indirect mood of the Second figure of syllogisms. (Here used to mock dry scholastic logic.)

45. '80: reasons *gross, manageable* and palpable. Since Philosophy . . .

46. In the myth of Hesiod, Virtue dwells on a fair plateau reached by a rugged and toilsome path. Cf. I, 20, 'To philosophize is to learn how to die'; note 7. (Seneca denied it, *De ira*, III, xiii.)

47. Venus, the goddess of love; Pallas, of wisdom.

48. Heroines in Ariosto's *Orlando furioso*.

shepherd.[49] The tutor will then be teaching him a new lesson: what makes true virtue highly valued is the ease, usefulness and pleasure we find in being virtuous: so far from it being difficult, children can be virtuous as well as adults; the simple, as well as the clever. The means virtue uses is control not effort. Socrates, the foremost of her darlings, deliberately renounced effort so as to glide along with her easy natural progress. She is a Mother who nurtures human pleasures: by making them just she makes them sure and pure; by making them moderate they never pant for breath or lose their savour; by cutting away those which she denies us she sharpens our appreciation of those she leaves us – an abundance of all those which Nature wills for us; Mother-like, she provides them not until we are satiated but until we are satisfied (unless, that is, we claim that her rule is the enemy of pleasure because she ordains drinking without drunkenness, eating without indigestion, and sex without the pox). If Virtue should lack the ordinary share of good fortune, she evades or does without it, or else she forges a private happiness of her own, neither floating nor changeable. She knows how to be rich, powerful and learned and how to lie on a perfumed couch; she does love life; she does love beauty, renown and health. But her own peculiar office is to know how to enjoy those good things with proper moderation and how to lose them with constancy: an office much more noble than grievous; without it the whole course of our life becomes unnatural, troubled, deformed; then you can indeed tie it to those rocky paths, those brambles and those spectres.

Were our pupil's disposition so bizarre that he would rather hear a tall story than the account of a great voyage or a wise discussion; that at the sound of the drum calling the youthful ardour of his comrades to arms he would turn aside for the drum of a troop of jugglers; that he would actually find it no more delightful and pleasant to return victorious covered with the dust of battle than after winning a prize for tennis or dancing: then I know no remedy except that his tutor should quickly strangle him when nobody is looking or apprentice him to make fairy-cakes in some goodly town – even if he were the heir of a Duke – following Plato's precept that functions should be allocated not according to the endowments of men's fathers but the endowments of their souls.[50]

49. Virgil, *Aeneid*, VII, 363: Paris who, in his famous judgement between Aphrodite, Hera and Athene, chose the more dainty and artificial Aphrodite (Venus). Montaigne opts for Bradamante.
50. This passage is toned down in ['95]. Cf. Plato, *Republic*, 415 BC; then, Persius, *Satires*, III, 23–4.

[A]   Since philosophy is the art which teaches us how to live, and since children need to learn it as much as we do at other ages, why do we not instruct them in it?

> [B]   *Udum et molle lutum est; nunc nunc properandus et acri*
> *Fingendus sine fine rota.*

[The clay is soft and malleable. Quick! hurry to fashion it on that potter's wheel which is for ever spinning.]

[A]   They teach us to live when our life is over. Dozens of students have caught the pox before they reach the lesson on temperance in their Aristotles.   [C]   Cicero said that even were he to live two men's lives he would never find enough time to study the lyric poets.[51] I find these chop-logic merchants even more gloomily useless. Our boy is too busy for that: to school-learning he owes but the first fifteen or sixteen years of his life: the rest is owed to action. Let us employ a time so short on things which it is necessary to know.   [A]   Get rid of those thorny problems of dialectics – they are trivial: our lives are never amended by them; take the simple arguments of philosophy: learn how to select the right ones and to apply them. They are easier to grasp than a tale in Boccaccio: a boy can do it as soon as he leaves his nanny; it is much easier than learning to read and write. Philosophy has arguments for Man at birth as well as in senility.

I share Plutarch's conviction[52] that Aristotle never spent much of the time of his great pupil Alexander on the art of syllogisms nor on the principles of geometry: he taught him, rather, sound precepts concerning valour, prowess, greatness of soul and temperance, as well as that self-assurance which fears nothing. With such an armoury he sent him still a child to conquer the empire of the world with merely thirty thousand foot-soldiers, four thousand horsemen and forty-two thousand crowns. As for the other arts and sciences, Plutarch says that he held them in esteem, praising their excellence and their nobility; but whatever pleasure he found in them he did not allow himself to be surprised by a desire to practise them himself.

> [B]   *Petite hinc, juvenesque senesque,*
> *Finem animo certum, miserisque viatica canis.*

[Seek here, young men and old, a lasting purpose for your mind and a provision for white-haired wretchedness.][53]

---

51. According to Seneca, *Epist. moral.*, XLIX, 5.
52. Plutarch (tr. Amyot), *De la fortune ou vertu d'Alexandre*, 308GH.
53. Persius, *Satires*, V, 64–5.

[C]   That is what Epicurus says at the beginning of his letter to Meniceus: 'Let the youngest not reject philosophy nor the oldest tire of it. Whoever does otherwise seems to be saying that the season for living happily has not yet come or is already past.'[54]

[A]   Despite all this I do not want to imprison the boy.[55] I do not want him to be left to the melancholy humour of a furious schoolmaster. I do not want to corrupt his mind as others do by making his work a torture, slaving away for fourteen or fifteen hours a day like a porter.   [C]   When you see him over-devoted to studying his books because of a solitary or melancholy complexion, it would not be good I find to encourage him in it: it unfits boys for mixing in polite society and distracts them from better things to do. And how many men have I known in my time made as stupid as beasts by an indiscreet hunger for knowledge! Carneades was turned so mad by it that he could not find time to tend to his hair or his nails.[56]

[A]   Nor do I wish to have his noble manners ruined by the uncouthness or barbarity of others. In antiquity French wisdom was proverbially good at the outset, but lacking in staying power.[57] And truly, still now, nothing is more gentlemanly than little French children; but they normally deceive the hopes placed in them, being in no ways outstanding once they are grown up. I have heard men of wisdom maintain that it is those colleges which parents send children to – and we have them in abundance – which make them so stupid.

For our boy any place and any time can be used to study: his room, a garden; his table, his bed; when alone or in company; morning and evening. His chief study will be philosophy, that Former of good judgement and character who is privileged to be concerned with everything.

It was an orator Isocrates who, being begged to talk about his art at a feast, replied (rightly we all think): 'What I can do, this is no time for: what this is time for, I cannot do!'[58] To present harangues and rhetorical debates to a company gathered for laughter and good cheer would be to mix together things too discordant.

You can say the same of all the other disciplines, but not of that part of

54. Diogenes Laertius, *Life of Epicurus*.
55. [A] until [C]: boy *in a college*. I do not . . .
56. Diogenes Laertius, *Life of Carneades*.
57. The Romans said this of the French (the Gauls') fighting-power (Erasmus, *Apophthegmata*, VI, *varie mixta*, CIII).
58. Plutarch (tr. Amyot), *Premier livre des Propos de Table*, 359F.

Philosophy which treats of Man, his tasks and his duties: by the common
consent of all the wise, she should not be barred from sports nor feastings
seeing that commerce with her is sweet. And Plato having invited her to
his *Banquet*, we can see how she entertained the guests in a relaxed manner
appropriate to time and place even when treating one of her most sublime
and most salutary themes:[59]

> *Æque pauperibus prodest, locupletibus æque;*
> *Et, neglecta, æque pueris senibüsque nocebit.*

[She is equally helpful to the poor and the rich: neglect her, and she equally harms
the young and the old.][60]

In this way he will certainly lie fallow much less than do others. Now
we can take three times as many steps strolling about a long-gallery and
still feel less tired than on a walk to a definite goal: so too our lessons will
slip by unnoticed if we apparently happen upon them, as, restricted to
neither time nor place, they intermingle with all our activities. The games
and sports themselves will form a good part of his studies: racing,
wrestling, [C] music-making, [A] dancing, hunting and the handling
of arms and horses. I want his outward graces, his social ease [C] and his
physical dexterity [A] to be moulded step by step with his soul. We are
not bringing up a soul; we are not bringing up a body: we are bringing up
a man. We must not split him into two. We must not bring up one
without the other but, as Plato said, lead them abreast like a pair of horses
harnessed together to the same shaft. [C] And does not Plato when you
listen to him appear to devote more time and care to exercising the body,
convinced that the mind may be exercised with the body but not vice
versa?

[A] This education is to be conducted, moreover, with a severe gentleness, not as it usually is.[61] Instead of children being invited to letters as
guests, all they are shown in truth are cruelty and horror. Get rid of
violence and force: as I see it, nothing so fundamentally stultifies and
bastardizes a well-born nature.

If you want the boy to loathe disgrace and punishment do not harden
him to them. Harden him to sweltering heat and to cold, to wind and sun

---

59. Plato's *Symposium* in French, and sometimes in English, is known as the
Banquet: its theme is the nature of love. Then Plutarch, ibid., 360E.
60. Horace, *Epistles*, I, i, 25–6.
61. [A] until [C]: usually is *in colleges, where* instead ... (Cf. Plutarch (tr.
Amyot), *Regles et Preceptes de Santé*, 302B.)

and to such dangers as he must learn to treat with contempt. Rid him of all softness and delicacy about dress and about sleeping, eating and drinking. Get him used to anything. Do not turn him into a pretty boy or a ladies' boy but into a boy who is fresh and vigorous.   [C]   Boy, man and now old man, I have always thought this. But I have always disliked, among other things, the way our colleges are governed. Their failure would have been less harmful, perhaps, if they had leant towards indulgence. They are a veritable gaol for captive youth. By punishing boys for depravity before they are depraved, you make them so.

Go there during lesson time: you will hear nothing but the screaming of tortured children and of masters drunk with rage. What a way to awaken a taste for learning in those tender timorous souls, driving them to it with terrifying scowls and fists armed with canes! An iniquitous and pernicious system. And besides (as Quintilian justly remarked)[62] such imperious authority can lead to dreadful consequences – especially given our form of flogging.

How much more appropriate to strew their classrooms with leaf and flower than with blood-stained birch-rods. I would have portraits of Happiness there and Joy, with Flora and the Graces, as Speucippus the philosopher did in his school.[63]

When they have something to gain, make it enjoyable. Health-giving foods should be sweetened for a child: harmful ones made to taste nasty.

It is amazing how concerned Plato is in his *Laws* with the amusements and pastimes of the youths of his City and how he dwells on their races, sports, singing, capering and dancing, the control and patronage of which has been entrusted, he said, in antiquity to the gods, to Apollo, the Muses and Minerva. His care extends to over a hundred precepts for his gymnasia, yet he spends little time over book-learning; the only thing he seems specifically to recommend poetry for is the music.[64]

[A]   In our manners and behaviour any strangeness and oddness are to be avoided as enemies of easy mixing in society –   [C]   and as monstrosities. Who would not have been deeply disturbed by Alexander's steward Demophon whose complexion made him sweat in the shade and shiver in the sun?   [A]   I have known men who fly from the smell of apples rather than from gunfire; others who are terrified of a mouse, who vomit at the

---

62. Quintilian, *Institutio*, I, iii, 13–16. Dismissing Chrysippus' belief in the value of flogging, Quintilian held that it can produce mental depression.
63. Diogenes Laertius, *Life of Speucippus*.
64. Plato, *Laws*, VII; then, for Demophon, Sextus Empiricus, *Hypotyposes*, I, xiv, and for Germanicus, Plutarch (tr. Amyot), *De l'envie et la haine*, 108A.

sight of cream or when a feather mattress is shaken up (like Germanicus who could not abide cocks or their crowing). Some occult property may be involved in this, but, if you ask me, if you set about it young enough you could stamp it out.

One victory my education has achieved over me (though not without some trouble, it is true) is that my appetite can be brought to accept without distinction any of the things people eat and drink except beer. While the body is still supple it should, for that very reason, be made pliant to all manners and customs. Provided that he can restrain his appetites and his will, you should not hesitate to make the young man suited to all peoples and companies, even, should the need arise, to immoderation and excess.

[C] His practice should conform to custom. [A] He should be able to do anything but want to do only what is good. (The very philosophers do not approve of Calesthenes for falling from grace with his master Alexander the Great, by declining to match drink for drink with him. He will laugh, fool about and be unruly with his Prince.) I would want him to outstrip his fellows in vigour and firmness even during the carousing and that he should refrain from wrongdoing not because he lacks strength or knowledge but because he does not want to do it. [C] '*Multum interest utrum peccare aliquis nolit aut nesciat.*' [There is a great difference between not wanting to do evil and not knowing how to.][65]

[A] My intention was to honour a nobleman who is as far removed from such excesses as any man in France when I asked him, in the presence of guests, how many times in his life he had had to get drunk while serving the King in Germany. He took it in the right spirit and said he had done it three times; and he told me about them. (I have known people who have run into real difficulties when frequenting that nation because they lacked this ability.)

I have often noted with great astonishment the extraordinary character of Alcibiades who, without impairing his health, could so readily adapt to diverse manners: at times he could outdo Persians in pomp and luxury; at others, Spartans in austerity and frugal living.[66] He was a reformed man in Sparta, yet equally pleasure-seeking in Ionia:

Omnis Aristippum decuit color, et status, et res.

[On Aristippus any colour, rank or condition was becoming.]

65. Seneca, *Epist. moral.*, XC, 46.
66. Plutarch, *Life of Alcibiades*.

Thus would I fashion my pupil:

> *quem duplici panno patientia velat*
> *Mirabor, vitæ via si conversa decebit,*
> *Personámque feret non inconcinnus utramqué.*

[One who is patiently clad in rags yet could also adapt to the opposite extreme, playing both roles becomingly: him I will admire.][67]

Such are my lessons.[68] [C] For him who draws most profit from them, they are acts, not facts. To see his deeds is to hear his word: to hear his word is to see his deeds. 'God forbid,' says someone in Plato,[69] 'that philosophy should mean learning a lot of things and then talking about the arts: *'Hanc amplissimam omnium artium bene vivendi disciplinam vita magis quam literis persequuti sunt.'* [The fullest art of all – that of living good lives – they acquired more from life than from books.][70]

Prince Leon of the Phliasians inquired of Heraclides of Pontus which art or science he professed. 'I know none of them,' he replied; 'I am a philosopher.' Diogenes was reproached for being ignorant yet concerned with philosophy. 'My concern is all the more appropriate,' he replied. When Hegesias begged him to read a certain book he replied, 'How amusing of you! You prefer real figs to painted ones, so why not true and natural deeds to written ones?'[71]

My pupil will not say his lesson: he will do it. He will rehearse his lessons in his actions. You will then see whether he is wise in what he takes on, good and just in what he does, gracious and sound in what he says, resilient in illnesses, modest in his sports, temperate in his pleasures, [A] indifferent to the taste of his food, be it fish or flesh, wine or water; [C] orderly in domestic matters: *'Qui disciplinam suam, non ostentationem scientiæ, sed legem vitæ putet, quique obtemperet ipse sibi, et decretis pareat'* [as a man who knows how to make his education into a rule of life not a means of showing off; who can control himself and obey

---

67. Horace, *Epistles*, I, xvii, 23, 25, 26, 29.
68. '80: lessons, *in which doing goes with saying. For what is the use of preaching at his mind if deeds do not go along with it? You will see from what he undertakes whether there is any wisdom there: if there is any goodness in his actions, if he is* indifferent . . .
69. Plato, *The Lovers* (*Erastai*) 137 A B (which shows Socrates discussing the nature of philosophy with schoolboys).
70. Cicero, *Tusc. disput.*, IV, iii, 5.
71. Cicero, ibid., IV, iii, 8; then, Diogenes Laertius, *Life of Diogenes*.

his own principles].[72] The true mirror of our discourse is the course of our lives.

[A] To a man who asked him why the Spartans never drew up written rules of bravery and gave them to their children, Zeuxidamus replied that they wished to accustom them to deeds not [C] words. [A] After[73] fifteen or sixteen years compare with that one of our college latinizers who has spent precisely as long simply learning to talk!

The world is nothing but chatter: I have never met a man who does not say more than he should rather than less. Yet half of our life is spent on that; they keep us four or five years learning the meanings of words and stringing them into sentences; four or five more in learning how to arrange them into a long composition, divided into four parts or five; then as many again in plaiting and weaving them into verbal subtleties.

Let us leave all that to those who make it their express profession.

When I was travelling to Orleans one day, on the plain this side of Cléry I met two college tutors who were coming from Bordeaux; there was about fifty yards between them; I could also make out some troops further away still, led by their officer (who was the Count de la Rochefoucault). One of my men asked the first of these tutors who was 'that gentleman coming behind him'? The tutor had not noticed the party following behind them and thought they were talking about his companion: 'He is not a gentleman,' he amusingly replied, 'but a grammarian. And I am a logician.' Now we who, on the contrary, are trying to form a gentleman not a grammarian or a logician should let them waste their own time: we have business to do elsewhere. Provided that our student be well furnished with *things*, words will follow only too easily: if they do not come easily, then he can drag them out slowly.

I sometimes hear people who apologize for not being able to say what they mean, maintaining that their heads are so full of fine things that they cannot deliver them for want of eloquence. That is moonshine. Do you know what I think? It is a matter of shadowy notions coming to them from some unformed concepts which they are unable to untangle and to clarify in their minds: consequently they cannot deliver them externally. They themselves do not yet know what they mean. Just watch them giving a little stammer as they are about to deliver their brain-child: you can tell that they have labouring-pains not at childbirth [C] but during

---

72. Cicero, *Tusc. disput.*, II, iv, 11.
73. Plutarch (tr. Amyot), *Dicts notables des Lacedaemoniens*, 217A.
 '80: deeds not *writings*. After . . .

conception! [A] They are merely licking an imperfect lump into shape.[74] For my part I maintain – [C] and Socrates is decisive – [A] that whoever has one clear living thought in his mind will deliver it even in Bergamask.[75] Or if he is dumb he will do so by signs.

> *Verbaque prævisam rem non invita sequentur.*

[Once you have mastered the things the words will come freely.][76]

And as another said just as poetically though in prose: '*Cum res animum occupavere, verba ambiunt.*' [When things have taken hold of the mind, the words come crowding forth.][77]   [C]   And another one: '*Ipsae res verba rapiunt.*' [The things themselves ravish the words.][78]

[A] 'But he does not know what an ablative is, a conjunctive, a substantive: he knows no grammar!' Neither does his footman or a Petit-Pont fishwife[79] yet they will talk you to death if you let them and will probably no more stumble over the rules of their own dialect than the finest Master of Arts in France.

'But he knows no rhetoric nor how to compose an opening *captatio benevolentiae* for his gentle reader!'[80] He does not need to know that. All those fine 'colours of rhetoric' are in fact easily eclipsed by the light of pure and naïve truth. Those elegant techniques (as Afer shows in Tacitus) merely serve to entertain the masses who are unable to [C]   take [A]   heavier solid meat.[81]

Ambassadors from Samos came to King Cleomenes of Sparta with a long prepared speech to persuade him to go to war against Polycrates the Tyrant. He let them have their say and then replied: 'As for your preamble

---

74. Like bears, the offspring of which were thought to be born without form but 'licked into shape' by their parents.
75. Bergamask – the dialect of Bergamo (in Venice). The inhabitants and their language were considered rustic and uncouth. (In the context of imagery drawn from childbirth there is possibly also a play on *boucler à la bergamasque*, to shut up one's wife in a chastity-belt.)
76. Horace, *Ars poetica*, 311.
77. Marcus Annaeus Seneca, *Controversiae*, III.
78. Cicero, *De finibus*, III, v. 19.
79. *Petit-Pont* – the 'Billingsgate' of Paris.
80. A *captatio benevolentiae* is a literary device designed to catch the reader's sympathetic attention. It was taught as part of rhetoric and dialectic.
81. [A]: unable to *appreciate* heavier . . .
   Tacitus, *Dialogus an sui saeculi oratores antiquioribus concedant*, XIX.

and preface, I no longer remember it; nor of course your middle bit. As for your conclusion, I will do none of it.'[82] An excellent answer, it seems to me, with a blow on the nose of those speechifiers.

[B] And what about this other case. The Athenians had to choose between two architects to take charge of a large building project. The first one was the more fly and presented himself with a fine prepared speech about the job to be done; he won the favour of the common people. The other architect merely spoke two or three words: 'Gentlemen of Athens: what he said, I will do.'[83]

[A] At the height of his eloquence Cicero moved many into ecstasies of astonishment. But Cato merely laughed:'Quite an amusing consul we have,' he said.[84]

Now a useful saying or a pithy remark is always welcome wherever it is put. [C] If it is not good in the context of what comes before it or after it, it is good in itself. [A] I am not one of those who hold that good scansion makes a good poem: let the poet lengthen a short syllable if he wants to. That simply does not count. If the invention of his subject-matter is happy and if his wit and judgement have done their jobs, then I shall say: 'Good poet: but bad versifier.'

> *Emunctæ naris, durus componere versus.*

> [He has the flair, though his verses are harsh.]

Take his work (says Horace) and pull its measured verse apart at the seams —

> [B] *Tempora certa modosque, et quod prius ordine verbum est,*
> *Posterius facias, præponens ultima primis,*
> *Invenias etiam disjecti membra poetæ*

[Take away rhythm and measure; change the order of the words putting the first last and the last first: you will still find the poet in those scattered remains] —

[A] he will still not belie himself for all that: even bits of it will be beautiful.[85]

That is what Menander replied when the day came for his promised comedy and people chided him for not yet putting it in hand: 'It is already

82. Plutarch (tr. Amyot), *Dicts notables des Lacedaemoniens*, 218B.
83. Plutarch (tr. Amyot), *Instructions pour ceux qui manient les affaires d'Estat*, 163F.
84. Erasmus, *Apophthegmata*, V, *Cato Uticensis*, III.
85. Horace, *Satires*, I, iv, 8; 58–60.

composed,' he said. 'All I have to do is to put it into verse.'[86] Having thought the things through and arranged them in his mind, he attached little importance to the remainder. Since Ronsard and Du Bellay have brought renown to our French poetry, every little apprentice I know is doing more or less as they do, using noble words and copying their cadences. [C] *'Plus sonat quam valet.'* ['More din than sense.']ptember[87] [A] Ordinary people think there never have been so many poets. But easy as it has proved to copy their rhymes they all fall short when it comes to imitating the rich descriptions of the one and the delicate invention of the other.

'Yes. But what will he do when they harass him with some sophistical syllogistic subtlety:

> Bacon makes you drink;
> Drinking quenches your thirst:
> Therefore bacon quenches your thirst?'

[C] Let him simply laugh at it: it is cleverer to laugh at it than to answer it. Or let him borrow Aristippus's amusing rejoinder: 'Why should I unravel that? It is bad enough all knotted up!' Someone challenged Cleanthes with dialectical trickeries; Chrysippus said to him: 'Go and play those conjuring tricks on children: do not interrupt the serious thoughts of a grown-up.'[88] [A] If this verbal jugglery – [C] *'contorta et aculeata sophismata'* [these contorted prickly sophisms][89] – [A] should persuade him to accept an untruth, that is dangerous: but if they do not result in action and simply move him to laughter, I really do not see why he should pay attention to them.

Some people are so daft that they will go a mile or so out of their way to hunt for a good word: [C] *'aut qui non verba rebus aptant, sed res extrinsecus arcessunt, quibus verba conveniant!'* [they do not fit words to things but look for irrelevant things to fit to their words!] Or again: *'Sunt qui alicujus verbi decore placentis vocentur ad id quod non proposuerant scribere.'* [There are authors who are led by the beauty of some attractive word to write what they never intended.][90] I myself am more ready to distort

---

86. Plutarch (tr. Amyot), *Si les Atheniens ont esté plus excellents en armes qu'en lettres*, 525DE.

87. Seneca, *Epistles*, XL, 5.

88. Both from Diogenes Laertius, *Life of Aristippus*. (Cf. also Erasmus, *Apophthegmata*, III, *Aristippus*, XIII.)

89. Cicero, *Academica*, II (*Lucullus*), xxiv, 75.

90. Quintilian, *Institutiones oratoriae*, VIII, iii, 30 (adapted); then, Seneca, *Epist. moral.*, LIX, 5.

a fine saying in order to patch it on to me than to distort the thread of my argument to go in search of one.

[A] It is, on the contrary, for words to serve and to follow: if French cannot get there, let Gascon do so. I want *things* to dominate, so filling the thoughts of the hearer that he does not even remember the words. I like the kind of speech which is simple and natural, the same on paper as on the lip; speech which is rich in matter, sinewy, brief and short; [C] not so much titivated and refined as forceful and brusque –

Haec demum sapiet dictio, quae feriet

[The good style of speaking is the kind which strikes home][91] –

[A] gnomic rather than diffuse, far from affectation, uneven, disjointed and bold – let each bit form a unity – not schoolmasterly, not monkish, not legalistic, but soldierly, rather as Sallust described Julius Caesar's [C] (though I do not quite see why he did so).[92] [B] I like to imitate the unruly negligence shown by French youth in the way they are seen to wear their clothes,[93] [C] with their mantles bundled round their neck, their capes tossed over one shoulder or [B] with a stocking pulled awry: it manifests a pride contemptuous of the mere externals of dress and indifferent to artifice. But I find it even better applied to speech. [C] All affectation is unbecoming in a courtier, especially given the hearty freedom of the French: and under a monarchy every gentleman is inevitably schooled in court manners. So we do well to lean towards the careless and natural. [A] I have no love for textures where the joins and seams all show (just as you ought not to be able to count the ribs or the veins in a beautiful body). [C] '*Quae veritati operam dat oratio, incomposita sit et simplex.*' [Speech devoted to truth should be straightforward and plain.][94] '*Quis accurate loquitur, nisi qui vult putide loqui?*' [Who can speak carefully unless he wants to sound affected?][95]

91. From the Epitaph of Lucan (the poet of the *Pharsalia*).
92. A very perspicacious remark. Suetonius' alleged remark arises from a poor manuscript reading of a passage in his *Life of Caesar* which is corrected in modern editions but was accepted during the Renaissance.
   [B] until [C]: Julius Caesar's. *Let us boldly hold against him what was held against Seneca: his style was quick-lime, but without the sand. I like to . . .*
93. '88: clothes, *letting themselves be taken for German mercenaries, wearing a cape and with a stocking . . .*
94. Seneca, *Epist. moral.*, XL, 4 (on the style fit for a philosopher).
95. Ibid., LXXV, 1.

When eloquence draws attention to itself it does wrong by the substance of *things*.

Just as in dress it is the sign of a petty mind to seek to draw attention by some personal or unusual fashion, so too in speech; the search for new expressions and little-known words derives from an adolescent schoolmaster-ish ambition. If only I could limit myself to words used in Les Halles in Paris! That grammarian Aristophanes did not know the first thing about it when he criticized Epicurus for his simple words and for having perspicuity of language as his sole rhetorical aim.[96]

To imitate speech is easy: an entire nation can do it: to imitate judgement and the research for your material takes rather more time! Most readers think similar styles, when they find them, clothe similar bodies. But you cannot borrow strength or sinews: you can borrow mantles and finery. Most of the people who haunt my company talk like these *Essays*:[97] I cannot tell whether they think like them . . .

[A] Athenians (says Plato) take copious and elegant speech as their share; Spartans, brevity; Cretans, fecundity of thought not speech – and they are the best.[98] Zeno said that he had two sorts of followers: those he termed *philologous*, who cared for real learning (they were his favourites) and those he termed *logophilous*, whose concern was with words.[99]

That does not mean that speaking well is not a fine thing or a good thing, but that it is not as good as we make it out to be. It irritates me that our life is taken up by it. I would prefer first to know my own language well and then that of the neighbours with whom I have regular dealings.

There is no doubt that Greek and Latin are fine and great accomplishments; but they are bought too dear. I will tell you a cheaper way of buying them: it was assayed on me. Anyone is welcome to use it. My late father, after having made all possible inquiries among the learned and the wise about the choicest form of education, was warned about the disadvantages of the current system: they told him that the length of time we spend learning languages, [C] which cost the Ancients nothing, [A] is the sole reason why we cannot attain to the greatness of mind and knowledge of those old Greeks and Romans. I do not believe that to be the sole reason. Nevertheless the expedient found by my father

96. Diogenes Laertius, *Life of Epicurus*.
97. That is, they talk in French (not Gascon).
98. Plato, *Laws*, I, 641E.
99. A pun known only from John Stobaeus' compendium of Greek sayings (xxxvi). There is a play on the two senses of *logos* in Greek: *reason* and *word*.

was to place me, while still at the breast and before my tongue was untied, in the care of a German (who subsequently died in France as a famous doctor); he was totally ignorant of our language but very well versed in Latin. He had been brought over expressly and engaged at a very high fee: he had me continuously on his hands. There were two others with him, less learned: their task was to follow me about and provide him with some relief. They never addressed me in any other language but Latin. As for the rest of the household, it was an inviolable rule that neither he nor my mother nor a manservant nor a housemaid ever spoke in my presence anything except such words of Latin as they had learned in order to chatter a bit with me. It is wonderful how much they all got from it. My father and my mother learned in this way sufficient Latin to understand it and acquired enough to be able to talk it when they had to, as did those other members of the household who were most closely devoted to my service. In short we became so latinized that it spilled over into the neighbouring villages, where, resulting from this usage, you can still find several Latin names for tools and for artisans. As for me, I was six years old before I knew French any more than I know the *patois* of Périgord or Arabic. And so, without art, without books, without grammar, without rules, without whips and without [C] tears,[100] [A] I had learned Latin as pure as that which my schoolteacher knew – for I had no means of corrupting it or contaminating it. So if they wanted me to assay writing a prose (as other boys do in the colleges by translating from French) they had to give me some bad Latin to turn into good. And Nicholas Grouchy (who wrote *De comitiis Romanorum*), Guillaume Guerente (who wrote a commentary on Aristotle), George Buchanan, that great Scottish poet, [A1] Marc-Antoine Muret [C] whom France and Italy acknowledge to be the best prose-writer in his day, [A] who were my private tutors, have often told me that in my infancy I had that language so fluent and so ready that they were afraid to approach me.[101]

Buchanan, whom I subsequently met in the retinue of the late Lord Marshal de Brissac, told me that he was writing a book on educating children and was taking my education as his model, for he was then the tutor of Count de Brissac whom we have since seen so valiant and brave.

As for Greek (which I scarcely understand at all) my father planned to have it taught to me as methodically, but in a new way, as a sort of game

100. '80: without *constraint*, I had learned . . .
101. All these great Latinists were masters at the Collège de Guyenne in Bordeaux, to which Montaigne was sent after studying at home.

or sport. We would bounce declensions about, rather like those who use certain board-games as a means of learning arithmetic and geometry. For among other things he had been counselled to bring me to love knowledge and duty by my own choice, without forcing my will, and to educate my soul entirely through gentleness and freedom. He was so meticulous about this that since some maintain that it disturbs the tender brains of children to wake them up with a start and to snatch them suddenly and violently out of their sleep (in which they are far more deeply plunged than we are) he would have me woken up by the sound of a musical instrument;   [A1]   and I was never without someone to do this for me.[102]

This example will suffice to judge all the rest by, and also to emphasize the wisdom and love of so good a father who is by no means to be criticized because he harvested no fruits worthy of so choice a husbandry. There were two causes for that: first, my soil was ill-suited and barren, for, though I enjoyed solid good health together with a quiet and amenable nature, I was, despite that, so heavy, passive and dreamy that nobody could drag me out of my idleness, not even to make me play. Whatever I could perceive I saw well and, beneath my heavy complexion, I nursed bold ideas as well as opinions old for my age. My mind was lazy and would only budge so long as it was led; I was slow to understand and my inventiveness was   [C]   slack.[103]   [A]   To top it all, my memory was incredibly unreliable.

Considering all that it is no wonder that my father could make nothing of me.

The second reason was as follows: just as people who are frantic about finding a cure go and consult anybody, that good man was extremely frightened of failure in a matter which meant so much to him: he finally let himself be carried away by the common opinion (which always merely follows the leader as cranes do); he fell in with standard practice (no longer having about him the men who had given him his original educational ideas, which he had brought back from Italy) and sent me, at the age of six, to the Collège de Guyenne, then in full flourish as the best school in France. There too it is impossible to exaggerate the trouble he took over choosing good personal tutors for me and over all the other details of my education, preserving several idiosyncrasies opposed to the usual practices

102. [A]: for me: *and there was always at hand someone who played the spinet for this purpose*. This example . . .
103. '80: was *dull*. To top . . .

of the College. But for all that, it was still school. My Latin was at once corrupted and, since then, I have lost all use of it from lack of practice. And all my novel education merely served to enable me to stride right into the upper forms: I left College at thirteen, having 'completed the course' (as they put it); and in truth I now have nothing to show for it.

My first taste for books arose from enjoying Ovid's *Metamorphoses*; when I was about seven or eight I used to sneak away from all other joys to read it, especially since Latin was my mother-tongue and the *Metamorphoses* was the easiest book I knew and the one most suitable by its subject to my tender age. (As for *Lancelot du lac*, [B] *Amadis*, [A] *Huon de Bordeaux* and so on, trashy books which children spend time on, I did not even know their titles – and still do not know their insides – so exact was the way I was taught.)

This rendered me a bit slacker about studying my set-books. I was particularly lucky at this stage to have to deal with an understanding tutor who adroitly connived at this and other similar passions: for I read in succession Virgil (the *Aeneid*), Terence, Plautus and the Italian comedies, ever seduced by the attractiveness of their subjects. Had he been mad enough to break this succession I reckon that I would have left school hating books, as most French aristocrats do. He acted most ingeniously. Pretending not to notice anything, he sharpened my appetite by making me devour such books in secret, while gently requiring me to do my duty by the other, prescribed, books. For the chief qualities which my father looked for in those who had charge of me were affability and an easy-going complexion: and my own complexion had no vices other than sluggishness and laziness. The risk was not that I should do wrong but do nothing. Nobody forecast that I would turn out bad, only useless. What they foretold was idleness not wickedness.

[C] I am aware that that is the way things have turned out. The complaints which ring in my ears confirm it: 'Lazy! No warmth in his duties as friend, relation or public official! Too much on his own!' Even the most insulting accusers never say, 'Why did he go and take that?' or 'Why has he never paid up?' What they say is, 'Why will he not write it off?' or 'Why will he not *give* it away?'

I would consider it flattering if people found me wanting only in such works of supererogation. Where they are unjust is in requiring that I exceed my obligations – more rigorously, indeed, than they require of themselves their mere fulfilment. By so requiring they destroy the gratuitous nature of the deed and therefore the gratitude which would be my due; whereas any active generosity on my part should be more highly appreciated, seeing that I have never been the recipient of any. I am all the more free to dispose of my fortune in that it is thoroughly mine. Yet if I were a great burnisher-up of my actions I might well beat off such reproaches. I would teach some of these people that they are not annoyed because I do not do a lot for them but because I could do a lot more.

[A]   For all that, my soul was not wanting in powerful emotions of her own,   [C]   nor in sure and open judgements about subjects which she knew,   [A]   digesting them alone, without telling anyone else. Among other things, I truly believe that she was incapable of surrendering to force and violence.

[B]   Should I include another of my characteristics as a child? I had an assured countenance and a suppleness of voice and gesture when I undertook to act in plays; for, in advance of my age,

> *Alter ab undecimo tum me vix ceperat annus,*

[The following year had scarcely plucked me from my eleventh,][104]

I played the chief characters in the Latin tragedies of Buchanan, Guerente and Muret, which were put on in our Collège de Guyenne with dignity.[105] In such matters Andreas Gouveanus, our principal, was incomparably the best principal in France, as he was in all other aspects of his duties; and I was held to be a past master. Acting is an activity which is not unpraiseworthy in the children of good families; I have subsequently seen our Princes actively involved in it (following the example of the ancients) and winning honour and praise.   [C]   In Greece it was open even to gentlemen to make acting their profession: '*Aristoni tragico actori rem aperit: huic et genus et fortuna honesta erant; nec ars, quia nihil tale apud Græcos pudori est, ea deformabat.*' [He disclosed his project to Ariston, the tragic actor, a gentleman respected for his birth and his fortune; his profession in no ways impaired this respect, since nothing like that is a source of shame among the Greeks.][106]

[B]   Those who condemn such entertainments I have even accused of lack of perspicacity; and of injustice, those who deny entry into our goodly towns to worthwhile troops of actors, begrudging the people such public festivities. Good governments take the trouble to bring their citizens

104. Virgil, *Eclogue*, VIII, 39 (adapted).
105. These plays were all in Latin; they included no doubt Muret's *Julius Caesar* and Buchanan's *Jephthes*. Guerante's plays are not known.
106. Livy, XXIV, xxiv.

together and to assemble them for sports and games just as they do for serious acts of worship: a sense of community and good-will is increased by this. And you could not allow citizens any amusements better regulated than those which take place in the presence of all and in full view of the magistrate. I would find it reasonable that the magistrate or the monarch should occasionally offer such amusements to the people for nothing, with a kind of fatherly goodness and affection, [C] and that in the bigger towns there should be places set aside and duly appointed for such spectacles, which would be a diversion from worse and secret goings-on.

[A] Now, to get back to my subject, there is nothing like tempting the boy to want to study and to love it: otherwise you simply produce donkeys laden with books. They are flogged into retaining a pannierful of learning; but if it is to do any good, Learning must not only lodge with us: we must marry her.

't is madness to judge the true and ...ne false from our own capacities

====

[Curiosity when applied to strange or miraculous events is both vain and arrogant. Since men are lulled by habit, they cease to wonder at the glory of the heavens yet they claim to know the limits of the whole order of Nature – and so to judge from their own parochial experience what is miraculous and what is not. Only the authority of the Church and of God's saints can recognize miracles for what they are and vouch for them. Once the Church has decided any issue of fact or doctrine, Roman Catholics must never deviate from her teachings. A man may reject her authority altogether, but he is not free to pick and choose among doctrines, especially during discussions with heretics.]

[A] It is not perhaps without good reason that we attribute to simple-mindedness a readiness to believe anything and to ignorance the readiness to be convinced, for I think I was once taught that a belief is like an impression stamped on our soul: the softer and less resisting the soul, the easier it is to print anything on it: [C] *'Ut necesse est lancem in libra ponderibus impositis deprimi, sic animum perspicuis cedere.'* ['For just as a weight placed on a balance must weigh it down, so the mind must yield to clear evidence.']¹ The more empty a soul is and the less furnished with counterweights, the more easily its balance will be swayed under the force of its first convictions. [A] That is why children, the common people, women and the sick are more readily led by the nose.

On the other hand there is a silly arrogance in continuing to disdain something and to condemn it as false just because it seems unlikely to us. That is a common vice among those who think their capacities are above the ordinary.

I used to do that once: if I heard tell of ghosts walking or of prophecies, enchantments, sorcery, or some other tale which I could not get my teeth into –

> *Somnia, terrores magicos, miracula, sagas,*
> *Nocturnos lemures portentaque Thessala*

1. Cicero, *Academica*, II, ii, 127.

[Dreams, magic terrors, miracles, witches, nocturnal visits from the dead or spells from Thessaly][2]

– I used to feel sorry for the wretched folk who were taken in by such madness. Now I find that I was at least as much to be pitied as they were. It is not that experience has subsequently shown me anything going beyond my original beliefs (nor is it from any lack of curiosity on my part), but reason has taught me that, if you condemn in this way anything whatever as definitely false and quite impossible, you are claiming to know the frontiers and bounds of the will of God and the power of Nature our Mother; it taught me also that there is nothing in the whole world madder than bringing matters down to the measure of our own capacities and potentialities.

How many of the things which constantly come into our purview must be deemed monstrous or miraculous if we apply such terms to anything which outstrips our reason! If we consider that we have to grope through a fog even to understand the very things we hold in our hands, then we will certainly find that it is not knowledge but habit which takes away their strangeness;

> [B] *jam nemo, fessus satiate videndi,*
> *Suspicere in cœli dignatur lucida templa;*

[Already now, tired and satiated with seeing, nobody bothers to gaze up at the shining temples of the heavens;]

[A] such things, if they were newly presented to us, would seem as unbelievable as any others;

> *si nunc primum mortalibus adsint*
> *Ex improviso, ceu sint objecta repente,*
> *Nil magis his rebus poterat mirabile dici,*
> *Aut minus ante quod auderent fore credere gentes.*

[supposing that now, for the first time, they were suddenly shown to mortal men: nothing could be called more miraculous; such things the nations would not have dared to believe.][3]

He who had never actually seen a river, the first time he did so took it for the ocean, since we think that the biggest things that we know represent the limits of what Nature can produce in that species.

2. Horace, *Epistles*, II, ii, 208–9.
3. Lucretius, II, 1037–8; 1032–5.

[B]   *Scilicet et fluvius, qui non est maximus, eii est*
       Qui non ante aliquem majorem vidit, et ingens
       Arbor homoque videtur;   [A]   *et omnia de genere omni*
       Maxima quæ vidit quisque, hæc ingentia fingit.

[B] [Just as a river may not be all that big, but seems huge to a man who has never seen a bigger one, so, too, the biggest tree or biggest man or   [A]   the biggest thing of any kind which we know is considered huge by us.]

[C] *'Consuetudine oculorum assuescunt animi, neque admirantur, neque requirunt rationes earum rerum quas semper vident.'* [When we grow used to seeing anything it accustoms our minds to it and we cease to be astonished by it; we never seek the causes of things like that.][4] What makes us seek the cause of anything is not size but novelty.

[A] We ought to judge the infinite power of [C] Nature [A] with more reverence[5] and a greater recognition of our own ignorance and weakness. How many improbable things there are which have been testified to by people worthy of our trust: if we cannot be convinced we should at least remain in suspense. To condemn them as impossible is to be rashly presumptuous, boasting that we know the limits of the possible. [C] If we understood the difference between what is impossible and what is unusual, or between what is against the order of the course of Nature[6] and what is against the common opinion of mankind, then the way to observe that rule laid down by Chilo, *Nothing to excess*, would be, Not to believe too rashly: not to disbelieve too easily.

[A] When we read in Froissart that the Comte de Foix knew the following morning in Béarn of the defeat of King John of Castille at Juberoth, and when we read of the means he is alleged to have used, we can laugh at that;[7] we can laugh too when our annals tell how Pope Honorius, on the very same day that King Phillip-Augustus died at Mante, celebrated a public requiem for him and ordered the same to be done

---

4. Lucretius, VI, 674–7; Cicero, *De natura deorum*, II, XXXVIII, 96.
5. '80: power of *God* with more reverence . . .
6. In Christian theology it is only an event which occurs against the *whole order* of Nature which constitutes a miracle.
7. In 1385 the Comte de Foix took to his rooms and then was able to announce that there had just occurred in Portugal a huge slaughter of soldiers from Béarn. It was believed that he had a familiar spirit, either one called Orthon or another like him, who, in an earlier period, had deserted the local *curé* to serve the Seigneur de Corasse (Froissart, III, 17).

throughout Italy;[8] for the authority of such witnesses is not high enough to rein us back.

But wait. When Plutarch (leaving aside the many examples which he alleges from Antiquity) says that he himself knows quite definitely that, at the time of Domitian, news of the battle lost by Antony several days' journey away in Germany was publicly announced in Rome and spread through all the world on the very day that it was lost; and when Caesar maintains that it was often the case that news of an event actually anticipated the event itself: are we supposed to say that they were simple people who merely followed the mob and who let themselves be deceived because they saw things less clearly than we do![9]

Can there be anything more delicate, clear-cut and lively than the judgement of Pliny when he pleases to exercise it? Is there anything further from triviality? (I am not discussing his outstanding erudition; I put less store by that: but in which of those two qualities are we supposed to surpass him?) And yet every little schoolboy convicts him of lying and lectures him about the march of Nature's handiwork.[10]

When we read in Bouchet about miracles associated with the relics of Saint Hilary we can shrug it off:[11] his right to be believed is not great enough to take away our freedom to challenge him. But to go on from there and condemn all similar accounts seems to me to be impudent in the extreme. Such a great saint as Augustine swears that he saw:[12] a blind child restored to sight by the relics of Saint Gervaise and Saint Protasius at Milan; a woman in Carthage cured of a cancer by the sign of the cross made by a woman who had just been baptized; his close friend Hesperius driving off devils (who were infesting his house) by using a little soil taken from the sepulchre of our Lord, and that same soil, borne into the Church, suddenly curing a paralytic; a woman who, having touched the reliquary of Saint Stephen with a posy of flowers during a procession, rubbed her eyes with them afterwards and recovered her sight which she had recently lost – as well as several other miracles which occurred in his presence. What are we to accuse him of – him and the two holy bishops, Aurelius and Maximinus, whom he calls on as witnesses? Is it of ignorance, simple-

8. Nicole Gilles, *Annales des moderateurs des belliqueuses Gaulles*; the event 'happened' in 1233.

9. Plutarch, *Life of Paulus Aemilius*. The reference to Caesar is puzzling.

10. Such works as the *De Plini erroribus* of Nicolaus Leonicenus had helped spread criticisms of Pliny.

11. Jean Bouchet, *Annales d'Acquitaine*, Poitiers, 1567 etc., pp. 21–30.

12. St Augustine, *City of God*, XII, viii.

mindedness, credulity, deliberate deception or imposture? Is there any man in our century so impudent as to think he can be compared with them for virtue, piety, scholarship, judgement and ability? [C] *'Qui, ut rationem nullam afferent, ipsa authoritate me frangerent.'* [Why, even if they gave no reasons, they would convince me by their very authority.][13]

[A] Apart from the absurd rashness which it entails, there is a dangerous boldness of great consequence in despising whatever we cannot understand. For as soon as you have established the frontiers of truth and error with that fine brain of yours and then discover that you must of necessity believe some things even stranger than the ones which you reject, you are already forced to abandon these frontiers.

Now it seems to me that what brings as much disorder as anything into our consciences during our current religious strife is the way Catholics are prepared to treat some of their beliefs as expendable. They believe they are being moderate and well-informed when they surrender to their enemies some of the articles of faith which are in dispute. But, apart from the fact that they cannot see what an advantage you give to an adversary when you begin to yield ground and beat a retreat, or how much that excites him to follow up his attack, the very articles which they select as being less weighty are sometimes extremely important ones.

We must either totally submit to the authority of our ecclesiastical polity or else totally release ourselves from it. It is not for us to decide what degree of obedience we owe to it.

Moreover I can say that for having assayed it; in the past I made use of that freedom of personal choice and private selection in order to neglect certain details in the observances of our Church because they seemed to be rather odd or rather empty; then, when I came to tell some learned men about it, I discovered that those very practices were based on massive and absolutely solid foundations, and that it is only our ignorance and animal-stupidity which make us treat them with less reverence than all the rest.

Why cannot we remember all the contradictions which we feel within our own judgement, and how many things which were articles of belief for us yesterday are fables for us today?

Vainglory and curiosity are the twin scourges of our souls. The former makes us stick our noses into everything: the latter forbids us to leave anything unresolved or undecided.

---

13. Cicero, *Tusc. disput.*, I, xxi, 49, adapted: Cicero wrote, 'For even though Plato gave no reasons – note what tribute I pay to him – he would convince me by his very authority.'

31. On the Cannibals

═══

[The cannibals mentioned in this chapter lived on the coasts of Brazil. Montaigne had read many accounts of the conquest of the New World, including Girolamo Benzoni's Historia del mondo novo *(Venice, 1565) in the French translation by Urbain Chauveton, the very title of which emphasizes the dreadful treatment of the natives by the Conquistadores:* A New History of the New World containing all that Spaniards have done up to the present in the West Indies, and the harsh treatment which they have meted out to those peoples yonder . . . Together with a short History of a Massacre committed by the Spaniards on some Frenchmen in Florida *(two editions in 1579).*

Montaigne's 'primitivism' (his respect for barbarous peoples and his admiration for much of their conduct, once their motives are understood) has little in common with the 'noble savages' of later centuries. These peoples are indeed cruel: but so are we. Their simple ways have much to teach us: they can serve as a standard by which we can judge Plato's Republic, *the myth of the Golden Age, the cruelty, the corruption and the culture of Europe, and show up that European insularity which condemns peoples as barbarous merely because their manners and their dress are different.]*

[A] When King Pyrrhus crossed into Italy, after noting the excellent formation of the army which the Romans had sent ahead towards him he said, 'I do not know what kind of Barbarians these are' (for the Greeks called all foreigners Barbarians) 'but there is nothing barbarous about the ordering of the army which I can see!' The Greeks said the same about the army which Flaminius brought over to their country, [C] as did Philip when he saw from a hill-top in his kingdom the order and plan of the Roman encampment under Publius Sulpicius Galba.[1] [A] We should be similarly wary of accepting common opinions; we should judge them by the ways of reason not by popular vote.

I have long had a man with me who stayed some ten or twelve years in that other world which was discovered in our century when Villegaignon made his landfall and named it *La France Antartique*.[2] This discovery of a

1. Plutarch, *Life of Pyrrhus* and *Life of Flaminius*.
2. Durand de Villegagnon struck land, in Brazil, in 1557. Cf. *Lettres sur la navigation du chevalier de Villegaignon es terres de l'Amérique*, Paris, 1557, by an author who calls himself simply N.B.

boundless territory seems to me worthy of reflection. I am by no means sure that some other land may not be discovered in the future, since so many persons, [C] greater than we are, [A] were wrong about this one! I fear that our eyes are bigger than our bellies, our curiosity more[3] than we can stomach. We grasp at everything but clasp nothing but wind.

Plato brings in Solon to relate that he had learned from the priests of the town of Saïs in Egypt how, long ago before the Flood, there was a vast island called Atlantis right at the mouth of the Straits of Gibraltar, occupying an area greater than Asia and Africa combined; the kings of that country, who not only possessed that island but had spread on to the mainland across the breadth of Africa as far as Egypt and the length of Europe as far as Tuscany, planned to stride over into Asia and subdue all the peoples bordering on the Mediterranean as far as the Black Sea. To this end they had traversed Spain, Gaul and Italy and had reached as far as Greece when the Athenians withstood them; but soon afterwards those Athenians, as well as the people of Atlantis and their island, were engulfed in that Flood.[4]

It is most likely that that vast inundation should have produced strange changes to the inhabitable areas of the world; it is maintained that it was then that the sea cut off Sicily from Italy –

> [B]   *Hæc loca, vi quondam et vasta convulsa ruina,*
> *Dissiluisse ferunt, cum protinus utraque tellus*
> *Una foret.*

[Those places, they say, were once wrenched apart by a violent convulsion, whereas they had formerly been one single land.][5]

– [A] as well as Cyprus from Syria, and the island of Negropontus from the Boeotian mainland, while elsewhere lands once separated were joined together by filling in the trenches between them with mud and sand:

> *sterilisque diu palus aptaque remis*
> *Vicinas urbes alit, et grave sentit aratrum.*

3. '80: our bellies, *as they say, applying it to those whose appetite and hunger make them desire more meat than they can manage: I fear that we too have* curiosity *far* more . . .
4. Plato, *Timaeus*, 24E etc., and Girolamo Benzoni, *Historia del mondo novo*, Venice 1565. Cf. also Plato, *Critias*, 113 A ff.
5. Virgil, *Aeneid*, III, 414–17.

[Barren swamps which you could row a boat through now feed neighbouring cities and bear the heavy plough.]⁶

Yet there is little likelihood of that island's being the New World which we have recently discovered, for it was virtually touching Spain; it would be unbelievable for a flood to force it back more than twelve hundred leagues to where it is now; besides our modern seamen have already all but discovered that it is not an island at all but a mainland, contiguous on one side with the East Indies and on others with lands lying beneath both the Poles – or that if it is separated from them, it is by straits so narrow that it does not deserve the name of 'island' on that account.

[B] It seems that large bodies such as these are subject, as are our own, to changes, [C] some natural, some [B] feverish.⁷ When I consider how my local river the Dordogne has, during my own lifetime, been encroaching on the right-hand bank going downstream and has taken over so much land that it has robbed many buildings of their foundation, I realize that it has been suffering from some unusual upset: for if it had always gone on like this or were to do so in the future, the whole face of the world would be distorted. But their moods change: sometimes they incline one way, then another: and sometimes they restrain themselves. I am not discussing those sudden floodings whose causes we know. By the coast-line in Médoc, my brother the Sieur d'Arsac can see lands of his lying buried under sand spewed up by the sea: the tops of some of the buildings are still visible: his rents and arable fields have been changed into very sparse grazing. The locals say that the sea has been thrusting so hard against them for some time now that they have lost four leagues of land. These sands are the sea's pioneer-corps: [C] and we can see those huge shifting sand-dunes marching a half-league ahead in the vanguard, capturing territory.

[A] The other testimony from Antiquity which some would make relevant to this discovery is in Aristotle – if that little book about unheard wonders is really his.⁸ He tells how some Carthaginians struck out across the Atlantic beyond the Straits of Gibraltar, sailed for a long time and finally discovered a large fertile island entirely clothed in woodlands and watered by great deep rivers but very far from any mainland; they and others after them, attracted by the richness and fertility of the soil,

6. Horace, *Ars poetica*, 65–6.
7. '88: changes *sickly* and feverish. When . . .
8. The *Secreta secretorum* is supposititious. Montaigne is following Girolamo Benzoni.

emigrated with their wives and children and started living there. The Carthaginian lords, seeing that their country was being gradually depopulated, expressly forbade any more to go there on pain of death and drove out those new settlers, fearing it is said that they would in time increase so greatly that they would supplant them and bring down their State.

But that account in Aristotle cannot apply to these new lands either.

That man of mine was a simple, rough fellow – qualities which make for a good witness: those clever chaps notice more things more carefully but are always adding glosses; they cannot help changing their story a little in order to make their views triumph and be more persuasive; they never show you anything purely as it is: they bend it and disguise it to fit in with their own views. To make their judgement more credible and to win you over they emphasize their own side, amplify it and extend it. So you need either a very trustworthy man or else a man so simple that he has nothing in him on which to build such false discoveries or make them plausible; and he must be wedded to no cause. Such was my man; moreover on various occasions he showed me several seamen and merchants whom he knew on that voyage. So I am content with what he told me, without inquiring what the cosmographers have to say about it.

What we need is topographers who would make detailed accounts of the places which they had actually been to. But because they have the advantage of visiting Palestine, they want to enjoy the right of telling us tales about all the rest of the world! I wish everyone would write only about what he knows – not in this matter only but in all others. A man may well have detailed knowledge or experience of the nature of one particular river or stream, yet about all the others he knows only what everyone else does; but in order to trot out his little scrap of knowledge he will write a book on the whole of physics! From this vice many great inconveniences arise.

Now to get back to the subject, I find (from what has been told me) that there is nothing savage or barbarous about those peoples, but that every man calls barbarous anything he is not accustomed to; it is indeed the case that we have no other criterion of truth or right-reason than the example and form of the opinions and customs of our own country. There we always find the perfect religion, the perfect polity, the most developed and perfect way of doing anything! Those 'savages' are only wild in the sense that we call fruits wild when they are produced by Nature in her ordinary course: whereas it is fruit which we have artificially perverted and misled from the common order which we ought to call savage. It is in the first kind that we find their true, vigorous, living, most natural and most useful properties and virtues, which we have bastardized in the other kind by merely adapting them to our corrupt tastes. [C] Moreover, there is a delicious savour which even our taste finds excellent in a variety of fruits produced in those countries without cultivation: they rival our own. [A] It is not sensible that artifice should be reverenced more than Nature, our great and powerful Mother. We have so overloaded the richness and beauty of her products by our own ingenuity that we have smothered her entirely. Yet wherever her pure light does shine, she wondrously shames our vain and frivolous enterprises:

> [B] *Et veniunt ederæ sponte sua melius,*
> *Surgit et in solis formosior arbutus antris,*
> *Et volucres nulla dulcius arte canunt.*

[Ivy grows best when left untended; the strawberry tree flourishes more beautifully in lonely grottoes, and birds sing the sweeter for their artlessness.][9]

[A] All our strivings cannot even manage to reproduce the nest of the smallest little bird, with its beauty and appropriateness to its purpose; we cannot even reproduce the web of the wretched spider. [C] Plato says that all things are produced by nature, fortune or art, the greatest and fairest by the first two, the lesser and least perfect by the last.[10]

[A] Those peoples, then, seem to me to be barbarous only in that they have been hardly fashioned by the mind of man, still remaining close neighbours to their original state of nature. They are still governed by the laws of Nature and are only very slightly bastardized by ours; but their purity is such that I am sometimes seized with irritation at their not having been discovered earlier, in times when there were men who could have appreciated them better than we do. It irritates me that neither Lycurgus nor Plato had any knowledge of them, for it seems to me that what experience has taught us about those peoples surpasses not only all the descriptions with which poetry has beautifully painted the Age of Gold[11] and all its ingenious fictions about Man's blessed early state, but also the very conceptions and yearnings of philosophy. They could not even imagine a state of nature so simple and so pure as the one we have learned about from experience; they could not even believe that societies of men could be maintained with so little artifice, so little in the way of human

9. Propertius, I, ii, 10–12.
10. Plato, *Laws*, X, 889A–C.
11. Cf. Elizabeth Armstrong, *Ronsard and the Age of Gold*, Cambridge, 1968.

solder. I would tell Plato that those people have no trade of any kind, no acquaintance with writing, no knowledge of numbers, no terms for governor or political superior, no practice of subordination or of riches or poverty, no contracts, no inheritances, no divided estates, no occupation but leisure, no concern for kinship – except such as is common to them all – no clothing, no agriculture, no metals, no use of wine or corn. Among them you hear no words for treachery, lying, cheating, avarice, envy, backbiting or forgiveness. How remote from such perfection would Plato find that Republic which he thought up – [C] *'viri a diis recentes'* [men fresh from the gods].[12]

[B]   *Hos natura modos primum dedit.*

[These are the ways which Nature first ordained.][13]

[A]   In addition they inhabit a land with a most delightful countryside and a temperate climate, so that, from what I have been told by my sources, it is rare to find anyone ill there;[14] I have been assured that they never saw a single man bent with age, toothless, blear-eyed or tottering. They dwell along the sea-shore, shut in to landwards by great lofty mountains, on a stretch of land some hundred leagues in width. They have fish and flesh in abundance which bear no resemblance to ours; these they eat simply cooked. They were so horror-struck by the first man who brought a horse there and rode it that they killed him with their arrows before they could recognize him, even though he had had dealings with them on several previous voyages. Their dwellings are immensely long, big enough to hold two or three hundred souls; they are covered with the bark of tall trees which are fixed into the earth, leaning against each other in support at the top, like some of our barns where the cladding reaches down to the ground and acts as a side. They have a kind of wood so hard that they use it to cut with, making their swords from it as well as grills to cook their meat. Their beds are woven from cotton and slung from the roof like hammocks on our ships; each has his own, since wives sleep apart from their husbands. They get up at sunrise and have their meal for the day as soon as they do so; they have no other meal but that one. They drink

12. Seneca, *Epist. moral.*, XC, 44. (This epistle is a major defence of the innocence of natural man before he was corrupted by philosophy and progress.)
13. Virgil, *Georgics*, II, 208.
14. One of Montaigne's sources was Simon Goulart's *Histoire du Portugal*, Paris, 1587, based on a work by Bishop Jeronimo Osorio (da Fonseca) and others.

nothing with it, [B] like those Eastern peoples who, according to Suidas,[15] only drink apart from meals. [A] They drink together several times a day, and plenty of it. This drink is made from a certain root and has the colour of our claret. They always drink it lukewarm; it only keeps for two or three days; it tastes a bit sharp, is in no ways heady and is good for the stomach; for those who are not used to it it is laxative but for those who are, it is a very pleasant drink. Instead of bread they use a certain white product resembling coriander-cakes. I have tried some: it tastes sweet and somewhat insipid.

They spend the whole day dancing; the younger men go off hunting with bow and arrow. Meanwhile some of the women-folk are occupied in warming up their drink: that is their main task. In the morning, before their meal, one of their elders walks from one end of the building to the other, addressing the whole barnful of them by repeating one single phrase over and over again until he has made the rounds, their building being a good hundred yards long. He preaches two things only: bravery before their enemies and love for their wives. They never fail to stress this second duty, repeating that it is their wives who season their drink and keep it warm. In my own house, as in many other places, you can see the style of their beds and rope-work as well as their wooden swords and the wooden bracelets with which they arm their wrists in battle, and the big open-ended canes to the sound of which they maintain the rhythm of their dances. They shave off all their hair, cutting it more cleanly than we do, yet with razors made of only wood or stone. They believe in the immortality of the soul: souls which deserve well of the gods dwell in the sky where the sun rises; souls which are accursed dwell where it sets. They have some priests and prophets or other, but they rarely appear among the people since they live in the mountains. When they do appear they hold a great festival and a solemn meeting of several villages – each of the barns which I have described constituting a village situated about one French league distant from the next. The prophet then addresses them in public, exhorting them to be virtuous and dutiful, but their entire system of ethics contains only the same two articles: resoluteness in battle and love for their wives. He foretells what is to happen and the results they must expect from what they undertake; he either incites them to war or deflects them from it, but only on condition that if he fails to divine correctly and if things turn out other than he foretold, then – if they can catch him – he is condemned as a false prophet and hacked to pieces. So the prophet who gets it wrong once is seen no more.

15. Suidas, *Historica, caeteraque omnia quae ad cognitionem rerum spectant*, Basle, 1564.

[C] Prophecy is a gift of God.[16] That is why abusing it should be treated as a punishable deceit. Among the Scythians, whenever their soothsayers got it wrong they were shackled hand and foot and laid in ox-carts full of bracken where they were burned.[17] Those who treat subjects under the guidance of human limitations can be excused if they have done their best; but those who come and cheat us with assurances of powers beyond the natural order and then fail to do what they promise, should they not be punished for it and for the foolhardiness of their deceit?

[A] These peoples have their wars against others further inland beyond their mountains; they go forth naked, with no other arms but their bows and their wooden swords sharpened to a point like the blades of our pig-stickers. Their steadfastness in battle is astonishing and always ends in killing and bloodshed: they do not even know the meaning of fear or flight. Each man brings back the head of the enemy he has slain and sets it as a trophy over the door of his dwelling. For a long period they treat captives well and provide them with all the comforts which they can devise; afterwards the master of each captive summons a great assembly of his acquaintances; he ties a rope to one of the arms of his prisoner [C] and holds him by it, standing a few feet away for fear of being caught in the blows,   [A]   and allows his dearest friend to hold the prisoner the same way by the other arm: then, before the whole assembly, they both hack at him with their swords and kill him. This done, they roast him and make a common meal of him, sending chunks of his flesh to absent friends. This is not as some think done for food – as the Scythians used to do in antiquity – but to symbolize ultimate revenge. As a proof of this, when they noted that the Portuguese who were allied to their enemies practised a different kind of execution on them when taken prisoner – which was to bury them up to the waist, to shoot showers of arrows at their exposed parts and then to hang them – they thought that these men from the Other World, who had scattered a knowledge of many a vice throughout their neighbourhood and who were greater masters than they were of every kind of revenge, which must be more severe than their own; so they began to abandon their ancient method and adopted that one. It does not sadden me that we should note the horrible barbarity in a practice such as theirs: what does sadden me is that, while judging correctly of their wrong-doings we should be so blind to our own. I think there is more

16. Cf. Cicero, De divinatione, I, i.1; I Peter 1:2; I Corinthians 12:20; 13:2.
17. Herodotus, History, IV, lxix.

barbarity in eating a man alive than in eating him dead; more barbarity in lacerating by rack and torture a body still fully able to feel things, in roasting him little by little and having him bruised and bitten by pigs and dogs (as we have not only read about but seen in recent memory, not among enemies in antiquity but among our fellow-citizens and neighbours – and, what is worse, in the name of duty and religion) than in roasting him and eating him after his death.

Chrysippus and Zeno, the leaders of the Stoic school, certainly thought that there was nothing wrong in using our carcasses for whatever purpose we needed, even for food – as our own forebears did when, beleaguered by Caesar in the town of Alesia, they decided to relieve the hunger of the besieged with the flesh of old men, women and others who were no use in battle:

> [B] *Vascones, fama est, alimentis talibus usi*
> *Produxere animas.*

[By the eating of such food it is notorious that the Gascons prolonged their lives.][18]

[A] And our medical men do not flinch from using corpses in many ways, both internally and externally, to cure us.[19] Yet no opinion has ever been so unruly as to justify treachery, disloyalty, tyranny and cruelty, which are everyday vices in us. So we can indeed call those folk barbarians by the rules of reason but not in comparison with ourselves, who surpass them in every kind of barbarism. Their warfare is entirely noble and magnanimous; it has as much justification and beauty as that human malady allows: among them it has no other foundation than a zealous concern for courage. They are not striving to conquer new lands, since without toil or travail they still enjoy that bounteous Nature who furnishes them abundantly with all they need, so that they have no concern to push back their frontiers. They are still in that blessed state of desiring nothing beyond what is ordained by their natural necessities: for them anything further is merely superfluous. The generic term which they use for men of the same age is 'brother'; younger men they call 'sons'. As for the old men, they are the 'fathers' of everyone else; they bequeath all their goods, indivisibly, to all these heirs in common, there being no other entitlement

18. Sextus Empiricus, *Hypotyposes*, III, xxiv; Caesar, *Gallic Wars*, VII, lvii–lviii; Juvenal, *Satires*, XV, 93–4.
19. Mummies were imported for use in medicines. (Othello's handkerchief was steeped in 'juice of mummy'.)

than that with which Nature purely and simply endows all her creatures by
bringing them into this world. If the neighbouring peoples come over the
mountains to attack them and happen to defeat them, the victors' booty
consists in fame and in the privilege of mastery in virtue and valour: they
have no other interest in the goods of the vanquished and so return home
to their own land, which lacks no necessity; nor do they lack that great
accomplishment of knowing how to enjoy their mode-of-being in happiness and to be content with it. These people do the same in their turn: they
require no other ransom from their prisoners-of-war than that they should
admit and acknowledge their defeat – yet there is not one prisoner in a
hundred years who does not prefer to die rather than to derogate from the
greatness of an invincible mind by look or by word; you cannot find one
who does not prefer to be killed and eaten than merely to ask to be spared.
In order to make their prisoners love life more they treat them generously
in every way,[20] but occupy their thoughts with the menaces of the death
awaiting all of them, of the tortures they will have to undergo and of the
preparations being made for it, of limbs to be lopped off and of the feast
they will provide. All that has only one purpose: to wrench some weak or
unworthy word from their lips or to make them wish to escape, so as to
enjoy the privilege of having frightened them and forced their constancy.[21]

Indeed, if you take it the right way, true victory[22] consists in that alone:

[C]   *victoria nulla est*
Quam quæ confessos animo quoque subjugat hostes.

[There is no victory unless you subjugate the minds of the enemy and make them
admit defeat.][23]

In former times those warlike fighters the Hungarians never pressed their
advantage beyond making their enemy throw himself on their mercy.
Once having wrenched this admission from him, they let him go without
injury or ransom, except at most for an undertaking never again to bear
arms against them.[24]

[A]   Quite enough of the advantages we do gain over our enemies are
mainly borrowed ones not truly our own. To have stronger arms and legs

20. '80: generously in every way, *and furnish them with all the comforts they can devise*
but . . .
21. '80: their *virtue and their* constancy . . .
22. '80: true *and solid* victory . . .
23. Claudian, *De sexto consulatu Honorii*, 248–9.
24. Nicolas Chalcocondylas (tr. Blaise de Vigenère), *De la décadence de l'empire grec*,
V, ix.

is the property of a porter not of Valour; agility is a dead and physical quality, for it is chance which causes your opponent to stumble and which makes the sun dazzle him; to be good at fencing is a matter of skill and knowledge which may light on a coward or a worthless individual. A man's worth and reputation lie in the mind and in the will: his true honour is found there. Bravery does not consist in firm arms and legs but in firm minds and souls: it is not a matter of what our horse or our weapons are worth but of what we are. The man who is struck down but whose mind remains steadfast, [C] *'si succiderit, de genu pugnat'* [if his legs give way, then on his knees doth he fight];[25] [B] the man who relaxes none of his mental assurance when threatened with imminent death and who faces his enemy with inflexible scorn as he gives up the ghost is beaten by Fortune not by us: [C] he is slain but not vanquished.[26] [B] Sometimes it is the bravest who may prove most unlucky. [C] So there are triumphant defeats rivalling victories; Salamis, Plataea, Mycale and Sicily are the fairest sister-victories which the Sun has ever seen, yet they would never dare to compare their combined glory with the glorious defeat of King Leonidas and his men at the defile of Thermopylae.[27] Who has ever run into battle with a greater desire and ambition for victory than did Captain Ischolas when he was defeated? Has any man ever assured his safety more cleverly or carefully than he assured his destruction?[28] His task was to defend against the Arcadians a certain pass in the Peleponnesus. He realized that he could not achieve this because of the nature of the site and of the odds against him, concluding that every man who faced the enemy must of necessity die in the battlefield; on the other hand he judged it unworthy of his own courage, of his greatness of soul and of the name of Sparta to fail in his duty; so he chose the middle path between these two extremes and acted thus: he saved the youngest and fittest soldiers of his unit to serve for the defence of their country and sent them back there. He then determined to defend that pass with men whose loss would matter less and who would, by their death, make the enemy purchase their breakthrough as dearly as possible. And so it turned out. After butchering the Arcadians who beset them on every side, they were all put to the sword. Was ever a trophy raised to a victor which was not better due to those who were vanquished?

25. Seneca, *De constantia*, II.

26. '80: by us: *he is vanquished in practice but not by reason; it is his bad luck which we may indict not his cowardice.* Sometimes . . .

27. Cf. Cicero, *Tusc. disput.*, I, xli, 100 for the glory of Leonidas' death in the defile of Thermopylae.

28. Diodorus Siculus, XV, xii.

True victory lies in your role in the conflict, not in coming through safely: it consists in the honour of battling bravely not battling through.

[A] To return to my tale, those prisoners, far from yielding despite all that was done to them during the two or three months of their captivity, maintain on the contrary a joyful countenance: they urge their captors to hurry up and put them to the test; they defy them, insult them and reproach them for cowardice and for all the battles they have lost against their country. I have a song made by one such prisoner which contains the following: Let them all dare to come and gather to feast on him, for with him they will feast on their own fathers and ancestors who have served as food and sustenance for his body. 'These sinews,' he said, 'this flesh and these veins – poor fools that you are – are your very own; you do not realize that they still contain the very substance of the limbs of your forebears: savour them well, for you will find that they taste of your very own flesh!' There is nothing 'barbarous' in the contriving of that topic. Those who tell how they die and who describe the act of execution show the prisoners spitting at their killers and pulling faces at them. Indeed, until their latest breath, they never stop braving them and defying them with word and look. It is no lie to say that these men are indeed savages – by our standards; for either they must be or we must be: there is an amazing gulf between their [C] souls [A] and ours.[29]

The husbands have several wives: the higher their reputation for valour the more of them they have. One beautiful characteristic of their marriages is worth noting: just as our wives are zealous in thwarting our love and tenderness for other women, theirs are equally zealous in obtaining them for them. Being more concerned for their husband's reputation than for anything else, they take care and trouble to have as many fellow-wives as possible, since that is a testimony to their husband's valour.

– [C] Our wives will scream that that is a marvel, but it is not: it is a virtue proper to matrimony, but at an earlier stage. In the Bible Leah, Rachel, Sarah and the wives of Jacob all made their fair handmaidens available to their husbands; Livia, to her own detriment, connived at the lusts of Augustus, and Stratonice the consort of King Deiotarus not only provided her husband with a very beautiful chambermaid who served her but carefully brought up their children and lent a hand in enabling them to succeed to her husband's rank.[30]

---

29. '80: their *constancy* and ours . . .
30. Standard examples: cf. Tiraquellus, *De legibus connubialibus*, XIII, 35, for all these un-jealous wives. (But Leah and Sarah were in fact Jacob's wives.)

– [A] Lest anyone should think that they do all this out of a simple slavish subjection to convention or because of the impact of the authority of their ancient customs without any reasoning or judgement on their part, having minds so dulled that they could never decide to do anything else, I should cite a few examples of what they are capable of.

Apart from that war-song which I have just given an account of, I have another of their songs, a love-song, which begins like this:

> O Adder, stay: stay O Adder! From your colours
>   let my sister take the pattern for a girdle
>   she will make for me to offer to my love;
> So may your beauty and your speckled hues be for
>   ever honoured above all other snakes.

This opening couplet serves as the song's refrain. Now I know enough about poetry to make the following judgement: not only is there nothing 'barbarous' in this conceit but it is thoroughly anacreontic.[31] Their language incidentally is [C] a pleasant one with an agreeable sound [A] and has terminations[32] rather like Greek.

Three such natives, unaware of what price in peace and happiness they would have to pay to buy a knowledge of our corruptions, and unaware that such commerce would lead to their downfall – which I suspect to be already far advanced – pitifully allowing themselves to be cheated by their desire for novelty and leaving the gentleness of their regions to come and see ours, were at Rouen at the same time as King Charles IX.[33] The King had a long interview with them: they were shown our manners, our ceremonial and the layout of a fair city. Then someone asked them what they thought of all this and wanted to know what they had been most amazed by. They made three points; I am very annoyed with myself for forgetting the third, but I still remember two of them. In the first place they said (probably referring to the Swiss Guard) that they found it very odd that all those full-grown bearded men, strong and bearing arms in the King's entourage, should consent to obey a boy rather than choosing one of themselves as a Commander; secondly – since they have an idiom in their language which calls all men 'halves' of one another – that they had noticed that there were among us men fully bloated with all sorts of

31. Anacreon was the great love-poet of Teos (*fl.* 540 BC).
32. '80: their language *is the pleasantest language in the world; its* sound *is agreeable to the ear* and has terminations . . .
33. In 1562, when Rouen was retaken by Royalist forces.

comforts while their halves were begging at their doors, emaciated with poverty and hunger: they found it odd that those destitute halves should put up with such injustice and did not take the others by the throat or set fire to their houses.

I had a very long talk with one of them (but I used a stupid interpreter who was so bad at grasping my meaning and at understanding my ideas that I got little joy from it). When I asked the man (who was a commander among them, our sailors calling him a king) what advantage he got from his high rank, he told me that it was to lead his troops into battle; asked how many men followed him, he pointed to an open space to signify as many as it would hold – about four or five thousand men; questioned whether his authority lapsed when the war was over, he replied that he retained the privilege of having paths cut for him through the thickets in their forests, so that he could easily walk through them when he visited villages under his sway.

Not at all bad, that. – Ah! But they wear no breeches . . .

32. Judgements on God's ordinances must be embarked upon with prudence

[*The theme that God's counsel is a secret which Man should not try to scan was a common one in the Renaissance. Montaigne applies that dogma to the ups and downs of the Wars of Religion: we cannot say that God is on the side of the victors in battle. Montaigne asserts that even the pagan Indians of the New World know that better than warring Christians do.*]

[A] The real field and subject of deception are things unknown: firstly because their very strangeness lends them credence; second, because they cannot be exposed to our usual order of argument, so stripping us of the means of fighting them. [C] Plato says that this explains why it is easier to satisfy people when talking of the nature of the gods than of the nature of men: the ignorance of the hearers provides such hidden matters with a firm broad course for them to canter along in freedom.[1] [A] And so it turns out that nothing is so firmly believed as whatever we know least about, and that no persons are more sure of themselves than those who tell us tall stories, such as alchemists and those who make prognostications: judicial astrologers, chiromancers, doctors and '*id genus omne*' [all that tribe].[2] To which I would add if I dared that crowd of everyday chroniclers and interpreters of God's purposes who claim to discover the causes of everything that occurs and to read the unknowable purposes of God by scanning the secrets of His will; the continual changes and clash of events drive them from corner to corner and from East to West, but they still go on chasing the tennis-ball and sketching black and white with the same crayon. [B] In one Indian tribe they have a laudable custom: when they are worsted in a skirmish or battle they publicly beseech the Sun their god for pardon for having done wrong, attributing their success or failure to the divine mind, to which they submit their own judgement and discourse.

[A] For a Christian it suffices to believe that all things come from God,

1. Plato, *Critias*, 107B.
2. Horace, *Satires*, I, ii, 2.

to accept them with an acknowledgement of His holy unsearchable wisdom and so to take them in good part, under whatever guise they are sent to him. What I consider wrong is our usual practice of trying to support and confirm our religion by the success or happy outcome of our undertakings. Our belief has enough other foundations without seeking sanction from events: people who have grown accustomed to such plausible arguments well-suited to their taste are in danger of having their faith shaken when the turn comes for events to prove hostile and unfavourable. As in the religious wars which we are now fighting, after those who had prevailed at the battle of La Rochelabeille had had a great feast-day over the outcome, exploiting their good fortune as a sure sign of God's approval for their faction, they then had to justify their misfortunes at Moncontour and Jarnac as being Fatherly scourges and chastisements:[3] they would soon have made the people realize (if they did not have them under their thumb) that that is getting two kinds of meal from the same bag and blowing hot and cold with the same breath. It would be better to explain to the people the real foundations of truth.

That was a fine naval engagement which we won against the Turk a few months ago, led by Don John of Austria: yet at other times it has pleased God to make us witness other such battles which cost us dear.[4]

In short it is hard to bring matters divine down to human scales without their being trivialized. Supposing someone sought to explain why Arius and Leo his Pope (who were the main proponents of the Arian heresy) both died at different times of deaths so strange and similar, for they both had to leave the debates because of pains in their stomach and go to the lavatory, where both promptly died; and supposing they emphasized God's vengeance by insisting on the nature of the place where this happened: well, they could add the example of the death of Heliogabalus who was also killed in a privy. Why, Irenaeus himself met the same fate.[5]

[C] God wishes us to learn that the good have other things to hope for and the wicked other things to fear than the chances and mischances of this

3. The Reformers won at La Rochelabeille (1562) and lost at Jarnac and Moncontour (1569). Both sides attributed their defeats to God's 'fatherly' chastisement, on the authority of II Samuel 7:14 and Hebrews 12:5–6.
4. Don John of Austria's Catholic Spanish navy won at Lepanto (1571); but the Spanish Invincible Armada was scattered and defeated in 1588, a defeat attributed throughout Protestant Europe to God's intervention on the side of true religion.
5. Ravisius Textor in his *Officina* lists under the heading *Dead or killed in latrines* Heliogabalus and also the martyrs Irenaeus and Albundius who were tossed alive into the latrines by Valerianus, where they died.

world, which his hands control according to his hidden purposes: and so he takes from us the means of foolishly exploiting them. Those who desire to draw advantage from them by human reason delude themselves. For every hit which they make, they suffer two in return. St Augustine amply proved that against his opponents: the arms which decide that wrangle are not those of reason but of memory.[6]

[A] We must be content with the light which the Sun vouchsafes to shed on us by its rays: were a man to lift up his eyes to seek a greater light in the Sun itself, let him not find it strange if he is blinded as a penalty for his presumption. [C] *'Quis hominum potest scire consilium dei? aut quis poterit cogitare quid velit dominus?'* [For what man can know the counsel of God: or who shall conceive what the Lord willeth?][7]

6. Cf. St Augustine, *City of God*, I, viii.
7. Wisdom of Solomon 9:13.

39. On solitude

====

[Montaigne himself had withdrawn in solitude to his estates, as many an ancient philosopher and statesman had done, with leisure to seek after wisdom, goodness and tranquillity of mind. His advice that we should set aside for ourselves a 'room at the back of the shop' is a reminder that true solitude is a spiritual withdrawal from the world. Living in solitude did not mean living as a hermit but living with detachment – if possible away from courts and the bustle of the world. Living as though always in the presence of a great and admired figure was a Renaissance practice (Sir Thomas More lived as though always in the company of the elder Pico). Montaigne draws a sharp distinction between the solitude of rare saintly ecstatics and that of ordinary men.]

[A]   Let us leave aside those long comparisons between the solitary life and the active one;[1] and as for that fine adage used as a cloak by greed and ambition, 'That we are not born for ourselves alone but for the common weal,'[2] let us venture to refer to those who have joined in the dance: let them bare their consciences and confess whether rank, office and all the bustling business of the world are not sought on the contrary to gain private profit from the common weal. The evil methods which men use to get ahead in our century clearly show that their aims cannot be worth much.

Let us retort to ambition that she herself gives us a taste for solitude, for does she shun anything more than fellowship? Does she seek anything more than room to use her elbows?

The means of doing good or evil can be found anywhere, but if that quip of Bias is true, that 'the evil form the larger part', or what Ecclesiasticus says, 'One good man in a thousand have I not found'[3] –

> [B]   *Rari quippe boni: numero vix sunt totidem, quot*
> *Thebarum portæ, vel divitis ostia Nili.*

[Good men are rare: just about as many as gates in the walls of Thebes or mouths to the fertile Nile.] –

---

1. From early Christian times such comparisons were legion.
2. The great Platonic adage spread by Cicero in its Latin form and stating that 'No man is born for himself alone, but partly for his country and partly for those whom he loves.' (Erasmus, *Adages*, IV, VI, VIII, *Nemo sibi nascitur*.)
3. Ecclesiasticus 7:28; then, Juvenal, *Satires*, XIII, 26–7.

[A]   then contagion is particularly dangerous in crowds. Either you must loathe the wicked or imitate them. It is dangerous both to grow like them because they are many, or to loathe many of them because they are different.

[C]   Sea-going merchants are right to ensure that dissolute, blasphemous or wicked men do not sail in the same ship with them, believing such company to be unlucky. That is why Bias jested with those who were going through the perils of a great storm with him and calling on the gods for help: 'Shut up,' he said, 'so that they do not realize that you are here with me.'⁴ And (a more pressing example) when Albuquerque, the Viceroy of India for Emmanuel, King of Portugal, was in peril from a raging tempest, he took a boy on his shoulders for one reason only: so that by linking their fates together the innocence of that boy might serve him as a warrant and intercession for God's favour and so bring him to safety.

[A]   It is not that a wise man cannot live happily anywhere nor be alone in a crowd of courtiers, but Bias says that, if he has the choice, the wise man will avoid the very sight of them. If he has to, he will put up with the former, but if he can he will choose the other. He thinks that he is not totally free of vice if he has to contend with the vices of others. [B]   Those who haunted evil-doers were chastised [C]   as evil [A] by Charondas.⁵

[C]   There is nothing more unsociable than Man, and nothing more sociable: unsociable by his vice, sociable by his nature. And Antisthenes does not seem to me to have given an adequate reply to the person who reproached him for associating with the wicked, when he retorted that doctors live among the sick: for even if doctors do help the sick to return to health they impair their own by constantly seeing and touching diseases as they treat them.⁶

[A]   Now the end I think is always the same: how to live in leisure at our ease. But people do not always seek the way properly. Often they think they have left their occupations behind when they have merely changed them. There is hardly less torment in running a family than in running a whole country. Whenever our soul finds something to do she is

---

4. Diogenes Laertius, *Life of Bias*. (The subsequent references to Bias are also from this work.) His remark became proverbial; cf. Erasmus, *Apophthegmata*, VII, *Bias Prienaeus*, II. Then, Simon Goulart, *Histoire du Portugal*, VIII, ix.
5. Charondas the lawgiver of Sicily and follower of Pythagoras (Seneca, *Epist. moral.*, XC, 6).
    '80: chastised *with great punishments* by . . .
6. Erasmus, *Apophthegmata*, VII, *Antisthenes Atheniensis*, XXII.

there in her entirety: domestic tasks may be less important but they are no
less importunate. Anyway, by ridding ourselves of Court and market-place
we do not rid ourselves of the principal torments of our life:

> *ratio et prudentia curas,*
> *Non locus effusi late maris arbiter, aufert.*

[it is reason and wisdom which take away cares, not places affording wide views
over the sea.][7]

Ambition, covetousness, irresolution, fear and desires do not abandon us
just because we have changed our landscape.

> *Et post equitem sedet atra cura.*

[Behind the parting horseman squats black care.][8]

They often follow us into the very cloister and the schools of philosophy.
Neither deserts nor holes in cliffs nor hair-shirts nor fastings can disentangle
us from them:

> *haerit lateri letalis arundo.*

[in her side still clings that deadly shaft.][9]

Socrates was told that some man had not been improved by travel. 'I am
sure he was not,' he said. 'He went with himself!'[10]

> *Quid terras alio calentes*
> *Sole mutamus? patria quis exul*
> *Se quoque fugit?*

[Why do we leave for lands warmed by a foreign sun? What fugitive from his
own land can flee from himself?][11]

If you do not first lighten yourself and your soul of the weight of your
burdens, moving about will only increase their pressure on you, as a ship's
cargo is less troublesome when lashed in place. You do more harm than
good to a patient by moving him about: you shake his illness down into
the sack, [A1] just as you drive stakes in by pulling and waggling them
about. [A] That is why it is not enough to withdraw from the mob,

7. Horace, *Epistles*, I, xi, 25–6.
8. *Odes*, III, i, 40.
9. Virgil, *Aeneid*, IV, 73.
10. Seneca, *Epist. moral.*, CIV, 7, Erasmus, *Apophthegmata*, III, *Socrates*, XLIV.
11. Horace, *Odes*, II, xvi, 18–20. (The ideas in general are indebted here to Seneca.)

not enough to go to another place: we have to withdraw from such attributes of the mob as are within us. It is our own self we have to isolate and take back into possession.

> [B]   *Rupi jam vincula dicas:*
> *Nam luctata canis nodum arripit; attamen illi,*
> *Cum fugit, a collo trahitur pars longa catenæ.*

['I have broken my chains,' you say. But a struggling cur may snap its chain, only to escape with a great length of it fixed to its collar.][12]

We take our fetters with us; our freedom is not total: we still turn our gaze towards the things we have left behind; our imagination is full of them.

> *Nisi purgatum est pectus, quæ prælia nobis*
> *Atque pericula tunc ingratis insinuandum?*
> *Quantæ conscindunt hominem cuppedinis acres*
> *Sollicitum curæ, quantique perinde timores?*
> *Quidve superbia, spurcitia, ac petulantia, quantas*
> *Efficiunt clades? quid luxus desidiesque?*

[But if our breast remains unpurged, what unprofitable battles and tempests we must face, what bitter cares must tear a man apart, and then what fears, what pride, what sordid thoughts, what tempers and what clashes; what gross gratifications; what sloth!][13]

   [A]   It is in our soul that evil grips us: and she cannot escape from herself:

> *In culpa est animus qui se non effugit unquam.*

   [That mind is at fault which never escapes from itself.][14]

So we must bring her back, haul her back, into our self. That is true solitude. It can be enjoyed in towns and in kings' courts, but more conveniently apart.

   Now since we are undertaking to live, without companions, by ourselves, let us make our happiness depend on ourselves; let us loose ourselves from the bonds which tie us to others; let us gain power over ourselves to live really and truly alone – and of doing so in contentment.

   Stilpo had escaped from the great conflagration of his city in which he had lost wife, children and goods; when Demetrius Poliorcetes saw him in the midst of so great a destruction of his homeland, yet with his face

12. Persius, *Satires*, V, 158–60.
13. Lucretius, V, 43–8.
14. Horace, *Epistles*, I, xiv, 13.

undismayed, he asked him if he had suffered no harm. He said, No. Thank God he had lost nothing of his.[15]   [C]   The philosopher Antisthenes put the same thing amusingly when he said that a man ought to provide himself with unsinkable goods, which could float out of a shipwreck with him.[16]

[A]   Certainly, if he still has himself, a man of understanding has lost nothing.

When the city of Nola was sacked by the Barbarians, the local Bishop Paulinus lost everything and was thrown into prison; yet this was his prayer: 'Keep me O Lord from feeling this loss. Thou knowest that the Barbarians have so far touched nothing of mine.' Those riches which did enrich him and those good things which made him good were still intact.[17]

There you see what it means to choose treasures which no harm can corrupt and to hide them in a place which no one can enter, no one betray, save we ourselves. We should have wives, children, property and, above all, good health ... if we can: but we should not become so attached to them that our happiness depends on them. We should set aside a room, just for ourselves, at the back of the shop, keeping it entirely free and establishing there our true liberty, our principal solitude and asylum. Within it our normal conversation should be of ourselves, with ourselves, so privy that no commerce or communication with the outside world should find a place there; there we should talk and laugh as though we had no wife, no children, no possessions, no followers, no menservants, so that when the occasion arises that we must lose them it should not be a new experience to do without them. We have a soul able to turn in on herself; she can keep herself company; she has the wherewithal to attack, to defend, to receive and to give. Let us not fear that in such a solitude as that we shall be crouching in painful idleness:

[B]   *in solis sis tibi turba locis.*

[in lonely places, be a crowd unto yourself.][18]

[C]   'Virtue,' says Antisthenes, 'contents herself, without regulations, words or actions.'   [A]   Not even one in a thousand of our usual activities has anything to do with our self.

15. Seneca, *Epist. moral.*, IX, 18.
16. Diogenes Laertius, *Life of Antisthenes* (with later references also to this work).
17. St Augustine, *City of God*, I, x.
18. Tibullus, IV, xiii, 12 (adapted).

That man you can see over there, furiously beside himself, scrambling high up on the ruins of that battlement, the target of so many volleys from harquebuses; and that other man, all covered with scars, wan, pale with hunger, determined to burst rather than open the gate to him: do you think they are in it for themselves? It could well be for someone they have never seen, someone plunged meanwhile in idleness and delights, who takes no interest in what they are doing. And this man over here, rheumy, filthy and blear-eyed, whom you can see coming out of his work-room at midnight! Do you think he is looking in his books for ways to be better, happier, wiser? Not a bit. He will teach posterity how to scan a verse of Plautus and how to spell a Latin word, or else die in the attempt.

Is there anyone not willing to barter health, leisure and life itself against reputation and glory, the most useless, vain and counterfeit coinage in circulation? Our own deaths have never frightened us enough, so let us burden ourselves with fears for the deaths of our wives, children and servants. Our own affairs have never caused us worry enough, so let us start cudgelling and tormenting our brains over those of our neighbours and of those whom we love.

> *Vah! quemquamne hominem in animum instituere, aut*
> *Parare, quod sit charius quam ipse est sibi?*

[Eh? Should a man prepare a settled place in his soul for something dearer than himself!][19]

[C] It seems to me that solitude is more reasonable and right for those who, following the example of Thales, have devoted to the world their more active, vigorous years.

[A] We have lived quite enough for others: let us live at least this tail-end of life for ourselves. Let us bring our thoughts and reflections back to ourselves and to our own well-being. Preparing securely for our own withdrawal is no light matter: it gives us enough trouble without introducing other concerns. Since God grants us leave to make things ready for our departure, let us prepare for it; let us pack up our bags and take leave of our company in good time; let us disentangle ourselves from those violent traps which pledge us to other things and which distance us from ourselves. We must unknot those bonds and, from this day forth, love this or that but marry nothing but ourselves. That is to say, let the rest be ours, but not so

19. Terence, *Adelphi*, I, i, 13–14.

glued and joined to us that it cannot be pulled off without tearing away a piece of ourselves, skin and all. The greatest thing in the world is to know how to live to yourself.

[C] It is time to slip our knots with society now that we can contribute nothing to it. A man with nothing to lend should refrain from borrowing. Our powers are failing: let us draw them in and keep them within ourselves. Whoever can turn round the duties of love and fellowship and pour them into himself should do so. In that decline which makes a man a useless encumbrance importunate to others, let him avoid becoming an encumbrance, importunate and useless to himself. Let him pamper himself, cherish himself, but above all control himself, so respecting his reason and so fearing his conscience that he cannot stumble in their presence without shame: 'Rarum est enim ut satis se quisque vereatur.' [It is rare for anybody to respect himself enough.][20] Socrates says that youth must get educated; grown men employ themselves in good actions; old men withdraw from affairs, both civil and military, living as they please without being bound to any definite duties.[21]

[A] There are complexions more suited than others to these maxims [C] about retirement. [A] Those who hold on to things slackly and weakly, and whose will and emotions are choosy, accepting neither slavery nor employment easily – and I am one of them, both by nature and by conviction – will bend to this counsel better than those busy active minds which welcome everything with open arms, which take on everything, get carried away about everything and which are always giving themselves, offering themselves, putting themselves forward. When any good things happen to come to us from outside we should make use of them, so long as they remain pleasurable; we must not let them become our principal base, for they are no such thing: neither reason nor Nature will have them so. Why do we go against Nature's laws and make our happiness a slave in the power of others?

Yet to go and anticipate the injuries of Fortune, depriving ourselves of such good things as are still in our grasp, as several have done out of devotion and a few philosophers out of rational conviction, making slaves of themselves, sleeping rough, poking out their own eyes, chucking their wealth into rivers, going about looking for pain – the first to acquire blessedness in the next life because of torment in this one, the others to ensure against tumbling afresh by settling for the bottom rung – are actions

20. Quintilian, X, 7.
21. The source of this saying is unknown to me.

of virtue taken to excess. Let tougher sterner natures make even their hiding-places glorious and exemplary.

> *tuta et parvula laudo,*
> *Cum res deficiunt, satis inter vilia fortis:*
> *Verum ubi quid melius contingit et unctius, idem*
> *Hos sapere, et solos aio bene vivere, quorum*
> *Conspicitur nitidis fundata pecunia villis.*

[When I lack money, I laud the possession of a few things which are sure; I show fortitude enough among paltry goods: but – still the same person – when anything better, more sumptuous, comes my way, then I say that only they are wise and live right well whose income is grounded in handsome acres.][22]

I have enough to do without going that far. When Fortune favours me, it is enough to prepare for her disfavour, picturing future ills in comfort, to the extent that my imagination can reach that far, just as we train ourselves in jousts and tournaments, counterfeiting war in the midst of peace. [C] I do not reckon that Arcesilaus the philosopher had reformed his mind any the less because I know he used such gold and silver vessels as the state of his fortune allowed: for using them frankly and in moderation I hold him in greater esteem than if he had got rid of them.

[A] I know how far our natural necessities can extend; and when I reflect that the indigent beggar at my door is often more merry and healthy than I am, I put myself firmly in his place and make an assay at giving my soul a slant like his. Then by running similarly through other examples, though I may think that death, poverty, contempt and sickness are dogging my heels, I can readily resolve not to be terrified by what a man of lesser estate than mine can accept with such patience. I cannot believe that a base intelligence can do more than a vigorous one or that reason cannot produce the same effects as habit. And since I realize how insecure these adventitious comforts are, my sovereign supplication, which I never fail to make to God, is that, even while I enjoy them fully, He may make me content with myself and with such goods as are born within me. I know healthy young men who travel with a mass of pills in their baggage to swallow during an attack of rheum, fearing it less since they know they have a remedy to hand. That is the way to do it, only more so: if you know yourself subject to some grave affliction, equip yourself with medicines to benumb and deaden the part concerned.

The occupation we must choose for a life like this one should be neither

22. Horace, *Epistles*, I, xv, 42–6.

toilsome nor painful (otherwise we should have vainly proposed seeking such leisure). It depends on each man's individual taste. My taste is quite unsuited to managing my estates: those who do like it, should do it in moderation:

> *Conentur sibi res, non se submittere rebus.*

[They should try to subordinate things to themselves, not themselves to things.][23]

Otherwise management, as Sallust puts it, is a servile task.[24] (Some aspects of it are more acceptable, such as an interest in gardening – which Xenophon attributes to Cyrus.)[25] A mean can be found between that base unworthy anxiety, full of tension and worry, seen in those who immerse themselves in it, and that profound extreme neglect one sees in others, who let everything go to rack and ruin:

> *Democriti pecus edit agellos*
> *Cultaque, dum peregre est animus sine corpore velox.*

[Democritus left his herds to ravage fields and crops, while his speeding soul was wandering outside his body.][26]

But let us just listen to the advice about solitude which Pliny the Younger gave to his friend Cornelius Rufus: 'I counsel you in that ample and thriving retreat of yours, to hand the degrading and abject care of your estates over to those in your employ, and to devote yourself to the study of letters so as to derive from it something totally your own.'[27] By that, he means a good reputation, his humour being similar to Cicero's who said he wanted to use his withdrawal and his repose from the affairs of State to gain life everlasting through his writings!

> [B]   *Usque adeo ne*
> *Scire tuum nihil est, nisi te scire hoc sciat alter?*

[Does *knowing* mean nothing to you, unless somebody else knows that you know it?][28]

[C]   It seems logical that when you talk about withdrawing from the

23. Horace, *Epistles*, I, i, 19.
24. Sallust, *Catilenae conjuratio*, IV.
25. Cicero, *De Senectute*, XVI, 59.
   [A]: more *noble* and acceptable . . .
26. Horace, *Epistles*, I, xii, 12–13.
27. Pliny the Younger, *Epistles*, I, i. no. 3.
28. Persius, *Satires*, I, xxiii.

world you should be contemplating things outside it; they only half do that: they do indeed arrange their affairs for when they will no longer be in the world, yet the fruits of their project they claim to draw from the world they have left: a ridiculous contradiction.

The thought of those who seek solitude for devotion's sake, filling their minds with the certainty of God's promises for the life to come, is much more sane and appropriate. Their objective is God, infinite in goodness and power: the soul can find there matters to slake her desires in perfect freedom. Pains and afflictions are profitable to them, being used to acquire eternal healing and joy; death is welcome as a passing over to that perfect state. The harshness of their Rule is smoothed by habit; their carnal appetites are rejected and lulled asleep by their denial – nothing maintains them but practising them and using them. Only this end, another life, blessedly immortal, genuinely merits our renunciation of the comforts and sweetnesses of this life of ours. Whoever can, in reality and constancy, set his soul ablaze with the fire of this lively faith and hope, builds in his solitude a life of choicest pleasures, beyond any other mode of life.

[A] Neither the end, then, nor the means of Pliny's counsel satisfy me: we are always jumping from feverish fits into burning agues. Spending time with books has its painful side like everything else and is equally inimical to health, which must be our main concern; we must not let our edge be blunted by the pleasure we take in books: it is the same pleasure as destroys the manager of estates, the miser, the voluptuary and the man of ambition.

The wise men teach us well to save ourselves from our treacherous appetites and to distinguish true wholesome pleasures from pleasures diluted and crisscrossed by pain. Most pleasures, they say, tickle and embrace us only to throttle us, like those thieves whom the Egyptians called *Philistae*.[29] If a hangover came before we got drunk we would see that we never drank to excess: but pleasure, to deceive us, walks in front and hides her train. Books give pleasure: but if frequenting them eventually leads to loss of our finest accomplishments, joy and health, then give up your books. I am one who believes that their fruits cannot outweigh a loss such as that.

As men who have long felt weakened by illness in the end put themselves at the mercy of medicine and get that art to prescribe a definite diet never to be transgressed: so too a man who withdraws pained and disappointed with the common life must rule his life by a diet of reason, ordering it and arranging it with argument and forethought. He should have taken leave of toil and travail, no matter what face they present, and should flee from

29. Seneca, *Epist. moral.*, LI, 13; the *Philistae* (or *Philetai*) were assassins.

all kinds of passion which impede the tranquillity of his body and
soul,   [B]   and choose the way best suited to his humour.

> *Unusquisque sua noverit ire via.*

[Let each man choose the road he should take.][30]

[A]   Whether we are running our home or studying or hunting or
following any other sport, we should go to the very boundaries of pleasure
but take good care not to be involved beyond the point where it begins to
be mingled with pain. We should retain just enough occupations and
pursuits to keep ourselves fit and to protect ourselves from the unpleasant-
ness which comes in the train of that other extreme: slack and inert idleness.

There are branches of learning both sterile and prickly, most of them
made for the throng: they may be left to those who serve society.
Personally I only like pleasurable easy books which tickle my interest, or
those which console me and counsel me how to control my life and death.

> *Tacitum sylvas inter reptare salubres,*
> *Curantem quidquid dignum sapiente bonoque est.*

[Walking in silence through the healthy woods, pondering questions worthy of
the wise and good.][31]

Wiser men with a strong and vigorous soul can forge for themselves a
tranquillity which is wholly spiritual. Since my soul is commonplace, I
must help sustain myself with the pleasures of the body – and since age has
lately robbed me of those more pleasing to my fancy I am training and
sharpening my appetite for those which are left, more suited to my later
season. We must cling tooth and claw to the use of the pleasures of this life
which the advancing years, one after another, rip from our grasp.

> [B]   *Carpamus dulcia; nostrum est*
> *Quod vivis: cinis et manes et fabula fies.*

[Let us pluck life's pleasures: it is up to us to live; you will soon be ashes, a ghost,
something to tell tales about.][32]

30. Propertius, II, xxv, 38.
31. Horace, *Epistles*, I, iv, 4–5.
32. Persius, *Satires*, V, 151–2.
   '80 (instead of this quotation): grasp, *and prolong them with all our power:*
Quamcunque Deus tibi fortunaverit horam, Grata sume manu, nec dulcia differ in annum
[Whatever happy hour God has allotted you, accept with a grateful hand and do
not put off delights for a year] . . . (Did Montaigne strike out this because he had
confused, in his quotation from Horace, *Epistles* I, xi, 22, *God* with *Fortuna*? All
editions of Horace read *Fortuna* not *Deus*.)

[A]   As for glory – the end proposed by Pliny and Cicero – that is right outside my calculations. Ambition is the humour most contrary to seclusion. Glory and tranquillity cannot dwell in the same lodgings. As far as I can see, those authors have withdrawn only their arms and legs from the throng: their souls, their thoughts, remain even more bound up with it.

[B]   *Tun', vetule, auriculis alienis colligis escas?*

[Now then, old chap, are you collecting bait to catch the ears of others?][33]

[A]   They step back only to make a better jump, and, with greater force, to make a lively charge through the troops of men.

Would you like to see how they fall just a tiny bit short of the target? Let us weigh against them the counsels of two philosophers – and from two different schools at that – one of them writing to his friend Idomeneus and the other to his friend Lucilius, to persuade them to give up the management of affairs of state and their great offices and to withdraw into solitude:[34]

'You have (they said) lived up to the present floating and tossing about; come away into the harbour and die. You have devoted your life to the light: devote what remains to obscurity. It is impossible to give up your pursuits if you do not give up their fruits. Renounce all concern for name and glory. There is the risk that the radiance of your former deeds may still cast too much light upon you and pursue you right into your lair. Among other gratifications give up the one which comes from other people's approval. As for your learned intelligence, do not worry about that: it will not lose its effect if you yourself are improved by it. Remember the man who was asked why he toiled so hard at an art which few could ever know about: "For me a few are enough; one is enough; having none is enough." He spoke the truth. You and one companion are audience enough for each other; so are you for yourself. For you, let the crowd be one, and one be a crowd. It is a vile ambition in one's retreat to want to extract glory from one's idleness. We must do like the beasts and scuff out our tracks at the entrance to our lairs. You should no longer be concerned with what the world says of you but with what you say to yourself. Withdraw into yourself, but first prepare yourself to welcome yourself there. It would be madness to entrust yourself to yourself, if you did not know how to govern yourself. There are ways of failing in solitude as in society. Make

33. Persius, *Satires*, I, 19–20.
34. The first is Epicurus. The second is Seneca. The following epistle is largely composed of borrowings from various epistles of Seneca.

yourself into a man in whose sight you would not care to walk awry; feel shame for yourself and respect for yourself, — [C] *"observentur species honestae animo"* [let your mind dwell on examples of honour];[35] until you do, always imagine that you are with Cato, Phocion and Aristides, in whose sight the very madmen would hide their faults; make them recorders of your inmost thoughts, which, going astray, will be set right again out of reverence for them.[36]

'The path they will keep you on is that of being contented with yourself, of borrowing all from yourself, of arresting and fixing your soul on thoughts contained within definite limits where she can find pleasure; then, having recognized those true benefits which we enjoy the more the more we know them, content yourself with them, without any desire to extend your life or fame.'

That is the advice of a philosophy which is natural and true, not like that of those other two,[37] all verbiage and show.

35. Cicero, *Tusc. disput.*, II, xxii, 52.
36. Modelled on Seneca, *Epist. moral.*, XXV, 6. The 'companions' proposed there are Cato, Scipio and Laelius. Montaigne prefers Phocion, the great Athenian general, and Aristides, a statesman renowned for his integrity.
37. Pliny the Younger and Cicero, condemned above for seeking glory from their withdrawal from the world.

56. On prayer

=====

[*We are given here a deeper insight into the austerer, rigorist side of Montaigne's Catholicism. The additions, which are numerous, beginning with those of 1582, marked [A1], are partly designed to meet the criticisms raised by the Maestro di Palazzo at the Vatican about Montaigne's assertion 'that a man when he prays must be free of sinful inclinations during that time'. Such a doctrine savours of that 'puritanism' of which the Roman Catholic Church was ever suspicious. Together with III, 2, 'On repenting' we can see here how demanding Montaigne's Catholicism was beneath its urbane exterior. We can also understand his work better: he is writing philosophy not theology; and philosophy has its own rules and its own language. As usual Montaigne is suspicious of words, even liturgical words, without deeds. To many in his Church his theological position appeared rigorous to the point of heresy where sin-free prayer was concerned. But he himself presents his thoughts as a kind of disputabilis opinio, that is, as analogous to an unresolved topic or paradox, subject to open debate in the universities.*]

[A1] The notions which I am propounding have no form and reach no conclusion. (Like those who advertise questions for debate in our Universities I am seeking the truth not laying it down.) I submit them to the judgement of those whose concern it is to govern not only my actions and my writings but my very thoughts. Both condemnation and approbation will be equally welcome, equally useful, [C] since I would loathe to be found saying anything ignorantly or inadvertently against the holy teachings of the Church Catholic, Apostolic and Roman, in which I die and in which I was born.[1] [A1] And so, while ever submitting myself to the authority of their censure, whose power over me is limitless, I am emboldened to treat all sorts of subjects – as I do here.

[A] I may be mistaken but, seeing that we have been granted by special grace and favour a set form of prayer prescribed and dictated to us, word by word, by God's own mouth, it has always seemed to me that we

---

1. All churches claim to be catholic. Roman Catholics in Montaigne's time often stressed the 'Roman' so as to avoid any ambiguity.

should use it more commonly.[2] If it depended on me I would like to
see Christians saying the Lord's Prayer as a grace before and after meals,
when we get up and go to bed and on all those special occasions where
we normally include prayers, [C] saying it always if not exclusively.
[A] The Church may lengthen or vary prayers according to her need
to instruct us; for I am well aware that the matter is identical and always
substantially the same. But this prayer ought to have the prerogative
of being on people's lips at all times, since it is certain that it says everything necessary and that it is always most appropriate on all occasions.
[C] It is the only prayer that I say everywhere; instead of varying it
I repeat it. That explains why it is the only prayer I can ever remember.

[A] I was wondering recently how the error arose which leads us to
have recourse to God in all our doings and designs, [B] calling upon
him in every kind of need and in any place whatsoever where our
weakness needs support, without once considering whether the occasion is
just or unjust. No matter how we are or what we are doing – however
sinful it may be – we invoke God's name and power. [A] He is of
course our only and unique Protector, [C] able to do anything whatever
to help us; [A] but even though he does vouchsafe to grant us that
sweet honour of being our Father by adoption,[3] he is as just as he is
good [C] and powerful; but he uses his justice more often than his
power; [A] and he grants us his favours according to [C] its criteria
not our petitions.[4]

In his *Laws*, Plato lists three kinds of belief which are insulting to the
gods: that there are none; that they do not concern themselves with our
affairs; that they never refuse to answer our prayers, oblations and sacrifices.
He believes that the first error never remains stable in anyone from
childhood to old age but that the other two do allow of constancy.[5]

[A] God's power and his justice are inseparable. If we implore him to
use his power in a wicked cause it is of no avail. Our soul must be pure, at
least for that [C] instant [A] when we make our prayer, free from

---

2. The Lord's Prayer (Matthew 6:9–13; Luke 11:2–4). Montaigne always presents
the Bible as divinely inspired by the Holy Ghost. Here, by special grace, the
incarnate Son ensures the absolute verbal accuracy of the central prayer of
Christendom.
3. Romans 8:14–17, etc.
4. '80: According to *the* criteria *of his justice, not according to our inclinations and
wishes.* God's . . .
5. Plato, *Laws*, X, 885 B–C.

the weight of vicious passions; otherwise we offer him rods for our own chastisement.[6] Instead of amending our faults we redouble them by offering God (from whom we ought to be begging forgiveness) emotions full of irreverence and hatred. That is why I do not approve of those whom I see praying to God frequently and regularly if deeds consonant with their prayers do not bear me witness of some reformation and amendment[7] –

[B] *si, nocturnus adulter,*
Tempora Sanctonico velas adoperta cucullo.

[if, for your nightly adultery, you hide beneath an Aquitanian cowl.][8]

[C] The position of a man who mingles devotion with a detestable life seems somehow to deserve condemnation more than that of a man who is self-consistent, dissolute in everything. That is why our Church daily excludes all stubborn notorious evildoers from entry into our fellowship.

[A] We say our prayers out of habit and custom, or to put it better, we merely read and utter the words of our prayers. It amounts, in the end, to [C] outward show. [B] And it displeases me to see a man making three signs of the cross at the *Benedicite* and three more at grace – displeasing me all the more since [C] it is a sign which I revere and continually employ, not least when I yawn – [B] only[9] to see him devoting every other hour of the day to [C] hatred, covetousness and injustice.[10] [B] Give vices their hours, then one hour to God – a sort of barter or arrangement! What a miracle it is to see actions so incompatible proceeding at so even a course that at the very point where they pass from one to the other you can notice no break or hesitation.

[C] What monstrous a conscience it is that can find rest while nurturing together in so peaceful and harmonious a fellowship both the crime and the judge in the same abode. If a man has his head full of the demands of lechery, judging it to be something most odious in the sight of God, what

6. '80: at least for that *time* when ... (This passage was raised by the Maestro del Palazzo. Consult Malcolm Smith, *Montaigne and the Roman Censors*, Geneva, 1981. Montaigne's assertion is rigorist and neo-Augustinian. Some still judge it hyperorthodox.)

7. Cf. Matthew 3:8.

8. Juvenal, *Satires*, VIII, 144–5.

9. The *Benedicite* precedes dinner; grace follows it.
   '80: It amounts in the end to *pretence*. And it ...
   '88: since *they are practices which I honour and often imitate*, only ...

10. '80: to *usury, venality and lechery*. Give ... [Montaigne strengthens his case, replacing sinful practices by the infinitely more serious inward sins of the mind].

does he say to God when he tells him of it? He repents, only to fall again –
at once. If as he claims the concept of divine Justice really did strike home,
scourging and chastising his soul, then however short his repentance fear
itself would force him to cast his mind back to it, making him thenceforth
master of those bloated vices which were habitually his.

And what about those men whose whole life reposes on the fruits and
profits of what they know to be a mortal sin? How many trades and vocations are there which gain acceptance, yet whose very essence is vicious?

And then there is the man who confided to me how, all his life, he had
professed and practised a religion which he believed to be damnable, quite
opposite to the one dear to him, so as not to lose favour or the honour of
his appointments. How did he defend such reasoning in his mind? When
men address God's Justice on such matters, what do they say? Since their
repentance requires a visible and tangible reparation, they forfeit all means
of pleading it before God or men. Do they go so far as to dare to beg
forgiveness without making satisfaction, without repentance? I hold that
the first ones I mentioned are in the same state as these; but their obstinacy
is far less easy to overcome.

Those sudden violent changes and veerings of opinion that they feign for
us are a source of wonder to me. They reveal a state of unresolved conflict.
And how fantastical seem to me the conceptions of those who, in recent
years, have habitually accused anyone who showed a glimmer of intelligence yet professed the Catholic faith of only feigning to do so – even
maintaining, to do him honour, that whatever he might actually say for
show, deep down inside he could not fail to hold the religion as 'reformed'
by their standards! What a loathsome malady it is to believe that you are so
right that you convince yourself that nobody can think the opposite. And
most loathsome still, to convince yourself that such a mind may prefer
some chance but present advantage to the hopes and fears of eternal life.
They can take my word for it: if anything could have tempted me in
youth, a large part would have been played by an ambition to share in the
hazards and hardships attendant upon that fresh young enterprise.

[A] It is not without good reason, it seems to me, that the Church has
forbidden the indiscriminate, thoughtless and indiscreet use of those venerable sacred songs which the Holy Ghost dictated through David.[11] We

---

11. '80: the *Catholic* Church has forbidden ... (Psalm-singing, often in the
translation of the French poet Clément Marot, had been a practice in the Court of
Margaret of Navarre but had become for many the sign of the Reformed
Church.)

must only bring God into our activities with reverence and attentiveness full of honour and respect. That Word is too holy to serve merely to exercise our lungs and to please our ears; it must be rendered by our hearts not by our tongues. It is unreasonable to permit some shop-boy to amuse himself playing about with it while his mind is on silly frivolous matters. [B] Nor, certainly, is it right to see the Sacred Book of the holy mysteries of our faith dragged about through hall or kitchen[12] – [C] they used to *be* mysteries: now they serve as amusements and pastimes.

[B] A study so serious, a subject so revered, should not be handled incidentally or hurriedly. It should always be a considered calm activity, prefaced as in our liturgy by the *Sursum corda*;[13] we should bring to it even our bodies disposed in such attitudes as bear witness to a special attentiveness and reverence. [C] It is not a study for just anybody: it is a study for those who are dedicated to it, for people whom God calls to it. It makes the wicked and the ignorant grow worse. It is not a story to be told but a story to be reverenced, feared, adored.

How silly they are who think they have made it accessible to the vulgar simply by translating it into the vulgar tongues! When people fail to understand everything they read is it only the fault of the words! I would go further. By bringing Scripture that little bit nearer they actually push it further away. Pure ignorance, leaving men totally dependent on others, was much more salutary and more learned than such vain verbal knowledge, that nursery of rashness and presumption.

[B] I also believe that the liberty everyone takes of[14] broadcasting so religious and so vital a text into all sorts of languages is less useful than dangerous. Jews, Mahometans and virtually all the others have reverently espoused the tongue in which their mysteries were first conceived; any changes or alterations are forbidden; not, it seems, without reason. Can we be sure that in the Basque country or in Brittany there are enough good judges, men adequate enough to establish the right translation in their languages? Why, the Catholic Church has nothing more difficult to do than to decide such matters – and nothing more solemn. When it is a case of preaching or speaking our translations can be vague, free, variable and partial: that is not at all the same thing.

12. '80: kitchen, *in the hands of everybody.* A study . . .
13. 'Lift up your hearts' – the liturgical summons to prayer.
14. '88: of *translating and* broadcasting . . .

[C]   One of our Greek historians[15] justly accused his own time of
having so scattered the secrets of the Christian religion about the
market-place and into the hands of the meanest artisans that everybody
could argue and talk about them according to his own understanding: 'It is
deeply shameful,' he added, 'that we who by God's grace enjoy the pure
mysteries of our pious faith should allow them to be profaned in the
mouths of persons ignorant and base, seeing that the Gentiles forbade even
Socrates, Plato and the wisest men to talk or to inquire about matters
entrusted to the priests at Delphi.' He also said that, where Theology is
concerned, the factions of princes are armed with anger not with zeal; that
zeal itself does partake of the divine Reason and Justice when it behaves
ordinately and moderately but that it changes into hatred and envy
whenever it serves human passions, producing then not wheat and the fruit
of the vine but tares and nettles. And there was another man who rightly
advised the Emperor Theodosius that debates never settled schisms in the
Church but rather awakened heresies and put life into them; therefore he
should flee all contentiousness and all dialectical disputations, committing
himself to the bare prescriptions and formulas of the Faith established of
old. And when the Emperor Andronicus came across two great men
verbally skirmishing in his palace against Lopadius over one of the more
important points of our religion, he reprimanded them, even threatening
to have them thrown into the river if they still went on.

Nowadays women and children read lectures about ecclesiastical law to
the oldest and most experienced of men whereas the first of Plato's laws
forbids them to inquire even into the reason for merely civil ones, which
must be regarded as divine ordinances; he allowed only the older men to
discuss laws among themselves and with the Magistrate – adding, 'provided
that it is not done in the presence of the young and the uninitiated'.[16]

A bishop has testified in writing[17] that there is, at the other end of the
world, an island which the Ancients called Dioscorides, fertile and favoured
with all sorts of fruits and trees and a healthy air; the inhabitants are
Christian, having Churches and altars which are adorned with no other
images but crosses; they scrupulously observe feast-days and fasts, pay their

15. All this paragraph of Nicetas comes directly from Justus Lipsius' *De una
religione*.
16. Plato forbade youths, not women, to discuss the laws (Plato, *Laws*, I, 634 D– E).
Here, as often in the Renaissance, *Law* includes religion. (Christianity was termed
'the law of Christians' from medieval times.)
17. Bishop Jeronimo Osorio (da Fonseca), *De rebus Emanuëlis Lusitaniae Regis gestis*,
Cologne, 1581 (1586).

tithes meticulously and are so chaste that no man ever lies with more than one woman for the whole of his life; meanwhile, so happy with their lot that, in the middle of the ocean, they know nothing about ships, and so simple that they do not understand a single word of the religion which they so meticulously observe – something only unbelievable to those who do not know that pagans, devout worshippers of idols, know nothing about their gods apart from their statues and their names. The original beginning of Euripides' tragedy *Menalippus* went like this:

> *O Juppiter, car de toy rien sinon*
> *Je ne connois seulement que le nom . . .*

[O Jupiter – for I know nothing of thee but thy Name . . .][18]

[B]   I have also seen in my time criticisms laid against some books for dealing exclusively with the humanities or philosophy without any admixture of Theology. The opposite case would not be totally indefensible, namely: that Christian Doctrine holds her rank better when set apart, as Queen and Governor; that she should be first throughout, never ancillary nor subsidiary; that Grammar, Rhetoric and Logic should [C] perhaps [B] choose their examples from elsewhere not from such sacred materials, as also should the subjects of plays for the theatre, farces and public spectacles; that Divinity is regarded with more veneration and reverence when expounded on its own style rather than when linked to human reasoning; that the more frequent fault is to see Theologians writing like humanists rather than humanists like Theologians (Philosophy, says St Chrysostom, has long been banished from the School of Divinity as a useless servant judged unworthy of glimpsing, even from the doorway when simply passing by, the sanctuary of the holy treasures of sacred doctrine); that the language of men has its own less elevated forms and must not make use of the dignity, majesty and authority of the language of God. I myself let it say –   [C]   *verbis indisciplinatis* [using undisciplined words] –   [B]   fortune, destiny, accident, good luck, bad luck, the gods and similar phrases, following its own fashion.[19]

[C]   I am offering my own human thoughts as human thoughts to be considered on their own, not as things established by God's ordinance,

18. Euripides *apud* Plutarch (tr. Amyot), *De l'amour*, 604B.
19. St Augustine, *City of God*, X, xxix. This was current Renaissance practice. For some reason the Maestro di Palazzo raised the question of the use of 'fortune' in the *Essays*. Montaigne changed a few passages but held his ground and explains why. (The passage of Chrysostom remains untraced.)

incapable of being doubted or challenged; they are matters of opinion not matters of faith: what I reason out *secundum me*, not what I believe *secundum Deum*[20] – like schoolboys reading out their essays, not teaching but teachable, in a lay not a clerical manner but always deeply devout.

[B] And might it not be said, apparently reasonably, that a decree forbidding anyone to write about religion (except very reservedly) unless expressly professing to do so would not lack some image of usefulness and justice – as perhaps would one requiring me too to hold my peace on the subject?

[A] I have been told that for reasons of reverence even those who are not of our Church forbid the use among themselves of the name of God in their everyday speech.[21] They do not want it to be used as a kind of interjection or exclamation, nor to support testimony nor when making contracts; in that I consider they are right. Whenever we bring God's name into our affairs or our society let it be done seriously and devoutly.

I believe there is a treatise in Xenophon somewhere in which he shows that we ought to pray to God less often, since it is not easy for us to bring our souls so frequently into that controlled, reformed and supplicatory state needed to do so; without that, our prayers are not only vain and useless: they are depraved. 'Forgive us,' we say, 'as we forgive them that trespass against us.' What do those words mean if not that we are offering God our souls free from vengeance and resentment? Yet we call on God and his help to connive at wrongdoings   [C]   and to invite him to be unjust:

> [B]   *Quæ, nisi seductis, nequeas committere divis.*

[Things which you would not care to entrust to the gods, except when drawing aside.][22]

[A] The miser prays God for the vain and superfluous preservation of his hoard; the ambitious man, for success and the achievement of his desires; the thief uses God to help him overcome the dangers and difficulties which obstruct his nefarious designs or else thanks God when he finds it easy to slit the gizzard of some passer-by.   [C]   At the foot of the mansion which

20. Montaigne's terms are technical. He is giving his *opinions* (i.e. his unproven notions) 'according to himself', 'selon moy' (*secundum me*). Anything which is said *secundum quid* ('according to anything') is not stated *simpliciter* (absolutely, simply) but in some partial respect only. Anything stated 'selon Dieu', 'according to God' (*secundum Deum*) would be infallible and a matter of absolute faith.
21. That was the practice of the Reformed Church. (Cf. Joachim Du Bellay, *Regrets*, 136, on the Genevan Calvinists.)
22. Persius, *Satires*, II, 4; glossing a petition from the Lord's Prayer.

they are about to climb into and blow up, men say their prayers, while their purposes and hopes are full of cruelty, lust and greed.

> [B] *Hoc ipsum quo tu Jovis aurem impellere tentas,*
> *Dic agedum, Staio, pro Juppiter, ô bone clamet,*
> *Juppiter, at se se non clamet Juppiter ipse?*

[Try telling Statius what you are up to, what you have just whispered to Jove: 'By Jove!' he'll say: 'How dreadful!' – 'Well, cannot Jove say *By Jove!* to Himself?']²³

[A] Queen Margaret of Navarre relates the tale of a young 'prince' – and, even though she does not name him his exalted rank is quite enough to make him recognizable; whenever he was out on an assignation (lying with the wife of a Parisian barrister) he would take a short-cut through a church and never failed to make his prayers and supplications in that holy place, both on the way there and on the way back. I will leave you to judge what he was asking God's favour for when his soul was full of such fair cogitations! Yet she cites that as evidence of outstanding devotion. But that is not the only proof we have of the truth that it hardly befits women to treat Theological matters.

A devout reconciliation with God, a true prayer, cannot befall a soul which is impure and, at that very time, submissive to the domination of Satan. A man who calls God to his aid while he is actually engaged in vice is like a cutpurse calling on justice to help him or like those who produce the name of God to vouch for their lies:

> [B] *tacito mala vota susurro*
> *Concipimus.*

[we softly murmur evil prayers.]²⁴

[A] Not many men would care to submit to view the secret prayers they make to God:

> *Haud cuivis promptum est murmurque humilesque susurros*
> *Tollere de templis, et aperto vivere voto.*

[It is hardly everyone who could take his murmured prayers whispered within the temples and say them aloud outside.]

That is why the Pythagoreans believed that prayer should be public and

---

23. Persius, *Satires*, II, 21–31. The young monarch (or '*prince*') in the next paragraph is Francis I (cf. Margaret of Navarre, *Heptaméron*, III, 25). *Prince* regularly means *King* in the Renaissance, as a current Latinism.
24. Lucan, *Pharsalia*, V, 104–5.

heard by all, so that God should not be begged for things unseemly or unjust – like the man in this poem:

> clare cum dixit: Apollo!
> Labra movet, metuens audiri: pulchra Laverna,
> Da mihi fallere, da justum sanctumque videri.
> Noctem peccatis et fraudibus objice nubem.

[he first exclaims, 'Apollo!' loud and clear; then he moves his lips, addressing the goddess of Theft and fearing to be overheard: 'O fair Laverna: do not let me get found out; let me appear to be just and upright; cloak my sins with night and my lies with a cloud.']25

[C] The gods heavily punished the unrighteous prayers of Oedipus by granting them: he prayed that his children should fight among themselves to decide who should succeed to his inheritance; he was wretched enough to be taken literally.

We should not ask that all things should comply with our will but that they should comply with wisdom.

[A] It really does seem that we use prayer [C] as a sort of jingle and [A] like those who exploit God's holy words in sorcery and practical magic.26 As for their effect, we apparently count on their structure, their sound and the succession of words, [A1] or on our outward appearance. [A] For, with our souls still full of concupiscence, untouched by repentance or by any fresh reconciliation with God, we offer him such words as memory lends to our tongue, hoping in that way to obtain the expiation of our sins.

Nothing is so gentle, so sweet, so gracious as our Holy Law:27 she calls us to her, all sinful and abominable as we are; she stretches forth her arms and clasps us to her bosom, however base, vile and besmirched we may be now and shall be once again. But we on our part must look favourably upon her. We must also receive her absolution with thanksgiving and – at least for that instant when we address ourselves to her – have a soul loathing its own shortcomings and hostile to those [C] passions [A] which28 drove us to offend her.

---

25. Persius, *Satires*, II, 6–7; Horace, *Epistles*, III, i, 16–19.
26. For Oedipus, cf. Plato, *Second Alcibiades*, 138 B–C. Then, for prayer, cf. the 'magic' prayers of Panurge during the Storm in the *Quart Livre* of Father Rabelais. Montaigne's point is theologically sound and, at the time, not difficult to grasp.
27. That is, Christianity.
28. '80: those *concupiscences* which . . .

[C]   Neither the gods nor good men, Plato says, accept gifts from a wicked man:[29]

> [B]   *Immunis aram si tetigit manus,*
> *Non sumptuosa blandior hostia*
> *Mollivit aversos Penates,*
> *Farre pio et saliente mica.*

[If the hands which have touched the altar are undefiled, then, even when they are not commended by some costly sacrifice, they can appease the hostile household gods with a simple cake of meal sprinkled with salt.][30]

29. Plato, *Laws*, IV, 717E.
30. Horace, *Odes*, III, xxxiii, 13–16.

57. On the length of life

=====

[Montaigne, who published the first two books of his Essays when he was forty-seven, looks back at youth and sees thirty as the watershed dividing vigour from decline. The last word of this chapter, and so of Book I, is 'apprenticeship'. At thirty a wise man's 'apprenticeship' should doubtless be over, but, for those who make good use of their time, can knowledge and experience grow with the years?]

[A] I cannot accept the way we determine the span of our lives.[1] I note that wise men shorten it considerably compared to the common opinion. 'What!' said Cato the Younger to those who wanted to stop him killing himself: 'Am I still at the age when you can accuse me of leaving life too soon?'[2] Yet he was only forty-eight. He reckoned, considering how few men reach it, that his age was fully mature and well advanced. And those who keep themselves going with the thought that some span of life or other which they call 'natural' promises them a few years more could only do so provided that there was some ordinance exempting them personally from those innumerable accidents (which each one of us comes up against and is subject to by nature) which can rupture the course of life which they promise themselves.

What madness it is to expect to die of that failing of our powers brought on by extreme old age and to make that the target for our life to reach when it is the least usual, the rarest kind of death. We call that death, alone, a natural death, as if it were unnatural to find a man breaking his neck in a fall, engulfed in a shipwreck, surprised by plague or pleurisy, and as though our normal condition did not expose us to all of those harms. Let us not beguile ourselves with such fine words: perhaps we ought, rather, to call natural anything which is generic, common to all and universal. Dying of old age is a rare death, unique and out of the normal order and therefore less natural than the others. It is the last, the uttermost way of dying; the farther it is from us, the less

1. Presumably the biblical 'three-score years and ten', held to be the norm.
2. Plutarch, *Life of Cato of Utica*.

we can hope to reach it; it is indeed the limit beyond which we shall not go and which has been prescribed by Nature's law as never to be crossed: but it is a very rare individual law of hers which makes us last out till then. It is an exemption which she grants as an individual favour to one man in the space of two or three centuries, freeing him from the burden of those obstacles and difficulties which she strews along the course of that long progress.

Therefore my opinion is that we should consider whatever age we have reached as an age reached by few. Since in the normal course of events men never reach that far, it is a sign that we are getting on. And since we have crossed the accustomed limits – and that constitutes the real measure of our days – we ought not to hope to get much farther beyond them; having escaped those many occasions of death which have tripped up all the others, we ought to admit that an abnormal fortune such as that which has brought us so far is indeed beyond the usual procedure and cannot last much longer.

It is a defect in our very laws to hold that false idea, for they do not admit that a man be capable of managing his affairs before the age of twenty-five, yet he can scarcely manage to make his life last that long! Augustus lopped five years off the old Roman ordinances and decreed that it sufficed to be thirty for a man to assume the office of judge. Servius Tullius exempted knights who had passed the age of forty-seven from obligatory war-service; Augustus remitted it at forty-five.[3] Sending men into inactivity before fifty-five or sixty does not seem very right to me. I would counsel extending our vocations and employments as far as we could in the public interest; the error is on the other side, I find: that of not putting us to work soon enough. The man who had power to decide everything in the whole world at nineteen[4] wanted a man to be thirty before he could decide where to place a gutter!

Personally I reckon that our souls are free from their bonds at the age of twenty, as they ought to be, and that by then they show promise of all they are capable of. No soul having failed by then to give a quite evident pledge of her power ever gave proof of it afterwards. By then – or never at all – natural qualities and capacities reveal whatever beauty or vigour they possess.

---

3. Suetonius, *Life of Augustus*.
4. The Emperor Augustus.

[B]   *Si l'espine nou pique quand nai,*
      A peine que pique jamai

[If a thorn pricks not at its birth,
It will hardly prick at all]

as they say in Dauphiné.

[A]   Of all the fair deeds of men in ancient times and in our own which have come to my knowledge, of whatever kind they may be, I think it would take me longer to enumerate those which were made manifest before the age of thirty than after.   [C]   Yes, and often in the lives of the very same men: may I not say that with total certainty in the case of Hannibal and his great adversary Scipio? They lived a good half of their lives on the glory achieved in their youth: they were great men later compared with others, but not great compared with themselves.   [A]   As for me, I am convinced that, since that age, my mind and my body have not grown but diminished, and have retreated not advanced.

It may well be that (for those who make good use of their time) knowledge and experience grow with the years but vitality, quickness, firmness and other qualities which are more truly our own, and more important, more ours by their essence, droop and fade.

[B]   *Ubi jam validis quassatum est viribus ævi*
      Corpus, et obtusis ceciderunt viribus artus,
      Claudicat ingenium, delirat linguaque mensque.

[When the body is shattered by the mighty blows of age and our limbs shed their blunted powers, our wits too become lame and our tongues and our minds start to wander.][5]

Sometimes it is the body which is the first to surrender to old age, sometimes too the soul; and I have known plenty of men whose brains grew weak before their stomachs or their legs; and it is all the more dangerous an infirmity in that the sufferer is hardly aware of it and its symptoms are not clear ones.

But now   [A]   I am complaining not that the laws allow us to work so late but that they are so late in putting us to work.

It seems to me that, considering the frailty of our life and the number of

5. Lucretius, III, 452–4.

natural hazards to which it is exposed, we should not allow so large a place in it to being born, to leisure and to our apprenticeship.[6]

6. Montaigne's next-to-last noun, *oisiveté* probably renders the classical Latin word *otium*; in which case he is not thinking of 'idleness' but of that 'leisure' time, when learning, study and culture took precedence over 'business' (*negotium*), which included all duties and employments.

1. On the inconstancy of our actions

===

[In Montaigne's French inconstance *is a term which includes fickleness and variability as well as inconsistency of conduct. In Latin,* constantia *(inner consistency and steadfast constancy) were the ideals of Stoic philosophy. Montaigne, having finished Book I with the notion of apprenticeship, now moves more boldly into new areas of exploration of himself and the nature of Man, both of which he finds subject to fickleness and marked by inconsistent qualities.]*

[A]   Those who strive to account for a man's deeds are never more bewildered than when they try to knit them into one whole and to show them under one light, since they commonly contradict each other in so odd a fashion that it seems impossible that they should all come out of the same shop. Young Marius now acts like a son of Mars, now as a son of Venus. They say that Pope Boniface VIII took up his duties like a fox, bore them like a lion and died like a dog. And who would ever believe that it was Nero, the very image of cruelty, who when they presented him with the death-sentence of a convicted criminal to be duly signed replied, 'Would to God that I had never learned to write!' so much it oppressed his heart to condemn a man to death?[1]

Everything is so full of such examples (indeed each man can furnish so many from himself) that I find it strange to find men of understanding sometimes taking such trouble to match up the pieces, seeing that vacillation seems to me to be the most common and blatant defect of our nature: witness the famous line of Publius the author of farces:

> *Malum consilium est, quod mutari non potest!*
>
> [It's a bad resolution which can never be changed!][2]

[B]   It seems reasonable enough to base our judgement of a man on the more usual features of his life: but given the natural inconstancy of our behaviour and our opinions it has often occurred to me that even sound authors are wrong in stubbornly trying to weave us into one invariable and solid fabric.

1. Plutarch, *Life of Marius*; Bouchet, *Annales d'Acquitaine*; Seneca, *De Clementia*.
2. Publius Syrus cited by Aulus Gellius, *Attic Nights*, XVII, 14.

They select one universal character, then, following that model, they classify and interpret all the actions of a great man; if they cannot twist them the way they want they accuse the man of insincerity. Augustus did get away from them: for there is in that man throughout his life a diversity of actions so clear, so sudden and so uninterrupted that they had to let him go in one piece, with no verdict made on him by even the boldest judges. Of Man I can believe nothing less easily than invariability: nothing more easily than variability. Whoever would judge a man in his detail, [C] piece by piece, separately, [B] would hit on the truth more often.

[A] It is difficult to pick out more than a dozen men in the whole of Antiquity who groomed their lives to follow an assured and definite course, though that is the principal aim of wisdom. To sum it all up and to embrace all the rules of Man's life in one word, 'Wisdom,' said an Ancient, 'is always to want the same thing, always *not* to want the same thing.' I would not condescend to add, he said, 'provided that your willing be right. For if it is not right, it is impossible for it to remain ever one and the same.'[3]

I was once taught indeed that vice is no more than a defect and irregularity of moderation, and that consequently it is impossible to tie it to constancy. There is a saying attributed to Demosthenes: the beginning of all virtue is reflection and deliberation: its end and perfection, constancy. If by reasoning we were to adopt one definite way, the way we chose would be most beautiful of all; but nobody has thought of doing that.

> *Quod petiit, spernit, repetit quod nuper omisit;*
> *Æstuat, et vitae disconvenit ordine toto.*

[Judgement scorns what it yearned for, yearns again for what it recently spurned; it shifts like the tide and the whole of life is disordered.][4]

Our normal fashion is to follow the inclinations of our appetite, left and right, up and down, as the winds of occasion bear us along. What we want is only in our thought for the instant that we want it: we are like that creature which takes on the colour of wherever you put it. What we decided just now we will change very soon; and soon afterwards we come back to where we were: it is all motion and inconstancy:

3. Seneca, *Epistles*, XX, 5.
4. Demosthenes (?), *On the Fallen at Chaeronea*; then, Horace, *Epistles*, I, i, 98–9.

Ducimur ut nervis alienis mobile lignum.

[We are led like a wooden puppet by wires pulled by others.]

We do not *go*: we are borne along like things afloat, now bobbing now lashing about as the waters are angry or serene.

[B]   *Nonne videmus*
Quid sibi quisque velit nescire, et quærere semper,
Commutare locum, quasi onus deponere possit?

[Surely we see that nobody knows what he wants, that he is always looking for something, always changing his place, as though he could cast off his burden?]

[A]   Every day a new idea: and our humours change with the changes of weather:

Tales sunt hominum mentes, quali pater ipse
Juppiter auctifero lustravit lumine terras.

[The minds of men are such as Father Jupiter changes them to, as he purifies the world with his fruitful rays.]⁵

[C]   We float about among diverse counsels: our willing of anything is never free, final or constant.

[A]   If a man were to prescribe settled laws for a settled government established over his own brain, then we would see, shining throughout his whole life, a calm uniformity of conduct and a faultless interrelationship between his principles and his actions.

– [C]   (The defect in the Agrigentines noted by Empedocles was their abandoning themselves to pleasure as though they were to die the next day, while they built as though they would never die at all.)⁶ –

[A]   It would be easy enough to explain the character of such a man; that can be seen from the Younger Cato: strike one of his keys and you have struck them all; there is in him a harmony of sounds in perfect concord such as no one can deny. In our cases on the contrary every one of our actions requires to be judged on its own: the surest way in my opinion would be to refer each of them to its context, without looking farther and without drawing any firm inference from it.

During the present debauchery of our wretched commonwealth I was told about a young woman near where I then was who had thrown herself from a high window to avoid being forced by some beggarly soldier

---

5. Horace, *Satires*, II, vii, 82; Lucretius, III, 1070–3; Homer, cited in Latin by St Augustine, *City of God*, V, xxxviii.
6. Diogenes Laertius, *Life of Empedocles*. Also cited in Erasmus' *Apophthegmata*.

billeted on her. She was not killed by her fall and repeated her attempt by trying to slit her own throat with a knife; she was stopped from doing so, but only after she had given herself a nasty wound. She herself admitted that the soldier had not yet gone beyond importuning her with requests, solicitations and presents, but she was afraid that he would eventually use force. And above all this, there were the words she used, the look on her face and that blood testifying to her chastity, truly like some second Lucretia. Now I learned as a fact that both before and after this event she was quite wanton and not all that hard to get. It is like the moral in that tale: 'However handsome and noble you may be, when you fail to get your end in do not immediately conclude that your lady is inviolably chaste: it does not mean that the mule-driver is not having better luck with her.'

Antigonus had grown to love one of his soldiers for his virtue and valour and ordered his doctors to treat him for a malignant internal complaint which had long tormented him; he noticed that, once the soldier was cured, he set about his work with much less ardour and asked him who had changed him into such a coward. 'You yourself, Sire,' he replied, 'by freeing me from the weight of those pains which made me think life was worth nothing.'[7]

Then there was the soldier of Lucullus who had been robbed of everything by the enemy and who, to get his own back, made a fine attack against them. After he had plucked enough enemy feathers to make up for his loss Lucullus, who had formed a high opinion of him, began urging some hazardous exploit upon him with all the fairest expostulations he could think of:

> *Verbis quae timido quoque possent addere mentem.*

> [With words enough to give heart to a coward.]

'You should try urging that,' he replied, 'on some wretched soldier who has lost everything' –

> *quantumvis rusticus ibit,*
> *Ibit eo, quo vis, qui zonam perdidit, inquit*

[yokel though he was, he replied: 'The man who will go anywhere you like is the one who has just lost his money-belt'] –

and he absolutely refused to go.[8]

7. Erasmus, *Apophthegmata*, IV, *Antigonus Rex Macedonum*, XXXIII.
8. Horace, *Epistles*, II, ii, 36; 26–40 (where the soldier's tale is told).

[C] When we read that after Mechmet[9] had insulted and berated Chasan the chief of his Janissaries for allowing his line of battle to be broken by the Hungarians and for fighting faint-heartedly, Chasan's only reply was, alone and just as he was, weapon in hand, to charge madly against the first group of enemy soldiers to come along, who promptly overwhelmed him: that may well have been not so much an act of justification as a change of heart; not so much natural bravery as a new feeling of distress.

[A] That man you saw yesterday so ready to take risks: do not think it odd if you find him craven tomorrow. What had put heart into his belly was anger, or need, or his fellows, or wine, or the sound of a trumpet. His heart had not been fashioned by reasoned argument: it was those factors which stiffened it; no wonder then if he has been made quite different by other and contrary factors.

[C] The changes and contradictions seen in us are so flexible that some have imagined that we have two souls, others two angels who bear us company and trouble us each in his own way, one turning us towards good the other towards evil, since such sudden changes cannot be accommodated to one single entity.[10]

[B] Not only does the wind of chance events shake me about as it lists, but I also shake and disturb myself by the instability of my stance: anyone who turns his prime attention on to himself will hardly ever find himself in the same state twice. I give my soul this face or that, depending upon which side I lay it down on. I speak about myself in diverse ways: that is because I look at myself in diverse ways. Every sort of contradiction can be found in me, depending upon some twist or attribute: timid, insolent; [C] chaste, lecherous; [B] talkative, taciturn; tough, sickly; clever, dull; brooding, affable; lying, truthful; [C] learned, ignorant; generous, miserly and then prodigal — [B] I can see something of all that in myself, depending on how I gyrate; and anyone who studies himself attentively finds in himself and in his very judgement this whirring about and this discordancy. There is nothing I can say about myself as a whole simply and completely, without intermingling and admixture. The most universal article of my own Logic is DISTINGUO.[11]

9. That is, Mechmet II. Cf. Nicolas Chalcocondylas (tr. Blaise de Vigenère), *De la décadence de l'empire grec*, 1584.
10. That each individual is swayed by a good guardian angel and a bad angel derives from platonizing interpretations of Matthew 18:10; Rabelais accepts it (*Tiers Livre*, TLF, VII). (Cf. Erasmus, *Adages*, I, I, LXXII, *Genius malus*.)
11. 'I make a distinction', a term used in formal debates to reject or modify an opponent's assertion.

[A] I always mean to speak well of what is good, and to interpret favourably anything that can possibly be taken that way; nevertheless, so strange is our human condition that it leads to our being brought by vice itself to 'do good', except that 'doing good' is to be judged solely by our intentions. That is why one courageous action must not be taken as proof that a man really is brave; a man who is truly brave will always be brave on all occasions. If a man's valour were habitual and not a sudden outburst it would make him equally resolute in all eventualities: as much alone as with his comrades, as much in a tilt-yard as on the battlefield; for, despite what they say, there is not one valour for the town and another for the country. He would bear with equal courage an illness in his bed and a wound in battle, and would no more fear dying at home than in an attack. We would never see one and the same man charging into the breach with brave assurance and then raging like a woman over the loss of a lawsuit or a son. [C] If he cannot bear slander but is resolute in poverty; if he cannot bear a barber-surgeon's lancet but is unyielding against the swords of his adversaries, then it is not the man who deserves praise but the deed. Cicero says that many Greeks cannot even look at an enemy yet in sickness show constancy: the Cimbrians and the Celtiberians on the contrary; *'nihil enim potest esse æquabile, quod non a certa ratione proficiscatur.'* [For nothing can be called constant which does not arise out of a fixed principle.][12]

[B] There is no valour greater in its kind than Alexander's; yet it is but one kind of valour; it is not in all cases sufficiently whole or all-pervasive. [C] Absolutely incomparable it may be, but it has its blemishes, [B] with the result that we see him worried to distraction over the slightest suspicion he may have that his men are plotting against his life, and see him conducting his investigations with an injustice so chaotic and ecstatic and with a fear which overturned his natural reason. Then there is the superstition from which he so markedly suffered: it bears some image of faint-heartedness. [C] And the excessive repentance he showed for murdering Clytus is another testimony to the inconstancy of his mind.[13]

[A] We are fashioned out of oddments put together – [C] *'voluptatem contemnunt, in dolore sunt molliores; gloriam negligunt, franguntur infamia'* [they despise pleasure but are rather weak in pain; they

12. Cicero, *Tusc. disput.*, II, xxvii, 65.
13. Ibid., IV, xxxvii, 79. Alexander murdered Clitus when drunk.

are indifferent to glory, but are broken by disgrace][14] – [A] and we wish to win honour under false flags. Virtue wants to be pursued for her own sake: if we borrow her mask for some other purpose then she quickly rips it off our faces. Virtue, once the soul is steeped in her, is a strong and living dye which never runs without taking the material with her.

That is why to judge a man we must follow his tracks long and carefully. If his constancy does not rest firmly upon its own foundations; [C] 'cui vivendi via considerata atque provisa est'; [the path which his life follows having been thought about and prepared for beforehand;] [A] if various changes make him change his pace – I mean his *path*, for his pace may be hastened by them or made heavy and slow – then let him go free,[15] for that man will always 'run with the wind', *A vau le vent*, as the crest of our Lord Talbot puts it.

No wonder, said an Ancient, that chance has so much power over us, since it is by chance that we live. Anyone who has not groomed his life in general towards some definite end cannot possibly arrange his individual actions properly. It is impossible to put the pieces together if you do not have in your head the idea of the whole. What is the use of providing yourself with paints if you do not know what to paint? No man sketches out a definite plan for his life; we only determine bits of it. The bowman must first know what he is aiming at: then he has to prepare hand, bow, bowstring, arrow and his drill to that end. Our projects go astray because they are not addressed to a target.[16] No wind is right for a seaman who has no predetermined harbour. I do not agree with the verdict given in favour of Sophocles in the action brought against him by his son, which argued, on the strength of seeing a performance of one of his tragedies, that he was fully capable of managing his domestic affairs.[17] [C] Neither do I agree that the inferences drawn by the Parians sent to reform the Milesian government justified the conclusion they reached: visiting the island they looked out for the best-tended lands and the best-run country estates and, having noted down their owners' names, summoned all the citizens of the town to assemble and appointed those owners as the new governors and magistrates, judging that those who took care of their private affairs would do the same for the affairs of state.[18]

14. Cicero, *De officiis*, I, xxi, 71.
15. Cicero, *Paradoxa*, V, i; Seneca, *Epist. moral.*, XX, 2–3.
16. Several echoes of Seneca, *Epist. moral.*, LXXI and XCII and of other Epistles throughout this chapter.
17. Cicero, *De senectute*, VII.
18. Herodotus, *Historia*, V, xxix.

[A] We are entirely made up of bits and pieces, woven together so diversely and so shapelessly that each one of them pulls its own way at every moment. And there is as much difference between us and ourselves as there is between us and other people. [C] *'Magnam rem puta unum hominem agere'* [Let me convince you that it is a hard task to be always the same man.][19] [A] Since ambition can teach men valour, temperance and generosity – and, indeed, justice; since covetousness can plant in the mind of a shop-boy, brought up in obscurity and idleness, enough confidence to cast himself on the mercy of the waves and angry Neptune in a frail boat, far from his hearth and home, and also teach him discernment and prudence; and since Venus herself furnishes resolution and hardiness to young men still subject to correction and the cane, and puts a soldier's heart into girls still on their mothers' knees:

> [B] *Hac duce, custodes furtim transgressa jacentes,*
> *Ad Juvenem tenebris sola puella venit:*

[With Venus as her guide, the maiden, quite alone, comes to the young man, sneaking carefully through her sleeping guardians:][20]

it is not the act of a settled judgement to judge us simply by our outward deeds: we must probe right down inside and find out what principles make things move; but since this is a deep and chancy undertaking, I would that fewer people would concern themselves with it.

19. Seneca, *Epist. moral.*, CXX, 22. In the following sentence 'ambition', as often, means inordinate ambition; so too covetousness ('*avarice*' in the French original) means an inordinate desire to obtain, and retain, not only wealth but honour: its sense is close to that of inordinate ambition. Montaigne holds that bad motives can produce admirable qualities.
20. Tibullus, II, i, 75–6.

2. On drunkenness

===

[Drunkenness was considered a form of ecstasy, in which body and soul became separated or loosely joined. From Ancient times it was associated with the higher ecstasies (those of mystics, poets, prophets and lovers) as well as with the ecstasy of wonder, of bravery and of fear. (In his Paraphrases on the New Testament *Erasmus has a long section explaining the rapture of the disciples at Pentecost by analogy with the effects of drunkenness, of which the disciples were accused.) Montaigne is wary of ecstasy and despises excessive drinking, which is for him a rapture not of the mind but the body.]*

[A] The world is all variation and dissimilarity. Vices are all the same in that they are vices – and doubtless the Stoics understand matters after that fashion: but even though they are equally vices they are not equal vices. That a man who has overstepped by a hundred yards those limits

> *quos ultra citraque nequit consistere rectum,*
>
> [beyond which, and short of which, there is no right way,]

should not be in a worse condition than a man who has only overstepped them by ten yards is not believable; nor that sacrilege should be no worse than stealing a cabbage from our garden:

> *Nec vincet ratio, tantumdem ut peccet idemque*
> *Qui teneros caules alieni fregerit horti,*
> *Et qui nocturnus divum sacra legerit.*

[Reason cannot convince me that there is equal sinfulness in trampling down someone's spring cabbages and in robbing the temple-treasures in the night.][1]

There is as much diversity in vice as in anything else.

[B] It is dangerous to confound the rank and importance of sins: murderers, traitors and tyrants gain too much by it. It is not reasonable that they should be able to salve their consciences because somebody else is lazy, lascivious or not assiduous in his prayers. Each man comes down heavily on

1. For Stoics all vices are equally evil; all virtues equally good. Horace (as cited) denies that: *Satires*, I, i, 107; I, iii, 115–17.

his neighbours' sins and lessens the weight of his own. Even the doctors of the Church often rank sins badly to my taste.

[C]   Just as Socrates said that the prime duty of wisdom is to distinguish good from evil,[2] we, whose best always partakes of vice, should say the same about knowing how to distinguish between the vices: if that is not done exactingly, the virtuous man and the vicious man will be jumbled unrecognizedly together.

[A]   Now drunkenness, considered among other vices, has always seemed to me gross and brutish. In others our minds play a larger part; and there are some vices which have something or other magnanimous about them, if that is the right word. There are some which are intermingled with learning, diligence, valour, prudence, skill and *finesse*: drunkenness is all body and earthy. Moreover the grossest nation of our day is alone in honouring it.[3] Other vices harm our intellect: this one overthrows it;   [B]   and it stuns the body:

> *cum vinis vis penetravit,*
> *Consequitur gravitas membrorum, præpediuntur*
> *Crura vacillanti, tardescit lingua, madet mens,*
> *Nant oculi; clamor, singultus, jurgia gliscunt.*

[when the strength of the wine has sunk in, our limbs become heavy, we stagger and trip over our legs; our speech becomes slow; our mind, sodden; our eyes are a-swim. Then comes the din, the hiccoughs and the fights.][4]

[C]   The worst state for a man is when he loses all consciousness and control of himself.

[A]   And among other things they say that, just as the must fermenting in the wine-jar stirs up all the lees at the bottom, so too does wine unbung the most intimate secrets of those who have drunk beyond measure:

> [B]   *tu sapientium*
> *Curas et arcanum jocoso*
> *Consilium retegis Liæo.*

[in those jolly Bacchic revels you, my wine-jar, uncover worries and the secret counsels of the wise.][5]

2. Erasmus, *Apophthegmata*, III, *Socratica*, XXXIII.
3. The Germanic peoples.
4. Lucretius, III, 475–8.
5. Seneca, *Epist. moral.*, LXXXIII, 16; Horace, *Odes*, III, xxi, 14–17.

[A]   Josephus[6] tells how he wheedled secrets out of an ambassador sent to him by his enemies by making him drink a lot. Nevertheless Augustus confided his most private secrets to Lucius Piso, the conqueror of Thrace, and was never let down; nor was Tiberius let down by Cossus on whom he unburdened all of his plans: yet we know that those two men were so given to drinking that they had often to be carried out of the Senate, both drunk,[7]

> *Externo inflatum venas de more Lyæo.*
>
> [With veins swollen with others' wine, as usual.][8]

[C]   And the plan to kill Caesar was well kept when confided to Cassius, who drank water, but also when confided to Cimber, who often got drunk; which explains his joking reply: 'Should I bear the weight of a tyrant, when I cannot bear the weight of my wine!'[9]   [A]   Even our German mercenaries when drowned in their wine remember where they are quartered, the password and their rank:

> [B]   *nec facilis victoria de madidis, et*
> *Blæsis, atque mero titubantibus.*

[it is not easy to beat them, even when they are sodden-drunk, incoherent and staggering about.][10]

[C]   I would never have thought anybody could be buried so insensibly in drunkenness if I had not read the following in the history books. With the purpose of inflicting on him some notable indignity, Attalus invited to supper that Pausanias who, on this very subject, later killed Philip King of Macedonia (a king whose fine qualities nevertheless bore witness to the education he had received in the household and company of Epaminondas). He got him to drink so much that he could bring him, quite unaware of what he was doing, to abandon his fair body to mule-drivers and to many of the most abject scullions in his establishment, as if it were the body of some whore in a hedgerow.[11]

And then there is the case told me by a lady whom I honour and hold in

---

6. Flavius Josephus (the Jewish historian): *De vita sua.*
7. Seneca, *Epist. moral.*, LXXXIII, 14–15 (for both Piso and Cossa).
8. Virgil, *Bucolica*, VI, 15 (adapted).
9. Seneca, *Epist. moral.*, LXXXIII, 12–13.
10. Juvenal, *Satires*, XV, 47–8.
11. Diodorus Siculus, XV, xxvi.

the greatest esteem: towards Castres, near Bordeaux, where her house is, there was a village woman, a widow of chaste reputation, who, becoming aware of the first hints that she might be pregnant, told the women of the neighbourhood that if only she had a husband she would think she was expecting. But as the reason for her suspicions grew bigger every day and finally became evident, she was reduced to having a declaration made from the pulpit in her parish church, stating that if any man would admit what he had done she promised to forgive him and, if he so wished, to marry him. One of her young farm-labourers took courage at this proclamation and stated that he had found her one feast-day by her fireside after she had drunk her wine freely; she was so deeply and provocatively asleep that he had been able to have her without waking her up. They married each other and are still alive.

[A] Antiquity, certainly, did not greatly condemn this vice. The very writings of several philosophers speak of it indulgently; even among the Stoics there are those who advise you to let yourself drink as much as you like occasionally and to get drunk so as to relax your soul:

> [B] *Hoc quoque virtutum quondam certamine, magnum*
> *Socratem palmam promeruisse ferunt.*

[They say that Socrates often carried off the prize in this trial of strength too.][12]

[C] That Censor and corrector of others,[13] [A] Cato was reproached for his heavy drinking:

> [B] *Narratur et prisci Catonis*
> *Sæpe mero caluisse virtus.*

[It is told how the virtue of old Cato was often warmed with wine].[14]

[A] Such a famous King as Cyrus cited among the praiseworthy qualities which made him preferable to his brother Artaxerxes the fact that he knew how to drink better. Even among the best regulated and best governed peoples it was very common to assay men by making them drunk. I have heard one of the best doctors in Paris, Silvius, state that it is a good thing once a month to arouse our stomachs by this excess so as to stop their powers from getting sluggish and to stimulate them in order to prevent

12. Pseudo-Gallus, I, 47–8.
13. [A]: *That true portrait of Stoic virtue*, Cato... (Montaigne had first confused Cato of Utica with Cato the Censor).
14. Horace, *Odes*, III, xxi, 11–12.

their growing dull.   [B]   And we can read that the Persians discussed their most important affairs after drinking wine.[15]

[A]   My taste and my complexion are more hostile than my reason to this vice. For, leaving aside the fact that I readily allow my beliefs to be captive to the Ancients, I find this vice base and stultifying but less wicked and a cause of less harm than the others, which virtually all do more direct public damage to our society. And if, as they maintain, we can never enjoy ourselves without it costing us something, I find that this vice costs our conscience less than the others: besides it is not a negligible consideration that it is easy to provide for and easy to find.

[C]   A man advanced in years and rank told me that he counted drink among the three main pleasures left to him in this life.[16] But he set about it in the wrong way; for fine palates and an anxious selecting of wine are to be absolutely avoided. If you base your pleasure on drinking good wine you are bound to suffer from sometimes drinking bad. Your taste ought to be more lowly and more free. To be a good drinker you must not have too tender a palate. The Germans enjoy drinking virtually any wine. Their aim is to gulp it rather than to taste it. They get a better bargain. Their pleasure is more abundant and closer at hand.

Secondly, to drink in the French style at both meals, but moderately for fear of your health, is too great a restraint on the indulgence of god Bacchus: more time and constancy are required. The Ancients spent entire nights in this occupation and often went on into the next day. So we should train our habit in wider firmer ways. I have seen in my time a great lord, a person famous for his successes in several expeditions of high importance, who effortlessly and in the course of his ordinary meals never drank less than two gallons of wine and who, after that, never showed himself other than most sage and well-advised in the conduct of our affairs.

We should allow more time to that pleasure which we wish to count on over the whole of our lives. Like shop-apprentices and workmen we ought to refuse no opportunity for a drink; we ought always to have the desire for one in our heads: it seems that we are cutting down this particular one all the time and that, as I saw as a boy, dinner parties, suppers, and late-

---

15. '88: dull. *Plato attributes to it the same effect on the mind.*   [B]   And we can ...
(Cf. Erasmus, *Adages*, IV, III, LVIII, *Non est dithyrambus qui bibit aquam*; Rabelais, *Tiers Livre*, TLF, *Prologue*, 175ff.; Plutarch (tr. Amyot), *Propos de Table*, 364B; 420A.) Joannes Sylvius (Dubois) was a doctor and pharmacologist of note. He died in 1576.

16. '95: life: *and where do you hope more rightly to find them among the natural pleasures?* But ...

night feasts used to be much more frequent and common in our houses than they are now. Could we really be moving towards an improvement in something at least! Certainly not. It is because we throw ourselves into lechery much more than our fathers did. Those two occupations impede each other's strength. On the one hand lechery has weakened our stomachs: on the other, sober drinking has rendered us vigorous and lively in our love-making.

It is wonderful what accounts I heard my father give of the chastity of his times. He had the right to say so, as he was both by art and nature most graceful in the company of ladies. He talked little and well; he intermingled his speech with elegant references to books in the vernacular, especially Spanish, and among the Spanish he frequently cited the so-called *Marco Aurelio*.[17] His face bore an expression of gentle seriousness, humble and very modest; he took particular care to be respectable and decent in his person and his dress both on horse and on foot. He was enormously faithful to his word and, in all things, conscientious and meticulous, tending rather towards over-scrupulousness. For a small man he was very strong, straight and well-proportioned; his face was pleasing and rather brown; he was skilled and punctilious in all gentlemanly sports. I have also seen some canes filled with lead with which he is said to have exercised his arms for throwing the bar and the stone or for fencing, as well as shoes shod with lead to improve his running and jumping. Folk recall little miracles of his at the long-jump. When he was over sixty I remember him laughing at our own agility by vaulting into the saddle in his furry gown, by putting his weight on his thumb and leaping over a table and by never going up to his room without jumping three or four steps at a time. But more to my subject, he said that there was hardly one woman of quality in the whole province who was ill-spoken of, and he would tell of men – especially himself – who were on remarkably intimate terms with decent women without a breath of suspicion. In his own case he solemnly swore that he came virgin to his marriage-bed; and yet he had long done his bit in the transalpine wars, leaving a detailed diary of events there, both public and personal. And he married on his return from Italy in 1528 at the mature age of thirty-three.

Let us get back to our bottles.

[A] The disadvantages of old age (which has need of support and renewal) could reasonably give birth to a desire for drink, since a capacity for wine is virtually the last pleasure which the passing years steal from us.

17. The *Libro aureo del emperador Marco Aurelio* of Bishop Antonio de Guevara.

According to our drinking fraternity natural heat first gets a hold on our feet; that concerns our childhood; from there it rises to our loins where it long settles in, producing there if you ask me the only true bodily pleasures of this life: [C] in comparison, the other pleasures are half asleep. [A] Finally, like a mist rising and evaporating, it lands in the gullet and makes there its last abode.

[B] For all that, I do not understand how anyone can prolong the pleasure of drinking beyond his thirst, forging in his mind an artificial appetite which is contrary to nature. My stomach would never get that far: it has enough bother dealing with what it takes in for its needs. [C] I am so constituted that I care little for drink except at dessert; that is why my last draught is usually my biggest. Anacharsis was amazed that the Greeks should drink out of bigger glasses at the end of their meals;[18] it was I think for the same reason that the Germans do: that is when they start their drinking contests.

Plato forbids young people to drink before the age of eighteen and to get drunk before forty. But men over forty he tells to enjoy it and to bring copiously into their banquets the influence of Dionysius, that kind god who restores gaiety to grown men and youth to the old ones, who calms and softens the passions of the soul just as iron is softened by the fire. And in his *Laws* he considers convivial drinking to be useful (provided that the group has a leader to ensure that order is maintained), since getting drunk is a good and certain trial of each man's character and, at the same time, has the property of giving older men the idea of enjoying themselves in music and dancing, useful pastimes which they would not dare to engage in when of settled mind. Wine also has the capacity of tempering the soul and giving health to the body. Nevertheless he liked the following restrictions, partly borrowed from the Carthaginians: that it should be done without on military expeditions; that all statesmen and judges should abstain when about to perform their duties and to deliberate on matters of public concern; that the daytime should be avoided – that is owed to other activities – as well as any night when we intend to beget children.[19]

They say that the philosopher Stilpo, weighed down by old age, deliberately hastened his death by drinking his wine without water. A similar cause suffocated the failing powers of the aged philosopher Arcesilaus, but that was unintentional.[20]

18. Diogenes Laertius, *Life of Anacharsis*.
19. Cf. Tiraquellus, *De legibus connubialibus*, XIII, §147, citing Plato's *Laws*.
20. Diogenes Laertius, *Lives of Stilpo* and of *Arcesilaus*.

[A]   Whether the soul of a wise man should be such as to surrender to the power of wine is an old and entertaining question:

> *Si 'munitae adhibet vim sapientiae'.*

> [Whether 'wine should be able to make an assault on secure wisdom'.][21]

To what inanities are we driven by that good opinion we men have of ourselves! The best governed Soul in the world has quite enough to do to stay on her feet and to keep herself from falling to the ground from her own weakness. Not one in a thousand can stand up calm and straight for one instant in her life; it can even be doubted, given her natural condition, whether she ever can. But if you add constancy as well, then that is her highest perfection: I mean if nothing should shake it, something which hundreds of events can do. It was no good that great poet Lucretius philosophizing and bracing himself: a love-potion drove him insane. Do they think that an apoplexy will not make Socrates lose his wits as much as a porter? Some have forgotten their own names by the force of an illness, and a light wound has struck down the judgement of others. A man can be as wise as he likes: he is still a man; and what is there more frail, more wretched, more a thing of nothing, than man? Wisdom cannot force our natural properties:

> [B]   *Sudores itaque et pallorem existere toto*
> *Corpore, et infringi linguam, vocemque aboriri,*
> *Caligare oculos, sonere aures, succidere artus,*
> *Denique concidere ex animi terrore videmus.*

[Then we see sweat and pallor take over his whole body, his tongue grows incoherent, his voice fails, his eyes are troubled, his ears begin to ring, his legs give way and he falls to the ground, as panic seizes his mind.][22]

[A]   When he is threatened with a blow nothing can stop a man closing his eyes, or trembling if you set him on the edge of a precipice,   [C]   just like a child, Nature reserving to herself these signs of her authority, signs slight but unattackable by reason or Stoic virtue, in order to teach Man that he is mortal and silly.   [A]   He becomes livid with fear; he reddens with shame; he bewails an attack of colic paroxysms if not with a loud cry of despair at least with a cry which is broken and wheezing.

> *Humani a se nihil alienum putet!*

> [Let him realize that nothing human is a stranger to him!][23]

21. Horace, *Odes*, III, xxviii, 4.
22. Lucretius, III, 155–8.
23. Terence, *Heautontimorumenos*, I, i, 25.

Poets [C] who can make up anything they like [A] dare not relieve their heroes even of the burden of weeping:

> *Sic fatur lachrymans, classique immittit habenas.*

[Thus spoke Aeneas through his tears and his fleet sailed unbridled away.][24]

It suffices that a man should rein in his affections and moderate them, for it is not in his power to suppress them. And my very own Plutarch – so perfect, so outstanding a judge of human actions – when confronted by Brutus and Torquatus killing their children was led to doubt whether virtue could really get that far, and whether those great men had not in fact been shaken by some passion or other.[25] All actions which exceed the usual limits are open to sinister interpretations, since higher things are no more to our taste than inferior ones.

[C] Let us leave aside that other School which makes an express profession of pride.[26] Yet even in that third School which is reckoned to be the most indulgent of them all we hear similar boastings from Metrodorus:[27] *'Occupavi te, Fortuna, atque cepi; omnesque aditus tuos interclusi, ut ad me aspirare non posses.'* [I have forestalled you, O Fortune, and I have caught you; I have blocked off all your approaches, you cannot get near me.]

When Anaxarchus, on the orders of Nicocreon, Tyrant of Cyprus, was put into a stone mortar and beaten to death with blows from an iron pestle, he never ceased to cry, 'Go on! Strike, bash on, you are not pounding Anaxarchus but his casing';[28] [A] when we hear our Christian martyrs shouting out to the tyrant from the midst of the flames, 'It is well roasted on this side; chop it off and eat it; it is cooked just right: now start on the other side'; when we hear in Josephus[29] of the boy who was torn to pieces with clawed pincers and bored through by the bradawls of Antiochus, yet who still defied him, crying out in a firm assured voice: 'Tyrant! You are wasting your time! I am still here, quite comfortable! Where is this pain, where are those tortures you were threatening me with? Is this all you can do? My constancy hurts you more than your cruelty hurts me!

24. Virgil, *Aeneid*, VI, 1.
25. Plutarch (tr. Amyot), *Publicola*, III.
26. The Stoics.
27. The Epicureans; Cicero, *Tusc. disput.*, V, ix, 27, citing Metrodorus the pupil of Epicurus.
28. Diogenes Laertius, *Lives of Philosophers*, I, civ.
29. Flavius Josephus, *De Macabaeorum martyrio*.

You cowardly beggar! It is you who are surrendering: I am growing stronger! Make me lament, make me give way, make me surrender, if you can! Goad on your henchmen and your hangmen: they have lost heart and can do nothing more! Give them weapons! Egg them on!' – then we have to admit that there is some change for the worse in their souls, some frenzy, no matter how holy.

When we hear such Stoic paradoxes as, 'I would rather be raging mad than a voluptuary' [C] – that is the saying of Antisthenes,[30] [A] Μανείειν μᾶλλον ἢ ἡθείειν – when Sextius tells us that he would rather be transfixed by pain than by pleasure; when Epicurus decides to treat gout as though it were tickling him, refuses rest and good health, light-heartedly defies ills and, despising less biting pains, will not condescend to struggle in combat against them but summons and even wishes for pains which are strong and anguishing and worthy of him:

> *Spumantemque dari pecora inter inertia votis*
> *Optat aprum, aut fulvum descendere monte leonem;*

[Amidst his placid flock he prays to be vouchsafed some slavering boar, or that some wild lion will come down from the mountain;][31]

who does not conclude that those are the cries of a mind which is leaping out of its lodgings? Our Soul cannot reach so high while remaining in her own place. She has to leave it and rise upwards and, taking the bit between her teeth, bear her man off, enrapture him away so far that afterwards he is amazed by what he has done; just as in war, the heat of the combat often makes the valiant soldiers take such hazardous steps that they are the first to be struck with astonishment once they have come back to themselves; so too the poets are often seized by amazement by their own works and no longer recognize the defiles through which they had passed at so fine a gallop. In their case too it is called frenzy and mania. And just as Plato says that a sedate man knocks in vain at poetry's door, so too Aristotle says that no outstanding soul is free from a mixture of folly.[32] He is right to call *folly* any leap – however praiseworthy it might be – which goes beyond our reason and our discourse. All the more so in that wisdom is a controlled handling of our soul, carried out, on our Soul's responsibility, with measure and proportion.

30. Erasmus, *Apophthegmata*, VII, *Antithenes Atheniensis*, III; other examples from Aulus Gellius, IX, v, and Sextus Empiricus, *Hypotyposes*, III, xx.
31. Virgil, *Aeneid*, IV, 158–9.
32. Seneca, *De tranquillite*, XV (a major borrowing).

[C]   Plato contends that the faculty of prophesying is 'above ourselves'; that we must be 'outside ourselves' when we accomplish it; our prudence must be darkened by some sleep or illness, or else snatched out of its place by a heavenly rapture.[33]

33. Plato, *Timaeus*, 71D–72A.

5. On conscience

[Conscience originally meant connivance. Conscience in the sense of our individual consciousness of right and wrong or of our own guilt or rectitude fascinated Montaigne. It became a vital concern of his during the Wars of Religion with their cruelties, their false accusations and their use of torture on prisoners. Such moral basis as there was for the 'question' (judicial torture) seems, curiously enough, to have been a respect for the power of conscience – of a man's inner sense of his guilt or innocence which would strengthen or weaken his power to withstand pain. A major source of Montaigne's ideas here is St Augustine and a passionate note by Juan Luis Vives in his edition of the City of God designed to undermine confidence in torture.]

[A] During our civil wars I was travelling one day with my brother the Sieur de la Brousse when we met a gentleman[1] of good appearance who was on the other side from us; I did not know anything about that since he feigned otherwise. The worst of these wars is that the cards are so mixed up, with your enemy indistinguishable from you by any clear indication of language or deportment, being brought up under the same laws, manners and climate, that it is not easy to avoid confusion and disorder. That made me fear that I myself would come upon our own troops in a place where I was not known, be obliged to state my name and wait for the worst. [B] That did happen to me on another occasion: for, from just such a mishap, I lost men and horses. Among others, they killed one of my pages, pitifully: an Italian of good family whom I was carefully training; in him was extinguished a young life, beautiful and full of great promise.

[A] But that man of mine was so madly afraid! I noticed that he nearly died every time we met any horsemen or passed through towns loyal to the King; I finally guessed that his alarm arose from his conscience. It seemed to that wretched man that you could read right into the very secret thoughts of his mind through his mask and the crosses on his greatcoat.[2] So

---

1. '80: an honourable gentleman.
2. Reformers often considered the cross, when used as a symbol, to be idolatrous and blasphemous. Here it is used as a disguise.

wondrous is the power of conscience! It makes us betray, accuse and fight
against ourselves. In default of an outside testimony it leads us to witness
against ourselves:

> *Occultum quatiens animo tortore flagellum.*

> [Lashing us with invisible whips, our soul torments us.][3]

The following story is on the lips of children: a Paeonian called Bessus
was rebuked for having deliberately destroyed a nest of swallows, killing
them all. He said he was right to do so: those little birds kept falsely
accusing him of having murdered his father! Until then this act of parricide
had been hidden and unknown; but the avenging Furies of his conscience
made him who was to pay the penalty reveal the crime.[4]

Hesiod corrects that saying of Plato's, that the punishment follows hard
upon the sin. He says it is born at the same instant, with the sin itself; to
expect punishment is to suffer it: to merit it is to expect it. Wickedness
forges torments for itself,

> *Malum consilium consultori pessimum,*

> [Who counsels evil, suffers evil most,][5]

just as the wasp harms others when it stings but especially itself, for it loses
sting and strength for ever:

> *Vitasque in vulnere ponunt.*

> [In that wound they lay down their lives.][6]

The Spanish blister-fly secretes an antidote to its poison, by some mutual
antipathy within nature. So too, just when we take pleasure in vice, there is
born in our conscience an opposite displeasure, which tortures us, sleeping
and waking, with many painful thoughts.[7]

---

3. Juvenal, *Satires*, XIII, 195 (adapted).
4. Plutarch (tr. Amyot), *Pourquoy la justice divine differe la punition des malefices*,
261 E–G (a major borrowing).
5. Erasmus, *Adages*, I, II, XIV, *Malum consilium*.
6. Virgil, *Georgics*, IV, 238. Montaigne wrote *Mousches guespes* (wasps), but clearly
means 'bees'.
7. This Spanish fly was particularly poisonous. Cf. Cicero, *Tusc. disput.*, V, xl, 117;
Pliny, XXIX, iv, 30; XI, xxv, 41.

[B] *Quippe ubi se multi, per somnia sæpe loquentes,*
Aut morbo delirantes, procraxe ferantur,
Et celata diu in medium peccata dedisse.

[Many indeed, often talking in their sleep or delirious in illness, have proclaimed, it is said, and betrayed long-hidden sins.][8]

[A] Apollodorus dreamed that he saw himself being flayed by the Scythians then boiled in a pot while his heart kept muttering, 'I am the cause of all these ills.' No hiding-place awaits the wicked, said Epicurus, for they can never be certain of hiding there while their conscience gives them away.[9]

Prima est hæc ultio, quod se
Judice nemo nocens absolvitur.

[This is the principal vengeance: no guilty man is absolved: he is his own judge.][10]

Conscience can fill us with fear, but she can also fill us with assurance and confidence. [B] And I can say that I have walked more firmly through some dangers by reflecting on the secret knowledge I had of my own will and the innocence of my designs.

[A] *Conscia mens ut cuique sua est, ita concipit intra*
Pectora pro facto spemque metumque suo.

[A mind conscious of what we have done conceives within our breast either hope or fear, according to our deeds.][11]

There are hundreds of examples: it will suffice to cite three of them about the same great man.

When Scipio was arraigned one day before the Roman people on a grave indictment, instead of defending himself and flattering his judges he said: 'Your wishing to judge, on a capital charge, a man through whom you have authority to judge the Roman world, becomes you well!'

Another time his only reply to the accusations made against him by a Tribune of the People was not to plead his cause but to say: 'Come, fellow citizens! Let us go and give thanks to the gods for the victory they gave me over the Carthaginians on just such a day as this!' Then as he started to walk towards the temple all the assembled people could be seen following after him – even his prosecutor.

8. Lucretius, V, 1157–9.
9. Plutarch (tr. Amyot), *Pourquoi la justice divine diffère*, 262 D–E; Seneca, *Epist. moral.*, XCVII, 13.
10. Juvenal, *Satires*, XIII, 2–3.
11. Ovid, *Fasti*, I, 485–6. Cf. also Cognatus, *Adages, Conscientia crimen prodit*.

Again when Petilius, under the instigation of Cato, demanded that Scipio account for the monies that had passed through his hands in the province of Antioch, Scipio came to the Senate for this purpose, took his account-book from under his toga and declared that it contained the truth about his receipts and expenditure; but when he was told to produce it as evidence he refused to do so, saying that he had no wish to act so shamefully towards himself; in the presence of the Senate he tore it up with his own hands. I do not believe that a soul with seared scars could have counterfeited such assurance. [C] He had, says Livy, a mind too great by nature, a mind too elevated by Fortune, even to know how to be a criminal or to condescend to the baseness of defending his innocence.[12]

[A] Torture is a dangerous innovation; it would appear that it is an assay not of the truth but of a man's endurance. [C] The man who can endure it hides the truth: so does he who cannot. [A] For why should pain make me confess what is true rather than force me to say what is not true? And on the contrary if a man who has not done what he is accused of is able to support such torment, why should a man who has done it be unable to support it, when so beautiful a reward as life itself is offered him?

I think that this innovation is founded on the importance of the power of conscience. It would seem that in the case of the guilty man it would weaken him and assist the torture in making him confess his fault, whereas it strengthens the innocent man against the torture. But to speak the truth, it is a method full of danger and uncertainty. What would you *not* say, what would you *not* do, to avoid such grievous pain?

> [C]   *Etiam innocentes cogit mentiri dolor.*
>
> [Pain compels even the innocent to lie.]

This results in a man whom the judge has put to the torture lest he die innocent being condemned to die both innocent and tortured.[13] [B] Thousands upon thousands have falsely confessed to capital charges. Among them, after considering the details of the trial

12. Plutarch (tr. Amyot), *Comment on se peut louer soy-mesme*, 139 F; Aulus Gellius, *Attic Nights*, IV, xviii; Livy, *Annales*, XXXVIII. Erasmus gives these anecdotes s.v. *Scipio Africanus Major* in his *Apophthegmata*.
13. St Augustine, *City of God*, XIX, vi (against torture) with Vives' comments (in which Vives cites *Etiam innocentes* [from Publius Syrus] and apologizes for turning a commentary into a plea against torture). Montaigne is deeply indebted to him for what follows.

which Alexander made him face and the way he was tortured, I place Philotas.[14]

[A] All the same it is [C], so they say, [B] the least bad[15] [A] method that human frailty has been able to discover. [C] Very inhumanely, however, and very ineffectually in my opinion. Many peoples less barbarous in this respect than the Greeks and the Romans who call them the Barbarians reckon it horrifying and cruel to torture and smash a man of whose crime you are still in doubt.[16] That ignorant doubt is yours: what has it to do with him? You are the unjust one, are you not? who do worse than kill a man so as not to kill him without due cause! You can prove that by seeing how frequently a man prefers to die for no reason at all rather than to pass through such a questioning which is more painful than the death-penalty itself and which by its harshness often anticipates that penalty by carrying it out.

I do not know where I heard this from, but it exactly represents the conscience of our own Justice: a village woman accused a soldier before his commanding general – a great man for justice – of having wrenched from her little children such sops as she had left to feed them with, the army having laid waste all the surrounding villages. As for proof, there was none. That general first summoned the woman to think carefully what she was saying, especially since she would be guilty of perjury if she were lying; she persisted, so he had the soldier's belly slit open in order to throw the light of truth on to the fact. The woman was found to be right.[17] An investigatory condemnation!

---

14. Quintus Curtius, VI ff.
15. '80: it is the *best* method that . . .
16. Vives (cf. note 13 above).
17. Anecdote from Froissart in H. Estienne's *Apologie pour Hérodote*.

8. On the affection of fathers for their children

===

[This is one of the most moving and revealing of the chapters: it starts with the bout of melancholy which upset Montaigne's complexion and led him to write his Essays; it ends with thoughts of the mad frenzy which can lead fathers to fall in love with their own children or brain-children. Some of the examples he cites of strange behaviour concern chagrin (manic-depression) and melancholy itself. The shift from real children to brain-children (a vital platonic commonplace) is given greater urgency by the fact that Montaigne's children all died in infancy, one daughter excepted. His final examples emphasize that great deeds and books can be not only a man's 'sons' but his 'daughters' too.

The irritability which transpires through his discussion of wills and inheritances reminds us of tensions between him and his mother over the dispositions in Pierre de Montaigne's last will and testament. An earlier will (1560–61) had left great financial authority to the mother; the last will simply followed the relevant practices of the customary law of Bordeaux, which treated widows generously, though less so than some other legal systems within France. The widow (who died in 1601) harboured resentment until the end, in her own will bitterly accusing Michel de Montaigne's only daughter, her own granddaughter, of enjoying wealth which ought to have been hers. (See R. M. Calder, 'Montaigne and Customary Law', in Bibliothèque d'Humanisme et Renaissance, XLVII, 1985, pp. 79–85). In this chapter we are far from that balanced serenity which Montaigne often achieves. There are deletions in the Bordeaux manuscript probably not made by the author himself. Two have been reinserted here.

Incidentally, Michel de Montaigne's own marriage-settlement, doubtless principally drawn up by his father, Pierre, did not follow the customary law of Bordeaux and was less generous in its provisions for his widow than customary law allowed.]

For Madame d'Estissac

[A] Madame: unless I am saved by oddness or novelty (qualities which usually give value to anything) I shall never extricate myself with honour from this daft undertaking; but it is so fantastical and presents an aspect so totally unlike normal practice that it may just get by.

It was a melancholy humour (and therefore a humour most inimical to my natural complexion) brought on by the chagrin caused by the solitary retreat I plunged myself into a few years ago, which first put into my head this raving concern with writing.[1] Finding myself quite empty, with nothing to write about, I offered myself to myself as theme and subject matter. It is [C] the only book of its kind in the world, [A] in its conception wild and [C] fantastically eccentric.[2] [A] Nothing in this work of mine is worthy of notice except that bizarre quality, for the best craftsman in the world would not know how to fashion anything remarkable out of material so vacuous and base.

Now, Madame, having decided to draw a portrait of myself from life, I would have overlooked an important feature if I had failed to portray the honour which I have always shown you for your great merits.[3] I particularly wanted to do so at the head of this chapter, since of all your fine qualities one of the first in rank is the love you show your children.

Anyone who knows how young you were when your husband Monsieur d'Estissac left you a widow; the proposals which have been made to you by such great and honourable men (as many as to any lady of your condition in France); the constancy and firmness of purpose with which you have, for so many years and through so many difficulties, carried the weight of responsibility for your children's affairs (which have kept you busy in so many corners of France and still besiege you); and the happy prosperity which your wisdom or good fortune have brought to those affairs: he will readily agree with me that we have not one single example of maternal love today more striking than your own.

I praise God, Madame, that your love has been so well employed. For the great hopes of himself raised by your boy, Monsieur d'Estissac, amply assure us that when he comes of age you will be rewarded by the duty and gratitude of an excellent son.[4] But he is still a child, unable to appreciate the innumerable acts of devotion he has received from you: so I should like him, if this book should fall into his hands one day, to be able to learn something from me at a time when I shall not even have a mouth to tell it

---

1. Montaigne's *complexion* (balance of humours) was melancholy modified by sanguine elements. An access of melancholy *humour* would unbalance his complexion, plunging him into a depression (*chagrin*).
2. '80: wild and *monstrous*. Nothing . . .
3. '80: until [C]: the honour *and particular reverence* which [. . .] merits *and virtues*. I . . .
4. Montaigne took him as a youth to Italy.

to him – something I can vouch for quite truthfully and which will be made even more vigorously evident, God willing, by the good effects he will be aware of in himself: namely, that there is no nobleman in France who owes more to his mother than he does, and that in the future he will be able to give no more certain proof of his goodness and virtue than by acknowledging your qualities.

If there truly is a Law of Nature – that is to say, an instinct which can be seen to be universally and permanently stamped on the beasts and on ourselves (which is not beyond dispute) – I would say that, in my opinion, following hard on the concern for self-preservation and the avoidance of whatever is harmful, there would come second the love which the begetter feels for the begotten. And since Nature seems to have committed this love to us out of a concern for the effective propagation of the successive parts of the world which she has contrived, it is not surprising if love is not so great when we go backwards, from children to fathers.   [C]   To which we may add a consideration taken from Aristotle,[5] that anyone who does a kindness to another loves him more than he is loved in return; that anyone to whom a debt is owed feels greater love than the one by whom the debt is owed; and that every creator loves what he has made more than it would love him if it were capable of emotions. This is especially true because each holds his *being* dear: and *being* consists in motion and activity; in a sense, therefore, everyone is, to some degree, within anything he does: the benefactor has performed an action both fair and noble: the recipient, on the other hand, has only performed a useful one, and mere usefulness is less lovable than nobility. Nobility is stable and lasting, furnishing the one who has practised it with a constant satisfaction. Usefulness, however, can easily disappear or diminish, and the memory of it is neither so refreshing nor so sweet. The things which have cost us most are dearest to us – and it costs us more to give than to receive.

[A]   Since it has pleased God to bestow some slight capacity for discursive reasoning on us so that we should not be slavishly subject to the laws of Nature as the beasts are but should conform to them by our free-will and judgement, we should indeed make some concessions to the simple authority of the common laws of Nature but not allow ourselves to be swept tyrannously away by her: Reason alone must govern our inclinations.

For my part, those propensities which are produced in us without the command and mediation of our judgement taste strangely flat. In the case

5. Aristotle, *Nicomachaean Ethics*, IX, vii, 4–6.

of the subject under discussion, I am incapable of finding a place for that emotion which leads people to cuddle new-born infants while they are still without movements of soul or recognizable features of body to make themselves lovable. [C] And I have never willingly allowed them to be nursed in my presence. [A] A true and well-regulated affection should be born, and then increase, as children enable us to get to know them; if they show they deserve it, we should cherish them with a truly fatherly love, since our natural propensity is then progressing side by side with reason; if they turn out differently, the same applies, *mutatis mutandis*: we should, despite the force of Nature, always yield to reason.

In fact, the very reverse often applies; we feel ourselves more moved by the skippings and jumpings and babyish tricks of our children than by their activities when they are fully formed, as though we had loved them not as human beings but only as playthings [C] or as pet monkeys. [A] Some fathers will give them plenty of toys when they are children but will resent the slightest expenditure on their needs once they have come of age. It even looks, in fact, as if we are jealous of seeing them cut a figure in the world, able to enjoy it just when we are on the point of leaving it, and that this makes us miserly and close-fisted towards them: it irritates us that they should come treading on our heels, [C] as if to summon us to take our leave. [A] Since in sober truth things are so ordered that children can only have their being and live their lives at the expense of our being and of our lives, we ought not to undertake to be fathers if that frightens us.

For my part, I find it cruel and unjust not to welcome them to a share and fellow-interest in our property – giving them full knowledge of our domestic affairs as co-partners when they are capable of it – and not to cut back on our own interests, economizing on them so as to provide for theirs, since we gave them birth for just such a purpose. It is unjust to see an aged father, [B] broken [A] and only half alive,[6] stuck in his chimney-corner with the absolute possession of enough wealth to help and maintain several children, allowing them all this time to waste their best years without means of advancement in the public service and of making themselves better known. They are driven by despair to find some way, however unjust, of providing for their needs: I have seen in my time several young men of good family so addicted to larceny that no punishment could turn them from it. I know one young man, very well connected, with whom I had a word about just such a matter at the earnest

6. '80: father, *in his dotage* and only half alive . . .

request of his brother, a brave and most honourable nobleman. In reply the young man admitted quite openly that he had been brought to such vile conduct by the unbending meanness of his father, adding that he had now grown so used to it that he could not stop himself. He had just been caught stealing rings from a lady whose morning reception he was attending with several others. It reminded me of a story I had heard about another nobleman who had so adapted himself to the exigencies of that fine profession that when he did become master of his inheritance and decided to give up this practice he nevertheless could not stop himself from stealing anything he needed when he passed by a stall, despite the bother of having to send somebody to pay for it later. I have known several people so trained and adapted to thieving that they regularly steal from their close companions things which they intend to return.

[B] I may be a Gascon but there is no vice I can understand less. My complexion makes me loathe it rather more than my reason condemns it: I have never even wanted to steal anything from anyone. [A] It is true that my part of the world is rather more infamous for theft than the rest of our French nation: yet we have all seen in our time, on several occasions, men of good family from other provinces convicted of many dreadful robberies. I am afraid that we must partly attribute such depravity to the fault of their fathers.

If anyone then tells me, as a very intelligent nobleman once did, that the only practical advantage he wanted to get from saving up all his money was to be honoured and courted by his children (since now that age had deprived him of strength that was the only remedy he had left against being treated with neglect and contempt by everybody, and so maintaining his authority over his family – [C] and truly, not only old age but all forms of weakness are, according to Aristotle, great encouragements to miserliness)[7] – [A] then there is something in that. But it is medicine to cure an illness the birth of which ought to have been prevented. A father is wretched indeed if he can only hold the love of his children – if you can call it love – by making them depend on his help.

We should make ourselves respected for our virtues and our abilities and loved for our goodness and gentlemanliness. The very ashes of a rare timber have their value, and we are accustomed to hold in respect and reverence the very bones and remains of honourable people. In the case of someone who has lived his life honourably, no old age can be so decrepit and smelly that it ceases to be venerable – especially to the children, whose

7. Aristotle, *Nicomachaean Ethics*, IV, i, 37.

souls should have been instructed in their duty not by need and want, nor by harshness nor force, but by reason:

> *et errat longe, mea quidem sententia,*
> *Qui imperium credat esse gravius aut stabilius*
> *Vi quod fit, quam illud quod amicitia adjungitur.*

[if you ask my opinion, it is quite untrue that authority is firmer or more stable when it relies on force than when it is associated with affection.][8]

[B] I condemn all violence in the education of tender minds which are being trained for honour and freedom. In rigour and constraint there is always something servile, and I hold that you will never achieve by force what you cannot achieve by reason, intelligence and skill.[9]

That was the way I was brought up. They tell me that I tasted the [C] rod [B] only twice[10] during all my childhood, and that was but lightly. I owed the same treatment to the children born to me; they all die, though, before they are weaned. But [C] Léonor, [B] an only daughter who has escaped that calamity, has reached the age of six or more (her mother's gentleness readily predisposing her that way) without our having used in her upbringing and in the punishment of her childish faults anything but words – gentle ones at that. And even if my hopes for her turn out to be frustrated, there are other causes in plenty to blame for that without finding fault with my method of upbringing, which I know to be just and natural.

I would have been even more punctilious with boys, who are less born to serve and whose mode-of-being is freer: I would have loved to make their hearts overflow with openness and frankness. I have never seen caning achieve anything except making souls more cowardly or more maliciously stubborn.

[A] Do we want to be loved by our children? Do we want to remove any occasion for their wishing us dead? – though no occasion for so horrible a wish could ever be right or pardonable: [C] *'nullum scelus rationem habet'* [no crime has rational justification][11] – then let us within reason enrich their lives with whatever we have at our disposal. To achieve

---

8. Terence, *Adelphi*, I, i, 40–3.
9. The gentlemanly idea of education, as in Rabelais, who also loathed corporal punishment.
10. '80: tasted the *whip* only twice . . .
11. Cf. *Adagia*, Frankfurt, 1656, *Appendix Erasmi*, p. 313, *Scelera non habent consilia*, cited after Livy, XXVIII, xxviii.

that we ought not to get married so young that our adult years almost become confounded with theirs. Such unseemliness can plunge us into many great difficulties – I mean especially in the case of the nobility, whose way of life is one of leisure and who can live, as we say, on their income. In other cases, where life is a struggle for money, the fellowship of a great many children is a help to the whole family; they are so many new ways and means of helping to enrich it.

[B] I was thirty-three when I married; and I approve of thirty-five – the opinion attributed to Aristotle. [C] Plato does not want any man to marry before thirty; he is also right to laugh at spouses who lie together after fifty-five, judging their offspring unworthy to live and eat.[12]

It was Thales who gave the right ages; his mother pressed him to get married when he was young: 'Too soon,' he said. When he was older: 'Too late!' Accept no time as opportune for any inopportune activity!

[A] The Ancient Gauls reckoned it to be extremely reprehensible for a man to lie with a woman before he was twenty, particularly advising those who wanted to train for war to remain chaste well into adulthood, [A1] because sexual intercourse makes minds soft and deflects them.

> Ma hor congiunto a giovinetta sposa,
> Lieto homai de' figli, era invilito
> Ne gli affetti di padre e di marito.

[But now, married to a young wife, happy to have children, he was weakened by his love as father and husband.][13]

[C] The history of Greece notes how Iccus of Tarentum, Chryso, Astylus, Diopompus and others deprived themselves of any sort of sexual activity during all the time they were getting their bodies in trim for the races, wrestling and other contests at the Olympic Games.[14]

Muley Hassan, the Dey of Tunis (the one whom the Emperor Charles V restored to his throne) was critical of his father's memory because he was always with his wives, calling him a weak effeminate spawner of children.

[B] In a certain province in the Spanish Indies men were allowed to marry only after forty, yet girls could marry at ten.[15]

12. Aristotle, *Politics*, VII, xvi (age of thirty-seven not thirty-five); Plato, *Republic*, V, 460A ff.; cf. Tiraquellus, *De legibus connubialibus*, VI, §§ 44–7; 52.
13. Plutarch, *Life of Thales*; Caesar, *Gallic Wars*, VI (cf. Tiraquellus, ibid., VI, § 47); Torquato Tasso, *Gierusalemme liberata*, X, 39–41.
14. Tiraquellus, ibid., XV, § 26, citing Plato, *Laws*, VIII, 839E–840A.
15. Paolo Giovio, *Historia sui temporis*, on 'Muleasses' (Muley Hassan); Lopez de Gomara, *Histoire générale des Indes*.

[A] If a nobleman is only thirty-five it is too soon for him to make way for a twenty-year-old son: he has still got to achieve a reputation in military expeditions or at the Court of his monarch: he needs his cash; he should allow his son a share but not forget himself. Such a man can rightly give the answer which fathers often have on their lips: 'I have no wish to be stripped bare before I go and lie down.' But a father who is brought low by age and illness, whose weakness and ill-health deprive him of ordinary human fellowship, does wrong to himself and to his family if he broods over a great pile of riches. If he is wise, he has reached the period when he really ought to want to get stripped and lie down – not stripped to his shirt but down to a nice warm dressing-gown. He has no more use for all the remaining pomp: he should give it all away as a present to those whom it ought to belong to by Nature's ordinance.

It is right that he should let them use what Nature deprives him of: otherwise there is certainly an element of malice and envy. The finest gesture the Emperor Charles V ever made was when, [C] in imitation of some ancient holders of his rank, [A] he was able to recognize that reason clearly commands us to strip off our garments when they weigh us down and get in our way, and to go and lie down when our legs fail us.[16] Once he began to feel deficient in the strength and energy needed to continue to conduct his affairs with the glory he had earned, he handed over his wealth, his rank and his power to his son:

> *Solve senescentem mature sanus equum, ne*
> *Peccet ad extremum ridendus, et ilia ducat.*

[Be wise enough to unharness that tired old nag lest it ends up short-winded, stumbling while men jeer at it.][17]

This defect of not realizing in time what one is, of not being aware of the extreme decline into weakness which old age naturally brings to our bodies and our souls – to them equally in my opinion unless the soul actually has the larger share – has ruined the reputation of most of the world's great men. I have seen in my lifetime and intimately known great men in authority who had clearly declined amazingly from their former

16. Charles V resigned his crown and entered a monastery in 1557 (cf. J. Du Bellay, *Regrets*, 111).
17. Horace, *Epistles*, I, i, 8. (The 'old nag' is his Muse: hence the following development.)

capacities, which I knew of from the reputation they had acquired in their better years. For their honour's sake I would deeply have wished that they had withdrawn to their estates, dropping the load of public or military affairs which were no longer meant for their shoulders.

There was a nobleman whose house I used to frequent who was a widower, very old but still with some sap in him. He had several daughters to marry and a son already old enough to enter society, so that his house was burdened with considerable expenditure and quite a lot of outside visitors; he took little pleasure in this, not only out of concern for economy but even more because, at his age, he had adopted a mode of life far different from ours. In that rather bold way I have[18] I told him one day that it would be more becoming if he made room for us youth, leaving his principal residence to his son (for it was the only one properly equipped and furnished) and withdrew to a neighbouring estate of his where nobody would trouble his rest, since, given his children's circumstances, there was no other way he could avoid our unsuitable company. He later took my advice and liked it.

That is not to say we should make a binding gift of our property and not be able to go back on it. I am old enough to have to play that role now, and would leave the young the use of my house and property but be free to withdraw my consent if they gave me cause. I would let them have use of them because they no longer gave me pleasure, but I would retain as much general authority over affairs as I wanted to, for I have always thought that it must be a great happiness for an old father to train his own children in the management of his affairs; he could then, during his lifetime, observe how they do it, offering advice and instruction based on his own experience in such things, and personally arranging for the ancient honour and order of his house to come into the hands of his successors, confirming in this way the hopes he could place in their future management of them.

To do this I would not avoid their company; I would like to be near so as to watch them and to enjoy their fun and festivities as much as my age permitted. Even if I did not live among them (as I could not do without embarrassing the company by the gloominess of my age and by my being subject to illnesses — and also without being forced to restrict my own rules and habits), I would at least like to live near them in some corner of my house — not the fanciest but the most comfortable. Not (as I saw a few

18. [A] until [C]: I have *of bringing forth whatever comes to my lips* I told him . . .

years ago) a dean of St-Hilaire-de-Poitiers[19] brought to such a pitch of solitude by the troublesome effects of his melancholy that, when I went into his room, he had not set foot outside it for twenty-two years; yet he could still move about freely and easily, apart from a rheumatic flux discharging into his stomach. He would let scarcely anyone in to see him even once a week; he always stayed shut up in that room all by himself except for a valet who brought him his food once a day and who merely went in and out. His only occupation was to walk about reading a book (for he had some acquaintance with literature), obstinately determined as he was to die in those conditions – as soon afterwards he did.

I would try to have gentle relations with my children and so encourage in them an active love and unfeigned affection for me, something easily achieved in children of a well-born nature; of course if they turn out to be wild beasts   [C]   (which our century produces in abundance)   [A]   then you must hate them and avoid them as such.

I am against the custom   [C]   of forbidding children to say 'Father' and requiring them to use some other, more respectful title, as though Nature had not sufficiently provided for our authority. We address God Almighty as Father and scorn to have our own children call us by that name.

It is also unjust, and mad, to   [A]   deprive our grown-up children of   [C]   easy relations   [A]   with their[20] fathers by striving to maintain   [C]   an austere and contemptuous   [A]   frown, hoping[21] by that to keep them in fear and obedience. That is a quite useless farce which makes fathers loathsome to children and, what is worse, makes them ridiculous. Since youth and vigour are in their children's hands they enjoy the current favour of the world; they treat with mockery the fierce tyrannical countenance of a man with no blood left in his veins or his heart – scarecrows in a field of flax! Even if I were able to make myself feared I would rather make myself loved.[22]

[B]   There are so many drawbacks in old age, so much powerlessness; it so merits contempt that the best endowment it can acquire is the fond love of one's family: its arms are no longer fear and commands.

I know one man who had a most imperious youth. Now that old age is

19. Jean d'Estissac, who died in 1576. Such symptoms of melancholy as Montaigne describes are not rare in Renaissance medical treatises.
20. '80: children of *private intercourse and easy understanding* with . . .
21. '80: maintain *a severe and distant frown, full of rancour and contempt*, hoping . . .
22. Cf. Erasmus' similar reaction in his *Adages*, II, IX, LXII, *Oderint dum metuant*.

coming upon him, despite trying to accept it as well as he can, he slaps and bites and swears − [C] the stormiest master in France; [B] he frets himself with cares and watchfulness: but it is all a farce which the family conspire in; the others have access to the best part of his granary, his cellar and even his purse: meanwhile he keeps the keys in his pouch, dearer to him than sight itself. While he is happy to keep so spare and thrifty a table, in various secret places in his house all is dissipation, gambling, prodigality and tales about his fits of temper and his precautions. Everybody is on the lookout against [C] him.[23] [B] If some wretched servant happens to become devoted to him, suspicion is immediately thrown on to him − a quality which old age is only too ready to ruminate upon. How many times has that man boasted to me of keeping his family on a tight rein, of the meticulous obedience and reverence he received because of it, and of the lucid watch he kept over his affairs:

> *Ille solus nescit omnia!*
>
> [He alone is unaware of the lot!][24]

No man of my acquaintance can claim more qualities, natural and acquired, proper for maintaining his mastery; yet he had failed completely, like a child. That is why I have picked him out as an example from several other cases that I know.

[C] It would make a good scholastic debate: whether or not he is better off as he is. In his presence, all things defer to him; his authority runs its empty course: nobody ever resists him; they believe what he says, they fear and respect him . . . as much as he could wish! Should he dismiss a servant he packs his bag and is off at once − but only out of his presence. Old people's steps are so slow and their senses so confused that the valet can live a full year in the house doing his duty without their even noticing it. At the appropriate time a letter arrives from distant parts, a pitiful one, a submissive one, full of promises to do better in the future; the valet then finds himself back in favour.

Does my Lord strike a bargain and send a missive which the family do not like? They suppress it, sometimes inventing afterwards reasons to explain the lack of action or reply. Since no letters from outside are ever brought to him first, he only sees the ones which it seems convenient for him to know. If he happens to get hold of any, he always has to rely on

23. '88: against *that poor man*. If . . .
24. Terence, *Adelphi*, IV, ii, 9.

somebody else to read them for him, so they invent things on the spot: they are always pretending that someone is begging his pardon in the very letter that contains abuse. In short he sees his affairs only through some counterfeit image designed to be as pleasing to him as they can make it so as not to awake his spleen or his anger.

Under various guises, but all to the same effect, I have seen plenty of households run long and steadily in this way.

[B] Wives are always disposed to disagree with their husbands.[25] [C] With both hands they grasp at any pretence for contradicting them; any excuse serves as full justification. I know one who used to rob her husband wholesale – in order, she told her confessor, to 'fatten up her almsgiving'. (There's a religious spendthrift for you to trust!) Whatever their husbands agree to never provides them with enough dignity. To give it grace and authority they must have usurped it by ruse or by force, but always unjustly. When, as in the case I am thinking of, they are acting against some poor old man on behalf of the children, they seize on this pre-text and are honoured for serving their own passions; and, as though they were all slaves together, readily plot against his sovereignty and government. [B] If the children are male and grown-up, in the bloom of youth, then their mothers gang up with them and corrupt the steward, the bursar and everyone else by force or favour.

Old men without wives and children fall into this evil less easily but more cruelly and with less dignity. [C] Cato the Elder already said in his time, 'So many valets: so many enemies.' Given the gulf separating the purity of his century from ours, just think whether he was not really warning us that wife, sons and valet are all 'so many enemies' in our case.[26]

[B] It is a good thing that decrepitude furnishes us with the sweet gifts of inadvertency, ignorance and a readiness to be cheated. If we were to resist, what would happen to us, especially nowadays when the judges who settle our quarrels are usually on the side of the children – and venal?

[C] The cheating may escape my sight, but it does not escape my sight that I am very cheatable. ✶✶ Thrice and four times blessed is he who can entrust his pitiful old age into the hands of a friend. ✶✶[27] And

---

25. '88: husbands, *especially if they are old and irascible: but when it is a matter of favouring their children they grasp that pretext and glory in it.* If the children . . .
26. Cf. Seneca, *Epist. moral.*, XLVII, 5; but it was not Cato who said it. (The proverb applied to slaves, not valets or servants.)
27. This and the following passage between stars have been restored. In the Bordeaux manuscript they are deleted, but not certainly by Montaigne himself.

shall we have ever said enough about the value of a friend and how totally different it is from bonds based on contracts! Even that counterpart to a friend which I see between beasts, how devoutly I honour it!   ** Am I better or worse off for having savoured a friend? Better off, certainly. My regret for him consoles me and honours me. Is it not a most pious and pleasant task in life to be ever performing his obsequies? Can any pleasure possessed equal that pleasure lost? I would readily let myself be rapt insensible lingering over so caressing a notion.   **

[C] Others may deceive me, but at least I do not deceive myself into thinking that I can protect myself against it; nor do I cudgel my brains for ways of making myself able to do so. Only in my own bosom can I find salvation from treachery like this – not in disquieting and tumultuous inquisitiveness but in diversion and constancy. Whenever I hear of the state that some other man is in, I waste no time over that but immediately turn my eyes on to myself to see how I am doing. Everything which touches him touches me too. What has happened to him is a warning and an alert coming from the same quarter. Every day, every hour, we say things about others which ought more properly to be addressed to ourselves if only we had learned to turn our thoughts inward as well as widely outward. Similarly many authors inflict wounds on the cause they defend by dashing out against the attackers, hurling shafts at their enemies which can properly be hurled back at them.

[A] The late Monsieur de Monluc, the Marshal, when talking to me of the loss of his son (a truly brave gentleman of great promise who died on the island of Madeira), among other regrets emphasized the grief and heartbreak he felt at never having revealed himself to his son and at having lost the pleasure of knowing and savouring him, all because of his fancy to appear with the gravity of a stern father; he had never told him of the immense love he felt for him and how worthy he rated him for his virtue. 'And all that poor boy saw of me,' he said, 'was a frowning face full of scorn; he is gone, believing I was unable to love him or to judge him as he deserved. Whom was I keeping it for, that knowledge of the special love I harboured for him in my soul! Should not he have felt all the pleasure of it, and all the bonds of gratitude? I forced myself, I tortured myself, to keep up that silly mask, thereby losing the joy of his company – and his good-will as well, which must have been cold towards me: he had never received from me anything but brusqueness or known anything but a tyrannous façade.'

I find that lament to be reasonable and rightly held: for as I know only too well from experience when we lose those we love there is no consolation sweeter than the knowledge of having remembered to tell them everything and to have enjoyed the most perfect and absolute communication with them.

[B]   As much as I can I open myself to my own folk, and am most ready to tell them or anyone else what I intend towards them and what is the judgement I make on them. I hasten to reveal myself, to make myself known, for I do not want them to be misled about me in any way whatsoever.

[A]   According to Caesar, among the customs peculiar to our ancient Gauls there was the following: sons were not presented to their fathers and never dared to appear in public with them until they had begun to bear arms, as if to signify that the time had now come for the fathers to admit them to their intimate acquaintance.[28]

Yet another abuse of paternal discretion which I have seen in my time is when fathers are not content with having deprived their children of their natural share of the property during their long lifetime, but then go and leave authority over all of it after their death to their widows, free to dispose of it at their pleasure. One lord I have known (among the highest officers of the Realm) could rightfully have expected to come into property worth fifty thousand crowns a year: yet he died in need, overwhelmed with debts at the age of fifty, while his mother, despite advanced senility, still enjoyed rights over the entire property under the will of his father, who himself had lived to be eighty.

To me that seems in no way reasonable.

[B]   For all that, I cannot see it helps much when a man whose affairs are prospering goes and seeks a wife who burdens him with a large dowry: no debt contracted outside the family is more ruinous to a household. My ancestors have all followed this precept, most fittingly; so have I.

[C]   Yet those who warn us against marrying rich wives out of fear that they might be less beholden to us and more difficult wrongly lose a real advantage for a frivolous conjecture.[29] If a woman is unreasonable it costs her no more to jump over one reason than another. Such women are most pleased with themselves when they are most in the wrong: it is the injustice which allures them; whereas for good women it lies in their virtuous deeds: the richer they are the more gracious they are, just as beautiful women are more willingly and more triumphantly chaste.

28. Caesar, *Gallic Wars*, VI, xviii.
29. Cf. Tiraquellus, *De legibus connubialibus*, V, § 1 ff., repeating Aristotle's warning against wives who dominate because of their wealth.

[A]   It is reasonable to let mothers run affairs until the sons are legally old enough to assume the responsibility; but the father has brought them up wrongly if (considering the normal weakness of the female) he could not expect them to be wiser and more competent than his wife once they have reached that age. But it would be even more unnatural to make mothers depend on the discretion of their sons. They should be given a provision generous enough to maintain their state according to the condition of their family and their age, especially since want or indigence are far more difficult for them to bear with decorum than for males: that burden ought to be put on the sons rather than on the mother.

[C]   On the whole, the soundest way of sharing out our property when we die is (I believe) to follow local customary law. The Law has thought it out better than we have, so it is better to let the Law make the wrong choice than rashly hazard doing so ourselves. The property does not really belong to us personally, since without our leave it is entailed by civil law to designated heirs. And even though we have some discretion as well, I hold that it would take a great and very clear reason to justify our depriving anyone of what he was entitled to by the fortune of his birth and of what common law leads him to expect; it would be an unreasonable abuse of that freedom to make it serve whims both frivolous and private.

Fate has been kind, sparing me opportunities which might have tempted me to change my predilection for the dictates of common law. I know people whom it would be a waste of time to serve long and dutifully: one word taken the wrong way can wipe out ten years of merit. Anyone able to butter them up when they are just about to go is lucky indeed! The latest action scoops the lot: it is not the best and most frequent services which prove efficacious but recent ones, present ones.

There are people who exploit their wills as sticks and carrots to punish or reward every action of those who may claim an interest in the inheritance. But this is a matter of long-lasting consequence; it is too weighty to be changed from moment to moment: wise men settle it once and for all – and have regard for the reasonable customs of the community.

We are a little too fond of male entail; we foresee a ridiculous eternity for our family name and attach too much weight to silly conjectures about the future based on the minds of little boys. Somebody might easily have been unjust to me, ousting me from my place because I was more lumpish, more leaden, more slow and more unwilling to learn than any of my brothers (indeed, than all the children in my province), whether I was being taught to exercise mind or body. It is madness to make such selections, interrupting the succession on the faith of such fortune-telling which has so often deceived us. If we can ever infringe that rule and correct the choice of heirs made by destiny, it would probably be out of consideration for some huge noticeable physical deformity, of a permanent and incurable kind, one which those of us who are great admirers of beauty believe to be highly deleterious.

There is an agreeable dialogue between Plato's Lawgiver and his citizens which may honour my pages here: 'What!' they say, feeling their end draw near: 'Can we not bequeath our own property to anyone we please? What cruelty, O gods, that it be not lawful to give more or to give less just as we like, depending on how our heirs have helped us in our affairs, our illnesses or our old age!' The Legislator made this reply: 'My dear friends; you are certain to die soon: so it is difficult for any of you to "Know Thyself" (according to that Delphic inscription) and to know what is yours. I make these laws and maintain that you do not belong to yourselves, nor do the things of which you enjoy the use actually belong to you. You and your goods belong to your family, both past and future. And still more do your family and your goods belong to the commonwealth. Therefore if on your sickbed or in your old age some flatterer tries to persuade you to make an unjust will (or if a fit of temper does) I will protect you. Out of respect for the general concerns of our City and of your family, I will establish laws which make it known that private interests must reasonably yield to those of the community. Go, gently and willingly, whither human necessity bids you. It is for me, who favour all things equally and who take care of the people in general, to take care also of what you leave behind you.'[30]

To return to my subject, [A] it seems to me right, somehow, that women should have no mastery over men save only the natural one of motherhood – unless it be for the chastisement of those who have wilfully submitted to them out of some feverish humour; but that does not apply to old women, the subject of our present discussion. It is the manifest truth of this consideration which has made us so ready to invent and entrench that Salic Law – which nobody has ever seen – which debars women from succeeding to our throne;[31] and though Fortune has lent it more credence in some places than others, there is scarcely one jurisdiction in the world where that law is not cited as here, because of the genuine appearance of reason which gives it authority.

30. Plato, *Laws*, XI, 922 D–924 A.
31. The English claim to the French crown was based on the irrelevance of the mythical Salic Law. (Guillaume Postel maintained that it specifically applied to France, its real name being the 'Gallic' Law: *La Loi Salique*, Paris, 1552.)

It is dangerous to leave the superintendence of our succession to the judgement of our wives and to their choice between our sons, which over and over again is iniquitous and fantastic. For those unruly tastes and physical cravings which they experience during pregnancy are ever-present in their souls. They regularly devote themselves to the weakest and to the feeblest, or to those (if they have any) who are still hanging about their necks. Since women do not have sufficient reasoning-power to select and embrace things according to their merits they allow themselves to be led to where natural impressions act most alone – like animals, which only know their young while they are still on the teat.[32]

Incidentally, experience clearly shows us that the natural love to which we attach such importance has very shallow roots. For a very small sum of money we daily tear their own children out of women's arms and get them to take charge of our own; we make them entrust their babes to some wretched wet-nurse to whom we have no wish to commit our own or else to a nanny-goat; then we forbid them not only to give suck to theirs no matter what harm it might do them but even to look after them; they must devote themselves entirely to the service of our children. And then we see that in most cases custom begets a kind of bastard love more distracted than the natural kind; they are far more worried about the preservation of those foster-children than of the children who really belong to them.

I mentioned nanny-goats because the village-women where I live call in the help of goats when they cannot suckle their children themselves; I have now two menservants who never tasted mothers' milk for more than a week. These nanny-goats are trained from the outset to suckle human children; they recognize their voices when they start crying and come running up. They reject any other child you give them except the one they are feeding; the child does the same to another nanny-goat. The other day I saw an infant who had lost its own nanny-goat as the father had only borrowed it from a neighbour: the child rejected a different one which was provided and died, certainly of hunger.

The beasts debase and bastardize maternal affection as easily as we do.

[C] Herodotus tells of a certain district of Libya where men lie with women indiscriminately, but where, once a child can toddle, it recognizes its own father out of the crowd, natural instinct guiding its first footsteps.[33] There are frequent mistakes, I believe . . .

---

32. '80: their young, *or savour their kinship* while . . .
33. Tiraquellus, *De legibus connubialibus*, VII, § 51; Herodotus, *History*, IV.

[A] Now once we consider the fact that we love our children simply because we begot them, calling them our second selves, we can see that we also produce something else from ourselves, no less worthy of commendation: for the things we engender in our soul, the offspring of our mind, of our wisdom and talents, are the products of a part more noble than the body and are more purely our own. In this act of generation we are both mother and father; these 'children' cost us dearer and, if they are any good, bring us more honour. In the case of our other children their good qualities belong much more to them than to us: we have only a very slight share in them; but in the case of these, all their grace, worth and beauty belong to us. For this reason they have a more lively resemblance and correspondence to us. [C] Plato adds that such children are immortal and immortalize their fathers – even deifying them, as in the case of Lycurgus, Solon and Minos.[34]

[A] Since our history books are full of exemplary cases of the common kind of paternal love, it seemed to me not inappropriate to cite a few examples of this other kind too.

[C] Heliodorus, that good bishop of Tricca, preferred to forgo the honour of so venerable a bishopric with its income and its dignity rather than to destroy his 'daughter', who still lives on – a handsome girl but attired perhaps with a little more care and indulgence than suits the daughter of a priest, of a clerk in holy orders – and fashioned in too erotic a style.[35]

[A] In Rome there was a figure of great bravery and dignity called Labienus;[36] among other qualities he excelled in every kind of literature; he was, I think, the son of that great Labienus who was the foremost among captains who served under Caesar in the Gallic Wars, subsequently threw in his lot with Pompey the Great and fought for him most bravely until Caesar defeated him in Spain. There were several people who were jealous of the Labienus I am referring to; he also probably had enemies among the courtiers and favourites of the contemporary Emperors for his frankness and for inheriting his father's innate hostility towards tyranny, which we

34. Plato, *Phaedrus*, 258 C, dealing with a man's writings, his 'brain-children'; but Montaigne has transcribed *Minos* for *Darius*.
35. His Greek novel, *An Ethiopian History*, tells of the loves of Theagenes and Chariclea. It was translated into French by Amyot (Paris, 1547) and often reprinted.
36. Labienus was, for the ferocious nature of his controversial style, nicknamed *Rabienus* (the Fierce One). (Cf. Marcus Annaeus Seneca, *Controversiae*, 10, Preface; Suetonius, *Caligula*, 16.)

may believe coloured his books and writing. His enemies prosecuted him before the Roman magistrates and obtained a conviction, requiring several of the books he had published to be burnt. This was the very first case of the death-penalty being inflicted on books and erudition; it was subsequently applied at Rome in several other cases. We did not have means nor matter enough for our cruelty unless we also let it concern itself with things which Nature has exempted from any sense of pain, such as our renown and the products of our minds, and unless we inflicted physical suffering on the teachings and the documents of the Muses.

Labienus could not bear such a loss nor survive such beloved offspring; he had himself borne to the family vault on a litter and shut up alive; there he provided his own death and burial. It is difficult to find any example of fatherly love more vehement than that one. When his very eloquent friend Cassius Severus saw those books being burnt, he shouted that he too ought to be burnt alive with them since he actively preserved their contents in his memory.

[B] A similar misfortune happened to Greuntius Cordus who was accused of having praised Brutus and Cassius in his books.[37] That slavish, base and corrupt Senate (worthy of a worse master than Tiberius) condemned his writings to the pyre: it pleased him to keep his books company as they perished in the flames by starving himself to death.

[A] Lucan was a good man, condemned by that blackguard Nero; in the last moments of his life, when most of his blood had already gushed from his veins (he had ordered his doctors to kill him by slashing them) and when cold had already seized his hands and feet and was starting to draw near to his vital organs, the very last thing he remembered were some verses from his *Pharsalian War*; he recited them, and died with them as the last words on his lips. Was that not saying farewell to his children tenderly and paternally, the equivalent of those adieus and tender embraces which we keep for our children when we die, as well as being an effect of that natural instinct to recall at our end those things which we held dearest to us while we lived?

When Epicurus lay dying, tormented they say by the most extreme colic paroxysms, he found consolation only in the beauty of the philosophy he had taught to the world;[38] are we to believe that he would have found happiness in any number of well-born, well-educated children (if he had

37. Or rather, *Cremutius* Cordus, an historian honoured for his frankness: Tacitus, *Annals*, IV, xxxiv; Marcus Annaeus Seneca, *Suasoria*, VII; Quintilian, X, i, 104.
38. Cicero, *De finibus*, II, xxx, 96.

had any) to equal what he found in the abundant writing which he had brought forth? And if he had had the choice of leaving either an ill-conceived and deformed child behind him or a stupid and inept book, would – not he alone but any man of similar ability – have preferred to incur the first tragedy rather than the other?

It would probably have been impious of Saint Augustine (for example) if someone had obliged him to destroy either his children (supposing he had had any) or else his writings (from which our religion receives such abundant profit) and he had not preferred to destroy his children.[39]

[B] I am not at all sure whether I would not much rather have given birth to one perfectly formed son by commerce with the Muses than by commerce with my wife. [C] As for this present child of my brain, what I give it I give unconditionally and irrevocably, just as one does to the children of one's body; such little good as I have already done it is no longer mine to dispose of; it may know plenty of things which I know no longer, and remember things about me that I have forgotten; if the need arose to turn to it for help, it would be like borrowing from a stranger. It is richer than I am, yet I am wiser than it.

[A] Few devotees of poetry would not have been more gratified at fathering the *Aeneid* than the fairest boy in Rome, nor fail to find the loss of one more bearable than the other. [C] For according to Aristotle, of all artists the one who is most in love with his handiwork is the poet.[40]

[A] It is hard to believe that Epaminondas (who boasted that his posterity consisted in two 'daughters' who would bring honour to their father one day – he meant his two noble victories over the Spartans) would have agreed to exchange them for daughters who were the most gorgeous in the whole of Greece; or that Alexander and Caesar had ever wished they could give up the greatness of their glorious feats in war in return for the pleasure of having sons and heirs however perfect, however accomplished; indeed I very much doubt whether Phidias or any other outstanding sculptor would have found as much delight in the survival and longevity of his physical children as in some excellent piece of sculpture brought to completion by his long-sustained labour and his skill according to the rules of his art.

And as for those raging vicious passions which have sometimes inflamed fathers with love for their daughters, or mothers for their sons, similar ones

39. St Augustine did have an illegitimate son. If Montaigne had read the *Confessions* he would have known of him.
40. Aristotle, *Nicomachaean Ethics*, IX, vii, 3.

can be found in this other kind of parenthood: witness the tale of Pygmalion who, having carved the statue of a uniquely beautiful woman, was so hopelessly ravished by an insane love for his own work that, for the sake of his frenzy, the gods had to bring her to life:

> *Tentatum mollescit ebur, positoque rigore*
> *Subsedit digitis.*

[He touches the ivory statue; it starts to soften; its hardness gone, it yields to his fingers.][41]

41. Ovid, *Metamorphoses*, X, 243 ff., citing 283–4.

11. On cruelty

[In the previous chapter, 'On books', Montaigne had praised Froissart for admitting that he had changed his mind at whatever point of his book that the change actually occurred. In this chapter Montaigne follows suit, letting us see how he suddenly realized that virtue as conceived by Hesiod or by Cato is inadequate to explain the virtue of Socrates, which Montaigne had come to prefer to the sterner kind. Cruelty, which Montaigne loathed, is not one of the seven deadly sins and was not widely considered wrong in itself. Montaigne sees cruelty as arising from ecstasies of anger or from ecstatic sexual encounters. Even worse are cruelty and torture done for the fun of it.

The extension of Montaigne's sensitivity to the rest of creation, especially to Man's fellow-creatures the animals, is a skilful preparation for one of the major themes of the following chapter, 'An apology for Raymond Sebond'.]

[A] It seems to me that virtue is something other, something nobler, than those tendencies towards the Good which are born in us. Such souls as are well-endowed and in control of themselves adopt the same gait as virtuous ones and, in their actions, present the same face: but the word virtue has a ring about it which implies something greater and more active than allowing ourselves to be gently and quietly led in reason's train by some fortunate complexion.

A man who, from a naturally easy-going gentleness, would despise injuries done to him would do something very beautiful and praiseworthy; but a man who, stung to the quick and ravished by an injury, could arm himself with the arms of reason against a frenzied yearning for vengeance, finally mastering it after a great struggle, would undoubtedly be doing very much more. The former would have acted well: the latter, virtuously; goodness is the word for one of these actions; virtue, for the other; for it seems that virtue presupposes difficulty and opposition, and cannot be exercised without a struggle. That is doubtless why we can call God good, mighty, bountiful and just, but we cannot call him virtuous: his works are his properties and cost him no struggle.

Among the philosophers take the Stoics, and even more so the Epicureans – and I borrow that 'even more so' from the common opinion, which is wrong, [C] despite the clever retort which Arcesilaus made to the

philosopher who reproached him with the fact that many people crossed
over from his school to the Epicurean one, but never the other way round:
'I am sure that is so,' he said; 'you can make plenty of cocks into capons,
but never capons into cocks!'[1] –   [A]   for in truth the Epicurean School
in no wise yields to the Stoic in firmness of opinion and rigour of doctrine.
A Stoic (who showed better faith than those disputants who, to oppose
Epicurus and to make the game easy for themselves, put into his mouth
things he never even thought of, sinisterly twisting his words and by the
rules of grammar claiming to find other senses in his way of speaking, and
beliefs different from those which he showed in mind and manners)
declared that he ceased being an Epicurean for this reason among others,
that he found their path too steep and unapproachable;   [C]   *'et ii qui*
φιλήδονοι vocantur, sunt φιλόκαλοι et φιλοδίκαιοι, omnesque virtutes et colunt et
retinent.' [and those who were called 'lovers of pleasure' are in fact 'lovers
of honour' and 'lovers of justice', cultivating and practising all the
virtues].[2]

[A]   Among the Stoic and Epicurean philosophers there were, I say,
many who judged that it was not sufficient to have our soul in a good
state, well under control and ready for virtue; that it was not sufficient to
have our powers of reason and our thoughts above all the strivings of
Fortune, but that we must do more, seeking occasions to put them to the
test. They wish to go looking for pain, hardship and contempt, in order to
combat them and to keep our souls in fighting trim: [C]   *'multum sibi*
adjicit virtus lacessita.' [virtue gains much by being put to the proof.][3]

[A]   That is one of the reasons why Epaminondas, who belonged to a
third School, rejected the wealth which Fortune put in his hands in the
most legitimate of ways, in order, he said, to have to fence against
poverty; and he remained extremely poor unto the end. Socrates, it
seems to me, assayed himself even more roughly: to exercise his virtue
he put up with the malevolence of his wife, which is to assay yourself
in good earnest.[4]

Metellus alone among all the Roman Senators undertook to withstand
by the force of his virtue the violence of Saturninus (the Tribune of the
People of Rome, intent on forcing through an unjust law in favour of the

---

1. Erasmus, *Apophthegmata*, VII, *Arcesilaus*, II.
2. Cicero, *Epistulae ad familiares*, XV, 19.
3. Seneca, *Epist. moral.*, XIII, 3.
4. Epaminondas was a Pythagorean; Socrates' wife Xanthippe was, for Plato, the
archetypal shrew.

plebs); having incurred the death penalty which Saturninus had decreed for those who rejected it, he conversed with those who were escorting him to the Forum in this extremity, saying that to act badly was too easy and too cowardly; to act well when there was no danger, too commonplace; but to act well when danger threatened, was the proper duty of a virtuous man.[5]

Those words of Metellus show us clearly what I wanted to prove: that virtue rejects ease as a companion, and that the gentle easy slope up which are guided the measured steps of a good natural disposition is not the path of real virtue. Virtue demands a rough and thorny road:[6] she wants either external difficulties to struggle against (which was the way of Metellus) by means of which Fortune is pleased to break up the directness of her course for her, or else inward difficulties furnished by the disordered passions [C] and imperfections [A] of our condition.

I have got this far quite easily. But by the end of the above argument the thought occurs to me that the soul of Socrates, which is the most perfect to have come to my knowledge, would be by my reckoning a soul with little to commend it, for I cannot conceive in that great man any onslaught from vicious desires. I cannot imagine any difficulty or any constraint in the progress of his virtue; I know that his reason was so powerful and sovereign within him that it would never have even let a vicious desire be born in him. I cannot put anything face to face with so sublime a Virtue as his: it seems I can see her striding victoriously and triumphantly along, stately and at her ease, without let or hindrance. If Virtue can only be resplendent when fighting opposing desires are we therefore to say that she cannot manage without help from vice, to whom she at least owes the fact that she is held in esteem and honour? And what would become of that bold and noble-minded Pleasure of the Epicureans, who prides herself on nursing Virtue gently in her lap and making her sport there, giving her shame and fevers and poverty and death and tortures to play with? If I postulate that perfect Virtue makes herself known by fighting pain and bearing it patiently, by sustaining attacks from the gout without being shaken in her seat; if I make her necessarily subject to hardship and difficulty, what becomes of that Virtue who has reached such a pinnacle that she not only despises pain but delights in it, taking the stabbings of a strong colic paroxysm as tickling pleasures? Such was the virtue established by the Epicureans, of which several of them have left us by their actions proofs which are absolutely certain.

5. Plutarch, *Life of Marius*.
6. As in the myth of Hesiod, *Works and Days*, 289 f.

So have many others whom, in their actions, I find surpassing the very rules of their doctrines. Witness the Younger Cato. When I see him dying and ripping out his entrails I cannot be satisfied with the belief that he then simply had his soul totally free from trouble and dismay; I cannot believe that he merely remained in that state which the rules of the Stoic School ordained for him: calm, without emotion, impassible. There was, it seems to me, in the virtue of that man too much panache and green sap for it to stop there. I am convinced that he felt voluptuous pleasure in so noble a deed and that he delighted in it more than in anything else he did in his life: [C] *'Sic abiit e vita ut causam moriendi nactum se esse gauderet.'* [He quitted this life, rejoicing that a reason for his dying had been born.][7] [A] I am so convinced by this that I begin to doubt whether he would have wished the opportunity for so fine an exploit to be taken from him. And, if that goodness which led him to embrace public interests rather than his own did not rein me back, I would readily concur with the opinion that he was grateful to Fortune for having put his virtue to so fine a proof and for having favoured that brigand[8] who was to trample the ancient freedom of his country underfoot. I seem to read in his action some unutterable joy in his Soul, an access of delight beyond the usual order and a manly pleasure, when she considered the sublime nobility of his deed:

[B]   *Deliberata morte ferocior;*

[She was all the more ferocious for having chosen death;][9]

[A] she was not pricked on by any hope of glory (as the base and womanish judgements of some men have opined), for such a consideration is too low to touch so generous a mind, so high and unbending; he did it for the beauty of the thing itself, which he, who could handle such motives better than we can, saw much more clearly in all its perfection.

[C] It pleases me that philosophy decreed that so beautiful a deed would become no other life than Cato's and that it was for his life alone to end that way. That is why he rightly ordered his son and the senators who bore him company to provide some other way in their own case: *'Catoni cum incredibilem natura tribuisset gravitatem, eamque ipse perpetua constantia roboravisset, semperque in proposito consilio permansisset, moriendum potius quam tyranni vultus aspiciendus erat.'* [To Cato Nature had attributed an

7. Cicero, *Tusc. disput.*, I, xxx, 74.
8. Julius Caesar; defeated by him at Pharsalia, Cato killed himself later at Utica.
9. Horace, *Odes*, I, xxxvii, 29.

unbelievable dignity; he himself had strengthened it by his unfailing constancy; he had remained ever loyal to the principles which he had adopted, so he had to die rather than look on the face of a tyrant.][10]

Every man's death should be one with his life. Just because we are dying we do not become somebody else. I always interpret a man's death by his life. And if I am given an account of an apparently strong death linked to a weakling life, I maintain that it was produced by some weakling cause in keeping with that life.

[A] So are we to say that the ease with which Cato died, and that power which he acquired by the strength of his soul to do so without difficulty, should somehow dim the splendour of his virtue? And who among those whose brain is even slightly tinged with true philosophy can be satisfied with imagining a Socrates merely free from fear and anguish when his lot was prison, shackles and a verdict of guilty? And who fails to recognize in him not merely firmness and constancy (that was his ordinary state) but some new joy and a playful rapture in his last words and ways? [C] When he scratched his leg after the shackles were off he trembled with pleasure: does that not suggest a similar sweet joy in his Soul at being unshackled from her past hardships and capable of entering into a knowledge of things to come? [A] Cato must please forgive me: his death is more taut and more tragic but Socrates' is somehow even more beautiful. [C] To those who deplored it, Aristippus replied: 'May the gods send me one like it!'[11]

In the souls of those two great men and in those who imitated them (for I very much doubt if any were actually like them) you can see such a perfect acquisition of the habit of virtue that it became a matter of their complexion. It was no longer a painful virtue nor a virtue ordained by reason, virtues which they had to stiffen their souls to maintain: it was the very being of their souls, their natural ordinate manner. They rendered them thus by a long practice of the precepts of philosophy encountering beautiful and richly endowed natures. Those vicious passions which are born in us can find no entry into them; the force and rectitude of their souls stifle and snuff out concupiscence as soon as it begins to stir.

That it is more beautiful to prevent the birth of temptations by a sublime and god-like resolve and to be so fashioned to virtue that even the seeds of vices have been uprooted rather than to prevent their growing by active force and, once having been surprised by the first stirrings of the

10. Cicero, *De officiis*, I, xxxi, 112.
11. Erasmus, *Apophthegmata*, III, *Aristippus*, XXXV.

passions, to arm and tense oneself to halt their progress and to vanquish them; or that this second action is nevertheless more beautiful than to be simply furnished with an easy affable nature which of itself finds indulgence and vice distasteful: cannot I think be doubted. For this third and last manner may seem to produce an innocent man but not a virtuous one; a man exempt from doing evil but not one apt for doing good. Added to which such a mode of being is so close to imperfection and weakness that I cannot easily unravel and distinguish what separates them. That is why the very terms 'goodness' and 'innocence' are somewhat pejorative. I note that several virtues – chastity, sobriety and temperance – can come to us as our bodies grow weaker. Staunchness in the face of danger (if that is the right name for it), together with contempt for death and patience in affliction, can come to men (and are often found in them) by a defect in their assessment of such misfortunes, by a failure to conceive them as they are. A lack of intelligence or even animal-stupidity can counterfeit virtuous deeds: I have often seen men praised for deeds which deserved blame.

An Italian nobleman once spoke as follows in my presence at the expense of his nation: the subtlety of the Italians and the vividness of their minds are so great that they can foresee far ahead the dangers and mishaps that may befall them, so that in war we should not consider it strange if we often find them providing for their safety even before reconnoitring the danger; whereas we French and the Spaniards, who were nothing like as subtle, would press on; we had to be made to see danger with our own eyes and to handle it before we took fright: then there was no holding us; whereas the Germans and the Swiss, grosser and stolider men, scarcely had enough sense to change their ideas even when they were being struck down. Perhaps it was said for a laugh. It is nevertheless true that apprentices to the craft of war often leap into dangers more thoughtlessly than they do once they have been mauled:

> [B]   *haud ignarus quantum nova gloria in armis,*
> *Et prædulce decus primo certamine possit.*

[I was not unaware of what can be achieved by a man coming fresh to battle seeking glory and by the sweet honour of a first engagement.][12]

[A]   That then is why, when we make a judgement of any individual action, we must consider a great many circumstances as well as the man as a whole who performed it before we give it a name.

Now a word about myself.   [B]   I have sometimes seen my friends

12. Virgil, *Aeneid*, XI, 154–5.

speak of wisdom in me when it was really luck, or attribute something to
my courage and endurance when it was really due to my judgement or to
my opinion, attributing one quality to me instead of another, sometimes to
my advantage, sometimes to my detriment. Meanwhile, [A] so far am I
from having reached that first degree of excellence where virtue becomes
an acquired habit that I have hardly given any proof of the second. I have
not made much of a struggle to bridle any of my pressing desires. My
virtue is a virtue – or rather a state of innocence – which is incidental
and fortuitous. If I had been born with a more unruly complexion I am
afraid my case would have been deserving of pity. Assays of myself
have not revealed the presence in my soul of any firmness in resisting
the passions whenever they have been even to the slightest degree ecstatic. I do
not know how to sustain inner conflicts and debates. So I cannot congratulate
myself much if I do find that I am exempt from many of the vices:

> *si vitiis mediocribus et mea paucis*
> *Mendosa est natura, alioqui recta, velut si*
> *Egregio inspersos reprehendas corpore nævos;*

[if, in my nature, which is otherwise straight, there are a few trivial vices, just as
you might criticize an otherwise beautiful body for having a few moles;][13]

I owe that more to my Fortune than to my reason.

Fortune caused me to be born from a stock famous for its honourable
conduct and from an excellent father. Did some of his humours flow into
me? Was it the examples in the home and the good education I received as
a boy which contributed to it without my knowledge? Was it due to some
other accident of birth? I cannot tell:

> [B] *Seu libra, seu me scorpius aspicit*
> *Formidolosus, pars violentior*
> *Natalis horæ, seu tyrannus*
> *Hesperiæ Capricornus undæ?*

[Was I born under the constellation of the Balance? Or was it dread Scorpio with
violent power over the hour of birth? Or was it Capricorn, who rules as tyrant
over the Hesperian waves?][14]

[A] it is at all events true that, of my own self, I am horrified by most of
the vices. [C] ('To unlearn evil', the reply which Antisthenes made to

13. Horace, *Satires*, I, vi, 65–7.
14. Horace, *Odes*, II, xvii, 13–16. (To be born under the equable Balance, Libra,
was to be learned and judicious: cf. Manilius, *Astronomica*, IV, 202 ff.)

the man who asked him what was the best way to be initiated, seems to centre on that idea.)[15] I am, I repeat, horrified by them, [A] out of a native conviction so thoroughly my own that I have retained the impulses and character which I bore away with me when I was weaned; no other factors have made me worsen them – not even my own arguments which, since they have in some things broken ranks and left the common road, would readily license actions in me which my natural inclinations make me loathe. [B] I shall be saying something monstrous but I will say it all the same: I find, [C] because of this, in many cases [B] more rule and order in my morals than in my opinions, and my appetites less debauched than my reason.

[C] Aristippus laid down opinions about pleasure and riches which were so bold that the whole of philosophy rose and stormed against him. Yet where his morals were concerned, when Dionysius the Tyrant presented him with three beautiful young women to choose from, he said he would choose all three, since things had gone badly for Paris when he preferred one woman to her two companions: but having escorted them to his home he sent them away without laying a finger on them. And when his man-servant found the load of coins he was carrying too heavy to manage, he told him to pour out as many of them as he found too heavy.[16]

Epicurus too, whose doctrines are free from religious scruple and favour luxury, in fact behaved in real life most devoutly and most industriously. He wrote to a friend of his that he lived on nothing but coarse bread and water, asking him to send him a bit of cheese for when he wanted to give himself an extra special treat.[17]

Can it possibly be true that to be good in practice we must needs be so from some inborn, all-pervading property hidden within us, without law, without reason and without example?

[A] By God's mercy any excesses in which I have found myself implicated have not been of the worst. In my own case, I have condemned them at their true value, since my judgement was never infected by them. I have made the case for the prosecution against myself more rigorously than against anyone else. But that is not the whole story: despite all this, I bring too little resistance to bear on them, letting myself readily come down on the opposite side of the scales, except that I do control my vices, preventing them from being contaminated by others: for unless you are on your guard

15. Erasmus, *Apophthegmata*, VII; *Antisthenes Atheniensis*, XXVII.
16. Erasmus, *Apophthegmata*, III; *Aristippus*, III and XXXVII.
17. Diogenes Laertius, *Life of Epicurus*.

one vice leads to another; and most support each other. I prune my own vices and train them to be as isolated and as uncomplicated as possible.

> [B]   *Nec ultra*
> *Errorem foveo.*

[Beyond that point I do not indulge my faults.][18]

[A]   As for the opinion of the Stoics, who say that when the Wise Man acts he acts through all his virtues together even though there is one virtue which is more in evidence depending on the nature of the action (and a comparison with the human body is of some service to them in that, since choler cannot be exercised in action unless all our humours come to our aid, even though the choler predominates): if they then proceed to draw the parallel consequence that when the bad man does wrong he does so through all his vices together, then I do not believe it to be simple – or else I fail to understand what they mean, for I know the contrary to be true by experience.[19]

[C]   Such are the insubstantial pin-point subtleties which philosophy occasionally lingers over.

Some vices I follow: others I flee as much as any saint could do. And the Peripatetics reject the idea of any such indissoluble interconnection and bonding: Aristotle maintains that a man may be wise and just yet intemperate and lacking in restraint.[20]   [A]   Socrates confessed to those who recognized in his physiognomy some inclination towards vice that such was indeed his natural propensity but he had corrected it by discipline. [C]   And the intimate friends of Stilpo the philosopher said that he was born subject to wine and women but had trained himself to be most abstemious in both by study.[21]   [A]   Any good that I may have in me I owe on the contrary to the luck of my birth. I do not owe it to law, precept or apprenticeship.   [B]   Such innocence as there is in me is an unfledged innocence: little vigour, no art.

[A]   Among the vices, both by nature and judgement I have a cruel

18. Juvenal, *Satires*, VIII, 164–5.

19. For Stoics the virtues are individually impossible without all the others. Cf. Cicero, *De finibus*, IV, xxviii, 77 ff. Augustine, *Catalogus hereseon* considers that this doctrine favours the Jovinian heresy.

20. Diogenes Laertius, *Life of Aristotle*.

21. Zopyrus the Physiognomist judged from Socrates' features that he was lecherous and a dullard. Socrates agreed: he was born such, but had 'reformed' his soul: see Erasmus, *Apophthegmata*, III; *Socratica*, LXXX; and Cicero, *De fato*, V, 10 for both Socrates and Stilpo.

hatred of cruelty, as the ultimate vice of them all. But I am so soft that I cannot even see anyone lop the head off a chicken without displeasure, and cannot bear to hear a hare squealing when my hounds get their teeth into it, even though I enjoy the hunt enormously.

Those who have to write against sensual pleasure like to use the following argument to show that it is entirely vicious and irrational: when its force is at its climax it overmasters us to such an extent that reason has no way to come into it; they go on to cite what we know of that from our experience of lying with women –

> *cum jam præsagit gaudia corpus,*
> *Atque in eo est venus ut muliebria conserat arva*

[as when the body already anticipates its joy, and Venus is about to scatter seeds broadcast in the woman's furrows][22] –

in which it seems to them that the delight so transports us outside ourselves that our reason could not possibly perform its duty then, being entirely transfixed and enraptured by the pleasure.

But I know that it can go otherwise and that, if we have the will, we can sometimes manage, at that very instant, to bring our soul back to other thoughts. But we must vigilantly ensure that our soul is taut and erect. I know it is possible to master the force of that pleasure; and   [C]   I am quite knowledgeable about the subject; I have never found Venus to be as imperious a goddess as several people, chaster than I am, attest her to be.   [A]   I do not regard it as a miracle, as the Queen of Navarre does in one of the tales in her *Heptaméron* (which is a noble book for its cloth), nor even as a matter of extreme difficulty, to spend nights at a time with a mistress long yearned for, in complete freedom and with every opportunity, while keeping my promised word to her to content myself with simple kisses and caresses.[23]

[C]   I think a more appropriate example would be that of hunting (in which there is less pleasure but more ecstasy and rapture by which our reason is stunned, so losing the ability of preparing and bracing itself for the encounter),   [A]   when,[24] after a long chase, our quarry suddenly

---

22. Lucretius, IV, 1099–10.
23. Margaret of Navarre, *Heptaméron*, IIIe *Journée, conte* 30; she states that St Ambrose had to forbid such tests of virtue.
24. '80: I think a more appropriate *comparison would be with* hunting, *in which there seems to be more rapture: not in my opinion that the pleasure in itself is greater but because it affords us no leisure to brace and prepare ourselves against it, and that it surprises us when* . . .

pops up and reveals itself where we were perhaps least expecting it. The shock of this [C] and the heat of the view-halloo strike us so, that it would be difficult for those who love this sort of hunt to bring their thoughts at this point back to anything else. That is why the poets [A] make Diana[25] to triumph over Cupid's flames and arrows:

> *Quis non malarum, quas amor curas habet,*
> *Haec inter obliviscitur?*

[Is there anyone who, in the joys of the hunt, does not forget the ills which love's cares bring?][26]

To return to my subject, I feel a most tender compassion for the afflictions of others and would readily weep from fellow-feeling – if, that is, I knew how to weep at anything at all. [C] Nothing tempts my tears like tears – not only real ones but tears of any kind, in feint or paint.

[A] I scarcely ever lament for the dead: I would be more inclined to envy them; but I do make great lamentations for the dying. Savages do not upset me so much by roasting and eating the bodies of the dead as those persecutors do who torture the bodies of the living. However reasonable lawful public executions may be, I cannot even look fixedly at them. Someone, having to bear witness to the clemency of Caesar, wrote the following:[27] 'He was so mild in his vengeance that, having forced surrender on the pirates who had formerly taken him prisoner and held him to ransom, he did indeed condemn them to be crucified since he had threatened them with that fate, but he first had them strangled. His secretary Philemon, who had tried to poison him, he punished with nothing severer than simple death.' Without my even naming the author who ventures to allege as evidence of clemency the mere killing of those who have injured us, it is easy enough to guess that he was shocked by the base and horrifying examples of cruelty which the Roman tyrants introduced. As for me, even in the case of Justice itself, anything beyond the straightforward death-penalty seems pure cruelty, and especially in us Christians who ought to be concerned to dispatch men's souls in a good state, which cannot be so when we have driven them to distraction and despair by unbearable tortures.

---

25. '80: The shock of this *pleasure* strikes us so *furiously* that it would be difficult for those who love the hunt to bring their *soul* at this point back *from its rapture. Love gives way to the pleasure of the chase, say the poets: that is why they* make Diana . . .

26. Horace, *Epodes*, II, 37–8.

27. The author is Suetonius (*Life of Julius Caesar*). Related by Erasmus, *Apophthegmata*, IV; *Julius Caesar*, I.

['95]   A few days ago[28] a soldier in prison noticed from the tower in which he was held that a crowd was gathering in the square and that the carpenters were at work constructing something; he concluded that this was for him; he determined to kill himself, but found nothing which could help him to do so save a rusty old cart-nail which Fortune offered to him. He first of all gave himself two big jabs about the throat, but finding that this was not effective he soon afterwards gave himself a third one in his stomach, leaving the nail protruding. The first of his gaolers to come in found him in this state, still alive but lying on the ground weakened by the blows. So as not to waste time before he swooned away, they hastened to pronounce sentence on him. When he had heard it and learned that he was to be decapitated, he seemed to take new heart; he accepted the wine which he had previously refused and thanked his judges for the unhoped for mildness of their sentence, saying that he had made up his mind to appeal personally to death because he had feared a death more cruel and intolerable, having formed the opinion that the preparations which he had seen being made in that square meant that they wanted to torture him with some horrifying torment. This change in the way he was to die seemed to him like a deliverance from death.

[A]   My advice would be that exemplary severity intended to keep the populace to their duty should be practised not on criminals but on their corpses: for to see their corpses deprived of burial, boiled or quartered would strike the common people virtually as much as pains inflicted on the living, though in reality they amount to little or nothing – [C] as God says, 'Qui corpus occidunt, et postea non habent quod faciant.' [Who kill the body and after that have nothing that they can do.][29] And the poets particularly emphasize the descriptions of such horrors as something deeper than death.

> Heu! relliquias semiassi regis, denudatis ossibus,
> Per terram sanie delibutas fæde divexarier.

[O grief! that the remains of a half-burnt king, his flesh torn to the bone, and spattered with mud and blood, should be dragged along in shame.][30]

---

28. The text of the Bordeaux manuscript addition is partly damaged, but clearly tells of the same event in much the same words. Here ['95] replaces [C] as being more reliable.
29. Luke 12:4. (Christ's own words, but cited inexactly from memory).
30. Cicero, Tusc. disput., I, xliv, 106 (citing Ennius)

[A1]   I found myself in Rome at the very moment when they were dispatching a notorious thief called Catena. The crowd showed no emotion when he was strangled, but when they proceeded to quarter him the executioner never struck a blow without the people accompanying it with a plaintive cry and exclamation, as if each person had transferred his own feelings to that carcass.[31]

[B]   Such inhuman excesses should be directed against the dead bark not the living tree. In somewhat similar circumstances Artaxerxes tempered the harshness of the ancient laws of Persia: he ordained that noblemen who had failed in their tasks should not be whipped as they used to be but stripped naked and their clothes whipped instead, and that whereas they used to have their hair torn out by the root they should merely be deprived of their tall headdresses.[32]

[C]   The scrupulously devout Egyptians reckoned that they adequately satisfied divine justice by sacrificing swine in figure and effigy; it was a bold innovation to wish to pay in shadow and effigy God whose substance is very essence.[33]

[A]   I live in a season when unbelievable examples of this vice of cruelty flourish because of the licence of our civil wars; you can find nothing in ancient history more extreme than what we witness every day. But that has by no means broken me in. If I had not seen it I could hardly have made myself believe that you could find souls so monstrous that they would commit murder for the sheer fun of it; would hack at another man's limbs and lop them off and would cudgel their brains to invent unusual tortures and new forms of murder, not from hatred or for gain but for the one sole purpose of enjoying the pleasant spectacle of the pitiful gestures and twitchings of a man dying in agony, while hearing his screams and groans. For there you have the farthest point that cruelty can reach: [C]   *'Ut homo hominem, non iratus, non timens, tantum spectaturus occidat.'* [That man should kill man not in anger or in fear but merely for the spectacle.][34]

[A]   As for me, I have not even been able to witness without displeasure an innocent defenceless beast which has done us no harm being hunted to the kill. And when as commonly happens the stag, realizing that it has

31. Described in Montaigne's *Journal de Voyage.*
32. Erasmus, *Apophthegmata*, V, *Artoxerxes*, XVIII. (Similarly cited in Amyot's Plutarch, but as Artaxerxes).
33. Herodotus, *History*, II, xlvii.
34. Seneca, *Epist. moral.*, XC, 45.

exhausted its breath and its strength, can find no other remedy but to surrender to us who are hunting it, throwing itself on our mercy which it implores with its tears:

[B]   *quæstuque, cruentus*
Atque imploranti similis;

[all covered with blood, groaning, and seeming to beg for grace;][35]

[A]   that has always seemed to me the most disagreeable of sights.

[B]   I hardly ever catch a beast alive without restoring it to its fields. Pythagoras used to do much the same, buying their catches from anglers and fowlers:

[A]   *primoque a cæde ferarum*
Incaluisse puto maculatum sanguine ferrum.

[it was, I think, by the slaughter of beasts in the wild that our iron swords were first spattered with warm blood.][36]

Natures given to bloodshed where beasts are concerned bear witness to an inborn propensity to cruelty.

[B]   In Rome, once they had broken themselves in by murdering animals they went on to men and to gladiators. I fear that Nature herself has attached to Man something which goads him on towards inhumanity. Watching animals playing together and cuddling each other is nobody's sport: everyone's sport is to watch them tearing each other apart and wrenching off their limbs.

[A]   And lest anyone should laugh at this sympathy which I feel for animals,[37] Theology herself ordains that we should show some favour towards them; and when we consider that the same Master has lodged us in this palatial world for his service, and that they like us are members of his family, Theology is right to enjoin upon us some respect and affection for them.

Pythagoras borrowed his metempsychosis from the Egyptians, but it was subsequently accepted by many peoples including our Druids:[38]

35. Virgil, *Aeneid,* VII, 501.
36. Erasmus, *Adages,* I, I, II, *Amicitia aequalis;* section *Pythagorae Symbolae: A pisces abstineto;* then, Ovid, *Metamorphoses,* XV, 106–7.
37. '80: sympathy *and love* [amitié] which I confess that I feel for *them . . .*
    An echo of the Pythagorean adage of Erasmus, *Amicitia aequalis* (see note 36).
38. The Druids were the priests and philosophers of the Ancient Gauls: Caesar, *Gallic Wars,* V, xiii ff.

> *Morte carent animæ; semperque, priore relicta*
> *Sede, novis domibus vivunt, habitantque receptæ.*

[Souls have no death: they live for ever welcome in new abodes, having left their former ones.][39]

The religion of our Ancient Gauls included the belief that souls, being eternal, never cease changing and shifting from one body to another. In addition the Gauls attached to this idea some concern with divine justice: they said that for the Soul which had made her home in, say, Alexander there was ordained by God, depending on how she had behaved, a different body, more [C] painful [A] or less so,[40] according to her behaviour:

> [B] *muta ferarum*
> *Cogit vincla pati, truculentos ingerit ursis,*
> *Prædonesque lupis, fallaces vulpibus addit;*
> *Atque ubi per varios annos, per mille figuras*
> *Egit, lethæo purgatos flumine, tandem*
> *Rursus ad humanæ revocat primordia formæ.*

[He compels those souls to accept the mute fetters of the beasts: the merciless are imprisoned in bears; thieves, in wolves; cheats in foxes; then, having driven them over many a year through thousands of shapes, He at last purges them in the waters of Lethe and summons them back to their original human shape].[41]

[A] If the Soul had been valiant, she was lodged in the body of a lion; if a voluptuary, in a pig's; if a coward, in a stag's or a hare's; if cunning, in a fox's; and so on until, purified by such chastisement, she took on the shape of some other man.

> *Ipse ego, nam memini, Trojani tempore belli*
> *Panthoides Euphorbus eram.*

[For I, Pythagoras, as I remember well, was Euphorbus, son of Pantheus, during the Trojan War.][42]

39. Ovid, *Metamorphoses*, XV, 106–7. The Egyptian origin of metempsychosis is mentioned by Ovid's commentators (e.g., among many, the Venice edition, 1586, p. 295).
40.   [A]: body more *vile*, or less so . . .
41. Claudius Claudianus, *In Ruffinum*, II, 482–7.
42. Ovid, *Metamorphoses*, XV, 160–1 – from the verses which sympathetically expound Pythagoras' ideas.

I do not attach much importance to such cousinship between us and the beasts;[43] nor to the fact that many nations, particularly some of the oldest and noblest, not only welcomed animals to companionship and fellowship with themselves but even ranked them far above themselves, sometimes reckoning that they were the familiar friends and favourites of their gods, respecting them and reverencing them as above mankind, sometimes acknowledging no other god nor godhead but them: [C] *'belluæ a barbaris propter beneficium consecratæ.'* [beasts were sacred to the Barbarians because of the blessings they bestowed.][44]

> [B]   *Crocodilon adorat*
> *Pars hæc, illa pavet saturam serpentibus Ibin;*
> *Effigies hic nitet aurea cercopitheci;*
>   *hic piscem fluminis, illic*
> *Oppida tota canem venerantur.*

[This region worships the crocodile; another trembles before the ibis, gorged with snakes; here on the altar stands a golden image of a long-tailed monkey; in this town they venerate a river-fish; in another, a dog.][45]

[A]   And the actual interpretation which Plutarch makes of this error (which is a very sound one) is to their honour. For he states that it was not the cat or (for example) the bull which the Egyptians worshipped: what they worshipped in those beasts was an image of the divine attributes: in the bull, patience and utility; in the cat, quickness,[46] [C] or, like our neighbours the Burgundians as well as all the Germans, its refusal to let itself be shut in: by the cat they represented that freedom which they loved and adored above any other of God's attributes. And so on.

[A]   But when among other more moderate opinions I come across arguments which assay to demonstrate the close resemblance we bear to the animals, and how much they share in our greatest privileges and how convincingly they can be compared to us, I am led to abase our presumption considerably and am ready to lay aside that imaginary kingship over other creatures which is attributed to us.

---

43. Such 'cousinship' is briefly mentioned by Brassicanus in his remarks on Pythagoras' adage *Ab animalibus abstine*, with an allusion to Ovid's 'truly golden' verses in the *Metamorphoses*, XV, which, throughout the Renaissance, is the source always cited or followed.
44. Cicero, *De nat. deorum*, I, xxxvi, 101.
45. Juvenal, *Satires*, XV, 2–6.
46. Plutarch (tr. Amyot), *De Isis et Osiris*, 333F–334H.

Even if all of that remained unsaid, there is a kind of respect and a duty in man as a genus which link us not merely to the beasts, which have life and feelings, but even to trees and plants. We owe justice to men: and to the other creatures who are able to receive them we owe gentleness and kindness. Between them and us there is some sort of intercourse and a degree of mutual obligation. [C] I am not afraid to admit that my nature is so childishly affectionate that I cannot easily refuse an untimely gambol to my dog wherever it begs one.

[A1] The Turks have charities and hospitals for their beasts. [A] The Romans had a public duty to care for geese, by the vigilance of which their Capitol had been saved;[47] the Athenians commanded that the he-mules and she-mules which had been used in building the temple named the Hecatompedon should be set free and allowed to graze anywhere without hindrance.[48]

[C] It was the usual practice of the citizens of Agrigentum to give solemn burial to the beasts they loved, such as to horses of some rare merit, to working birds and dogs or even to those which their children had played with. And their customary magnificence in all things was particularly paraded in the many splendid tombs which they erected for that purpose; they remained on display many centuries afterwards. The Egyptians buried wolves, bears, crocodiles, dogs and cats in hallowed places; they embalmed their corpses and wore mourning at their deaths. [A] Cimon gave honourable burial to the mules which had thrice won him the prize for racing in the Olympic Games. In Antiquity Xantippus had his dog buried on a coastal headland which has borne its name ever since.[49] And Plutarch says that it offended his conscience to make a little money by sending to the slaughter-house an ox which had long been in his service.[50]

---

47. Plutarch (tr. Amyot), *Les demandes des choses Romaines*, 475E. The geese heard the Barbarians scaling the walls while the guard-dogs slept (*Quels animaux sont les plus advisez*, 514 D–E).

48. The Hecatompedon ('the Hundred-feet long') was the regular name for the Parthenon (the temple of Athena Parthenos in the citadel of Athens). It was rebuilt by Pericles on the site of a previous temple of that name.

49. Same examples in Ravisius Textor, *Officina* (*Bruta animalia honorata sepulchris aut statuis*).

50. Plutarch, *Life of Cato*.

32. In defence of Seneca and Plutarch

=====

[In this chapter Montaigne reveals not only how he reads his books but dares to give the great Bodin, the author of the famous Method *for studying history, a lesson in historical interpretation. That makes this one of his more personally revealing chapters, as well as once again emphasizing Montaigne's lasting preoccupation with philosophical and moral ecstasy.]*

[A] My intimacy with those two great men and the help they give to me in my old age, [C] as well as to my book which is built entirely out of their spoils, [A] bind me to espouse their honour.

As for Seneca, among the thousands of little pamphlets that those of the Religion Allegedly Reformed[1] circulate in defence of their cause (which come sometimes from the hands of good writers which it is a pity not to find occupied on a better subject) I saw one, long ago, which extended and filled out the similitude it intended to establish between the rule of our poor late King Charles IX and that of Nero, by comparing the late Cardinal of Lorraine to Seneca – including their destinies (which made them both first men in the governments of their monarchs), their morals, endowments and conduct.[2] In this, in my opinion, he does too much honour to my Lord the Cardinal; for while I am one of those who rate highly his intelligence, his eloquence, his zeal for religion and for the King's service as well as his good fortune in being born in an age when it was so new, so rare and so necessary for the public good to have a great Churchman of such nobility, so worthy and capable of his office: nevertheless, to tell the truth, I do not think that his ability was anywhere near Seneca's nor that his virtue was as pure and as inflexible as his.

1. The official French Roman Catholic name for the religion of the Reformed Church of the 'Calvinists' was *la Religion Prétendue Réformée*, often abbreviated to RPR.
2. When Nero became Emperor in AD 54, Seneca, who had been his tutor, became his counsellor and minister; the Cardinal of Lorraine was counsellor to Charles IX.

Now that pamphlet which I am talking about,[3] so as to attain its purpose, has a description (which is deeply insulting) borrowed from the strictures on Seneca by Dion the historian, whose testimony I simply do not believe; for Dion, apart from being inconsistent in first calling Seneca very wise and also a mortal enemy of Nero's vices, nevertheless makes him mean, given to usury, ambitious, cowardly, pleasure-seeking and a counterfeit philosopher under false colours. Seneca's virtue is so evidently alive and vigorous in his writings, which themselves provide such a manifest defence against such insinuations as his being excessively rich and spendthrift, that I could never accept any witness to the contrary. Moreover in matters such as these it is more reasonable to trust the Roman historians than foreign Greek ones.[4] Now Tacitus speaks most honourably of his life and of his death, portraying him in all things as a great man, most excellent and most virtuous. And it will be enough for me to make no criticism but this of Dion's power of judgement – an unavoidable one: his judgement of matters Roman was so diseased that he ventured to champion the causes of Julius Caesar against Pompey, and of Antony against Cicero.

Now for Plutarch.

Jean Bodin is a good contemporary author, endowed with far better judgement than the mob of scribblers of his time: he merits our own considered judgement. I find him a bit rash in that passage of his *Method of History* where he accuses Plutarch not only of ignorance (on that he can say what he likes: I do not hunt that game) but also of frequently writing 'things which are incredible and entirely fabulous' (those are his very words).[5] If he had simply said 'things otherwise than they are', that would have been no great censure, since we have to take on trust from the hands of others things we have not ourselves witnessed, and I can see that he occasionally relates the same event differently, well aware that he is doing so: for example, the judgement of the three best Captains that there ever were, which Hannibal made, appears differently in his life of Flaminius and in his life of Pyrrhus. But to charge him with having accepted as valid currency things unbelievable and impossible is to accuse the most judicious author in the world of lack of judgement.

3. Perhaps the *Memoires de l'Estat de France, sous Charles Neufiesme* of Simon Goulart.
4. Dion Cassius' censures in his Greek *Roman History* (which was widely read in Xylander's Latin translation) are normally accepted now as justified. (But cf. Tacitus, *Annals*, XIII, 1, XIV, liii, etc.)
5. Jean Bodin, *Methodus ad facilem historiarum cognitionem*, 1566, IV, p. 58.

Here is Bodin's example. 'As,' he says, 'when he relates that a Spartan boy allowed his entire stomach to be torn out by a fox-cub which he had stolen and kept hidden under his tunic until he died rather than reveal his theft.' In the first place I find that a badly chosen example, since it is hard indeed to prescribe limits to the powers of the faculties of our souls, whereas in the case of bodily strength we have more means of knowing them and of setting bounds to them. For that reason if I had to choose an example I would rather have taken one from the second category, where some facts are harder to believe – among others what he narrates about Pyrrhus: that, gravely wounded as he was, he gave so great a blow with his sword to an enemy clad in full armour that, from the top of his head downwards, he clove him in two.

In Bodin's own example I find no great miracle; nor do I accept the excuse that he makes for Plutarch, that he added the words 'So they say', to warn us to keep a bridle on our credulity. For apart from such things as are accepted on the authority of Antiquity or out of respect for religion, Plutarch would not himself have accepted to believe things intrinsically incredible nor would he have proposed that we should. And as for the phrase, 'So they say', he does not employ it in this context with that sense: that is easy to see, since he relates elsewhere other examples touching the powers of endurance of the boys of Sparta which happened in his own time and which are even harder to accept, such as the one to which Cicero bore witness before him, having, he says, been there himself: some boys were undergoing that test of endurance by which the Spartans assayed them before the altar of Diana; they allowed themselves to be flogged until they were all over blood, without uttering cry or groan, some having sufficient strength of will to lose their lives there.[6]

Then there is the one which Plutarch relates with a hundred other witnesses; during the sacrifice a hot coal slipped up the sleeve of a Spartan boy while he was swinging the incense; he let the whole of his arm be burnt until the smell of cooked flesh reached the congregation.

By Spartan custom nothing more directly affected your reputation nor made you suffer more shame and disgrace than being caught out stealing.[7] I am so imbued with the greatness of those men of Sparta that not only

6. Cicero, *Tusc. disput.*, II, xiv, 34; cf. Erasmus, *Apophthegmata*, II, *Prisca Lacedaemoniorum Instituta*, XXXIV.
7. Spartan boys were underfed and taught to steal food: i) to increase their hardihood and skill at foraging in war; ii) to make Spartans defend their property. Any boy *caught* stealing was flogged. (Erasmus, *Apophthegmata*, XII.)

does it not seem incredible to me as it does to Bodin: it does not even seem rare or unusual. [C] The history of Sparta is full of hundreds of harsher and rarer examples: by Bodin's standards it is all miracle. [A] On this subject of theft, Marcellinus reports that nobody in his time had yet found any kind of torture which could force any Egyptians surprised in this crime to tell you even their own name.[8]

[B] A Spanish peasant who was put to the rack to make him reveal his accomplices in the murder of the praetor Lucius Piso yelled out in the midst of his tortures that his friends should not go away but stay and watch in full confidence, since it was not in the power of pain to force a single word of confession from him. And on the first day that was all they did get out of him. The next day, as they were escorting him back to start torturing him again, he struggled violently in the hands of his guards and killed himself by bashing his head against a wall.

[C] Epicharis, having glutted and exhausted the cruelty of Nero's attendants and withstood for one full day their burning brands, their beatings and their instruments of torture without revealing a word of her conspiracy, was brought back to the rack the next day with her limbs all shattered: she slipped the cord from her dress through the arm of a chair, made a running knot, thrust her head through it and hanged herself by the weight of her body. Having as she did the courage to die thus after having endured those first tortures, does she not appear to have deliberately lent herself to that trial of her endurance in order to mock that tyrant and to encourage others to make a plot against him similar to her own?

[A] And if anyone would go and ask our mounted riff-raff about the experiences which they have had in these civil wars of ours, he will hear of acts of endurance, of obstinate resistance and of stubbornness even among that rabble – effeminate though it is with a more than Egyptian sensuality[9] – worthy of being compared with those which we have just rehearsed of Spartan valour.

I know that there are cases of simple peasants who were prepared to allow the soles of their feet to be burnt, their fingertips to be smashed with the butt of a pistol, their eyes to be forced all bloody from their sockets by having a thick cord twisted tight around their foreheads, before they would even think about putting themselves to ransom. I myself saw one who was left for dead, naked in a ditch, with his neck all swollen and bruised by a halter which still dangled down from it and by which he had

8. Ammanius Marcellinus, XXII, xvi; then Tacitus, *Annals*, IV, xlv and XV, lvii.
9. Cf. Cognatus' Adage, *Miles Romane, Aegyptum cave*.

been dragged all night behind a horse, his body stabbed through by
daggers in a hundred places – not to kill him but to make him feel pain and
fear – and who had suffered all that until he had lost all power of speech,
all consciousness, determined (as he told me) to die a thousand deaths (as
indeed, so far as suffering is concerned, he had died one whole death
already) rather than promise them anything; yet he was one of the richest
husbandmen of the entire region. How many have we seen patiently
suffering to be roasted or burnt for opinions which, without understanding
or knowledge, they have taken from others!

[B]   I have known hundreds and hundreds of women (for they say that
Gascon heads have some special gift for this) whom you would have more
easily made to bite a red-hot iron than made to let go of an opinion
conceived in a fit of choler once they have got their teeth into it. Women
are rendered intractable by blows and constraint. That man who forged the
tale of the goodwife who would not stop calling her husband lice-ridden
however much she suffered correction by threats and cudgelings, who was
thrown into a pond and, even while she was drowning, thrust her hands
out of the water high above her head and made the sign for squashing lice,
forged indeed a tale the express image of which we can see every day in the
stubbornness of women.[10] And stubbornness is the sister of constancy, in
vigour and inflexibility at least.

[A]   We must not judge what is possible and impossible according to
what seems credible or incredible to our own minds (as I have said
elsewhere). It is nevertheless a major fault into which most people fall –
[C]   and I do not say that of Bodin –   [A]   to make difficulties about
believing of another anything which they could not   [C]   or would
not   [A]   do themselves.[11] It seems to each man that the master Form of
Nature is in himself, as a touchstone by which he may compare all the

10. A well-known tale in Poggio's *Facetiae*.
11. A reworked passage revealing Montaigne's conception of philosophical ecstasy:
i) '80: do themselves. I consider *some of those souls of the Ancients to be raised up to
Heaven when valued against mine;* and even though I realize that I am powerless to
follow them, I do not give up judging the principles which raise *and lift* them thus
aloft. I admire . . .

ii) ['95] . . . that the master Form of *human* nature is in himself *and that all the others
must be regulated in accordance with it. Attitudes which do not correspond to his own are
feigned and false. Do you set before him some details of the deeds or capacities of another
man? The first thing which he calls upon to guide his judgement is himself as a standard: as
things go with him, thus must they go with the Order of the world. O dangerous and
intolerable asininity!* I consider . . .

other forms. Activities which do not take his form as their model are feigned and artificial. What brute-like stupidity! I consider some men, particularly among the Ancients, to be way above me and even though I clearly realize that I am powerless to follow them on my feet I do not give up following them with my eyes and judging the principles which raise them thus aloft, principles the seeds of which I can just perceive in myself, as I also can that ultimate baseness in minds which no longer amazes me and which I do not refuse to believe in either. I can clearly see the spiral by which those great souls wind themselves higher. [A] I admire the greatness of those souls; those ecstasies which I find most beautiful I clasp unto me; though my powers do not reach as far, at least my judgement is most willingly applied to them.

The other example which Bodin cites of 'things which are incredible and entirely fabulous' in Plutarch is the statement that Agesilaus was condemned to pay a fine by the Ephors for having attracted to himself the hearts and minds of his fellow-citizens. I do not know what mark of falsehood he discovers in that, but at any rate Plutarch on this occasion was writing of things which must have been far better known to him than to us, and it was no novelty in Greece for men to be punished and exiled merely because they were too well-liked by their citizens: witness their ostracism and their petalism.[12]

In the same passage there is another accusation which irritates me on Plutarch's behalf: it is where Bodin says that Plutarch showed good faith in his parallels between Roman and Roman or Greek and Greek but not between Roman and Greek. Witness, he says, Demosthenes and Cicero; Cato and Aristides; Sylla and Lysander; Marcellus and Pelopidas; Pompey and Agesilaus, reckoning as he does that he favoured the Greeks by matching them so unfairly. That is precisely to attack what is most excellent and commendable in Plutarch: for in those parallel lives (which are the most admirable part of his works and to my mind the one he took most pleasure in) the faithfulness and purity of his judgements equals their weight and profundity. He is a philosopher who teaches us what virtue is. Let us see whether we can save him from this accusation of falsehood and prevarication.

12. Bodin, *Methodus*, IV, 58 (here and also later in the chapter). Over-popular leaders were indeed banished for five or ten years: i) by *ostracism* in Athens, signified by writing the leader's name on a potsherd; ii) by *petalism* in Syracuse, signified by writing the name on an olive leaf.

The only thing I can think of which can have given occasion for Bodin's judgement is that great and dazzling lustre of the Roman names which we have in our heads. It does not seem possible to us that Demosthenes could ever equal the glory of a man who was Consul, Proconsul and Quaestor of that great Republic. But whoever would consider the truth of the matter and the men themselves (which was Plutarch's chief aim, namely to weigh against each other their morals, their natures, their competencies rather than their destinies) will find, I think, contrary to Bodin, that Cicero and the Elder Cato weigh lighter than their parallels.

For Bodin's purpose I would have chosen the parallel between Cato the Younger and Phocion: for in that pair there could with verisimilitude be found an inequality – to the advantage in the Roman.

As for Marcellus, Sylla and Pompey, I quite see that their exploits in war are more expansive, more glorious and more splendid than those of the Greeks whom Plutarch puts in parallel to them; but, no less in war as elsewhere, the most beautiful and most virtuous deeds are not always the most celebrated ones. I often find the names of Captains overshadowed by the splendour of other names of lesser merit: witness Labienus, Ventidius, Telesinus and many others. And if I had to look at things in such a way as to complain on behalf of the Greeks, might I not say that Camillus is far less to be compared to Themistocles; the Gracchi to Agis and Cleomenes; Numa to Lycurgus?

But it is lunacy to wish to judge from one aspect things which present so many facets. When Plutarch compares men he does not thereby make them equal. Who could ever bring out their differences more clearly and conscientiously! When he comes to match the victories, the martial exploits and the might of the armies led by Pompey, and his triumphs, against those of Agesilaus, this is what he says: 'I do not believe that even Xenophon, had he been alive, would have dared to judge them comparable to those of Agesilaus, even if he had been allowed to write all he wished in his favour.' Does he talk of matching Lysander to Sylla? 'There is,' he says, 'no comparison, neither in the number of victories nor the hazards run in battle: for Lysander only won two naval victories . . .' and so on.

In that, he is not cheating the Romans out of anything: he cannot have wronged them merely by placing them beside the Greeks, no matter what disparity there was between them. Plutarch does not weigh them in the lump; he does not prefer one to the other over all: one after the other he matches piece against piece, circumstance against circumstance. So if you wanted to convict him of partiality you would have to take one particular judgement of his and tease it out or else make a general criticism: that he was wrong to match this Roman against that Greek since there were others which more closely resembled each other and were better fitted for comparison.

35. On three good wives

[A chapter which in some ways is a pendant to II, 10, 'On books'. History, true history, can be a source of both aesthetic delight and of moral profit. It is potentially a valuable alternative to moral fiction, to tales (such as those of Boccaccio). Montaigne's preoccupation with great-souled suicides in the Stoic mould is rarely more visible than in this chapter; it is given prominence by coming near the end of Book II and so having (until Book III was published) the air of leading up to the conclusion.]

[A] As every man knows, they are not counted in dozens, especially in performing their matrimonial obligations: for marriage is a business full of so many thorny conditions that a woman cannot keep her intentions in it for long. Even the men (who are there under slightly better terms) find it hard to do so.

[B] The touchstone of a good marriage, the real test, concerns the time that the association lasts, and whether it has been constant – sweet, loyal and pleasant. In our century wives usually reserve their displays of duty and vehement love for when they have lost their husbands;   [C]   then at least they bear witness to their good intentions – a laggardly, unseasonable witness, by which they prove that they love their husbands only once they are dead.   [B] Life is full of inflammatory material: death, love and social duties. Just as fathers hide their love for their sons so as to keep themselves honoured and respected, so do wives readily hide theirs for their husbands. That particular mystery-play is not to my taste! It is no good widows tearing their hair and clawing their faces: I go and whisper straight in the ear of their chambermaid or private secretary, 'How did they get on? What were they like when living together?' I always remember that proverbial saying: *'Jactantius moerent, quae minus dolent.'* [Women who weep most ostentatiously grieve least.][1] Their lamentations are loathed by living husbands and useless to the dead ones. We husbands will willingly let them laugh afterwards if they will only laugh with us while we are alive.

1. Tacitus, *Annals*, II, lxxvii.

[C]   Is it not enough to raise a man from the dead out of vexation, if a wife who had spat in my face while I was still there were to come and massage my feet once I am beginning to go!   [B]   If some honour resides in weeping for husbands it belongs to widows who laughed with them in life; let those widows who wept when they were alive laugh outwardly and inwardly once they are dead. Moreover, take no notice of those moist eyes and that pitiful voice: but do note the way they carry themselves and the colour of those plump cheeks beneath their veils! That way they speak to us in the kind of French we can understand! There are few widows who do not go on improving in health: and health is a quality which cannot lie. All that dutiful behaviour does not regard the past as much as the future: it is all profit not loss. When I was a boy an honest and most beautiful lady, a prince's widow who is still alive, began to wear some little extras not allowed by our convention of widowhood. To those who reproached her with this she replied, 'It is because I meet no new suitors now: I have left behind the desire to remarry.'

So as not to be totally out of keeping with our customs, I have selected three wives who, on the death of their husbands, did show the force of their goodness and their love. They are however rather diverse examples of pressing cases which resulted in a bold sacrifice of life.

[A]   In Italy Pliny the Younger had a man living near one of his houses who was appallingly tormented by ulcers which appeared on his private parts. His wife watched him languishing in pain; she begged him to allow her enough time to examine the symptoms of his disease: she would then tell him more frankly than anyone else what hope he could have. She obtained this of him and carefully examined him; she found that it was impossible for him to be cured and that all he could expect was, over a long period, to drag out a painful and languishing life. And so she advised him, as the surest, sovereign remedy, to kill himself. Finding him a little hesitant about so stark a deed she said: 'You must never think, my Beloved, that the pains which I see you suffer do not affect me as much as you, or that to deliver myself from them I am unwilling to use the same remedy that I am prescribing for you. I wish to be your companion in your cure as I am in your illness: lay aside your fears and think only that we shall have the pleasure of that journey into death which must free us from such torments. We shall go happily away together.' Having finished speaking and bringing new warmth to her husband's heart, she resolved that they should cast themselves into the sea from a window in their house which gave on to it. And so as to maintain unto the end that loyal and vehement love by which she had clung to him in life, she wanted him also to die in her arms. But fearing that those arms might fail her and that the clasp of her embrace might be loosened by the terror of the fall, she had herself tied to him, tightly bound by their waists. And thus she gave up her life for the repose of her husband.[2]

That woman was from a lowly class; among people of that condition it is not all that new to find signs of rare goodness.

> *Extrema per illos*
> *Justitia excedens terris vestigia fecit.*

[When Justice finally left this earth, she left her last vestiges with them.][3]

The other two are rich and noble; examples of virtue rarely make their home among people like that.

Arria was the wife of Caecinna Paetus, a great man of consular rank; she was the mother of another Arria, the wife of Thrasea Paetus who was so renowned for his virtue during the time of Nero; through this son-in-law she was the grandmother of Fannia. The similarity of name and fortune of these men and women has often led to confusion. This first Arria (when her husband Caecinna Paetus had been taken prisoner by the supporters of the Emperor Claudius after the defeat of Scribonianus whose faction he had supported) begged the men who were transferring their prisoner to Rome to take her aboard their ship, where she would be much less expense and trouble than the many people they would need to look after her husband since she alone would take care of his room, his cooking and all other chores. They refused this to her; so she leapt into a fisherman's boat which she had immediately hired and in this manner followed her husband from Sclavonia.

One day in Rome in the presence of the Emperor she was familiarly approached by Junia, the widow of Scribonianus, because of their shared misfortunes; but she roughly thrust her away with these words: 'Should I even talk to you or listen to you when Scribonianus, the husband of your bosom, is dead. Yet you are still alive!' Such words and several other indications brought her relations to realize that, unable to endure her husband's misfortune, she intended to do away with herself.

On hearing those words her son-in-law Thrasea begged her not to desire to kill herself, saying: 'What? If I incurred a similar misfortune to Caecinna's, would you want my wife, your daughter, to do likewise?' – 'What do you mean, would I!' she replied. 'Yes. Yes of course I would, if she had lived as long and as peacefully together with you as I did with my

2. Pliny the Younger, *Epist.*, VI, xxiv.
3. Virgil, *Georgics*, II, 473–4 (of happy rustics).

husband.' Such answers increased their worries about her and led to their watching her behaviour closely.

One day she said to those who were set to guard her: 'It is no good, you know. You can force me to make the death I die much harsher: you cannot stop me from dying.' She madly darted out of the chair she was sitting in and, with all her might, bashed her head against the nearby wall. The blow felled her to the ground, severely wounded and unconscious. They just managed to bring her round with great difficulty. 'I told you plainly,' she said, 'that if you refuse me the means to kill myself easily, then I shall choose some other way, no matter how hard it might be.'

The end of so amazing a virtue came like this: by himself Paetus her husband did not have courage enough to kill himself, as the Emperor's cruelty would force him to do some day or other; so having first used the appropriate arguments and exhortations for the counsel which she was giving him to bring him to do so, she seized the dagger which her husband was wearing, drew it, held it in her hand and concluded her exhortation thus: 'This is the way to do it, Paetus.' And that same instant, having struck herself a mortal blow in the bosom, she wrenched the dagger from her wound and offered it to him, ending her life as she did so with these noble, great-souled, immortal words: *'Paete, non dolet.'* Those three words so full of beautiful meaning were all she had time to utter: 'You see, Paetus: it doesn't hurt.'[4]

> *Casta suo gladium cum traderet Arria Pæto,*
> *Quem de visceribus traxerat ipsa suis:*
> *Si qua fides, vulnus quod feci, non dolet, inquit;*
> *Sed quod tu facies, id mihi, Pæte, dolet.*

[When chaste Arria proffered the blade to Paetus which she had torn from her very entrails, she said: 'Believe me, that wound I have given myself does not hurt me. What hurts me, Paetus, is the wound you will give to yourself.']

But it has much more living force in the original and a much richer meaning. Far from being depressed by the thought of her husband's wound and death, or of her own, she was the one who advised and encouraged them; so, having performed that high courageous deed solely in the interest of her husband, even with the final words of her life her only thought was of removing from him his fear of following her by taking his life. Paetus at once struck himself through with that same blade, feeling shame, in my judgement, at having needed so costly and so precious a lesson.

4. Retold after Pliny the Younger. *Epistles*, III, xvi; then, Martial, *Epigrams*, I, xiv.

There was a young and very high-born Roman matron called Pompeia
Paulina. She had wedded Seneca in his extreme old age. Nero, that fine
pupil of his, sent one of his courtiers to him to announce that he was
sentenced to death.[5] (Such sentences used to be executed in this way: when
the Emperors of Rome had condemned any man of quality, they dispatched
their officials to tell him to choose which death he would prefer and to see
that he carried it out within such time as they caused to be prescribed,
shorter or longer depending on how finely tempered their choleric humour
was: it was a concession designed to allow him to put his affairs in order,
though too short on occasions to permit him to do so. If the condemned
person resisted their command they brought in suitable men to carry it out,
either by slashing the veins in his arms and legs or forcing him to swallow
poison. Men of honour did not wait for such compulsion but used their
own doctors and surgeons to do the deed.) With a peaceful resolute
expression Seneca listened to the order brought by Nero's henchmen, then
asked for paper to write his will. That was refused by the Captain, so
Seneca turned to those who loved him and said: 'Since I can bequeath you
nothing else, out of gratitude for what I owe you I shall at least bequeath
you the most beautiful thing I possess: the portrait of my morals, of my
life, which I pray you to conserve in your memory; by doing so you will
acquire the reputation of ones who loved me purely and truly.' At the
same time with gentle words he quietened the bitter anguish which he saw
that they were suffering, though sometimes speaking more firmly to
rebuke them: 'Where are all those beautiful precepts of philosophy?' he
asked. 'What has happened to that store which we have set aside over so
many years against the accidents of Fortune? Did we not know of Nero's
cruelty? What could we expect from a man who had killed his mother and
his brother, except that he would also kill his tutor who had looked after
him and brought him up?'

Having addressed them all in general, he turned aside to his wife; and
since her heart and strength were yielding under the weight of her grief he
held her tight in his arms; he prayed her that, for love of him, she should
bear this misfortune a little more patiently, since the hour had come when
he had to show the fruit of his studies not by speeches and arguments but
by deeds, and since he, without the slightest doubt, was welcoming death
not merely without grief but with joy. 'Wherefore my Beloved do not
dishonour it by your tears,' he said, 'lest it should seem that you love
yourself more than my reputation. Quieten your grief and console yourself

5. Retold from Tacitus, *Annals*, XV, lvii–lxiv.

with the knowledge that you have of me and of my actions, consecrating the rest of your life to those honourable occupations to which you are so devoted.'

Paulina replied, having somewhat recovered her composure and brought warmth again to her magnanimous heart by her noblest love: 'No, Seneca. I am not one to leave you companionless in such great need. I do not want you to think that the virtuous examples of your life have not yet taught me to know how to make a fine death. When could I ever die better, or more honourably, or more as I would wish to, than together with you? Rest assured that it is with you that I shall go.' Whereupon Seneca, welcoming such a beautiful and glorious resolve in his wife, and also to rid himself of his fear of leaving her to the tender mercies of his enemies after his death, replied: 'I once taught you, Paulina, such things as served you to live your life contentedly. Now you prefer the honour of death: truly I will never begrudge you that. The constancy and the resolve of our common end may be equal: but allow that on your side the beauty and the glory are greater.'

That done they both together slashed the veins in their arms; but since Seneca's veins had become constricted by old age[6] and abstemious diet they merely allowed the blood to trickle out slowly, so he gave orders to slash the veins in his thighs as well. Then, fearing that the torment he was suffering might sadden the heart of his wife, and also to deliver himself from the grief he bore at seeing her in so pitiful a state, after taking leave of her most lovingly he begged her to permit them to carry him away to another room; which they did. But as all those incisions were still insufficient to cause his death, he commanded Statius Annaeus his doctor to administer the poisoned drink; that too had little effect, since it could not reach his heart because his limbs were weak and chill. So they further prepared a very hot bath for him; as he felt his end approaching he continued, as long as he had breath, to deliver most excellent discourses on the subject of his present state, which his secretaries took down as long as they could hear his voice; and for years afterwards his final words remained honoured and respected, circulating in the hands of men. (It is a most regrettable loss that they have not come down to us.) As he felt the last pangs of death he took the blood-drenched waters of the bath and asperged his head with them saying, 'This water I consecrate to Jove the Liberator.'

Nero, warned of all this, fearing that he might be criticized for the death of Paulina (who was one of the most nobly-connected of Roman matrons)

6. [A] Until [A]: old age *(for he was then about one hundred and forty years old)* and . . .

and having no particular reason to hate her, sent back orders with all speed that her wounds were to be bound. Her people did so – without her knowledge, since she was half-dead already and quite without sensation. And so against her own design she lived her remaining span most honourably, as behoved her virtue, showing by the pallor of her face how much life-blood she had shed through her wounds.

There you have my three very true tales, which I find as pleasing in their tragedy as those fictions which we forge at will to give pleasure to the many. I am amazed that those who engage in that activity do not decide to choose some of the ten thousand beautiful historical accounts to be found in our books. In that they would have less toil and would afford more pleasure and profit. If any author should wish to construct them into a single interconnected unity he would only need to supply the links – like soldering metals together with another metal. He could by such means make a compilation of many true incidents of every sort, varying his arrangement as the beauty of his work required, more or less as Ovid in his *Metamorphoses* made a patchwork of a great number of varied fables.

In the case of my last couple it is also worth pondering on the fact that Paulina willingly gave up her life for love of her husband, and that formerly, for love of her, he had once given up dying. There is little equivalence in that for the likes of us: but to his Stoic humour I believe that he thought he had done as much for her by prolonging his life to please her as if he had died for her. In one of his letters to Lucilius,[7] after telling him how he had caught a fever in Rome and promptly climbed into his coach to go off to one of his houses in the country against the wish of his wife who wanted to prevent him, he tells how he replied that his fever was not physical but geographical. He went on: 'She then let me go, telling me to look after my health. So I, who know that her life is lodged in mine, now begin to take care of myself so as to take care of her. The privilege which old age had bestowed on me, making me more firmly resolved on many things, I am losing now that I remember that, in this old man, there is a young woman to whom I am of some use. Since I cannot bring her to love me more courageously, she brings me to love myself more carefully. For we must allow some place to honourable affections; so sometimes when opportunities pressingly invite us the other way, we must summon our life back – yes, even in torment. We must cling by our teeth to our souls since, for moral men, the law of life is not "as long as they please" but "as long as

7. Seneca, *Epist. moral.*, CIV, 2–6.

they should". The man who does not think enough of his wife or of his friend to prolong his life for them and who is determined to die is too fastidious, too self-indulgent. Our souls must order themselves to die when the interests of our dear ones require it. Sometimes we must make a loan of ourselves to those we love: even when we should wish to die for ourselves we should break off our plans on their account. It is a sign of greatness of mind to lay hold of life again for the sake of others, as several great and outstanding men have done. And it is a mark of particular goodness to prolong one's old age (the greatest advantage of which is to be indifferent to its duration and to be able to use life more courageously and contemptuously) if one knows that such a duty is sweet, delightful and useful to someone who loves us dearly. And we ourselves receive a most delightful recompense: for what can be more delightful than to be so dear to your wife that you become dearer to yourself for her sake? Thus my Paulina has laid upon me not only her fears for me but my fears for myself as well. It is not enough for me to consider with what resolution I could die: I also have to consider how irresolutely she would bear it. So I have compelled myself to go on living. Sometimes there is magnanimity in doing so.'

Those are his words, [C] as excellent as are his deeds.

n the resemblance of children to their fathers

[This is the final chapter of Book II and so, until 1588, the final chapter of the whole work, which ended therefore with two dominant notions: that the Essays are a portrait of Montaigne's character, opinions and bearing destined for his immediate descendants and friends; that the most marked characteristic of Nature is diversity and discordance.

Montaigne was convinced that he had inherited from his forefathers not only an antipathy to medicine but also the stone (that is, to the suicide pains of colic paroxysms). He explains how he fortified his inherited antipathy to the art of medicine with often contrived arguments, so giving us insights into his mind and incidentally providing a lively picture of life in watering-places. Spa-waters, being natural, might cure the stone and can probably do no harm. But how experimental medicine is ever supposed to be led to a cure for melancholy is another matter . . .

A major source of Montaigne's scepticism here about professional arts and sciences is Henry Cornelius Agrippa's book On the Vanity of all Sciences and on the Excellence of the Word of God.]

[A] All the various pieces of this faggot are being bundled together on the understanding that I am only to set my hand to it in my own home and when I am oppressed by too lax an idleness. So it was assembled at intervals and at different periods, since I sometimes have occasion to be away from home for months on end. Moreover I never correct my first thoughts by second ones – [C] well, except perhaps for the odd word, but to vary it, not to remove it. [A] I want to show my humours as they develop, revealing each element as it is born. I could wish that I had begun earlier, especially tracing the progress of changes in me.

One of the valets I used for dictation stole several pages of mine which were to his liking and thought he had acquired great plunder. It consoles me that he will no more gain anything by it than I shall lose.

Since I began I have aged by some seven or eight years – not without some fresh gain, for those years have generously introduced me to colic paroxysms. Long commerce and acquaintance with the years rarely proceed without some such benefit! I could wish that, of all those gifts which the years store up for those who haunt them, they could have chosen a present more acceptable to me, for they could not have given me anything that since childhood I have held in greater horror. Of all the misfortunes of old age, that was precisely the very one I most dreaded. I often thought to myself that I was travelling too far and that on such a long road I was eventually bound to be embroiled in some nasty encounter; I realized, and much proclaimed, that it was time for me to go. Following the surgeon's rule when he cuts off a limb,   [C]   I declared that life should be amputated at the point where it is alive and healthy; he who repays not his debt to Nature in good time usually finds she exacts interest with a vengeance.

[A]   But my declarations were in vain. I was so far from being ready to go then that even now, after about eighteen months in this distasteful state, I have already learnt how to get used to it. I have made a compact with this colical style of life; I can find sources of hope and consolation in it. So many men have grown so besotted with their wretched existence that no circumstances are too harsh, provided that they can cling on.   [C]   Just listen to Maecenas:

> *Debilem facito manu,*
> *Debilem pede, coxa,*
> *Lubricos quate dentes:*
> *Vita dum superest bene est.*

[Lop off a hand; lop off a foot and a thigh; pull out all my teeth: I am all right though: I am still alive.][1]

And it was with the philanthropy of a lunatic that Tamberlane cloaked his arbitrary cruelty against lepers when he put to death all those that came to his knowledge – 'In order,' he said, 'to free them from so painful a life.' Any of them would rather have been thrice a leper than to cease to be.[2] When Antisthenes the Stoic was extremely ill he cried out, 'Who will make me free from these ills?' Diogenes, who had come to see him, gave him a knife: 'If you so desire, this soon will,' he said. There came the reply: 'I never said *from this life*: I said, *from these ills*.'

[A]   Sufferings which touch the soul alone afflict me much less than they do most men; that is partly from judgement (for the majority think many things to be dreadful and to be avoided even at the cost of their life

---

1. Seneca, *Epist. moral.*, CI, ll, citing 'the most vile prayer of Maecenas'.
2. Nicolas Chalcocondylas, *De la décadence de L'Empire Grec*, III, x; then, Erasmus, *Apophthegmata*, III, *Diogenes Cynicus*, CCXVII.

which are almost indifferent to me); it is also partly because of my stolid complexion which is insensitive to anything which does not come straight at me; I believe that complexion to be one of the best of my natural characteristics. But bodily sufferings – which are very real – I feel most acutely. And yet, formerly, when I used to foresee them through eyes made weak, fastidious and flabby by the enjoyment of that long and blessed health and ease which God had lent me for the greater part of my life, I thought of them as so unbearable that in truth my fear of them exceeded the suffering they now cause me: that fact further increases my belief that most of the faculties of our soul, [C] as we employ them, [A] disturb our life's repose rather than serve it.

I am wrestling with the worst of all illnesses, the most unpredictable, the most painful, the most fatal and the most incurable. I have already assayed five or six very long and painful attacks. Yet either I am flattering myself or else, even in this state, a man can still find things bearable if his soul has cast off the weight of the fear of dying and the weight of all the warning threats, inferences and complications which Medicine stuffs into our heads. Even real pain is not so shrill, harsh and stabbing that a man of settled temperament must go mad with despair. I draw at least one advantage from my colic paroxysms: whatever I had failed to do to make myself familiar with death and reconciled to it that illness will do for me: for the more closely it presses upon me and importunes me the less reason I shall have to be afraid to die. I had already succeeded in holding on to life only for what life has to offer: my illness will abrogate even that compact; and may God grant that at the end, if the harsh pain finally overcomes my strength, it may not drive me to the other extreme (no less wrong) of loving and yearning to die.

Summum nec metuas diem, nec optes.

[Neither be afraid of your last day nor desire it.][3]

Both emotions are to be feared, though one has its remedy nearer at hand.

Moreover I have always considered that precept to be sheer affectation which so rigorously and punctiliously ordains that, when we are enduring pain, we must put on a good countenance and remain proud and calm. Why should Philosophy (whose concerns are with deeds and with inner

3. Martial, *Epigrams*, X, xlvii, 3. (Having inscribed this maxim in his library, Montaigne later painted another over it.)

motions) waste her time over external appearances?[4] [C] Let her leave such worries to actors in farces and to masters of rhetoric, who make such a fuss about our gesticulations. Let Philosophy have enough courage to concede that pain may act cowardly so long as the cowardice remains a matter of words, being neither heartfelt nor visceral. Let her classify such plaints (even if they do come from our will) with those sighs, sobs, tremblings and drainings of colour which Nature has placed beyond our control. So long as our minds know no terror and our words no despair, let Philosophy be contented. What does it matter if our arms flay about as long as our thoughts do not? Philosophy put us through our training not for others but for ourselves, so that we may *be* thus, not seem thus.

[A] Let her limit herself to controlling our intellect, which she has undertaken to instruct. Against the onslaught of colic paroxysms let her enable us to have souls capable of knowing themselves and following their accustomed courses, souls fighting pain and sustaining it, not shamelessly grovelling at her feet, souls stirred and aroused for battle, not cast down and subdued, [C] able to communicate and to some extent able to converse.

[A] In such extreme misfortunes it is cruelty to require of us too studied a comportment. If we play our role well, it matters little if we put a bad face on things! If the body finds relief in lamentations, let it; if it wants to toss about, let it writhe and contort as much as it likes; if the body believes that some of the pain can be driven off as vapour by forcing out our cries – or if doing so distracts us from the anguish, as some doctors say it helps pregnant women in their deliveries – just let it shout out. [C] Do not order the sound to come but allow it to do so. Epicurus does not merely allow his wise man to yell out in torment, he counsels him to: '*Pugiles etiam, quum feriunt in jactandis coestibus, ingemiscunt, quia profundenda*

---

4. '80 ... Philosophy (whose concerns are with *life and substance*) waste her time over external appearances *as though she was rehearsing men for the actions of a play, or as though it was of her jurisdiction to restrain movements and changes which we are required by Nature to accept? Let her restrain Socrates, then, from blushing with emotion or shame, from blinking when threatened with a blow, or trembling and sweating under the shakings of a fever: the descriptions of Poetry (who is free and freely willed) dare not deprive of tears even those persons whom she would present as perfect and complete: 'Et se n'aflige tanto/Che se mordi le man, morde le labbia,/Sperge le guancie di continuo pianto': Philosophy should leave such a duty to those whose profession it is to rule our deportment and outward show.* Let her limit ... (The Italian verse means: 'Her pain is such that she wrings her hands, bites her lips, while her cheeks are bathed in a flood of tears.')'

voce omne corpus intenditur, venitque plaga vehementior.' [Even the wrestlers grunt when lashing out with their boxing-gloves, because uttering such sounds makes the whole body tense, driving the blow home with greater vehemence.][5] [A] We have pangs enough from the pain without the pangs caused by clinging to superfluous rules.

It is usual to see men thrown into turmoil by the [C] attacks and [A] assaults of this illness; it is for them that I have said all this; for in my own case I have up till now put on a slightly better countenance: not that I take any trouble to maintain a decent appearance, for I do not think much of such an achievement and, in this respect, concede whatever my illness demands: but either the pain in my case is not so excessive or else I can show more steadfastness than most. I moan and groan when the stabbing pains hurt most acutely but I do not [C] lose control like this fellow:

> *Ejulatu, questu, gemitu, fremitibus*
> *Resonando multum flebiles voces refert.*

[Re-echoing with his tearful voice, wailing, groaning, lamenting, sighing.][6]

At the darkest moment of the paroxysm I explore myself and have always found that I am still capable of talking, thinking and replying as sensibly as at any other time but not as imperturbably, since the pain disturbs me and distracts me. When those around me start to spare me, thinking that I am at my lowest ebb, I often assay my strength and broach a subject as completely removed as possible from my condition. I can bring off anything with a sudden effort. But do not ask it to last . . .

If only I were like that dreamer in Cicero who dreamed he had a woman in his arms and had the faculty of ejaculating his gallstone in the bedclothes![7] My own gallstones monstrously unlecher me!

[A] In the intervals between these extremes of anguish, [C] when my urinary ducts are sick but without the stabbing pains, [A] I return at once to my accustomed form, since my soul knows no call to arms without bodily feeling – I definitely owe that to the care I once took to prepare myself by reason for such misfortunes:

> [B] *laborum*
> *Nulla mihi nova nunc facies inopinaque surgit;*
> *Omnia præcepi atque animo mecum ante peregi.*

5. Diogenes Laertius, *Epicurus*, X, cxviii; then, Cicero, *Tusc. disput.*, II, xxiii, 50.
6. Cicero, *De finibus*, II, xxix, 94; equally condemned by Cicero.
  '80: show despair and rage . . .
7. Cicero, *De divinatione*, II, lxix, 143.

[No toils present themselves new or unforeseen: I have seen them coming and been through them already in my mind.][8]

[A] But I have been assayed rather too roughly for an apprentice; the blow was indeed sudden and rough, for I fell all at once from a most gentle and happy mode of life into the most painful and distressing one imaginable: for, leaving aside the fact that the stone is an illness itself to be dreaded, its onset was in my case unusually difficult and harsh. Attacks recur so frequently that nowadays I hardly ever feel perfectly well. Yet if only I can add duration to the state in which I now maintain my spirits, I shall be in very much better circumstances than hundreds of others who have no fever nor illness except the ones which they inflict on themselves by defect of reason.

There is a certain kind of wily humility which is born of presumption. This for instance: we admit there are many things we do not understand; we confess frankly enough that within the works of Nature there are some qualities and attributes which we find incomprehensible, the means or the causes of which cannot be discovered by capacities such as ours. With so frank and scrupulous an admission we hope to make people believe what we say about the ones we do claim to understand. Yet there is no need to go picking over strange problems or miracles; it seems to me that among the things which we see quite regularly there are ones so strange and incomprehensible that they surpass all that is problematic in miracles.

What a prodigious thing it is that within the drop of semen which brings us forth there are stamped the characteristics not only of the bodily form of our forefathers but of their ways of thinking and their slant of mind. Where can that drop of fluid lodge such an infinite number of Forms? [B] How does it come to transmit these resemblances in so casual and random a manner that the great-grandson is like his great-grandfather, the nephew like his uncle? In the family of Lepidus in Rome there were born three children (not all at once; there were gaps between them) with cartilage over the very same eye.[9] There was a whole family in Thebes whose members all bore birthmarks shaped like a lance-head; any child who did not do so was held to be illegitimate. According to Aristotle there is a certain nation where they have wives in common and where children were assigned to fathers by resemblances.

[A] We can assume that it is to my father that I owe my propensity to the stone, for he died dreadfully afflicted by a large stone in the bladder.

---

8. Virgil, *Aeneid*, VI, 103–5.
9. Pliny, *Hist. nat.*, VII, xii; then, Plutarch (tr. Amyot) *Pourquoy la justice divine differe . . .* 267 B; Aristotle, *Politics*, II, i, 1262 a (this nation was in Upper Libya).

He was not aware of it until he was sixty-seven; he had experienced no sign or symptom of it beforehand, in his loins or his sides or anywhere else. Until then he had not been subject to much illness and had in fact enjoyed excellent health; he lasted another seven years with that affliction, lingering towards a very painful end.

Now I was born twenty-five years and more before he fell ill, during his most vigorous period: I was his third child. During all that time where did that propensity for this affliction lie a-brooding? When his own illness was still so far off, how did that little piece of his own substance which went to make me manage to transmit so marked a characteristic to me? And how was it so hidden that I only began to be aware of it forty-five years later – so far the only one to do so out of so many brothers and sisters, all from the same mother? If anyone can tell me how this comes about I will trust his explanations of as many other miracles as he likes – providing that he does not fob me off (as they usually do) with a theory which is more difficult and more fanciful than the thing itself.

Doctors will have to pardon my liberty a while, but from that same ejaculation and penetration I was destined to receive my loathing and contempt for their dogmas: my antipathy to their Art is hereditary; my father lived to seventy-four, my grandfather to sixty-nine, my great-grandfather to nearly eighty, none having swallowed any kind of drug. 'Medicine' for them meant anything they did not use regularly.

The Art of Medicine is built from examples and experience. So are my opinions. Is that not a very clean and profitable experience! I doubt if they will find me in their records three such, born, living and dying in the same hearth, under the same roof, who had lived so long subject to the laws of Medecine. Doctors will have to concede that on my side there is either reason or luck. And with them luck is a more valuable commodity then reason . . .

But they must not take advantage of me now, and certainly not threaten me after I have been struck down: that would not be fair. I have truly won a solid victory over them with that example of the rest of my family, even if it stops with them. Human affairs allow of no greater constancy: we have assayed our beliefs now for two centuries minus eighteen years: my great-grandfather was born in the year one thousand four hundred and two. It is only right that this experiment of ours should begin to run out on us. Let them not quote against me the illness which has got a stranglehold on me now. Is it not enough that even I stayed healthy for forty-seven years? Even if it should prove to be the end of our course, it has been longer than most.

My forebears disapproved of medicine because of some unexplained natural inclination. The very sight of medicine horrified my father. The Seigneur de Gaviac was one of my uncles on my father's side; he was in holy orders, a weakling from birth, who nevertheless struggled on to sixty-seven; once he did fall victim of a grave and delirious attack of Continual Fever; the doctors ordered that he be informed that he would definitely die if he did not call in aid – (what they call 'aid' is more often than not an impediment). Terrified though he was by this dreadful sentence of death, that good man replied: 'I am dead then.' But soon afterwards God showed the vanity of their prognosis.

[B] I had four brothers; the youngest, born a long time after the others, was the Sieur de Bussaguet; he was the only one to submit to the Art of medicine, doing so I think because of his contacts with practitioners of other arts, since he was counsellor in the Court of Parliament. It turned out so badly for him that, despite apparently having the strongest of complexions, he died way before all the others with the sole exception of the Sieur de Saint-Michel.

[A] Though it is possible that I inherited this natural aversion from my ancestors I would have assayed ways of countering it if that had been the only factor, since all non-rational inborn tendencies are a kind of disease which ought to be fought against. It may well be that I inherited the disposition, but I have supported it, fortified it, and corroborated my opinions, by reasoned argument: I loathe such motives as refusing medicine just because it tastes bitter. My temperament is not at all like that: I believe health to be so precious that I would buy it at the cost of the most agonizing of incisions and cauterizations. [C] Following Epicurus I believe pleasures are to be avoided if they result in greater pain, and pain is to be welcomed if it results in greater pleasure.[10]

[A] Health is precious. It is the only thing to the pursuit of which it is truly worth devoting not only our time but our sweat, toil, goods and life itself. Without health all pleasure, scholarship and virtue lose their lustre and fade away. The most firmly supported arguments against this that Philosophy seeks to impress on us can be answered by this hypothesis: imagine Plato struck down by epilepsy or apoplexy; then challenge him to get any help from all those noble and splendid faculties of his soul.

No road leading to health can be called rough or expensive for me. But there are other likely reasons too which make me suspicious of all such trafficking. I do not deny that there may be an element of art in medicine. It is quite certain that among all the works of Nature things may be found with properties which can preserve our health. [B] I mean that there are

10. Cicero, *Tusc. disput.*, V, xxxiii, 95.

simples which moisten and desiccate; I know from experience that horse-radish produces flatulence and that senna-pods act as an aperient. Experience has taught me other things too; so that I know that mutton nourishes me and wine warms me (Solon used to say that eating was like other remedies: it was a cure for a disease called hunger).[11] I do not reject practices drawn from the natural world; I do not doubt the power and fecundity of Nature nor her devotion to our needs. I can see that the pike and the swallows do well under her. What I am suspicious of are the things discovered by our own minds, our sciences and by that Art of theirs in favour of which we have abandoned Nature and her rules and on to which we do not know how to impose the limits of moderation.

[C] What we call justice is a farrago of any old laws which fall into our hands, dispensed and applied often quite ineptly and iniquitously; those who mock at this and complain of it are not reviling that noble virtue itself but only condemning the abuse and the profanation of that venerable name of justice. So too with medicine: I honour its glorious name, its aim and its promises, so useful to the human race; but what that name actually designates among us I neither honour nor esteem.

[A] In the first place experience makes me afraid of it, for as far as I can see no tribe of people are more quickly ill nor more slowly well than those who are under the jurisdiction of medicine. The constraints of their diets impair and corrupt their health. Doctors are not content with treating illness; they make good health ill too so as to stop us ever escaping from their jurisdiction. Do they not assert that long and continuous good health argues future illness?

I have been ill quite frequently; without help from doctors I have found my illnesses – and I have assayed virtually all of them – quite easy to bear and as short-lasting as anyone else's; and I have done this without bringing in the bitter taste of their prescriptions. My health is complete and untrammelled, with no rule but my habits, no discipline but my good pleasure. Any place is good enough for me to stay in: I need no more comforts when I am ill than when I am well. I do not get worked up because there is no doctor or no apothecary nearby to come to my aid (something which I can see to be a greater affliction for some people than the illness itself). Yet are the lives of doctors themselves so long and so happy that they can witness to the manifest effectiveness of their discipline?

Every nation existed without medicine for centuries (that was the first age of Man, the best and the happiest centuries); even now less than a tenth of the world makes use of it. Nations without number have no knowledge

11. Diogenes Laertius, *Epicurus*, CXXIX.

of medicine and live longer and more healthily than we do here. And among us the common folk manage happily without it. The Roman People were six hundred years old before they adopted it; then, having assayed it, they drove it out of their city at the instance of Cato the Censor who showed how easily he could do without it, having lived to be eighty-five himself and helping his wife to live to an extreme old age – not without medicine but without medical practitioners. (Anything at all which promotes good health can be called medicine.)

Plutarch says that Cato kept his family in good health by making use, [A1] it appears, [A] of the hare, just as the Arcadians, according to Pliny, cured all illnesses with cow's milk.[12] [C] Herodotus asserts that the Libyan people all enjoy a rare degree of good health owing to their custom of searing the veins in the head and temples of their children with cauteries at the age of four, thus blocking the way for the rest of their lives to all morbid defluxions of mucus. [A] And the villagers round here when they are ill never use anything but the strongest wine they can get, mixed with plenty of saffron and spice. And they all work equally well.

Truly, among all that confusing diversity of prescriptions is there any practical result except the evacuation of the bowels? Hundreds of homely simples can produce that. [B] And I am not convinced that the action of the bowels is as beneficial as they claim; perhaps our nature needs, up to a point, the residue of its excreta just as wine must be kept on its lees if you want to preserve it. You can often see healthy men succumbing, from some external cause, to attacks of vomiting or diarrhoea: they have a big turn-out of excrement without any prior need or subsequent benefit: indeed it does harm; they get worse. [C] It is from the great Plato himself that I recently learned that of the three motions which apply to men, the last and the worst is the motion of purgations; no man, unless he is a fool, should undergo one except of extreme necessity.[13] We set about disturbing and activating our illnesses by fighting them with contraries: yet it ought to be our way of life which gently reduces them and brings them to an end. Those violent clashes between the illness and the medicine always cost us dear since the quarrel is fought out in our inwards, while drugs give us unreliable support, being by their nature the enemy of our health and gaining access into our estates only through disturbances.

Let us leave things alone for a while: that Order which provides for the flea and the mole also provides for all men who suffer themselves to be

12. Henry Cornelius Agrippa's *De Vanitate omnium scientiarum et de excellentia verbi Dei* LXXXIII, is a major source here.
13. Plato, *Timaeus*, 8 B.

governed by it as the flea and the mole are. We shout *Gee up* in vain: it will make our throats sore but not make that Order go faster, for it is proud and knows no pity. Our fear and despair repel it and delay its help for us rather than summoning it. It owes it to disease as to health that each should run its course. It will not be bribed to favour one at the expense of the rights of the other: for then it would become Disorder. For God's sake let us follow. I repeat, follow. That Order leads those who follow: those who will not follow will be dragged along,[14] medicine, terror and all. Get them to prescribe an aperient for your brain; it will be better employed there than in your stomach.

[A] When a Spartan was asked what made him live so long, 'Ignorance of medicine,' he replied. And the Emperor Hadrian kept repeating as he lay dying that 'all those doctors' had killed him.[15] [B] When a bad wrestler became a doctor Diogenes said, 'That's the spirit. You are right. Now you can pin to the ground all those who used to do it to you.' [A] But doctors are lucky [B] according to Nicocles: [A] the sun shines on their successes and the earth hides their failures; on top of that they have a way of turning anything which happens to their own advantage: medicine claims the right to take credit for every improvement or cure brought about by Fortune, Nature or any other external cause (and the number of those is infinite). When a patient is under doctor's orders anything lucky which happens to him is always due to them. Take those opportune circumstances which have cured me and hundreds of others who never call in medical help: in the case of their patients doctors simply usurp them. And when anything untoward happens they either disclaim responsibility altogether or else blame it on the patient, finding reasons so vacuous that they need never fear they will ever run out of them: 'he bared his arm'; [B] 'he heard the noise of a coach' –

> *rhedarum transitus arcto*
> *Vicorum inflexu;*
> [wagons passing at the bends in narrow streets;][16]

14. The great Renaissance commonplace, deriving from Seneca, *Epist. moral.*, CVIII, 11: Greek verses of Cleanthes, translated by Seneca and ending, 'The Fates lead the willing but drag the unwilling.' St Augustine cites them (*City of God*, V, 8) in the context of the will of God.
15. Quips from H. C. Agrippa's *De Vanitate*, LXXXIII (from which work several subsequent borrowings are made); also, Diogenes Laertius, *Diogenes*, VI, lxii.
16. Juvenal, *Satires*, III, 236–7.

- [A] 'somebody opened a window'; 'he has been lying on his left side'; 'he has let painful thoughts run through his head'. In short a word, a dream, a glance, all appear to be sufficient excuses for shrugging off the burden of responsibility.

Or when we get worse they take advantage of that too if they want to, profiting from another ploy which can never fail: when their poultices merely help to inflame the illness they palm us off with assertions that without their remedies things would have been even worse. They take a man with a bad cold, turn it into a recurrent fever, then claim that without them it would have been a continual fever. No need to worry that business should be bad: when an illness grows worse it means greater profits for them. They are certainly right to require their patients to favour them with their trust. It truly has to be trust – and a pliant trust too – to cling to notions so hard to believe.

[B] Plato put it well when he allowed freedom to lie to no one but doctors, since their promises are empty and vain but our health depends on them.[17]

[A] Aesop is an author of the choicest excellence, though few people discover all his beauties; he agreeably portrays the tyrannous authority which doctors usurp over wretched souls weakened by sickness and prostrated by fear when he tells how a patient was asked by his doctor what effects he felt from a medicine he had given him: 'I sweated a lot,' said the patient. 'Good,' said the doctor. Another time he asked him how he had fared since then: 'I felt extremely cold and shivery,' he said. – 'Good,' replied the doctor. On a third occasion he again asked him how he felt: 'All puffy and swollen up,' he said, 'as though I had dropsy.' – 'Excellent!' said the doctor. Then one of the patient's close friends came to ask how things were with him. 'I am dying of good health, my friend,' he replied.[18]

They used to have a more equitable contract in Egypt: for the first three days the doctor took on the patient at the patient's risk and peril: when the three days were up, the risks and perils were the doctor's. Is it right that Aesculapius, the patron of medicine, should have been struck down by a thunderbolt for having brought the dead ['95] Hippolytus[19] [A] back to life–

17. Plato, *Republic*, 389 BC (cf. 382 D).
18. Aesop, *Fables*.
19. Until ['95]: not *Hippolytus* but, erroneously, *Helen*. (Then, Virgil, *Aeneid*, VII, 770–3.)

[B]   *Nam pater omnipotens, aliquem indignatus ab umbris*
Mortalem infernis ad lumina surgere vitæ,
Ipse repertorem medicinæ talis et artis
Fulmine Phæbigenam stygias detrusit ad undas

[For the Father Almighty, angry that a mortal should rise from the Shades of the Underworld to the light of the living, struck down the discoverer of the Art of Medicine, the son of Apollo, and with his thunderbolt cast him into the waters of Styx]

– [A]   while his followers who send so many souls from life to death find absolution!   [B]   A doctor was boasting to Nicocles that his Art had great prestige. Nicocles retorted: 'It must indeed be so, if you can kill so many people with impunity.'

[A]   Meanwhile if they had asked my advice I would have rendered their teachings even more mysterious and awesome. They began well but did not keep it up to the end. A good start that, making gods and daemons the authors of their doctrines and then adopting a specialized language and style of writing –   [C]   even though Philosophy may think that it is madness to give a man good counsel which is unintelligible: '*Ut si quis medicus imperat ut sumat: "Terrigenam, herbigradam, domiportam, sanguine cassam"* . . .' [As though a doctor's prescription for a diet should say: 'Take terrigenous herbigressive autodomiciled desanguinated gasteropods . . .']²⁰

[A]   It has proved a rule good for the Art (found in all vain fantastical supernatural arts) that the patient must first trust in the remedy with firm hope and assurance before it can work effectively. They cling to that rule so far as to hold that a bad doctor whom a patient trusts is better than the most experienced one whom he does not know.

The very constituents selected for their remedies recall mystery and sorcery: the left foot of a tortoise, the urine of a lizard, the droppings of an elephant, the liver of a mole, blood drawn from under the right wing of a white pigeon; and for those of us with colic paroxysms (so contemptuously do they abuse our wretchedness) triturated rat-shit and similar apish trickery which look more like magic spells than solid knowledge. I will not even mention pills to be taken in odd numbers; the designation of particular days and festivals as ominous; the prescribing of specific times for gathering the herbs for their ingredients; and the severe, solemn expression on doctors' faces which even Pliny laughs at.

Where doctors went wrong (I mean after such a good start) is that they did not also make their assemblies more religious and their deliberations

---

20. Cicero, *De divinatione*, II, lxiv, 133. The doctor is prescribing a diet of snails!

more secret: no profane layman ought to have access to them, no more than to the secret ceremonies of Aesculapius. Because of this error their uncertainties and the feebleness of their arguments, of their guesswork and of their premises, as well as the bitterness of their disagreements (full of hatred, of envy and personal considerations), have all been revealed to everybody, so that a man must be wondrously blind if he does not feel at risk in their hands.

Did you ever find a doctor taking over a colleague's prescription without putting in something extra or cutting something out? That gives their Art away and reveals that they are more concerned with their own reputation (and therefore with their fee) than with the well-being of their patients. The wisest of them all was he who decreed that each patient should be treated by only one doctor:[21] for if he does no good the failure of one single man would be no great reproach to the whole Art of medicine, but if on the contrary he does strike lucky, then great is the glory; whereas when many are involved, they discredit their trade at every turn, especially since they normally manage to do more harm than good. They ought to have remained satisfied with the constant disagreements to be found among the opinions of the great masters and ancient authorities of their Art – only the bookish know about those – without letting everybody know of their controversies and the intellectual inconsistencies which they still foster and prolong among themselves.

Do we want to see an example of medical disagreement among the Ancients? Hierophilus locates the original cause of illness in the humours; Erasistratus, in arterial blood; Asclepiades, in invisible atoms flowing through the pores; Alcmaeon, in the exuberancy or deficiency of bodily strength; Diocles, in the imbalance of our corporeal elements and the balance of the air that we breathe; Strato, in the quantity, crudity and decomposition of the food we eat; and Hippocrates locates it in our spirits.[22]

A friend of the doctors, whom they know better than I do, exclaims in this connection that it is a great misfortune that the most important of all the sciences we use, the one with responsibility for our health and preservation, should be the most uncertain, the most unstable and the one shaken by the most changes.

There is no great harm done if we miscalculate the height of the sun or

21. Rasis (Al Razi); after H. C. Agrippa.
22. Again, from H. C. Agrippa, as is the following list of medical variations; also Pliny (*Hist. nat.*, XXIX, i). The following 'friend of the doctors' is Pliny.

the fractions in some astronomical computation: but here, when it is a matter of the whole of our being, there is no wisdom in abandoning ourselves to the mercy of so many contrary gales.

Nothing much was heard of this science before the Peloponnesian War. It was brought into repute by Hippocrates. Everything he established was overturned by Chrysippus; everything Chrysippus wrote was then overturned by Erasistratus, the grandson of Aristotle. After that lot there came the Empirics who in their Art adopted a method quite different from the Ancients; when their reputation began to grow shaky, Herophilus succeeded in getting a new kind of medicine accepted, which Asclepiades came and attacked, destroying it in his turn. Then successively the opinions of Themison gained authority, then Musa's, then later still those of Vexius Valens (the doctor famous for his intimacy with Messalina). At the time of Nero, the empire (of medicine) fell to Thessalus, who condemned and destroyed everything taught before him. His teachings were subsequently struck down by Crinas of Massilia, whose new contribution was to regulate all the workings of medicines by ephemerides and astral movements, making men eat, sleep and drink at the times which suited the Moon or Mercury. His authority was soon supplanted by that of Charinus, also a doctor in Massilia; he not only fought against Ancient medicine but also against the centuries-old public institution of hot baths. He made his patients take cold baths even in winter, immersing the sick in streams of fresh water.

Before Pliny's time no Roman had ever condescended to practise medicine; that was done by Greeks and foreigners – as among us French it is practised by spouters of Latin. As a very great doctor has said, we do not easily accept treatments we can understand, any more than we [C] trust the simples we ourselves gather.[23]   [A] If those nations where we find our guaiacum, sarsaparilla and china-root have doctors of their own, just think how exoticism and costliness must make them esteem our cabbages and our parsley: who would dare to despise plants sought in such distant lands at the risk of long and perilous journeys!

Since those medical upheavals among the Ancients there have been innumerable others up to our own times, mostly total fundamental revolu-

23. Latin was the usual language of doctors throughout the sixteenth century. For the first doctor in Rome see Polydore Vergil, *De Inventoribus rerum*, I, xx, citing Livy, XVI.

'80: we *could value drugs which are known to us: if a drug does not come from overseas and has not been brought to us from far-off regions it has no efficacy. If* ... (I cannot identify the 'very great doctor'.)

tions like those recently produced by Paracelsus, Fioravanti and Argenterius; I am told that they do not only change the odd prescription but the woof and web and the government of the medical corpus, accusing those who professed it before them of being ignorant charlatans.[24]

I leave you to imagine where that leaves the wretched patient.

If we could only be sure that their mistakes did us no harm even if they did no good it would be a reasonable bet to chance gaining something without risk of losing everything. [B] But Aesop tells how a man bought a Moorish slave and thought that his colour was incidental, brought on by ill-treatment from his former master; so he had him carefully physicked with baths and medical concoctions. As a result the Moor was not cured of swarthiness but he did lose his good health. [A] How often have we found doctors blaming each other for the deaths of their patients! I remember the local epidemic a few years ago: it was fatally dangerous. When the storm was over (having swept away innumerable people) one of the most celebrated doctors in the land published a booklet on the subject in which he regretted having prescribed blood-letting, admitting that it was one of the principal sources of the harm that was done.[25]

Moreover their authors maintain that there is no medicine without harmful side-effects: if those which do us some good do us some harm as well, what must the other ones do when applied to us quite abusively?

As for those who loathe the taste of medicine, I personally feel that, even if for no other reason, it would be dangerous and harmful for them to make themselves force it down at so inappropriate a time: just when they need rest it constitutes, I think, an unacceptable assay of their strength. Besides when I consider the factors which are said to occasion our illnesses I find them so slight and so specific that I am forced to conclude that even a tiny error in the prescribed dosage could do us great harm.

Now things go very bad indeed for us if our doctor's mistake is a dangerous one, for it is difficult for him not to go on falling into yet more errors. To aim at the right target his treatment must embrace very many

24. The most famous (and infamous) of these was Bombast von Hohenheim (Paracelsus) whose chemical and mystical therapeutics reject medical tradition. One of Leonardo Fioravanti's books appeared in English in 1582 as *A compendium of Rational Secrets . . .*; Johannes Argenterius wrote critical commentaries on Galen and Hippocrates.

25. Aesop's fable gave rise to the expression, 'to wash an Ethiop white'. Ambroise Paré questioned the validity of phlebotomy in his treatise on the plague.

factors, circumstances and elements: he must know his patient's complexion, his temperament, his humours, his inclinations, his actions, even his thoughts and his ideas; he must take into account external circumstances such as the nature of the locality, the condition of the air and the weather, the position of the planets and their influences; then he must know what causes the illness, its symptoms and their effects and the day when the crisis is reached. Where the drugs themselves are concerned he must know their dosage and their strength, their country of origin, appearance and maturity as well as the right prescription. And then he must know how to combine those elements together in the right proportions so as to produce a perfect balance. If he gets any one of them slightly wrong, or if one of his principles is slightly awry, that is enough to undo us. Only God knows how difficult it is to understand most of these elements; for example, how can a doctor discover the proper symptoms of your illness when each illness can comport an infinite number of them? How many hesitations and disputes do they have over the analysis of urines? Otherwise, how could we explain their ceaseless wranglings over their diagnoses? How else could we excuse their 'mistaking sables for foxes' – the fault they fall into so often? In such illnesses that I have had, as soon as there was the slightest complication I never found three doctors to agree.

I am most impressed by the examples which could affect me.

Recently there was a nobleman in Paris who was cut on doctor's orders: the surgeon found he no more had a stone in his bladder than in the palm of his hand.

Then there was a close friend of mine, a bishop; most of the doctors he consulted urgently pressed him to be cut; trusting in the others, I too joined in the persuasion; once he was dead they opened him up and found he only had vague kidney trouble. They have less excuse in the case of the stone, which, to some extent, can be felt by probing. That is why surgery always seems to me to be more exact: it sees and feels its way along; there is less conjecture and guesswork: medicine has no vaginal prod which can open up the passages of our brains, our lungs or our livers.

The very promises of medicine pass belief; for doctors have to treat several maladies which afflict us at the same time and which, almost of necessity, are interconnected – for example, a heated liver and a chilled stomach; they try to persuade us that some of their ingredients warm the stomach while others refresh the liver: one is said to go straight to the liver or even to the very bladder without displaying its powers on the way and while conserving its efficacy and virtues throughout that long journey with all its pitfalls, until it arrives where its occult properties are destined to apply. This one desiccates the brain while the other humidifies the lungs. Is it not a kind of raving madness to think you can mix a draught out of all those remedies and then hope that all the virtues of the drugs contained in that chaotic mixture will split themselves up, sort themselves out and rush each to its divergent task? I would have endless fears that the instructions on their labels might get lost or switched round so that they confuse their destinations! And how can anyone think that the various properties in that liquid jumble would not corrupt, counteract and subvert each other? Then again the prescription has to be made up by another expert and our lives placed at the mercy of his good faith too.

[C] When it comes to clothing ourselves we have tailors specializing in doublets or breeches; they serve us better because each sticks to his trade and his restricted area of competence; when it comes to food, great households employ cooks who are specialists in soups or in roasts: no cook with an overall responsibility can make them so exquisitely. The same applies to cures: the Egyptians were right to reject general practitioners and to split the profession up, one man working on each illness and each part of the body, which were then treated more appropriately and less indiscriminately since each doctor was only concerned with his speciality.[26] Our doctors never realize that he who provides for all provides for none and that the overall organization of our human microcosm is too much for them to digest. While they were frightened to stop a dysentery lest it brought on a fever, they killed a friend of mine who was worth more than the lot of them, however many there may be. They attach more weight to their guesses about the future than to present illnesses; so as not to cure the brain at the expense of the stomach, they harm the stomach and aggravate the brain with their tumultuous and dissident drugs.

[A] The rational bases of this particular Art are more feeble, clearly, and contradictory than those of any other: *aperient substances are good for a patient suffering from colic paroxysm*, because they dilate and distend the tubes and so facilitate the passage of the glutinous matter which can build up into gravel or stone, so evacuating whatever is beginning to gather and to harden in the kidneys; *aperient substances are dangerous for a patient suffering from colic paroxysm*, because by dilating and distending the tubes they facilitate the passage towards the kidneys of substances whose property is to build up the gravel, for which the kidneys have a propensity, so that it is

26. Cf. Polydore Vergil, *De inventoribus rerum*, I, xx: a probable source of part of Montaigne's erudition and arguments about medicine. (The following case is the death of Etienne de La Boëtie.)

difficult to stop them retaining much of what passes through them; moreover if there should happen to be some solid body a trifle too large to pass through the narrows which have to be navigated if the gravel is to be expelled, this body may be set in motion by the aperient and forced into these narrow channels, bunging them up and causing inevitable and painful death.

They show the same certainty in the advice they give us about healthy living: *it is good to pass water frequently*, for experience shows us that by allowing it to stand we let its lees and impurities settle; they then serve to build up stones in the bladder; *it is good not to pass water frequently*: since the heavier impurities borne along in the urine will be discharged only if evacuated violently (we know from experience that a rushing torrent scours the bed it passes through more thoroughly than a sluggish, debilitated stream). Similarly: *it is good to lie frequently with our wives*, because it dilates the tubes and carries away the sand and gravel; *but it is bad*, since it overheats the kidneys, tires them and weakens them.[27]

27. [A] until [A1] (instead of the next seven paragraphs): weakens them. *To sum up, they have no reasons which do not allow of such counter-arguments. As for the judgement about the effectiveness of the drugs, it is as much or more uncertain. I have twice been to drink the hot waters of our local mountains, accepting to do so because it is a natural drink, simple, with no additives, which is at least not dangerous even if useless and which fortunately turned out to be not inimical to my taste (it is true that I take it according to my own rules, not the doctors'); moreover the pleasure of visiting several relatives and friends on the way and of the company which gathers there, as well as the beauty of the countryside, attract me there. Those waters, without a doubt, work no miracle. And I do not believe all the wonderful effects told about them: for while I was there several rumours were spread which I discovered to be false when I informed myself rather carefully about them. But people deceive themselves easily about things they desire. You should not, though, deny that the waters stimulate appetite, aid digestion and give you a new gaiety, provided that you do not go there weak and exhausted. But I never went there, and was determined never to go there, other than hale and happy. Now, as for what I was saying about the difficulty which presents itself in judging their effectiveness, here is an example: I first went to Aigues-Caudes; from the waters I felt no effect, no evident purgation while I was there: but, for a year after my return I was without any pain from the colic on account of which I went there. Since then I went to Bagnères: those waters made me void a deal of gravel and left me long afterwards with a very loose stomach. Yet they did not protect my health more than two months, after which I was most maltreated by my malady. I would ask my doctor which of the two waters he considers, on this evidence, I should put my faith in, having as we do opposing arguments and circumstances for each of them. People should stop yelling against those who, in such uncertainty, let themselves be guided by their inclination and by the simple advice of Nature. Thus, when they themselves advise one water rather than another, prescribing aperients such as those hot waters or forbidding them, they act with the same uncertainty; without a doubt they entrust to the mercy of Fortune the*

[A1] *It is good to take hot baths at the spas*, because they relax and soften the places where the sand or stone is lurking: *it is bad*, because such an application of external heat encourages the kidneys to concoct, harden and then petrify the matter which is deposited therein. Once you are at the spa, *it is healthier to eat little during the evenings*, so that when you take the waters in the morning they can work more effectively because they encounter a stomach empty and unclogged; but, on the contrary, *it is better not to eat much at midday*, so as not to confuse the workings of the spa-water which are not yet completed and so as not to overload the stomach too soon after such a labour: it is wiser to allow food to digest overnight, which is better than the daytime, during which the mind and body are in ceaseless movement and agitation.

That is how they juggle and trifle with reason – to our detriment. [B] They cannot give me a single proposition against which I could not construct an opposing one equally valid. [A1] Stop railing then at those who, amid such confusion, allow themselves to be gently led by their feelings and by the counsels of Nature, entrusting themselves to common fate.

My travels have provided occasions for seeing virtually all the famous baths of Christendom; I have been using them for some years now, for I reckon that bathing in general is salubrious and I believe that our health has suffered several quite serious inconveniences since we lost the habit (which was formerly observed by virtually all peoples and still is by many) of washing our bodies every day; I can only think that we are all the worse for having our limbs encrusted and our pores blocked up with filth.

As for drinking the waters, fortunately that is in the first place not inimical to my taste; secondly it is both natural and simple and so, at the very least, not dangerous even if it does no good. To support that I can refer to the huge crowds which assemble there, people of every condition and every complexion. Although I have never seen any miraculous or extraordinary cures there – on the contrary whenever I have bothered to investigate a little more carefully than is usual I have found all the rumours of cures which are scattered about such places to be ill-founded and false

---

outcome of their advice, since it is not within their power nor their Art to answer for the quantity of gravelly substances which are being nurtured in our loins, whereas a very slight difference in their size can produce contrasting results affecting our health. You can judge their form of argument from this example. But to press them more vigorously, you would need a man who was not so ignorant of their Art as I am. Poets . . .

(despite their being believed, since people easily deceive themselves when they want to) – nevertheless I have also hardly met anyone who was made worse by taking the waters; and you cannot honestly deny that they stimulate the appetite, help the digestion and liven us up a bit (unless you are already too weak when you go there, something I would advise you against). They cannot rebuild massy ruins but they can shore up a tottering wall or forestall the threat of something worse.

If you cannot come with enough spriteliness to enjoy the company gathered there or the walks and relaxations to which we are tempted by the beauty of the countryside in which most of these spas are situated, you certainly lose the better and surer part of their effect. For this reason I have so far chosen to stay and take the waters at the more beautifully situated spas where you find more pleasant lodgings, food and company, such as the baths at Bagnères in France, Plombières on the border between Germany and Lorraine, Baden in Switzerland and Lucca in Tuscany (especially the Spa at Della Villa, which I have used most often and at various seasons).

Each country has its own peculiar opinions about how to make use of the waters as well as their own rules and methods. In my experience the effects are virtually identical. In Germany it is not done to drink them; for all illnesses people stay in the waters from sunrise to sunset like frogs. In Italy, for every nine days they drink they bathe at least thirty; they usually drink the waters mixed with additional medicinal substances to help them to work. Here in France people are told to go for a walk to help digest the water; elsewhere they make you stay in the bed where you drank it until you have voided it, while keeping your stomach and feet warm. The peculiarity of the Germans is to use cupping-horns or cupping-glasses in the bath, accompanied by scarification; the Italians have their *doccie*, which are showers of hot water conveyed through pipes; for a whole month they douse their head or their stomach, or whatever part is to be treated, for an hour in the morning and the same in the afternoon. There are innumerable differences in the customs of each country or, more correctly, virtually no agreement whatsoever between them.

So much then for the only branch of medicine which I have frequented; it is the least artificial but has its fair share of the confusion and uncertainty you see everywhere else in that Art.[28]

28. The long re-writing in 1582 from seven paragraphs back ends here. The following epigrams are from Ausonius, LXXIV, and Martial, VI, liii.

[A]   Poets can choose how to say it with more eloquence and grace; witness these two epigrams:

> *Alcon hesterno signum Jovis attigit. Ille,*
> *Quamvis marmoreus, vim patitur medici.*
> *Ecce hodie, jussus transferri ex æde vetusta,*
> *Effertur, quamvis sit Deus atque lapis.*

[Alcon touched Jove's statue yesterday. It was of marble, but it felt that doctor's power! You see, god of stone though it was, they bore it out of its hallowed temple today and buried it.]

And the second one:

> *Lotus nobiscum est hilaris, cænavit et idem,*
> *Inventus mane est mortuus Andragoras.*
> *Tam subitæ mortis causam, Faustine, requiris?*
> *In somnis medicum viderat Hermocratem.*

[Andragoras was laughing and bathing with us yesterday; he dined with us too. This morning he was found dead. Do you want to know, Faustinus, why he died so suddenly? He had a dream about Dr Hermocrates.]

I can add two stories to that.

The Baron de Caupène, in Chalosse, is joint patron with me of a benefice called Lahontan at the foot of our mountains; it covers a wide area. There befell to the inhabitants of this region what they also tell of the inhabitants of the valley of Angrougne. Once upon a time they lived cut off, with their own peculiar ways, dress and manners, ruled by their own peculiar institutions and governed by their own customs which were handed down from father to son and to which they were bound by no constraint other than respect for tradition. This tiny state had lasted from ancient times in such happy circumstances that no neighbouring judge had ever been troubled to inquire into the affairs of its inhabitants, no lawyer had ever earned fees by giving them advice, no outsider had ever been called in to settle a quarrel, and nobody in the whole region was ever known to beg. They avoided all leagues and dealings with the outside world so as not to soil the purity of their institutions, until eventually, so they tell, one of their number, as their fathers could remember, was spurred on by an ambition for nobility and decided to increase the honour and reputation of his name by educating one of his sons to become a lawyer, Maître Jean or Maître Pierre. He had him taught to write in a neighbouring town and turned him into a fine village notary-public. As he rose higher he began to despise their ancient customs and to stuff the locals' heads with thoughts of the glorious world beyond. The first of his companions to be tricked out of a goat he counselled to seek satisfaction from the King's judges nearby; then, from one thing on to another he bastardized everything.

This corruption, so they tell, was soon followed by another with graver results when a doctor conceived a desire to marry one of their maidens and to dwell among them. First he taught them the names of their fevers, rheums and swellings; he told them where their hearts were, their livers and their intestines (something quite unknown to them before). Instead of the garlic which they had formerly used to cure any ills, no matter how harsh or serious they were, he taught them to take strange mixtures for their coughs and colds and began to do good business not only out of their health but out of their deaths.

They swear that only after he came did they realize that the air at nightfall gives them heavy heads,[29] that drinking when overheated does them harm, that the winds of autumn are more unhealthy than those of spring. Only since they started following this medicine of his have they found themselves overwhelmed by a legion of unaccustomed maladies and noticed a general decline in their former vigour. Their lives have been shortened by half.

That is the first of my tales.

The other is that, before I fell victim to the stone, I heard a fuss being made about billy-goats' blood, which many considered to be like manna from heaven vouchsafed to Man in recent centuries to protect and preserve our human lives; many intelligent people talked of it as an infallible wonder-cure. Being a man convinced that I may well fall prey to any misfortune which strikes another, it was my pleasure to produce this wonder while I was yet in full health; I ordered a billy-goat on my farm to be fed as prescribed; it has to be segregated during the hottest months of summer and given only aperient herbs to eat and white wine to drink. I happened to return home the very day it was slaughtered; they came and told me that my cook discovered in its paunch, among all the edible parts, two or three large balls which rattled together. I was careful to have all the entrails brought to me and got them to slit open the great heavy paunch; three large objects fell out; light as sponges, they looked hollow yet were hard and tough on the outside and mottled in several dullish colours. One

29. Contemporary French gentlefolk feared the *serein*, the cool dewy air of a summer evening. The mass of peasants ignored it!

was perfectly round, as big as a bowling-wood: the other two were smaller, not so perfectly round but apparently still growing. When I asked those who regularly slaughter such beasts I was told that such things are unusual and rarely found. It is probable that they were stones related to our own kind, and that it is vain for a sufferer from the gravel to hope to be cured by the blood of a goat about to die of a similar illness. As for asserting that the blood itself is not affected by such contact and that its usual virtues are not impaired, it is more likely that nothing is engendered within a body but by the conspiring of all the parts working together; the whole mass is involved, although one member may contribute more than another depending on the various ways they work. It seems very probable that in all the members of that billy-goat there was some quality of petrification.

I was curious about this experiment, not so much   [C]   for myself or from fears of the future   [A]   but because,[30] in my home as in many others, the womenfolk make a store of such remedies to help the local people, prescribing the same remedy for some fifty illnesses; they never take it themselves yet exult when it works well.

In the meanwhile I honour doctors, less as the precept goes 'for the need' (since against that may be set the example of the prophet reproving King Asa for having 'sought to the physicians') but because I like the men themselves, having known several honourable and likeable ones.[31] I have nothing against doctors, only against their Art; I do not blame them much for taking advantage of our follies: most people do; many vocations, both less honourable and more so, have no other base or stay than the abuse of a trusting public. When I am ill I call them in if they happen to be around at the right time: I ask them for treatment and pay up like anyone else. I grant them leave to order me[32]   [C]   to wrap up warm ... if I prefer it that way;   [A]   they can prescribe either leeks or lettuce to make me my broth or can limit me to white wine or claret – and so on, for anything

---

30. '80: petrification. *And if that beast is subject to that malady, I find that it was badly chosen to serve us as a medicine for it.* I was curious about this experiment not so much *for my own use* but ...

(This account and its argument incensed some doctors.)

31. The famous praise of medicine in Ecclesiasticus 38:1, 'Honour a physician according to the need' (*propter necessitatem* – that is, 'according to thy need of him'). For Asa's equally famous counter-example, see II Chronicles 16:12; Asa 'was diseased in his feet, until his disease was exceeding great: yet in his disease he sought not to the Lord but to the physicians.'

32. '80: order me to *sleep on my right side, if I like that as well as sleeping on my left*; they can prescribe ...

which my appetite or habits judge indifferent. [A1] I know that that does not really help them, since bitterness and rareness are essential properties of all medicines. Why did Lycurgus order sick Spartans to drink wine? Because when in health they hated it, just as a gentleman in my neighbourhood uses wine as a successful cure for fever precisely because by nature he hates the very taste of it.

[A] How many of the doctors we know share this humour of mine, never condescending to use medicine themselves but living untrammelled lives, flat contrary to what they prescribe for others? If that is not openly mocking our simple-mindedness what is? For their life and health are as dear to them as ours to us and they would practise what they preach if they did not know it to be false. What blinds us is our fear of pain and death, our inability to put up with illness and an insane indiscriminate thirst for cures; what makes our credulity so pliant and impressionable is pure funk. [C] Even then, most people do not so much believe in it as tolerate it; I hear them talking and complaining about medicine as I do; but they end up saying, 'What else can I do?' As though lack of endurance were superior to endurance.

[A] Is there a single case of anyone who subjects himself to such wretchedness who does not also give way to all sorts of imposters, putting himself at the mercy of anyone shameless enough to promise him a cure?

[C] The Babylonians used to carry their sick into the market-place: the people were their doctors, each passer-by asking how they felt and giving them advice on getting better based on their own experience.[33] We do much the same. [A] There is hardly one silly little woman whose spells and amulets we fail to use; and my own humour would lead me to accept such remedies (if I had to accept any): at least there are no ill-effects to fear from them. [C] What Homer and Plato said of Egyptians, that they were all doctors, applies to all nations; there is nobody who does not boast of his nostrum and risk it on a neighbour who trusts him.

[A] The other day I was in company when a fellow-sufferer brought news of a new kind of pill, compounded from literally over a hundred ingredients. He made quite a to-do about it and felt singularly alleviated: for what boulder could withstand the blows of such a numerous battering! Yet from those who assayed those pills I understand not even the tiniest grain of gravel deigned to be dislodged.

I cannot give up this piece of paper without saying just one more word about the way doctors guarantee the reliability of their cures by citing

33. Herodotus, I, lxxxviii. Then, Diogenes Laertius, *Plato*, III, vii; Homer, *Odyssey*, IV, 231. (Cf. Polydore Vergil, *De inventoribus rerum*, I, xx.)

personal experience. The greater part (perhaps over two-thirds) of the
virtues of medicines consists in the latent properties or the quintessences of
simples; only practical usage can tell us about that, for quintessence is,
precisely, a quality the cause of which our reason cannot explain.[34]

Those of their proofs which doctors say they owe to revelations from
some daemon or other,[35] I am content just to accept (I never touch
miracles); the same goes for proofs based on things we use every day for
other purposes – if for example they stumble on to some latent powers of
desiccation in the wool we use to clothe us and then cure the blisters on our
heels with it; or they may discover some aperient action in the horseradish
we eat every day for [C] food. Galen gives an account [A] of a
leper[36] cured by drinking wine from a jar into which a viper had chanced
to slip. That example shows how our experimental knowledge is likely to
increase, as do those cures which doctors claim to have been put on to by
the example of certain animals. But for most of the rest of the experimental
knowledge to which they claim to have been guided by fortune or luck, I
find it impossible to believe that they actually advanced their knowledge
that way. I think of a doctor looking round at the infinite variety of
matter: plants, animals, metals. What should he assay, to start with? I
cannot tell. Supposing his thought first lights, say, on an elk's horn – and
one's credulity must be soft and compliant to suppose that![37] His next task
is equally difficult. He has to confront so many illnesses, so many attendant
circumstances, that before he can advance to the point where his experiment
reaches certainty the human intellect runs out of words. Before he can
discover, among the infinite number of objects, what that horn actually is;
then, among the infinite number of illnesses, what epilepsy actually is; then,

34. The 'fifth essence' (quintessence) is the substance of which the heavenly bodies
were thought to be composed; it was held to be latent in all things and extractable
by distillation.
35. Such claims were made, for example, for Hippocrates, who, it was claimed,
learned by inspiration the way that semen was produced by the brain. This led his
Renaissance followers to claim that, while not omniscient, he was incapable of
error or of misleading others.
36. '80: for *its taste: just as* Galen gives an account (*so I have been told*) of a leper . . .
I do not know the source of Galen's alleged account, but Polydore Vergil (*De
Inventoribus rerum*, I, xxi) gives accounts of how the medical qualities of herbs were
discovered which support Montaigne's contentions.
37. This doctor's researches are concerned with epilepsy (a 'holy sickness' in
ancient Rome), melancholy and the conjunction of Venus with Saturn (which
aggravates melancholy). Montaigne starts with the horn of an *ellend* (elk), an
animal described by Cotgrave in his *Dictionarie* as a 'fearful melancholike beast,
much troubled by the falling sicknesse', that is, by epilesy.

from among all the complexions, identify melancholy, then, from all the seasons, winter; then, from so many peoples, the French; then, from so many stages of life, old age; then, from so many motions in the heavens, the conjunction of Venus and Saturn; then, from so many parts of the body, the finger: being guided in all that not by argument, not by conjecture, not by example, not by divine inspiration but only as moved by Fortuna: well, before all that can happen, he would need a Fortuna who was a perfect practitioner of the Art, with her rules and method.

And then, even if a cure is achieved, how can the doctor be certain that the malady had not simply run its course or that it was not a chance effect or produced by something else which the patient had eaten, drunk or touched that day – or by the merits of his grandmother's prayers?

Furthermore, even if that proof were absolutely convincing, how many times was it repeated and how often was the doctor able to string such chance encounters together again, so as to establish a rule?[38]

[B] And if that rule is to be established, who does it? Only three men out of so many millions are concerned to keep records of their experiments. Did Chance happen to come across precisely one of those? Supposing another man – or a hundred men – make opposing experiments. Perhaps we could see a little light if all the judgements and reasonings of all men were known to us. But that three witnesses – three doctors – should make rules for the whole human race is not reasonable: for that to happen our human Nature would have to select them, depute them and then have them declared our Syndics,   [C] by express letters of procuration.[39]

[A] TO MADAME DE DURAS.[40]

My Lady:

You caught me just at that point when you called to see me recently. Since these ineptitudes may fall into your hands one day I would also like them to testify that their author feels most honoured by the favour you will be doing them. In them you will find the same mannerisms and attitudes which you have known in your commerce with him. Even if I could have adopted some style other than my usual one or some form better or more honourable I would not have done so; I want nothing from these writings except that they should recall me to your memory as

---

38. Aristotle insists at the outset in his *Metaphysics* that an 'art' (such as medicine) is not based on experience (or experiment) as such, but on reflection on experience, by which general rules are established.

39. Renaissance medicine was, in the orthodox schools, still dominated by Hippocrates, Galen and Avicenna.

40. Marguerite d'Aure de Gramont, an intimate of Marguerite de Valois.

sketched from nature. I want to take those very same characteristics and attributes which you, My Lady, have known, welcoming them with more honour and courtesy than they deserve, and lodge them (without change or alteration) within some solid body which is able to outlive me by a few years – or a few days – in which you will be able to find them again, refreshing your memory of them whenever you want to, without having the burden of otherwise keeping them in mind (they would not be worth that). I desire that you will go on favouring me with your affection for the same qualities which first aroused it. I have no wish to be better loved or better valued when dead than when alive. [B] That humour of Tiberius which made him[41] more concerned to be widely honoured in the future than to make himself esteemed or liked in his own day is ridiculous, though common enough. [C] If I were one of those to whom the world may owe a debt of praise, I would rather be paid in advance, please, and wipe off the debt. Let praise rush to pile up round me, thickly not thinly spread, plentiful rather than long-lasting. Then, when its sweet voice can strike my ears no more, it can be bold enough to disappear with my own consciousness. [A] Now that I am ready to give up all commerce with men it would be an insane humour to parade myself before them decked in some new subject of esteem. I will not acknowledge any receipt for goods not delivered for use during my lifetime. Whatever I may be like, I have no desire to exist only on paper! My art and industry have been employed to make this self of mine worth something; my studies, to teach me not to write but to act. All my effort has gone into the forming of my life: that is my trade and vocation. Any other job is more for me than the scribbling of books. I have wanted merely to be clever enough for my present and essential comforts, not to store up a reserve for my heirs.

[C] If anyone is worth anything, let it appear in his behaviour, in his ordinary talk when loving or quarrelling, in his pastimes, in bed, at table, in the way he conducts his business and runs his house. Those men whom I see writing good books while wearing torn breeches would first mend their breeches if they took my advice. Ask a Spartan if he would rather be a good orator or a good soldier; why, I would rather be a good cook, if I did not have a fine one serving me already.

[A] Good God, My Lady, how I would hate the reputation of being clever at writing but stupid and useless at everything else! I would rather be stupid at both than to choose to employ my good qualities as badly as that. Far from expecting to acquire some new honour by this silly nonsense, I

41. '80: which made him, *said Tacitus*, more concerned . . .
    Tacitus, *Annals*, VI, xlvi.

shall have achieved a lot if it does not make me lose the little I have. Leaving aside the fact that this dumb *nature morte* will be an impoverished portrait of my natural being, it is not even drawn from my state at its best but only after it has declined from its original joy and vigour, now seeming withered and rancid. I have reached the bottom of the barrel which readily stinks of lees and sediment.

Moreover I would never have dared, My Lady, to be bold at disturbing the mysteries of Medicine (seeing the trust that you and so many others place in her), if I had not been helped along by the medical authorities themselves. There are only two among the Latins: Pliny and Celsus. If you take a look at them sometime you will find that they treat Medicine more rudely than I do. I give her a pinch: they slit her gizzard. Among other things Pliny mocks doctors who, when they have come to the end of their tether, have found a fine way of ridding themselves of their patients after they have racked them with their potions and tormented them with their diets, all to no avail: they pack some of the sick off to be succoured by vows and miracles, and the rest of them to hot-spring resorts. (Do not be offended, My Lady: he did not mean the ones on our own mountain-slopes which are all under the protection of your family, all devoted to the Gramonts.)

Doctors have a third way[42] of getting rid of us, driving us away and freeing themselves of the weight of our reproaches for the lack of improvement in our illnesses which they have been treating for so long that they can devise nothing new to spin out more time: they send us away to some other region to discover how good the air is there!

Enough of this, My Lady. You will allow me now to pick up the thread of my subject which I had digressed from in order to converse with you.

It was I think Pericles who was asked how he was getting on and replied, 'You can tell from all this,' pointing to the amulets tied to his neck and his arms. He wanted to imply that, since he had been reduced to having recourse to such silly things and to allow them to be used as protection, he was ill indeed.[43]

I do not mean that I may not one day be swept away by the ridiculous idea of entrusting my life to the mercy of the doctors and my health to their ordinances; I might well fall into such raving madness (I cannot vouch for my future constancy); but if I do, like Pericles I shall say to anyone who

---

42. Pliny, *Hist. nat.*, XXIX, xlvi.

    '80: Gramonts.) *Our own doctors are bolder still: for they* have a third way . . .

43. Plutarch, *Life of Pericles*.

asks how I am, 'You can tell from all this,' showing him my palm burdened with six drams of opiate. That will be a manifest symptom of violent illness.[44] My judgement will have miraculously flown off the handle. If fear and intolerance of pain ever make me do that, you may diagnose a very harsh fever in my soul.

I have bothered to plead this case (which I do not well understand) in order to lend a little support and reinforcement to that natural aversion for our medical drugs and practices which has been handed on to me by my ancestors, so that it should be more than some thoughtless, senseless tendency but an aversion with a little more form. I also want those who see me firmly set against the persuasions and menaces addressed to me when my afflictions oppress me not to take it for pure stubbornness nor be so hasty as to conclude that I am pricked on by vainglory. What a well-placed blow that would be, to wish to squeeze honour from a practice common to me, my gardener and my mule-driver![45] I certainly do not have a mind so distended and flatulent that I would go and swap a solid flesh-and-marrow joy like health for some fancied joy all wind and vapour. For a man of my humour even glory such as that of the *Four Sons of Aymon* is purchased too dear if the price is three good attacks of the stone. Health! For God's sake!

Those who like our medicine may also have their own good, great, powerful arguments: I do not loathe ideas which go against my own. I am so far from shying away when others' judgements clash with mine, so far from making myself unsympathetic to the companionship of men because they hold to other notions or parties, that, on the contrary, just as the most general style followed by Nature is variety – [C] even more in minds than in bodies, since minds are of a more malleable substance capable of accepting more forms – [A] I find it much rarer to see our humours and [C] purposes [A] coincide. In the whole world there has never been two identical opinions, any more than two identical [C] hairs or seeds. [A] Their most universal characteristic is diversity.[46]

---

44. '80: violent illness, *which will have disturbed the seat of my understanding and my reason.* My judgement . . .

45. Neither of whom could afford doctors' fees and so went without doctors.

46. '80: humours and *thoughts* coincide. *And perhaps* there has never been two identical opinions any more than two identical *faces.* Their most universal characteristic is diversity *and discordance* . . .

In [C], *hairs or seeds* replace *faces* under the influence of Cicero, *Academica*, II (Lucullus), xxvi, 85, where a case is marshalled against the assertion made here, which is presented as a Stoic one. With this phrase Montaigne discreetly emphasizes the Stoic savour of his argument.

2. On repenting

[Montaigne does not deal here primarily with the sacrament of repentance but with the act of repenting in domains religious, moral and practical. In this sense repenting consists not in regret but in denying the rightness of what one had formerly willed. Like Rabelais's good giant Gargantua, Montaigne knows that a man may live as a Christian gentleman: 'without reproach though not of course without sin'. And Montaigne's sense of sin is not a matter of wishing in old age that he had not committed the sins (especially the sensual sins) of his youth nor the worse sins of old men; neither is it a matter of wishing that he had been vouchsafed a higher Form than Man (that of an angel) or a better human Form than his own botched one (a Form like Cato's). In practical affairs, however they turn out, Montaigne sees no cause for repenting of decisions honourably made within Man's limitations; in his dealings with others in peace and civil war he knows he has acted as an honourable gentleman, far better than most. Where sins against the Christian God are concerned, Montaigne never hid from himself the ugly face which lurks behind their stormy beauty; that is where repentance comes in; real repentance – of the demanding, ultimate kind which alone moves Montaigne – is an agonizing matter: we must see ourselves throughly, as with the eyes of God who searches the reins and the bowels and from whom no secrets are hidden. To do that 'God must touch our hearts' – an act of grace which became the superscription of a religious emblem.]

[B]   Others form Man; I give an account of Man and sketch a picture of a particular one of them who is very badly formed and whom I would truly make very different from what he is if I had to fashion him afresh. But it is done now. The brush-strokes of my portrait do not go awry even though they do change and vary. The world is but a perennial see-saw. Everything in it – the land, the mountains of the Caucasus, the pyramids of Egypt – all waver with a common motion and their own.[1] Constancy itself is nothing but a more languid rocking to and fro. I am unable to stabilize my subject: it staggers confusedly along with a natural drunkenness. I grasp it as it is now, at this moment when I am lingering over it. I am not portraying being but becoming: not the passage from one age to another

---

1. Propertius, II, i, 69. (For the theme, cf. Erasmus, *Opera*, 1703–6, V, 488F–461E. Montaigne's theme of the perennial flux of all things is Heracleitan.)

(or, as the folk put it, from one seven-year period to the next) but from day to day, from minute to minute. I must adapt this account of myself to the passing hour. I shall perhaps change soon, not accidentally but intentionally. This is a register of varied and changing occurrences, of ideas which are unresolved and, when needs be, contradictory, either because I myself have become different or because I grasp hold of different attributes or aspects of my subjects. So I may happen to contradict myself but, as Demades said, I never contradict truth.[2] If my soul could only find a footing I would not be assaying myself but resolving myself. But my soul is ever in its apprenticeship and being tested. I am expounding a lowly, lacklustre existence. You can attach the whole of moral philosophy to a commonplace private life just as well as to one of richer stuff. Every man bears the whole Form of the human condition.[3] [C] Authors communicate themselves to the public by some peculiar mark foreign to themselves; I – the first ever to do so – by my universal being, not as a grammarian, poet or jurisconsult but as Michel de Montaigne. If all complain that I talk too much about myself, I complain that they never even think about their own selves.

[B] But is it reasonable that I who am so private in my habits should claim to make public this knowledge of myself? And is it also reasonable that I should expose to a world in which grooming has such credit and artifice such authority the crude and simple effects of Nature – and of such a weakling nature too? Is writing a book without knowledge or art not like building a wall without stones and so on? The fancies of the Muses are governed by art: mine, by chance. But I have one thing which does accord with sound teaching: never did man treat a subject which he knew or understood better than I know and understand the subject which I have undertaken: in that subject I am the most learned man alive! Secondly, no man ever [C] went more deeply into his matter, ever stripped barer its own peculiar members and consequences, or ever [B] reached more precisely or more fully the goal he had proposed for his endeavour. To finish the job I only need to contribute fidelity: and fidelity is there, as clean and as pure as can be found. I tell the truth, not enough to make me replete but as much as I dare – and as I grow older I dare a little more, for

2. Plutarch, *Life of Demosthenes*.
3. Aristotle's opinion was normative: all human beings have the same form (soul), the form of Man. What distinguishes each individual person is the union of one particular example of that form with one particular body.

custom apparently concedes to old age a greater licence to chatter more indiscreetly about oneself. What cannot happen here is what I often find elsewhere: that the craftsman and his artefact thwart each other: 'How can a man whose conversation is so decent come to write such a scurrilous book?' or 'How can such learned writings spring from a man whose conversation is so weak?'

[C] When a man is commonplace in discussion yet valued for what he writes that shows that his talents lie in his borrowed sources not in himself. A learned man is not learned in all fields: but a talented man *is* talented in all fields, even in ignorance. [B] Here, my book and I go harmoniously forward at the same pace. Elsewhere you can commend or condemn a work independently of its author; but not here: touch one and you touch the other. Anyone who criticizes it without knowing that will harm himself more than me; anyone who does know it has satisfied me completely. I shall be blessed beyond my merit if public approval will allow me this much: that I have made intelligent people realize that I would have been capable of profiting from learning if I had had any and that I deserved more help from my memory.

Let me justify here what I often say: that I rarely repent   [C]   and that my conscience is happy with itself – not as the conscience of an angel is nor of a horse, but as behoves the conscience of a man[4] –   [B]   ever adding this refrain (not a ritual one but one of simple and fundamental submission): that I speak as an ignorant questioning man: for solutions I purely and simply abide by the common lawful beliefs.[5] I am not teaching, I am relating.

There is no vice that is truly a vice which is not odious and which a wholesome judgement does not condemn; for there is so much evident ugliness and impropriety in it that perhaps those philosophers are right who maintain that it is principally the product of stupidity and ignorance, so hard it is to imagine that anyone could recognize it without loathing it.[6] [C] Evil swallows most of its own venom and poisons itself. [B] Vice leaves repentance in the soul like an ulcer in the flesh which is forever scratching itself and bleeding.[7] For reason can efface other

---

4. In the 'chain of being', Man comes between the beasts and the angels.
5. 'Lawful' by the law of the Church.
6. Socrates and his fellows. Cf. II, 12, 'An apology for Raymond Sebond' (beginning); then [C], from Seneca, *Epist. moral.*, LXXXI, 22.
7. Image and development from Plutarch (tr. Amyot), *De la tranquillité de l'ame*, 75 G.

griefs and sorrows, but it engenders those of repentance which are all the more grievous for being born within us, just as the chill and the burn of our fevers are more stinging than such as come to us from outside. I hold to be vices (though each according to its measure) not only those vices which are condemned by reason and nature but even those which have been forged by the opinions of men, even when false or erroneous, provided that law and custom lend them their authority.

Likewise there is no goodness which does not rejoice a well-born nature. There is an unutterable delight in acting well which makes us inwardly rejoice; a noble feeling of pride accompanies a good conscience. A soul courageous in its vice can perhaps furnish itself with composure but it can never provide such satisfaction and happiness with oneself. It is no light pleasure to know oneself to be saved from the contagion of a corrupt age and to be able to say of oneself: 'Anyone who could see right into my soul would even then not find me guilty of any man's ruin or affliction, nor of envy nor of vengeance, nor of any public attack on our laws, nor of novelty or disturbance, nor of breaking my word. And even though this licentious age not only allows it but teaches it to each of us, I have nevertheless not put my hand on another Frenchman's goods or purse but have lived by my own means, in war as in peace; nor have I exploited any man's labour without due reward.' Such witnesses to our conscience are pleasant; and such natural rejoicing is a great gift: it is the only satisfaction which never fails us.

Basing the recompense of virtuous deeds on another's approbation is to accept too uncertain and confused a foundation – [C] especially since in a corrupt and ignorant period like our own to be in good esteem with the masses is an insult: whom would you trust to recognize what was worthy of praise! May God save me from being a decent man according to the self-descriptions which I daily see everyone give to honour themselves: *'Quae fuerant vitia, mores sunt.'* [What used to be vices have become morality.][8]

Some of my friends have occasionally undertaken to lay bare my heart, to charge me and put me through the assizes, either on their own initiative or else summoned by me; of all the offices of friendship that is not only the most useful for a well-turned mind but also the sweetest. I have always welcomed it with the most courteous and grateful of embraces. But speaking of it now in all conscience I have often found such false measure in their praise and blame that, judging from their standards, I would not have been wrong to do wrong rather than right.

8. Seneca, *Epist. moral.*, XXXIX, 6.

[B]   Especially in the case of people like us who live private lives which only go on parade before ourselves, we must establish an inner model to serve as touchstone of our actions, by which we at times favour ourselves or flog ourselves. I have my own laws and law-court to pass judgement on me and I appeal to them rather than elsewhere. I restrain my actions according to the standards of others, but I enlarge them according to my own. No one but you knows whether you are base and cruel, or loyal and dedicated. Others never see you: they surmise about you from uncertain conjectures; they do not see your nature so much as your artifice. So do not cling to their sentence: cling to your own.   [C]   *'Tuo tibique judicio est utendum.'* [You must use your own judgement of yourself.][9] *'Virtutis et vitiorum grave ipsius conscientiae pondus est: qua sublata, jacent omnia.'* [Your own conscience gives weighty judgement on your virtues and vices: remove that, and all lies sprawling.]

[B]   Yet the saying that 'repentance follows hard upon the sin' does not seem to me to concern sin in full apparel, when lodged in us as in its own home. We can disown such vices as take us by surprise and towards which we are carried away by our passions; but such vices as are rooted and anchored in a will which is strong and vigorous brook no denial. To repent is but to gainsay our will and to contradict our ideas; it can lead us in any direction. It makes that man over there disown his past virtue and his continence!

> *Quæ mens est hodie, cur eadem non puero fuit?*
> *Vel cur his animis incolumes non redeunt genæ*

[Alas! Why did I not want to do as a young man what I want to do now? Or why, thinking as I do now, cannot my radiant cheeks return?][10]

Rare is the life which remains ordinate even in privacy. Anyone can take part in a farce and act the honest man on the trestles: but to be right-ruled within, in your bosom, where anything is licit, where everything is hidden – that's what matters. The nearest to that is to be so in your home, in your everyday actions for which you are accountable to nobody; there is no striving there, no artifice.[11] That is why Bias when portraying an excellent family state said it was one where the head of the family was of his own

9. Cicero, *Tusc. disput.*, II, lxiii; then, *De nat. deorum*, III, xxxv.
10. Horace, *Odes*, IV, x, 7–8.
11. Cf. the adage attributed variously to Socrates and to Diogenes: *'Aedibus in nostris quae prava aut recta geruntur'* (It is in our own home that good or evil are done): Erasmus, *Adages*, I, VI, LXXXV.

volition, the same indoors as he was outdoors for fear of the law and the comments of men: and it was a worthy retort of Julius Drusus to the builders who offered for three thousand crowns to re-plan his house so that his neighbours could no longer see in as they did: 'I will give you six thousand, and you can arrange for them to see in everywhere!' We comment with honour on Agesilaus' practice of taking up lodgings in the temples when on a journey, so that the people and the very gods could see what he did in private.[12] A man may appear to the world as a marvel: yet his wife and his manservant see nothing remarkable about him. Few men have been wonders to their families.

[C] 'No man has been a prophet not only in his own home but in his own country,' says the experience of history.[13] The same applies to trivialities. You can see an image of greater things in the following lowly example: in my own climate of Gascony they find it funny to see me in print; I am valued the more the farther from home knowledge of me has spread. In Guienne I pay my printers: elsewhere, they pay me. That consideration is the motive of those who hide away when alive and present, so as to enjoy a reputation when they are dead and gone. I would rather have a lesser one: I throw myself upon the world for the one that I can enjoy now. Once I am gone I acquit the world of its debt.

[B] That man over there is escorted to his door ecstatically by a public procession: he doffs that role when he doffs his robes; the higher he has climbed the lower he falls. Once at home he is all tumult and baseness within. And even if right-rule is to be found in him, you need a quick and highly selected judgement to perceive it in his humble private actions. Besides, to be ordinate is a glum and sombre virtue. Storming a breach, conducting an embassy, ruling a nation are glittering deeds. Rebuking, laughing, buying, selling, loving, hating and living together gently and justly with your household – and with yourself – not getting slack nor belying yourself, is something more remarkable, more rare and more difficult. Whatever people may say, such secluded lives sustain in that way duties which are at least as hard and as tense as those of other lives. [C] And Aristotle says that private citizens serve virtue as highly and with as much difficulty as those who hold office.[14] [B] We prepare

---

12. Plutarch (tr. Amyot), *Le banquet des sept sages*, 155 E (Bias), and *Instruction pour ceulx qui manient affaires d'Estat*, 162 G (Julius Caesar); then, *Life of Agesilas*.
13. Matthew 13:57; Mark 6:4; Luke 4:24; John 4:44.
14. Aristotle, *Nicomachaean Ethics*, X, vii, 10 (1179 a).

ourselves for great occasions more for the glory than for good conscience. [C] The quickest road to glory would be to do for conscience what we do for glory. [B] And the virtue of Alexander seems to me to act out less virtue on its stage than that of Socrates in his humble obscure role. I can easily conceive of Socrates in Alexander's place: but Alexander in Socrates' place, I cannot. Ask Alexander what he can do and he will reply: 'Subdue the whole world.' Ask Socrates, and he will answer, 'Live the life of man in conformity with his natural condition': knowledge which is much more general, onerous and right.

The soul's value consists not in going high but in going ordinately. [C] Its greatness is not displayed in great things but in the Mean.

Just as those who judge us by the touchstone of our motives do not rate highly the sparkle of our public deeds and see that it is no more than thin fine jets of water spurting up from the depths (which are moreover heavy and slimy), so too those who judge us from our brave outward show conclude that our inward disposition corresponds to it: they cannot couple ordinary talents just like their own with those other talents, so far beyond their ken, which amaze them. That is why we give savage shapes to demons. And who does not give Tamberlane arching eyebrows, gaping nostrils, a ghastly face and an immense size proportionate to the idea we have conceived of him from the spreading of his name? Once, if anyone had brought me to meet Erasmus it would have been hard for me not to take for adages and apophthegms everything he said to his manservant or to his innkeeper's wife. We can with more seemliness imagine an artisan on his jakes or on his wife than a great lord chancellor venerated for his dignity and wisdom. It seems to us that they never come down from their lofty thrones, even to live.

[B] As vicious souls are often incited to do good by some outside instigation, so are virtuous souls to do evil. We must therefore judge souls in their settled state, when they are at home with themselves – if they ever are – or at least when they are nearest to repose in their native place. Natural tendencies are helped and reinforced by education, but they can hardly be said to be altered or overmastered. In my lifetime hundreds of natures have escaped towards virtue, or vice, despite teaching to the contrary:

> *Sic ubi desuetæ silvis in carcere clausæ*
> *Mansuevere feræ, et vultus posuere minaces,*
> *Atque hominem didicere pati, si torrida parvus*

Venit in ora cruor, redeunt rabiesque furorque,
Admonitæque tument gustato sanguine fauces;
Fervet, et a trepido vix abstinet ira magistro.

[As when wild beasts, shut up in a cage, forget their forests and are tamed, losing their menacing looks and learning to be ruled by men, yet if a tiny drop of blood falls on their avid lips, back come their snarls and their ragings; they have tasted blood; their jaws yawn wide; they are in turmoil and can hardly be stopped from venting their wrath on their trembling tamer.][15]

We cannot extirpate the qualities we were originally born with; we cover them and we hide them. Latin is a native tongue for me: I understand it better than French; yet it is forty years now since I used it for speaking or writing. Nevertheless on those two or three occasions in my life when I have suffered some extreme and sudden emotion – one was when my perfectly healthy father collapsed back on to me in a dead faint – the first words which I have dredged up from my entrails have always been in Latin – [C] nature, against long nurture, breaking forcibly out and finding expression. [B] And this example applies to many others.

Those who have sought in my time to improve the morals of the world with their new opinions reform the vices which show: the essential vices they leave us as they are – if they do not make them grow bigger. And such growth is to be feared: we are ready to take a holiday from all other good deeds on the strength of those uncertain surface reformations which cost us less and which gain us more esteem; and we thereby cheaply give satisfaction to our other vices: those which are inborn, of one substance with us and visceral.

Just take a little look at what our own experience shows. Provided that he listen to himself there is no one who does not discover in himself a form entirely his own, a master-form which struggles against his education as well as against the storm of emotions which would gainsay it. In my case I find that I am rarely shaken by shocks or agitations; I am virtually always settled in place, as heavy ponderous bodies are. If I should not be 'at home' I am always nearby. My indulgences do not catch me away very far: there is nothing odd or extreme about them, though I do have some sane and vigorous changes of heart.

The real condemnation which applies to the common type of men nowadays is that their very retreat is full of filth and corruption, that their amendment of life is vague, and their repentance nearly as sickly and guilt-

15. Lucan, *Pharsalia*, 237–42.

ridden as their sinning. Some of them are so stuck to their vices by long
habit or some natural bonding that they no longer find them ugly. There
are others – and I am one of that regiment – for whom vice does have
some weight but who counterbalance it by the pleasure it gives or by some
other factor; they put up with it and give themselves over to it, but at a
definite price – viciously though and basely. Yet a vastly disproportionate
measure could be imagined between the vice and the price, one where the
pleasure could with justice compensate for the sin (as expediency is said to
do) – not when the pleasure is incidental, forming no part of the sin, as in
theft, but as in lying with women where the pleasure resides in performing
the sin and where the drive is violent and, so it is said, irresistible.

The other day when I was in Armagnac on the estates of one of my
relations I met a peasant whom everybody called Pincher. He gave me this
account of his life: being born to beggary and finding that he would never
succeed in earning his bread and warding off indigence by the labour of his
hands, he took the decision to become a thief and had spent his entire
youth safely in that trade because he was so physically strong; for he used
to harvest the corn and grapes on other men's lands, but so far off and in
such huge quantities that it was unthinkable that one man could have
loaded so much on his back in one single night. He also took care to spread
the damage equally about, so that each of his victims found the loss less
hard to bear. Now, in his old age, he is rich for a man of his station –
thanks to that trafficking, which he openly admits. To come to terms with
God for his gains he declares that, by making free-gifts, he is always keen
to compensate the heirs of all the men he robbed, and that if he does not
finish this (for he simply cannot provide for all at once) he will charge his
heirs to do so, based on the knowledge which he alone has of the evil he
had done to each individual. From this account, be it true or false, that man
regards theft as a dishonest deed; and he hates it . . . less than he hates
poverty. He indeed repents of the theft as such, but he does not feel any
repentance for its being counterbalanced and counterweighed. We do not
find in this case that habitual practice which makes us fellows-incorporate
with vice and brings our mind itself to conform to it; nor is it that violent
gale which batters and blinds our soul and sweeps us for a while into the
power of vice, judgement and all.

My custom is to be entirely given to what I do, marching forward all of
a piece. There is hardly an emotion in me which sneaks away and hides
from my reason or which is not governed by the consent of almost all my
parts, without schism or inner strife. The entire blame or praise for that
belongs to my judgement; and once it accepts that blame it has it for ever,

because virtually since birth it has always been one: the same bent, the same route, the same strength. And as for all my general opinions, I have since childhood lodged me where I was to remain.

There are sins which are violent, quick and sudden. Let us leave them aside. But as for those other sins, so often repeated, deliberated and meditated upon, those sins which are rooted in our complexions [C] and, indeed, in our professions or vocations, [B] I cannot conceive that they could be rooted so long in one identical heart without the reason and conscience of him who is seized of them being constant in his willing and wanting them to be so; and the repentance which he boasts to come to him at a particular appointed instant is hard for me to imagine or conceive. [C] I cannot follow the Pythagorean dogma that men take on a new soul when they draw near to the statues of the gods to gather up their oracles, unless Pythagoras meant that their soul must actually be a new one, foreign to them and lent for the occasion, since their own soul showed so little sign of being cleansed by purification and condign for that duty.[16] [B] What they do is flat contrary to the Stoics' precepts, which do indeed command us to correct any vices or imperfections which we acknowledge to be in us but forbid us to be sorry or upset about them. But these men would have us believe that they do feel deep remorse and regret within; yet no amendment or improvement, [C] no break, [B] ever becomes apparent. But if you do not unburden yourself of the evil there has been no cure. If repentance weighed down the scales of the balance it would do away with the sin. I can find no quality so easy to counterfeit as devotion unless our morals and our lives are made to conform to it; its essence is hidden and secret: its external appearances are easy and ostentatious.

As for me, I can desire to be entirely different, I can condemn my universal form and grieve at it and beg God to form me again entirely and to pardon my natural frailty. But it seems to me that that should not be called repenting any more than my grieving at not being an angel or Cato.[17] My doings are ruled by what I am and are in harmony with how I was made. I cannot do better: and the act of repenting does not properly touch such things as are not within our power – *that* is touched by regretting. I can imagine countless natures more sublime and better ruled than my own: by doing that I do not emend my own capacities, any more

16. Seneca, *Epist. moral.*, XCIV, 42.
17. Angels have souls higher than men's in the chain-of-being: Cato had a soul higher than Montaigne's within the human scale.

than my arm or my intelligence becomes more strong because I can imagine others which are. If imagining and desiring actions nobler than ours made us repent of our own we would have to go repenting of our most innocent doings, since we can rightly judge that they would have been brought to greater perfection and grandeur in a nature far excelling our own. When I reflect on my behaviour as a young man and as an old one I find that I have mainly behaved ordinately *secundum me*.[18] My power of resistance can do no more. I do not flatter myself: in like circumstances I would still be thus. It is no spot but a universal stain which soils me. I do not know any surface repentance, mediocre and a matter of ceremony. Before I call it repentance it must touch me everywhere, grip my bowels and make them yearn – as deeply and as universally as God does see me.[19]

In my business dealings several good opportunities have escaped me for want of the happy knack of conducting them: yet my decisions were well chosen *secundum quid* (that is, according to the events which they ran up against); my decisions are so fashioned as always to take the easiest and the surest side. I find that I proceeded wisely, according to my rule, in my previous deliberations given the state of the subject as set before me: and in the same circumstances I would do the same a thousand years from hence. I pay no regard to what it looks like now but to how it was when I was examining it.

[C] The force of any advice depends upon the time: circumstances endlessly alter and matters endlessly change. I have made some grievous mistakes in my life – important ones – for want of good luck not for want of good thought. In the subjects which we handle, and especially in the natures of men, there are hidden parts which cannot be divined, silent characteristics which are never revealed and which are sometimes unknown even to the one who has them but which are awakened and brought out by subsequent events. If my wisdom was unable to penetrate through to them and foresee them I bear it no grudge: there are limits to its obligations. What defeats me is the outcome, and   [B]   if it favours the side I rejected, that cannot be helped. I do not find fault with myself: I blame not what I did but my fortune. And that is not to be called repenting.

18. That is, even ordinate actions and reactions are relative insofar as they must be judged 'according to' one's capacities and judgements.
19. Each man is, in God's sight, sinful (Romans 3:23; 5:12), and God is the *scrutator cordium*, 'He who searches all hearts' (I Chronicles 28:9); 'He who searcheth the heart and knoweth the mind' (Romans 8:27); 'He that searcheth the reins and the heart' (Revelations 2:23).

Phocion gave a certain piece of advice to the Athenians which was not acted upon. When the affair turned out successfully against his advice somebody asked him, 'Well now, Phocion, are you pleased that things are going so well?' 'Of course,' he said, 'I am happy that it has turned out this way, but I do not repent of the advice that I gave.'[20] When my friends come to me for advice I give it freely and clearly, without (as nearly everyone does) dwelling on the fact that, since the matter is chancy, things can turn out contrary to what I think, so that they may well have cause to reproach me for my advice. That never bothers me, for they will be in the wrong: I *ought* not to have refused them such service.

[C] I have hardly any cause to blame anyone but myself for my failures or misfortunes, for in practice I rarely ask anyone for advice save to honour them formally; the exception is when I need learned instruction or knowledge of the facts. But in matters where only my judgement is involved, the arguments of others rarely serve to deflect me though they may well support me; I listen to them graciously and courteously – to all of them. But as far as I can recall I have never yet trusted any but my own. According to my standards they are but flies and midges buzzing over my will. I set little store by my own opinions but just as little by other people's. And Fortune has treated me worthily. I receive little counsel: I give even less. I am very rarely asked for it: I am even less believed, and I know of no public or private undertaking which has been set right or halted on my advice. Even such persons as chance to be somewhat dependent on my advice have readily allowed themselves to be swayed by some completely different mind. Since I am just as jealous of my right to peace and quiet as of my right to authority, I prefer it that way. By leaving me out they are acting on my own principles, which consist in being settled and contained entirely within myself: it is a joy for me to be detached from others' affairs and relieved of protecting them.

I have few regrets for affairs of any sort, no matter how they have turned out, once they are past. I am always comforted by the thought that they had to happen that way: there they are in the vast march of the universe and in the concatenation of Stoic causes; no idea of yours, by wish or by thought, can change one jot without overturning the whole order of Nature, both past and future.[21]

Meanwhile I loathe that consequential repenting which old age brings.

---

20. Plutarch (tr. Amyot), *Dicts notables des anciens Roys . . .*, 197 E.
21. For the Stoics, causation was absolute: everything is fated and unalterable.

That Ancient who said that he was obliged to the passing years for
freeing him from sensual pleasures held quite a different opinion from
mine: I could never be grateful to infirmity for any good it might do
me. [C] 'Nec tam aversa unquam videbitur ab opere suo providentia, ut
debilitas inter optima inventa sit.' [And Providence will never be found so
hostile to her work as to rank debility among the best of
things.]²² [B] Our appetites are few when we are old: and once they are
over we are seized by a profound disgust. I can see nothing of conscience in
that: chagrin and feebleness imprint on us a lax and snotty virtue. We must
not allow ourselves to be so borne away by natural degeneration that it
bastardizes our judgement. In former days youth and pleasure never made
me fail to recognize the face of vice within the sensuality: nor does the
distaste which the years have brought me make me fail to recognize now
the face of pleasure within the vice.

I have nothing to do with it now, but I judge it as though I
did. [C] Personally, when I give my reason a lively and attentive shake,
I find that [B] it is just the same as in my more licentious years, except
that it has perhaps grown more feeble and much worse with
age; [C] and I find that, although it declines to stoke up such pleasures
out of consideration for the interests of my physical health, it would not do
that, even now, any more than it once did, for the sake of my spiritual
health. [B] I do not think it any braver for seeing it drop out of the
battle. My temptations are so crippled and enfeebled that they are not
worth opposing. I can conjure them away by merely stretching out my
hands. Confront my reason with my former longings and I fear that it will
show less power of resistance than once it did. I cannot see that, of itself, it
judges in any way differently now than it did before, nor that it is freshly
enlightened. So if it has recovered it is a botched recovery. [C] A
wretched sort of cure, to owe one's health to sickliness.

It is not for our wretchedness to do us that service: it is for the happy
outcome of our judgement. As for whacks and afflictions, you can make
me do nothing but curse them: they are meant for men whose desires are
aroused only by a good whipping. Indeed my reason runs freer when
things go well: it is far more distracted and occupied when digesting
misfortunes than pleasures. I can see much more clearly when the weather
is serene. Health counsels me both more actively and usefully than illness
does. I had progressed as far as I could towards right-rule and reformation

22. Sophocles, criticized by Epicurus: Plutarch (tr. Amyot), Que l'on ne sçauroit
vivre heureusement selon la doctrine d'Epicurus, 283 DE; Quintilian, V, xii.

when I had health to enjoy. I would be ashamed and jealous if the wretched lot of my decrepitude were to be preferred above the years when I was healthy, aroused and vigorous, and if men had to esteem me not for what I was but for ceasing to be like that. It is my conviction that what makes for human happiness is not, as Antisthenes said, dying happily but living happily.[23] I have never striven to make a monster by sticking a philosopher's tail on to the head and trunk of a forlorn man, nor to make my wretched end disavow and disclaim the more beautiful, more wholesome and longer part of my life. I want to show myself to have been uniform and to be seen as such. If I had to live again, I would live as I have done; I neither regret the past nor fear the future. And unless I deceive myself, things within have gone much the same as those without. One of my greatest obligations to my lot is that the course of my physical state has brought each thing in due season. I have known the blade, the blossom and the fruit; and I now know their withering. Happily so, since naturally so. I can bear more patiently the ills that I have since they come in due season, and since they also make me recall with more gratitude the long-lasting happiness of my former life.

My wisdom may well have had the same stature in both my seasons, but it was far more brilliant and graceful then, green-sprouting, gay and naïve; now it is bent double, querulous and wearisome.

I disclaim those incidental reformations based on pain. [B] God must touch our hearts.[24] Our conscience must emend itself by itself, by the strengthening of our reason not by the enfeebling of our appetites. Sensual pleasure, of itself, is neither so pale nor so wan as to be perceived by bleared and troubled eyes. We must love temperance for its own sake and out of respect for God who has commanded it to us; and chastity too: what we are presented with by rheum, and what I owe to the grace of my colic paroxysms, are neither chastity nor temperance.[25]

You cannot boast of despising and of fighting pleasure if you cannot see her and if you do not know her grace and power, or her beauty at its most

23. Plutarch, *Life of Antisthenes*; Erasmus, *Apophthegmata*, VII, *Antisthenes*, XIV.

24. I Samuel 10: 26, 'whose hearts God hath touched'. Adapted for the motto of her emblematic picture FRUSTRA ('in Vain') by the Protestant author Georgette de Montenay in her *Emblemes ou devises chrestiennes* (Lyons, 1571).

25. Temperance is Aristotle's *sōphrosyne* (the Mean between two vices, one of excess and one of defect) (*Nicomachaean Ethics*, II, vi, 3). This Classical virtue, as well as the four Cardinal virtues, were held to apply to Christians, though all needed completing by the three theological virtues (Faith, Hope and Charity). St Paul in Philippians 4:5 counselled, 'Let your moderation be known to all men.'

attractive. I know them both: and I am the one to say so. But it seems to me that our souls are subject in old age to ills and imperfections more insolent than those of youth. I said so when I was young, and they cast my beardless chin in my teeth. And I still say so now that my [C] grey [B] hair lends me credit. What we call wisdom is the moroseness of our humours and our distaste for things as they are now. But in truth we do not so much give up our vices as change them – for the worse, if you ask me. Apart from silly tottering pride, boring babble, prickly unsociable humours, superstition and a ridiculous concern for wealth when we have lost the use of it, I find that there are more envy and unfairness and malice; age sets more wrinkles on our minds than on our faces. You can find no souls – or very few – which as they grow old do not stink of rankness and of rot. It is the man as a whole that marches towards his flower and his fading.

[C] When I see the wisdom of Socrates and several of the circumstances surrounding his condemnation, I would venture to conclude that to some degree he connived at it and deliberately put up a sham defence, since at seventy years of age he soon had to suffer the benumbing of his splendid endowments and the clouding over of his habitual clarity.

[B] What transformations do I daily see wrought by old age in those I know. It is a powerful illness which flows on naturally and imperceptibly. You must have a great store of study and foresight to avoid the imperfections which it loads upon us – or at least to weaken their progress. I know that, despite all my entrenchments, it is gaining on me foot by foot. I put up such resistance as I can. But I do not know where it will take me in the end. Yet come what may, I should like people to know from what I shall have declined.

3. On three kinds of social intercourse

[One of the most personal of the chapters so far. The 'trois commerces' examined by Montaigne are the three forms of social intercourse which enrich his private life and make it worth living: 1) loving-friendship — even though ordinary friendships become rather insipid when judged against his perfect friendship with La Boëtie; 2) loving relationships with 'ladies', beautiful and, if possible, intelligent; 3) reading books. The one adjective common to the friends, women and books discussed here and in 'On books' is honnête *(honourable and decent). Montaigne's ideal social intercourse would engage the whole man, body and soul. By themselves none of these three fully does so, and the first two engage the body and the soul in widely differing proportions, while books hardly engage the body at all.*

Montaigne speaks of women in a gruffly humorous way, but it will be noted that the reading he would concede to them corresponds closely to what he says of his own reading in the chapter 'On books'.

There is an important insistence that sexual intercourse is more than a physical 'necessity' and so not merely a hunger to be satisfied physically without the involvement of the higher faculties.

The disease Montaigne caught from prostitutes was syphilis.]

[B] We should not nail ourselves so strongly to our humours and complexions. Our main talent lies in knowing how to adapt ourselves to a variety of customs. To keep ourselves bound by the bonds of necessity to one single way of life is to be, but not to live. Souls are most beautiful when they show most variety and flexibility. [C] Here is a testimony which honours Cato the Elder: *'Huic versatile ingenium sic pariter ad omnia fuit, ut natum ad id unum diceres, quodcumque ageret.'* [His mind was so versatile, and so ready for anything, that whatever he did you could say he was born for that alone].[1]

[B] If it was for me to train myself my way, there would be no mould in which I would wish to be set without being able to throw it off. Life is a rough, irregular progress with a multitude of forms. It is to be no friend of yourself — and even less master of yourself — to be a slave endlessly following yourself, so beholden to your predispositions that you cannot

1. Livy, XXXIX, xl.

stray from them nor bend them. I am saying this now because I cannot easily escape from the state of my own Soul, which is distressing in so far as she does not usually know how to spend her time without getting bogged down nor how to apply herself to anything except fully and intensely. No matter how trivial the subject you give her she likes to magnify it and to amplify it until she has to work at it with all her might. For this reason her idleness is an activity which is painful to me and which damages my health. Most minds have need of extraneous matter to make them limber up and do their exercises: mine needs rather to sojourn and to settle down: '*Vitia otii negotio discutienda sunt*' [We must dispel the vices of leisure by our work];[2] my own mind's principal and most difficult study is the study of itself. [C] For it, books are the sort of occupation which seduces it from such study. [B] With the first thoughts which occur to it it becomes agitated and makes a trial of its strength in all directions, practising its control, sometimes in the direction of force, sometimes in the direction of order and gracefulness, [C] controlling, moderating and fortifying itself. [B] It has the wherewithal to awaken its faculties by itself: Nature has given it (as she has given them all) enough matter of its own for its use and enough subjects for it to discover and pass judgement upon.

[C] For anyone who knows how to probe himself and to do so vigorously, reflection is a mighty endeavour and a full one: I would rather forge my soul than stock it up. No occupation is more powerful, or more feeble, than entertaining one's own thoughts – depending on what kind of soul it is. The greatest of souls make it their vocation, '*quibus vivere est cogitare*' [for them, to think is to live];[3] there is nothing we can do longer than think, no activity to which we can devote ourselves more regularly nor more easily: Nature has granted the soul that prerogative. It is the work of the gods, says Aristotle, from which springs their beatitude and our own.[4] Reading, by its various subjects, particularly serves to arouse my discursive reason: it sets not my memory to work but my judgement. [B] So, for me, few conversations are arresting unless they are vigorous and powerful. It is true that grace and beauty occupy me and fulfil me as much as or more than weight and profundity. And since I doze off during any sort of converse and lend it only the outer bark of my attention, it often happens that during polite conversation (with its flat,

2. Seneca, *Epist. moral.*, LVI, 9 (adapted).
3. Cicero, *Tusc. disput.*, V, XXXVIII, 113 (of the learned and erudite).
4. Aristotle, *Nicomachaean Ethics*, X, viii, 1178 b (referring to *theōrētikē*, contemplation, intellectual activity).

well-trodden sort of topics) I say stupid things unworthy of a child, or make silly, ridiculous answers, or else I remain stubbornly silent which is even more inept and rude. I have a mad way of withdrawing into myself as well as a heavy, puerile ignorance of everyday matters. To those two qualities I owe the fact that five or six true anecdotes can be told about me as absurd as about any man whatsoever.

Now to get on with what I was saying: this awkward complexion of mine renders me fastidious about mixing with people: I need to handpick my companions; and it also renders me awkward for ordinary activities. We live and deal with the common people; if their commerce wearies us, if we disdain to apply ourselves to their humble, common souls – and the humble, common ones are often as well-governed as the most refined [C] (all wisdom being insipid which does not adapt to the common silliness) – [B] then we must stop dealing with our own affairs and anyone else's: both public and personal business involves us with such people. The most beautiful motions of our soul are those which are least tense and most natural: and the best of its occupations are the least forced. O God! What good offices does Wisdom do for those whose desires she ranges within their powers! No knowledge is more useful. 'According as you can' was the refrain and favourite saying of Socrates, a saying of great substance.[5] We must direct our desires and settle them on the things which are easiest and nearest. Is it not an absurd humour for me to be out of harmony with the hundreds of men to whom my destiny joins me and whom I cannot manage without, in order to restrict myself to one or two people who are beyond my ken? Or is it not rather a mad desire for something I cannot get?

My mild manners, which are the enemies of all sharpness and contentiousness, may easily have freed me from the burden of envy and unfriendliness: never did man give more occasion – I do not say to be loved but certainly not to be hated? But the lack of warmth in my converse has rightly robbed me of the good-will of many, who can be excused for interpreting it differently, in a worse sense.

Most of all I am able to make and keep exceptional and considered friendships, especially since I seize hungrily upon any acquaintanceship which corresponds to my tastes. I put myself forward and throw myself into them so eagerly that I can hardly fail to make attachments and to leave

5. Cited by Xenophon (*Memorabilia*, I, iii, 3). In the Latin form *'secundum quod potes'* it lends force to Montaigne's conviction that all is not simple but *secundum quid*.

my mark wherever I go. I have often had a happy experience of this. In commonplace friendships I am rather barren and cold, for it is not natural to me to proceed except under full sail. Besides, the fact that as a young man I was brought to appreciate the delicious savour of one single perfect friendship has genuinely made the others insipid to me and impressed on my faculty of perception that (as one ancient writer said) friendship is a companionable, not a gregarious, beast.[6] I also, by nature, find it hard to impart myself by halves, with limitations and with that suspicious vassal-like prudence prescribed to us for our commerce with those multiple and imperfect friendships[7] – prescribed in our time above all, when you cannot talk to the world in general except dangerously or falsely.

Yet I can clearly see that anyone like me whose aim is the good things of life (I mean those things which are of its essence) must flee like the plague from such moroseness and niceness of humour. What I would praise would be a soul with many storeys, one of which knew how to strain and relax; a soul at ease wherever fortune led it; which could chat with a neighbour about whatever he is building, his hunting or his legal action, and take pleasure in conversing with a carpenter or a gardener. I envy those who can come down to the level of the meanest on their staff and make conversation with their own servants. [C] I have never liked Plato's advice to talk always like a master to our domestics, without jests or intimacy, whether addressing menservants or maidservants.[8] For, apart from what my own reason tells me, it is ill-bred and unjust to give such value to a trivial privilege of Fortune: the most equitable polities seem to me to be those which allow the least inequality between servants and masters.

[B] Other men study themselves in order to wind their minds high and send them forth: I do so in order to bring mine lower and lay it down. It is vitiated only when it reaches out:

> *Narras, et genus Æaci,*
> > *Et pugnata sacro bella sub Ilio:*
> *Quo Chium pretio cadum*
> > *Mercemur, quis aquam temperet ignibus,*

6. Plutarch (tr. Amyot), *De la pluralité des amis*, 103 B–C, stressing that great friendships come in pairs, not in groups.
7. The most famous prudential maxim was, 'So have a friend that he may be your enemy.' Aristotle attributes it to Bias, one of the Seven Sages of Greece. In I, 28, Montaigne attributes it to Chilon.
8. Plato, *Laws*, VI, 778 A (of slaves, not servants).

> *Quo præbente domum, et quota,*
> *Pelignis caream frigoribus, taces.*

[You sing of Aeacus' line and the wars beneath the sacred walls of Ilium: but you do not say how much I must pay for a jar of Chian wine, who will heat my water on his fire, where I shall find shelter and when I shall escape from the cold of the Pelignian mountains.][9]

Thus, just as Spartan valour needed moderating by the gentle gracious playing of flutes to calm it down in war lest it cast itself into rashness and frenzy[10] (whereas all other peoples normally employ shrill sounds and powerful voices to stir and inflame the hearts of their warriors), so it seems to me that, in exercising our minds, we for the most part – contrary to normal practice – have greater need of lead-weights than of wings, of cold repose rather than hot agitation.

Above all, to my mind, it is to act like a fool to claim to be in the know amidst those who are not, and to be ever speaking guardedly – *'favellar in punta di forchetta'* [speaking daintily, 'with the prongs of your fork']. You must come down to the level of those you are with, sometimes even affecting ignorance. Thrust forceful words and subtleties aside: when dealing with ordinary folk it is enough if you maintain due order. Meanwhile, if they want you to, creep along at ground-level. That is the stone which scholars frequently trip up over. They are always parading their mastery of their subject and scattering broadcast whatever they have read. Nowadays they have funnelled so much of it into the ears of the ladies in their drawing-rooms that, even though those ladies of ours have retained none of the substance, they look as though they have: on all sorts of topics and subjects, no matter how menial or commonplace, they employ a style of speaking and writing which is newfangled and erudite:

> *Hoc sermone pavent, hoc iram, gaudia, curas,*
> *Hoc cuncta effundunt animi secreta; quid ultra?*
> *Concumbunt docte.*

[This is the style in which they express their fears, their anger, their joy and their cares. This is the style in which they pour forth all their secrets; why, they even lie with you eruditely.][11]

9. Horace, *Odes*, III, xix, 3–8.
10. Plutarch (tr. Amyot), *Comment il faut refrener la colère*, 59F; cf. 51G–H.
11. Juvenal, *Satires*, VI, 189–91 (adapted).

They cite Plato and St Thomas Aquinas for things which the first passer-by could serve to support. That doctrine which they have learned could not reach their minds so it has stayed on their tongues. However well-endowed they are, they will, if they trust me, be content to make us value the natural riches proper to them. They hide and drape their own beauties under borrowed ones. There is great simpleness in such smothering of their own light so as to shine with borrowed rays; they are dead and buried under artifice: [C] *'De capsula totae.'* [All out of the clothes-press.][12]

[B] That is because they do not know enough about themselves: there is nothing in the whole world as beautiful; they it is who should be lending honour to art and beauty to cosmetics. What more do they want than to live loved and honoured? They have enough, and know enough, to do that. All that is needed is a little arousing and enhancing of the qualities which are in them. When I see them saddled with rhetoric, judicial astrology, logic and such-like vain and useless trash, I begin to fear that the men who counsel them to do so see it as a way of having a pretext for manipulating them. For what other excuse can I find for them?

It suffices that ladies (without our having to tell them how) can attune the grace of their eyes to gaiety, severity and gentleness; season a 'No! No!' with rigour, doubt or favour; and seek no hidden meanings in the speeches with which we court them. With knowledge like that it is they who wield the big stick and dominate the dominies and their schools.

Should it nevertheless irk them to lag behind us in anything whatsoever; should they want a share in our books out of curiosity: then poetry is a pastime rightly suited to their needs: it is a frivolous, subtle art, all disguise and chatter and pleasure and show, like they are. They will also draw a variety of benefits from history; and in philosophy – the part which helps us to live well – they will find such arguments as train them to judge of our humours and our attributes, to shield them from our deceptions, to control the rashness of their own desires, to cultivate their freedom and prolong the pleasure of this life, and to bear with human dignity the inconstancy of a suitor, the moroseness of a husband and the distress of wrinkles and the passing years. That sort of thing.[13]

That – at most – is the share of learning that I would assign to them.

---

12. Seneca, *Epist. moral.*, CXV, 2, condemning the affected style of clothes and speech of dandies.
13. Much the same reading as Montaigne likes himself (II, 10, 'On books'), though doubtless presupposing that the books are in French not Latin.

Some natures are withdrawn, enclosed and private. The proper essence of my own form lies in imparting things and in putting them forth: I am all in evidence; all of me is exposed; I was born for company and loving relationships. The solitude which I advocate is, above all, nothing but the bringing of my emotions and thoughts back to myself, restricting and restraining not my wandering footsteps but my anxiety and my desires, abandoning disquiet about external things and fleeing like death from all slavery and obligation, [C] and running away not so much from the throng of people as from the throng of affairs.

[B] To tell the truth, localized solitude makes me reach out and extend myself more: I throw myself into matters of State and into the whole universe more willingly when I am alone. In a crowd at the Louvre I hold back and withdraw into my skin; crowds drive me back into myself and my thoughts are never more full of folly, more licentious and private than in places dedicated to circumspection and formal prudence. It is not our folly which makes me laugh: it is our wisdom.

I am not by complexion hostile to the jostlings of the court: I have spent part of my life there and am so made that I can be happy in large groups provided that it be at intervals and at my own choosing. But that lax judgement I am speaking of forces me to bind myself to solitude even in my own home, in the midst of a crowded household which is among the most visited. I meet plenty of people there, but rarely those whom I love to converse with; and I reserve an unusual degree of liberty there for myself and for others. There we have called a truce with all etiquette, welcomings and escortings and other such painful practices decreed by formal courtesy. (Oh what servile and distressing customs!) Everybody goes his own way; anyone who wants to can think his own thoughts: I remain dumb, abstracted and inward-looking – no offence to my guests.

I am seeking the companionship and society of such men as we call honourable and talented: my ideal of those men makes me lose all taste for the others. It is, when you reflect on it, the rarest of all our forms; and it is a form which is mainly owed to nature. The ends of intercourse with such men are simply intimacy, the frequenting of each other and discussion – exercising our souls with no other gain. In our conversation any topic will do: I do not worry if they lack depth or weight: there is always the grace and the appropriateness: everything in it is coloured by ripe and sustained judgement mingled with frankness, goodwill, gaiety and affection. Our minds do not merely show their force and beauty on the subject of entailed property or our kings' business: they show it just as well in our private discussions together. I recognize my kind of men by their very silences or their smiles; and I perhaps discover them better at table than in their work-rooms. Hippomachus said that he could tell a good wrestler simply by seeing him walk down the street.[14]

If Erudition wants to mingle in our discussions, then she will not be rejected, though she must not be, as she usually is, professorial, imperious and unmannerly, but courting approval, herself ready to learn. We are merely seeking a pastime: when the time comes to be lectured to and preached at we will go and seek her on her throne. Let her be kind enough to come down to us on this occasion, please! For, useful and desirable as she is, I presume that if we had to we could get on quite well in her absence and achieve our effect without her. A well-endowed Soul, used to dealing with men, spontaneously makes herself totally agreeable. Art is but the register and accounts of the products of such souls.

There is for me another delightful kind of converse: that with [C] beautiful and [B] honourable women: [C] *'Nam nos quoque oculos eruditos habemus.'* [For we too have well-taught eyes.][15] [B] Though there is less here for our souls to enjoy than in the first kind, our physical senses, which play a greater part in this one, restore things to a proportion very near to the other – though for me not an equal one. But it is a commerce where we should remain a bit on our guard, especially men like me over whom the body has a lot of power. I was scalded once or twice in my youth and suffered all the ragings which the poets say befall men who inordinately and without judgement let go of themselves in such matters. It is true that I got a beating which taught me a lesson:

> *Quicunque Argolica de classe Capharea fugit,*
> *Semper ab Euboicis vela retorquet aquis.*

[Anyone in the Grecian fleet who escaped from that shipwreck on the promontory of Caphareus ever thereafter turns his sails away from the waters of Euboea.][16]

It is madness to fix all our thoughts on it and to engage in it with a frenzied singleminded passion. On the other hand to get involved in it without love or willing to be bound, like actors, so as to play the usual part expected from youth, contributing nothing of your own but your words, is indeed to provide for your safety; but it is very cowardly, like a man who would

14. Plutarch, *Life of Dion*; Hippomachas was a teacher of athletics.
15. Cicero, *Paradoxa Stoicorum*, V, 38 (the wise can appreciate objects of artistic beauty but should not be enslaved by them).
16. Ovid, *Tristia*, I, i, 83–4.

jettison his honour, goods and pleasure from fear of danger. For one thing is certain: those who set such a snare can expect to gain nothing by it which can affect or satisfy a soul of any beauty. We must truly have desired any woman we wish truly to enjoy possessing; I mean that, even though fortune should unjustly favour play-acting – as often happens, since there is not one woman, no matter how ugly she may be, who does not think herself worth loving   [C]   and who does not think herself attractive for her laugh, her gestures or for being the right age, since none of them is universally ugly any more than universally beautiful. (When the daughters of the Brahmans have nothing else to commend them, the town-crier calls the people together in the market-place expressly for them to show off their organs of matrimony to see whether they at least can be worth a husband to them.)   [B]   It follows that there is not one who fails to let herself be convinced by the first oath of devotion sworn by her suitor. Now from the regular routine treachery of men nowadays there necessarily results what experience already shows us: to escape us, women turn in on themselves and have recourse to themselves or to other women; or else they, on their side, follow the example we give them, play their part in the farce and join in the business without passion, concern or love.   [C] *'Neque affectui suo aut alieno obnoxiae'* [Beholden to no love, their own or anyone else's];[17] following the conviction of Lysias in Plato and reckoning that the less we love them the more usefully and agreeably they can devote themselves to it.   [B]   It will go as in comedies: the audience will have as much pleasure as the comedians, or more.

As for me, I no more know Venus without Cupid than motherhood without children: they are things whose essences are interdependent and necessary to each other. So such cheating splashes back on the man who does it. The *affaire* costs him hardly anything, but he gets nothing worthwhile out of it either.

Those who turned Venus into a goddess considered that her principal beauty was not a matter of the body but of the spirit: yet the 'beauty' such men are after is not simply not human, it is not even bestial. The very beasts do not desire it so gross and so earth-bound: we can see that imagination and desire often set beasts on heat and arouse them before their body does; we can see that beasts of both sexes choose and select the object of their desires from among the herd and that they maintain long affection-ate relationships. Even beasts which are denied physical powers by old age still quiver, whinny and tremble with love. We can see them full of hope

17. Tacitus, *Annals*, XIII, xlv; then, Plato, *Phaedrus*, 227 B–228 C.

and fire before copulation, and, once the body has played its part, still tickling themselves with the sweet memory of it; some we see which swell with pride as they make their departure and which produce songs of joy and triumph, being tired but satisfied. A beast which merely wished to discharge some natural necessity from its body would have no need to bother another beast with such careful preparations: we are not talking about feeding some gross and lumpish appetite.[18]

Being a man who does not ask to be thought better than I am, I will say this about the errors of my youth: I rarely lent myself to venal commerce with prostitutes, not only because of the danger [C] to my health (though even then I did not manage to escape a couple of light anticipatory doses) [B] but also because I despised it. I wanted to sharpen the pleasure by difficulties, by yearning and by a kind of glory; I liked the style of the Emperor Tiberius (who in his love-affairs was attracted more by modesty and rank than by any other quality)[19] and the humour of Flora the courtesan (who was also attracted by a dictator, a consul or a censor, delighting in the official rank of her lovers). Pearls and brocade certainly add to the pleasure; so do titles and retainers. Moreover I set a high value on wit, provided however that the body was not wanting; for if one of those two qualities had to be lacking, I must admit in all conscience that I would have chosen to make do without the wit; it has use in better things. But where love is concerned – a subject which is mainly connected with sight and touch – you can achieve something without the witty graces but nothing without the bodily ones.

Beauty is the true privilege of noblewomen.   [C]   It is so much more proper to them than ours is to us men, that even though ours requires slightly different traits, at its highest point it is boyish and beardless, and therefore confounded with theirs. They say that in the place of the Grand Seigneur males chosen to serve him for their beauty – and they are countless in number – are sent away at twenty-two at the latest.[20] [B] Reasoning powers, wisdom and the offices of loving-friendship are rather to be found in men: that is why they are in charge of world affairs.

18. Philosophy classified sexual intercourse among the physical necessities. Montaigne does not deny that it is so, but insists that sexual fulfilment is more than the physical slaking of an appetite.
19. Tacitus, *Annals*, VI, i; then a tale of Flora recounted among others by Brantôme in *Les Dames Galantes* (Deuxième Discours).
20. Guillaume Postel, *Histoire des Turcs*.

Those two forms of converse[21] depend on chance and on other people. The first is distressingly rare, the second withers with age, so they could not have adequately provided for the needs of my life. Converse with books (which is my third form) is more reliable and more properly our own. Other superior endowments it concedes to the first two: its own share consists in being constantly and easily available with its services. This converse is ever at my side throughout my life's course and is everywhere present. It consoles me in my old age and in my retreat; it relieves me of the weight of distressing idleness and, at any time, can rid me of boring company. It blunts the stabs of pain whenever the pain is not too masterful and extreme. To distract me from morose thought I simply need to have recourse to books; they can easily divert me to them and rob me of those thoughts. And yet there is no mutiny when they see that I only seek them for want of other benefits which are more real, more alive, more natural: they always welcome me with the same expression.

It is all very well, we say, for a man to go on foot when he leads a ready horse by the bridle! And our James, King of Naples, manifested a kind of austerity which was still delicate and vacillating, when, young, handsome and healthy, he had himself wheeled about the land on a bier, lying on a cheap feather-pillow, clad in a robe of grey cloth with a bonnet to match, followed meanwhile by great regal pomp with all sorts of litters and horses to hand, and by officers and noblemen.[22] 'No need to pity an invalid who has a remedy up his coat-sleeve!' All the profit which I draw from books consists in experiencing and applying that proverb (which is a very true one). In practice I hardly use them more than those who are quite unacquainted with them. I enjoy them as misers do riches: because I know I can always enjoy them whenever I please. My soul is satisfied and contented by this right of possession. In war as in peace I never travel without books. Yet days and even months on end may pass without my using them. 'I will read them soon,' I say, 'or tomorrow; or when I feel like it.' Thus the time speeds by and is gone, but does me no harm; for it is impossible to describe what comfort and peace I derive from the thought that they are there beside me, to give me pleasure whenever I want it, or from recognizing how much succour they bring to my life. It is the best protection which I have found for our human journey and I deeply pity men of intelligence who lack it. I on the other hand can accept any sort of pastime, no matter how trifling, because I have this one which will never fail me.

21. Intercourse with friends and with ladies.
22. Olivier de La March, *Mémoires*, 1561.

At home I slip off to my library a little more often; it is easy for me to oversee my household from there. I am above my gateway and have a view of my garden, my chicken-run, my backyard and most parts of my house. There I can turn over the leaves of this book or that, a bit at a time without order or design. Sometimes my mind wanders off, at others I walk to and fro, noting down and dictating these whims of mine.

[C] It is on the third storey of a tower. The first constitutes my chapel; the second, a bed-chamber with a dressing-room, where I often sleep when I want to be alone. Above that there is a large drawing-room. It was formerly the most useless place in my house: I spend most days of my life there, and most hours of each day, but I am never there at night. It leads on to quite an elegant little chamber which can take a fire in winter and agreeably lets in the light. If I feared the bother as little as the expense – and the bother drives me away from any task – I could erect a level gallery on either side, a hundred yards long and twelve yards wide, having found all the walls built (for some other purpose) at the required height. Every place of retreat needs an ambulatory. My thoughts doze off if I squat them down. My wit will not budge if my legs are not moving – which applies to all who study without books.

My library is round in shape, squared off only for the needs of my table and chair; as it curves round it offers me at a glance every one of my books ranged on five shelves all the way along. It has three splendid and unhampered views and a circle of free space sixteen yards in diameter. I am less continuously there in winter since my house is perched on a hill (hence its name) and no part of it is more exposed to the wind than that one. By being rather hard to get at and a bit out of the way it pleases me, partly for the sake of the exercise and partly because it keeps the crowd from me. There I have my seat. I assay making my dominion over it absolutely pure, withdrawing this one corner from all intercourse, filial, conjugal and civic. Everywhere else I have but a verbal authority, one essentially impure. Wretched the man (to my taste) who has nowhere in his house where he can be by himself, pay court to himself in private and hide away! Ambition well rewards its courtiers by keeping them always on display like a statue in the market-place: *'Magna servitus est magna fortuna.'* [A great destiny is great slavery.][23] They cannot even find privacy on their privy! I have never considered any of the austerities of life which our monks delight in to be harsher than the rule that I have noted in some of their foundations:

23. Seneca, *Consolatio ad Polybium*, XXVI.

to be perpetually with somebody else and to be surrounded by a crowd of people no matter what they are doing. And I find that it is somewhat more tolerable to be always alone than never able to be so.

[B] If anyone says to me that to use the Muses as mere playthings and pastimes is to debase them, then he does not know as I do the value of pleasure, [C] plaything or pastime. [B] I could almost say that any other end is laughable. I live from day to day; and, saving your reverence, I live only for myself. My plans stop there. In youth I studied in order to show off; later, a little, to make myself wiser; now I do it for amusement, never for profit. A silly spendthrift humour that once I had for furnishing myself with books, [C] not to provide for my needs but three paces beyond that, [B] so as to paper my walls with them as decorations, I gave up long ago.

Books have plenty of pleasant qualities for those who know how to select them. But there is no good without ill. The pleasure we take in them is no purer or untarnished than any other. Reading has its disadvantages – and they are weighty ones: it exercises the soul, but during that time the body (my care for which I have not forgotten) remains inactive and grows earth-bound and sad. I know of no excess more harmful to me in my declining years, nor more to be avoided.

There you have my three favourite private occupations. I make no mention of the ones I owe to the world through my obligations to the state.

5. On some lines of Virgil

[*Montaigne now breaks totally new ground. A concern for marriage and human sexuality was widespread in the Renaissance, partly because of the Reformation with its respect for marriage and the demands made on it, partly because of ferment within the Roman Catholic Church, the universities, legal and medical circles and among moralists. (A good example of such ferment in a comic setting is* The Third Book of Pantagruel *by Rabelais.) Montaigne's achievement can be compared and contrasted with that of a friend of Rabelais, the great jurisconsult Andreas Tiraquellus in his ever-expanding Latin* Laws of Marriage. *But Montaigne is partly making a general confession; partly (for the first time ever) giving a self-portrait in which the sexual drive is openly portrayed; partly showing how old age may come to terms with dwindling physical potency yet powerful erotic dreams and memories. The development of sexuality in his own time from (in Montaigne's view) the courteous chastity of his father's days to his own youth with its tolerance of the courtly service of love in extramarital love-affairs (especially between young unmarried gentlemen and married ladies) to the brutality which he believed to mark French sexuality in his declining years was doubtless (if true) one of the results of the moral collapse brought about by the Wars of Religion. Montaigne, as usual, sees men and women as body-plus-'soul' (or 'spirit' or 'mind'). Love-affairs, primarily but by no means exclusively, concern the body. The love,* amour, *which Montaigne discusses here is not* amitié, *that loving-friendship proper to marriage at its best; after his own wedding he himself was much more loyal to his marriage-vows than he had ever dreamt possible. Virgil and Lucretius lead him to stress the poetry of erotic love and to contrast and compare it with the outspoken quasi-pornographic verses of the classical Priapics and their Renaissance imitators, who included religious leaders such as Beza. The chapter is marked by statements of anti-feminism and of jaundiced views of marriage: these are in fact often humorous in ways not always clear to modern readers. Medieval and Renaissance convention often made such attitudes comic or ironical: there is much of that here; but Horace is cited: 'What can stop us from telling the truth with a laugh!' Montaigne was warned before publication that his ironies might be taken seriously. That did not worry him: this is a self-portrait and he was indeed given to irony. But while Montaigne presents men and women as a case of 'us' and 'them', he frequently gives examples of men to support a statement of allegedly female vice or virtue, and of women to exemplify allegedly masculine ones. In Rabelais or Tiraquellus, men and women are almost different creatures, their sexual drives deriving from different causes and producing different effects (men being able to control their sexuality without risk to life and health, women not). Montaigne goes back to the very passage of Plato's* Timaeus *where doctors had for a millennium and a half found justification for that conviction and quietly shows that Plato made men and women equally subject to analogous sexual drives. The conclusion of Montaigne is an arresting one: women should be allowed more freedom: men and women share a common 'mould' – both have the common form of human kind. And that is nowhere more obvious than in our sexuality.*

The element of confession in this chapter is emphasized by Montaigne's reminder that God sees through society's conventions and what are nowadays called taboos, seeing us not clad in evasive words but in the cankered nakedness of soul and body, 'with our tattered rags ripped off our pudenda'.]

[B] The more our moral thoughts are abundant and solid the more engrossing they are and oppressive. Vice, death, poverty, illness are weighty subjects and they do indeed weigh on us. We need our Soul to be instructed in the means of sustaining evils and of fighting them off, instructed too in the rules of right-living and right-believing; and we need to awaken her to practise so fine an endeavour. But in the case of a soul of the common sort this must be done with moderation and some laxity: keep her continually tensed and you drive her mad. In my youth I needed to arouse myself and counsel myself if I were to remain dutiful: liveliness and good health do not agree all that well, [C] they say, [B] with serious and sagacious discourse. Nowadays I am in a different state: the properties of old age give me too many counsels, making me wise and preaching at me. I have fallen from excessive gaiety into excessive seriousness which is more bothersome. That is why I deliberately go in for a bit of debauchery at times by employing my Soul on youngish wanton thoughts over which she can linger a while. From now on I am all too stale, heavy and ripe. Every day the years read me lectures on lack of ardour and on temperance. My body flees from excess: it is afraid of it. It is its turn now to guide my mind towards amendment of life. It is its turn now to act the professor, and it does so more harshly and imperiously. For one single hour, sleeping or waking, it never allows me to take time off from learning about death, suffering and penitence. I now defend myself against temperance as I used to do against voluptuousness. Now it is my body which pulls me back, to the point of numbness. Yet I want to be in every way master of myself. Wisdom has its excesses and has no less need of moderation than folly. So, fearing that in the intervals which my ills allow me, I may be desiccated, dried up and weighed down by wisdom –

mens intenta suis ne siet usque malis

[Lest my mind should dwell intensely on its ills][1]

1. Ovid, *Tristia*, IV, i, 4 (adapted); then, Petronius, *Satyricon*, 128.

I turn very gently aside and make my eyes steal away from such stormy, cloud-wracked skies as lie before me: which, thanks be to God, I can contemplate without terror but not without strain and effort; and I find myself spending my time recalling periods of my past youth:

> *animus quod perdidit optat,*
> *Atque in præterita se totus imagine versat*

[My mind prefers what it has lost and gives itself entirely over to by-gone memories.]

Let babes look ahead, old age behind: is that not what was meant by the double face of Janus?[2] The years can drag me along if they will, but they will have to drag me along facing backwards. While my eyes can still make reconnaissances into that beautiful season now expired, I will occasionally look back upon it. Although it has gone from my blood and veins at least I have no wish to tear the thought of it from my memory by the roots:

> *hoc est*
> *Vivere bis, vita posse priore frui.*

[To be able to enjoy your former life again is to live twice.][3]

[C] Plato tells old men to go and watch the exercises, dancing and sports of the young, to enjoy in others that beauty and suppleness of body which they have no longer and to recall to their memory the grace and privileges of those years of bloom; and he desires that they should award the victory in those sports to the young man who has given most joy and gladness to the greatest number of the old.

[B] Once upon a time I used to mark as exceptional the dark, depressing days: those days are now my routine ones; it is the ones which are beautiful and serene which are extraordinary now. I am close to the point when I shall jump for joy and accept anything which does not actually hurt as some new favour. Tickle myself I may, but I cannot force a laugh out of this vile body. I make myself delight in dream and fantasy so as to divert by ruse the chagrin of old age. But it would take a different remedy to cure it. What a feeble struggle of art against nature!

There is great silliness in extending by anticipation our human ills; I do

---

2. Janus, the god of the beginning of the year, had two faces, one looking back, the other forward (Ovid, *Fasti*, I, 345 etc.).
3. Martial, *Epigrams*, X, xxiii, 7; then, Plato, *Laws*, II, 657 D–E.

not want to be old before my time; I prefer to be old for a shorter one. I grab hold of even the slightest occasions of pleasure that I come across. I know from hearsay that there are several species of pleasure which are wise, strong and laudable; but rumour has not enough power over me to arouse an appetite for them in me. [C] I do not so much want noble, magnificent and proud pleasures as sweetish ones, easy and ready to hand: '*A natura discedimus; populo nos damus, nullius rei bono auctori*' [We are departing from what is natural, surrendering ourselves to the plebs, who are never a good guide in anything.][4]

[B] My philosophy lies in action, in natural [C] and present [B] practice, and but little in ratiocination. Would that I could enjoy tossing hazelnuts and whipping tops!

Non ponebat enim rumores ante salutem

[Not for him did common report take precedence over his welfare.][5]

As a quality, pleasure-seeking is not very ambitious; of itself it reckons it is rich enough without bringing in the prize of reputation; it likes itself more in the shadows. If a man spends time savouring the tastes of wine and sauces when he is young, we ought to give him a good hiding. There is nothing I knew or valued less. I am learning about them now, I am ashamed to say: but what else can I do? I am even more ashamed and angry at the causes which drive me to it. It is for us to act the madman over trifles: young men ought to stand to their reputation and in the best places; youth is making its way forward in the world and seeking a name: we are on our way back. [C] '*Sibi arma, sibi equos, sibi hastas, sibi clavam, sibi pilam, sibi natationes et cursus habeant; nobis senibus, ex lusionibus multis, talos relinquant et tesseras.*' [Let them have their arms, their horses, their spears and their fencing-foils; let them toss balls and swim and race: and from the many pastimes let old men choose dice and knuckle-bones.][6] [B] The very laws send us back to our homes. The least I can do on behalf of this wretched state into which my age has thrust me is to furnish it, as we do childhood, with toys and playthings: for that is what we are declining into. Wisdom and folly both will have plenty to do if they are to support and succour me alternately in disastrous old age:

4. Seneca, *Epist. moral.*, CXIX, 17.
5. Cicero, *De officiis*, I, xxiv, 84: from lines of Ennius, the ancient Latin poet. In context the word *salutem* means not 'his welfare' but 'the safety' of the State.
6. Cicero, *De senectute*, XVI, 58.

Misce stultitiam consiliis brevem.

[Mix a little brief folly in your counsels.][7]

I similarly flee from the slightest pin-pricks: those which once would have scarcely scratched me now run right through me. My mode of being is beginning to like dwelling on the pain. [C] '*In fragili corpore odiosa omnis offensio est.*' [To a frail body every shock is vexatious.][8]

[B]   *Mensque pati durum sustinet ægra nihil.*

[A mind that is ill can tolerate no hardships whatsoever.][9]

I have always been delicately sensitive to attacks of pain; I am more tender still now and in every way defenceless.

Et minimæ vires frangere quassa valent.

[The least shock will shatter a cracked vessel.]

My judgement prevents me from kicking and muttering against the indignities which Nature orders me to tolerate, but it does not stop me from feeling them. I would run from one end of the world to the other to seek a single twelve-month of gay and pleasant tranquillity: I have no other end but to live and enjoy myself. There is enough sombre and dull tranquillity for me now, but it sends me to sleep and dulls my brain: I can never be satisfied by it. If there is any man or any good fellowship of men in town or country, in France or abroad, sedentary or gadabout, whom my humours please and whose humours please me, they have but to whistle through their fingers and I'll come to them, furnishing them with 'essays' in flesh and blood.

Since it is the privilege of the mind to escape from old age I counsel it to do so with all my might: let it meanwhile sprout green and flourish, if it can, like mistletoe on a dead tree. But it is a traitor, I fear: it is so closely bound in brotherhood to the body that it is constantly deserting me to follow my body in its necessity. In vain do I try to divert it from this attachment; I set before it Seneca and Catullus and the ladies and their *dances royales*: but if its comrade has colic paroxysms it thinks it has them too! The very activities which are proper and peculiar to it cannot then

7. Horace, *Odes*, IV, xii, 27.
8. Cicero, *De senectute*, XVIII, 65.
9. Ovid, *Ex Ponto*, I, v, 18, and *Tristia*, IV, xi, 22.

raise it up: they too manifestly reek of snot. There is no alacrity about what the mind brings forth when there is none in its body at the very same time.

[C] *Magistri Nostri*[10] are wrong when they seek to explain the extraordinary transports of our spirit. Leaving aside the attribution of some of them to divine rapture, to love, to the harshness of war, to poetry, to wine, they do not allow the part played in them by good health, by boiling vigorous health, whole and idle, such as from time to time in former days my verdant years, so free from care, provided for me. That joyful fire gives rise to flashes in our spirit; they are lively and bright beyond our natural reach; they are some of our most lively enthusiasms, even though they are not the most frenzied. No wonder then if the opposite state overburdens my spirit, hammers it down and produces opposite results:

> [B] *Ad nullum consurgit opus, cum corpore languet.*

> [No task can make it struggle to its feet: it languishes with the body.][11]

Furthermore my spirit wants me to be beholden to it for its allegedly showing much less complicity in all this than is usually the practice among men. Let us at least drive away ills and hardships from our human intercourse while we are enjoying a truce:

> *Dum licet, obducta solvatur fronte senectus.*

> [So while it can, let old age smooth away the wrinkles on its brow.]

'*Tetrica sunt amoenenda jocularibus.*' [Gloomy thoughts should be made pleasant by jests.] I like the kind of wisdom which is gay and companionable; I fly from grating manners and from sourness; I am suspicious of grim faces.

> [C] *Tristemque vultus tetrici arrogantiam;*

> [The sad arrogance of a gloomy face;]

> [B] *Et habet tristis quoque turba cynaedos.*

> [And buggers too are found in groups of sombre men.]

---

10. The title of university professors, especially theologians. Here they are explaining various forms of ecstasy and rapture.
11. Pseudo-Gallus, I, 125; then, Horace, *Epodes*, XIII, 7; Bishop Caius Sollius Apollinaris (Sidonius), *Epist.*, I, ix; George Buchanan, *Joannes Baptista* (prologue); Martial, *Epigrams*, VII, lvii, 8.

[C] I wholeheartedly believe Plato when he says that great portents of the goodness or evil of a soul are easy or difficult humours. Socrates had a set expression but a serene and laughing one: it was not set as was that of the aged Crassus who was never known to laugh.[12] [B] As a quality virtue is pleasing and gay. I know that few of those who will glower at the unrestrained freedom of my writings do not have greater cause to glower at the unrestrained freedom of their thoughts. I am certainly in harmony with their sentiments: it is their eyes I offend! What a well-ordered mind that is which can gloss over the writings of Plato burying all knowledge of his alleged affairs with Phaedo, Dion, Stella and Archeanassa! 'Non pudeat dicere quod non pudeat sentire.' [Let us be not ashamed to say whatever we are not ashamed to think.][13]

[B] I loathe a morose and gloomy mind which glides over life's pleasures but holds on to its misfortunes and feeds on them – like flies which cannot get a hold on to anything highly polished and smooth and so cling to rough and rugged places and stay there; or like leeches which crave to suck only bad blood.[14] I have moreover bidden myself to dare to write whatever I dare to do: I am loath even to have thoughts which I cannot publish. The worst of my deeds or qualities does not seem to me as ugly as the ugly cowardice of not daring to avow it. Everybody is circumspect about confessing, whereas they ought to be circumspect about doing: daring to do wrong is to some extent counterweighted and bridled by the courage needed to confess it. [C] Any man who would bind himself to tell all would bind himself to do nothing which we are forced to keep quiet about. God grant that my excessive licence may draw men nowadays to be free, rising above those cowardly counterfeit virtues which are born of our imperfections, and also grant that I may draw them to the pinnacle of reason at the expense of my own lack of moderation! If you are to tell of a vice of yours you must first see it and study it. Those who conceal it from others usually do so from themselves as well: they hold that it is not sufficiently hidden if they can see it, so they disguise it and steal it from their own moral awareness. 'Quare vitia sua nemo confitetur? Quia etiam nunc in illis est; somnium narrare vigilantis est.' [Why does nobody confess his

---

12. Cicero, Tusc. disput., III, xv, 31; Ravisius Textor, Officina (for both Socrates and Crassus): Severissimi et maxime tetrici.
13. Source not identified.
14. Plutarch (tr. Amyot), De la tranquillité de l'âme, 73 H (for the flies); Du banissement, ou de l'exil, 125 AB (for the leeches).

faults? Because even now he remains within them: only after men have awakened can they relate their dreams.][15]

The body's ills become clearer as they grow bigger: we discover that what we called a sprain or a touch of rheumatism is the gout. But as the soul's ills grow in strength they are wrapped in greater obscurity: the more ill a man is, the less he realizes it. That is why the maladies of the soul need to be often probed in daylight, cut and torn from our hollow breasts by a pitiless hand. What applies to the benefactions we receive applies to the evils that we do: sometimes the only way to requite them is to acknowledge them. Is there some ugliness in our wrong-doing which dispenses us from the duty of acknowledging it?

[B]   I suffer such pains whenever I dissemble that I avoid being entrusted with another man's secret, having no mind to deny what I know. I can keep quiet about it but I cannot deny it without strain and unease. To be really able to keep a secret you need to be made that way by nature, not doing so because you are under bond. When serving princes it is not enough to keep a secret: you need to be a liar as well. To the man who inquired of Thales of Milesia whether he should deny on oath that he had been a lecher I would have replied that he should not do so, for lying has always seemed worse to me than lechery. Thales gave quite different advice, telling him to swear the oath so as to cloak a bad vice by a lesser one. Yet this counsel means not so much choosing between vices as increasing their number.[16]

Be it said *en passant* that if you present a man of conscience with the need to weigh an awkward situation against a vice he can easily strike the right bargain, but if you imprison him between two vices you oblige him to make a harsh choice – as happened to Origen who had either to commit idolatry or submit to being carnally assaulted by an ugly great Ethiopian paraded before him. He suffered the first alternative. Wrongly, it is said. So those women nowadays who protest to us that they would rather have ten lovers on their conscience than a single Mass would – by their false standards – not be making a bad choice.[17]

---

15. Seneca, *Epist. moral.*, LIII, 8; he continues: 'Similarly a confession of one's evils is proof of a healthy mind'; Montaigne then develops LIII, 6.
16. Erasmus, *Apophthegmata*, VII, *Milesii Thaletis*, VII. (Erasmus is also puzzled by this counsel.)
17. Nicephoros Callistos Xanthopoullos, *Ecclesiastical History*, V, who asserts that Origen uselessly damned his soul by this act. Montaigne compares Origen's choice to that of those women of the Reformed Church (the 'Calvinists'), who would rather consent to commit fornication than consent to the 'idolatry' of the

There may be a lack of discretion in publishing one's defects this way but there is no great danger of it becoming customary by example, for Ariston said that the winds which men most fear are those which uncover them.[18] We must truss up those silly rags which cover over our morals. Men dispatch their consciences to the brothels and regulate their appearances. Even traitors and murderers are wedded to the laws of etiquette and dutifully stick to them. Yet it is not for injustice to complain of discourtesy [C] nor for wickedness to complain of indiscretion. It is a pity that a wicked man should not also be a boor and that his vice should be palliated by politeness. Such stucco belongs rightly to good healthy walls which are worth whitening or preserving.

[B] As a courtesy to the Huguenots who damn our private auricular confession I make my confession here in public, sincerely and scrupulously. St Augustine, Origen and Hippocrates publicly admitted the error of their opinions; I do more; I include my morals.[19] I hunger to make myself known. Provided I do so truly I do not care how many know it. Or, to put it better, I hunger for nothing, but I go in mortal fear of being mistaken for another by those who happen to know my name. If a man does all for honour and glory what does he think he gains by appearing before the world in a mask, concealing his true being from the people's knowledge? If you praise a hunchback for his fine build he ought to take it as an insult. Are people talking about *you* if they honour you for valour when you are really a coward? They mistake you for somebody else. It would amuse me as much if such a person were to be gratified when men raised their caps to him, thinking that he was the master of the band when he was merely one of the retainers. When King Archelaus of Macedonia was going along the street somebody threw water over him. His entourage wanted to punish the man. 'Ah yes,' he replied, 'but he never threw it at me but at the man he mistook me for.'[20] [C] When somebody told Socrates that people were gossiping about him he said, 'Not at all. There is nothing of me in what they are saying.'[21] [B] In my case, if a man were

---

Roman Catholic mass, which was indeed often assimilated by their ministers (in Old Testament terms) to 'whoremongering after strange gods'. All theologians of all Churches agreed that physical sins are far, far less serious than spiritual ones.

18. Plutarch (tr. Amyot), *De la curiosité*, 64 C–D.

19. This may well imply that Montaigne had never read the *Confessions* of St Augustine, though he knew the *City of God* in detail.

20. Erasmus, *Apophthegmata*, V, *Archelaus*, V.

21. Diogenes Laertius, *Life of Socrates*.

to praise me for being a good navigator, for being very proper or very chaste I would not owe him a thank you. Similarly, if anyone should call me a traitor, a thief or a drunkard I would not think that it was me he attacked. Men who misjudge what they are like may well feed on false approval: I cannot. I see myself and explore myself right into my inwards; I know what pertains to me. I am content with less praise provided that I am more known. [C] People might think that I am wise with the kind of wisdom which I hold to be daft.

[B] It pains me that my *Essays* merely serve ladies as a routine piece of furniture – something to put into their *salon*. This chapter will get me into their private drawing-rooms; and I prefer my dealings with women to be somewhat private: the public ones lack intimacy and savour.

When saying our goodbyes we feel warmer affection than usual for whatever we are giving up. I am taking a last farewell of this world's sports: these are our final embraces. But now let us get round to my subject.

The genital activities of mankind are so natural, so necessary and so right: what have they done to make us never dare to mention them without embarrassment and to exclude them from serious orderly conversation? We are not afraid to utter the words *kill*, *thieve* or *betray*; but those others we only dare to mutter through our teeth. Does that mean that the less we breathe a word about sex the more right we have to allow it to fill our thoughts?

[C] It is interesting that the words which are least used, least written and the least spoken are the very ones which are best known and most widely recognized. No one of any age or morals fails to know them as well as he knows the word for bread. They are printed on each one of us without being published; they have no voice, no spelling. It is interesting too that they mean an act which we have placed under the protection of silence, from which it is a crime to tear it even to arraign it and to judge it. We dare not even flog it except by periphrasis and similitude. A criminal is greatly favoured if he is so abominable that even the laws think it illicit to touch him or to see him: he is freed by the beneficence of his condemnation and saved by its severity. Is it not the same concerning books, which become more saleable and publicized once they are suppressed? Personally I intend to take Aristotle's advice literally: he says that coyness serves as an ornament in youth and a defect in old age.[22]

22. Aristotle, *Nicomachaean Ethics*, IV, ix, 1128 b. (His term, aidōs, covers modesty, bashfulness and shamefacedness. It keeps young men in check: old men should not need it, since they should do nothing shameful.)

[B]   In the school of the Ancients – the school I cling to far more than
to the modern,   [C]   its virtues seeming greater to me and its vices less –
[B]   they preach these words at you:

> [B]   *Ceux qui par trop fuyant Venus estrivent*
> *Faillent autant que ceux qui trop la suivent.*

[Those who excessively strive to flee from Venus fail just like those who follow
her excessively.][23]

> *Tu, Dea, tu rerum naturam sola gubernas,*
> *Nec sine te quicquam dias in luminis oras*
> *Exoritur, neque fit lætum nec amabile quicquam.*

[Thou alone, O goddess, rulest over the totality of nature; without thee nothing
comes to the heavenly shores of light, nothing is joyful, nothing lovable.]

I do not know who managed to make Pallas and the Muses fall out with
Venus and chill their ardour for Cupid;[24] yet I can find no deities who
become each other more or who owe more to each other. Anyone who
removed their amorous thoughts from the Muses would rob them of the
most beauteous entertainment they provide and of the noblest subject-
matter of their works; and anyone who made Cupid lose contact with
poetry and its services would weaken him by depriving him of his
weapons. In that way we charge both the god of sexual relationships and of
tenderness, and the tutelary goddesses of elegance and justice, with the vices
of ingratitude and churlishness.

I have been struck off the roll of Cupid's attendants but not for so long
that my memory is not still imbued with his powers and his values:

> *agnosco veteris vestigia flammæ.*

[I can recognize the tracks of my former passions.][25]

There are still some traces of heat and emotion after the fever,

> *Nec mihi deficiat calor hic, hiemantibus annis*

[And let me not lack that warmth in my winter years.]

23. Plutarch (tr. Amyot), *Qu'il fault qu'un Philosophe converse avec les Princes*, 134 C;
then, Lucretius, I, 6 and 23–4.
24. Among others Joachim Du Bellay regretted that Ronsard devoted so much
time and genius to love-poetry; cf. *Regrets*, XXIII.
25. Virgil, *Aeneid*, IV, 23; then, Johannes Secundus, *Elegies*, III, 29; Tasso,
Gierusalemme liberata, XII, 63–6; Juvenal, *Satires*, VI, 196.

All gross and dried up as I am, I can still feel some lukewarm remnants from that bygone ardour:

> Qual l'alto Ægeo, per che Aquilone o Noto
> Cessi, che tutto prima il vuolse et scosse,
> Non s'accheta ei pero: ma'l sono e'l moto,
> Ritien de l'onde anco agitate è grosse.

[As the Aegean sea when the North Wind and the South have dropped, which first had whipped and churned it up, does not at once grow calm but retains the roar and surge of the waves, huge still and thrashing.]

To the best of my knowledge the powers and values of that god are found more alive and animated in poetry than in their proper essence:

> Et versus digitos habet.

> [Poetry has playful fingers too.]

Poetry can show us love with an air more loving than Love itself. Venus is never as beautiful stark naked, quick and panting, as she is here in Virgil:

> Dixerat, et niveis hinc atque hinc diva lacertis
> Cunctantem amplexu molli fovet. Ille repente
> Accepit solitam flammam, notusque medullas
> Intravit calor, et labefacta per ossa cucurrit.
> Non secus atque olim tonitru cum rupta corusco
> Ignea rima micans percurrit lumine nimbos.
> . . . Ea verba loquutus,
> Optatos dedit amplexus, placidumque petivit
> Conjugis infusus gremio per membra soporem.

[Venus fell silent; and as he hesitates she encircles him in her snow-white arms and warms him in her soft embrace. Soon he was welcoming the accustomed flame; its well-known heat struck him to the marrow and coursed through the bones of his trembling limbs. It was like unto the brilliant lightning which, with a thunder-clap, flashes through the clouds . . . He spoke to her, gave her the embraces that she yearned for, and then his limbs sought quiet repose as he lay flowing around his wife's bosom.][26]

What I find worth stressing is that Virgil in these lines portrays her as a little too passionate for a married Venus. Within that wise contract our

26. These are the lines of Virgil alluded to in the chapter heading (*Aeneid*, VIII, 387–92; 404–6). Cf. below, note 99.

sexual desires are not so madcap; they are darkened and have lost their edge. Cupid hates that couples should be held together except by himself, and only slackly comes into partnerships such as marriage which are drawn up and sustained by different title-deeds. In marriage, alliances and money rightly weigh at least as much as attractiveness and beauty. No matter what people say, a man does not get married for his own sake: he does so at least as much (or more) for his descendants, for his family. The customary benefits of marriage go way beyond ourselves and concern our lineage. That is why I like the practice of having marriages arranged at the hands of a third party rather than our own, not by our own judgement but by someone else's. How contrary all that is to amorous compacts. Moreover there is a kind of lewdness (as I think I have said already) in deploying the rapturous strivings of Love's licentiousness within such a relationship, which is sacred and to be revered.[27] Aristotle says that we should approach our wives wisely and gravely for fear lest we unhinge their reason by arousing them too lasciviously. What he says for our moral sense the doctors say for our health's sake, namely that too hot, voluptuous and unremitting a pleasure is deleterious to the sperm and impedes conception.[28] They go on to say that in the case of the kind of intercourse which is feeble by nature (as the married kind is) we should undertake it rarely, at stated intervals, so as to fill it with a just and fruitful heat,

> *quo rapiat sitiens venerem interiusque recondat.*

[by which the mare avidly seizes on Venus' seed and buries it deep inside her.][29]

I know no marriages which fail and come to grief more quickly than those which are set on foot by beauty and amorous desire. Marriage requires foundations which are solid and durable; and we must keep on the alert. That boiling rapture is no good at all.

Those who think to honour marriage by associating passion with it are like those (it seems to me) who to promote virtue hold rank to be none other than a virtue: there is some cousinship between rank and virtue but great differences as well; there is no gain in confusing their names and title-deeds: we wrong them both by confounding them that way. Noble rank is a beautiful quality and was rightly instituted; but, since it is a quality

27. Then a commonplace of traditional Christian morality.
28. Cf. Andreas Tiraquellus, *De legibus connubialibus*, XV, 23 ff.; but the reference to Aristotle is puzzling.
29. Virgil, *Georgics*, III, 137.

dependent on others and can fall to a vicious man of naught, it is well below virtue in esteem. It is a 'virtue' – if indeed it be one – which is artificial and visible, dependent on time and fortune, differing in style in various countries; it lives, yet is mortal, having no more origin than the river Nile. Genealogical and not individual, it depends on succession; it is drawn from sequency – and a feeble sequency at that! Knowledge, fortitude, goodness, beauty, riches, indeed all other qualities, are subject to communication and sharing; rank is self-devouring and of no utility in the service of others. It was explained to one of our kings that a choice had to be made between two candidates for the same office: one of them was a nobleman, the other certainly not. He commanded that they should choose, irrespective of rank, the man with the greater merit; but should they prove to be of exactly equal worth, they should in that case take rank into account. That was to assign to it its just importance. When a young unproven man asked Antigonus for the position held by his father (a valiant man who had just died), he replied: 'My friend, in such promotions I do not so much have regard for the rank of my soldiers as for their prowess.'[30]

[C] It really should not be done as it was for the office-holders of the kings of Sparta – trumpeters, minstrels and cooks – who were succeeded in their charges by their sons, no matter how ignorant they might be, taking precedence over men best skilled at the craft.[31] The people of Calicut make their nobility into a species higher than Man. Marriage is forbidden them, as is any profession but war. They can have their fill of concubines, and their women may have as many studs; jealousy is unknown between them; but it is an unforgivable crime punishable by death to lie with anyone of a different rank; they feel defiled if they are even touched by them as they go by; and since their noble state is marvellously polluted and tainted by it, they slaughter those who draw even a little too close to them; the untouchables are therefore forced to cry out at street corners as they walk along, like gondoliers in Venice, to avoid colliding. And persons of rank can order them to get out of their way whenever they want to. By such means the nobility avoid a disgrace which they consider indelible; the others avoid certain death. No stretch of time, no princely favour, no office, valour or wealth can entitle a commoner to become a nobleman. This is reinforced by their custom of forbidding marriages across trades: a woman descended from cobblers cannot marry a woodworker; and parents

30. Erasmus, *Apophthegmata*, V, *Antigonus Secundus*, IV.
31. Herodotus, VI, lx.

are under the obligation of training their sons for their father's calling –
exactly that one: no other will do. By such means they maintain permanent
distinctions in their lot.[32]

[B] A good marriage (if there be such a thing) rejects the company and
conditions of Cupid: it strives to reproduce those of loving-friendship. It
is a pleasant fellowship for life, full of constancy, trust and an infinity of
solid useful services and mutual duties. No wife who has ever savoured its
taste –

optato quam junxit lumine tæda

[whom the marriage-torch has joined with its long-desired light][33]

– would ever wish to be the beloved mistress of her husband. If she is lodged
in his affection as a wife then her lodging is far more honourable and
secure. Even when he is swept off his feet with passion for another, just ask
him whether he would prefer some disgrace to befall his wife or his
mistress; whose misfortune would grieve him more? for which of them he
desires the greater respect? In a healthy marriage such questions admit of no
doubt. The fact that one sees so few good ones is a token of its value and
price. Shape it and accept it rightly and there is no more beautiful element
in our society. We cannot do without it yet we go and besmirch it, with
the result that it is like birds and cages: the ones outside despair of getting
in: the ones inside only care to get out. [C] When Socrates was asked
whether it was more appropriate to take or not to take a wife, he replied,
'Whichever you do you will be sorry.'[34] [B] It is a contractual engagement to which can be exactly applied the proverb: Man is god or wolf to
Man. Many elements have to coincide to construct it. In our times it is
considered to be more rewarding for those with uncomplicated everyday
souls which are not so troubled by frivolity, curiosity and sloth. Roving
humours such as mine which loathe all forms of tie or bond are not so
proper for it:

Et mihi dulce magis resoluto vivere collo.

[For me too it is sweeter far to live with no chain about my neck.][35]

---

32. Montaigne's account of the Hindu caste-system is based on Simon Goulart's
Histoire du Portugal, II, iii.
33. Catullus, LXIV, 79.
34. Erasmus, *Apophthegmata*, III, *Socratica*, XL; then, *Adages*, I, I, LXIX, *Homo
homini lupus*, and I, I, LXX, *Homo homini Deus*.
35. Pseudo-Gallus, I, 61.

By my own design I would have fled from marrying Wisdom herself if she would have had me. But no matter what we may say, the customs and practices of life in society sweep us along. Most of my doings are governed by example not choice. Nevertheless I did not, strictly speaking, invite myself to the feast: I was led there, brought to it by external considerations.

There is nothing so awkward – in fact nothing at all, no matter how ugly, vitiated or repugnant – but can become bearable under certain conditions and in certain circumstances, so vain is our human situation. When I was borne into marriage I was less broken in and more recalcitrant than I am now that I have made an assay at it. And, womanizer though I am held to be, I have, in truth, more rigidly observed the laws of matrimony than I ever vowed or hoped. It is no longer the time for kicking over the traces once they have tied your legs together! We should tend our freedom wisely; but once we have submitted to the marriage-bond we must stay there under the laws of our common duty (or at least strive to). The actions of those husbands who accept the bargain and then show hatred and contempt are harsh and unjust. Equally unfair and intolerable is that fine counsel which I see passed from hand to hand among our women:

> *Sers ton mary comme ton maistre,*
> *Et t'en guarde comme d'un traistre.*

[Serve him like a master: watch him like a traitor.]

That is a challenge and a call to battle, meaning, 'Act towards him with a constrained respect, hostile and suspicious.'

I am too easy-going for such prickly designs. To tell the truth I have yet to attain to that perfect intellectual elegance and cunning which confound right and injustice and which ridicule any rule and order which may not accord with my desires. Just because I loathe superstition I do not go straightway mocking religion. Though we may not always do our duty we must always at least love and acknowledge it. [C] To take a wife without espousing her is treachery.

[B] Let us get on.

Our poet Virgil portrays a marriage full of concord and harmony, in which however there is not much fidelity. Did he mean to say that it is not impossible to surrender to the attacks of Cupid and yet nevertheless to keep a sense of duty towards one's marriage; that one may injure marriage without tearing it totally apart? [C] A valet can diddle his master without hating him!

[B]   A wife may be attracted to an unknown man by beauty, opportune-
ness and destiny – for destiny plays its role in it:

> fatum est in partibus illis
> Quas sinus abscondit: nam, si tibi sidera cessent,
> Nil faciet longi mensura incognita nervi

[The privy parts hidden in your toga are fated: if the stars forsake you, it will do
you no good to have a tool of unprecedented size][36]

– yet she may not be so totally attracted that there remain no bonds still
holding her to her husband. We are dealing with two projects which each
go their own distinct separate ways. A wife may give herself to another
man whom – not because of the state of his finances but because of his
very personality – she would never wish to marry. Few men have
married their mistresses without repenting of it.   [C]   That even applies
to the other world! What a wretched household, that of Jupiter and a wife
whom he had seduced and had enjoyed having little affairs with! That,
as the saying goes, is shitting in the basket and then plonking it on your
head.
   [B]   I have in my time seen a highly placed love-affair shamefully and
dishonourably cured by a marriage. The motives of both are quite distinct.
We can, without difficulty, love two very different and incompatible
things.
   Isocrates said that the City of Athens was pleasing in the same way as a
mistress served for love: all men took pleasure in spending their time and
walking with her, but no man loved her well enough to wed her (that is,
to make his home and habitation there).[37]
   It has angered me to see husbands hating their wives precisely because
they are doing them wrong: at very least we should not love them less
when the fault is ours; at very least they ought to be made dearer to us by
our regrets and our sympathy.
   Isocrates meant that, while the ends were different, they were in certain
circumstances not incompatible. For its part marriage has usefulness, justice,
honour and constancy: a level but more universal pleasure. A love-affair

---

36. Juvenal, Satires, IX, 32–4.
37. Isocrates, the pupil of Gorgias and the friend of Plato. I do not know what
Montaigne drew upon for his saying, unless it be a confused memory of Zeno and
Cleanthes' reasons for not becoming citizens of Athens (Plutarch tr. Amyot),
Contredicts des Stoïques, 561 F).

is based on pleasure alone: and in truth its pleasure is more exciting, lively and keen: a pleasure set ablaze by difficulties. It must have stabs of pain and anguish. Without darts and flames of desire Cupid is Cupid no longer. In marriage the ladies are so lavish with their presents that they dull the edge of our passion and desire. [C] You merely need to see the trouble that Lycurgus and Plato give themselves in order to avoid this incongruity.

[B] Women are not entirely wrong when they reject the moral rules proclaimed in society, since it is we men alone who have made them. There is by nature always some quarrelling and brawling between women and men: the closest union between us remains turbulent and tempestuous. In the opinion of our poet we treat women without due consideration. That is seen by what follows.

We realize that women have an incomparably greater capacity for the act of love than we do and desire it more ardently – and we know that this fact was attested in Antiquity by that priest who had been first a man and then a woman:

> *Venus huic erat utraque nota.*

> [He knew Venus from both angles.][38]

Moreover we have learned from their own lips such proof as in former ages was provided by an Emperor and Empress of Rome, both infamous past masters on the job: he managed to deflower ten captive Sarmatian virgins in one night, but she in one night furnished the means of five-and-twenty engagements, changing her partners according to her needs and preferences:

> *adhuc ardens rigide tentigine vulve,*
> *Et lassata viris, nondum satiata, recessit.*

[at last she retired, inflamed by a cunt stiffened by tense erections, exhausted by men but not yet satisfied.]

Then there was that plea lodged in Catalonia by a wife as plaintiff against her husband's excessively assiduous love-making: not I think because she was actually troubled by it (except within the Faith I believe in

---

38. Tiresias, who changed sex; a frequently cited example: cf. Ovid, *Metamorphoses*, III, 323; then, Juvenal, *Satires*, VI, 128–9; the Emperor was Proculus, the Empress, Messalina, the consort of Claudius. (Cf. Tiraquellus, *De legibus connubialibus*, IX, 94 for Messalina, and XV, 92 for Proculus.)

no miracles) but rather to have a pretext for pruning back and curbing the authority of husbands over their wives even in the very deed which forms the basic act of marriage, and also to show that the nagging and spitefulness of wives extend over the marriage-bed and trample under heel the sweet delights of Venus. Her husband, a really depraved brute of a fellow, made the rejoinder that even on days of abstinence he could not manage with less than ten times. Whereupon intervened that notable judgement of the Queen of Aragon: after mature deliberation in her counsel that good Queen (wishing to provide for all time an example of the moderation required in a proper marriage and a measuring-rod for temperance) ordained that it is necessary to limit and restrict intercourse to six times a day – sacrificing much of women's needs and surrendering many of their desires in order to establish a scale which would be unexacting and therefore durable and unchanging.[39] At which the doctors exclaim: 'If that is the rate assessed by a reasoned moral reformation, what must be the lusts and the appetites of women?' [C] Just think of the disparity of judgements on our appetites: Solon, the head of the school of lawgivers, with the aim of avoiding failure, sets the rate for such conjugal intimacy at three times a month.[40]

We believe all that and teach all that. And then we go and assign sexual restraint to women as something peculiarly theirs, under pain of punishments of the utmost severity. No passion is more urgent than this one, yet our will is that they alone should resist it – not simply as a vice with its true dimensions but as an abomination and a curse,[41] worse than impiety and parricide. Meanwhile we men can give way to it without blame or reproach.

Those men who have made an assay at overcoming it, employing purely material remedies to cool down the body, to weaken it and to subdue it, have adequately vouched for the difficulty, or rather the impossibility, of achieving it. Yet we men on the other hand want our wives to be in good health, energetic, radiant, buxom . . . and chaste at the same time, both hot and cold at once.

As for marriage (which has the duty, we say, of stopping them from burning)[42] it brings them but little respite given our manners: if they do

---

39. Tiraquellus, *De legibus connubialibus*, XV, 1.
40. Plutarch (tr. Amyot), *De l'amour*, 612 C; Tiraquellus, XV, 83.
41. Perhaps an echo of Leviticus 26.
42. St Paul, I Corinthians 7:9; then, Martial, *Epigrams*, XII and Diogenes Laertius, *Life of Polemaon*.

take a husband in whom the vigour of youth is still a-boil he will boast of scattering it elsewhere:

> *Sit tandem pudor, aut eamus in jus:*
> *Multis mentula millibus redempta,*
> *Non est hæc tua, Basse; vendidisti.*

[A little more propriety, please, or I'll take you to law. I paid a few thousand for your cock. It is not yours now, Bassus: you sold it to me.]

[C] And Polemon the philosopher rightly received a legal summons from his wife because he scattered on a barren field the fruitful seed he owed to her fertile one.

[B] If they take one of those broken-down husbands, there they are, fully wed yet worse off than virgins and widows. (We assume that they are furnished with all they need because they have a man about the place, just as the Romans assumed that a Vestal Virgin called Clodia Laeta had been raped simply because Caligula had made an approach to her, even though it was proved that he had done no more than that.)[43] Their needs are then not satisfied but increased, since their ardour, which would have remained calm in their single state, is awoken by contact with any male company whatsoever. That explains why those monarchs of Poland, Boleslaus and Kinge his consort, agreed together to take the vow of chastity on their very wedding-day as they lay side by side, maintaining it in the teeth of the pleasure which marriage offers: such considerations and circumstances made their chastity more meritorious.[44]

We train women from childhood for the practices of love: their graces, their clothes, their education, their way of speaking regard only that one end. Those in charge of them impress nothing on them but the face of love, if only to put them off it by continually portraying it to them. My daughter − I have no other children − is of an age when the more passionate girls are legally allowed to marry. She is slender and gentle; by complexion she is young for her age, having been quietly brought up on her own by her mother; she is only just learning to throw off her childish innocence. She was reading from a French book in my presence when she came across the name of that well-known tree *fouteau* [a beech].[45] The

---

43. Clodia Laeta was buried alive. The emperor was in fact Caracalla.
44. Jan Herburt, *Histoire des Roys de Pologne*, 1573.
45. *Fouteau* evoked *foutre*, then the usual vulgar word for 'to have sexual intercourse', a meaning almost submerged by other usages in modern French.

woman she has for governess pulled her up short rather rudely and made her jump over that awkward ditch. I let her be, so as not to interfere with women and their rules, for I play no part at all in that sort of education: feminine polity goes its own mysterious way: we must leave it entirely to them. But unless I am mistaken the company of twenty lackeys would not in half a year have imprinted on her mind an understanding of what those naughty syllables mean, how they are used and what they imply, as did that good old crone by her one reprimand and prohibition.

> *Motus doceri gaudet Ionicos*
> *Matura virgo, et frangitur artubus*
> *Fam nunc, et incestos amores*
> *De tenero meditatur ungui.*

[The marriageable maiden loves to learn the steps of the Ionic dance; she twists her limbs and from a tender age trains herself for unchaste loves.][46]

Just let them dispense with a little ceremony and become free to develop their thoughts: in knowledge of such things we are babes compared with them. Just listen to them describing our pursuit of them and our rendezvous with them. They will soon show you that we contribute nothing but what they have known and already assimilated independently of us. [C] Could Plato be right when he said that in a former existence girls had been lascivious boys![47]

[B] I happened to be one day in a place where my ear could unsuspectedly catch part of what they were saying to each other. I wish I could tell you! 'By our Lady,' I said, 'let us go, after this, and study the language of Amadis and tales in Boccaccio and Aretino so as to appear sophisticated.' What a good use of our time! There is no word, no exemplary tale and no stratagem which women do not know better than our books do. The doctrines which nature, youth and good health (those excellent schoolmasters) ceaselessly inspire in their souls are born in their veins:

> *Et mentem Venus ipsa dedit.*

[Venus herself inspired their frenzy.][48]

They do not need to learn them: they give birth to them.

---

46. Horace, *Odes*, III, vi, 21–4.
47. Cf. Plato, *Timaeus*, 42 B–C.
48. Virgil, *Georgics*, 42 B–C.

> *Nec tantum niveo gavisa est ulla columbo*
> *Compar, vel si quid dicitur improbius,*
> *Oscula mordenti semper decerpere rostro,*
> *Quantum præcipue multivola est mulier.*

[Never did white dove nor any more lascivious bird which you could name invite love's kisses with its pecking beak as much as a woman yearning for a host of men.][49]

If the ferocity of their desires were not somewhat reined in by that fear for their honour with which all women are endowed, we would all be laughing-stocks. The whole movement of the world tends and leads towards copulation. It is a substance infused through everything; it is the centre towards which all things turn. We can still read some of the ordinances made by that wise Rome of old to regulate love-affairs, as well as Socrates' precepts for the education of courtesans.[50]

> *Nec non libelli Stoici inter sericos*
> *Jacere pulvillos amant.*

[And there are little books which love to lie strewn about in silken cushions: some of them are Stoic ones.]

There are enactments among Zeno's Laws covering penetration and opening up for deflowering.[51]   [C]   I wonder what was the drift of that book by Strato the philosopher entitled *On carnal knowledge;*[52] what did Theophrastes treat of in those books of his which bore the titles *The Lover* and *On Love-affairs*; and what did Aristippus treat in his work *On Antique Delights*? What was Plato's intention in his long and vivid descriptions of the most controversial love-affairs of the day? Then there are *The Book of the Love-maker* by Demetrius Phalereus; *Cliniasor, or the Lover Raped*, by Heraclides of Pontus; *On Marriage: or How to make Children*, and another, *On Master and Lover*, by Antisthenes; *On Amorous Exploits* by Ariston; two by Cleanthes, *The Art of Loving* and *On Love*; *Lovers' Dialogues* by Sphaerus;

49. Catullus, LXVI, 125–8.
50. For the laws of Rome, cf. Tiraquellus, *De legibus connubialibus*, XIII, 12 ff. But I do not know what Socrates' precepts were. Then, Horace, *Epodes*, VIII, 15–16 (adapted).
51. Cf. Plutarch (tr. Amyot), *Propos de table*, III, question 6, p. 384 C (blaming Zeno).
52. All these books are lost. (Cf. Tiraquellus, *De legibus connubialibus*, XV, 91.)

The Fable of Jupiter and Juno, intolerably pornographic, by Chrysippus, with his *Fifty Lecherous Letters*. And I am not counting the writings of philosophers who followed the Epicurean School. [B] In bygone days fifty gods were tied to this job; and a nation was discovered who kept male and female prostitutes in their temples all ready to be enjoyed, so as to lull to sleep the lusts of those who came to worship there. [C] '*Nimirum propter continentiam incontinentia necessaria est; incendium ignibus extinguitur.*' [Sexual excesses are doubtless needed for sexual restraint, as fire is doused by fire.][53]

[B] In most parts of the world that member of our male bodies was turned into a god.[54] In a single province some peeled off the skin and consecrated part of it as an oblation while others offered up their sperm and consecrated it. In another province the youths bored holes through it in public, prised gaps between the flesh and the skin and then threaded through them the longest thickest skewers which they could stand. They afterward made a bonfire of those skewers as an offering to their gods, and if they were stunned by the violence of the ferocious pain they were reckoned unchaste and lacking in vigour. Elsewhere the revered symbol of the most hallowed magistrate was the sexual organ; and in many processions an effigy of it was borne in pomp, in honour of a variety of gods. During the feast of Bacchus the ladies of Egypt wore such an effigy about their necks; it was of wood, exquisitely fashioned and as big and heavy as each could manage. In addition the statue of their god had a carved member which was bigger than the rest of his body. The married women near my place twist their headscarves into the shape of one to revel in the enjoyment they derive from it; then on becoming widows they push it back and bury it under their hair. The wisest of the Roman matrons were granted the honour of offering crowns of flowers to the god Priapus; when their maidens came to marry, they were required to squat over its less decent parts.[55]

I even wonder whether I have not seen in my own lifetime practices recalling similar devotions: what was the sense of that silly flap on our fathers' flies which you can still see worn by our Swiss guards?[56] Why do

---

53. Tertullian (known to Montaigne only at second-hand?); cf. Villey, *Sources et évolution des 'Essais' de Montaigne*, p. 256.
54. Cf. Coelius Richerius Rhodiginus, *Antiquae lectiones*, VII, xvi, *Dionysiorum ritus. Qui sunt phalle. Phallogogia Sacra.*
55. St Augustine, *City of God*, VI, ix; note of J. L. Vives on this passage.
56. The codpiece.

we parade our genitals even now behind our loose-breeches, and, what is worse, cheat and deceive by exaggerating their natural size? [C] I would like to believe that such styles of clothing were invented in better and more moral times so that people should in fact not be deceived, each man gallantly rendering in public an account of his endowments; the more primitive peoples do still display it somewhere near its real size. In those days they supplied details of man's working member just as we give the measurements of our arm or foot.

[B] That fine fellow who when I was young castrated so many beautiful ancient statues in his City so as not to corrupt our gaze,[57] [C] following the counsel of that other fellow in Antiquity:

> *– Flagitii principium est nudare inter cives corpora*

[Baring the body among our citizens is the beginning of shameful deeds] –

[B] ought to have recalled that (as in the mysteries of the *Bona Dea* in which all signs of the male were banned) nothing is achieved unless you also geld horses, donkeys and finally everything in nature:

> *Omne adeo genus in terris hominumque ferarumque,*
> *Et genus æquoreum, pecudes, pictæque volucres,*
> *In furias ignemque ruunt.*

[All species on earth, both man and brute, and dwellers in the sea, and flocks and painted birds, all dash madly into the flames of desire.][58]

[C] The gods, says Plato, have furnished men with a rebellious and tyrannical member which tries to force everything to submit to its appetite like an animal on the rampage. So too the women have an animal, avid and greedy: if you deny it in due season, it becomes frenzied and can brook no delay; its own raging madness is inhaled into their bodies; it stops all respiration by blocking up the tubes, so causing hundreds of kinds of illness which last until after it has drawn inwards with its breath the product of our common desire and scattered it broadcast, planting it in the ground of the womb.[59]

57. Just possibly Pope Paul IV; then, Cicero, *Tusc. disput.*, IV, xxxiii, 70, citing Ennius.
58. Virgil, *Georgics*, III, 242–4. *Bona Dea* (the Good Goddess) was worshipped by Roman women as the patron of fertility and chastity. No man might enter her temple.
59. Plato made both men and women subject to sexual organs which were deaf to reason. Ancient medical writers isolated the women in this context, with the result

[B]   Now that lawgiver of mine[60] ought also to have recalled that it is perhaps a more chaste and fruitful practice to bring women to learn early what the living reality is rather than to allow them to make conjectures according to the licence of a heated imagination: instead of our organs as they are their hopes and desires lead them to substitute extravagant ones three times as big.   [C]   And one man I know lost out by exposing his somewhere while they were still unready to perform their most serious task.

[B]   What great harm may be done by those graffiti of enormous genitals which boys scatter over the corridors and staircases of our royal palaces! From them arise a cruel misunderstanding of our natural capacities. [C]   Who knows whether that explains why Plato decreed (following the practice of other states with sound institutions) that both men and women, old and young, should appear naked before each other during exercises in the gymnasia?[61]   [B]   Those Indian women who see their men in the nude have at least cooled off their visual senses.

[C]   The women of that great Kingdom of Pegu wear below the belt nothing but a kirtle slit in the front and so tight that, no matter what formal decency they may seek to preserve, they reveal everything they have got with every step they take. They maintain that this fashion was created in order to attract the men to them and to distract them from that taste for males to which that nation has entirely surrendered. Yet it could be said that they lose more than they gain and that a complete hunger is sharper than one where at least the eyes are satisfied.[62]   [B]   Livia said, moreover, that to a moral woman a naked man means no more than a statue.   [C]   And the women of Sparta, who as wives were more virginal than our daughters, saw every day the young men of their city take everything off for their exercises; they themselves were not very particular

---

that women – but not men – were, on the highest medical authority, for centuries thought to be subject to an irrational 'animal' (the womb), the frustrations of which could cause a form of hysteria ('womb-disease') all but indistinguishable from death. Rabelais makes this medical belief central to his doctor's judgement on women in the *Tiers Livre du Pantagruel*, XXXII. Montaigne, unlike Rabelais, shows great independence of mind by going back to Plato himself (*Timaeus*, 91 B–C), so putting men and women essentially on a par, sexually speaking, both being subject to the irrational demands of their genitalia (which were defined in both sexes as 'animals' in accordance with criteria long accepted by doctors).
60. The 'fine fellow' who put fig leaves on the Roman statues.
61. Plato, *Republic*, V, 452.
62. G. Balbi, *Viaggio del' Indie*, then, for Livia, Dion Cassius, *Life of Tiberius*.

about keeping their thighs covered as they went about, believing, says Plato, that they were sufficiently veiled with virtue without needing a 'virtue-guard'.[63] Yet Saint Augustine is our witness for there once having been men who attributed such wonderful powers of temptation to nudity that they doubted whether, at the General Resurrection, women would rise again as women rather than in our sex so as not to go on tempting us in that blessed state![64]

[B] In short we bait and lure women by every means. We are constantly stimulating and overheating their imagination. And then we gripe about it.

Let us admit it: there is hardly one of us who is not more afraid of the disgrace which comes to him from his wife's immorality than from his own; hardly one who is not so amazingly charitable that he worries more about his dear wife's conscience than he does about his; hardly one who would not rather commit theft and sacrilege – or that his wife were a murderer or a heretic – than to have her be no chaster than he is.

And our women would much rather volunteer to go and earn their fees in the law-courts or their reputations on the battlefield than to have to mount so difficult a guard in the midst of idle pleasures. Our women can see, can they not, that there is no merchant, no barrister, no soldier who does not drop what he is doing so as to hurry and get on with 'the job' – no porter or cobbler either, however weary with toil or faint with hunger.

> *Num tu, que tenuit dives Achœmenes,*
> *Aut pinguis Phrygiœ Mygdonias opes,*
> *Permutare velis crine Licinniœ,*
>   *Plenas aut Arabum domos,*
>
> *Dum fragrantia detorquet ad oscula*
> *Cervicem, aut facili sœvitia negat,*
> *Quœ poscente magis gaudeat eripi,*
>   *Interdum rapere occupet?*

[Would you really exchange – even for all the wealth of Achaemenes or all the riches of Mygdon, King of fertile Phrygia, or the treasure-boxes of Araby – a

63. The *vertugade* (farthingale) was a structure worn beneath the skirts. Obviously, it 'got in the way'. Montaigne therefore derives *vertugade* from '*virtue-guard*'.
64. St Augustine, *City of God*, XXII, xvii; St Paul (Romans 8:29) teaches that God will raise Christians from the dead to be 'conformed to the image of His Son'. Augustine denies that this means that all Christians, male and female, will arise again as males.

single one of Licinnia's tresses when she bends her neck towards you for a fragrant kiss or when, with sweet severity, she denies what she in fact desires far more than you do, and will soon be snatching from you?][65]

[C]   We do not weigh the vices fairly in our estimation. Both men and women are capable of hundreds of kinds of corrupt activities more damaging than lasciviousness and more disnatured. But we make things into vices and weigh them not according to their nature but our self-interest: that is why they take on so many unfair forms. The ferocity of men's decrees about lasciviousness makes the devotion of women to it more vicious and ferocious than its characteristics warrant, and engages it in consequences which are worse than their cause.

[B]   I am not even sure that the campaigns of Caesar and Alexander surpass the stern resolve of a beautiful young woman, brought up our way, in the light of society's social norms and battered by numerous examples to the contrary, who, in the midst of hundreds of unending and forceful suitors yet remains pure. No attaining so bristles with difficulties as her abstaining; nor is any more active. I think it easier to keep on a suit of armour all your life than to keep a maidenhead. And so the vow of virginity is the noblest of all the vows and also the harshest.   [C]   As Saint Jerome says, 'Diaboli virtus in lumbis est.' [The Devil's power is in the loins.][66]

[B]   We have certainly assigned to the ladies the most exacting and arduous of human duties and we let them have all the glory. It ought to serve them as a singular goad to help them stubborn it out that this is a subject in which they can challenge that vain pre-eminence in virtue and valour which men claim over them and can trample it underfoot. If they take care over it, they will find that not only are they most highly thought of but also better loved. No gentleman abandons his suit because he is refused, provided that the refusal is based on chastity not on preference for another. In vain do we swear oaths and make menaces and lamentations. We lie. We love them all the better for it. There is no lure like wise conduct when not brusque and glowering. There is cowardice and a lack of feeling in stubbornly continuing despite loathing and contempt: but when up against a constant and virtuous resolve mingled with an appreciative good-will it is an exercise fit for a noble and magnanimous soul.

65. Horace, Odes, II, xii, 21–8 (the text is corrected from the posthumous printed editions of Montaigne).
66. St Jerome, Contra Jovinianum, II – a work so rhetorically hostile to marriage that Erasmus prefaced it with an 'Antidote'.

They can, up to a point, show their appreciation of our courtship and make us realize that in all honour they do not disdain us. [C] For that rule which ordains that they must detest us because we worship them and hate us because we love them is indeed cruel, if only for the hardship it causes. Why should ladies not lend an ear to our requests and offers of service provided we do not go beyond the bounds of propriety, and why do we go on assuming that their doing so suggests some inner licentiousness of thought? A Queen in our own days wittily said that to exclude such advances was a sign of frailty and an indication of one's own levity, adding that no lady who had not been tempted could boast of her chastity.

[B] The boundaries of honour are by no means so narrowly drawn. There are means of being relaxed and showing some initiative without infringing them. Along its frontiers there is a stretch of neutral territory where a woman is free to show some discretion. If a man has been able to pursue her honour and to bring it to bay in its own corner of its fortress, then he is a silly fellow if he is not satisfied with his fortune. The prize of victory is valued for its difficulty. Do you want to know what impact your courtship and your merits have had on her heart? Measure it by her morals. Some women grant much who grant little: it is entirely in relation to the will of the one who grants it that we judge her gratitude for a kindness. The other attributes which apply to love's favours are fortuitous and are deaf and dumb. That little which one lady grants you costs her more than it costs her companions to grant you her all. If rarity is worth esteeming in anything it must be so in this case: do not consider the smallness of the favour but the small number of those who receive it. Money is valued according to its stamp and hallmark. Whatever some men may be brought to say by frustration and bad judgement at the height of their distress, truth and virtue always regain the advantage.

I have known ladies whose reputation was unjustly compromised over a long period but who, without careful planning, were later restored to the unanimous esteem of mankind by their constancy alone. Everybody is sorry and denies what he once believed. After being young women who were just a little suspect they now hold the foremost rank among good and honoured noblewomen. When someone said to Plato, 'They are all gossiping about you,' he said, 'Let them. I will so live that I will compel them to change their style.'[67] But apart from the fear of God and the winning of

67. Source unknown. Cf. (not very close!) Plutarch (tr. Amyot), *Comment on pourra recevoir utilité de ses ennemis*, 110 EF.

the prize of so rare a glory (which must incite women to protect themselves) the corrupt state of our century drives them to do so; and if I were in their place there is nothing I would not do rather than commit my reputation to such dangerous hands. In my day the pleasure of telling of an affair (a pleasure scarcely less delightful than having one) was conceded only to such as had one single faithful friend; nowadays the most usual talk at table and when men get together turns to boasting about favours received and the secret bounties of the ladies, who really do show abject baseness of mind to allow such tender gifts to be thus cruelly hunted, grabbed and plundered by men so ungrateful, so indiscreet and so inconstant.

It is our exaggerated and improper harshness towards this vice which gives birth to jealousy, the most vain and turbulent distemper which afflicts our human souls:

> *Quis vetat apposito lumen de lumine sumi?*

[Whatever stops us lighting one torch from another's light?][68]

> *Dent licet, assidue, nil tamen inde perit.*

[They can go on giving, on and on: they lose nothing in the process.]

Jealousy and Envy her sister seem to me to be the most absurd of the bunch. About Envy I can say virtually nothing: that passion which is portrayed as so powerful and violent has no hold on me (and I thank her for it). As for Jealousy, I know her – by sight at least. Beasts can feel it too. When the shepherd Crastis fell in love with a nanny-goat her billy charged him while he lay asleep, butting his head and smashing it.[69]

We have raised the temperature of jealousy's fevered climax, following in that some of the Barbarian nations. The better educated nations have been touched by jealousy – that is reasonable – but not caught away by it:

> *Ense maritali nemo confossus adulter*
> *Purpureo stygias sanguine tinxit aquas.*

[There, never did adulterer stain with his blood the waters of Styx while he lay pierced by a husband's sword.][70]

Lucullus, Caesar, Pompey, Antony, Cato and other fine men were all cuckolds and knew it: they never made a commotion about it. In those

68. Ovid, *Ars amandi*, III, 93; then a verse from the *Priapeia*.
69. A tale related, after Aelianus, by Coelius Richerius Rhodiginus, *Antiquae Lectiones*, XXV, xxxii.
70. Johannes Secundus, *Elegiae*, I, vii, 71–2.

days there was only one man who died of distress over it: Lepidus; and he was a fool:[71]

> *Ah! tum te miserum malique fati,*
> *Quem attractis pedibus, patente porta,*
> *Percurrent mugilesque raphanique.*

[Ah! You wretched man caught out on the job! They will bind your legs together and stuff mullet and Greek radishes up your back passage.]

But when that god in our poet[72] surprised one of his comrades lying with his wife he was satisfied with exposing them both to shame;

> *atque aliquis de Diis non tristibus optat*
> *Sic fieri turpis!*

[but one of the other gods, not the most severe, wished he was shamed as well!]

And that did not stop him from being inflamed by the sweet kisses she gave him as she lamented that, for so little a thing, she had begun to doubt his love for her:

> *Quid causas petis ex alto, fiducia cessit*
> *Quo tibi, diva, mei?*

[Why, my goddess, do you seek such far-fetched arguments? Have you lost your faith in your husband?][73]

More. She begs him a favour for one of her bastards –

> *Arma rogo genitrix nato*

[I, a mother for her son, am begging you for his armour]

– and it is generously granted to her, Vulcan speaking honourably of Aeneas:

> *Arma acri facienda viro.*

[Arms must be forged for such a man.]

71. Plutarch, *Life of Pompey* (Lepidus intercepted a love-letter and died of grief); then, Catullus, XV, 17–19. (For this use of mullet to punish adulterers, cf. Juvenal, *Satires*, X, 317.)
72. Vulcan, in the verse of Virgil cited, p. 271; then, Ovid, *Metamorphoses*, IV, 187–8.
73. Virgil, *Aeneid*, VII, 395–6; then, VIII, 383; VIII, 441.

Humane kindness surpassing humankind! And I do agree that we can leave such excessive bounty to the gods.

Nec divis homines componier æquum est

[Nor is it right to compare men to deities.][74]

As for the confounding of children, [C] apart from the fact that the gravest of lawgivers want it and legislate for it in their republics,[75] [B] it does not affect the women, yet it is precisely in them that jealous passion is somehow more at home.

Sæpe etiam Juno, maxima cælicolum,
Conjugis in culpa flagravit quotidiana.

[Even Juno, the greatest goddess among the dwellers in heaven, feels the scourge of jealousy over her consort's daily wrongs.][76]

When jealousy seizes hold of the feeble, defenceless souls of such women it is pitiful to see how it bowls them over and cruelly tyrannizes them. It slips into them, under the title of loving affection: but as soon as it gets possession of them, those same causes which served as a basis for benevolence now serve as a basis for deadly hatred. [C] Of all the spiritual illnesses, jealousy is the one which has more things which feed it and fewer things which cure it. [B] The manly virtue, the health, the merit and the reputation of their husbands then kindle the flames of their wives' maleficent frenzy:

Nullæ sunt inimicitiæ, nisi amoris, acerbæ.

[No hatreds so bitter than those of love.][77]

It is a feverish passion which turns all that is beautiful in them ugly and corrupts what is good; in a jealous woman, no matter how chaste and thrifty she may be as a wife, there is nothing which does not reek of bitterness and savagery. It is an insane perturbation which drives them to the other extreme, to the contrary of what causes it.

An interesting example of this was a man called Octavius in Rome. After lying with Pontia Posthumia, his delight in it so increased his love that he persistently begged her to marry him. When he could not win her

---

74. Catullus, LXVIII, 141.
75. Above all, Plato and, presumably, those who follow him.
76. Catullus, LXVIII, 138–9.
77. Propertius, II, viii, 3.

over, his extreme love hurled him headlong into deeds of most cruel and mortal hatred; and he killed her.[78]

Similarly the regular symptoms of this kind of love-sickness are domestic discord, plottings and conspiracies –

> *notumque furens quid fœmina possit*
>
> [we all know what a woman's rage can do][79]

– and a fury which is all the more gnawing for being compelled to justify itself by loving affection.

Now the duty of chastity is wide-ranging. What is it that we want women to bridle? Their wills? But the will is a seductive and active quality: it is too quick to let itself be restrained. Supposing their dreams sometimes so hold them in pawn that they cannot redeem them? It is not in their power to protect themselves from sexual desire and lust – not even perhaps in the power of Chastity herself: she is a woman. So if our sole concern is with their will, where do we stand? Just think of the press of assignations if a man were to have the privilege of being borne on wings (with no eyes to see him and no tongue to gossip) to the lap of every woman who would have him!

[C] The Scythian women used to poke out the eyes of all their slaves and prisoners of war in order to avail themselves of them more freely and secretly.[80]

Oh, what a mad advantage lies in the opportune moment! If anyone were to ask me what is the first quality needed in love I would reply: knowing how to seize an opportunity. It is the second and the third as well. It is the factor which can achieve anything. I have often lacked good fortune but also occasionally lacked initiative. God help those who can mock me for it! In our days you need to be more inconsiderate – which our young men justify under the pretence of ardour; but if women looked into it closely they would find that it arises rather from lack of respect. I myself devoutly feared to give offence and am always inclined to respect whomever I love. Besides in this sort of business if you remove the respect

---

78. Tacitus, *History*, IV, xliv.

79. Virgil, *Aeneid*, V, 6.

80. A misunderstanding of Herodotus, IV; cf. Plutarch (tr. Amyot), *Que la vertu se peult enseigner et apprendre*, 399: the Scythian women blinded slaves to stop them from stealing milk. (Montaigne had certainly read this passage, the following sentence of which concerning Iphicrates he used in I, 40 'Reflections on Cicero'.)

you dowse the lustre. I like a lover to play the timid youth serving his lady. Not in this situation precisely but in other ones, I do have something of that awkward shyness which Plutarch speaks of;[81] the course of my life has been in varying ways bespattered and harmed by it. It is a quality which ill becomes my overall character: but then, what are we but dissension and discord?

I am as sensitive about giving a refusal as receiving one, and my eyes show it. It so weighs on me to weigh on others that when duty forces me to assay the intentions of a man in a matter of doubt which could cost him some bother I hold back and skimp it. But if it concerns my own interests – [C] though Homer says truly that in a beggar shyness is a stupid virtue[82] – [B] I usually charge a third person to blush in my stead. I find it equally difficult to deny those who ask a service of me: I have occasionally had the will to refuse but not the capacity.

It is therefore madness to assay restraining [C] so blazing [B] a desire, so natural to women. And when I hear them boasting that their very wills are coldly chaste and virginal I laugh at them: that really is backing away too far. It may still not be credible, but there is at least some appearance of plausibility in the case of a toothless old hag or a young girl wasted by consumption. But women who are still alive and breathing worsen the terms of the bargain by saying so, since ill-advised excuses serve as accusations. Like one of the gentlemen in my neighbourhood who was suspected of impotence:

> *Languidior tenera cui pendens sicula beta*
> *Nunquam se mediam sustulit ad tunicam.*

[whose tiny dagger, drooping like a flabby parsnip, never stuck halfway up his underwear.][83]

Two or three days after his wedding, to prove his masculinity he went about boasting that he had ridden his wife twenty times the previous night. That was cited later to convict him of absolute ignorance and to annul the marriage.

Besides, those women are saying nothing worthwhile: for where there is no struggle there is neither continence nor virtue. 'That is true,' they should say, 'but I have no intention of giving way.' The very saints put it thus.

---

81. Plutarch sees it as the sign of a good marriage (*Les preceptes de mariage*, 146 A).
82. Homer, *Odyssey*, XVII, 347, cited by Plato (*Charmides*, 161 A).
83. Catullus, LXVII, 21–2.

I am of course talking of women who seriously boast of their cold chastity and indifference, who keep a straight countenance and want us to believe what they say. For when they put on a studied countenance (with eyes which belie their looks) and make their profession with cant phrases which imply the contrary to what they say, I like that. I am the obedient servant of naïve frankness: nevertheless I cannot refrain from saying that, unless it is absolutely innocent and childlike, it does not become a lady and is inappropriate to courtship: it at once slips into provocativeness. Women's affectations and grimaces deceive only idiots. Lying is then in the seat of honour: it is a diversion which brings us to the right truth through the wrong door.

Now if we cannot bridle their thoughts, what is it we want from women? Action? But plenty of their actions which corrupt chastity escape the knowledge of others:

> *Illud sæpe facit quod sine teste facit.*

> [She often does it without testes to testify.][84]

Such actions as we fear the least are perhaps the most to be feared: silent sins are the worst:

> *Offendor mæcha simpliciore minus.*

> [A straightforward whore offends me less.]

[C] And then there are actions by which women can lose their maidenheads without their maidenhood – and, what is more, without their knowing it: '*Obstetrix, virginis cujusdam integritatem manu velut explorans, sive malevolentia, sive inscitia, sive casu, dum inspicit, perdidit.*' [Sometimes the obstetrician while examining with her fingers whether the hymen is intact, has ruptured it – by ignorance or malice or bad luck.][85] Some maidens have lost their maidenhead while feeling for it: others have ruptured it while out riding.

[B] We could never delimit precisely what are the actions we forbid to them. We must frame our law in vague general terms.

The very ideal which men forge of their chastity is ridiculous: among the most extreme models of it that I know are Fatua the wife of Faunus,

---

84. Martial, *Epigrams*, VII, lxi, 6; then, VI, vii, 6.
85. St Augustine, *City of God*, I, xviii (stressing that modesty is a matter of the mind not the body).

who after her wedding never let herself be seen by any man whatever, and the wife of Hiero, who never realized that her husband's breath stank, thinking that it was a quality common to all men.[86]

To satisfy us they have to be invisible and insensate.

So now let us admit that the crucial element in judging this duty in women lies mainly in the intention. There have been husbands who have suffered adultery not only without feeling reproach or hostility for their wives but specifically bound to acknowledge their virtue. Many a woman who loved her honour more than her life has nevertheless prostituted herself to the insane lusts of a deadly enemy in order to save her husband's life, doing for him what she would never have done for herself. This is not the place to dwell on such *exempla*. They are too splendid and sublime to be rehearsed in the light of this chapter: let us keep them for a nobler place.

[C] But to give some examples here which do shine with a more vulgar light, are there not wives who daily lend their bodies to others solely to help on their husbands – and with their express command and pandering? In ancient times, for ambition's sake, Phaulius of Argos offered his wife to King Philip;[87] so too when Galba was entertaining Maecenas to dinner he noticed that his wife and his guest were beginning to ogle and to make signs and advances to each other, so he slipped down on his cushions and acted like a man heavy with sleep in order, for hospitality's sake, to lend a hand to their arrangements. And he let this be known, not without some elegance: for when the wine-steward ventured to reach out for the wine-jars on the table he shouted: 'Can you not see, you dolt, that I have only fallen asleep for Maecenas?'

[B] A woman may behave loosely yet have a will which she has reformed more than another whose conduct is hidden by a more orderly appearance: just as we know of women who complain that they were dedicated to chastity before the age of discretion, I know of some who sincerely complain that, before the age of discretion, they were dedicated to debauchery. Vicious parents may be the cause, or the force of necessity which is a cruel counsellor.

In the East Indies, although chastity is singularly valued there, custom

---

86. Fatua's case was a commonplace; Plutarch tells of Hiero's wife (*Comment on pourra recevoir utilité de ses ennemis*, 111 D–E). So does Tiraquellus, *De legibus connubialibus*, IV, 1.

87. Plutarch (tr. Amyot), *De l'amour*, 606 E–F; then, for Galba, 606 D–E and Erasmus, *Apophthegmata*, VI, *Varie mixta*, LVIII.

suffers a married woman to give herself to any man who presents her with an elephant – and not without glory for being so highly prized.[88]

[C] A man of good family, Phaedo the philosopher, when his country of Elis was captured, professionally prostituted his youthful beauty (as long as it lasted) to anyone who would pay for it, so as to earn his living.[89] And Solon, they say, was the first legislator in Greece to give women the right to provide for the necessities of life at the expense of their modesty, a practice which Herodotus however says was accepted earlier by several polities.

[B] Then what do we hope to gain from such painful disquiet: for however justified the jealousy we still have to see whether that passion enraptures us to any purpose! Is there one man who believes that he is clever enough to buckle up his women?

> *Pone seram, cohibe; sed quis custodiet ipsos*
> *Custodes? Cauta est, et ab illis incipit uxor!*

[Lock her up; shut her in. But who will guard your guardians? Your wife is clever: she will start with them!]

In so ingenious a century any occasion will suffice.

Curiosity is always a fault; here it is baleful. It is madness to want to find out about an ill for which there is no treatment except one which makes it worse and exacerbates it; one the shame of which is spread abroad and augmented chiefly by our jealousy; one which to avenge means hurting our children rather than curing ourselves. You wither and die while hunting for such hidden truth. How wretched are those husbands in my days who manage to find out!

If the man who warns you of it does not also at once supply a remedy and his help, his warning is noxious, deserving your dagger more than if he called you a liar. We mock the husband who cannot put things right no less than the one who knows nothing about it. Cuckoldry has an indelible stamp: once a man is branded with it he has it for ever; chastising cuckoldry emphasizes it more than the defect. A fine thing to tear our private misfortunes from the shadow of doubt and trumpet them abroad like tragedians on the trestles – especially misfortunes which hurt only when they are related. Marriages and wives are called good not because they *are* good but because they are not talked about.

---

88. Flavius Arrian, *Alexander the Great*, VII.
89. The usual accounts say Phaedo was compelled to do so (cf. Aulus Gellius, *Attic Nights*, II, xviii, 1). Then, cf. for Solon, Coelius Richerius Rhodiginus, *Antiquae lectiones*, XIV, iv, and Juvenal, *Satires*, VI, 347–8.

We should use our ingenuity to avoid making such useless discoveries which torture us. It was the custom of the Romans when returning home from a journey to send a messenger ahead to announce their arrival to their womenfolk so as not to take them unawares. That is why there is a certain people where the priest welcomes the bride and opens the proceedings on the wedding-night to remove from the groom any doubts and worries about whether she came to him virgin or already blighted by an *affaire*.[90]

'Yes. But people talk!' I know a hundred men who are cuckolds yet honoured and not unrespected. A decent man is sympathized with for it, not discredited by it. See to it that your misfortune is smothered by your virtue, so that good folk curse the cause of it and the man who wrongs you trembles to think of it.

And then who is never gossiped about for this, from the least to the greatest?

> *Tot qui legionibus imperitavit, . . .*
> *Et melior quam tu multis fuit, improbe, rebus!*

[Even the general who commanded all those legions . . . and was a far better man than you, you reprobate!][91]

When so many honourable men have been included in this opprobrium in your presence, do you think you are spared elsewhere?

'But even the ladies will laugh at me!' Well, what do they laugh at nowadays more readily than a peaceful, orderly marriage?   [C]   Each one of you has cuckolded somebody: and Nature is ever like, alternating and balancing accounts.   [B]   The frequency of this misfortune ought by now to have limited its bitter taste: why, it will soon be customary.

In addition that wretched misery is one you cannot even tell anyone about:

> *Fors etiam nostris invidit questibus aures.*

[Even Fortune refuses to listen to our woes.][92]

For what friend can you dare to confide your worries to? Even if he does not laugh at you, will he not be put on the track and shown how to join in the kill?

---

90. Plutarch (tr. Amyot), *Demandes des choses Romaines*, IX, 462 B–L; S. Goulart, *Hist. générale des Indes*, in which the priests are called *Piates*.
91. Lucretius, III, 1041 (adapted) and III, 1039.
92. Catullus, LXIV, 170.

[C] Wise men keep secret both the sweets of marriage and its bitter-nesses. For a talkative man like me, of all the distressing disadvantages of marriage one of the principal is the fact that custom has made it indecorous and obnoxious to discuss with anyone whatever all that we know and feel about it.

[B] It would be a waste of time to give women the same advice in order to make jealousy distasteful to them. Their essence is so pickled in suspicion, vanity and curiosity that you must not hope to do so by legitimate means. They often cure this infirmity by a species of well-being which is more to be feared than the malady. Just as there are magic spells which can only remove an evil by loading it on to someone else, so too wives readily pass this fever of jealousy on to their husbands, once they themselves have lost it.

All the same, to tell the truth, I do not know whether one can ever suffer anything worse than their jealousy: it is the most dangerous of their characteristics, as the head is of the anatomy. Pittacus said that every man has his curse: his was his wife's bad temper; if it were not for that he would think himself entirely happy. Seeing that so just, so wise, so valiant, so great a man should feel the whole state of his life corrupted by it, it must indeed be a grievous clog.[93] So what are we to do about it, little men like us!

[C] The Senate of Marseilles[94] was right to accede to the request of a husband for permission to kill himself so as to escape his wife's petulance, for it is an evil which can never be removed except by removing the whole limb: you can make no worthwhile arrangement with it except by fleeing from it or putting up with it: both are fraught with difficulties. [B] That man knew what he was talking about, it seems to me, who said that a good marriage needs a blind wife and a deaf husband.[95]

We also need to ensure that the great and intense harshness of the obligations which we lay on women should not produce two results hostile to our ends: namely, that it does not whet the appetites of their suitors nor make the wives more ready to surrender. As for the first point, by raising the value of a redoubt we raise the value of conquering it and the desire to do so. May not Venus herself cunningly have raised the cost of her merchandise by making the laws pimp for her, realizing that it is a silly

93. Plutarch (tr. Amyot), *De la tranquillité de l'ame et de l'esprit*, 72 C.
94. Cf. II, 3, 'A custom of the Isle of Cea', p. 406.
95. Erasmus, *Apophthegmata*, VIII, *Alphonsus Aragonum Rex*, IV, commented upon in Montaigne's sense.

pleasure for anyone who does not enhance it by imagination and by buying it dear?

In short, as Flaminius' host said, 'it is all pork with different sauces.'[96] Cupid is a mischievous god: his sport is to wrestle with loyalty and justice; glory for him means clashing his strength against all others' strength, all rules yielding to his.

> *Materiam culpæ prosequiturque suæ.*

[He is always hunting for occasion to do wrong.][97]

And as for my second point, would we be cuckolded less often if we were less afraid of being so, thus conforming to the complexion of women? For interdicts provoke and incite them.

> *Ubi velis, nolunt; ubi nolis, volunt ultro.*

[What you want they don't: what you don't, they do.]

> *Concessa pudet ire via.*

[They feel disgraced if they go the way we permit them.]

What better interpretation can we find for the case of Messalina? At the start she cuckolded her husband in secret, as one does; but as she carried on her affairs too easily because of her husband's dull unawareness, she suddenly felt contempt for that practice. So there she was being openly courted, acknowledging her lovers, welcoming them and granting her favours in sight of everyone. She was determined that he should know of it. When that dull brute could not even be aroused by all that (so rendering her pleasures weak and insipid by his excessive complaisance, which seemed to permit them and to legitimize them) what else could she do? Well, one day when her husband was out of the City, she – the consort of an Emperor alive and in good health, at noon, in Rome the theatre of the world, with public pomp and festivity – married Silius, the man she had long since enjoyed.

Does it not appear that either she had set herself on the road to becoming chaste because of the indifference of her husband, or else that she had sought another husband who would stimulate her desire by his jealousy [C] and excite her by standing up to her?

[B] However, the first trouble she had to face was also her last. That

---

96. Plutarch (tr. Amyot), *Dicts notables des anciens Roys . . .*, 203 B.
97. Ovid, *Tristia*, IV, i, 34; then, Terence, *Eunuch*, IV, viii, 43 and Lucan, *Pharsalia*, II, 446.

brute of hers did wake up with a start. You often get the worst treatment
from such dozing dullards. Experience has shown me that such excessive
tolerance once it bursts apart produces the harshest of vengeances, for then
wrath and frenzy fuse into one and fire their whole battery during the first
assault;

> *irarumque omnes effundit habenas.*
>
> [it looses anger's every rein.][98]

He put her to death, together with a large number of those who were in
complicity with her, even including some who had had no option, having
been driven to her marriage-bed with leathern scourges.

What Virgil sings of Venus and Vulcan, Lucretius sings more fittingly of
stolen joys between her and Mars:

> *belli fera mœnera Mavors*
> *Armipotens regit, in gremium qui sæpe tuum se*
> *Rejicit, æterno devinctus vulnere amoris:*
> *Pascit amore avidos inhians in te, Dea, visus,*
> *Eque tuo pendet resupini spiritus ore:*
> *Hunc tu, diva, tuo recubantem corpore sancto*
> *Circunfusa super, suaveis ex ore loquelas*
> *Funde.*

[Mars, mighty in arms, ruler of the savage works of war, now wounded by an
everlasting wound of love, flees to thy bosom. He feeds his eyes on thee with
gaping lips, O goddess, his breath now hanging on thy mouth. While he rests
upon thy sacred body as it flows around him, pour from thine own lips, O
goddess, thy sweet complaints.][99]

When I chew over those words, *rejicit, pascit, inhians*, and then *molli fovet,
medullas, labefacta, pendet, percurrit*, and Lucretius' noble *circunfusa* mother
to Virgil's elegant *infusus*, I feel contempt for those little sallies and verbal
sports which have been born since then. Those fine poets had no need for

98. Virgil, *Aeneid*, XII, 499. The standard source about Messalina is Tacitus, XI,
xvi–xvii. She is given as an example of 'prodigious lust' by Tiraquellus and,
indeed, by almost everyone.
99. Lucretius, I, 33–40. The first three of the following Latin words are from
Lucretius, and so is *pendet*. The rest are from the lines of Virgil which are alluded
to in the title of this chapter and cited above (cf. p. 271). Montaigne believed that
Lucretius' use of the word *circunfusa* (literally 'poured like water around' the body
of Mars in a close embrace) was imitated by Virgil when he used *infusus* in a
similar sense.

smart and cunning word-play; their style is full, pregnant with a sustained and natural power. With them not the tail only but everything is epigram: head, breast and feet. Nothing is strained. Nothing drags. Everything progresses steadily on its course: [C]   *'Contextus totus virilis est; non sunt circa flosculos occupati.'* [The whole texture of their work is virile: they were not concerned with little purple passages.][100]   [B]   Here is not merely gentle eloquence where nothing offends: it is solid and has sinews; it does not so much please you as invade you and enrapture you. And the stronger the mind the more it enraptures it. When I look upon such powerful means of expression, so dense and full of life, I do not conclude that it is said well but thought well. It is the audacity of the conception which fills the words and makes them soar: [C]   *'Pectus est quod dissertum facit.'* [It is the mind which makes for good style.][101]   [B]   Nowadays when men say judgement they mean style, and rich concepts are but beautiful words.

Descriptions such as these are not produced by skilful hands but by having the subject vividly stamped upon the soul. Gallus writes straightforwardly because his concepts are straightforward. Horace is not satisfied with some superficial vividness; that would betray his sense; he sees further and more clearly into his subject: to describe itself his mind goes fishing and ferreting through the whole treasure-house of words and figures of speech; as his concepts surpass the ordinary, it is not ordinary words that he needs. Plutarch said that he could see what Latin words meant from the things which they signified.[102] The same applies here: the sense discovers and begets the words, which cease to be breath but flesh and blood.   [C]   They signify more than they say.   [B]   Even the weaker brethren have some notion of this: when I was in Italy I could express whatever I wanted to say in everyday conversation, but for serious purposes I would not have dared to entrust myself to a language which I could neither mould nor turn on my lathe beyond the common idiom. I want to add something of my own.

What enriches a language is its being handled and exploited by beautiful minds – not so much by making innovations as by expanding it through more vigorous and varied applications, by extending it and deploying it. It is not words that they contribute: what they do is enrich their words, deepen their meanings and tie down their usage; they teach it unaccustomed rhythms, prudently though and with ingenuity.

100. Seneca, *Epist. moral.*, XXXIII, 1.
101. Quintilian, X, vii, 15.
102. Plutarch, *Life of Demosthenes*.

That such a gift is not vouchsafed to everybody can be seen from many of the French authors of our time. They are bold enough and proud enough not to follow the common road; but their want of invention and power of selection destroys them. All we can see is some wretched affectation of novelty, cold and absurd fictions which instead of elevating their subject batter it down. Provided they are clad in new-fangled apparel they care nothing about being effective. To seize on some new word they quit the usual one which often has more sinew and more force.

In our own language there is plenty of cloth but a little want of tailoring. There is no limit to what could be done with the help of our hunting and military idioms, which form a fruitful field for borrowing; locutions are like seedlings: transplanting makes them better and stronger. I find French sufficiently abundant but not sufficiently [C] tractable and [B] vigorous. It usually collapses before a powerful concept. If you are taut as you proceed, you can often feel it weakening and giving way under you; in default your Latin comes to your aid – and Greek to the aid of others.

It is hard for us to perceive the power of some of the words I have just selected because use has somewhat cheapened their grace, and familiarity has made it commonplace. So too in our vulgar tongue there are some excellent expressions whose beauty is fading with age and metaphors whose colour is tarnished by too frequent handling. But by that they lose nothing of their savour for a man who has a good nose for them; nor does it detract from the glory of those ancient authors who were (as seems likely) the first to shed such lustre on those words.

Erudite works treat their subjects too discreetly, in too artificial a style far removed from the common natural one. My page-boy can court his lady and understands how to do so. Read him Leone Ebreo and Ficino: they are talking about him, about what he is thinking and doing. And they mean nothing to him![103] I cannot recognize most of my ordinary emotions in Aristotle: they have been covered over and clad in a different gown for use by the schoolmen. Please God they know what they are doing! If I were in that trade, [C] just as they make nature artificial, I would make art natural.[104]

---

103. Authors of treatises on Renaissance Platonic love: Ficino, *Commentary on Plato's Symposium*; Leone Ebreo (Judah Abravanel), *Dialogues of Love*.
104. '88: trade, I would *treat art as naturally as I could*. Let us . . .
   Allusions follow to Pietro Bembo, *Gli Asolani* and Mario Equicola, *On the Nature of Love*: two more Renaissance Platonists.

[B]   Let us skip over Bembo and Equicola.

When I am writing I can well do without the company and memory of my books lest they interfere with my style. Also (to tell the truth) because great authors are too good at beating down my pretensions: they dishearten me. I am tempted to adopt the ruse of that painter who, having wretchedly painted a portrait of some cocks, forbade his apprentices to let any natural cock enter his workshop.[105]   [C]   And to lend me some lustre I would need to adopt the device of Antinonides the musician[106] who, whenever he had to perform, arranged that, either before him or after him, his audience should have their fill of some bad singers.   [B]   But I cannot free myself from Plutarch so easily. He is so all-embracing, so rich that for all occasions, no matter how extravagant a subject you have chosen, he insinuates himself into your work, lending you a hand generous with riches, an unfailing source of adornments. It irritates me that those who pillage him may also be pillaging me: [C]   I cannot spend the slightest time in his company without walking off with a slice of breast or a wing.

[B]   For this project of mine it is also appropriate that I do my writing at home, deep in the country, where nobody can help or correct me and where I normally never frequent anybody who knows even the Latin of the Lord's Prayer let alone proper French. I might have done it better somewhere else, but this work would then have been less mine: and its main aim and perfection consists in being mine, exactly. I may correct an accidental slip (I am full of them, since I run on regardless) but it would be an act of treachery to remove such imperfections as are commonly and always in me. When it is said to me, or I say to myself: 'Your figures of speech are sown too densely'; 'This word here is pure Gascon'; 'This is a hazardous expression' – I reject no expressions which are used in the streets of France: those who want to fight usage with grammar are silly – 'Here is an ignorant development'; 'Here your argument is paradoxical'; 'This one is too insane';   [C]   'You are often playing about; people will think that you are serious when you are only pretending':   [B]   'Yes,' I reply, 'but I correct only careless errors not customary ones. Do I not always talk like that? Am I not portraying myself to the life? If so, that suffices! I have achieved what I wanted to: everyone recognizes me in my book and my book in me.'

---

105. Plutarch (tr. Amyot), *Comment on peult discerner le flatteur d'avec l'amy*, 49 H.
106. Or rather, *Antigenides*. Cf. Coelius Richerius Rhodiginus, *Antiquae Lectiones*, XV, x.

Now I have a tendency to ape and to imitate: when I took up writing verse – I wrote it exclusively in Latin – it always manifestly betrayed who was the last poet I had been reading; and some of my earliest essays are somewhat redolent of others' work. [C] When in Paris I talk rather differently than at Montaigne. [B] Anyone I look at with attention easily stamps something of his on me. Whatever I contemplate I make my own – a silly expression, a nasty grimace, a ridiculous turn of speech. Faults, even more so: as soon as they strike me they cling to me and will not leave me unless shaken off; I have more often been heard using swear-words from conformity than by complexion.

[C] Such imitation kills, like that of those monkeys terrifying in strength and size which King Alexander had to confront in a certain country in India.[107] He would have found it hard to get the better of them, but they showed him the way to do so by their tendency to imitate everything they saw being done. This inspired those who were hunting them to put on their boots, tying many knots in the laces, while the monkeys looked on; then to deck themselves in headgear with dangling nooses and to pretend to daub their eyes with bird-lime. And so those poor creatures were led to their doom by their apish complexions: they too daubed themselves with bird-lime, tied themselves in knots and garotted themselves. Yet the talent for cleverly imitating intentionally the words and gestures of another is no more in me than in a tree-stump. When I swear my own way it is always 'By God' – which is the most direct of all the oaths. They say that Socrates used to swear 'By dog'; Zeno 'By goats' (the same exclamation used today by the Italians, *Cappari*); Pythagoras, 'By air and by water'.

[B] I am marked so easily by surface impressions that, having *Sire* or *Your Majesty* [C] thoughtlessly [B] on my lips for three days in a row, those terms slip out a full week later instead of *Your Excellency* or *My Lord*. And any expression which I have fallen into saying in jest or for fun I will say the following day seriously. That is why I am loath to write on well-trodden topics: I am afraid I might treat them with another man's substance. All topics are equally productive to me. I could write about a fly! (God grant that the topic I now have in hand be not chosen at the behest of a will which is as light as a fly's.) I may begin with any subject I please, since all subjects are linked to each other.

But what displeases me about my soul is that she usually gives birth

107. Diodorus Siculus, XVII, xxv.

quite unexpectedly, when I am least on the lookout for them, to her profoundest, her maddest ravings which please me most. Then they quickly vanish away because, then and there, I have nothing to jot them down on; it happens when I am on my horse or at table or in bed – especially on my horse, the seat of my widest musings.

When speaking I have a fastidious zeal for attention and silence if I am in earnest; should anyone interrupt me he stops me dead. On journeys the very exigencies of the roads cut down my conversation; moreover I most often journey without the proper company for sustained conversation, which enables me to be free to think my own thoughts. What happens is like what happens to my dreams: during them I commend them to my memory (for I often dream I am dreaming); next morning I can recall their colouring as it was – whether they were playful or sad or weird – but as for all the rest, the more I struggle to find it the more I bury it in forgetfulness. It is the same with those chance reflections which happen to drop into my mind: all that remains of them in my memory is a vague idea, just enough to make me gnaw irritably away, uselessly seeking for them.

Well now, leaving books aside and talking more simply and plainly, I find that sexual love is nothing but the thirst for the enjoyment of that pleasure   [C]   within the object of our desire, and that Venus is nothing but the pleasure of unloading our balls;[108] it becomes vitiated by a lack either of moderation or discretion:[109] for Socrates love is the desire to beget by the medium of Beauty.[110]

[B]   Reflecting as I often do on the ridiculous excoriations of that pleasure, the absurd, mindless, stupefying emotions with which it disturbs a Zeno or a Cratippus,[111] that indiscriminate raging, that face inflamed with frenzy and cruelty at the sweetest point of love, that grave, severe, ecstatic face in so mad an activity,   [C]   the fact that our delights and our waste-matters are lodged higgledy-piggledy together;   [B]   and that its highest

108. '95: balls, *analogous to the pleasure which Nature vouchsafes to us when we are unloading other organs of ours;* it becomes. . .
  Montaigne's word for balls, *vases*, represents the Latin word *vas (tool)* used in this sense in the Priapics and, for example, by Plautus, *Poenulus* IV, ii.
109. Aristotle, *Nicomachaean Ethics*, II, ii, 1104 a ff.
110. Plato, *Symposium*, 203 ff.
111. Zeno, the founder of the Stoic School; Cratippus, the Peripatic who taught the son of Cicero; both admitted the effects of terrifying emotion: cf. St Augustine, *City of God*, IX, iv.

pleasure has something of the groanings and distraction of pain, I believe [C] that what Plato says is true: [B] Man is the plaything of the gods[112] –

> *quænam ista jocandi*
> Sævitia!

[what a ferocious way of jesting!]

– and that it was in mockery that Nature bequeathed us this, the most disturbing of activities, the one most common to all creatures, so as to make us all equal, bringing the mad and the wise, men and beasts, to the same level.

When I picture to myself the most reflective and the most wise of men in such postures, I hold it as an effrontery that he should claim to be reflective and wise; like the legs on a peacock, they humble pride;

> *ridentem dicere verum*
> Quid vetat?

[what can stop us telling the truth with a laugh?][113]

[C] Those who reject serious opinions in the midst of fun are, it is said, like the man who refuses to venerate the statue of a saint because it wears no drapery.

[B] We eat and drink as the beasts do, but those activities do not hamper the workings of our souls. So in them we keep our superiority over the beasts. But that other activity makes every other thought crawl defeated under the yoke; by its imperious authority it makes a brute of all the theology of Plato and a beast of all his philosophy. Everywhere else you can preserve some decency; all other activities accept the rules of propriety: this other one can only be thought of as flawed or ridiculous. Just try and find a wise and discreet way of doing it! Alexander said that he acknowledged he was a mortal because of sleep and this activity: sleep stifles and suppresses the faculties of our souls; the 'job' similarly devours and disperses them.[114] It is indeed a sign of our original Fall, but also of our inanity and ugliness. On the one hand Nature incites us to it, having attached to this desire the most noble, useful and agreeable of her labours: on the other hand she lets us condemn it as immoderate and flee it as indecorous, lets us blush at it and recommend abstaining from it.

---

112. Plato, *Laws*, VII, 803 E and I, 644 D; then, Claudius Claudianus, *In Eutropium*, I, 24.
113. Horace, *Satires*, I, i, 24.
114. Tiraquellus, *De legibus connubialibus*, XV, 63–4.

[C]   Are we then not beasts to call the labour which makes us bestial?

[B]   In their religions all peoples have several similarities which coincide, such as sacrifices, lights, incense, fastings, offertories and, among others, the condemnation of this act. All their opinions come to it, not to mention the widespread practice of cutting off the foreskin [C] which is a punishment for it. [B] Perhaps we are right to condemn ourselves for giving birth to such an absurd thing as a man; right to call it an act of shame and the organs which serve to do it shameful. [C] (It is certain that mine may now properly be called shameful and wretched.)

The Essenes whom Pliny mentions were maintained for several centuries without wet-nurses or swaddling-clothes by the arrival of outsiders who, attracted by the beauty of their doctrines, constantly joined them. An entire people risked self-extermination rather than engage in woman's embraces, risked having no successors rather than create one.[115] It is said that Zeno lay with a woman only once in his entire life; and that that was out of politeness, so as not to seem to have too stubborn a contempt for that sex.[116]

[B]   No man likes to be in on a birth: all men rush to be in on a death. [C]   To unmake a human being we choose an open field in broad daylight: to make one, we hide away in a dark little hollow. When making one we must hide and blush: but glory lies in unmaking one, and it produces other virtues. One act is unwholesome: the other, an act of grace, for Aristotle says that in his country there is a saying 'To do a man a favour', which means to kill him.[117] The Athenians showed those two activities to be equally blemished when they were required ritually to purge the island of Delos and to seek reconciliation with Apollo: within its coasts they forbade both childbirth and burial:[118]

[B]   *Nostri nosmet pœnitet.*

[We are embarrassed by our very selves.]

---

115. The Essenes forbade procreation, depending on proselytes to continue their community (Pliny, V, xvii).
116. Diogenes Laertius, *Life of Zeno.*
117. Plutarch (tr. Amyot), *Demandes des choses Romaines*, 469 A: not a general statement, but Aristotle's gloss on a term in a peace-treaty between the Arcadians and the Spartans.
118. Diodorus Siculus, XII, xvii; then, Terence, *Phormio*, I, iii, 20.

'88: poenitet. *We condemn in hundreds of ways the circumstances of our being.* There are . . .

[C]   We regard our very being as vitiated.

[B]   There are some nations where they hide to eat. I know one lady (among the greatest) who shares the opinion that chewing distorts the face, derogating greatly from women's grace and beauty; when hungry she avoids appearing in public. And I know a man who cannot tolerate watching people eat nor others watching him do so: he shuns all company even more when he fills his belly than when he empties it.   [C]   In the Empire of the Grand Turk you can find many men who, to rise above their fellows, never allow themselves to be seen eating a meal; they eat but once a week; they slash and disfigure their faces and limbs and never talk to anyone – ['95] fanatics   [C]   all – folk who believe they are honouring their nature by defacing it; who pride themselves on their contempt; who seek to make themselves better by making themselves worse.

[B]   What a monstrosity of an animal,[119] who strikes terror in himself,   [C]   whose pleasures are a burden to him and who thinks himself a curse.   [B]   Those there are who hide their existence –

Exilioque domos et dulcia limina mutant

[They give up their homes and domestic delights to go into exile][120]

– stealing away from the sight of other men; they shun health and happiness as harmful and inimical qualities. There are not merely several sects but whole peoples for whom birth is a curse, death a blessing. [C]   And some there are who loathe the sunlight and worship the darkness.

[B]   We show our ingenuity only by ill-treating ourselves: that is the real game hunted by the power of our mind –   [C]   an instrument dangerous in its unruliness.

[B]   *O miseri! quorum gaudia crimen habent.*

[O pitiful men, who hold their joys a crime.]

Alas,   wretched   Man,   you   have   enough   [C]   necessary   [B] misfortunes[121] without increasing them by inventing others. Your condition is wretched enough already without making it artificially so. You

119. '88: What a *disnatured* animal . . .
   (Cf. the similar change in note 121.)
120. Virgil, *Georgics*, II, 511.
121. Pseudo–Gallus, I, 180.
   '88: enough *natural* misfortunes . . . ('Necessary' misfortunes are those entailed by the human condition and its *necessitates*.)

have uglinesses enough which are real and of your essence without fabricating others in your mind. [C] Do you really think that you are too happy unless your happiness is turned to grief? [B] Do you believe that you have already fulfilled all the necessary duties in which Nature involves you and that, unless you bind yourself to new ones, Nature is [C] defective and [B] idle within you? You are not afraid to infringe her universal and undoubted laws yet preen yourself on your own sectarian and imaginary ones: the more particular, [C] uncertain and [B] controverted they are, the more you devote your efforts to them. [C] The arbitrary laws of your own invention – your own parochial laws – engross you and bind you: you are not even touched by the laws of God and this world. [B] Just run through a few *exempla* of that assertion: why, all your life is there.

Those lines of our two poets,[122] treating sexual pleasure as they do with reserve and discretion, seem to me to reveal it and throw a closer light upon it. Ladies cover their bosoms with lace-work; priests similarly cover many sacred objects; painters paint shadows in the pictures to emphasize the light; and it is said that the sun and wind beat down more heavily on us when deflected than when they come direct. When that Egyptian was asked, 'What are you carrying there, hidden under your cloak?' he gave a wise reply: 'It is hidden under my cloak so that you should not know what it is.'[123] Nevertheless some things are hidden in order to reveal them more.

Just listen to this man writing more openly:

> *Et nudam pressi corpus adusque meum.*
>
> [Nude against my body did I press her.][124]

I can feel him gelding me!

Let Martial, as he does, pull up Venus' skirts: he does not succeed in revealing her all that completely. The poet who tells all, gluts us and puts us off: the one who is timid about expressing his thoughts leads us in our thoughts to discover more than is there. There are revelations in that sort of modesty; especially when, as they do, they half-open such a beautiful highway for our imagination. Both that act and its portrayal should savour of theft.[125]

122. Virgil and Lucretius, cited earlier.
123. Plutarch (tr. Amyot), *De la curiosité*, 64 C.
124. Ovid, *Amores*, I, v, 24.
125. As, for example, in 'stolen' kisses.

For the Spaniard and the Italian sex-love is more timid and respectful, more coy and less open: I like that. (In ancient times someone or other wished that his throat was as long as the neck of a crane so as to have more time to taste what he was swallowing.[126] Such a wish is more appropriate to this hasty and headlong pleasure, especially for natures such as mine whose fault is to be too quick.) For them, so as to stop its flight and to let it expand itself on preliminaries, everything serves as a grace and reward: a loving glance, a bow of the head, a word, a gesture.

Would anyone who could actually dine on the smell of roast beef not be making a fine saving?[127] Well, this is a passion which mingles very little essential solids with plenty of vanity and feverish madness: we should reward it and treat it accordingly. Let us instruct our ladies how to make themselves valued and esteemed, to keep us waiting and to be sweet deceivers. We French always make our last attack the first: there is always that impetuosity of ours.[128] If only our ladies were to string out love's favours, offering them retail, then each one of us, according to his worth and merit, would get a scrap even in our pitiful old age. A man who only enjoys enjoying a woman, a man who only wins if he takes the lot and who, in hunting, only likes the kill, is not made for joining our sect. The more the steps the greater the height, and the more the rungs the greater the honour, of that ultimate bastion. We should take delight in being conducted there as through splendid palaces, by varied portals and corridors, long and pleasant galleries and many a winding way. Such stewardship would turn to our advantage; there we would linger and love longer: without hope and desire we no longer achieve anything worthwhile. Women should infinitely fear our overmastery and entire possession. Their position is pretty perilous once they have totally thrown themselves on the mercy of our faith and constancy; those virtues are rare and exacting; as for the women, as soon as we have them, they no longer have us:

> *postquam cupidæ mentis satiata libido est,*
> *Verba nihil metuere, nihil perjuria curant.*

126. Aristotle, *Nicomachaean Ethics*, III, x, 1118a; Aristophanes, *The Frogs*, 934.
127. Allusion to a famous legal tale related by Rabelais (*Tiers Livre*, TLF, xxxvii, after Tiraquellus, *De legibus connubialibus*, XI, 5): a chef complained that a poor man was savouring the smell of his roast beef: a fool, called in to judge, ordered the smell to be paid by the jangle of coins.
128. An ancient Roman gibe against the Gauls (referring to military not amorous ventures): Erasmus, *Apophthegmata*, VI, *Varie mixta*, CIII.

[as soon as eager longing is satisfied, our minds fear not for their pledged word nor care about perjury.][129]

[C]   A young Greek called Thrasonides was so in love with love that, having won his lady's heart, he refused to enjoy her so as not to weaken, glut and deaden by the joy of lying with her that unquiet ardour in which he gloried and on which he fed.

   [B]   Foods taste better when they are dear. Think how far kisses, the form of greeting peculiar to our nation, have had their grace cheapened by availability: Socrates thought they were most powerful and dangerous at stealing our hearts.[130] Ours is an unpleasant custom which wrongs the ladies who have to lend their lips to any man, however ugly, who comes with three footmen in his train.

> *Cujus livida naribus caninis*
> *Dependet glacies rigetque barba:*
> *Centum occurrere malo culilingis.*

[Cold leaden snot drips from his dog-like conk and bedews his beard. Why, I would a hundred times rather go and lick his arse.][131]

And we men gain little from it: for as the world is made we have to kiss fifty ugly women for every three beauties. And for the delicate gullets of men of my age, a bad kiss outweighs a good one.

   In Italy they play the swooning suitor even with women who sell their favours. They defend themselves thus: there are degrees in enjoying a woman; by such courtship they want to obtain for themselves the fullest enjoyment of all. Such women sell only their bodies; their wills cannot be up for sale: they are too free, too autonomous. It is her will that the Italians are after, they say. And they are right. What must be courted and ensnared is the will. I am horrified by the thought of a body given to me but lacking love. To me such raging madness is analogous to that of the boy who sullied with his love that beautiful statue of Venus sculpted by Praxiteles, or to that of the Egyptian madman who was inflamed with love for the corpse of a dead woman he was embalming while wrapping it in its shroud, and who gave rise to the law subsequently proclaimed in Egypt that the corpses of beautiful young women and of women of noble families

129. Catullus, LXIV, 147–8; then, Diogenes Laertius, *Life of Zeno*.
130. Platonic theories of mutual love held that by kissing one another lovers exchange souls and so literally 'live in' each other. Ficino had made such a belief current during the Renaissance.
131. Martial, *Epigrams*, VII, cxv, 10–12.

should be kept for three days before being handed over to those whose task it was to bury them. Periander acted more horrifyingly still when he prolonged his conjugal love (itself most proper and legitimate) by enjoying his departed wife Melissa.[132]

[C] And was Luna's humour not clearly lunatic when, being unable to enjoy in any other way her beloved Endymion, she went and put him to sleep for several months, feasting herself on the enjoyment of a boy who never stirred but in her dreams?[133]

[B] I claim that we are similarly loving a body deprived of soul and sensation when we make love to one without its agreement and desire. All enjoyings of women are not the same. Some are thin and languid: hundreds of causes other than tenderness can obtain that privilege from women. It is not in itself a sufficient proof of affection: deceiving can be found in that as in anything else; sometimes they only set about it with one cheek of their arse:

> *tanquam thura merumque parent:*
> *Absentem marmoreamve putes.*

[as cool as though preparing an offertory of incense and wine; you would think she was somewhere else, or made of marble.][134]

Some ladies I know would rather lend you 'that' than their carriage: it is the only way they know how to converse. You need to see whether your company pleases them for some other end also (or, as does some hulking great stable-boy, only for 'that'), and in what rank, and at what price, you are accepted:

> *tibi si datur uni*
> *Quo lapide illa diem candidiore notet.*

[whether she gives herself to you alone, and marks that day with her whitest milestone.]

What if she is eating your bread with a sauce derived from more pleasing thoughts!

> *Te tenet, absentes alios suspirat amores.*

132. Ravisius Textor, *Officina: Animalium et aliarum rerum amatores* (for the statue); *amor conjugalis* (for Periander); Herodotus, II, lxxxix (for the Egyptian law).
133. Erasmus, *Adages*, I, IX, LXIII, *Endymionis somnium dormis*, alluding to the tale of the shepherd Endymion in Cicero, *Tusc. disput.*, I, xxxviii, 92; Plato, *Phaedo*, 72 C; Aristotle, *Nicomachaean Ethics*, VI, viii.
134. Martial, X, ciii; XI, lix; then, Catullus, LXVIII, 147–8 and Tibullus, I, vi, 35.

[She holds you close while sighing for the loves of an absent lover.]

What! Do we not know of a man who in our own day used this activity as a means of horrifying vengeance, so as to inject poison into a decent woman and kill her?[135]

Those who know Italy will never find it odd if, while on this subject, I do not go anywhere else for *exempla*, since that natiòn can claim to be the world's professor in such matters. They have more routinely beautiful women than we do and fewer ugly ones, though for rare and outstanding beauties we are on a par. And I think the same applies to wit: of routinely fine ones they have more and it is obvious that brutish stupidity is incomparably more rare. But in matchless minds, those of the highest rank, we owe them [C] nothing.[136] [B] Were I to have to extend that comparison it could probably be said, on the contrary, that, by their standards, valour is commonplace and natural with us: yet sometimes you can see it so full and vigorous as they handle it that it surpasses all the stern examples which we have. Italian marriages are crippled: by their customs, so harsh and slavish a rule is imposed on their wives that the slightest acquaintance with another man is as capital an offence as the most intimate. The result of this rule is that any approach to their wives becomes, of necessity, basic; and since whatever they do amounts to the same, the choice is made for them already.   [C]   And once they have broken out of their pens, believe you me, they are all ablaze: *'luxuria ipsis vinculis, sicut fera bestia, irritata, deinde emissa.'* [sexual desire then breaks loose, like a wild beast first provoked and then set free.][137]   [B]   They really ought to give them a little more rein.

> *Vidi ego nuper equum, contra sua frena tenacem,*
> *Ore reluctanti fulminis ire modo.*

[Of late I saw a horse, straining at the bit, pulling with its mouth and careering along like lightning.]

We can weaken the desire for such companionship by allowing them a mite of freedom.[138]

---

135. Brantôme relates a case of a French nòbleman who poisoned his wife through her genitals in the hope of marrying another woman (*Dames galantes*, ed. M. Rat, Paris, 1947, pp. 14–15).
136. '88: We owe them *hardly anything . . .*
137. Cato, in Livy, XXIV, iv; then, Ovid, *Amores*, III, iv, 13–14.
138. '88: freedom. *They are, in their social life, ladies of many parts. We put them on the way to using the ultimate one, since we rate them all the same.* Both run . . .

Both run more or less equal risks. They are excessive in restraint: we, in freedom. One of the fine customs of our nation is that the boys of good families are taken in as pages to be educated and brought up, schooled for nobility. It is said to be rude and discourteous to refuse a young gentleman. I have noted (but there are as many fashions as there are different homes) that ladies who have sought to impose the most austere of rules on the girls in their entourage have not produced any better results. What we need is moderation. We should leave a good bit of the behaviour of girls to their own discretion; whatever you do, there is no training that can bridle them in all the time; but what is true is that a girl who has bolted, bag and baggage, from a dressage in freedom inspires much more confidence than one who emerges with propriety from an austere prison of a school.

Our forefathers trained their daughters' countenances to be bashful and timorous; their minds and desires were alike: we, knowing nothing about the matter, train them to be bold. [C] That is for Sauromatians who are forbidden to lie with a man until they have killed one with their own hands in war.[139] [B] It suffices me (who have no rights in the matter except to be heard) that they retain me as a counsellor, according to the privilege of my age. So I would counsel them – [C] and us too – [B] to refrain; but if this age is too inimical to that, at least to show discretion and moderation. [C] As in the story told of Aristippus: some young men blushed at seeing him go in to the house of a courtesan: he said to them: 'The error lies not in going in but in never coming out.'[140] [B] If a woman cannot save her conscience let her at least save her reputation: even if the base is not worth it let appearances hold out. I advocate gradualness and stringing things out when dispensing of love's favours. [C] Plato demonstrates that surrendering easily or quickly is forbidden to the defenders in loves of all kinds.[141] [B] To yield all, so inadvisedly and so hastily, is a sign of voracity,[142] which they must hide with all their art. By acting ordinately and with measure when distributing their gifts they succeed far better in tempting our desires and hiding their own. Let them ever flee before us – I mean even those who intend to be

139. Also called *Sarmatae*; cf. Herodotus, IV, cxvii; Coelius Richerius Rhodiginus, *Antiquae lectiones*, IX, xii, who assimilates them to the Amazons.
140. Erasmus (*Apophthegmata*, III, *Aristippus*, XIII), who adds a caution, restricting the saying to legitimate relationships.
141. Implied in Plato's *Symposium*.
142. '88: voracity *and hunger*, which . . .

caught: like the Scythians they beat us best when retreating. By the law which Nature gives them, it is truly not for them to wish and to desire: their role is to accept, to obey, to consent. That is why Nature has made them able to do it at any time: we men are only able to do it occasionally and unreliably. The time is always right for them, so that they will be always ready when our time comes along: [C] *'pati natae'* [they are born to be passive].[143] [B] And whereas Nature has so arranged it that men's desires should declare themselves by a visible projection, theirs are hidden and internal and she has furnished them with organs [C] unsuited to making a display and [B] strictly defensive.

[C] We should leave to the licence of the Amazons events like the following: when Alexander was marching through Hircania, Queen Thalestris of the Amazons came to meet him with three hundred warriors of her sex, well mounted and well armed, having left beyond the nearby mountains the rest of a big army which followed her leadership; she told him, aloud and in public, that the rumour of his victories and of his valour had brought her there to see him and to offer him her might and her support to forward his campaigns; she added that as she found him to be so beautiful, young and full of vigour she, who was perfection itself in all her qualities, advised him that they should lie together, so that there should be born from the most valiant woman in the world and the most valiant man then alive some great and rare offspring for the future. For the rest Alexander merely thanked her kindly, but he remained for thirteen days to allow time to fulfil her last request, days which he celebrated with all possible eagerness to please so courageous a princess.[144]

[B] In virtually everything we men are as unjust judges of women's actions as they are of ours – I confess the truth when it goes against me just as when it serves me. It is a base disorder which drives them to change so frequently and which impedes them from settling their affections firmly on any person whatsoever; as we can see in that goddess Venus to whom is attributed so many changes of lovers. Yet it is true that it is against the nature of sex-love not to be impetuous, and it is against the nature of what is impetuous to remain constant: so those men who are amazed by this and who denounce and seek the causes of this in women as unbelievable and unnatural, ought to ask themselves why that distemper finds acceptance in

143. Seneca, *Epist. moral.*, CXV, 21.
144. Diodorus Siculus, XVII, xvi.

themselves, without their being stunned as by a miracle. It would perhaps be more odd to find any fixity in it. It is not a passion of the body alone. Just as there is no end to covetousness and ambition, so there is no end to lust. It still lives on after satiety: you can prescribe to it no end, no lasting satisfaction: it always proceeds beyond possession. And fickleness is perhaps somewhat more excusable in them than in us. Like us they can cite in their defence the penchant we both have for variety and novelty; secondly they can cite, what we cannot, that they buy a pig in a poke [C] (Queen Joanna of Naples caused her first husband Andreosso to be hanged from the grill of her window by a gold and silver cord, plaited by her own hands, once she discovered that neither his organs nor his potency corresponded to the hopes she had conceived of his matrimonial duties from his stature, his beauty, his youth and his disposition, by which he had won her and deceived her);[145] [B] they can also cite the fact that since the active partner is required to make more effort than the passive one, they at least can always provide for this necessity while we cannot. [C] That is why Plato wisely established in his laws that those making a judgement on the suitability of a marriage should see the youths who were ambitious to marry stark naked but the maidens naked only down to the girdle.[146] [B] By assaying us that way the women might perhaps find us not worth the choosing:

> *Experta latus, madidoque simillima loro*
> *Inguina, nec lassa stare coacta manu,*
> *Deserit imbelles thalamos.*

[She deserts his impotent bed after exploring his thighs and his prick which, like a damp leather thong, refuses an erection to her exhausted hand.][147]

It is not enough to have the will to drive straight up: in law impotence and an inability to consummate annul a marriage –

> *Et querendum aliunde foret nervosius illud,*
> *Quod posset zonam solvere virgineam*

[You had to look elsewhere for a more sinewy one, capable of unsealing her maidenly girdle][148]

145. Jacques de Lavardin, *Scanderbeg*; cf. Tiraquellus, *De legibus connubialibus*, IX, 99.
146. Plato, *Laws*, XI, 925 A.
147. Martial, *Epigrams*, VII, lvii, 3–5.
148. Catullus, LXVII, 27–8.

– so why should a proportionally more wanton and active sexual skill not do so,

> *si blando nequeat supresse labori?*

[if it proves unequal to its pleasant task?][149]

But it is most unwise (is it not?) to bring our inadequacy and our weaknesses to a place where what we would leave behind is a good reputation and a good impression. For the little that I need nowadays –

> *ad unum*
> *Mollis opus*

[limp, even for one go]

– I would not embarrass any lady whom I should hold in reverence and awe:

> *Fuge suspicari,*
> *Cujus heu denum trepidavit aetas,*
> *Claudere lustrum.*

[Suspect not a man whose life has staggered to its fiftieth year.][150]

Nature ought to be satisfied with making that age pitiful without making it ridiculous as well. I hate to see old age with an inch of paltry vigour which arouses it three times a week dashing about and bragging with the same vehemence as if it had a good day's legitimate work in its belly. Straw on fire![151] Truly. [C] And I am always shocked when its lively and quivering fire is promptly quenched and frozen cold. That appetite was meant for the flower of beauteous youth. [B] Just to see, try relying on old age to further that tireless, full constant and great-souled ardour that is in you! It will leave you stranded halfway there! Venture to cede it to some gawky gentle dazzled youth, still quaking before his wand and blushing at it,

> *Indum sanguineo veluti violaverit ostro*
> *Si quis ebur, vel mista rubent ubi lilia multa*
> *Alba rosa*

---

149. Virgil, *Georgics*, III, 127 (adapted).
150. Horace: *Epodes*, XII, 15; then, *Odes*, II, iv, 22–4. The text of '95 reads *undenum*, not *heu denum*, that is, 'fifty-five', not 'alas fifty'. Horace wrote *octavum* (forty). Horace is counting by five-year units (*lustra*).
151. Allusion to the proverb (listed by Cotgrave): A whore's love is but straw on fire (*Amour de putain, feu d'estoupe*).

[like Indian ivory stained blood-red, or even as white lilies arranged among red roses reflect their hue.][152]

Any man who can without dying of shame await the morning which brings disdain from a pair of lovely eyes, conscious of his flaccidity and irrelevance,

> *Et taciti fecere tamen convitia vultus,*

> [her silent features eloquent with loud reproach,]

has never known the happy pride of turning them glazed and dim by the vigorous exercises of a fulfilled and active night. When I have found a woman discontented with me I have not immediately gone and railed at her fickleness: I have asked myself, rather, whether I would be right to rail against Nature.

> *Si non longa satis, si non bene mentula crassa,*

> [Should my cock be not long enough nor good and thick,][153]

then Nature has indeed treated me unlawfully and unjustly –

> *Nimirium sapiunt, videntque parvam*
> *Matronae quoque mentulam illibenter*

> [Even good matrons know all too well and do not gladly see a tiny cock]

– [C] and inflicted the most enormous injury. Every one of my members, each as much as another, makes me myself: and none makes me more properly a man than that one. I owe to the public my portrait complete.

The wisdom to be found in my account lies in truth, in frankness and in essentials – entirely; it disdains to count among its real duties those little made-up rules based on provincial custom; it is natural, unvarying, universal; its daughters are indeed courtesy and respect, but they are bastard ones. Apparent defects we shall get the better of all right once we have got the better of those which are of the essence. After we have finished with the latter here, we will fall upon the others – if we find we still need to do so. For there is a danger that we will think up imaginary new duties so as to excuse our neglect of our natural ones and to jumble them up together.

152. Virgil, *Aeneid*, XII, 67–9; then, Ovid, *Amores*, I, vii, 21.
153. *Priapeia*, LXXX, 1; then VIII, 4–5.

That can be shown: you can see that wherever peccadillos are treated as crimes, crimes are treated as peccadillos; that among the peoples whose laws of politeness are fewest and slackest, the more basic laws, those common to all, are best observed since the countless multitude of those other obligations smother our concern, weaken it and disperse it. Applying ourselves to petty things diverts us from the pressing ones. Oh what an easy, favoured route such superficial men follow compared with ours! Such things are but shadowy pretences with which we bedaub each other and repay our mutual debts; but we cannot repay with them, but increase rather, the debt owed to that Great Judge who rips our tattered rags from off our pudenda and really sees us through and through, right down to our innermost and most secret filth. Our maidenly bashfulness would be useful and fitting if it could order that Judge not to uncover us!

To sum up: whoever could make Man grow out of an over-nice dread of words would do no great harm to this world. Our life consists partly in madness, partly in wisdom: whoever writes about it merely respectfully and by rule leaves more than half of it behind. I address no apologies to myself; were I to do so I would apologize for those apologies more than anything else. My apology is addressed to those of certain kinds of temperament (who are I believe numerically greater than those siding with me). I would like to please everyone, even though it is a difficult thing *'esse unum hominem accommodatum ad tantum morum ac sermonum et voluntatum varietatem'* [for one single man to conform to so great a variation in manners, speech and intentions];[154] so out of consideration for them I will add this: that they cannot justifiably complain that I am putting words into the mouths of authors accepted with approval for many centuries, nor can they deny me, because I lack verse, the freedom enjoyed by some of the greatest clerical cocks-of-the-walk of our own days. Here are two examples:

Rimula, dispeream, ni monogramma tua est;

[Strike me dead if your slit is more than one sketchy line;][155]

154. Cicero, *De petitione consulatus*, xiv. Montaigne's manuscript jottings at this point, eventually crossed out, show that he was aware of going beyond the limits of decency which he had set himself in his Preface: that was because he had been emboldened by the welcome given to his book.
155. A line from the erotic *Juvenilia* of Theodore Beza, the great Reformer and successor to Calvin. The next is by Octavian de Saint-Gelais, a Roman Catholic cleric and court poet.

and:

Un vit d'amy la contente et bien traicte.

[A lover's cock services and delights her.]

And what about all the others?

I like modesty. It is not my judgement which makes me choose this shocking sort of talk: Nature chose it for me. I am no more praising it than I am praising any behaviour contrary to the accepted norms; but I *am* defending it, lessening the indictment by citing individual and general considerations.

Let us get on.

Similarly, [B] from what do you derive that sovereign authority you assume over any ladies who, to their own cost, grant you their favours –

Si furtiva dedit nigra munuscula nocte

[If she gives you some little stolen present in the black of night][156]

– so that you immediately invest yourselves with rights, cold disapproval and husbandly authority? It is a covenant freely entered into: why do you not stick to it if you want to hold them to it? [C] Voluntary agreements grant no prescriptive rights.

[B] It was not good form, but nevertheless true, that in my day I kept this bargain (as far as its nature allows) as conscientiously as any other one, and with a sort of justice, since I never showed more affection to the woman than I felt, portraying to them in all simplicity its decline, its flourishing period and its birth, its accesses of fever and its relapses. We do not go about such things with an even stride. I was so mean with my promises that I think I kept more than I ever vowed or owed. They found faithfulness there, even to the extent of my serving their inconstancy – and I mean inconstancy admitted and at times repeated. I never broke with one of them as long as I was held there even by the tail-end of a thread. And no matter what occasions they gave me, I never broke it off even for hatred or disdain: for such intimacies still oblige me to show some kindness even when acquired by the most discreditable of covenants. I did sometimes show my choler and a somewhat undiscerning impatience at the high point of their trickery, their evasions and our quarrels, but then I am by complexion subject to sudden distempers which, despite being short and

156. Catullus, LXVIII, 145.

light, are often prejudicial to my affairs. If they wanted to make an assay of
my freedom of judgement, I never baulked at giving them bitingly
paternal advice and lancing them where it hurts. If I left them any room to
complain of me, it is rather for having found me to be, by modern
standards, a ridiculously scrupulous lover. I kept my word in cases where
anyone at all would have readily released me from it: women yielded in
those days while saving their reputations by terms of surrender which they
would readily have allowed their conqueror to infringe. In the interests of
their honour I have more than once made my pleasure strike its sails at the
point of a climax, and, when reason urged me, I have even armed them
against me, so well indeed that they acted more safely and soberly by my
rules, once they had frankly accepted them, than they would have done by
their own.

[C] As far as in me lay I personally assumed all the risks of our
assignations so as to take the load off them; and I managed our intrigues in
the most difficult and unforeseeable of ways, for they are the least open to
suspicion and, in my opinion, the most practical. Assignations are most
overt when they seem the most covert. What is least feared is least
protected, least observed; it is easy to dare what nobody thinks you will:
the difficulty makes it easy.

[B] No man's advances were ever more saucily genital. The way of
courting I have described is more in harmony with the rules: but does
anyone know better than I do how ridiculous it appears to folk nowadays
and how unsuccessful it is! Yet I shall never be brought to gainsay it: I have
nothing more to lose by it now,

> *me tabula sacer*
> *Votiva paries indicat uvida*
> *Suspendisse potenti*
> *Vestimenta maris Deo.*

[As is shown by my votive tablet, I have hung up my dripping garments on the
temple wall and dedicated them to the god of the sea.][157]

It is time, now, to talk of this openly. But as I might say to someone now,
'You are raving mad, my friend: love in these days of yours has nothing to
do with fidelity and loyalty' —

> *hæc si tu postules*
> *Ratione certa facere, nihilo plus agas,*
> *Quam si des operam, ut cum ratione insanias*

157. Horace, *Odes*, I, v, 13–16; then, Terence, *The Eunuch*, I, i, 16–18.

[if you try to reduce all this to rational rules you will simply give yourself the task of going rationally insane]

– so, on the other hand, if I had to start again, I would certainly adopt the same course and the same method, however fruitless that might prove for me. [C] Inexpertise and silliness are praiseworthy in an activity which deserves no praise. [B] The further I go from others' humours in this, the nearer I draw to my own.

Incidentally, I never allowed all of myself to be totally devoted to this business. I took delight in it but I never forgot *me*: both in the ladies' service and in mine I conserved, in its entirety, such little sense and discretion as Nature had allotted me: some passion but no raging madness. My conscience was compromised by it so far as to include lasciviousness and licentiousness, though never ingratitude, treachery, wickedness or cruelty. These are prices which I would not pay for the pleasures of this vice: I was happy to pay its proper honest price: [C] '*Nullum inter se vitium est.*'[158] [No vice is self-enclosed.] I have a virtually equal loathing of all cowering torpid idleness and all prickly painful bustle. One cuts into me, the other knocks me senseless: and I am no more fond of cuts than of bruises, of slashing blows than of blunt ones. In these affairs, when I was more fit for them, I found a just moderation between those two extremes. Love is a lively emotion, light-hearted and alert: I was neither confused nor afflicted by it but I was thrown into a heat by it and troubled. There you must stop: it is harmful only for fools.

When a youth asked Panaetius the philosopher whether it became a wise man to be in love, 'Let us leave aside the wise,' he replied, 'neither you nor I are that; but let us not pledge ourselves to an activity so violent and disturbing, one which makes us the slave of another and despicable to ourselves.'[159] He was telling the truth when he said that something so intrinsically impulsive should not be entrusted to a man's soul if it has no means of withstanding its assaults and of disproving by its deeds the assertion of Agesilaus, that wisdom and love cannot live together.[160]

It is a vain pastime, it is true, indecorous, shaming and wrong; but I reckon that, treated in this fashion, it is health-bringing and appropriate for loosening up a sluggish mind and body; as a doctor I would order it for a

---

158. Seneca, *Epist. moral.*, XCV, 33 (that is, one vice leads to another).
159. Ibid., CXVI, 5. (Panaetius was a Stoic.)
160. Erasmus, *Apophthegmata*, I, *Agesilaus*, XIX; Plutarch (tr. Amyot), *Dicts notables des Lacedaemoniens*, 210 EF (when duty required Agesilaus to leave a sick friend).

man of my mould and disposition as readily as any other prescription so as to liven him up and keep him in trim until he is well on in years and to postpone the onset of old age. While we are still only in its outskirts, while there is still life in our pulse,

> Dum nova canities, dum prima et recta senectus,
> Dum superest Lachesi quod torqueat, et pedibus me
> Porto meis, nullo dextram subeunte bacillo,

[while the hair is but newly grey, while old age is still fresh and erect, while there is still some yarn for Lachesis to spin, while I can stand on my own feet without leaning on a stick,][161]

we have need of being stirred and thrilled by some such perturbation as that: just think how it restored youth, vigour and merriness to wise Anacreon. And Socrates, when older than I am, said, in talking of someone he loved, 'When we touched shoulders and brought our heads together while looking at the same book I felt, I can assure you, a sudden jab in my shoulder like an insect's sting: it went on irritating for five whole days and poured into my mind a ceaseless longing.'[162] – A mere touch, by chance, on the shoulder, was enough to warm and disturb a soul chilled and enervated by age, a soul which was foremost among all human souls in its re-formation.[163]   [C] And why not? Socrates was a man: he never wanted to be, or to seem to be, anything else.

[B]   Philosophy does not do battle against such pleasures as are natural, provided that temperance accompanies them:[164]   [C] she teaches moderation in such things not avoidance;   [B]   her powers of resistance are used against bastard unnatural pleasures. She says that the body's desires must not be augmented by the mind and cleverly warns us   [C]   not to seek to stimulate our hunger by sating it, not to seek to stuff our bellies instead of filling them, as well as to avoid any enjoyment which brings us to penury,

---

161. Juvenal, *Satires*, I, 26–8.

162. Xenophon, *Symposium*, IV, 27–8. Socrates was consulting a book-scroll with Cleinias, bare shoulder to bare shoulder. Sage though he was, he was disturbed for five days as though he had been bitten by a wild beast. In his innocence he did not realize why, until Charmides twitted him about it.

163. '88: human souls, *in rule and* in its re-formation . . .

Socrates, as he told Zopyrus the physiognomist, had been born with a vicious, lecherous inferior 'form' (soul), but had re-formed it.

164. The Classic Aristotelian teaching (e.g. *Nicomachaean Ethics*, II, vii, 3; VIII, 2 ff.; III, x–xii, etc.).

all meats which increase hunger and all drinks that increase thirst, [B] just as[165] in the service of love she orders us to take a person who simply satisfies the needs of the body and who does not disturb the soul; the soul must not make love its concern, but follow nakedly along, accompanying the body.[166]

But am I not right to think that these precepts – which are by my standard nevertheless a trifle rigorous[167] – concern a body which is functioning properly, and that for a broken-down body (as for a prostrate stomach) we are allowed to use the art of medicine to prop it up and put a little heat into it by means of our imagination so as to restore its appetite and joy, since, left to itself, it has lost them for good? May we not say that there is nothing in us during this earthly prison either purely corporeal or purely spiritual and that it is injurious to tear a living man apart; and that it seems reasonable that we should adopt towards the enjoyment of pleasure at least as favourable an attitude as we do towards pain? Pain for example was vehement to the point of perfection in the Soul of the saints doing penance; the body naturally took part in it by right of the links binding it to her; yet it could have had little part in the cause.[168] But the saints were by no means content that the body should 'follow nakedly along, accompanying' the afflicted soul: they afflicted such horrifying punishment on it as was proper to it, in order that both body and soul should emulate each other, plunging the whole man into pain, most salutary when most atrocious.

[C] So, in the parallel case of bodily pleasures, is it not unjust to chill the Soul towards them and to maintain that she should be dragged towards them as to some compelling obligation or some slavish need? It is for the Soul, rather, to keep them warm like a broody hen and, since she has the responsibility of governing them, to come forward and welcome them;

165. '88: warns us *to avoid* all meats which increase hunger, *that is, which make us desire to be hungry afresh*, just as . . .

Cf. Plutarch (tr. Amyot), *De la curiosité*, 67 p.
166. Cf. the advice of the giant heroes in Rabelais, *Tiers Livre*, TLF, XXXV, 46 ff. and notes. Cf. Tiraquellus, *De legibus connubialibus*, XV, 56 ff, with references to Thomas Aquinas, etc.
167. '88: rigorous *and inhumane* – concern . . .

The ensuing notion that the soul is 'imprisoned' in the body is a Platonic commonplace. (The usual corollary was that the soul should strive, in ecstasy and rapture, to escape from the body. Montaigne does not accept it for most men.)
168. The temptations of saints are not so much grossly corporeal as spiritual and mental.

just as in my opinion it is also her duty in the case of such pleasures as are proper to her to inject and pour into the body every sense-impression which their attributes allow and to see that they are made sweet to it and salutary. For it is, as they say, right that the body should never follow its appetites to the prejudice of the Soul. Why is it not right, then, that the Soul should not follow hers to the prejudice of the body?

[B] I have absolutely no other passion than that to keep me going. What covetousness, ambition, quarrels and lawsuits do for men who, like me, have no other allotted task, love would do more suitably: it would restore me to vigilance, sober behaviour, graceful manners and care about my person; love would give new strength to my features so that the distortions of old age, pitiful and misshapen, should not come and disfigure them; [C] it would bring me back to wise and healthy endeavours by which I could make myself more esteemed and more loved, banishing from my mind all sense of hopelessness about itself and about its application, while bringing it to know itself again: [B] it would divert me away from a thousand painful thoughts, [C] from a thousand melancholy sorrows [B] which idleness burdens us with in old age, [C] as does the poor state of our health; [B] it would, at least in dream, restore some heat to my blood – this blood of mine which Nature is foresaking; it would lift up the chin, and prolong for a while the powers, vigour and joy of the soul [B] for this poor fellow who is on his way out, rushing towards disintegration.

But I am well aware that love is a good thing very hard to recover. Our tastes have, through weakness, become more delicate and, through experience, more discriminating. We demand more when we have less to offer: we want the maximum of choice just when we least deserve to find favour. Realizing we are thus, we are less bold and more suspicious; knowing our own circumstances – and theirs – nothing can assure us we are loved.

I feel shame for myself to be found among fresh-green, boiling youth

> *Cujus in indomito constantior inguine nervus,*
> *Quam nova collibus arbor inhæret.*

[in whose indomitable groin there is a tendon firmer far than a young tree planted on the hillside.][169]

Why should we go and show our wretchedness among such eager joy,

169. Horace, *Epodes*, XII, 19–20; then, *Odes*, IV, xiii, 26–8.

Possint ut juvenes visere fervidi,
Multo non sine risu,
Dilapsam in cineres facem?

[so that burning youth, not without many a laugh, may see our nuptial torch decayed into ashes?]

They have strength and reason on their side; let us make room for them; we can hold out no longer.

[C] That sprig of budding beauty will not suffer itself to be handled by hands benumbed, nor seduced by purely material means. For, as that ancient philosopher replied to one who was laughing at him for being unable to win the favour of some tendril he was pursuing: 'My friend, the hook will not bite when the curd is so fresh.'[170]

[B] Now love is a commerce which requires inter-relationship and reciprocity. We can show our appreciation of the other pleasures we receive by recompenses of a different nature: this one can only be repaid in the same coin. [C] Truly in this one the pleasure that I give stimulates my imagination more sweetly than the pleasure I receive. [B] A man who can receive pleasure when he gives none at all is in no wise generous: it is a base soul which will owe the lot and is pleased to nurse contacts with women who do all the paying. There is no beauty nor grace nor intimacy so exquisite that a gentleman should want them at that price. If they can only do us a good turn out of pity, then I would dearly prefer not to live at all than to live on charity. Would that I had the right to ask it of them in the style which I have seen beggars use in Italy: *'Fate ben per voi'* [Do a good turn for yourself]; [C] or in the manner which Cyrus adopted to exhort his soldiers: 'He who loves himself, let him follow me.'[171]

[B] Someone will say to me: 'Go back again to women who are now in the same state as you are: fellowship in the same misfortune will make them easier to get.' What absurd and dull terms for a truce!

Nolo
Barbam vellere mortuo leoni!

---

170. Erasmus, *Apophthegmata*, VII, *Bion Borythenites*, II. Cheese, curd, *Caseus*, was a Latin term of amorous endearment. (Erasmus chastely holds this expression to mean that Philosophy cannot 'hook' tender minds; Montaigne, more literally, that ageing philosophers cannot 'hook' tender lovers.)
171. A famous saying, parodied by Rabelais (*Gargantua*, XXXI, end) to mock Picrochole, his foolish, choleric monarch.

[I have no desire to pluck hairs from a dead lion's beard!][172]

[C] One of the reproaches and accusations that Xenophon makes about Meno is that in his love-affairs he only got on the job with partners past their bloom.[173] The sight of a young couple appropriately united in a tender embrace – or even the contemplation of it in imagination – contains I believe more sensual pleasure than being the second partner in a sad misshapen union. [B] I leave that fanciful appetite to the Emperor Galba who devoted himself only to tough and ancient flesh – or to that other pitiful wretched man:

> *O ego di' faciant talem te cernere possim,*
> *Charaque mutatis oscula ferre comis,*
> *Amplectique meis corpus non pingue lacertis!*

[O would the gods let me see you as you are, tenderly kiss your fading hair and clasp your withered body in my embrace!][174]

[C] And I count among the principal forms of ugliness all beauties due to artifice and constraint. A young lad of Chio called Hemon, hoping that fine clothes would procure him that handsomeness which Nature had denied him, came to the philosopher Arcesilaus and asked him if a philosopher could ever find himself in love. 'Oh yes,' he replied, 'provided it be not with a dishonest dressed-up beauty such as yours.'[175] An ugly old age when openly avowed is in my opinion less old and less ugly than one smoothed out and painted over.

[B] Shall I say it, on condition that you do not jump down my throat? Love never seems to me to be properly and naturally seasonable except in the age nearest boyhood:

> *Quem si puellarum insereres choro,*
> *Mille sagaces falleret hospites*
> *Discrimen obscurum, solutis*
> *Crinibus ambiguoque vultu.*

[A youth such that, if you put him among a band of maidens, those who knew

172. Martial, *Epigrams*, X, xc, 10–11.
173. Xenophon, *Anabasis*, II, vi; then, Suetonius, *Life of Galba*, XXII.
174. Ovid, wretched in unending exile on the orders of Augustus Caesar (*Ex Ponto*, I, iv, 49–51).
175. Diogenes Laertius, *Life of Arcesilaus*. (Cf. Erasmus, *Apophthegmata*, VII, *Arcesilaus*, VI.)

him not, for all their perspicacity, would fail to pick him out with his flowing hair and his hermaphrodite's face.][176]

[C] Nor handsomeness, either. For Plato himself noted that Homer prolongs it until there is a shadow of a beard on the chin, but remarks that such a flower is rare. (We all know why Dion the Sophist jokingly called the mossy beards of adolescence Aristogitons and Harmodians!)[177]

[B] I find love already out of place in adult manhood let alone in old age.

> *Importunus enim transvolat aridas*
> *Quercus.*

[For Cupid disdainfully flies past the withered oak.][178]

[C] Queen Margaret of Navarre (just like a woman) greatly extends the privileges of women when she ordains that it is time for them to change the title *beautiful* for *good* after they have reached thirty.[179]

[B] The shorter the tenancy we grant to Cupid in our lives the better off we are. Look at his deportment! And his chin is as smooth as a boy's! Who is unaware that in Cupid's school you do everything contrary to good order? There the novices are the professors: study, practice and experience lead to failure. [C] *'Amor ordinem nescit.'* [Cupid knows no order.][180] [B] The way Cupid conducts things is most in fashion when mingled with ingenuousness and awkwardness; mistakes and failures lend it charm and grace; provided it is sorrowful and yearning, it little matters whether it shows prudence. See how Cupid stumbles along, tripping over merrily; to guide him by art and wisdom is to clamp him in the stocks: you constrain his divine freedom when you lay hairy calloused hands upon him.

Moreover I often hear women portraying a relationship as being entirely of the mind, disdaining to take into consideration the interests which our senses have in it.[181] Everything helps in this case, but I should add that

176. Horace, *Odes*, II, V, 21–4; then, Plato, *Protagoras*, 309 AB, alluding to Homer, *Iliad*, XXIV, 348.
177. Conspirators who freed Athens from the tyranny of the Pisistratids. Similarly, a sprouting beard freed youths from the 'tyranny' of homosexual advances: Plutarch (tr. Amyot), *De l'amour*, 613 AB. Saying of Bion (not Dion).
178. Horace, *Odes*, IV, xiii, 9–10.
179. Margaret of Navarre, *Heptaméron*, Journée 4, nouvelle 35 (an unfair remark: Margaret does not 'ordain' it, but notes that it is usual).
180. St Jerome, *Letters, Ad Chromatium* (identified by Marie de Gournay).
181. This was the general drift of Renaissance 'platonic' love.

though I have often found that we men have overlooked weaknesses in their minds on account of the beauty of their bodies, I have yet to see one woman willing, on account of the beauty of a man's mind, however mature and wise, to lend a helping hand to his body once it has even begun to decline. Why is not one of them ever moved by desire for that noble [C] Socratic [B] bargain of body for mind, [C] purchasing at the price of her thighs a philosophical relationship and procreation through the soul – the highest price she could ever get for them![182]

Plato decrees in his laws that a man who has achieved some signal and useful exploit in a war may not, for the duration of that conflict, irrespective of his age or ugliness, be refused a kiss or any other of love's favours from anyone he pleases.[183] Can what he finds so just in commendation of a warrior's worth not also be used to commend worth of another kind? And why is no woman ever moved [B] to win, before her fellow-women do, the glory of a love so chaste? Yes, I do indeed say chaste:

> nam si quando ad prælia ventum est,
> Ut quondam in stipulis magnus sine viribus ignis
> Incassum furit.

[for when it comes to the clinch, its frenzied love serves no purpose; like burning stubble: lots of flame but no force.][184]

We do not rank among our worst vices those whose fire is smothered in our minds.

To bring to an end these infamous jottings which I have loosed in a diarrhoea of babble – a violent and at times morbid diarrhoea –

> Ut missum sponsi furtivo munere malum
> Procurrit casto virginis e gremio,
> Quod miseræ oblitæ molli sub veste locatum,
> Dum adventu matris prosilit, excutitur,
> Atque illud prono præceps agitur decursu;
> Huic manat tristi conscius ore rubor

[as when an apple, secretly given by her admirer breaks loose from the chaste bosom of a maiden as she starts to her feet on hearing her mother's footstep,

182. Cf. I, 28, 'On affectionate relationships'; Socratic philosophers paid with their teachings of virtue and wisdom for the homage of youthful disciples. Philosophers beget ideas (brain-children) rather than real children.
183. In Plato's Republic (not his Laws), V, 468.
184. Virgil, Georgics, III, 98–100 (of an aged stallion).

forgetting she had concealed it beneath her flowing robes; it lies there on the ground while a blush suffuses her troubled face and betrays her fault][185]

– I say that male and female are cast in the same mould: save for education and custom the difference between them is not great. [C] In *The Republic* Plato summons both men and women indifferently to a community of all studies, administrations, offices and vocations both in peace and war;[186] and Antisthenes the philosopher removed any distinction between their virtue and our own.[187]

[B] It is far more easy to charge one sex than to discharge the other. As the saying goes: it is the pot calling the kettle smutty.

185. Catullus, LXV, 19–24.
186. Plato, *Republic*, V, where no sex distinctions are allowed to affect eligibility for the offices of State.
187. Erasmus, *Apophthegmata*, VII, *Antisthenes*, LVII. Erasmus comments: 'So too did Socrates think women to be no less apt for instruction in all the duties of wisdom than men, provided they receive the same education. Yet the mob condemn women as though they cannot be taught virtue.'

6. On coaches

===

[A favourite chapter, linking the ideas of fantastic luxury, generosity and princely magnificence with fantastic cruelty, vulgarity and ostentation. Coaches (which for Montaigne means all sorts of wheeled vehicles including Roman chariots) were the symbols of luxury. They are contrasted with the simplicity of those American Indian cultures which had never invented the wheel, had no horses and used gold for its beauty alone. Their simplicity emphasized the horrors of the Spanish conquest of Peru, with its naked cruelty and avarice.

Montaigne's three main sources are a work of Pietro Crinito, De honesta disciplina; *another, by Justus Lipsius,* De amphitheatro; *a third by Francisco Lopez de Gomara, one of the Conquistadores, whom he read in the French translation by J. Fumée:* Histoire générale des Indes.*]*

[B] It is very easy to prove that, when great authors write about causes, they not only marshal those which they reckon to be true but also those which they do not believe, provided that they have some [C] originality and [B] beauty.[1] If what they say is ingenious they think that their words are sufficiently useful and true. We cannot be sure of the master-cause, so we pile cause upon cause, hoping that it may happen to be among them:

> *namque unam dicere causam*
> *Non satis est, verum plures, unde una tamen sit.*

[since it suffices not to give one single cause, many must be given, one of which only may be true.][2]

You ask me: 'What is the origin of our custom of saying *Bless you* when people sneeze?' Well, we break three sorts of wind: the one which issues lower down is very dirty; the one which issues from the mouth comports an element of reproach for gluttony; and the third is sneezing, to which, since it issues from the head and is blameless, we give that honourable greeting.

1. '88: some *appositeness* and beauty . . .
2. Lucretius, VI, 704–5.

Do not mock such subtle reasoning: it is (so they say) from Aristotle . . .³

I came across, in Plutarch I think (and he is of all the authors I know the one who has best blended art with nature and judgement with erudition), the explanation that the vomiting from the stomach which befalls men on sea-voyages is to be attributed to fear.⁴ (He had already found some reason or other to prove that fear can produce such an effect.) Now I am very subject to seasickness and I know that that cause does not apply to me; and I know it not by argument but compelling experience. I shall not cite what I have been told, that animals, especially pigs, which have no conception of danger, get seasick; nor what one of my acquaintances has told me about himself: he is much subject to it yet on two or three occasions when he was obsessed by fear during a great storm the desire to vomit disappeared –
[C] as it did to that man in Antiquity: *'Pejus vexabar quam ut periculum mihi succurreret.'* [I was too shaken for the danger to occur to me.]⁵
[B] Though many occasions for being afraid have arisen (if you count death as one) I have never felt, on water nor anywhere else, such fear as to confuse or to daze me. Fear can arise from lack of judgement as well as from lack of courage. All such dangers as I have encountered have been with my eyes open, with my sight free, sound and whole: besides, to feel fear you also need to have courage. Once when I did have to flee, I was able to manage my flight well and, compared with others, to maintain some order because I did so [C] if not without fear nevertheless [B] without ecstatic terror; fear was aroused, but not the kind which is thunderstruck or insane. The souls of great men can go far beyond that, showing us retreats which were not merely tranquil and sane but marked by pride.

Here let me quote the flight which Alcibiades relates: it concerns Socrates, his companion in arms:⁶ 'I came across him (he said) after the rout of our army; he and Laches were the last to retreat. I could watch him at leisure and in safety, since I was on a good horse while he was on foot; that is the way we had fought. I noted first his presence of mind and the resolve which he showed in contrast with Laches; next it was his confident walk, in no ways different from his usual one; then the controlled and steady eyes with which he weighed and evaluated what was going on about him, staring now at some who were friends, now at others who

3. In the *Problemata*, XXXIII, 9, attributed to Aristotle.
4. Plutarch (tr. Amyot), *Causes naturelles*, 536H–537A.
5. Seneca, *Epist. moral.*, LIII, 3 (of his own experience).
6. Plato, *Symposium*, 221A–B.

were foes, encouraging the friends and showing the others that he was a man to sell his life-blood very dear should any assay to take it from him. That saved them, for you do not willingly attack men like that: you hunt the fearful.'

There you have the testimony of a great Captain, teaching us (what we can assay every day) that nothing casts us into dangers so much as a rash hunger to get out of them: [C] *'Quo timoris minus est, eo minus ferme periculi est.'* [As a rule, where you feel less fear you experience less danger.][7]

[B] People today are wrong to say 'That man is frightened of dying,' when they really mean that he dwells on it and anticipates it. Anticipation equally concerns whatever affects us, for good or evil. In some ways, weighing and evaluating a danger is the opposite of being thrown into amazement by it. I do not think I am strong enough to sustain the violent onslaught of fear nor of any other passion which disturbs the mind. If ever I were once to be vanquished and thrown to the ground by it I would never wholly get up again; should anything make my soul lose her footing I could never set her back straight in place again. She is ever probing and feeling herself too vigorously and examining herself too deeply; consequently she would never allow the wound which had pierced her to grow together and become strong. It is a good thing for me that no malady has so far overthrown her. Each onslaught against me I confront and oppose equipped in full armour, so the first to get the better of me would leave me without resources. There is no question of doing anything twice: let the storm once breach my dyke anywhere and all of me is open, irremediably drowned. [C] Epicurus asserts that no wise man can become the opposite of wise.[8] I know something about that judgement the other way round: no man who has been a real fool once will ever be really wise again!

[B] God sends us cold according to our garment; he sends me emotions according to my means of sustaining them. Nature, having exposed me on one flank, has covered me on the other: having stripped me of fortitude she has equipped me with an inability to feel and with blunted balanced powers of anticipation.

Now I cannot put up for long with coach, litter or boat (and could do so less still in my youth). I loathe all means of conveyance but the horse, both for town and country. But litters I can tolerate less than coaches; and for

7. Livy, XXII, v.
8. Diogenes Laertius, *Life of Epicurus.*

the same reason I can better tolerate being thrown about on a rough sea — which produces fear — than I can the motion experienced during calm weather. Just as I cannot suffer a rickety chair under me, similarly I cannot suffer that slight jerk made by the oars as they pull the boat from under us without it somehow disturbing my brain and my stomach. Now, when sail or current bears us smoothly along or when we are towed, the unified motion in no wise bothers me; what upsets me is that series of broken movements, the more so when it is slow. I cannot describe its characteristics any other way. Doctors have prescribed binding a towel as a compress round the lower part of my belly; I have never assayed it, being used to fighting against my defects and vanquishing them by myself.

[C] If my memory were adequately furnished with them I would not regret time spent listing here the infinite variety of historical examples of the applications of coaches to the service of war, varying as they do from nation to nation and century to century; they are, it seems to me, most effective and very necessary. It seems a marvel to me that we have forgotten all about it. I will merely say this: quite recently in our fathers' time the Hungarians put them to excellent use against the Turks; in each coach a soldier with a round buckler was stationed beside a musketeer, together with a number of harquebuses in racks, already loaded. They clad the sides of each coach with rows of shields rather like a frigate. They drew up a line in front of their troops consisting of three thousand such coaches; after the cannon had played their part they either sent them ahead towards the enemy who had to swallow that salvo as a foretaste of what was to come (no slight advantage), or else they threw them against the enemy squadrons to break them up and open a way through. In addition there was the help they could give in covering the flanks of their troops when marching through ticklish country or in speedily defending an encampment by turning it into a fort.[9]

In my own day there was a gentleman living on one of our frontiers; he was an invalid and could find no horse able to bear his weight; he was involved in a feud and campaigned in a coach such as I have described and managed very well. But let us finish with those war-coaches.

The kings of our first Gaulish dynasty used to travel the land in a cart drawn by four oxen.[10] [B] Mark Antony was the first to be drawn

9. Nicolas Chalcocondylas, *Décadence de l'empire grec*, VII, vii (tr. Blaise de Vigenère).
10. Du Haillant, *Hist. des Roys de France*, II; then a series of examples from Pietro Crinito, *De honesta disciplina*, XVI, v.

through Rome – with a minstrel-girl beside him – by lions harnessed to a coach. Heliogabalus did the same somewhat later, claiming to be Cybele the Mother of the gods; then, drawn by tigers, he pretended to be the god Bacchus. On other occasions he harnessed two stags to his coach; once it was four dogs; then he stripped naked and was drawn in solemn procession by four naked girls. The Emperor Firmus had his coach drawn by ostriches of such extraordinary size that he seemed to fly rather than to roll along. The oddness of such novelties leads me on to the idea that it is a sort of lack of confidence in monarchs, a sign of not being sure of their position, to strive to make themselves respected and glorious through excessive expenditure. It would be pardonable abroad but among his subjects, where he is the sovereign power, the highest degree of honour to which he can attain is derived from the position he holds. Similarly it seems to me that it is superfluous for a gentleman to take a lot of trouble over how he dresses when at home: his house, his servants, his cuisine are enough to vouch for him there.

[C] Isocrates' advice to his king does not seem to lack good sense: let his furniture and his tableware be magnificent, for such expenditure is of lasting value and is passed on to his successors: let him avoid all magnificence which drains away immediately from use or memory.[11]

[B] When I was a young man, in default of other glories I gloried in fine clothes. In my case they were quite becoming; but there are folk on whom fine clothes sit down and cry.

There are tales of the extraordinary meanness of some of our kings over both personal expenditure and donations – and they were kings great in reputation, wealth and fortune. Demosthenes fought unsparingly against one of his city's laws which authorized monies to be spent on parades of athletes and festivals (he wanted his city's greatness to be displayed in the number of its well-armed fighting-ships and in good, well-equipped forces). [C] And Theophrastus is rightly condemned for asserting the opposite doctrine in his book *On Riches*, in which he maintained that expenditure on festivals was the true fruit of opulence. Such pleasures, says Aristotle, have an effect only on the lowest of the low; they immediately vanish from their memory as soon as they have had enough of them; no serious man of judgement can hold them in esteem.[12]

11. Isocrates, *Nicocles*, VI, xix.
12. [C] all from Cicero, *De officiis*, II, xvi, 56–7. Aristotle's judgement otherwise unknown.

Such funds would seem to me to be more regal, useful, sensible and durable if spent on ports, harbours, fortifications and walls, on splendid buildings, on churches, hospitals and colleges, and on repairing roads and highways. In my time Pope Gregory XIII left a favourable reputation behind him by so doing; and, by so doing, our own Queen Catherine would for many a long year to come leave witnesses to her natural generosity and munificence, if only her means were sufficient for her desires.[13] Fortune deeply distressed me by interrupting the construction in our capital city of the Pont neuf, a beautiful bridge, so cheating me of the hope of seeing it in regular use before I die.

[B] Moreover to their subjects who form the spectators of these festivities, it seems that it is their own wealth that is being flaunted and that they are being feasted at their own expense. Their peoples are always ready to assume about kings what we assume about our servants: that their job is to provide abundantly for everything that we want but never to spend anything on themselves. That is why the Emperor Galba, when he was delighted by a musician during dinner, called for his chest, plunged in his hand and gave him a fistful of crowns saying, 'This is my own money not the government's.'[14] Be that as it may, the people are usually right: money earned to feed their bellies is used instead to feed their eyes.

Even munificence is not truly resplendent from a sovereign's hands: it more rightly belongs to private citizens; for strictly speaking a king has nothing which is properly his own: even his person belongs to others. [C] Sentences are not passed in the interests of the judge but of the plaintiffs. We never appoint our superiors for their own advantage but for that of their inferiors; we appoint a doctor for his patients not for himself. All public offices, like all professional skills, aim at something beyond themselves: 'nulla ars in se versatur' [no art is concerned with itself].[15]

[B] That is why those tutors of youthful princes who pride themselves on impressing upon them that there is virtue in lavishness, who exhort them not to know what it means to reject anything and to hold that money is never better spent than when given away (teaching, greatly honoured, I know, in my own lifetime), are either thinking more of their own good than that of their own master or else they do not know what they are talking about. It is all too easy to stamp ideas of generosity on a

13. The Queen Mother, Catherine de' Medici.
14. Plutarch, *Life of Galba*.
15. Cicero, *De finibus*, V, vi, 16.

man who has the means of fulfilling them with other people's money.
[C] And since generosity is measured not against the gift but the means
of the giver, in such powerful hands it always proves useless. To be
generous, they discover, they have to be prodigal. [B] So it is not
highly honoured compared to the other kingly virtues: it is, said Dionysius
the Tyrant, the only virtue to be fully compatible with tyranny itself.[16] I
would rather teach a king this line from one ancient ploughman:

$$Τῇ χειρὶ δεῖ σπείρειν, ἀλλὰ μὴ ὅλῳ τῷ θυλακῷ$$

that is, 'If you want a good crop, you must broadcast your seed not pour it
from your sack.'[17] [C] Seed must be drilled not spilled. [B] So
when a king has to make gifts or, to put it better, has to make payments to
so many persons for services rendered, he should distribute royally but
advisedly. If a prince's generosity is indiscriminate and immoderate I would
like him better as a miser.

It is in justice that kingly virtue seems mainly to consist. And what most
distinguishes a king is that kind of justice which is the companion of
generosity; kings readily dispense all other kinds of justice through
intermediaries: that one they reserve to themselves.

Liberality without moderation is a feeble means of acquiring good-will,
since it offends more people than it seduces. [C] 'Quo in plures usus sis,
minus in multos uti possis. Quid autem est stultius quam quod libenter facias,
curare ut id diutius facere non possis?' [The more people you have helped by
it, the fewer you can help in the future ... Is there a greater folly than
doing something you like in such a way that you can do it no
longer?][18] [B] And if it is exercised without due regard for merit, it
embarrasses the recipient, who receives it without gratitude. There have
been tyrants who have been sacrificed to the people's hatred by the very
men they have unjustly advanced, since [C] men of that sort [B]
reckon that[19] they can insure their possession of ill-gotten gains by showing
hatred and contempt for the one they got them from; in that way they
seek to placate the judgement and opinions of the people.

The subjects of a prince who is lavish in giving become lavish in their
demands. They base their assessments not on reason but example. We

16. Plutarch (tr. Amyot), Dicts notables des anciens Roys, 190 D–E.
17. In Amyot's Plutarch (525 F) this verse of Corinna's is cited in French, not
Greek. The original appears in Justus Lipsius, De amphitheatro.
18. Cicero, De officiis, II, xv, 52–3; 54.
19. '88: since clowns, pimps, fiddlers and other such riff-raff reckon that ...

certainly ought often to blush at our shamelessness. We are already overpaid by just standards once the reward is equal to our services. Do we owe nothing to our princes by natural obligation? If our prince meets our expenses he has already done a great deal. Should he contribute to them, that is enough: anything above that is called a bounty: as such it cannot be demanded. (The very word liberality has the sound of liberty.) By our fashion there is no end to it: goods already received do not figure in our accounts: we only love future liberality. So the more a prince exhausts his wealth in giving, the poorer he is in friends.   [C] How could he possibly slake desires which grow bigger the more he pours wealth into them? The man whose thoughts are set on getting thinks no longer of what he has got. The property of covetousness is, above all, ingratitude.[20]

The example of Cyrus would not fit in badly here to serve our kings today as a touchstone for discovering whether their gifts are well or ill bestowed (and to show them that that Emperor distributed his gifts better than they do; by their extravagance they are reduced to raising loans from subjects unknown to them or from those whom they have harmed rather than from those whom they have helped, receiving 'gratuities' from them which have nothing gratuitous about them but the name). Croesus reproached Cyrus for his bounty, calculating what his treasure would have amounted to if he had restrained his hands a little more. Cyrus sought to justify his liberality: so he dispatched messengers all over the place to those magnates of his empire whose interests he had individually advanced, begging each of them to help him with as much money as they could for some urgent need and to write to him disclosing the amount. When all the letters of credit were brought to him, none of his friends had reckoned that it was enough to offer merely as much as they had received from his munificence but included much of their own wealth. He found that the sum amounted to far more than Croesus' economies. Whereupon Cyrus said to him, 'I love riches no less than other princes do; if anything I am more sparing. You can see by what little outlay I have acquired the countless riches of so many friends, and how much better Chancellors of the Exchequer they are than hired men would be with no bonds of affection, and how my wealth is better lodged with them than in my own treasure-chests, calling down upon me the hatred, envy and contempt of other princes.'[21]

[B]   The Roman Emperors justified the lavishness of their public games

20. Seneca, *Epist. moral.*, LXXIII, 2–3.
21. Xenophon, *Cyropaedia*, VIII, ii.

and parades by the fact that their authority in some ways depended (in appearance at least) on the will of the people, who had ever been accustomed to be courted by such extravagant spectacles. Yet it was private citizens who had encouraged this custom of pleasing their fellow-citizens and their equals with such a profusion of magnificence drawn mainly from their own purses. It took on a quite different savour when their masters came to imitate them. [C] *'Pecuniarum translatio a justis dominis ad alienos non debet liberalis videri.'* [Taking money from rightful owners and giving it to others ought not to be regarded as liberality.][22] When his son assayed winning the support of the Macedonians by sending them gifts, Philip reprimanded him in a letter with these words: 'What? Do you desire that your subjects should consider you not their King but their bursar? If you want to seduce, seduce them by deeds of virtue not by deeds of your purse-strings.'

[B]   Yet there was beauty in providing a great quantity of mature trees, with thick green branches, and in planting them beautifully and symmetrically in the arena to make a great shady forest, and then, on the first day, in releasing within it a thousand ostriches, a thousand stags, a thousand wild boars and a thousand deer and in handing it over to the populace to pillage; then, on the following day, in killing off before them a hundred full-grown lions, a hundred leopards and three hundred bears; then, on the third day, in having three hundred pairs of gladiators fight to the finish, as did the Emperor Probus.[23] Beautiful too to see those great amphitheatres incrusted on the outside with marble and decorated with works of art and statuary, the inside gleaming with rare and precious stones –

> *Baltheus en gemmis, en illita porticus auro*

[Here is the circular partition clad in gems; here, the portico, daubed with gold]

– with all the sides surrounding that vast space completely encircled from top to bottom with sixty to eighty tiers of seats, also of marble, covered with cushions –

> *exeat, inquit,*
> *Si pudor est, et de pulvino surgat equestri,*
> *Cujus res legi non sufficit;*

22. Cicero, *De officiis*, I, xiv, 43 (on the liberality of Sylla and Gaius Caesar); then, II, xv, 53–4 (on Philip of Macedonia).
23. Related after Pietro Crinito, *De honesta disciplina*, XII, vii, with interpolated verses from Calpurnius' *Bucolica*, VII, 47; Juvenal, *Satires*, III, 153–5 and Calpurnius, *Bucolica*, VII, 64–75, taken (with much else) from Justus Lipsius' *De amphitheatro*.

['Shame him out,' they say: 'he has only paid for the cheapest seats, not for the cushioned ones of the knights]

– where you could seat a hundred thousand men in comfort; beauty, too, to have the base of the arena where the games took place dug up and divided into caverns representing lairs which spewed forth the animals destined for the spectacle; subsequently to flood it with a deep sea of water, sweeping along many a sea-monster and bearing armed warships to enact a naval engagement; then, thirdly, to flatten it and drain it out afresh for the gladiatorial combats; and then, for the fourth act, to strew it, not with sand but with vermilion and aromatic resin in order to prepare upon it a formal banquet for that infinite crowd of people – the final scene on one single day!

> *Quoties nos descendentis arenæ*
> *Vidimus in partes, ruptaque voragine terræ*
> *Emersisse feras, et iisdem sæpe latebris*
> *Aurea cum croceo creverunt arbuta libro.*
> *Nec solum nobis silvestria cernere monstra*
> *Contigit, æquoreos ego cum certantibus ursis*
> *Spectavi vitulos, et equorum nomine dignum,*
> *Sed deforme pecus.*

[How often have we beheld a section of the arena drop down, forming a gaping chasm from which emerged wild beasts and whole forests of golden trees with barks of saffron! Not only have we seen the denizens of the forests in our amphitheatres but sea-beasts set in the midst of fighting bears and those monstrous hippopotamuses honoured by the name of 'river-horses'.]

Sometimes they produced in the arena a great mountain covered with green trees, many bearing fruit, and a river running from its summit as from the source of a flowing stream. Sometimes they had a great ship sail into the arena; it opened up and fell apart automatically, spewed forth from its belly four or five hundred beasts of combat, reassembled itself unaided and vanished from sight. Sometimes down there in the arena they produced fountains and water-jets which spouted immensely high, sprinkling perfume over that vast multitude. To protect themselves from the hot weather they caused that immense area to be covered either with awnings of purple needlework or with variously coloured silks, which they drew or withdrew at will:

> *Quamvis non modico caleant spectacula sole,*
> *Vela reducuntur, cum venit Hermogenes.*

[Although the fierce sun beats down on the amphitheatre they draw back the awnings whenever Hermogenes appears.][24]

Even the netting erected in front of the crowd to protect them from the ferocity of the wild beasts once they were loosed was plaited with gold:

> auro quoque torta refulgent
> Retia.

[The very nets glisten with woven gold.]

If anything can justify such excesses, it is the cases where the amazement was caused not by the expense but by the originality and ingenuity.

Even in vanities such as these we can discover how those times abounded in more fertile minds than ours. The same applies to that sort of fertility as to any other which Nature produces. Which is not to say that she then employed her utmost forces.[25] [C] We cannot be said to progress but rather to wander about this way and that. We follow our own footsteps. [B] I am afraid that our knowledge is in every sense weak; we cannot see very far ahead nor very far behind; it grasps little, lives little, skimped in terms of both time and matter.

> Vixere fortes ante Agamemnona
> Multi, sed omnes illachrimabiles
> Urgentur ignotique longa
> Nocte.

[Great heroes lived before Agamemnon; many they were, yet none is lamented, being swept away unknown into the long night.]

> Et supera bellum Trojanum et funera Trojæ,
> Multi alias alii quoque res cecinere poetæ.

[Before the Trojan War and the death of Troy many other poets have sung of other wars.][26]

[C] And while on this subject I think we should not reject the testimony

24. Martial, *Epigrams*, XII, xxix, 15–16; then, Calpurnius, *Bucolica*, VII, 53–4, with other matter from Justus Lipsius.
25. '88: forces. *There is verisimilitude in saying that we neither go forward nor backwards, rolling, rather, spinning and changing.* I am afraid ... Then, Horace, *Odes*, IV, ix, 25–8.
26. Lucretius, V, 327–8.

of Solon's account of how he had learned from the priests of Egypt the long history of their State and their way of teaching and preserving the history of other peoples: '*Si interminatam in omnes partes magnitudinem regionum videremus et temporum, in quam se injiciens animus et intendens ita late longeque peregrinatur, ut nullam oram ultimi videat in qua possit insistere: in hac immensitate infinita vis innumerabilium appareret formarum.*' [If we were vouchsafed a sight of the infinite extent of time and space stretching away in every direction, and if our minds were allowed to wander over it far and wide, ranging about and hastening along without ever glimpsing a boundary where it could halt: from such an immensity we would grasp what almighty power lies behind those innumerable forms.][27]

[B] Even if everything that has come down to us about the past by report were true and known to someone, that would be nothing compared with what we do not know. And against the idea of a universe which flows on while we are in it, how puny and stunted is the knowledge of the most inquisitive men. A hundred times more is lost for us than what comes to our knowledge, not only of individual events (which sometimes are turned by Fortune into weighty *exempla*) but of the circumstances of great polities and nations. When our artillery and printing were invented we clamoured about miracles: yet at the other end of the world in China men had been enjoying them over a thousand years earlier.[28] If what we saw of the world were as great as the amount we now cannot see, it is to be believed that we would perceive an endless [C] multiplication and [B] succession of forms. Where Nature is concerned, nothing is unique or rare: but where our knowledge is concerned much certainly is, which constitutes a most pitiful foundation for our scientific laws, offering us a very false idea of everything.

Just as we vainly conclude today that the world is declining into decrepitude using arguments drawn from our own decline and decadence –

Jamque adeo affecta est ætas, affectaque tellus

[Our age lacks vigour now: even the soil is less abundant][29]

27. Cicero, *De natura deorum*, I, xx, 54 (changing Cicero's *atomorum* to *formarum*, thus linking the concept less to Lucretius than to Plato's Great Chain of Being).
28. Many, including Rabelais, believed that printing was invented under the inspiration of the Holy Ghost, so as to counteract the Devil's invention of gunpowder and artillery (cf. *Pantagruel*, TLF, VIII, 92–5). Knowledge of China was being spread especially by the Jesuits.
29. Lucretius, II, 1136; then, V, 331–5.

– so that same poet concluded that the world was yet newly born and young, from the vigour of the minds of his day, fertile in new inventions and the creation of various arts:

> Verum, ut opinor, habet novitatem summa, recensque
> Natura est mundi, neque pridem exordia cæpit:
> Quare etiam quædam nunc artes expoliuntur,
> Nunc etiam augescunt, nunc addita navigiis sunt
> Multa.

[In my opinion our universe is new; the origin of the world is recent: it is but newly born. That is why some arts are still developing nowadays and growing still; the art of navigation is even now progressing.]

Our world has just discovered another one: and who will answer for its being the last of its brothers, since up till now its existence was unknown to the daemons, to the Sibyls, and to ourselves? It is no less big and full and solid than our own; its limbs are as well developed: yet it is so new, such a child, that we are still teaching it its ABC; a mere fifty years ago it knew nothing of writing, weights and measures, clothing, any sort of corn or vine. It was still naked at the breast, living only by what its nursing Mother provided. If we are right to conclude that our end is nigh, and that poet is right that his world is young, then that other world will only be emerging into light when ours is leaving it. The world will be struck with the palsy: one of its limbs will be paralysed while the other is fully vigorous, yet I fear we shall have considerably hastened the decline and collapse of that young world by our contagion and that we shall have sold it dear our opinions and our skills.

That world was an infant: we whipped it and subjected it to our teaching, but not from any superior worth of ours or our natural energy; we neither seduced it by our justice and goodness nor subjugated it by our greatness of soul. Most of the responses of its peoples, and most of our negotiations with them, witness that they are in no ways beholden to us where aptitude and natural clarity of mind are concerned. The awe-inspiring magnificence of the cities of Cuzco and Mexico and, among similar things, the gardens of that king where all the trees and fruits and all the plants were, in size and arrangement, as in a normal garden, but all excellently wrought in gold, as were in his museum all the creatures which are born in his estates or in his seas;[30] the beauty of their

30. The Inca garden and museum described on hearsay by Lopez de Gomara (tr. Fumée), *Histoire générale des Indes*, V, xiii. Much of what follows is from that work.

works of art in precious stones, feathers and cotton as well as in painting shows that they were not behind us in craftsmanship either.

And as for their piety, observance of the laws, goodness, liberality, loyalty and frankness: well, it served us well that we had less of that than they did; their superiority in that ruined them, sold them and betrayed them.

As for bravery and courage; as for resolution, constancy and resistance to pain, hunger and death, I would not hesitate to compare the examples provided by them with the most celebrated ones of the Ancients written in the annals of our own world on this side of the seas.

As regards those men who subjugated them, were you to take from them the trickery and sleight-of-hand which they used to deceive them, the justified ecstasy of amazement which struck those peoples at the sight of the totally unexpected landing of bearded men, differing from them in language, religion, build and facial features, coming from a world so remote and from regions in which they had never even dreamed that there were any humans dwelling whatsoever; men mounted on big unknown monsters confronting men who had never seen not merely horses but any animal whatsoever trained to be ridden by man or to bear any other burden; men whose skin was shining and hard, men armed with a glittering cutting-instrument confronting men who would barter a vast wealth of gold or pearls for a looking-glass or a knife, the sheen of which to them appeared miraculous; men who, even if they had had the time, had neither the knowledge nor the materials to discover ways of piercing our steel; to which add the lightning flashes of our cannons, the thundering of our harquebuses (able to confuse the mind of Caesar himself in his day if they had surprised him when he was as ignorant of them as they were) opposed to people who were naked except in those areas which had been reached by the invention of a kind of woven cotton-cloth; peoples with no arms except (at the most) bows, stones, staves [C] or wooden shields; [B] peoples who, under pretence of friendship and good faith, were caught off their guard by their curiosity to see things strange and unknown: remove (I say) from the Conquistadores such advantages and you strip them of what made so many victories possible.

When I reflect on the indomitable ardour with which so many thousands of men, women and children came so many times and threw themselves into certain danger in defence of their gods and their freedom, and when I reflect on that great-souled stubborn determination to suffer any extremity, any hardship including death, rather than to submit to the domination of those who had so disgracefully deceived them – some of them preferring once they were captured to die slowly of hunger than to accept food from the hands of enemies so vilely victorious: I maintain that, if they had been attacked equal to equal in arms and experience and numbers, then the conflict would have been as hazardous (or more so) as any other that we know of.

Oh why did it not fall to Alexander and those ancient Greeks and Romans to make of it a most noble conquest; why did such a huge transfer of so many empires, and such revolutions in the circumstances of so many peoples, not fall into hands which would have gently polished those peoples, clearing away any wild weeds while encouraging and strengthening the good crops that Nature had brought forth among them, not only bringing to them their world's arts of farming the land and adorning their cities (in so far as they were lacking to them) but also bringing to the natives of those countries the virtues of the Romans and the Greeks? What a renewal that would have been, what a restoration of the fabric of this world, if the first examples of our behaviour which were set before that new world had summoned those peoples to be amazed by our virtue and to imitate it, and had created between them and us a brotherly fellowship and understanding. How easy it would have been to have worked profitably with folk whose souls were so unspoiled and so hungry to learn, having for the most part been given such a beautiful start by Nature. We, on the contrary, took advantage of their ignorance and lack of experience to pervert them more easily towards treachery, debauchery and cupidity, toward every kind of cruelty and inhumanity, by the example and model of our own manners. Whoever else has ever rated trade and commerce at such a price? So many cities razed to the ground, so many nations wiped out, so many millions of individuals put to the sword, and the most beautiful and the richest part of the world shattered, on behalf of the pearls-and-pepper business! Tradesmen's victories! At least ambition and political strife never led men against men to such acts of horrifying enmity and to such pitiable disasters.

While sailing along the coast on the lookout for the natives' mines there were some Spaniards who went ashore in a fertile, pleasant and densely populated countryside; they gave the inhabitants their usual warning, declaring that they were men of peace, coming to them after sailing far across the seas, sent on behalf of the King of Castile, the greatest monarch in the inhabited world, to whom the Pope, as Vicar of God on earth, had granted dominion over all the Indies; that, if they would pay that King tribute they would be most kindly treated; then they asked for victuals to eat, and for gold ... which they needed as a medicine; they incidentally insisted that there is only one God, that our religion is the true one which they advised them to adopt – adding a menace or two.

In reply they were told that, as for their being men of peace, if they were they did not look it; as for their King, he must be poor and needy since he came a-begging; as for that man who had apportioned that tribute, he was a man who loved dissension since he gave to a third party something which was not his to give, seeking to pick a quarrel with those who had long possessed it; as for victuals, they would supply some; as for gold, they had very little; it was something they did not highly value since it was of small practical use in life, whereas their aim was to live their lives in happiness and contentment; so the Spaniards could readily have whatever gold they could find, except the gold which was used in the service of their own gods. As for there being only one God, they were pleased by the argument but did not intend to change their religion, having so profitably followed their own for such a long time and being unaccustomed to taking advice from anyone but their friends and acquaintances. As for their menaces, it was a sign of lack of judgement in them to go about threatening people the nature of whose resources was unknown to them; so let them get out of their country, quickly, for they were not accustomed to take in good part such courtesies from armed men and warnings from foreigners. They would do to them what they had done to others – and they indicated the heads of men condemned to death and displayed about their city.

There is an example of their baby-talk for you!

So the Spaniards neither remained nor campaigned in that place nor in many others where they found none of the merchandise they were after, no matter what other delights could be found there. Witness my cannibals.[31]

The last two kings whom the Spaniards hounded were kings over many kings, the most powerful kings in that new world and perhaps also in our own.

The first was the King of Peru. He was captured in battle and put to so huge a ransom that it defies all belief; he paid it faithfully and showed by his dealings that he was of a frank, noble and steadfast heart, a man of honest and tranquil mind. The Conquistadores, having already extracted gold weighing one million three hundred and twenty-five thousand five hundred ounces (not counting silver and other booty amounting to no less,

31. I, 31, 'On the Cannibals', above, pp. 79–92.

so that afterwards they even used solid gold to shoe their horses), were seized with the desire to discover what remained of the treasures of that king, no matter what it cost them in bad faith, [C] and to make free with whatever he had kept back. [B] They fabricated false evidence, accusing him of planning to get his territories to rise up in revolt and to set him free. Whereupon – a beautiful sentence, delivered by those who had got up this act of treachery! – he was condemned to be publicly hanged until he was dead, having first been compelled to buy off the agony of being burned alive at the stake by accepting baptism – which was administered to him while he was being tortured.

A horrifying, unheard-of action, which he nevertheless bore without demeaning, by look or word, his truly regal gravity and comportment. And then to placate the people who were stunned into an ecstasy of amazement by so outlandish a deed, they counterfeited great grief at his death and arranged a costly funeral.

The second was the King of Mexico: he had long held out during the siege of his city, showing (if ever a people did so) what can be achieved by endurance and constancy, yet he had the misfortune to fall alive into the hands of his enemies, but on terms of being treated like a king. (And during his captivity he showed nothing unworthy of that title.) But the Spaniards, not finding after that victory as much gold as they had anticipated, pillaged and ransacked everything and then proceeded to seek information by inflicting on the prisoners they had taken the most painful tortures that they could devise. But since nothing of value could be extorted from them, their hearts being stronger than the tortures, the Spaniards finally fell into such a fit of madness that, contrary to their word and to the law of nations, they sentenced the King and one of the chief lords of his court to be tortured in each other's sight. That lord, overcome with pain, surrounded by blazing braziers, finally turned his gaze piteously towards his sovereign, as if to beg [C] forgiveness because he could stand it no longer. [B] That King[32] proudly and severely fixed his eyes on him to reproach him for his cowardice and faint-heartedness and simply said these words in a firm hoarse voice: 'What about me? Am I having a bath? Am I any more at ease than you are?' Straightway afterwards that lord succumbed to the pain and died where he was. The King was borne away, half-roasted, not so much out of pity (for what pity could ever touch the souls of men who, for dubious information about some golden

32. '88: to beg *leave to tell what he knew to redeem himself from the unbearable pain.* That King . . .

vessel or other that they would pillage, would grill a man before their very eyes, not to mention a King of so great a destiny and merit) but because his constancy rendered their cruelty more and more humiliating.

When he afterwards made a courageous attempt to effect an armed escape from so long a captivity and slavery, they hanged him; he made an end worthy of a prince so great of soul.

On another occasion they set about burning, at one time and in the same pyre, four hundred and sixty men – every one of them alive – four hundred from the common people, sixty from the chief lords of the land, all straightforward prisoners of war.

These accounts we have from the Spaniards themselves.[33] They do not merely confess to them, they [C] boast of them and proclaim them. [B] Could it be[34] in order to witness to their justice or to their religious zeal? Such ways are certainly too contrary, too hostile, to so holy a purpose. If their intention had simply been to spread our faith, they would have thought upon the fact that it grows not by taking possession of lands but of men, and that they would have had killings enough through the necessities of war without introducing indiscriminate slaughter, as total as their swords and pyres could make it, as though they were butchering wild animals, merely preserving the lives of as many as they intended to make pitiful slaves to work and service their mines: so that several of the leaders of the Conquistadores were punished by death in the very lands they had conquered by order of the Kings of Castile, justly indignant at their dreadful conduct, while virtually all the others were loathed and hated.[35] To punish them God allowed that their vast plunder should be either engulfed by the sea as they were shipping it or else in that internecine strife in which they all devoured each other, most being buried on the scene, in no wise profiting from their conquest.

The gold actually received, even into the hands of a wise and thrifty Prince, corresponds so little to the expectations aroused in his predecessors

33. Montaigne's main source throughout is Francisco Lopez de Gomara (tr. Fumée), *L'Histoire générale des Indes* (1578 and 1587). It is not known whether he had also read the blistering attacks on the Conquistadores or on Spanish policy by Bishop Bartolome de las Casas, e.g. his *Brevissima relación de la destruyción de Las Indias* (Seville, 1552) or the account of his dispute entitled *Aqui se contiene una disputa entre B. de las Casas y G. de Sepulveda* (Seville, 1552), with which he would have been in agreement.

34. '88: they *preach and proclaim them.* Could it be . . .

35. These included Pizarro, condemned to death in 1548.

and to the abundant riches discovered when men first came to these new lands (for while they draw great profit from them we can see that it is nothing compared with what they could have expected); that is because the Indians knew nothing about the use of coinage. Consequently all their gold was gathered in one place, used only for display and parade; their gold was moveable-goods handed on from father to son by several puissant kings who always worked their mines merely to make great quantities of vessels and statues to decorate their palaces and their temples. All our gold circulates in trade. We break it down, change it in a thousand ways, spread it about and so disperse it. Just imagine what it would be like if our kings, over several centuries, had likewise piled up all the gold they could find and kept it idle.

The peoples of the Kingdom of Mexico were somewhat more urban and more cultured than the other peoples over there.[36] In addition, like us, they judged that the world was nearing its end, taking as a portent of this the desolation that we visited upon them. They believed that the world's existence was divided into five periods, each as long as the life of five successive suns. Four suns had already done their time, the one shining on them now being the fifth. The first sun perished with all other creatures in a universal Flood; the second, by the sky falling on mankind and choking every living thing (to which age they ascribed giant men, showing the Spaniards bones of men of such proportion that they must have stood twenty spans high); the third, by a fire which engulfed and burnt everything; the fourth, by a rush of air and wind which flattened everything including several mountains; human beings were not killed by it but changed into baboons (what impressions cannot be stamped on the receptive credulity of men!). After the death of that fourth sun the world was in perpetual darkness for twenty-five years, during the fifteenth of which was created a man and a woman who remade the human race. Ten years later, on a particular day which they observe, the sun appeared, newly created; they count their years from that day. On the third day after it was created their old gods died; new gods were subsequently born from time to time. My authority[37] could learn nothing about how they believed this fifth sun

---

36. Montaigne's term *plus civilisez* probably means not 'more civilized', but 'more urban and hence more given to civic virtues' than the pastoral Indians; similarly his term *plus artistes* probably means 'more cultured' rather than 'more artistic': they had more developed arts and sciences.

37. Francisco Lopez de Gomara, *Histoire générale des Indes*, II, lxxv and (for the Royal road described later) V, lxxxvii.

will die. But their dating of that fourth change tallies with that great conjunction of the planets which (eight hundred years ago, according to the reckoning of our astrologers) produced many great changes and innovations in the world.[38]

As for that ostentatious magnificence which led me to embark on this subject, neither Greece nor Rome nor Egypt can compare any of their constructions, for difficulty or utility or nobility, with the highway to be seen in Peru, built by their kings from the city of Quito to the city of Cuzco — three hundred leagues, that is — dead-straight, level, twenty-five yards wide, paved, furnished on either side with a revetment of high, beautiful walls along which there flow on the inside two streams which never run dry, bordered by those beautiful trees which they call *molly*. Whenever they came across mountains and cliffs they cut through them and flattened them, filling in whole valleys with chalk and stone. At the end of each day's march there are beauteous palaces furnished with victuals and clothing and weapons, both for troops and travellers who have to pass that way.

My judgement on this construction takes account of the difficulty, which in that place is particularly relevant since they build using blocks never less than ten-foot square; they have no means of transporting them except to drag them along by the force of their arms: they do not even have the art of scaffolding, knowing no other method than to pile up earth against a building as it rises and then to remove it afterwards.

But let us drop back to those coaches of ours.

Instead of using coaches or vehicles of any kind they have themselves carried on the shoulders of men. The day he was captured, that last King of Peru[39] was in the midst of his army, borne seated on a golden chair suspended from shafts of gold. The Spaniards in their attempts to topple him (as they wanted to take him alive) killed many of his bearers, but

---

38. According to the teaching of Alkindi, Albumasar and other Islamic astrologers widely accepted in medieval and Renaissance Europe, when a 'great conjunction' (that of the planets Saturn and Jupiter) occurs in the first degree of the zodiacal sign of the Ram, it produces one single outstanding prophet, teacher or lawgiver. Such a great conjunction was calculated to occur every 960 years. Both Islamic and Christian astrologers often held that a great conjunction heralded the birth of Moses, Jesus and Mahomet. Cf., for example, Petrus de Abano, *Conciliator* (*Diff.* XVIII). The great conjunction mentioned by Montaigne was the one preceding the birth of the Prophet of Islam. The theory of the influence of conjunctions was, of course, challenged by many.

39. Attabalipa.

many more vied to take the places of the dead, so that, no matter how many they slaughtered, they could not bring him down until a mounted soldier dashed in, grabbed hold of him and yanked him to the ground.

11. On the lame

[*The human mind is capable of great self-deception. It can find reasons for anything –
even for non-existent phenomena and unreal 'facts'. Experience is no guard against
error: it can be conditioned by prior expectations. That is one of the considerations
which led Montaigne never to discuss alleged miracles and to remain unimpressed by
judicial certainties.*

*For us today Montaigne's scepticism about the reality of the powers of male and
female witches is arresting. (He was not alone in holding such views, though he
remained in the minority.) But he is determined to subordinate his own opinions to the
teachings of the Roman Catholic Church. For him the value of his opinions is that
they are opinions and that they are his: they tell us of his* forma mentis. *But since
men's opinions are never certainties, should we ever burn people on account of them,
unless God directly intervenes to order us to do so?*]

[B] In France, some two or three years ago now, they shortened the year
by ten days.[1] What changes were supposed to result from that reform! It
was, quite literally, to move both the heavens and the earth at the same
time. Yet nothing has been shoved out of place. My neighbours find that
seed-time and harvest, auspicious times for business, as well as ill-omened
or propitious days, come at precisely the same second to which they have
ever been assigned. The error of our practices was never felt beforehand:
no amendment is felt there now, so much uncertainty is there everywhere,
so gross is our faculty of perception,   [C] so darkened and so blunt.

[B] They say that this adjustment could have been made less awkwardly
by following the example of Augustus and omitting the extra day over a
period of several leap-years – it is a source of trouble and confusion
anyway – until we had paid back the missing time (something which we
have not even achieved by this correction: we are still a day or two in
arrears). By this means we could also have provided for the future,
declaring that after a specified number of years had rolled by that extra day
would be banished for ever, with the result that our miscalculation from
then on could not exceed twenty-four hours.

1. The Gregorian reform of the calendar (1582). Montaigne says that he could not
adapt to it (III, 10, 'On restraining your will').

Years are the only measure we have for time. The world has been using 'years' for many centuries, yet it is a unit which we have never succeeded in standardizing, so that we live in daily uncertainty about the incompatible forms given to it by other nations, and about how they apply them.

And what if (as some say) the heavens as they grow old are contracting downwards towards us, thereby casting our very hours and days into confusion? And what of our months too, since Plutarch says that even in his period the science of the heavens had yet to fix the motions of the moon?[2]

A fine position we are in to keep chronicles of past events!

I was recently letting my mind range wildly (as I often do) over our human reason and what a rambling and roving instrument it is. I realize that if you ask people to account for 'facts', they usually spend more time finding reasons for them than finding out whether they are true. They ignore the *whats* and expatiate on the *whys*.   [C]   Wiseacres!

To know causes belongs only to Him who governs things, not to us who are patients of such things and who, without penetrating their origin or essences, have complete enjoyment of them in terms of our own nature. Wine is no more delightful to the man who knows its primary qualities. Quite the reverse: by bringing in pretensions to knowledge the body infringes, and the soul encroaches upon, the rights which both of them have to enjoy the things of this world. To define, to know and to allow belong to professors and schoolmasters: to enjoy and to accept belong to inferiors, subordinates and apprentices.

Let us get back to that custom of ours.

[B] They skip over the facts but carefully deduce inferences. They normally begin thus: 'How does this come about?' But does it do so? That is what they ought to be asking. Our reason has capacity enough to provide the stuff for a hundred other worlds, and then to discover their principles and construction! It needs neither matter nor foundation; let it run free: it can build as well upon the void as upon the plenum, upon space as upon matter:

> *dare pondus idonea fumo.*
>
> [meet to give heaviness even to smoke.][3]

---

2. Plutarch (tr. Amyot), *Demandes des choses Romaines*, 464 B, drawing the same conclusions as Montaigne.
3. Persius, *Satires*, I, 20.

I find that we should be saying virtually all the time, 'It is not at all like that!' I would frequently make that reply but I dare not, since folk bellow that it is a dodge produced by ignorance and by weakness of intellect; so I am usually obliged to be a mountebank for the sake of good company, and to discuss trivial subjects and tales which I totally disbelieve. Moreover it is rather rude and aggressive flatly to deny a statement of fact; and (especially in matters where it is difficult to convince others) few people fail to assert that 'they have seen it themselves' or to cite witnesses whose authority puts a stop to our contradictions. By following this practice we know the bases and causes of hundreds of things which never were; the world is involved in duels about hundreds of questions where both the for and the against are false: [C] *'Ita finitima sunt falsa veris, ut in præcipitem locum non debeat se sapiens committere.'* [The false and the true are in such close proximity that the wise man should not trust himself to so steep a slope.][4] [B] Truth and falsehood are both alike in form of face and have identical stances, tastes and demeanours. We look on them with the same eye. I find that we are not merely slack about guarding ourselves from dupery, but we actually want to fall on its sword. We love to be entangled with vanity, since it corresponds in form to our own being.

I have seen in my time the birth of several miracles. Even if they are smothered at birth, that does not stop us from predicting the course they would have taken if they had grown up! We only need to get hold of the end of the thread: we then reel off whatever we want. Yet the distance is greater from nothing to the minutest thing in the world than it is from the minutest thing to the biggest. Now when the first people who drank their fill of the original oddity come to spread their tale abroad, they can tell by the opposition which they arouse what it is that others find difficult to accept; they then stop up the chinks with some false piece of oakum. [C] Moreover, *'insita hominibus libidine alendi de industria rumores'* [by man's inborn tendency to work hard at feeding rumours][5] we naturally feel embarrassed if what was lent to us we pass on to others without some exorbitant interest of our own. At first the individual error creates the public one: then, in its turn, the public error creates the individual one. [B] And so, as it passes from hand to hand, the whole fabric is padded out and reshaped, so that the most far-off witness is better informed about it than the closest one, and the last to be told more convinced than the first. It is a natural progression. For whoever believes anything reckons

4. Cicero, *Academica*, II (Lucullus), XXI, 68.
5. Livy, XXVIII, xxiv.

that it is a work of charity to convince someone else of it; and to do this he is not at all afraid to add, out of his own invention, whatever his story needs to overcome the resistance and the defects which he thinks there are in the other man's ability to grasp it. I myself am particularly scrupulous about lying and can scarcely be bothered to quote authority for what I say in order to make it believable: yet even I notice that when I get heated about a matter I have in hand,   [C]   either because of another's resistance to it or else because of the excitement of the actual telling,   [B]   I increase the importance of my subject and puff it up by tone of voice, gestures, powerful and vigorous words – and also by stretching it a bit and exaggerating it, not without some damage to native truth. But I do so with the proviso that I immediately give up the attempt for the first man who summons me back and demands the truth, bare and bold, which I then give to him without exaggeration, without bombast and without embroidery.   [C]   A loud and lively gab, such as mine habitually is, soon flies off into hyperbole.

[B]   There is nothing over which men usually strain harder than when giving free run to their opinions: should the regular means be lacking, we support them by commands, force, fire and sword. It is wretched to be reduced to the point where the best touchstone of truth has become the multitude of believers, at a time when the fools in the crowd are so much more numerous than the wise: [C]   *'quasi vero quidquam sit tam valde quam nil sapere vulgare'* [as though anything whatsoever were more common than lack of wisdom].[6] *'Sanitatis patrocinium est, insanientium turba.'* [A mob of lunatics now form the authority for sane truth.]

[B]   It is hard to stiffen your judgement against widely held opinions. At first simple folk are convinced by the event itself: it sweeps over them. From them it spreads to the more intelligent folk by the authority of the number and the antiquity of the testimonies. Personally, what I would not believe when one person says it, I would not believe if a hundred times one said it. And I do not judge opinions by their age.

Not long ago one of our princes, whose excellent natural endowments and lively constitution had been undermined by the gout, allowed himself to be so strongly convinced by the reports which were circulating about the wonderful treatments of a priest who, by means of words and gestures, cured all illnesses, that he made a long journey to go and consult him. By the force of his imagination he convinced his legs for a few hours to feel no

6. Cicero, *De divinatione*, II, xxxix, 81; then, St Augustine, *City of God*, VI, x. (Montaigne's context echoes Seneca, *Epist. moral.*, LXXXI, etc.)

pain, so that he made them serve him as they had long since forgotten how to do. If Fortune had allowed some five or six such events to happen one on top of the other, they would have sufficed to give birth to a miracle. Afterwards, there was found such simplemindedness and such little artifice in the inventor of this treatment that he was not judged worthy of any punishment. We would do the same for most such things if we examined them back in their burrows. [C] *'Miramur ex intervallo fallentia.'* [We are astounded by things which deceive us by their remoteness.][7] [B] Thus does our sight often produce strange visions in the distance which vanish as we draw near. *'Nunquam ad liquidum fama perducitur.'* [Rumour never stops at what is crystal-clear.]

It is wonderful how such celebrated opinions are born of such vain beginnings and trivial causes. It is precisely that which makes it hard to inquire into them: for while we are looking for powerful causes and weighty ends worthy of such great fame we lose the real ones: they are so tiny that they escape our view. And indeed for such investigations we need a very wise, diligent and subtle investigator, who is neither partial nor prejudiced.

To this hour all such miracles and strange happenings hide away when I am about. I have not seen anywhere in the world a prodigy more expressly miraculous than I am. Time and custom condition us to anything strange: nevertheless, the more I haunt myself and know myself the more my misshapenness amazes me and the less I understand myself.

The right to promulgate and to publish such phenomena is mainly reserved to Fortune. The day before yesterday I was on my way through a village two leagues from home when I found the market-place still hot and excited about a miracle which had just come to grief there. All the neighbourhood had been preoccupied with it for months; the excitement had spread to the neighbouring provinces and great troops of people of all classes came pouring in. One night a local youth had larked about at home, imitating the voice of a ghost; he intended no trickery beyond enjoying the immediate play-acting. He succeeded somewhat beyond his hopes, so, to heighten the farce and thicken the plot, he brought in a village maiden who was absolutely stupid and simple. Eventually there were three of them, all of the same age, all equally stupid. From sermons in people's homes they progressed to sermons in public, hiding under the altar in church, delivering them only at night and forbidding any lights to be brought in. They started with talk directed towards the conversion of the

7. Seneca, *Epist. moral.*, CVIII, 7; then, Quintus Curtius, IX, ii.

world and the imminence of the Day of Judgement (for imposture can more readily crouch behind our reverence for the authority of such subjects) and then progressed on to several visions and actions so silly and laughable there is hardly anything more crude in the games of little children. Yet if Fortune had chosen to lend them a little of her favour, who knows what that play-acting might have grown into? Those poor devils are even now in gaol and may easily have to pay the penalty for the public's gullibility. And who knows whether some judge or other may not revenge his own upon them?

This incident has been uncovered: we can see clearly into it this time; but in many similar kinds of case which surpass our knowledge I consider that we should suspend our judgement, neither believing nor rejecting. Many of this world's abuses are engendered – [C] or to put it more rashly, all of this world's abuses are engendered – [B] by our being schooled to fear to admit our ignorance [C] and because we are required to accept anything which we cannot refute. [B] Everything is proclaimed by injunction and assertion. In Rome, the legal style required that even the testimony of an eye-witness or the sentence of a judge based on his most certain knowledge had to be couched in the formula, 'It seems to me that . . .'[8]

You make me hate things probable when you thrust them on me as things infallible. I love terms which soften and tone down the rashness of what we put forward, terms such as 'perhaps', 'somewhat', 'some', 'they say', 'I think' and so on. And if I had had sons to bring up I would have trained their lips to answer with [C] inquiring and undecided [B] expressions such as, 'What does this mean?', 'I do not understand that', 'It might be so', 'Is that true?' so that they would have been more likely to retain the manners of an apprentice at sixty than, as boys do, to act like learned doctors at ten. Anyone who wishes to be cured of ignorance must first admit to it: [C] Iris is the daughter of Thaumantis: amazement is the foundation of all philosophy; inquiry, its way of advancing; and ignorance is its end.[9]

[B] Yes indeed: there is a kind of ignorance, strong and magnanimous, which in honour and courage is in no wise inferior to knowledge;

8. Cicero, Academica, II (Lucullus), xlvii, 146.
9. The Scholastic axiom, Admiratio parit scientiam. (Consult Signoriello, Lexicon peripateticum philosophico-theologicum, s.v. Admiratio, citing Thomas Aquinas.) The saying derives from Plato, Theaetetus, 155 D. (Plato derived the name of Thaumas, Iris' father, from thauma, wonder, prodigy. Montaigne's name for him, Thaumantis, is in fact the name of Isis herself.)

[C]   you need no less knowledge to beget such ignorance than to beget knowledge itself.

[B]   When I was a boy I saw the account of a trial of a strange event printed by Coras, a learned counsel in Toulouse, concerning two men who each passed himself off for the other. What I remember of it (and I remember nothing else) is that it seemed to me at the time that Coras had made the impersonation on the part of the one he deemed guilty to be so miraculous and so far exceeding our own experience and his own as judge, that I found a great deal of boldness in the verdict which condemned the man to be hanged.[10] Let us (more frankly and more simply than the judges of the Areopagus, who when they found themselves hemmed in by a case which they could not unravel decreed that the parties should appear before them again a hundred years later) accept for a verdict a formula which declares, 'The Court does not understand anything whatever about this case.'[11]

My local witches go in risk of their lives, depending on the testimony of each new authority who comes and gives substance to their delusions. The Word of God offers us absolutely certain and irrefragable examples of such phenomena,[12] but to adapt and apply them to things happening in our own times because we cannot understand what caused them or how they were done needs a greater intelligence than we possess. It may perhaps be the property of that almighty Witness[13] alone to say to us: 'This is an example of it; so is that; this is not.' We must believe God – that really is right – but not, for all that, one of ourselves who is amazed by his own

10. The case of Martin Guerre (now well-known from a film thanks to the scholarship of Professor Nathalie Zemon Davies). Cf. the *Arrest memorable du Parlement de Tholose contenant une histoire prodigieuse d'un supposé mary, advenüe de nostre temps . . . par M. Iean de Coras*, Paris, 1582. Coras (p. 129) justifies the sentence of strangulation by hanging followed by the public burning of the body but (pp. 130–3) makes a passionate plea against burning anyone alive and against cruel torturings as unworthy of Christians, since they are partly based on a desire to purge one's own guilt.

11. The Areopagus in Athens had to judge a wife who murdered her second husband who, with his own son, had murdered her child by her dead husband. (This became the classical example of a *casus perplexus*, a case with the maximum degree of moral difficulty.) The Areopagus decreed that the parties concerned were to return to the Court, in person, one hundred years later! Tiraquellus evokes this well-known *exemplum* in his treatise *De poenis temperandis* (*Opera*, 1597, VII, 14). Cf. Rabelais (*Tiers Livre*, TLF, XLIIII, 6–44).

12. Cf. II Chronicles 33; II Kings 9; I Samuel 28 (the Witch of Endor consulted by Saul).

13. The Holy Ghost who, for Montaigne, was the author of Scripture.

narration – necessarily amazed if he is not out of his senses – whether testifying about others or against himself. I am a lumpish fellow and hold somewhat to solid probable things, avoiding those ancient reproaches: *'Majorem fidem homines adhibent iis quae non intelligunt'* [Men place more trust in whatever they do not understand] and, *'Cupidine humani ingenii libentius obscura creduntur.'* [There is a desire in the mind of Man which makes it more ready to believe whatever is obscure.][14] I am well aware that folk get angry and forbid me to have any doubts about witches on pain of fearsome retribution. A new form of persuasion! Thanks be to God my credo is not to be managed by thumps from anyone's fists. Let them bring out the cane for those who maintain that their opinions are wrong; I merely maintain that their opinions are bold and hard to believe, and I condemn a denial as much as they do, though less imperiously. [C] *'Videantur sane: ne affirmentur modo.'* [Let us grant that things so appear, provided they be not affirmed.][15]

[B] Any man who supports his opinion with challenges and commands demonstrates that his reasons for it are weak. When it is a question of words, of scholastic disputations, let us grant that they apparently have as good a case as that of their objectors: but in the practical consequences that they draw from it the advantages are all with the latter. To kill people, there must be sharp and brilliant clarity; this life of ours is too real, too fundamental, to be used to guarantee these supernatural and imagined events.

As for the use of compounds and potions, I leave it out of account: that is murder of the worst sort.[16] Yet even there it is said that we should not always be content with the confessions of such folk, for they have been known to accuse themselves of killing people who have later been found alive and well. As for those other accusations which exceed the bounds of

---

14. The second from Tacitus, *Hist.*, I, xxii; the first is attributed by Marie de Gournay to Pliny, but remains untraced.

15. Cicero, *Academica*, II (Lucullus), xxvii, 87.

16. In law a *maleficus* (a witch, an 'evil-doer') was taken in general as one who harmed another and was not necessarily restricted to *incantatores* (workers of spells). (Cf. Spiegel, *Lexicon Juris*, s.v.) Montaigne here excludes those not allegedly working their evil through magic; thus strengthening and limiting his argument. The crucial biblical authority is Exodus 22:18, 'Thou shalt not suffer a witch to live.' But what does it mean? The Greek Septuagint uses the word *pharmakous* here, the Clementine Vulgate uses *maleficos*. Both words apply to both sexes. But Hebraists, since at least Nicolas of Lyra, insisted that the original term *kashaph* is used in the feminine. Liberal theologians clung to the Greek term and insisted that it means sorcerers who use potions to produce their wicked effects.

reason I would like to say that it is quite enough for any man – no matter how highly esteemed he is – to be believed about matters human: in the case of whatever is beyond his comprehension and produces supernatural results he should be believed only when supernatural authority confirms it.

That privilege which God has granted to some of our testimonies must not be debased or lightly made common.[17] They have battered my ears with hundreds of stories like this: three men saw him in the east on a particular day; the following morning, in such-and-such a time and place and dress, he was seen in the west. I would certainly never trust my own testimony over such a matter: how much more natural and probable it seems to me that two men should lie, rather than that, in twelve hours, one man should go like the wind from east to west; how much more natural that our mind should be enraptured from its setting by the whirl-wind of our own deranged spirit than that, by a spirit from beyond, one of us humans, in flesh and blood, should be sent flying on a broomstick up the flue of his chimney. We, who are never-endingly confused by our own internal delusions, should not go looking for unknown external ones. It seems to me that it is excusable to disbelieve any wonder, at least in so far as we can weaken its 'proof' by diverting it along some non-miraculous way. I am of Saint Augustine's opinion, that in matters difficult to verify and perilous to believe, it is better to incline towards doubt than certainty.[18]

A few years ago I was passing through the domains of a sovereign prince who, as a courtesy to me and to overcome my disbelief, graciously allowed me to see, in a private place when he was present, ten or a dozen of this kind of prisoner, including one old woman, truly a witch as far as ugliness and misshapenness was concerned, and who had long been most famous for professing witchcraft. I was shown evidence and voluntary confessions as well as some insensitive spot or other on that wretched old woman;[19] I talked and questioned till I had had enough, bringing to bear the most sane attention that I could – and I am hardly the man to allow my judgement to

17. As Montaigne is about to talk of physical rapture from one place to another he is doubtless thinking of the rapture of Philip (Acts 8:39) when the 'Spirit of the Lord caught away' Philip from the road to Gaza so that he was found at Azotus.
18. St Augustine, *City of God*, XIX, xviii, contrasting scriptural truth with human testimony. Vives comments that no human knowledge, since it is known through the senses, can have the certainty of Scripture.
19. The so-called *witches' spot*; when pricked the true witch felt no sensation there. Inquisitors made painful searches for such a spot on the body of anyone charged with witchcraft.

be muzzled by preconceptions – but in the end, and in all honesty, I would have prescribed not hemlock for them but hellebore:[20]   [C]   *'Captisque res magis mentibus, quam consceleratis similis visa.'* [Their case seemed to be more a matter of insane minds rather than of delinquents.][21]   [B]   Justice has its own remedies for such maladies.[22]

As for the objections and arguments put to me there, and often elsewhere, by decent men, none ever seemed to tie me fast: all seemed to have a solution more convincing than their conclusions. It is true, though, that I never attempt to unknot 'proofs' or 'reasons' based on   [C]   experience nor on   [B]   a fact: they have no ends that you can get hold of; so, like Alexander cutting his knot, I often slice through them.[23] After all, it is to put a very high value on your surmises to roast a man alive for them.

[C]   Praestantius – and we have various examples of similar accounts – tells how his father fell into a profound sleep, deeper far than normal sleep at its best: he thought that he was a mare, serving soldiers as a beast of burden. And he actually became what he thought he was.[24] Now even if wizards dream concrete dreams like that; even if dreams can at times take on real bodies: still I do not believe that our wills should be held responsible to justice for them.   [B]   I say that, as one who am neither a king's judge nor counsellor, and who consider myself far from worthy of being so; I am an ordinary man, born and bred to obey State policy in both word and deed. Anyone who took account of my ravings, to the prejudice of the most wretched law, opinion or custom of his village, would do great wrong to himself and also to me.   [C]   I warrant you no certainty for whatever I say, except that it was indeed my thought at the time . . . my vacillating and disorderly thought. I will talk about anything by way of

20. Hemlock (*cicuta*) was used by the Greeks to poison criminals – hence Socrates' death by it; hellebore was used to purge madness.
21. Livy, VIII, xviii.
22. From the earliest times, Roman law placed the insane in the primary care of their blood relations.
23. It was said that whoever undid the untieable knot in the temple of Gordius would conquer the East: Alexander sliced it through with his sword. Cf. Erasmus, *Adages*, I, I, VI, *Nodum solvere* and, I, IX, XLVIII, *Heraculanus nodus*. (Throughout this passage Montaigne plays on the double meaning of *solutio* in Latin: 'unloosening' and 'resolving'.)
24. St Augustine, *City of God*, XVIII, xviii, suggesting that the cause was diabolical deception working through a Platonizing philosopher. Vives has a long theological note on the subject, rejecting as fictional Apuleius' metamorphosis into a donkey in his *Golden Ass*.

conversation, about nothing by way of counsel. *'Nec me pudent, ut istos, fateri nescire quod nesciam.'* [Nor, like those other fellows, am I ashamed to admit that I do not know what I do not know.][25]

[B] I would not be so rash of speech if it were my privilege to be believed on this matter. And I replied thus to a great nobleman who complained of the sharpness and tension of my exhortations: 'Knowing that you are braced and prepared on one side, I set out the other side for you as thoroughly as I can, not to bind your judgement but to give it some light. God holds sway over your mind: he will allow you a choice. I am not so presumptuous as to desire that my opinions should weigh even slightly in a matter of such importance: it is not my lot to groom them to influence such mighty and exalted decisions.'

It is certain that I have not only a great many humours but also quite a few opinions which I would willingly train a son of mine to find distasteful, if I had one that is. Why! What if even the truest of them should not always be the most appropriate for Man, given that his make-up is so barbarous?

On the point or off the point, no matter; it is said as a common proverb in Italy that he who has not lain with a lame woman does not know Venus in her sweet perfection. Chance, or some particular incident, long ago put that saying on the lips of the common people. It is applied to both male and female, for the Queen of the Amazons retorted to the Scythian who solicited her: Ἄριστα χολός οἰφεῖ: 'The lame man does it best.'[26]

In that Republic of women, in order to avoid the dominance of the male, they crippled their boys in childhood – arms, legs and other parts which give men the advantage over women – and exploited men only for such uses as we put women to in our part of the world.

Now I would have said that it was the erratic movements of the lame woman which brought some new sensation to the job and some stab of pleasure to those who assayed it: but I have just learned that ancient philosophy itself has decided the matter: it says that the legs and the thighs of lame women cannot receive (being imperfect) the nourishment which is their due, with the result that the genital organs which are sited above them become more developed, better fed and more vigorous. Alternatively, since this defect discourages exercise, those who are marked by it dissipate

25. Cicero, *Tusc. disput.*, I, xxv, 60.
26. Erasmus, *Adages*, II, IX, XLIX, *Claudus optime virum agit.* Cf. also Septalius' note in his edition of Aristotle's (or Pseudo-Aristotle's) *Problemata* X, 25 (26); Coelius Richerius Rhodiginus, *Antiquae Lectiones*, XIV, v, *Cur claudi salaciores.* Cf. also Erasmus, *Apophthegmata*, VIII, *Thrasea*, second hundred, XXI.

their strength less and so come more whole to Venus' sports which is also why the Greeks disparaged women who worked at the loom, saying they were lustier than others because of their sedentary occupation which is without much physical exertion.

At this rate, what can we *not* reason about! Of those women weavers I could just as well say that the shuttling to and fro which their work imposes on them while they are squatting down stimulates and arouses them just as the jerking and shaking of their coaches do for our ladies.

Do not these examples serve to prove what I said at the outset: that our reasons often run ahead of the facts and enjoy such an infinitely wide jurisdiction that they are used to make judgements about the very void and nonentity. Apart from the pliancy of our inventive powers when forging reasons for all sorts of idle fancies, our imagination finds it just as easy to receive the stamp of false impressions derived from frivolous appearances: for on the sole authority of the ancient and widespread currency of that saying, I once got myself to believe that I had derived greater pleasure from a woman because she was deformed, even counting her deformity among her charms.

In his comparison between France and Italy Torquato Tasso says that he had noticed that we have skinnier legs than the gentlemen of Italy and attributes the cause of it to our being continually on our horses. Now that is the very same 'cause' which leads Suetonius to the opposite conclusion: for he says, on the contrary, that Germanicus had fattened his legs by the constant practice of that same exercise![27]

There is nothing so supple and eccentric as our understanding. It is like Theramenes' shoe: good for either foot.[28] It is ambiguous and faces both ways; matters, too, are ambiguous and facing both ways: 'Give me a silver penny,' said a Cynic philosopher to Antigonus. 'That is no present from a king,' he replied. 'Give me half a hundredweight of gold then' – 'That is no present for a Cynic!'[29]

> *Seu plures calor ille vias et cæca relaxat*
> *Spiramenta, novas veniat qua succus in herbas;*
> *Seu durat magis et venas astringit hiantes,*
> *Ne tenues pluviæ, rapidive potentia solis*
> *Acrior, aut Boreæ penetrabile frigus adurat.*

27. Torquato Tasso, *Paragon dell'Italia alla Francia*; Suetonius, *Life of Caligula*, III.
28. Cf. Erasmus, *Adages*, I, I, XCIV, *Cothurno versatilior*. Theramenes was an Athenian rhetorician who could find arguments for either party.
29. Erasmus, *Apophthegmata*, IV, *Antigonus Rex Macedonum*, XV.

[It is either because the heat opens up new ways through the secret pores in the soil, along which the sap rises to the tender plants, or else because it hardens that soil and constricts its gaping veins, thus protecting it from the drizzling rain, the heat of the burning sun and the penetrating cold of the north wind.][30]

'*Ogni medaglia ha suo riverso.*' [Every medal has its obverse.] That is why Clitomachus said in ancient times that Carneades had surpassed the labours of Hercules by having wrenched assent away from Man (that is, conjecturing and rashness in judging).[31]

That idea of Carneades – such a vigorous one – was born, I suggest, in antiquity because of the shamelessness of those whose profession was knowledge and their overweening arrogance.

Aesop was put on sale with two other slaves. The purchaser asked the first what he could do: he, to enhance his value, answered mountains and miracles: he could do this and he could do that. The second said as much or more of himself. When it was Aesop's turn to be asked what he could do he said, 'Nothing! These two have got in first and taken the lot: they know everything!'[32]

That is what happened in the school of philosophy. The arrogance of those who attributed to Man's mind a capacity for everything produced in others (through irritation and emulation) the opinion that it has a capacity for nothing. Some went to the same extreme about ignorance as the others did about knowledge, so that no one may deny that Man is immoderate in all things and that he has no stopping-point save necessity, when too feeble to get any farther.

30. Virgil, *Georgics*, I, 89–93 (two of several reasons why burning stubble is good for crops).
31. Translated from Cicero, *Academica*, II (*Lucullus*), xxxiv, 108: '*adsensionem, id est, opinationem et temeritatem.*'
32. From Maximus Planudes' *Life of Aesop*, frequently printed with the *Fables*.

13. On experience

===

[The end of Montaigne's quest. See the Introduction, pp. xix ff.]

[B]   No desire is more natural than the desire for knowledge.[1] We assay all the means that can lead us to it. When reason fails us we make use of experience –

> [C]   *Per varios usus artem experientia fecit:*
> *Exemplo monstrante viam.*

[By repeated practice, and with example showing the way, experience constructs an art.][2]

Experience is a weaker and   [C]   less dignified means: [B]   but truth[3] is so great a matter that we must not disdain any method which leads us to it. Reason has so many forms that we do not know which to resort to: experience has no fewer. The induction which we wish to draw from the   [C]   likeness   [B]   between events is unsure since they all show unlikenesses.[4] When collating objects no quality is so universal as diversity and variety.[5] As the most explicit example of likeness the Greeks, Latins and we ourselves allude to that of eggs, yet there was a man of Delphi among others who recognized the signs of difference between eggs and never mistook one for another;[6]   [C]   when there were several hens he could tell which egg came from which.   [B]   Of itself, unlikeness obtrudes into

1. The opening sentence of Aristotle's *Metaphysics*.
2. Manilius, *Astronomica*, I, 62–3.
3. '88: weaker and *baser* means: but truth . . .
4. '88: from the *comparison* between events . . .
   Montaigne is contesting Aristotle's assertion that arts and sciences derive from judgements upon experiences.)
5. 'Collating objects': Montaigne's term *image des choses* is technical and based on Latin usage: *imago* in this sense is the comparison of form with form by some likeness between them.
6. Erasmus, *Adages*, I, V, X, *Non tam ovum ovo simile* (as we say, 'As alike as two eggs'), citing Montaigne's example of the 'man at Delphi' (or, rather, the *men* at *Delos*) who had this skill, from Cicero, *Academica*, II, (Lucullus) xviii, 58–9.

anything we make. No art can achieve likeness. Neither Perrozet nor anyone else can so carefully blanch and polish the backs of his playing-cards without at least some players being able to tell them apart simply by watching them pass through another player's hands. Likeness does not make things 'one' as much as unlikeness makes them 'other': [C] Nature has bound herself to make nothing 'other' which is not unlike.

[B] That is why I am not pleased by the opinion of that fellow who sought to rein in the authority of the judges with his great many laws, 'cutting their slices for them'.[7] He was quite unaware that there is as much scope and freedom in interpreting laws as in making them. (And those who believe that they can assuage our quarrels and put a stop to them by referring us to the express words of the Bible cannot be serious: our minds do not find the field any less vast when examining the meanings of others than when formulating our own – as though there were less animus and virulence in glossing than inventing!)

We can see how wrong that fellow was: in France we have more laws than all the rest of the world put together – more than would be required to make rules for all those worlds of Epicurus; [C] *'ut olim flagitiis, sic nunc legibus laboramus'* [we were once distressed by crimes: now, by laws].[8] [B] And, even then, we have left so much to the discretion and opinion of our judges that never was there liberty so licentious and powerful. What have our legislators gained by isolating a hundred thousand categories and specific circumstances, and then making a hundred thousand laws apply to them? That number bears no relationship to the infinite variations in the things which humans do. The multiplicity of our human inventions will never attain to the diversity of our cases. Add a hundred times more: but never will it happen that even one of all the many thousands of cases which you have already isolated and codified will ever meet one future case to which it can be matched and compared so exactly that some detail or some other specific item does not require a specific judgement. There is hardly any relation between our actions (which are perpetually changing) and fixed unchanging laws.

The most desirable laws are those which are fewest, simplest and most general. I think moreover that it would be better to have none at all than to have them in such profusion as we do now. Nature always gives us

---

7. Tribonian, the 'architect of the Pandects' of Justinian. He 'cut their slices' by carving up the Roman laws into gobbets. For an attack on him in the same terms, cf. Rabelais, *Tiers Livre*, TLF, XLIIII, 82–94.

8. Tacitus, *Annals*, III, xxv.

happier laws than those we give ourselves. Witness that Golden Age portrayed by the poets[9] and the circumstances in which we see those peoples live who have no other laws. There is a nation who take as the judge of their disputes the first traveller who comes journeying across their mountains; another which chooses one of their number on market-days and he judges their cases there and then.[10] Where would be the danger if the wisest men among us were to decide our cases for us according to the details which they have seen with their own eyes, without being bound by case-law or by established precedent? For every foot its proper shoe.

When King Ferdinand sent colonies of immigrants to the Indies he made the wise stipulation that no one should be included who had studied jurisprudence, lest lawsuits should pullulate in the New World – law being of its nature a branch of learning subject to faction and altercation: he judged with Plato that to furnish a country with lawyers and doctors is a bad action.[11]

Why is it that our tongue, so simple for other purposes, becomes obscure and unintelligible in wills and contracts? Why is it that a man who expresses himself with clarity in anything else that he says or writes cannot find any means of making declarations in such matters which do not sink into contradictions and obscurity? Is it not that the 'princes' of that art,[12] striving with a peculiar application to select traditional terms and to use technical language, have so weighed every syllable and perused so minutely every species of conjunction that they end up entangled and bogged down in an infinitude of grammatical functions and tiny sub-clauses which defy all rule and order and any definite interpretation? [C] *'Confusum est quidquid usque in pulverem sectum est.'* [Cut anything into tiny pieces and it all becomes a mass of confusion.][13]

[B] Have you ever seen children making assays at arranging a pile of quicksilver into a set number of segments? The more they press it and knead it and try to make it do what they want the more they exasperate the taste for liberty in that noble metal: it resists their art and proceeds to

---

9. The poets stressed that in the Golden Age, 'there was no mine and thine'; and Ovid, in the *Metamorphoses*, I, 89 ff., stresses that no law was needed since each was guided by his innocent natural sense of right and wrong.

10. Given Montaigne's assimilation of Indians to happy primitive tribes in the Golden Age, those nations are doubtless to be sought in the Americas.

11. Guillaume Bouchet, *Serées*, IX; Plato, *Republic*, III, 405 A.

12. Experts in the 'art' of law were often, even on the title-pages of their own books, referred to as 'princes'.

13. Seneca, *Epist. moral.*, LXXXIX, 3.

scatter and break down into innumerable tiny parts. It is just the same here: for by subdividing those subtle statements lawyers teach people to increase matters of doubt; they start us off extending and varying our difficulties, stretching them out and spreading them about. By sowing doubts and then pruning them back they make the world produce abundant crops of uncertainties and quarrels,   [C]   just as the soil is made more fertile when it is broken up and deeply dug: *'difficultatem facit doctrina'* [it is learning which creates the difficulty].[14]

[B]   We have doubts on reading Ulpian: our doubts are increased by Bartolo and Baldus.[15] The traces of that countless diversity of opinion should have been obliterated, not used as ornaments or stuffed into the heads of posterity. All I can say is that you can feel from experience that so many interpretations dissipate the truth and break it up. Aristotle wrote to be understood: if he could not manage it, still less will a less able man (or a third party) manage to do better than Aristotle, who was treating his own concepts. By steeping our material we macerate it and stretch it. Out of one subject we make a thousand and sink into Epicurus' infinitude of atoms by proliferation and subdivision. Never did two men ever judge identically about anything, and it is impossible to find two opinions which are exactly alike, not only in different men but in the same men at different times. I normally find matter for doubt in what the gloss has not condescended to touch upon. Like certain horses I know which miss their footing on a level path, I stumble more easily on the flat.

Can anyone deny that glosses increase doubts and ignorance, when there can be found no book which men toil over in either divinity or the humanities whose difficulties have been exhausted by exegesis? The hundredth commentator dispatches it to his successor prickling with more difficulties than the first commentator of all had ever found in it. Do we ever agree among ourselves that 'this book already has enough glosses: from now on there is no more to be said on it'? That can be best seen from legal quibbling. We give force of law to an infinite number of legal authorities, an infinite number of decisions and just as many interpretations. Yet do we ever find an end to our need to interpret? Can we see any

14. Quintilian, X, iii, 16 (explaining why peasants and uneducated folk speak more directly and less hesitantly).
15. Ulpian, the great second-century jurisconsult; the other two are Italian medieval glossators. Criticisms of such glossators was common in France among partisans of certain schools of legal methodology who included Guillaume Budé and Rabelais (cf. *Pantagruel*, TLF, IX *bis*, 76–100, etc.).

progress or advance towards serenity? Do we need fewer lawyers and judges than when that lump of legality was in its babyhood?

On the contrary we obscure and bury the meaning: we can no longer discern it except by courtesy of those many closures and palisades. Men fail to recognize the natural sickness of their mind which does nothing but range and ferret about, ceaselessly twisting and contriving and, like our silkworms, becoming entangled in its own works: '*Mus in pice.*' [A mouse stuck in pitch.][16] It thinks it can make out in the distance some appearance of light, of conceptual truth: but, while it is charging towards it, so many difficulties, so many obstacles and fresh diversions strew its path that they make it dizzy and it loses its way. The mind is not all that different from those dogs in Aesop which, descrying what appeared to be a corpse floating on the sea yet being unable to get at it, set about lapping up the water so as to dry out a path to it,   [C] and suffocated themselves.[17] And that coincides with what was said about the writings of Heraclitus by Crates: they required a reader to be a good swimmer, so that the weight of his doctrine should not pull him under nor its depth drown him.[18]

[B] It is only our individual weakness which makes us satisfied with what has been discovered by others or by ourselves in this hunt for knowledge: an abler man will not be satisfied with it. There is always room for a successor – [C] yes, even for ourselves – [B] and a different way to proceed. There is no end to our inquiries: our end is in the next world.[19]

[C] When the mind is satisfied, that is a sign of diminished faculties or weariness. No powerful mind stops within itself: it is always stretching out and exceeding its capacities. It makes sorties which go beyond what it can achieve: it is only half-alive if it is not advancing, pressing forward, getting driven into a corner and coming to blows; [B] its inquiries are shapeless and without limits; its nourishment consists in [C] amazement, the hunt and [B] uncertainty,[20] as Apollo made clear enough to us by his speaking (as always) ambiguously, obscurely and obliquely, not glutting us but

16. Erasmus, *Adages*, II, III, LXVIII.

17. [B] instead of [C]: path to it, and *killed* themselves. It is . . .

18. Not Crates but Socrates, not the proverbially obscure Heraclitus, but a certain Delius; cf. Erasmus, *Adages*, I, III, XXXVI, *Davus sum non Oedipus*, linking the saying to Heraclitus and to Diogenes Laertius, *Life of Socrates*, II, xxii.

19. A step in the argument from the opening quotation from *Metaphysics*, I, i: see the Introduction, p. xlv.

20. '88: consists in *doubt* and uncertainty . . .

keeping us wondering and occupied.[21] It is an irregular activity, never-ending and without pattern or target. Its discoveries excite each other, follow after each other and between them produce more.

> *Ainsi voit l'on, en un ruisseau coulant,*
> *Sans fin l'une eau apres l'autre roulant,*
> *Et tout de rang, d'un eternel conduict,*
> *L'une suit l'autre, et l'une l'autre fuyt.*
> *Par cette-cy celle-là est poussée,*
> *Et cette-cy par l'autre est devancée:*
> *Tousjours l'eau va dans l'eau, et tousjours est-ce*
> *Mesme ruisseau, et toujours eau diverse.*

[Thus do we see in a flowing stream water rolling endlessly on water, ripple upon ripple, as in its unchanging bed water flees and water pursues, the first water driven by what follows and drawn on by what went before, water eternally driving into water – ever the same stream with its waters ever-changing.][22]

It is more of a business to interpret the interpretations than to interpret the texts, and there are more books on books than on any other subject: all we do is gloss each other. [C] All is a-swarm with commentaries: of authors there is a dearth. Is not learning to understand the learned the chief and most celebrated thing that we learn nowadays! Is that not the common goal, the ultimate goal, of all our studies?

Our opinions graft themselves on to each other. The first serves as stock for the second, the second for a third. And so we climb up, step by step. It thus transpires that the one who has climbed highest often has more honour than he deserves, since he has only climbed one speck higher on the shoulders of his predecessor.

[B] How often and perhaps stupidly have I extended my book to make it talk about itself: [C] stupidly, if only because I ought to have remembered what I say about other men who do the same: namely that those all-too-pleasant tender glances at their books witness that their hearts are a-tremble with love for them, and that even those contemptuous drubbings with which they belabour them are in fact only the pretty little rebukes of motherly love (following Aristotle for whom praise and dispraise of oneself often spring from the same type of pride).[23] For I am not sure that everyone will understand what entitles me to do so: that I must have

---

21. Cf. III, 11, 'On the lame', note 9. Apollo was surnamed *loxias*, 'obscure'.
22. Etienne de La Boëtie, *A Marguerite de Carle*.
23. Aristotle, *Nicomachaean Ethics*, II, vii, 12, 1108a.

more freedom in this than others do since I am specifically writing about myself and (as in the case of my other activities) about my writings.

[B]   I note that Luther has left behind in Germany as many – indeed more – discords and disagreements because of doubts about his opinions than he himself ever raised about Holy Scripture.²⁴ Our controversies are verbal ones. I ask what is nature, pleasure, circle or substitution. The question is about words: it is paid in the same coin. – 'A stone is a body.' – But if you argue more closely: 'And what is a body?' – 'Substance.' – 'And what is substance?' And so on; you will eventually corner your opponent on the last page of his lexicon. We change one word for another, often for one less known. I know what 'Man' is better than I know what is animal, mortal or reasonable.²⁵ In order to satisfy one doubt they give me three; it is a Hydra's head.²⁶ Socrates asked Meno what virtue is. 'There is,' said Meno, 'the virtue of a man, a woman, a statesman, a private citizen, a boy and an old man.' 'That's a good start,' said Socrates. 'We were looking for a single virtue and here is a swarm of them.'²⁷ We give men one question and they hand us back a hive-full.

Just as no event and no form completely resembles another, neither does any completely differ.   [C]   What an ingenious medley is Nature's: if our faces were not alike we could not tell man from beast: if they were not unalike we could not tell man from man.²⁸   [B]   All things are connected by some similarity; yet every example limps and any correspondence which we draw from experience is always feeble and imperfect;²⁹ we can nevertheless find some corner or other by which to link our comparisons. And that is how laws serve us: they can be adapted to each one of our concerns by means of some   [C]   twisted,   [B]   forced³⁰ or oblique interpretation.

Since the moral laws which apply to the private duties of all individuals

24. A true statement. Geneseolutherans, Philippists (Melanchthonians), etc. formed hostile schools.
25. *The* example of a perfect definition, which can be used both ways: you can start from the definition and arrive at Man: start from Man and arrive at this definition: Priscian, *Opera*, 1527, XVII, 1180.
26. Cf. Erasmus, *Adages*, I, X, IX, *Hydram Secas*; you cut off one head of the serpent Hydra and several others grow in its place. (Well-known from Plato in the *Republic*, I, 427 A, where it is applied to the multiplicity of laws in an ill-governed state.)
27. Plutarch (tr. Amyot), *De la vertu*, 31, CD.
28. St Augustine, *City of God*, XXI, viii.
29. Cf. Cicero, *Academica*, II (*Lucullus*), 56.
30. '88: some *fine drawn-out*, forced . . .

are so difficult to establish (as we see that they are), not surprisingly those laws which govern collections of all those individuals are even more so. Consider the form of justice which has ruled over us: it is a true witness to the imbecility of Man, so full it is of contradiction and error. Wherever we find favouritism or undue severity in our justice – and we can find so much that I doubt whether the Mean between them is to be found as frequently – they constitute diseased organs and corrupt members of the very body and essence of Justice. Some peasants have just rushed in to tell me that they have, at this very moment, left behind in a wood of mine a man with dozens of stab-wounds; he was still breathing and begged them of their mercy for some water and for help to lift him up. They say that they ran away fearing that they might be caught by an officer of the law and (as does happen to those who are found near a man who has been killed) required to explain this incident; that would have ruined them, since they had neither the skill nor the money to prove their innocence. What ought I to have said to them? It is certain that such an act of humanity would have got them into difficulties.

How many innocent parties have been discovered to have been punished – I mean with no blame attached to their judges? And how many have never been discovered? Here is something which has happened in my time: some men had been condemned to death for murder; the sentence, if not pronounced, was at least settled and determined. At this juncture the judges were advised by the officials of a nearby lower court that they were holding some prisoners who had made a clean confession to that murder and thrown an undeniable light on to the facts. The Court deliberated whether it ought to intervene to postpone the execution of the sentence already given against the first group. The judges considered the novelty of the situation; the precedent it would constitute for granting stays of execution, and the fact that once the sentence had been duly passed according to law they had no powers to change their minds. In short those poor devils were sacrificed to judicial procedures. Philip or somebody provided for a similar absurdity in the following manner.[31] He had condemned a man to pay heavy damages to another and the sentence had been pronounced. Some time afterwards the truth was discovered and he realized that he had made an unjust judgement. On one side there were the interests of the case as now proven: on the other, the interests of judicial procedure. To some extent he satisfied both, allowing the sentence to stand while reimbursing from his own resources the expenses of the condemned

31. Plutarch (tr. Amyot), *Dicts notables des anciens Roys*, 192 B.

man. But he was dealing with a reparable situation: those men of mine were irreparably hanged. [C] How many sentences have I seen more criminal than the crime . . .

[B] All this recalls to my mind certain opinions of the Ancients: that a man is obliged to do retail wrong if he wants to achieve wholesale right, committing injustices in little things if he wants to achieve justice in great things; that human justice is formed on the analogy of medicine, by which anything which is effective is just and honourable;[32] that, as the Stoics held, Nature herself acts against justice in most of her works;[33] [C] or, what the Cyrenaics hold, that nothing is just *per se*, justice being a creation of custom and law; and what the Theodorians hold: that the wise man, if it is useful to him, may justifiably commit larceny, sacrilege and any sort of lechery.[34]

[B] It cannot be helped. My stand is that of Alcibiades: never, if I can help it, will I submit to be judged by any man on a capital charge, during which my life or honour depend more on the skill and care of my barrister than on my innocence.[35]

I would risk the kind of justice which would take cognizance of good actions as well as bad and give me as much to hope for as to fear: not to be fined is an inadequate reward to bestow on a man who [C] has achieved better than simply doing no wrong. [B] Our justice[36] offers us only one of her hands, and her left one at that. No matter who the man may be, the damages are against him. [C] In China (a kingdom whose polity and sciences surpass our own exemplars in many kinds of excellence without having had any contact with them or knowledge of them and whose history teaches me that the world is more abundant and diverse than

---

32. Plutarch (tr. Amyot): of. Jason, Tyrant of Thessalia; *Instruction pour ceulx qui manient affaires d'estat*, 173 F; *Pourquoy la justice divine differe quelquefois la punition des malefices*, 265 C (analogy with medicine).

33. A surprising statement. The Stoics took Nature as their standard of value. But their conception of Nature was paradoxical and, as such, attacked by Plutarch (tr. Amyot), *Que les Stoïques disent des choses plus estranges que les poëtes* (560C – 561A); *Les contredicts des Philosophes Stoïques* (561A – 574 C); *Des communes conceptions contre les Stoïques* (574 C – 588 F). Montaigne's assertion may possibly be read into such objections, but one would expect him to have some definite authority behind him.

34. From Diogenes Laertius, *Life of Aristippus*, II, xciii and xcix; Coelius Richerius Rhodiginus, *Antiquae lectiones*, XIV, vi.

35. Cf. Henry Estienne, *Apophthegmata*, s. v. Alcibiades.

36. '88: on a man who *is not merely free from evil-doing but who acts better than others.* Our justice . . .

either the ancients or we ever realized), the officials dispatched by the prince to inspect the condition of his provinces do punish those who act corruptly in their posts but also make *ex gratia* rewards to those who have behaved above the common norm and beyond the obligations of duty. You appear before them not simply to defend yourself but to gain something, and not simply to receive your pay but to be granted bounties.[37]

[B] Thank God no judge has ever addressed me *qua* judge in any case whatsoever, my own or a third party's, criminal or civil. No prison has had me inside it, not even to stroll through it. Thinking about it makes the very sight of a prison even from the outside distressing to me. I so hunger after freedom that if anyone were to forbid me access to some corner of the Indies I would to some extent live less at ease. And as long as I can find earth or sky open to me elsewhere I will never remain anywhere cowering in hiding. My God, how badly would I endure the conditions of those many people I know of who, for having had an altercation with our laws, are pinned to one region of this Kingdom, banned from entering our main cities or our courts or from using the public highways. If the laws that I obey were to threaten me only by their finger-tips I would be off like a shot looking for other laws, no matter where they might be. All my petty little wisdom during these civil wars of ours is applied to stop laws from interfering with my freedom to come and go.

Now laws remain respected not because they are just but because they are laws. That is the mystical basis of their authority. They have no other. [C] It serves them well, too. Laws are often made by fools, and even more often by men who fail in equity because they hate equality:[38] but always by men, vain authorities who can resolve nothing.

No person commits crimes more grossly, widely or regularly than do our laws. If anyone obeys them only when they are just, then he fails to obey them for just the reason he must![39] [B] Our French laws, by their chaotic deformity, contribute not a little to the confused way they are

37. China, increasingly known, especially from Jesuit sources, vastly widened the horizons of Renaissance moralists. Montaigne's account doubtless derives from Juan Gonzalez, whose *Historia de las cosas mas notables de la China* (Rome, 1585) was rapidly translated into French by L. de la Porte (Paris, 1588).

38. Cicero contrasts justice with equity (*De oratore*, I, lvi, 240). It was a legal contention that, in law, equity is above all to be observed (Spiegel, *Lexicon Juris Civilis*, s.v. *Aequitas*).

39. [B] instead of [C]: no other. If anyone *obeys the law because it is just, obeys it not.* Our French laws ...

applied and the corrupt way in which they are executed. The fact that their authority is so vague and inconsistent to some extent justifies our disobeying them and our faulty interpretation, application and enforcement of them.

Whatever we may in fact get from experience, such benefit as we derive from other people's examples will hardly provide us with an elementary education if we make so poor a use of such experience as we have presumably enjoyed ourselves; that is more familiar to us and certainly enough to instruct us in what we need.

I study myself more than any other subject. That is my metaphysics; that is my physics.[40]

> *Qua Deus hanc mundi temperet arte domum,*
> *Qua venit exoriens, qua deficit, unde coactis*
> *Cornibus in plenum menstrua luna redit;*
> *Unde salo superant venti, quid flamine captet*
> *Eurus, et in nubes unde perennis aqua?*

[By what artifice God governs this world, our home; where the moon comes from, where she does go and how she does bring her horns together month after month and so grow full; whence the gales spring which rule the salty sea, and what dominion does the South Wind enjoy; whence come those waters which are ever in the clouds?][41]

[C] *Sit ventura dies mundi quæ subruat arces?*

[And will there come a day when our hills shall be made low?]

[B] *Quaerite quos agitat mundi labor.*

[It is for those who are worried by problems about how the world works to inquire into that.]

I, unconcerned and ignorant within this universe, allow myself to be governed by this world's general law, which I shall know sufficiently when I feel it. No knowledge of mine will bring it to change its course: it will not take a different road for my sake. It is madness to wish it to; greater madness to be upset by that fact, since such law is, of necessity, unvarying, generic and applied to all. The goodness and sway of the Ruler should

---

40. That is, a study of his own self replaces a study of Aristotle's *Metaphysics* and *Physics*.
41. Propertius, III, v, 26–30, 31; then a line interpolated from Lucan, *Pharsalia*, I, 417.

purely and utterly free us from any weight of anxiety about His rule. Scientific investigations and inquiries serve merely to feed our curiosity. They have nothing to do with knowledge so sublime: the philosophers are very right to refer us to the laws of Nature, but they pervert them and present Nature's face too sophistically, painted in colours which are far too exalted, from which arise so many diverse portraits of so uniform a subject. As Nature has furnished us with feet to walk with, so has she furnished us with wisdom to guide us in our lives. That wisdom is not as clever, strong and formal as the one which they have invented, but it is becomingly easy and beneficial; in the case of the man who is lucky enough to know how to use it simply and ordinately (that is, naturally) it does − very well − what the other *says* it will. The more simply we entrust ourself to Nature the more wisely we do so. Oh what a soft and delightful pillow, and what a sane one on which to rest a well-schooled head, are ignorance and unconcern! [B] I would rather be an expert on me than on [C] Cicero.[42]

[B] Were I a good pupil there is enough, I find, in my own experience to make me wise. Whoever recalls to mind his last bout of choler and the excesses to which that fevered passion brought him sees the ugliness of that distemper better than in Aristotle and conceives even more just a loathing for it. Anyone who recalls the ills he has undergone, those which have threatened him and the trivial incidents which have moved him from one condition to another, makes himself thereby ready for future mutations and the exploring of his condition. (Even the life of Caesar is less exemplary for us than our own; a life whether imperial or plebeian is always a life affected by everything that can happen to a man.) We tell ourselves all that we chiefly need: let us listen to it. Is a man not stupid if he remembers having been so often wrong in his judgement yet does not become deeply distrustful of it thereafter?

When I find that I have been convicted of an erroneous opinion by another's argument, it is not so much a case of my learning something new he has told me nor how ignorant I was of some particular matter − there is not much profit in that − as of my learning of my infirmity in general and of the treacherous ways of my intellect. From that I can reform the whole lump.

With all my other mistakes I do the same, and I think this rule is of great use to me in my life. I regard neither a class of error nor an example of it as one stone which has made me stumble: I learn to distrust my trot in

42. '88: than on *Plato*. Were I . . .

general and set about improving it.   [C]   To learn that we have said or done a stupid thing is nothing: we must learn a more ample and important lesson: that we are but blockheads.

[B]   The slips by which my memory so often trips me up precisely when I am most sure of it are not vainly lost: it is no use after that its swearing me oaths and telling me to trust it: I shake my head. The first opposition given to its testimony makes me suspend judgement and I would not dare then to trust it over any weighty matter nor to stand warrant for it when another is involved. Were it not that[43] others do even more frequently from lack of integrity what I do from lack of memory, I would on matters of fact as readily accept that truth is to be found on another's lips not mine.

If each man closely spied upon the effects and attributes of the passions which have rule over him as I do upon those which hold sway over me, he would see them coming and slow down a little the violence of their assault. They do not always make straight for our throat: there are warnings and degrees:

> *Fluctus uti primo cœpit cum albescere ponto,*
> *Paulatim sese tollit mare, et altius undas*
> *Erigit, inde imo consurgit ad æthera fundo.*

[At first the gale whips up the foam-topped wavelets, then little by little the sea begins to heave, the billows roll and the sea surges from the deep to the very heavens.][44]

Within me judgement holds the rector's chair, or at least it anxiously strives to do so. It permits my inclinations to go their own way, including hatred and love (even self-love) without itself being worsened or corrupted. Though it cannot reform those other qualities so as to bring them into harmony with itself, at least it does not let itself be deformed by them: it plays its role apart.

It must be important to put into effect the counsel that each man should know himself, since that god of light and learning had it placed on the tympanum of his temple as comprising the totality of the advice which he had to give us.[45]   [C]   Plato too says that wisdom is but the executing of that command, and Socrates in Xenophon proves in detail that it is

43. '88: Were it not that *I see nothing but lying and that* others do . . .
44. Virgil, *Aeneid*, VII, 528–30.
45. The *Know Thyself* of the Temple of Apollo at Delphi. Montaigne may be here drawing upon several *Adages* of Erasmus, including *Nosce Teipsum* (Know thyself).

true.[46] [B] The difficulties and obscurities of any branch of learning can be perceived only by those who have been able to go into it; for we always need some degree of intelligence to become aware that we do not know: if we are to learn that a door is shut against us we must first give it a shove. [C] From which springs that Platonic paradox: those who know do not have to inquire since they know already: neither do those who do not know, since to find out you need to know what you are inquiring into.[47] [B] And so it is with this knowing about oneself: the fact that each man sees himself as satisfactorily analysed and as sufficiently expert on the subject are signs that nobody understands anything whatever about it – [C] as Socrates demonstrates to Euthydemus in Xenophon.[48] [B] I who make no other profession but getting to know myself find in me such boundless depths and variety that my apprenticeship bears no other fruit than to make me know how much there remains to learn.

It is to my inadequacy (so often avowed) that I owe my tendency to moderation, to obeying such beliefs as are laid down for me and a constant cooling and tempering of my opinions as well as a loathing for that distressing and combative arrogance which has complete faith and trust in itself: it is a mortal enemy of finding out the truth. Just listen to them acting the professor: the very first idiocies which they put forward are couched in the style by which religion and laws are founded: [C] *'Nil hoc est turpius quam cognitioni et perceptioni assertionem approbationemque praecurrere.'* [There is nothing more shocking than to see assertion and approval dashing ahead of cognition and perception.][49]

[B] Aristarchus said that in olden days there were scarcely seven wise men to be found in the whole world whereas in his own days there were scarcely seven ignoramuses.[50] Have we not more reason to say that than he did? Assertion and stubbornness are express signs of animal-stupidity. This man over here has bitten the ground a hundred times a day: but there he is strutting about crowing *ergo*, as decided and as sound as before: you would say that some new soul, some new mental vigour has been infused into him, and that he was like that Son of Earth of old who, when thrown down, found fresh resolve and strength:

46. Cf. Erasmus, *Adages*, I, VII, XCV, *Nosce teipsum* (citing Plato, *Charmides*, 164 D); Xenophon, *Memorabilia*, IV, ii, 24 ff, and his portrait of Socrates in general.
47. Plato, *Meno*, XIV, 80.
48. Xenophon, *Memorabilia*, IV, ii, 29–40.
49. Cicero, *Academica*, I, xii, 45. (The standard reading today is *adsensionem*, assent, not *assertionem*, assertion.)
50. Plutarch (tr. Amyot), *De l'amitié fraternelle*, 81 F.

> *cui, cum tetigere parentem,*
> *Jam defecta vigent renovato robore membra.*

[whose failing limbs, when they touched the earth, his Mother, took on new strength and vigour.][51]

The unteachable, stubborn fool! Does he believe that he assumes a new mind with each new dispute? It is from my own experience that I emphasize human ignorance which is, in my judgement, the most certain faction in the school of the world. Those who will not be convinced of their ignorance by so vain an example as me – or themselves – let them acknowledge it through Socrates.   [C]   He is the Master of masters; the philosopher Antisthenes said to his pupils, 'Let us all go to hear Socrates: you and I will all be pupils there.' And when he was asserting the doctrine of his Stoic school that, to make a life fully happy, virtue sufficed without need of anything else, he added, 'except the strength of Socrates'.[52]

[B]   This application which I have long devoted to studying myself also trains me to judge passably well of others: there are few topics on which I speak more aptly or acceptably. I often manage to see and to analyse the attributes of my friends more precisely than they can themselves. There is one man to whom I told things about himself which were so apposite that he was struck with amazement. By having trained myself since boyhood to see my life reflected in other people's I have acquired a studious tendency to do so; when I give my mind to it, few things around me which help me to achieve it escape my attention: looks, temperaments, speech, I study the lot for what I should avoid or what I should imitate.

I similarly reveal to my friends their innermost dispositions by what they outwardly disclose. I do not however classify such an infinite number of diverse and distinct activities within genera and species, sharply distributing my sections and divisions into established classes or departments,

> *sed neque quam multæ species, et nomina quæ sint,*
> *Est numerus.*

[for there is no numbering of their many categories nor of the names given to them.][53]

51. Lucan, *Pharsalia*, IV, 599–60; of Anthaeus, one of the giants called Sons of Earth; cf. Du Bellay, *Antiquités de Rome*, TLF, 12 and 11.
52. Erasmus, *Apophthegmata*, VII, *Antisthenes* II and XLIV.
   [B] instead of [C]: through Socrates, *the wisest man there ever was by the testimony of the gods and men*. This application . . .
53. Virgil, *Georgics*, II, 103–4.

[C]   The learned do arrange their ideas into species and name them in detail. I, who can see no further than practice informs me, have no such rule, presenting my ideas in no categories and feeling my way – as I am doing here now;   [B]   I pronounce my sentences in disconnected clauses, as something which cannot be said at once all in one piece. Harmony and consistency are not to be found in ordinary   [C]   base⁵⁴   [B]   souls such as ours. Wisdom is an edifice solid and entire, each piece of which has its place and bears its hallmark: [C]   *'Sola sapientia in se tota conversa est.'* [Wisdom alone is entirely self-contained.]⁵⁵

[B]   I leave it to the graduates – and I do not know if even they will manage to bring it off in a matter so confused, intricate and fortuitous – to arrange this infinite variety of features into groups, pin down our inconsistencies and impose some order. I find it hard to link our actions one to another, but I also find it hard to give each one of them, separately, its proper designation from some dominant quality; they are so ambiguous, with colours interpenetrating each other in various lights.

[C]   What is commented on as rare in the case of Perses, King of Macedonia (that his mind, settling on no particular mode of being, wandered about among every kind of existence, manifesting such vagrant and free-flying manners that neither he nor anyone else knew what kind of man he really was), seems to me to apply to virtually everybody.⁵⁶ And above all I have seen one man of the same rank as he was to whom that conclusion would, I believe, even more properly apply: never in a middle position, always flying to one extreme or the other for causes impossible to divine; no kind of progress without astonishing side-tracking and back-tracking; none of his aptitudes straightforward, such that the most true-to-life portrait you will be able to sketch of him one day will show that he strove and studied to make himself known as unknowable.⁵⁷   [B]   You need good strong ears to hear yourself frankly judged; and since there are few who can undergo it without being hurt, those who risk undertaking it do us a singular act of love, for it is to love soundly to wound and vex a

54. '88: ordinary *vile* souls . . .
55. Cicero, *De finibus*, III, vii, 24.
56. King Perses (or Perseus, as Livy calls him) was the last king of Macedonia and was conquered by Paulus Aemilius. For his character cf. Livy, XLI, xx.
57. This bold judgement is made on the character of a king, doubtless Henry of Navarre (Henri Quatre). A rejected manuscript reading in the Bordeaux copy is: '*I have since seen one other king to whom* . . .' Henry (King of Navarre, 1572–1610) became King of France in 1589. He is sure of himself enough, it is suggested, to accept frank criticism.

man in the interests of his improvement. I find it harsh to have to judge anyone in whom the bad qualities exceed the good.   [C]   Plato requires three attributes in anyone who wishes to examine the soul of another: knowledge, benevolence, daring.[58]

[B]   Once I was asked what I thought I would have been good at if anyone had decided to employ me while I was at the right age:

> *Dum melior vires sanguis dabat, æmula necdum*
> *Temporibus geminis canebat sparsa senectus.*

[When I drew strength from better blood and when envious years had yet to sprinkle snow upon my temples.]

'Nothing,' I replied; 'and I am prepared to apologize for not knowing how to do anything which enslaves me to another. But I would have told my master some blunt truths and would, if he wanted me to, have commented on his behaviour – not wholesale by reading the Schoolmen at him (I know nothing about them and have observed no improvement among those who do), but whenever it was opportune by pointing things out as he went along, judging by running my eyes along each incident one at a time, simply and naturally, bringing him to see what the public opinion of him is and counteracting his flatterers.' (There is not one of us who would not be worse than our kings if he were constantly   [C]   corrupted by that riff-raff as they are.)   [B]   How else[59] could it be, since even the great king and philosopher Alexander could not protect himself from them?[60] I would have had more than enough loyalty, judgement and frankness to do that. It would be an office without a name, otherwise it would lose its efficacity and grace. And it is a role which cannot be held by all men indifferently, for truth itself is not privileged to be used all the time and in all circumstances: noble though its employment is, it has its limits and boundaries. The world being what it is, it often happens that you release truth into a Prince's ear not merely unprofitably but detrimentally and (even more) unjustly. No one will ever convince me that an upright rebuke may not be offered offensively nor that considerations of matter should not often give way to those of manner.

For such a job I would want a man happy with his fortune –

58. '88: without being hurt *and resentful*, those who risk . . .

  Then, Plato, *Gorgias*, 487 A; Virgil, *Aeneid*, V, 415–16.

59. '88: constantly *cheated and diddled* as they are. How else . . .

60. Cf. Erasmus, *Apophthegmata*, IV, *Alexander Magnus*, XV; LXIII, etc.

Quod si esse velit, nihilque malit

[Who would be what he is, desiring nothing extra][61]

– and born to a modest competence. And that, for two reasons: he would not be afraid to strike deep, lively blows into his master's mind for fear of losing his way to advancement; he would on the other hand have easy dealings with all sorts of people, being himself of middling rank.   [C] And only one man should be appointed; for to scatter the privilege of such frankness and familiarity over many would engender a damaging lack of respect. Indeed what I would require above all from that one man is that he could be trusted to keep quiet.[62]

A king   [B]   is not to be believed if he boasts of his steadfastness as he waits to encounter the enemy in the service of his glory if, for his profit and improvement, he cannot tolerate the freedom of a man who loves him to use words which have no other power than to make his ears smart, any remaining effects of them being in his own hands. Now there is no category of man who has greater need of such true and frank counsels than kings do. They sustain a life lived in public and have to remain acceptable to the opinions of a great many on-lookers: yet, since it is customary not to tell them anything which makes them change their ways, they discover that they have, quite unawares, begun to be hated and loathed by their subjects for reasons which they could often have avoided (with no loss to their pleasures moreover) if only they had been warned in time and corrected. As a rule favourites are more concerned for themselves than for their master: and that serves them well, for in truth it is tough and perilous to assay showing the offices of real affection towards your sovereign: the result is that not only a great deal of good-will and frankness are needed but also considerable courage.

In short all this jumble that I am jotting down here is but an account of the assays of my life: it is, where the mind's health is concerned, exemplary enough – if you work against its grain. But where the body's health is concerned no one can supply more useful experience than I, who present it pure, in no wise spoiled or adulterated by science or theory. In the case of medicine, experience is on its own proper dung-heap, where reason voids

---

61. Martial, *Epigrams*, X, xlvii, 12.
62. Henry IV did indeed ask Montaigne to become such a counsellor, but too late, for Montaigne was dying.

   '88: middling rank. A *prince* is not . . .

the field.[63] Tiberius said that anyone who had lived for twenty years ought to be able to tell himself which things are harmful to his health and which are beneficial and to know how to proceed without medicine.[64]   [C] Perhaps he learned that from Socrates who when advising his followers to devote themselves assiduously, with a most particular devotion, to their health added that if a man of intelligence was careful about his eating, drinking and exercise, it would be difficult for him not to discern what was good or bad for him better than his doctor could.[65]

[B] Certainly medicine professes always to have experience as the touchstone of its performance. Plato was therefore right to say that to be a true doctor would require that anyone who would practise as such should have recovered from all the illnesses which he claimed to cure and have gone through all the symptoms and conditions on which he would seek to give an opinion.[66] If doctors want to know how to cure syphilis it is right that they should first catch it themselves! I would truly trust the one who did; for the others pilot us like a man who remains seated at his table, painting seas, reefs and harbours and, in absolute safety, pushing a model boat over them. Pitch him into doing the real thing and he does not know where to start. They give the kind of description of our maladies as the town-crier announcing a lost horse or hound: this colour coat, so many span high, this kind of ears: but confront him with it, and for all that he cannot identify it. By God let medicine provide me with some good and perceptible help some day and I will proclaim in good earnest,

> *Tandem efficaci do manus scientiæ!*
> [At last I yield to thy effective Art!][67]

Those disciplines which promise to maintain our bodies in health and our souls in health promise a great deal:[68] yet none keeps their promises less than they do; and those who profess those Arts in our own time show the effects of them less than any other men. The most you can say of them is that they trade in the *materia medica* of those healing Arts: that they are

63. That is Aristotle's position on all arts at the outset of his *Metaphysics*. Renaissance scholars applied it particularly but not exclusively to medicine, the Art *par excellence*.
64. Cf. Erasmus, *Apophthegmata* VI, *Tiberius*, XIII (but referring not to 'twenty years' but to the age of sixty).
65. Xenophon, *Memorabilia*, IV, vii, 9.
66. Plato, *Republic*, III, 408 D–E.
67. Horace, *Epodes*, XVIII, 1.
68. Medicine and philosophy.

healers you cannot say. I have lived long enough now to give an account of the regimen which has got me thus far. Should anyone want to try it, I have assayed it first as his taster. Here are a few items as memory supplies them. [C] (There is no practice of mine which has not been varied according to circumstances, but I note here those which, so far, I have most often seen at work and which are rooted in me.)

[B] My regimen is the same in sickness as in health: I use the same bed, same timetable, same food and same drink. I add absolutely nothing except for increasing and decreasing the measure depending on my strength and appetite. Health means for me the maintaining of my usual route without let or hindrance. I can see that my illness has blocked one direction for me: if I put trust in doctors they will turn me away from the other, so there I am off my route either by destiny or their Art; there is nothing that I believe so certainly as this: that carrying on with anything to which I have so long been accustomed cannot do me harm. It is for custom to give shape to our lives, such shape as it will – in such matters it can do anything. It is the cup of Circe which changes our nature as it pleases. How many peoples are there, not three yards from us, who think that our fear of the cool evening air – which 'so evidently' harms us – is ludicrous; and our boatsmen and our peasants laugh at us too.

You make a German ill if you force him to lie in bed on a straw mattress, as you do an Italian on a feather one, or a Frenchman without bed-curtains or a fire. The stomach of a Spaniard cannot tolerate the way we eat: nor can ours the way the Swiss drink. I was amused by a German in Augsburg who attacked our open hearths, emphasizing their drawbacks with the same arguments which we normally use against their stoves! And it is true that those stoves give out an oppressive heat and that the materials of which they are built produce when hot a smell which causes headaches in those who are not used to them: not however in me. On the other hand since the heat they give out is even, constant and spread over-all, without the visible flame, the smoke and the draught produced for us by our chimneys, it has plenty of grounds for standing comparison with ours. (Why do we not imitate the building methods of the Romans, for it is said that in antiquity their house-fires were lit outside, at basement level; from there hot air was blown to all the house through pipes set within the thickness of the walls which surrounded the areas to be heated. I have seen that clearly suggested somewhere in Seneca, though I forget where.)[69] That man in Augsburg, on hearing me praise the advantages and beauties

69. Seneca, *Epist. moral.*, XC, 25 (regretting the luxury of civilized man).

of his city (which indeed deserved it) started to pity me because I had to leave it; among the chief inconveniences he cited to me was the heavy head I would get 'from those open hearths yonder'. He had heard somebody make this complaint and linked it with us, custom preventing him from noticing the same thing at home.

Any heat coming from a fire makes me weak and drowsy. Yet Evenus maintained that fire was life's condiment.[70] I adopt in preference any other way of escaping the cold.

We avoid wine from the bottom of the barrel; in Portugal they adore its savour: it is the drink of princes. In short each nation has several customs and practices which are not only unknown to another nation but barbarous and a cause of wonder.

What shall we do with those people who will receive only printed testimony, who will not believe anyone who is not in a book, nor truth unless it be properly aged?   [C]   We set our stupidities in dignity when we set them in print.   [B]   For these people there is far more weight in saying, 'I have read that . . .' than if you say, 'I have heard tell that . . .' But I (who have the same distrust of a man's pen as his tongue; who know that folk write with as little discretion as they talk and who esteem this age as much as any other former one) as willingly cite a friend of mine as Aulus Gellius or Macrobius, and what I have seen as what they have written.   [C]   And just as it is held that duration does not heighten virtue,[71] I similarly reckon that truth is no wiser for being more ancient.

[B]   I often say that it is pure silliness which sets us chasing after foreign and textbook exemplars. They are produced no less abundantly nowadays than in the times of Homer and Plato. But are we not trying to impress people by our quotations rather than by the truth of what they say? – as though it were a   [C]   greater thing   [B]   to borrow our proofs from the bookshops of Vascosan and Plantin than from our village?[72] Or is it that we do not have wit enough to select and exploit whatever happens in front of us or to judge it so acutely as to draw examples from it? For if we say that we lack the requisite authority to produce faith in our testimony we are off the point: in my opinion the most ordinary things, the most commonplace and best-known can constitute, if we know how to present

---

70. Plutarch (tr. Amyot), *Propos de table*, 410 B, etc. (cited several more times in the *Oeuvres morales*).
71. A Stoic contention.
72. '88: were a *more noble* thing to borrow . . .
    Vascosan and Plantin were two great printing-houses.

them in the right light, the greatest of Nature's miracles and the most amazing of examples, notably on the subject of human actions.[73]

Now on this topic of mine (leaving aside any examples I know from books   [C]   and what Aristotle said of Andros the Argive who traversed the arid sands of Lybia without once drinking),[74]   [B]   a nobleman who has acquitted himself with honour of several charges stated in my presence that he had journeyed without drinking from Madrid to Lisbon in the height of summer. He is vigorous for his age and there is nothing in his way of life which goes beyond the normal Order except that he can, so he told me, do without drinking for two or three months or even a year. He feels a little thirsty but lets it pass: he maintains that it is a craving which can easily weaken by itself. He drinks more on impulse than from necessity, or for enjoyment.

Here is another. Not long ago I came across one of the most learned men in France – a man of more than moderate wealth; he was studying in a corner of his hall which had been partitioned off with tapestries; around him were his menservants making the most disorderly racket. He told me – [C] and Seneca said much the same of himself[75] – [B] that he found their hubbub useful: it was as though, when he was being battered by that din, he could withdraw and close in on himself so as to meditate, and that those turbulent voices hammered his thoughts right in. When he was a student at Padua his work-room was for so long subject to the clatter of wagons and the tumultuous uproar of the market-place that he had trained himself not merely to ignore the noise but to exploit it in the service of his studies.   [C]   When Alcibiades asked in amazement how Socrates could put up with the sound of his wife's perpetual nagging, he replied: 'Just like those who get used to the constant grating of wheels drawing water from the well.'[76]   [B]   I am quite the opposite: I have a mind which is delicate and easy to distract: when it withdraws aside to concentrate, the least buzzing of a fly is enough to murder it!

[C]   When Seneca was a young man, having been keenly bitten by the example of Sextius, he ate nothing that had been slaughtered. For a whole year he did without meat – with great pleasure as he relates. He did give

73. 'Miracles of Nature' were unusual and most rare events but not in any theological sense miraculous: they were sources of wonder.
74. Diogenes Laertius, *Life of Pyrrho*, IX, lxxxi. (The contemporary nobleman next mentioned is Marquis Jean de Vivonne.)
75. Seneca, *Epist. moral.*, LVI.
76. Erasmus, *Apophthegmata*, III, *Socratica*, LX.

up that diet, but only to avoid the suspicion of being influenced by certain new religions which were disseminating it. He had adopted at the same time one of the precepts of Attalus: never to lie on soft mattresses; until his death he continued to use the kinds which do not yield to the body.[77] That which the customs of his day led him to count as an austerity our own make us think of as an indulgence.

[B] Consider the diversity between the way of life of my farm-labourers and my own. Scythia and the Indies have nothing more foreign to my force or my form. And this I know: I took some boys off begging into my service: soon afterwards they left me, my cuisine and their livery merely to return to their old life. I came across one of them gathering snails from the roadside for his dinner: neither prayer nor menace could drag him away from the sweet savour he found in poverty. Beggars have their distinctions and their pleasures as do rich men, and, so it is said, their own political offices and orders.

Such are the effects of Habituation: she can not only mould us to the form which pleases her (that is why, say the wise, we must cling to the best form, which she will straightway make easy for us)[78] but also mould us for change and variation (which are the noblest and most useful of her crafts). Of my own physical endowments the best is that I am flexible and not stubborn: some of my inclinations are more proper to me than others, more usual and more agreeable, but with very little effort I can turn away from them and glide easily into an opposite style. A young man ought to shake up his regular habits in order to awaken his powers and stop them from getting lazy and stale. And there is no way of life which is more feeble and stupid than one which is guided by prescriptions and instilled habit:[79]

> *Ad primum lapidem vectari cum placet, hora*
> *Sumitur ex libro; si prurit frictus ocelli*
> *Angulus, inspecta genesi collyria quærit.*

[Does he want to be borne as far as the first milestone? Then he consults his almanack to find out the best time. Has he got a sore in the corner of an eye? Then he consults his horoscope before buying some ointment.][80]

77. Seneca, *Epist. moral.*, CVIII, 17 f.
78. Erasmus, *Adages*, IV, IX, XXV, *Usus est altera natura.*
79. By using *discipline* for instilled habit, Montaigne may be echoing the usage of the Roman comedies, where *disciplina* has this sense.
80. Juvenal, *Satires*, VI, 576–8.

If he trusts me a young man will often jump to the other extreme: if he does not, the least excess will undermine him: he makes himself disagreeable and clumsy in society. The most incompatible quality in a gentleman is to be over-nicely bound to one fixed idiosyncratic manner: and idiosyncratic it is, if it is not pliable and supple. There is disgrace in being incapable or afraid of doing what your companions are up to. Such men should stay in their kitchens! Unbecoming it is, in everyone else: in a warrior it is vile and not to be endured; he, as Philopoemen said, must get accustomed to all kinds of this life's changes and hardships.[81]

Although I was brought up, as much as is humanly possible, for freedom and flexibility, nevertheless as I grow older I am becoming through indifference more fixed in certain forms (I am past the age for elementary schooling; now old age has no other concern than to look after itself); without my noticing it, custom has imprinted its stamp on me so well where some things are concerned that any departure from it I call excess; and I cannot, without turning it into an assay of myself, sleep by day, eat snacks between meals, nor eat breakfast, nor go to bed after supper without having a considerable gap, [C] say three hours or more, [B] nor have sexual intercourse except before going to sleep, nor do it standing up, nor remain soaking with sweat, nor drink either water or wine unmixed, nor remain for long with my head uncovered, nor have my hair cut after dinner. I would feel just as ill at ease without gloves or shirt, or without a wash on leaving the table and when getting up in the morning, or lying in a bed without canopy and curtains, as I would if forced to do without things which really matter.

I could dine easily enough without a tablecloth, but I feel very uncomfortable dining without a clean napkin as the Germans do. I dirty my napkins more than they or the Italians and rarely seek the aid of spoon or fork. I regret that we have not continued along the lines of the fashion started by our kings, changing napkins like plates with each course.

We are told that as Marius grew older, tough old soldier though he was, he became choosy about his wine and would only drink it out of his own special goblet. [C] I too incline[82] towards glasses of a particular shape and I no more like drinking out of a common cup than I would like eating

81. Plutarch, *Life of Philopoemen*, I.
82. [B] instead of [C]: special goblet: *earthenware and silver displease me compared with glass, as does being served by hands which I am unused to or which are not in my employ, or from* a common cup, *and* I incline *to choose* glasses of a particular shape. Several such foibles . . .

out of common fingers; and I dislike all metals compared with clear transparent materials. Let my eyes too taste it to the full.

[B]   Several such foibles I owe to habit: on the other hand Nature has contributed her own, such as my not being able to stand more than two proper meals a day without overloading my stomach, nor to go without a meal altogether without filling myself with wind, parching my mouth and upsetting my appetite; nor can I stand a long exposure to the evening dew. During these last few years when a whole night has to be spent (as often happens) on some military task, my stomach begins to bother me after five or six hours; I have splitting headaches and can never get through to morning without vomiting. Then, while the others go to breakfast, I have a sleep; after which I am quite happy again.

I had always been taught that evening dew formed only after night-fall, but upon frequenting a nobleman who was imbued with the belief that such dew is more dangerous and severe two or three hours before sunset (when he scrupulously avoids going out) he made such an impression on me that I almost not so much believed it as felt it. Well now, that very doubt and concern for our health can hammer our thought-process and change us. Those who slide precipitously down slopes such as that bring disaster upon themselves. There are several gentlemen for whom I feel pity: through the stupidity of their doctors they shut themselves up indoors while still young and healthy; it would be better to put up with a chill rather than forever to forgo joining in common everyday life outdoors. [C]   What a grievous skill medicine is, disparaging for us the more delightful hours of the day.   [B]   Let us extend our hold on things by every means we possess. Usually if you stubborn things out you toughen yourself up, correcting your complexion by despising it and seducing it, as Caesar did his epilepsy. We should give ourselves, but not enslave ourselves, to the best precepts, except in such cases (if there be any) in which constraint and slavery serve a purpose.

Kings and philosophers shit: and so do ladies.[83] The lives of public figures are devoted to etiquette: my life, an obscure and private one, can enjoy all the natural functions: moreover to be a soldier and to come from Gascony are both qualities given to forthrightness. And so of that activity I shall say that it needs to be consigned to a set hour – not daytime – to which we should subject ourselves by force of habit, as I have done, but not (as applies to me now that I am growing old) subject to the pleasures of a

83. '88: and so do ladies; *others have tact and competence as their qualities: I, frankness and freedom.* The lives . . . .

particular place and seat for this function, nor to making it uncomfortable by prolonging it or by being fastidious. All the same, is it not to some extent pardonable to require more care and cleanliness for our dirtiest functions? [C] *'Natura homo mundum et elegans animal est.'* [By Nature Man is a clean and neat creature.][84] Of all the natural operations, that is the one during which I least willingly tolerate being interrupted. [B] I have known many a soldier put out by the irregularity of his bowels. My bowels and I never fail to keep our rendezvous, which is (unless some urgent business or illness disturbs us) when I jump out of bed.

So, as I was saying, I can give no judgement about how the sick can be better looked after except that they should quietly hold to the pattern of life in which they have been schooled and brought up. Change of any kind produces bewilderment and trauma. Convince yourself if you can that chestnuts are harmful to the men of Périgord or Lucca, or milk and cheese to folk in the highlands! Yet the sick are constantly prescribed not merely a new way of life but an opposite one – such a revolution as could not be endured by a healthy man. Prescribe water for a seventy-year-old Breton; shut a sailorman up in a vapour-bath; forbid a Basque manservant to go for walks! They are deprived of motion and finally of breath and the light of day:

An vivere tanti est?

[Is life worth that much?][85]

Cogimur a suetis animum suspendere rebus,
Atque, ut vivamus, vivere desinimus.

Hos superesse rear, quibus et spirabilis aer
Et lux qua regimur redditur ipsa gravis?

[We are compelled to deprive our souls of what they are used to; to stay alive we must cease to live! Should I count among the survivors those men for whom the very air they breathe and the light which lightens them have become a burden?]

If doctors do nothing else, they do at least in plenty of time prepare their patients to die, sapping and retrenching their contacts with life.

Sound or sick I willingly let myself follow such appetites as become pressing. I grant considerable authority to my desires and predispositions. I do not like curing one ill by another; I loathe remedies which are more importunate than the sickness: being subjected to colic paroxysms and then

84. Seneca, *Epist. moral.*, XCII, 12.
85. Untraced. Then verses from Pseudo-Gallus, *Elegeia*, I.

made to abstain from the pleasure of eating oysters are two ills for the price of one. On this side we have the illness hurting us, on the other the diet. Since we must risk being wrong, let us risk what gives us pleasure, rather. The world does the reverse, thinking that nothing does you good unless it hurts: pleasantness is suspect. In many things my appetite, of its own volition, has most successfully accommodated and adapted itself to the well-being of my stomach. When I was young I liked the tartness and sharp savour of sauces: my stomach being subsequently troubled by them, my taste for them at once followed its lead.

[C] Wine is bad for the sick: it is the first thing I lose my taste for, my tongue finding it unpleasant, invincibly unpleasant. [B] Anything the taste of which I find unpleasant does me harm: nothing does me harm if I swallow it hungrily and joyfully. I have never been bothered by anything I have done in which I found great pleasure. And that is why I have, by and large, made all medical prescriptions give way to what pleases me.

When I was young –

> Quem circumcursans huc atque huc sæpe Cupido
> Fulgebat, crocina splendidus in tunica,

[when shining Cupid flew here and there about me, resplendent in his saffron tunic,][86]

– I yielded as freely and as thoughtlessly as anyone to the pleasure which then seized hold of me:

> Et militavi non sine gloria,

[and I fought not without glory,]

making it last and prolonging it, however, rather than making sudden thrusts.

> Sex me vix memini sustinuisse vices.

[I cannot recall managing it more than six times in a row.][87]

There is indeed some worry and wonder in confessing at what tender an age I happened to fall first into Cupid's power – 'happened' is indeed right, for it was long before the age of discretion and awareness – so long ago that I cannot remember anything about myself then. You can wed my

86. Catullus, LXVI, 133–4; then, Horace, Odes, III, xxvi, 2.
87. Ovid, Amores, III, vii, 26 (who says nine, not six, times).

fortune to that of Quartilla, who could not remember ever having been a virgin.[88]

Inde tragus celeresque pili, mirandaque matri
Barba meæ.

[My armpits had precocious hairs and stank like a goat: Mother was astonished by my early beard.]

The doctors usually bend their rules – usefully – before the violence of the intense cravings which surprise the sick: such a great desire cannot be thought of as so strange or vicious that Nature is not at work in it. And then, what a great thing it is to satisfy our imagination. In my opinion that faculty concerns everything, at least more than any other does: the most grievous and frequent of ills are those which imagination loads upon us. From several points of view I like that Spanish saying: *'Defienda me Dios de my.'* [God save me from myself.] When I am ill what I lament is that I have no desire then which gives me the satisfaction of assuaging it: Medicine would never stop me doing so! It is the same when I am well: I have scarcely anything left to hope or to wish for now. It is pitiful to be faint and feeble even in your desires.

The art of medicine has not reached such certainty that, no matter what we do, we cannot find some authority for doing it. Medicine changes according to the climate, according to the phases of the moon, according to Fernel and according to Scaliger. If your own doctor does not find it good for you to sleep, to use wine or any particular food, do not worry: I will find you another who does not agree with his advice. The range of differing medical arguments and opinions embraces every sort of variety. I knew one wretched patient, weak and fainting with thirst as part of his cure, who was later laughed at by another doctor who condemned that treatment as harmful. Had his suffering been to some purpose? Well there is a practitioner of that mystery who recently died of the stone and who had used extreme abstinence in fighting that illness: his fellow-doctors say that, on the contrary, such deprivation had desiccated him, maturating the sand in his kidneys.

I have noted that when I am sick or wounded talking excites me and does me as much harm as any of my excesses. Speaking takes it out of me and tires me, since my voice is so strong and booming that when I have needed to have a word in the ear of the great on a matter of some

88. Known from Petronius. Cf. Tiraquellus, *De legibus connubialibus*, IX, 98; then, Martial, *Epigrams*, XI, xxii, 7–8.

gravity I have often put them to the embarrassment of asking me to lower it.

The following tale is worth a digression: there was in one of the schools of the Greeks a man who used to talk loudly as I do. The Master of debate sent to tell him to speak lower: 'Let him send and tell me what volume he wants me to adopt,' he said. The Master replied that he should pitch his voice to the ears of the man he was addressing.[89] Now that was well said, provided that he meant, 'Speak according to the nature of your business with your hearer.' For if he meant, 'It is enough if people can catch what you say,' or, 'Let yourself be governed by your hearer,' then I do not believe that he was right. Volume and intonation contribute to the expression of meaning: it is for me to control them so that I can make myself understood. There is a voice for instructing, a voice for pleasing or for reproving. I may want my voice not simply to reach the man but to hit him or go right through him. When I am barking at my footman with a rough and harsh voice, a fine thing it would be if he came and said to me, 'Speak more softly, Master. I can hear you quite well.'   [C] *'Est quaedam vox ad auditum accommodata, non magnitudine sed proprietate.'* [There is a kind of voice which impresses the hearer not by its volume but its own peculiar quality.][90]   [B]   Words belong half to the speaker, half to the hearer. The latter must prepare himself to receive them according to such motion as they acquire, just as among those who play royal-tennis the one who receives the ball steps backwards or prepares himself, depending on the movements of the server or the form of his stroke.

Experience has also taught me that we are ruined by impatience. Illnesses have their life and their limits,[91]   [C]   their maladies and their good health. The constitution of illnesses is formed on the pattern of that of animals: from birth their lot is assigned limits, and so are their days. Anyone who makes an assay at imperiously shortening them by interrupting their course prolongs them and makes them breed, irritating them instead of quietening them down. I am of Crantor's opinion that we should neither resist illnesses stubbornly and rashly nor succumb to them out of weakness but yield to them naturally, according to our own mode of being and to theirs.[92]   [B]   We must afford them right-of-passage, and I find that they stay less long with me, who let them go their way; and through

89. Erasmus, *Apophthegmata*, VII, *Carneades*, XXXI.
90. Quintilian, XI, iii, 40.
91. '88: limits. We *should* afford them right-of-passage . . .
92. Paraphrased from Cicero, *Tusc. disput.*, III, v, 12.

their own decline I have rid myself of some which are held to be the most tenacious and stubborn, with no help from that Art and against its prescriptions. Let us allow Nature to do something! She understands her business better than we do. – 'But so-and-so died of it!' – So will you, of that illness or some other. And how many have still died of it with three doctors by their arses? Precedent is [C] an uncertain looking-glass, [B] all-embracing, [C] turning all ways.[93] [B] If the medicine tastes nice, take it: that is so much immediate gain at least. [C] I will not jib at its name or colour if it is delicious and whets my appetite for it. One of the principal species of profit is pleasure. [B] Among the illnesses which I have allowed to grow old and die of a natural death within me are rheums, fluxions of gout, diarrhoeas, coronary palpitations and migraines, which I lost just when I was half-resigned to having them batten on me. You can conjure them away better by courtesy than by bravado. We must quietly suffer the laws of Man's condition. Despite all medicine, we are made for growing old, growing weaker and falling ill. That is the first lesson which the Mexicans teach to their children when, on leaving their mother's womb, they greet them thus: 'Child: thou hast come into this world to suffer: suffer, endure and hold thy peace.'

It is unfair to moan because what can happen to any has happened to one: [C] *'indignare si quid in te inique proprie constitutum est'* [if anything is unjustly decreed against you alone, that is the time to complain].[94]

[B] Here you see an old man praying God to keep him entirely healthy and strong – that is to say, to make him young again:

> *Stulte, quid hæc frustra votis puerilibus optas?*

[You fool. What do you hope to gain by such useless, childish prayers?][95]

Is it not madness? His mode of being does not allow it. [C] Gout, gravel and bad digestion go with long years just as heat, wind and rain go with long journeys. Plato does not believe that Aesculapius should trouble to provide remedies to prolong life in a weak and wasted body, useless to its country, useless to its vocation and useless for producing healthy robust sons: nor does he find such a preoccupation becoming to the justice and wisdom of God who must govern all things to a useful purpose.[96] [B] It

---

93. '88: Precedent is *a free and* all-embracing *pattern. If the medicine . . .*
94. Seneca, *Epist. moral.*, XCI, 15, after listing the normality of war, illness and death, and stressing that if we do not obey the laws of the world we should quit it.
95. Ovid, *Tristia*, III, viii, 11.
96. Plato, *Republic*, III, 407 C.

is all over, old chap: nobody can put you back on your feet; they will [C] at most [B] bandage and prop you up for a bit, [C] prolonging your misery an hour or so:

> [B] *Non secus instantem cupiens fulcire ruinam,*
> *Diversis contra nititur obicibus,*
> *Donec certa dies, omni compage soluta,*
> *Ipsum cum rebus subruat auxilium.*

[As a man, desiring to keep a building from collapsing, shores it up with various props until there comes the day when all the scaffolding shatters and the props collapse together with the building.][97]

We must learn to suffer whatever we cannot avoid. Our life is composed, like the harmony of the world, of discords as well as of different tones, sweet and harsh, sharp and flat, soft and loud. If a musician liked only some of them, what could he sing? He has got to know how to use all of them and blend them together. So too must we with good and ill, which are of one substance with our life. Without such blending our being cannot be: one category is no less necessary than the other. To assay kicking against natural necessity is to reproduce the mad deed of Ctesiphon who, to a kicking-match, challenged his mule.[98]

I do not go in much for consultations over such deterioration as I feel: once those medical fellows have you at their mercy they boss you about: they batter your ears with their prognostics. Once, taking advantage of me when I was weak and ill, they abused me with their dogmas and their masterly [C] frowns,[99] [B] threatening me with great suffering and then with imminent death. They did not succeed in knocking me down or dislodging me from my fortress, but I was jolted and jostled: my judgement was neither changed nor troubled by them but it was at least preoccupied, and that means so much agitation and strife. I treat my imagination as gently as I am able, freeing it if I can from the load of any pain and conflict. Anyone who can should help it, stroke it, mislead it. My wit is well suited to such service: it never runs out of specious arguments about anything. If it could convince as well as it preaches its help would be most welcome.

Would you like an example? It tells me: that it is for my own good that

---

97. Pseudo-Gallus, *Eclogues*, I, 171–4; then, a development inspired by Plutarch (tr. Amyot), *De la tranquillité de l'ame*, 74 A–D.
98. Erasmus, *Adages*, I, III, XLVI, *Contra stimulum calces*, explaining the Classical and biblical maxim, *To kick against the pricks*, by Plutarch's example of a choleric athlete named Ctesiphon, unknown except for this incident.
99. '88: masterly *countenances*, threatening me . . .

I have the gravel; that structures as old as I am are naturally subject to seepage (it is time they began to totter apart and decay; that is a common necessity, otherwise would not some new miracle have been performed just for me? I am paying the debt due to old age and could not get off more lightly); that I should be consoled by the fact that I have company, since I have fallen into the most routine illness for men of my age (on all sides I can see men afflicted by a malady of the same nature as mine and their companionship honours me since that malady willingly strikes the aristocracy: its essence is noble and dignified); and that, of the men who are stricken with it few get off more lightly – and even then it is at the cost of having the bother of following a nasty diet and of taking troublesome daily doses of medicine, whereas I owe everything to my good fortune. (As for the few routine concoctions of eryngo or burstwort[100] which I have swallowed twice or thrice thanks to those ladies who gave me half of their own to drink (their courtesy exceeding in degree the pain of my complaint) they seemed to me to be as easy to take as they were ineffectual in practice.) For that easy and abundant discharge of gravel which I have often been vouchsafed by the bounty of Nature, those men had to pay a thousand vows to Aesculapius and as many crowns to their doctor.   [C]   (In normal company my comportment remains decorous, even, and is untroubled by my illness; and I can hold my urine for ten hours at a time – as long as the next man.)

[B] 'The fear of this illness,' (to go on), 'used to terrify you: that was when it was unknown to you; the screams and distress of those who make the pain more acute by their unwillingness to bear it engendered a horror of it in you. This illness afflicts those members of yours by which you have most erred. You are a man with some sense of right and wrong:

> *Quæ venit indigne pæna, dolenda venit.*
>
> [Only punishment undeserved comes with cause for anger.][101]

Reflect on this chastisement: it is mild indeed compared with others and shows a Fatherly kindness.[102] Reflect on how late it appeared: having first

---

100. Herbal laxatives and astringents.
101. Ovid, *Heroidum Epistolae*, V, 8.
102. Not least during the French Civil Wars of Religion, setbacks and afflictions were often seen as divinely sent punishments, proof of the Fatherly love of God correcting and purging his children with salutary chastisements. All could thus find strength and comfort in tribulation.

made a compact by which it gave free-play to the excesses and pleasures of
your youth, it occupies with its vexations only that season of your life
which, willy-nilly, is sterile and forlorn. The fear and pity felt by people
for this illness gives you something to glory about (you may have purged
your judgement and cured your reason of such glorying, but those who
love you still recognize some stain of it within your complexion). There is
pleasure in hearing them say about you: "There's fortitude for you! There's
long-suffering!" They see you sweating under the strain, turning pale,
flushing, trembling, sicking up everything including blood, suffering curious spasms and convulsions, sometimes shedding huge tears from your
eyes, excreting frightening kinds of urine, thick and black, or finding
that they are retained by some sharp stone, bristling with spikes which
cruelly jab into the neck of your prick and skin it bare: you, meanwhile,
chat with those about you, keeping your usual expression, occasionally
clowning about with   [C]   your servants,[103]   [B]   defending your corner
in a tense argument, apologizing for any sign of pain and understating your
suffering.

'Do you remember those men of yore who greatly hungered after ills so
as to keep their virtue in trim and practise it? Supposing Nature is pushing
and shoving you into that [C] proud [B] Sect[104] into which you
would never have entered on your own! If you tell me that yours is a
dangerous, killing affliction, which of the others is not? For it is medical
hocus-pocus to pick out some and say that they do not follow a direct line
towards death: what does it matter if they only lead there incidentally,
floundering along by-ways in the same direction as the road which leads us
thither?   [C]   You are not dying because you are ill: you are dying
because you are alive;[105] Death can kill you well enough without illness to
help her. In some cases illnesses have postponed death, the sick living
longer precisely because they thought they were a-dying; besides, just as
there are some wounds which cure you or make you better, so too there
are some illnesses.   [B]   Your colic is often no less tenacious of life than
you are: we know of men in whom it has lasted from childhood to
extreme old age: and it would have gone along with them further if they
themselves had not deserted its company. Men kill the stone more than it

103. '88: With *the ladies*, defending . . .
104. '88: that *noble* sect . . .
   (Certain Stoics.)
105. Seneca, *Epist. moral.*, LXXVIII, 6 (with a wider influence on Montaigne's
general context).

kills men. And if it did present you with the idea of imminent death, would it not be doing a good turn to a man of your age to bring him to meditate upon his end?

[C] 'And the worst of it is you have nobody left to be cured for. As soon as she likes, whatever you do, our common Fate is summoning you. [B] Reflect on how skilfully and gently your colic makes you lose your taste for life and detaches you from the world – not compelling you by some tyrannous subjection as do so many other afflictions found in old men which keep them continually fettered to weakness and unremittingly in pain but with intermittent warnings and counsels interspersed with long periods of respite, as if to give you the means to meditate on its lesson and to go over it again at leisure. And so as to give you the means to make a sound judgement and to be resolved like a sensible man, it shows you the state of the whole human condition, both good and bad, shows you, during one single day, a life at times full of great joy, at times unbearable. Although you may not throw your arms about Death's neck, you do, once a month, shake her by the hand. [C] That gives you more reason to hope that Death will snatch you one day without warning and that, having so often brought you as far as the jetty, one morning, unexpectedly, when you are trusting that you are still on the usual terms, you and your trust will have crossed the Styx. [B] You have no need to complain of ill-nesses which share their time fairly with health.'

I am obliged to Fortune for the fact that she so often uses the same sort of weapons to assail me: she forms me and schools me for them by habit, hardens me and makes me used to them: I more or less know now what it will cost me to be released from what I owe them. [C] (Lacking a natural memory I forge one from paper: whenever some new feature occurs in my affliction, I jot it down. And so by now, when I have gone through virtually every category of examples of such symptoms, whenever some appalling crisis threatens me I can without fail, by flipping through my notes (which are as loose as the leaves of the Sibyls), find grounds for consolation in some favourable prognosis based on past experience.) [B] Such habituation helps me to hope for better things in the future: this way of voiding the stone has continued for such a long time now that it is probable that Nature will not change the way of it and that nothing worse will happen than what I already know.

Moreover the properties of this Affliction of mine are not ill-suited to my complexion, which is quick and sudden. It is when she makes mild assaults on me that she frightens me, for that means a long spell: yet she is by nature a thing of violent and audacious bouts, giving me a thorough shaking up for a day or two. My kidneys held out for [C] an age [B] without deterioration: it will soon be [C] another age, now, [B] since[106] they changed their condition. Ills as well as blessings run their courses. Perhaps this misfortune is near its end. Old age reduces the heat of my stomach, which therefore digests things less perfectly and dispatches waste matter to my kidneys: so why should the heat of my kidneys, after a stated period has rolled by, not similarly be reduced, rendering them unable to continue to petrify my phlegm and obliging Nature to find some other means of purging it? It is clear that the passing years have exhausted some of my discharges: why not then those excretions which furnish the raw material for my gravel?

But is there anything so delightful as that sudden revolution when I pass from the extreme pain of voiding my stone and recover, in a flash, the beauteous light of health, full and free, as happens when our colic paroxysms are at their sharpest and most sudden? Is there anything in that suffered pain which can outweigh the joy of so prompt a recovery? Oh how much more beautiful health looks to me after illness, when they are such close neighbours that I can study both, each in her full armour, each in each other's presence, defying each other as though intending to stubborn it out and hold their ground! The Stoics say that the vices were introduced for a purpose – to second virtue and make her prized: we can say, with better justification and less bold conjecture, that Nature has lent us suffering in order that it may honour and serve the purposes of pleasure and of mere absence of pain. When Socrates was freed from the load of his fetters he enjoyed the delicate tingling in his legs that their pressure had produced and he delighted in thinking about the close confederacy that there is between pain and pleasure, so bound together in fellowship as they are by bonds of necessity that they succeed each other and mutually produce each other; and he exclaimed that that excellent man Aesop ought to have drawn from such factors the substance of a beautiful fable.[107]

For the worst feature of other maladies is that they are less grievous in what they do at the time than in what comes later: you spend a whole year convalescing, all the time full of fear and debility. There is so much hazard in recovery, so many levels involved, that there is no end to it all: before they let you strip off your scarves and then your nightcaps, before they have allowed you to avail yourself again of fresh air, wine, your wife – and of melons – it is quite something if you have not had a relapse into some

106. '88: for *forty years* [. . .] soon be *fourteen years* since . . .
107. Plato, *Phaedo*, 60 B–E.

new wretchedness. My illness is privileged to make a clean break: the others lend each other a hand: they always leave some dent and weakness in you which render your body susceptible to some fresh woe. We can condone such illnesses as are content with their own rights-of-possession over us without introducing their brood: but those whose journey through us produces some useful result are courteous and gracious. Since my stone I find that I have been freed from the load of other ailments and that I seem to feel better than I did before. I have not had a temperature since! I reason that the frequent and extreme vomiting which I suffer purges me and that, from another aspect, the losses of appetite and bizarre fastings which I go through disperse my offending humours, Nature voiding with those stones all her noxious superfluities. And do not tell me that such medicine is bought at too high a price. What about those stinking possets, those cauterizations, incisions, sweat-baths, drainings of pus, diets and those many forms of treatment which often bring death upon us when we cannot withstand their untimely onslaught! So when I suffer an attack I consider it to be a cure: when freed from it, I consider that to be a durable and complete deliverance.

Another specific blessing of my illness is that it all but gets on with its own business and (unless I lose heart) lets me get on with mine. I have withstood it, at the height of an attack, for ten hours at a time in the saddle. 'Just put up with it, that's all! You need no other prescription: enjoy your sports, dine, ride, do anything at all if you can: your indulgences will do you more good than harm.' Try saying that to a man with syphilis, the gout or a rupture! The constraints of other illnesses are more all-embracing: they are far more restricting on our activities, upsetting our normal ways of doing anything and requiring us to take account of them throughout the entire state of our lives. Mine does no more than pinch the epidermis: it leaves you free to dispose of your wit and your will as well as of your tongue, your hands and your feet. Rather than battering you numb, it stimulates you. It is your soul which is attacked by a burning fever, cast to the ground by epilepsy, dislodged by an intense migraine and, in short, struck senseless by those illnesses which attack all the humours and the nobler organs. Such are not attacked in my case: if things go ill for my soul, too bad for her! She is betraying, surrendering and disarming herself. Only fools let themselves be persuaded that a solid, massy substance concocted within our kidneys can be dissolved by draughts of medicine. So, once it starts to move, all you can do is to grant it right-of-passage: it will take it anyway.

There is another specific advantage that I have noticed: it is an illness which does not leave us guessing. It dispenses us from the turmoil into which other ills cast us because of uncertainties about their causes, properties and development – an infinitely distressing turmoil. We need have nothing to do with consulting specialists and hearing their opinions: our senses can show us what it is and where it is.

With such arguments, both strong and feeble, I try, as Cicero did with that affliction which was his old age, to benumb and delude my power of thought and to put ointment on its wounds. And tomorrow, if they grow worse, we will provide other escape-routes for them.

[C] To show that that is true, since I wrote that, the slightest movements which I make have begun to squeeze pure blood from my kidneys again. Yet because of that I do not stop moving about exactly as I did before and spurring after my hounds with a youthful and immoderate zeal. And I find that I have got much the better of so important a development, which costs me no more than a dull ache and heaviness in the region of those organs. Some great stone is compressing the substance of my kidneys and eating into it: what I am voiding drop by drop – and not without some natural pleasure – is my life blood, which has become from now on some noxious and superfluous discharge.

[B] Can I feel something disintegrating? Do not expect me to waste time having my pulse and urine checked so that anxious prognostics can be drawn from them: I will be in plenty of time to feel the anguish without prolonging things by an anguished fear. [C] Anyone who is afraid of suffering suffers already of being afraid. And then the hesitation and ignorance of those who undertake to explain the principles by which Nature operates and her inner progression (as well as the false prognoses of their Art) oblige us to recognize that she keeps her processes absolutely unknown. In her promises and threats there is great uncertainty, variability and obscurity. With the exception of old age (which is an undoubted prognostic of the approach of death), in all our other maladies I can find few prognostics of the future on which we should base our predictions.   [B] Judgements about myself I make from true sensation not from argument: what else? since all I intend to bring to bear are patience and endurance. 'What do I gain from that?' do you ask? Look at those who act otherwise and who rely on all that contradictory counsel and advice. How often does their imagination assail them, independently of the body! When safely delivered from a dangerous bout, I have often found pleasure in consulting doctors about it as though it were just starting. Fully at ease I would put up with the formulation of their terrifying diagnoses, and would remain that much more indebted to God for his mercy and better instructed in the vanity of that Art.

There is nothing which ought to be commended to youth more than being active and energetic. Our life is but motion: I am hard to budge and sluggish about everything, including getting up, going to bed and eating. For me, seven o'clock is early morning! And where I head the household I never lunch before eleven nor have supper after six. The causes of those feverish ailments which I formerly used to fall into I once ascribed to the heaviness and sluggishness brought on by prolonged sleep; and I have always regretted falling back to sleep again of a morning. [C] Plato is harder against excessive sleep than excessive drink.[108]

[B] I like a hard bed all to myself, indeed (as kings do) without my wife, with rather too many blankets. I never use a warming-pan, but, since I have grown old, whenever I need them they give me coverlets to warm my feet and stomach. The great Scipio was criticized for being a slug-a-bed, for no other reason, if you ask me, than that it irritated people that in him alone there was nothing to criticize.[109] If I am fastidious about an item in my regimen it is more about bed than anything else: but on the whole I yield to necessity as well as anyone [C] and adjust to it. [B] Sleeping has taken up a large slice of my life and even at my age I can sleep eight or nine hours at a stretch. I am finding it useful to rid myself of this propensity towards laziness and am clearly the better for it. I am feeling the shock of such a revolution, but only for two or three days. And I know hardly anyone who can do with less sleep when the need arises, who can keep on working more continuously or feel less than I do the weight of the drudgery of war. My body is capable of sustained exertions but not of sudden, violent ones. I avoid nowadays all violent activities including those which bring on sweat: before my limbs get hot they feel exhausted. I can be on my feet all day, and I never tire when walking. Over paved roads however, [C] since my earliest childhood [B] I have always preferred to go by horse:[110] when on foot I splatter mud right up to my backside; and in our streets little men are liable to being jostled [C] and elbowed aside, [B] for want of an imposing appearance. And I have always liked to rest, lying or seated, with my legs at least as high as the bench.

No occupation is as enjoyable as soldiering – an occupation both noble in its practice (since valour is the mightiest, most magnanimous and proudest of the virtues) and noble in its purpose: there is no service you can

108. On legislation against excessive sleep, cf. Plato, *Laws*, VII, 807 E–808 D; on milder condemnation of excessive drinking, cf. ibid. II, 673 E–674 D.
109. Plutarch (tr. Amyot), *Qu'il est requis qu'un Prince soit sçavant*, 137 A.
110. '88: however, I *can only* go by horse . . .

render more just nor more complete than protecting the peace and greatness of your country. You enjoy the comradeship of so many men who are noble, young and active, the daily sight of so many sublime dramas, the freedom of straightforward fellowship as well as a manly, informal mode of life, the diversions of hundreds of different activities, the heart-stirring sound of martial music which fills your ears and enflames your soul, as well as the honour of this activity,[111] its very pains and hardships, [C] which Plato rates so low in his *Republic* that he allocates a share in it to women and children. [B] You urge yourself to accept specific tasks or hazards, depending upon your judgement of their splendour or importance; [C] you are a volunteer [B] and can see when your life itself may justifiably be sacrificed to them:

> *pulchrumque mori succurrit in armis.*

> [it is indeed beautiful, I think, to die in battle.][112]

It is for a mind [C] weak [B] and base beyond all measure to be afraid of risks shared in common with a crowd of others, or not to dare to do what men of so many kinds of soul may dare. The comradeship gives confidence to the very boys. Others may surpass you in knowledge, grace, force or fortune: in that case you can put the responsibility for it on to a third party: but if you yield to them in fortitude of soul you alone are responsible. Death is more abject, lingering and painful in bed than in combat: fevers and catarrhs are as painful and as mortal as volleys from harquebuses. Any man who could bear with valour the mischances of ordinary life would have no need to be more courageous on becoming a soldier. [C] *'Vivere, mi Lucili, militare est.'* [To live, my dear Lucilius, is to do battle.][113]

I cannot recall ever having had scabies, but scratching is one of the most delightful of Nature's bounties: and it is always ready to hand! But its neighbour, inconveniently close, is regret for having done it. I mainly practise it on my ears, which from time to time itch inside.

[B] I was born with all my senses[114] intact and virtually perfect. My

---

111. '88: honour and *nobility* of this activity . . .
   Then Plato, *Republic*, V, etc.
112. Virgil, *Aeneid*, II, 317.
   Then '88: for a mind *vile* and base . . .
113. Seneca, *Epist. moral.*, XCVI, 5 (in Seneca a metaphor, not a statement about war).
114. '88: all my *bodily* senses . . .

stomach is as sound as you could wish; my head is, too: both usually remain so during my bouts of fever. The same applies to my respiration. I have exceeded [C] recently, by six years, that fiftieth birthday [B] which[115] some peoples have not unreasonably laid down as termination of life, one so just that nobody was permitted to go beyond it: yet I still have periods of reprieve which, despite being short and variable, are so flawless that they lack nothing of that pain-free health of my youth. I am not referring to liveliness and vigour: it is not reasonable that they should accompany me beyond their limits:

> *Non hæc amplius est liminis, aut aquæ*
> *Cælestis, patiens latus.*

[No longer can I endure waiting on my mistress's doorstep in the pouring rain.][116]

It is my face which gives the game away first; [C] so do my eyes: [B] all changes in me begin there, appearing rather more grim than they are in practice. I often find my friends pitying me before I am aware of any cause. My looking-glass never strikes me with terror, because even in my youth I would often take on a turbid complexion and a look which boded ill without much happening, with the result that the doctors, who could find no cause in my body which produced that outward deterioration, attributed it to my mind and to some secret passion gnawing away within me. They were in error. My body and I would have got on rather better if it had behaved *secundum me*, as did my Soul which was then not only free from turbidity but, better still, full of joy and satisfaction – as she usually is, half because of her complexion and half by design.

> *Nec vitiant artus ægræ contagia mentis.*

[The illnesses of my mind do not affect my joints.][117]

I maintain that this disposition of my Soul has repeatedly helped up my body after its falls: my body is often knocked low whereas she, even when not merry, is at least calm and tranquil. I once had a quartan fever for four or five months which put me right out of countenance, yet my mind still went not merely peacefully but happily on her way. Once the pain has gone I am not much depressed by weakness or lassitude. I know of several bodily afflictions which are horrifying even to name but which I fear less

115. '88: exceeded *the age at* which . . .
116. Horace, *Odes*, III, ix, 19–20.
117. Ovid, *Tristia*, III, viii, 25.

than hundreds of current disturbances and distresses of the mind. I have decided never again to run: it is enough for me if I can drag myself along. Nor do I lament the natural decline which has me in its grip:

> *Quis tumidum guttur miratur in Alpibus?*

> [In the Alps is anyone surprised to find goitres?][118]

– no more do I lament that my lifespan is not as long and massive as an oak's. I have no cause to complain of my thought-processes: few thoughts in my life have ever disturbed even my sleep, except when concerned with desire (which woke me up without distressing me). I do not dream much: when I do it is of grotesque things and of chimeras usually produced by pleasant thoughts, more laughable than sad. And although I maintain that dreams are loyal interpreters of our inclinations, there is skill in classifying them and understanding them.

> [C]   *Res quæ in vita usurpant homines, cogitant, curant, vident*
> *Quæque agunt vigilantes, agitantque, ea sicut in somno accidunt*
> *Minus mirandum est.*

[It is no miracle that men should find again in their dreams things which occupy them in their lives, things which they think about, worry about, gaze upon and do when they are awake.][119]

Plato further adds that it is wisdom's task to extract from them information telling of future events. I know nothing about that except the wondrous experiences related by Socrates, Xenophon and Aristotle – great men of irreproachable authority.[120] The history books tell us that the Atlantes never dream;[121] they add that they never eat anything which has been slaughtered, a fact which I mention because it may explain why they do not dream, since Pythagoras prescribed a certain preparatory diet designed to encourage dreams.[122] My dreams are weak things: they occasion no twitching of the body, no talking in my sleep. I have known in my time some who have been astonishingly troubled by them. Theon the

118. Juvenal, XIII, 162. (Lack of iodine produced goitres among the Swiss.)
119. Cited by Cicero, *De divinatione*, I, 45, xxii from a lost work of Accius.
120. Cited together by Cicero in the same work, I, xxv, 52–3. (The work of Aristotle referred to by Cicero is lost.)
121. The example of the Atlantes was standard (cf. Rabelais, *Tiers Livre*, TLF, XIII, 56; Coelius Richerius Rhodiginus, XXVII, 16).
122. Cicero, *De divinatione*, II, lviii, 119.

philosopher walked while he dreamed (as did the manservant of Pericles, on the tiles of the very roof-ridge of his house).[123]

[B]   At table I rarely exercise a choice, tackling the first and nearest dish; I do not like shifting about from one taste to another. I dislike a multitude of dishes and courses as much as any other multitude. I can be easily satisfied with a few items and loathe the opinion of Favorinus[124] that during a feast any dish you are enjoying should be whipped away from you and a new one always brought in instead, and also that it is a wretched supper at which the guests are not stuffed with rumpsteaks exclusively taken from a variety of birds – only the fig-pecker bird being worth eating whole. I frequently eat salted meats but prefer my bread unsalted: the baker in my own kitchen (contrary to local custom) serves no other at my table. When I was a boy I often had to be punished for refusing precisely those things which are usually best liked at that age: sweets, jams and pastries. My tutor opposed this hatred of fancy foods as being itself a kind of fancy. And indeed, no matter what it applies to, it is nothing but finicking over your food: rid a boy of a fixed private love of coarse-bread, bacon or garlic and you rid him of self-indulgence. There are men who groan and suffer for want of beef or ham in the midst of partridge! Good for them: that is to be a gourmet among gourmets: it is a weak ill-favoured taste which finds insipid those ordinary everyday foods, [C] *'per quae luxuria divitiarum taedio ludit'* [by the which luxury escapes from the boredom of riches].[125]   [B]   The essence of that vice consists in failing to enjoy what others do and in taking anxious care over your diet,

> *Si modica cœnare times olus omne patella.*

> [If you jib at an herb salad on a modest platter].

There is certainly a difference, in that it is better to shackle your appetite to whatever is easier to obtain: but such shackling is still a vice. I once called a relation of mine self-indulgent because he had forgotten, during a period in our galleys, how to undress at night and sleep in our beds.

If I had any sons I would readily wish them a fate like mine: God gave me a good father (who got nothing from me apart from my acknowledgement of his goodness – one cheerfully given); from the cradle he sent me to be suckled in some poor village of his, keeping me there until I was

123. Both cited together by Diogenes Laertius in his *Life of Pyrrho*.
124. Actually Favorinus criticized this view, which he reported (Aulus Gellius, *Attic Nights*, XV, viii).
125. Seneca, *Epist. moral.*, XVIII, 7. Then, Horace, *Epistles*, I, 52.

weaned – longer in fact, training me for the lowliest of lives among the people: [C] *'Magna pars libertatis est bene moratus venter.'* [Freedom consists, for a large part, in having a good-humoured belly.][126]

[B] Never assume responsibility for such upbringing yourself and even less allow your wives to do so: let boys be fashioned by fortune to the natural laws of the common people; let them become accustomed to frugal and severely simple fare, so that they have to clamber down from austerity rather than scrambling up to it. My father's humour had yet another goal: to bring me closer to the common-folk and to the sort of men who need our help; he reckoned that I should be brought to look kindly on the man who holds out his hand to me rather than on one who turns his back on me and snubs me. And the reason why he gave me godparents at baptism drawn from people of the most abject poverty was to bind and join me to them. His plan has not turned out too badly. I like doing things for lowly people, either because there is more glory in it or else from innate sympathy (which can work wonders with me). [C] The party I condemn in these wars of ours I would condemn more severely when it is flourishing and successful: it can almost reconcile me to it when I see it [B] wretched and overwhelmed.[127] How I love to reflect on that beautiful humour of Chelonis who was both daughter and wife of Kings of Sparta: while her husband Cleombrotus had the edge over her father Leonidas she was a good daughter, rallying to her father in his wretched exile and defying the victor. Then fortune veered about, did it not? Whereupon, as fortune changed she changed her mind, ranging herself courageously beside her husband, whom she followed no matter where his downfall drove him, having, it seems, no preference between them but leaping to the support of whichever party needed her more and to whom she could better show pity.[128] My nature is to follow the example of Flaminius (who lent his support to those who needed him, not to those who could help him) rather than that of Pyrrhus (who had the characteristic of being humble before the great and arrogant before the common-folk).

Long sittings at table [C] irritate me and [B] disagree with me, since, lacking restraint (doubtless because I formed the habit as a boy), I go

126. Seneca, *Epist. moral.*, CXXIII, 3.
127. '88: me.) *I condemn* in these *disturbances* of ours *the cause of one of the parties, but more so* when it is flourishing and successful: it [i.e. the cause] *has* almost *reconciled* me to it when I see it wretched and overwhelmed . . . [Pity, or sympathy, for the cause of the Reformers changes to pity for their faction.]
128. Condensed from Plutarch's *Life of Agis* and *Life of Cleomenes*; then, *Life of Flaminius* and *Life of Pyrrhus*.

on eating as long as I am there. That is why at home   [C]   (even though our meals are among the shorter ones)   [B]   I like to come in   [C]   a little   [B]   after the others, following the fashion of Augustus, although I do not imitate him in leaving before the others. On the contrary: I like to stay on a long time afterwards listening to the conversation, provided that I do not join it since I find it as tiring and painful to talk on a full stomach as I find it a healthy and pleasant exercise to argue and bellow before a meal.   [C]   The ancient Greeks and Romans were more reasonable than we are: unless some other quite unusual task intervened they assigned to eating (which is one of the chief activities of our lives) several hours a day and the best part of the night, eating and drinking less hurriedly than we do who gallop through everything; they extended both the leisureliness of this natural pleasure and its conviviality by interspersing it with various social duties both useful and pleasant.

[B]   Those who   [C]   ought to take care of me could,   [B]   at little cost[129] to themselves, cheat me of whatever they think harmful to me, for in such matters I neither want what is not there nor notice its absence: but they also waste their breath if they lecture me on abstaining from whatever is served. The result is that when I resolve to diet you have to put me apart from the other diners, serving me precisely what is sufficient for a moderate snack; for if I sit down at table I forget my resolution. When I order my servants to change the way they are serving up a dish they know that that means my appetite is gone and that I will not touch any. I prefer to eat rare any flesh that lends itself to it. I like it to be well-hung, even in many cases until it starts to smell high. Generally speaking toughness is the only quality which irritates me (towards all others I am as indifferent and long-suffering as anyone), so much so that, contrary to the usual whim, I find even some fish too fresh and firm. That is nothing to do with my teeth which have always been exceedingly good and which only now are starting to be threatened by old age. Since boyhood I learned to rub them on my napkin, both on rising and before and after meals.

God shows mercy to those from whom he takes away life a little at a time: that is the sole advantage of growing old; the last death which you die will be all the less total and painful: it will only be killing off half a man, or a quarter. Look: here is a tooth which has just fallen out with no effort or anguish: it had come to the natural terminus of its time. That part of my being, as well as several other parts, is already dead: others are half-dead, including those which were, during the vigour of my youth, the

129. '88: Those who take care of me *can* at little cost . . .

most energetic and uppermost. That is how I drip and drain away from myself. What animal-stupidity it would be if my intellect took for the whole of that collapse the last topple of an already advanced decline. I hope that mine will not.

[C] To tell the truth the principal consolation I draw from thoughts of my death is that it will be right and natural: from this day forth I could not beg or hope from Destiny any but a wrongful favour. People convince themselves that in former times man's lifespan, like his height, was bigger. Yet Solon, who belongs to those times, cuts off our extreme limit at three score years and ten.[130] I, who have in all things so greatly honoured that ἄριστον μέτρον [excellent Mean] of former ages and who have taken moderation as the most perfect measure, should I aspire to an immoderate and enormously protracted old age? Anything which goes against the current of Nature is capable of being harmful, but everything which accords with her cannot but be pleasant: *'Omnia quae secundum naturam fiunt, sunt habenda in bonis.'* [Everything that happens in accordance with Nature must be counted among the things which are good.][131] That is why Plato says that deaths caused by wounds and illnesses may be termed violent, but the death which, as Nature leads us toward her, takes us by surprise is of all deaths the lightest to bear and to some extent enjoyable. *'Vitam adolescentibus vis aufert, senibus maturitas.'* [Life is wrenched from young men: from old men it comes from ripeness.]

[B] Everywhere death intermingles and merges with our life: our decline anticipates its hour and even forces itself upon our very progress. I have portraits of myself aged twenty-five and thirty-five. I compare them with my portrait now: in how many ways is it no longer me! How far, far more different from them is my present likeness than from what I shall be like in death. It is too much an abuse of Nature to [C] flog[132] [B] her along so far that she is, for us, compelled to give up and abandon our guidance, our eyes, teeth, legs and so on to the mercy of remedies not our own but such as we can beg, relinquishing us, since she is weary of following us, into the hands of that 'Art'.

I am not over-fond of salads nor of any fruit except melons. My father loathed all kinds of sauces: I love them all. Overeating distresses me, but I am not aware that any food as such definitely disagrees with me, any more

130. Herodotus, I, xxxii.
131. Cicero, *De senectute*, xix, 71; then, Plato, *Timaeus*, 81E and Cicero, *De senectute*, ix, 71 (again).
132. '88: to *drag* her along ...

than I take note of full or crescent moons or of spring or autumn. There are fickle inexplicable changes which occur in us: for example I first of all found that radishes agreed with me; then they did not; now they do again. I have found my stomach and my tastes varying like this over several foods: I have replaced white wine by red, then red by white. I delight in fish, so that my days of abstinence are days of plenty and my fast-days are feast-days. I believe what some say: that fish is more easily digestible than flesh. It goes against my conscience to eat flesh on fish-days and against my preference to mix fish and flesh: there seems to be too wide a difference between them.

Since I was a young man I have occasionally gone without my dinner, either to whet my appetite for the next day (for, while Epicurus went without food or ate little in order to accustom his sense of enjoyment to do without abundance, I on the contrary do so in order to train it to profit from abundance and to make merry with it); or so as to husband my strength in the service of some physical or mental activity (since both grow cruelly sluggish within me through repletion: and I loathe above all that silly yoking together of so sane and merry a goddess as Venus with that little belching dyspeptic Bacchus, all blown up by the fumes of his wine);[133] or else to cure a sick stomach, or for want of appropriate company (since with that same Epicurus I say that we should be less concerned with what we eat than with whom we eat,[134] and I approve of Chilo's refusal to promise to come to a banquet at Periander's before finding out who the other guests were). No recipe is so pleasing to me, no sauce so appetizing, as those which derive from the company.

I believe it is healthier to eat more leisurely, less and at shorter intervals. But I would give precedence to appetite and hunger: I would find no pleasure in dragging through three or four skimped meals a day on doctor's orders: [C] who could assure me that at suppertime I would find again that frank appetite I have this morning? Especially we old men should seize the first opportune moment which comes along. Let us leave the prognostics of propitious times to the scribblers of almanacks and to the doctors.[135]   [B]   The ultimate benefit of my feeling well is pleasure: let

133. Montaigne is rejecting proverbial Classical wisdom, which made food and wine the precursors of love-making. Cf. Erasmus, *Adages*, II, III, XCVII, *Sine Cerere et Baccho friget Venus.*
134. Seneca, *Epist. moral.*, XIX, 10; then for Chilo, Plutarch (tr. Amyot), *Banquet des sept Sages*, 150H–151C.
135. Medical astrological almanacks (a legal monopoly of the medical profession) marked particular dates as propitious for certain foods, treatments and so on.

us cling to the first pleasure which is present and known. I refuse to stick for long to any prescriptions limiting my diet. A man who wants a regimen which serves him must not allow it to go on and on; for we become conditioned to it; our strength is benumbed by it; after six months you will have so degraded your stomach that it will have profited you nothing: you will merely have lost your freedom to do otherwise without harm.

My legs and thighs I cover no more in winter than in summer, wearing simple silken hose. I did let myself go, keeping my head warmer to help my rheum and my stomach warmer to help my stone, but within a day or two my ailments grew used to this and showed contempt for such routine provisions: so I moved on from a cap to a head-scarf and then from a bonnet to a fur hat. The padding of my doublet now only serves as decoration: it is pointless unless I add a layer of rabbit-fur or vulture-skin[136] and wear a skull-cap under my hat. Follow that gradation and you will go a long way! I will not do so and would willingly countermand what I have already done if only I dared. 'Are you feeling some fresh discomfort? Well, then, that reform of yours did you no good: you have grown used to it. Find another.' Thus are men undermined when they allow themselves to become encumbered with restricted diets and to cling to them superstitiously. They need to go farther and farther on, and then farther still. There is no end to it.

For both work and pleasure's sake it is far more convenient to do as the ancients did: go without lunch and, so as not to break up the day, put off the feast until the time comes to return home and rest. I used to do that once, but I have subsequently found from experience that, on the contrary, it is better for my health's sake to eat at lunchtime, since digestion is better when you are awake.

I rarely feel thirsty when I am in good health – nor when ill, though I do get a dry mouth then, yet without a thirst. Normally I drink only for the thirst which comes as I eat, well on into the meal. For a man of the ordinary sort I drink quite enough: even in summer and during an appetizing meal I not only exceed the limits set by Augustus (who drank exactly three glasses, no more), but so as not to infringe the rule of Democritus (who forbade you to stop at four as being an unlucky number) I down up to five if the occasion arises (that is about a pint and

---

136. Cotgrave's *Dictionarie of the French and English Tongues* confirms that vulture-skin was used in garments for warmth.

a quarter: for I favour smaller glasses and like draining them dry, something which others avoid as unseemly).[137] I water my wine, sometimes half and half, sometimes one-third water. When I am home I follow an ancient custom which my father's doctor prescribed for him (and for himself): I have what I need mixed for me in the buttery two or three hours before serving. [C] It is said that this custom of mixing wine and water was invented by Cranaus, King of Athens – I have heard arguments both for and against its usefulness. I think it more proper and more healthy that boys should not drink any wine until they are sixteen or eighteen. [B] The finest custom is the one most current and common: in my view all eccentricity is to be avoided; I would hate a German who put water in his wine as much as a Frenchman who drank it neat. The law in such things is common usage.

I am afraid of stagnant air and go in mortal fear of smells (the first repairs I hastened to make in my place were to the chimneys and lavatories – the usual flaws in old buildings and quite intolerable) and among the hardships of war I count those thick clouds of dust under which we are buried in summer during a long day's ride. My breath comes easily and freely and my colds usually clear away without affecting my lungs or giving me a cough.

The rigours of summer are more inimical to me than those of winter, for (apart from the inconvenience of the heat, less easy to remedy than the cold, and apart from sunstroke from the sun beating down on your head) my eyes are affected by any dazzling light: I could not lunch now facing a bright and flaming fire. At the time when I was more in the habit of reading I used to place a piece of glass over my book to soften the glare of the paper and found it quite a relief. Up till now[138] I have no acquaintance with spectacles and can see as well at a distance as ever I did or as anyone can. It is true that towards nightfall I begin to be aware that when reading my vision is weak and hazy: reading has strained my eyes at all times, but especially in the evening. [C] Though barely noticeable, that constitutes one step backwards. I shall take another step back, the second followed by a third, the third by a fourth, so gently that, before I am aware that my ageing sight is failing, I shall have become quite blind – so skilfully do the Fates spin the thread of our lives.

---

137. Erasmus, *Adages*, II, III, I, *Aut quinque bibis aut treis, aut ne quatuor*. Montaigne drinks three *démi-sétiés*. A *septier* (or *sétier*) was a variable measure, but for wine contained two Parisian *chopines*, each a little less than an English pint. Montaigne may have drunk as much as a pint and a half.
138. '88: now, *at the age of fifty-four, I have* . . .

I am similarly unwilling to admit that I am on the point of becoming hard of hearing, and you will find that when I am half-deaf I shall still be blaming it on the voices of those who are speaking to me. If we want our Soul to be aware of how she is draining away we must keep her on the stretch.

[B] My walk is quick and steady and I do not know whether I have found it harder to fix my mind in one place or my body. Any preacher who can hold my attention throughout an entire sermon must be a good friend of mine! In the midst of ceremonial, where everyone else maintains a fixed expression and where I have seen ladies keep their very eyes still, I have never succeeded in stopping at least one of my limbs from jigging about: seated I may be, but sedate, never. [C] Just as the chambermaid said of her master the philosopher Chrysippus that only his legs were drunk[139] (for he had this same habit of fidgeting them about, no matter what position he sat in, and she said it of him when the wine was exciting the others while he alone felt none the worse for it), so too people have been able to say of me since boyhood that I have 'mad' or 'quicksilver' feet: no matter where I put them, they are restless and never still.

[B] To eat ravenously as I do is not only unseemly: it is bad for your health, and indeed for your pleasure. In my haste I often bite my tongue and occasionally bite my fingers. When Diogenes came across a boy who was eating like that he slapped his tutor.[140] — [C] There were instructors in Rome who taught how to masticate and perambulate graciously. — [B] By eating thus I lose an occasion for talking, which is such a fine [C] seasoning[141] [B] at table – provided that both the meal and the topics are pleasant and brief. There is jealousy and rivalry among our pleasures: they clash and get in each other's way. Alcibiades was a man who well understood good living: he specifically banished music from his table so that it should not interfere with the conversation, [C] justifying this with the reason which Plato ascribes to him, that it is the practice of commonplace men to invite musicians and singers to their feasts since they lack that good talk and those pleasant discussions with which intelligent men understand how to delight each other.[142]

---

139. Erasmus, *Apophthegmata*, VII, *Chrysippus Solensis*, VI.
    '88: sedate, never: *and for gesticulation I am rarely to be found, on horse or on foot, without a stick in my hand.* To eat ravenously . . .
140. Erasmus, *Apophthegmata*, III, *Diogenes*, final hundred, XXIII.
141. '88: fine *condiment* at table . . .
142. Plato, *Protagoras*, 347.

[B]   The following are Varro's prescription for a banquet: an assembly of people of handsome presence who are agreeable to frequent and neither dumb nor talkative; clean and delightful food in a clean and delightful place; serene weather.[143]   [C]   An enjoyable dinner is a feast requiring no little skill and affording no little pleasure: neither great war-leaders nor great philosophers have declined to learn how to arrange one. My mind has entrusted to my memory three such feasts: they occurred at different times during the flower of my youth and chanced to give me sovereign pleasure (guests contributing to such sovereign delight according to the degree of good temper of body and soul in which each man chances to be). My present circumstances exclude me from such things.

[B]   I who am always down-to-earth in my handling of anything loathe that inhuman wisdom which seeks to render us   [C]   disdainful and   [B]   hostile towards the care of our bodies.[144] I reckon that it is as injudicious to set our minds against natural pleasures as to allow them to dwell on them.   [C]   Xerxes was an idiot to offer a reward to anyone who could invent some new pleasure for him when he was already surrounded by every pleasure known to Man:[145] but hardly less idiotic is the man who lops back such pleasures as Nature has found for him.   [B]   We should neither hunt them nor run from them: we should accept them. I do so with a little more zest and gratitude than that, and more readily follow the slope of Nature's own inclining.   [C]   There is no need for us to exaggerate their emptiness: that makes itself sufficiently known and sufficiently manifest, thanks to our morbid spoilsport of a mind which causes them all to taste as unpleasant to us as it does itself, treating both itself and everything it absorbs, no matter how minor, according to its own insatiable, roaming and fickle condition:

> *Sincerum est nisi vas, quodcunque infundis, acessit.*

> [If the jug is not clean, all you pour into it turns sour.][146]

I who boast that I so sedulously and so individually welcome the pleasures of this life find virtually nothing but wind in them when I examine them in detail. But then we too are nothing but wind. And the wind (more wise than we are) delights in its rustling and blowing, and is content with its

143. Aulus Gellius, *Attic Nights*, XIII, 11.
144. '88: care *and pleasure* of our bodies . . .
145. Cicero, *Tusc. disput.*, V, vii, 20.
146. Horace, *Epistles*, I, ii, 54.

own role without yearning for qualities which are nothing to do with it such as immovability or density.

Some say that the greatest pleasures and pains are those which, as was shown by the Balance of Critolaus, belong exclusively to the mind.[147] No wonder: the mind fashions them as it wills and tailors them for itself from the whole cloth. Everyday I see noteworthy and doubtless desirable examples of it. But I, whose constitution is composite and coarse, cannot so totally get a bite on such an indivisible single object that I do not tend heavily towards the immediate pleasures of that law of humans and their genus: things are sensed through the understanding, understood through the senses.[148]

The Cyrenaic philosophers held that the most intense pleasures and pains are those of the body, virtually double and more right.[149] [B] There are [C] those who, from an uncouth insensibility, hold (as Aristotle says) bodily pleasures in disgust.[150] I know some who do it from ambition. [B] Why do they not also give up breathing, so as to live on what is theirs alone,[151] [C] rejecting the light of day because it is free and costs them neither ingenuity nor effort? [B] Just to see, let Mars, Pallas or Mercury sustain them instead of Venus, Ceres and Bacchus.[152] [C] I suppose they think about squaring the circle while lying with their wives! [B] I hate being told to have our minds above the clouds while our

147. The balance of Critolaus, the peripatetic philosopher, always gave greater weight to the goods of the soul. (Cicero, *Tusc. disput.*, V, xvii, 51.)
148. For this much reworked sentence, I have followed the punctuation of ['95] etc. The general meaning is: Being a man (that is, body-plus-soul) and being weighted towards the body, Montaigne is unable fully to enjoy pure and simple intellectual pleasures. The law of Nature which applies to our genus (*animal*) makes the senses the gateway of cognition and cognition the means by which the senses are appreciated. (The ideas are consonant with Epicureanism: cf. Cicero, *Tusc. disput.*, V, xxxiii, 95–8.)
149. Cicero, *De officiis*, III, xxxi, 116; *Academica*, II (Lucullus), xlii, 131 and xxiv, 76.
150. Probably an allusion to Aristotle, *Nicomachaean Ethics*, III, xi, 7 (1119a): men insensible to pleasure are very few and such insensibility is not human.
   '88: There are *in our youth those who ambitiously claim to trample them underfoot*: why do they . . .
151. '88: theirs alone, *without help from their normal pattern.* Just to see, let Mars . . .
152. That is, let them live on war (Mars), wisdom (Pallas) or eloquence (Mercury) instead of sexual intercourse (Venus), corn (Ceres) and wine (Bacchus), the second three representing bodily 'necessities'.
   '88: Bacchus. Such *vaunting humours can forge themselves some contentment (for what power can our minds not have over us!) but of wisdom they have no tincture.* I hate . . .

bodies are at the dinner-table. It is not that I want the mind to be nailed to it or wallowing in it but I do want it to apply itself to it,   [C]   to sit at table, not to lie on it. Aristippus championed only the body, as though we had no soul: Zeno embraced only the soul, as though we had no body. Both were flawed.[153] They say that Pythagoras practised a philosophy which was pure contemplation: Socrates one which was all deeds and morals; between them both Plato found the Mean. But they are pulling our legs. The true Mean is to be found in Socrates; Plato is far more Socratic than Pythagorean, and it better becomes him.[154]

[B]   When I dance, I dance. When I sleep, I sleep; and when I am strolling alone through a beautiful orchard, although part of the time my thoughts are occupied by other things, for part of the time too I bring them back to the walk, to the orchard, to the delight in being alone there, and to me. Mother-like, Nature has provided that such actions as she has imposed on us as necessities should also be pleasurable, urging us towards them not only by reason but by desire. To corrupt her laws is wrong.

When, in the thick of their great endeavours, I see Caesar and Alexander so fully enjoying pleasures which are[155]   [C]   natural and consequently necessary and right,   [B]   I do not say that their souls are relaxing but giving themselves new strength, by force of mind compelling their violent pursuits and burdensome thoughts to take second place to the usages of everyday life,   [C]   wise if they were to believe that to be their normal occupation and the other one abnormal.

What great fools we are! 'He has spent his life in idleness,' we say. 'I haven't done a thing today.' – 'Why! Have you not lived? That is not only the most basic of your employments, it is the most glorious.' – 'I would have shown them what I can do, if they had set me to manage some great affair.' – If you have been able to examine and manage your own life you have achieved the greatest task of all. Nature, to display and show her powers, needs no great destiny: she reveals herself equally at any level of life, both behind curtains or without them. Our duty is to bring order to our morals not to the materials for a book: not to win provinces in battle but order and tranquillity for the conduct of our life. Our most great and

153. Cicero's contention, *Academica*, II (Lucullus), xlv, 139.
154. Probably an echo of St Augustine, *City of God*, VIII, iv; but while Augustine makes Plato combine Socrates' virtues with those of Pythagoras, he does not write of his being the mean between them. Montaigne's term for the Mean, *tempérament*, represents Aristotle's term *sophrosyne*.
155. '88: pleasures which are *human and bodily*, I do not say . . .

glorious achievement is to live our life fittingly. Everything else – reigning, building, laying up treasure – are at most tiny props and small accessories.   [B]   I delight in coming across a general in the field, at the foot of a breach which he means soon to attack, giving himself whole-heartedly to his dinner while chatting freely with his friends,   [C]   or across Brutus, with heaven and earth conspiring against him and the liberty of Rome, stealing an evening hour from his rounds of duty to jot down notes on his Polybius as he read him with complete composure.[156]   [B]   It is for petty souls overwhelmed by the weight of affairs to be unable to disentangle themselves for them completely, not knowing how to drop them and then take them up again:

> *O fortes pejoraque passi*
> *Mecum sæpe viri, nunc vino pellite curas;*
> *Cras ingens iterabimus æquor.*

[O ye strong men who have often undergone worse trials with me, banish care now with wine: tomorrow we will sail again over the vast seas.][157]

Whether as a joke or in earnest, 'theological wine' and   [C]   'Sorbonne [B] wine' have become proverbial, as have their gaudies;[158] but I find that the fellows are right to dine all the more indulgently and enjoyably in that they have seriously and usefully used their mornings for the concerns of their college: the shared awareness of having used those other hours well is a proper and piquant condiment for their table. That is how the sages lived. Thus too did the inimitable eager striving towards virtue which amazes us in both the Catos, as well as their severity of humour to the point of rudeness, mildly and happily submit to the laws of our human condition, to Venus and to Bacchus,[159]   [C]   following the precepts of their School which required the perfect sage to be as experienced and knowledgeable about the use of the natural pleasures as about all the rest of life's duties: *'Cui cor sapiat, ei et sapiat palatus'* [To a discriminating mind let him ally a discriminating palate.][160]

[B]   In a strong and great-souled man it is, it seems to me, wondrously honourable to be relaxed and approachable, and it is most befitting.

---

156. From Plutarch's *Life of Brutus*.
157. Horace, *Odes*, I, vii, 30–2.
158. '88: and *professorial* wine . . .
    The quality and quantity of the drinking in the Sorbonne (the Faculty of Theology) was indeed proverbial. Cf. Sainéan, *Langue de Rabelais*, I, 368.
159. Cf. Rabelais, *Tiers Livre*, TLF, *Prologue*, 182; Horace, *Odes*, III, xxi, 9–12.
160. Cicero, *De finibus*, II, viii, 24 (truncated and differently applied).

Epaminondas never thought that to join in the dance with the young men of his city, [C] to sing and strum with them, [B] and to bother to do it properly, in any way detracted from the honour of his glorious victories nor from the [C] perfect [B] reformation of morals [C] which was within him.[161] [B] And among all the remarkable actions of Scipio [C] – the grandfather, that great man worthy of having been thought to descend from the gods[162] – [B] none is more gracious than his having been seen idling along, unperturbed, choosing and collecting shells like a schoolboy, playing *Quick! Quick! Pick up sticks* with Laelius along the seashore and, when the weather was bad, passing his time enjoyably by writing comedies about the most plebeian and realistic activities of men;[163] [C] and, while his mind was full of that marvellous African campaign of his against Hannibal, visiting the philosophy schools in Sicily and attending the lectures, so providing his enemies at Rome with something to snap at in their blind envy.[164]

[B] Nor is there anything more striking about Socrates than his finding the time when he was old to learn how to dance and to play instruments, maintaining that it was time well spent. He was seen standing in an ecstatic trance for a day and a night in view of all the Grecian army, surprised and caught up by some deep thought. He was seen [C] to be the first of many brave men in that army to dash to the help of Alcibiades when he was overwhelmed by the enemy, shielding him with his body and pulling him out from under the weight of their numbers by the sheer force of his arms; and of all the people of Athens (outraged like him by such a shameful sight) he was the first to stand forth to rescue Theramenes from the Thirty Tyrants, whose henchmen were escorting him to his death and, although he was seconded by only two men, he did not give up that valiant attempt until Theramenes himself urged him to do so. When wooed by a person whose beauty had enthralled him, he was

---

161. Cornelius Nepos, *Life of Epaminondas*.
    '88: morals *there ever was in man.* And among . . .
162. '88: of Scipio *the Younger (when all is done the first man among the Romans)* none is . . .
163. Erasmus, *Adages*, V, II, XX, *Conchas legere*, citing, apropos of Scipio and Laelius, Valerius Maximus, VIII, viii, and Cicero, *De oratore*, II, vi. (Montaigne introduces a confusion in [C]: he means, as he first wrote, the Younger, not the Elder, Scipio. The error remains in the posthumous editions, with the result that anecdotes about Scipio Africanus Major and Scipio Aemilianus Africanus Minor are fused into one, as are these two Scipios themselves.)
164. Livy, XIX, xix, of Scipio Africanus Major.

seen to maintain, as was necessary, the strictest continence; he was seen helping up Xenophon at the battle of Delium, saving him when his horse had given him a tumble. He was seen [B] striding undeviatingly to war [C] trampling over the ice [B] in his bare feet; wearing the same gown in winter as in summer; surpassing all his comrades in his endurance of hardships and, at feasts, eating no differently from usual. [C] He was seen, unmoved in countenance, putting up for twenty-seven years with hunger and poverty, with loutish sons, with a cantankerous wife and finally with calumny, tyranny, imprisonment, leg-irons and poison. [B] Yet that very man, when the dictates of courtesy made him a guest at a drinking-match, was, from the entire army, the man who best acquitted himself. Nor did he refuse to play five-stones with the boys nor to run about with them astride a hobby-horse. And he did it with good grace: for Philosophy says that all activities are equally becoming in a wise man, all equally honour him. We have the wherewithal, so we should never tire of comparing the ideal of that great man against all patterns and forms of perfection.[165] [C] There are very few pure and complete exemplars of how to live; those who instruct us do wrong to set before us weak and faulty ones with scarcely a single good habitual quality, ones which are more likely to pull us backwards, corrupting us rather than correcting us.

[B] The many get it wrong: you can indeed, using artifice rather than nature, make your journey more easily along the margins, where the edges serve as a limit and a guide, rather than take the wide and unhedged Middle Way; but it is also less noble, less commendable. [C] Greatness of soul consists not so much in striving upwards and forwards as in knowing how to find one's place and to draw the line. Whatever is adequate it regards as ample; it shows its sublime quality by preferring the moderate to the outstanding. [B] Nothing is so beautiful, so right, as acting as a man should: nor is any learning so arduous as knowing how to live this life [C] naturally and [B] well. And the most uncouth of our afflictions is to [C] despise [B] our being.[166] If anyone desires to set his soul apart so as to free it from contagion, let him have the boldness to do so (if he can) while his body is unwell: otherwise, on the contrary, his soul should assist and applaud the body, not refuse to participate in its

---

165. A composite picture of Socrates from the standard sources: especially Plato's *Symposium*, 213A – 220D, with a borrowing from Diogenes Laertius' *Life of Socrates*.
166. '88: is to *hate and disdain* our being . . .

natural pleasures but delight in it as if it were its husband, contributing, if it is wise enough, moderation, lest those pleasures become confounded with pain through want of discernment.   [C]   Lack of temperance is pleasure's bane: temperance is not its chastisement but its relish. It was by means of temperance, which in them was outstanding and exemplary, that Eudoxus (who made pleasure his sovereign good) and his companions (who rated it at so high a price) savoured it in its most gracious gentleness.[167]

[B]   I so order my soul that it can contemplate both pain and pleasure with eyes equally   [C]   restrained – *'eodem enim vitio est effusio animi in laetitia quo in dolore contractio'* [for it is as wrong for the soul to dilate with joy as to contract with pain][168] – doing so with eyes equally   [B]   steady, yet looking merrily at one and soberly at the other and, in so far as it can contribute anything itself, being as keen to snuff out the one as to stretch out the other.   [C]   Look sanely upon the good and it follows that you look sanely upon evils: pain, in its tender beginnings, has some qualities which we cannot avoid: so too pleasure in its final excesses has qualities which we can avoid. Plato couples pain and pleasure together and wants it to be the duty of fortitude to fight the same fight against pain and against the seductive fascinations of immoderate pleasure. They form two springs of water: blessed are they, city, man or beast, that draw what they should, when they should and from the one they should. From the first we should drink more sparingly, as a medicine, as a necessity: from the second to slake our thirst, though not to the point of drunkenness. Pain and pleasure, love and hatred, are the first things a child is aware of: if, after Reason develops, they are guided by her, then that is virtue.[169]

[B]   I have a lexicon all to myself: I 'pass' the time when tide and time are sticky and unpleasant: when good, I do not want to 'pass' time, I   [C]   savour it and hold on to it.[170]   [B]   We must run the gauntlet through the bad and recline on the good. 'Pastimes' and 'to pass the time' are everyday expressions which correspond to the practice of those clever folk who think that they can use their life most profitably by letting it leak and slip away, by-passing it or avoiding it and (as far as they can manage to

167. Eudoxus maintained that pleasure is the Supreme Good, arguing that all creatures, rational and irrational, seek it and avoid pain. (Aristotle, *Nicomachaean Ethics*, X, ii, 1172 b.) Aristotle adds that Eudoxus had a reputation for exceptional temperance. (Cf. also ibid., I, xii.) His 'companions' are doubtless the Platonists, of whom he was an unorthodox associate.
168. Cicero, *Tusc. disput.*, IV, xxxi, 66.
169. Plato, *Laws*, I, 632C–634B; 6360; 653A–C.
170. '88: I *taste* it and *linger over* it. We must . . .

do so) ignoring it and fleeing from it as painful and contemptible. But I know life to be something different: I find it to be both of great account and delightful – even as I grasp it now [C] in its final waning; [B] Nature has given it into our hands garnished with such attributes, such agreeable ones, that if it weighs on us, if it slips uselessly from us, we have but ourselves to blame. [C] *'Stulti vita ingrata est, trepida est, tota in futurum fertur.'* [It is the life of the fool which is graceless, fearful and entirely sacrificed to the future.][171]

[B] That is why I so order my ways that I can lose my life without regret, not however because it is troublesome or importunate but because one of its attributes is that it must be lost. [C] Besides, finding it not unpleasant to die can only rightly become those who find life pleasant. [B] To enjoy life requires some husbandry. I enjoy it twice as much as others, since the measure of our joy depends on the greater or lesser degree of our attachment to it. Above all now, when I see my span so short, I want to give it more ballast; I want to arrest the swiftness of its passing by the swiftness of my capture, compensating for the speed with which it drains away by the intensity of my enjoyment. The shorter my lease of it, the deeper and fuller I must make it.

Others know the delight of happiness and well-being: I know it as they do, but not *en passant*, as it slips by. We must also study it, savour it, muse upon it, so as to render condign thanksgivings to Him who vouchsafes it to us. Other folk enjoy all pleasures as they enjoy the pleasure of sleep: with no awareness of them. Why, with the purpose of not allowing even sleep to slip insensibly away, there was a time when I found it worthwhile to have my sleep broken into so that I could catch a glimpse of it. I deliberate with my self upon any pleasure. I do not skim it off: I plumb it, and now that my reason has grown chagrin and squeamish I force it to accept it. Do I find myself in a state of calm? Is there some pleasure which thrills me? I do not allow it to be purloined by my senses: I associate my Soul with it, not so that she will [C] bind herself to it[172] [B] but take joy in it: not losing herself but finding herself in it; her role is to observe herself as mirrored in that happy state, to weigh that happiness, gauge it and increase it. She measures how much she owes to God for having her conscience and

---

171. '88: I grasp it now, in its *decadence*; Nature . . .

Seneca, *Epist. moral.*, XV, 9. (Seneca presents this saying as an 'excellent Greek proverb' uttered by Epicurus, warning that it applies not to the lives of obviously foolish men but to our own, with its unsatisfiable desires.)

172. '88: she will *get drunk on* it but take . . .

her warring passions at peace, with her body in its natural [C] state, [B] enjoying ordinately and [C] appropriately [B] those sweet and pleasant functions by which it pleases Him, through His grace, to counterbalance the pains with which His justice in its turn chastises us;[173] she gauges how precious it is to her to have reached such a point that, no matter where she casts her gaze, all around her the heavens are serene – no desire, no fear or doubt bring disturbing gales; nor is there any hardship, [C] past, present or future [B] on which her thoughts may not light without anxiety. This meditation gains a great splendour by a comparison of my condition with that of others. And so I [C] pass in review,[174] [B] from hundreds of aspects, those whom fortune or their own mistakes sweep off into tempestuous seas, as well as those, closer to my own case, who accept their good fortune with such languid unconcern. Those folk really do 'pass' their time: they pass beyond the present and the things they have in order to put themselves in bondage to hope and to those shadows and vain ghosts which their imagination holds out to them –

> *Morte obita quales fama est volitare figuras,*
> *Aut quæ sopitos deludunt somnia sensus*

[Like those phantoms which, so it is said, flit about after death or those dreams which delude our slumbering senses]

– the more you chase them, the faster and farther they run away. Just as Alexander said that he worked for work's sake –

> *Nil actum credens cum quid superesset agendum:*

[Believing he had not done anything, while anything remained to be done:]

– so too your only purpose in chasing after them, your only gain, lies in the chase.[175]

As for me, then, I love life and cultivate it as it has pleased God to vouchsafe it to us. I do not go yearning that it should be without the need to eat and drink: [C] indeed to wish that need redoubled would not seem to me a less pardonable error: '*Sapiens divitiarum naturalium quaesitor acerrimus*' [The wise man is the keenest of seekers after the riches of Nature];[176] nor [B] that we could keep up our strength by merely popping into our mouths a little of that drug by means of which Epimenides

---

173. '88: natural *health*, enjoying ordinately and *fully* those sweet . . .
174. '88: I *picture to myself*, from hundreds of aspects . . .
175. Virgil, *Aeneid*, X, 641–2; Lucan, *Pharsalia*, II, 657.
176. Seneca, *Epist. moral.*, CXIX, 5.

assuaged his appetite and kept alive;[177] nor that we could, without sensation, produce children by our fingers and our heels [C] but rather, speaking with reverence, that we could also do it voluptuously with our fingers and our heels as well; [B] nor that our body should be without desire or thrills. Such plaints are [C] ungrateful and iniquitous. [B] I accept wholeheartedly [C] and thankfully [B] what Nature has done for me: I delight in that fact and am proud of it. You do wrong to that great and almighty Giver to [C] refuse [B] His gift, to [C] nullify [B] it or disfigure it. [C] Himself entirely Good, he has made all things good: '*Omnia quae secundum naturam est, aestimatione digna sunt.*' [All things which are in accordance with Nature are worthy of esteem.][178]

[B] I embrace most willingly those of Philosophy's opinions which are most solid, that is to say, most human, most ours: my arguments, like my manners, are lowly and modest. [C] To my taste she is acting like a child when she starts crowing out *ergo*, preaching to us that it is a barbarous match to wed the divine to the earthy, the rational to the irrational, the strict to the permissive, the decent to the indecent; that pleasure is a bestial quality, unworthy that a wise man should savour it; that the only enjoyment he gets from lying with his beautiful young wife is the pleasure of being aware that he is performing an ordinate action – like pulling on his boots for a useful ride! May Philosophy's followers, faced with breaking their wife's hymen, be no more erect, muscular nor succulent than her arguments are![179]

That is not what Socrates says – Philosophy's preceptor as well as ours. He values as he should the body's pleasure but he prefers that of the mind as having more force, constancy, suppleness, variety and dignity. And, according to him, even that pleasure by no means goes alone (he is not given to such fantasies): it merely has primacy. For him temperance is not the enemy of our pleasures: it moderates them.[180]

[B] Nature is a gentle guide but no more gentle than wise and just: [C] '*Intrandum est in rerum naturam et penitus quid ea postulet*

---

177. Plutarch, (tr. Amyot), *Banquet des Sept Sages*, 156 G.
178. '88: plaints are *those of ingratitude.* I accept wholeheartedly and *thank her for it,* what Nature ... Giver to *despise* His gift, to *debase* it or disfigure it – Echoes of James 1:17, and of Genesis 1:25; then a conflation of phrases from Cicero, *De finibus*, III, vi, 20.
179. Montaigne is, textually, condemning Seneca here (*Epist. moral.*, XCII, 7–8). Cf. also Aristotle, *Nicomachaean Ethics*, III, x, 8–9; Cicero, *Paradoxes*, 1.
180. Erasmus, *Apophthegmata*, III, *Socrates*, LXXVI (among others); Plato, *Laws*, 728E; 892 AB; 896 C ff.

pervidendum.' [We must go deeply into the nature of things and find out precisely what Nature wants.] [B] I seek her traces everywhere: we have jumbled them together with the tracks of artifice; [C] and thereby that sovereign good of the Academics and Peripatetics, which is to live according to Nature, becomes for that very reason hard to delimit and portray; so too that of the Stoics which is a neighbour to it, namely, to conform to Nature.[181] [B] Is it not an error to reckon some functions to be less worthy because they are necessities? They will never beat it out of my head anyway that the marriage of Pleasure to Necessity [C] (with whom, according to an ancient, the gods ever conspire) [B] is a most suitable match.[182] What are we trying to achieve by taking limbs wrought together into so interlocked and kindly a compact and tearing them asunder in divorce? On the contrary let us tie them together by mutual duties. Let the mind awaken and quicken the heaviness of the body: let the body arrest the lightness of the mind and fix it fast: [C] *'Qui velut summum bonum laudat animae naturam, et tanquam malum naturam carnis accusat, profecto et animam carnaliter appetit et carnem carnaliter fugit, quoniam id vanitate sentit humana, non veritate divina.'* [He who eulogizes the nature of the soul as the sovereign good and who indicts the nature of the flesh as an evil desires the soul with a fleshly desire and flees from the flesh in a fleshly way, since his thought is based on human vanity not on divine truth.][183]

[B] There is no part unworthy of our concern in this gift which God has given to us; we must account for it down to each hair. It is not a merely [C] formal [B] commission to Man to guide himself according to Man's [C] fashioning: it is expressly stated, [B] inborn, [C] most fundamental, [B] and the Creator gave it to us seriously [C] and strictly. Commonplace intellects can be persuaded by authority alone, and it has greater weight in a foreign tongue; so, at this point, let us make another charge at it: *'Stultitiae proprium quis non dixerit, ignave et*

181. Cicero, *De senectute,* iii, 5 *De finibus,* V, xxiv, 69; III, vi, 44.
    '88: with *bastard* tracks of artifice. Is it not . . .
182. Cf. Erasmus, *Adages,* II, III, XLI, *Adversum necessitatem ne dii quidem resistunt,* citing Simonides' saying and, above all, Plato. Montaigne is strongly influenced by Cicero (*De finibus,* II, xi, 34; IV, x, 25 – IV, xi, 27–9). In I, ii, 7 Cicero notes that the three schools mentioned by Montaigne, the Academics (the Platonists), the Peripatetics (the Aristotelians) and the Stoics have the virtual monopoly of ethics. Current distortions of their principles therefore pervert virtually the whole of moral philosophy. (Cf. also, *De finibus,* III, vi, 20–3; ix, 25–6; *Laelius,* V, 19; etc.) The debt to Cicero is fundamental.
183. St Augustine, *City of God,* XIV, v; stressing that even Plato devalued the body in the life of Man, who is body plus soul.

contumaciter facere quae facienda sunt, et alio corpus impellere, alio animum,
distrahique inter diversissimos motus?' [Who would not say that it was really
foolish to do in a slothful, contumacious spirit something which has to be
done anyway, thrusting the body in one direction and the soul in another
where it is torn between totally conflicting emotions?][184]

[B] Go on then, just to see: get that fellow over there to tell you one of
these days what notions and musings he stuffs into his head, for the sake of
which he diverts his thoughts from a good meal and regrets the time spent
eating it. You will find that no dish on your table tastes as insipid as that
beautiful pabulum of his soul (as often as not it would be better if we fell
fast asleep rather than stayed awake for what we do it for) and you will
find that his arguments and concepts are not worth your rehashed
leftovers. Even if they were the raptures of Archimedes, what does it
matter?[185]

Here, I am not alluding to – nor am I confounding with the   [C] scrap-
ings of the pot   [B] that we are, and with the vain longings and
ratiocinations which keep us musing – those revered souls which, through
ardour of devotion and piety, are raised on high to a constant and
scrupulous anticipation of things divine;   [C] souls which (enjoying by
the power of a quick and rapturous hope a foretaste of that everlasting
food which is the ultimate goal, the final destination, that Christians long
for) scorn to linger over our insubstantial and ambiguous pleasurable
'necessities' and easily assign to the body the bother and use of the temporal
food of the senses.   [B] That endeavour is a privilege.[186]   [C] Among
the likes of us there are two things which have ever appeared to me to
chime particularly well together – supercelestial opinions: subterranean
morals.

That great man   [B] Aesop saw his master pissing as he walked along.
'How now?' he said. 'When we run shall we have to shit?'[187] Let us
husband our time; but there still remains a great deal fallow and underused.
Our mind does not willingly concede that it has plenty of other hours to

184. '88: merely a *farcical* commission . . . man's *natural* fashioning [. . .] it is *simple*
and inborn [. . .] seriously *and expressly* . . .
   Seneca, *Epist. moral.*, LXXIV, 32 (adapted).
185. Archimedes was ecstatic when he discovered his famous principle. In the next
sentence, for 'rabble', *voirie*, Montaigne substituted *marmaille*, a pejorative term
recalling to the ear both monkey (*marmot*) and stew-pot (*marmite*).
186. '88: privilege. *Our endeavours are all worldly and among the worldly ones the most*
natural are the most right. Aesop . . .
187. From Planudes' *Life of Aesop*, often printed with the *Fables*.

perform its functions without breaking fellowship during the short time the body needs for its necessities. They want to be beside themselves, want to escape from their humanity. That *is* madness: instead of changing their Form into an angel's they change it into a beast's; they crash down instead of winding high. [C] Those humours soaring to transcendency terrify me as do great unapproachable heights; and for me nothing in the life of Socrates is so awkward to digest as his ecstasies and his daemonizings, and nothing about Plato so human as what is alleged for calling him divine. [B] And of [C] our [B] disciplines it is those which ascend the highest which, it seems to me, are the most [C] base and [B] earth-bound. I can find nothing so [C] abject [B] and so mortal in the life of Alexander as his fantasies about [C] his immortalization. [B] Philotas, in a retort he made in a letter, showed his mordant wit when congratulating Alexander on his being placed among the gods by the oracle of Jupiter Ammon: 'As far as you are concerned I'm delighted,' he said, 'but there is reason to pity those men who will have to live with a man, and obey a man, who [C] trespasses beyond, and cannot be content with, [B] the measure of a man':[188]

[C] *Diis te minorem quod geris, imperas.*

[Because you hold yourself lower than the gods, you hold imperial sway.][189]

[B] The noble inscription by which the Athenians honoured Pompey's visit to their city corresponds to what I think:

> *D'autant es tu Dieu comme*
> *Tu te recognois homme.*

[Thou art a god in so far as thou recognizest that thou art a man.]

It is an accomplishment, absolute and as it were God-like, to know how to enjoy our being as we ought. We seek other attributes because we do not understand the use of our own; and, having no knowledge of what is

188. '88: of *human* disciplines [...] I can find nothing *so base* and so mortal ... about his *deification*. Philotas ... who *exceeds* the measure of a man. The noble inscription ...
('Deification' was used by Christian mystics for the highest rapture. Montaigne replaced it, no doubt, as potentially misleading, Alexander's 'deification' not being an ecstasy but an act of flattery.) For Philotas, cf. Quintus Curtius, VI, 9.
189. Horace, *Odes*, III, vi, 5; then the inscription greeting Pompey as he left Athens, according to Plutarch. (Cited from Amyot's translation of his *Life of Pompey the Great*.)

within, we sally forth outside ourselves. [C] A fine thing to get up on stilts: for even on stilts we must ever walk with our legs! And upon the highest throne in the world, we are seated, still, upon our arses.

[B] The most beautiful of lives to my liking are those which conform to the common measure, [C] human and ordinate, without miracles though and [B] without rapture.

Old age, however, has some slight need of being treated more tenderly. Let us commend it to that tutelary god of health – and, yes, of wisdom, merry and companionable:

> Frui paratis et valido mihi,
> Latoe, dones, et, precor, integra
> Cum mente, nec turpem senectam
> Degere, nec cythara carentem.

[Vouchsafe, O Son of Latona, that I may enjoy those things I have prepared; and, with my mind intact I pray, may I not degenerate into a squalid senility, in which the lyre is wanting.][190]

190. '88: common measure, without *marvel*, without rapture . . . more tenderly *and more delicately*. Let us commend . . .

Horace, *Odes*, I, xxxi, 17–20. Apollo, son of Jupiter and Latona, was the god of healing and presided over the Muses.

Index

Other than in the entry under his name, Michel de Montaigne is referred to as M.
Footnotes have not been indexed

belief in miracles, 74–8; *see also*
  miracles
Catholics treating some beliefs as
  expendable, 78
choice of vices, 267–8
condemnation of sexual intercourse,
  306
contempt for life, 30
forced on New World, 345–7
general law of God, 374–5
God's ordinances, judgements on,
  93–5
God's purpose, attributing success or
  failure to, 93–5
Man to guide himself according to
  Man's fashioning, 423
mercy of God, 407
M's human thoughts on, 115–16
mystery, as, 114–15
obedience to Church, 78
prayer: approach to, 113; excess of,
  116–17; as a jingle, 118; Lord's
  Prayer, 109–10; occasions for,
  110–11; outward show, 111;
  private and public, 117–18
psalm-singing, 112
repentance, 111–12
Roman Catholic Church: M's
  anxiety not to write against, 109
scriptural authority for witches, 357
scriptural certainty and human
  testimony, 358–61
sex, attitude to, 306
similarities of all, 306
solitary pursuit of, 105
translations of the Scriptures, 113–14
use of God's name, 116
women and, 117
repentance
  inadequate, 239–40
  M's easy conscience, 234
  no cure unless vice eschewed, 241
  regret contrasted, 241–2
  selective, 240
Rhegium (Italian city), 7
Romans and Greeks, Plutarch's
  comparisons, 191–3

Rome, capture by Duke of Bourbon
  (1527), 13–14
royal-tennis, 392

Saint-Michel, Sieur de (M's brother),
  209
Scanderbeg, Prince of Epirus (George
  Castriota), 6
scientific investigations, 375
Scipio Africanus, Publius Cornelius,
  Major, 145–6, 401, 417
scratching, 402
sea-sickness, 331, 333
secrets, 267
self-study
  knowing one's self, 51
  M's metaphysics and physics, 374
  wisdom from, 375–8
Seneca
  austere life, 385–6
  death, 198–200
  on: Roman central-heating, 383;
    solitude, 107–8
  studying methods, 385
  virtues defended, 186–7
servants
  conversing with, 250
  M's upbringing with, 405–6
Sextius Niger, Quintus, the Elder
  (Roman philosopher), 385
sexuality
  animal demands, 283–4
  excesses needed for restraint, 282
  impetuosity of, 314
  impotence in old age, 316–17
  inconstancy in women judged by
    inconstant men, 314–15
  intercourse: *affaires*, 255, 276–7; all
    creatures at same level, 305–6; by
    beasts, 255–6; books on, 281–2;
    death during, 22; divergent
    medical advice as to, 220; drinking
    and, 137; frequency of, 277–8;
    health-giving properties, 321–2;
    intensity of climax, 178; with lame
    women, 361–2; legislation for, 281;
    lingering over, 309; love necessary,

Summary of the Symbols

[A] and '80: the text of 1580
[A1]: the text of 1582 (plus)
[B] and '88: the text of 1588
[C]: the text of the edition being prepared by Montaigne when he died, 1592
'95: text of the 1595 posthumous printed edition

In the notes there is given a selection of variant readings, including most abandoned in 1588 and many from the printed posthumous edition of 1595.

By far the most scholarly account of the text is that given in R. A. Sayce, *The Essays of Montaigne: A Critical Exploration*, 1972, Chapter 2, 'The Text of the *Essays*'.

Contemporary ... Provocative ... Outrageous ...
Prophetic ... Groundbreaking ... Funny ... Disturbing ...
Different ... Moving ... Revolutionary ... Inspiring ...
Subversive ... Life-changing ...

What makes a modern classic?

At Penguin Classics our mission has always been to make the best
books ever written available to everyone. And that also means
constantly redefining and refreshing exactly what makes a 'classic'.
That's where Modern Classics come in. Since 1961 they have been an
organic, ever-growing and ever-evolving list of books from the last
hundred (or so) years that we believe will continue to be read over and
over again.

They could be books that have inspired political dissent, such as
Animal Farm. Some, like *Lolita* or *A Clockwork Orange*, may have
caused shock and outrage. Many have led to great films, from *In Cold
Blood* to *One Flew Over the Cuckoo's Nest*. They have broken down
barriers – whether social, sexual, or, in the case of *Ulysses*, the
boundaries of language itself. And they might – like *Goldfinger* or
Scoop – just be pure classic escapism. Whatever the reason, Penguin
Modern Classics continue to inspire, entertain and enlighten millions
of readers everywhere.

'No publisher has had more influence on reading habits than Penguin'
Independent

'Penguins provided a crash course in world literature'
Guardian

The best books ever written

PENGUIN 🐧 CLASSICS

SINCE 1946

Find out more at www.penguinclassics.com